NOTABLE BRITISH NOVELISTS

MAGILL'S CHOICE

NOTABLE BRITISH NOVELISTS

Volume 3

Thomas Love Peacock — Virginia Woolf

707 – 1050

Index

edited by

CARL ROLLYSON

SALEM PRESS, INC.

Pasadena, California   Hackensack, New Jersey

Essays originally appeared in *Critical Survey of Long Fiction, Second Revised Edition*, 2000; new material has been added.

∞ The paper used in these volumes conforms to the American National Standard for Permanence of Paper for Printed Library Materials, Z39.48-1992 (R1997).

Library of Congress Cataloging-in-Publication Data
Notable British novelists / editor, Carl Rollyson
         p.   cm. — (Magill's choice)
   Includes bibliographical references and index.
ISBN 0-89356-204-1 (set : alk. paper). —
ISBN 0-89356-208-4 (v. 1 : alk. paper). —
ISBN 0-89356-209-2 (v. 2 : alk. paper). —
ISBN 0-89356-237-8 (v. 3 : alk. paper)
   1. English fiction—Bio-bibliography—Dictionaries.   2. Novelists, English—Biography—Dictionaries. 3. English fiction— Dictionaries   I. Rollyson, Carl E. (Carl Edmund) II. Series.
PR821.N57   2001
820.9′0003—dc21
[B]   00-046380

First Printing

Contents – Volume 3

Complete List of Contents

Contents—Volume 1

Contents—Volume 2

Contents—Volume 3

NOTABLE BRITISH NOVELISTS

Thomas Love Peacock

Born: Weymouth, England; October 18, 1785
Died: Halliford, England; January 23, 1866

Principal long fiction · *Headlong Hall*, 1816; *Melincourt*, 1817; *Nightmare Abbey*, 1818; *Maid Marian*, 1822; *The Misfortunes of Elphin*, 1829; *Crotchet Castle*, 1831; *Gryll Grange*, 1860.

Other literary forms · Before turning his talents to the satirical novel, Thomas Love Peacock wrote poetry. His early works include *Palmyra and Other Poems* (1806), *The Genius of the Thames* (1810), *The Philosophy of Melancholy* (1812), and *Sir Proteus: A Satirical Ballad* (1814). When his principal efforts turned to prose, Peacock continued to produce the occasional elegant lyric or rousing song, many of them incorporated into his novels. His long narrative poem *Rhododaphne* (1818), "a nympholeptic tale," attracted considerable contemporary attention and has retained a measure of continued critical esteem; his satirical *Paper Money Lyrics* (1837), topical and crochety, is largely ignored. Early in his literary career Peacock also wrote two farces, *The Dilettanti* and *The Three Doctors*, both of which were unpublished. Throughout his life, and particularly during the periods when his responsibilities at the East India Company precluded sustained literary projects, Peacock wrote essays and reviews, the most famous being his unfinished but incisive "Essay on Fashionable Literature," in *The Four Ages of Poetry* (1820), the satirical critique of contemporary poetry's debasement that provoked Percy Bysshe Shelley's *A Defense of Poetry* (1840) and Peacock's four-part *Memoirs of Percy Bysshe Shelley* (1858-1862), which the reserved and fastidious Peacock, who deplored the publication of private matters, wrote grudgingly, as a corrective to the muddled enthusiasms and posthumous scandal-retailing that admirers and acquaintances of Shelley were offering as literary biography.

Achievements · From the beginning of his career as a satirical novelist, Peacock always had an attentive audience, but never a wide one. His career in several ways has invited comparison with that of his contemporary, Jane Austen. Each writer set out to please himself or herself, uninfluenced by desire for fame or gold. Each swam against the Romantic mainstream. Each produced a slim shelf of novels distinguished by elegance, irony, and—detractors might add—limited scope. Whereas Austen limited herself to matters suitable to the notice of a lady, Peacock restricted himself yet more narrowly. Except for *Maid Marian* and *The Misfortunes of Elphin*, respectively set in the picturesque past of "Merrie England" and Arthurian Wales, Peacock's novels take place in an idyllic country-house world where conversation, varied by singing, dining, drinking, flirtation, and sightseeing, is the chief activity. Even so, in this Pavonian realm, the reader who is able to read the signs aright can find, as critic Marilyn Butler reveals, serious and well-grounded discussion of moral, political, aesthetic, economic, and scientific concerns.

The dense if oblique topicality of these conversations is something of an obstacle for the twentieth century reader. Another hurdle for the general public in any age is Peacock's learning: Only those who share Peacock's passion for the past, especially classical antiquity, can enjoy the novels' esoterica and allusions, and only readers nurtured in Greek and Latin (or possessing editions whose annotations compensate for such deficiency) can smile at the puns and scholarly jokes Peacock presents in the names and adventures of his characters. Writing for a few congenial spirits, Peacock attained in his own time the respect of Shelley, George Gordon, Lord Byron, and John Cam Hobhouse. He has retained the appreciative but limited audience Shelley's lines from *Letter to Maria Gisbourne* (1820) seem to prophesy: "his fine wit/ Makes such a wound, the knife is lost in it;/ A strain too learned for a shallow age,/ Too wise for selfish bigots."

Biography · Thomas Love Peacock was born at Weymouth in Dorset, England, in 1785. His father, Samuel, was a London merchant, his mother, Sarah, a woman of Devonshire. He attended a private school at Englefield Green until he was thirteen. After leaving school, he served for some time as a clerk at a mercantile house and as a private secretary. In his youth, Peacock found employment uncongenial, however, and his private resources, although insufficient to send him to a university, did preclude his having to work. Peacock used his leisure well. An apt and diligent student, he became a sound classicist through his independent reading. In 1812, Peacock met Percy Bysshe Shelley through the agency of a mutual friend, Thomas Hookham. For the next few years he was often a part of the Shelley circle. Closely involved in Shelley's tangled domestic affairs, Peacock attempted to be true to his friend, fair to the poet's wife, Harriet, and civil to Shelley's new love, Mary Godwin. When Shelley went abroad, Peacock corresponded with him and transacted business for him. When Shelley died, Peacock, along with Byron, was named executor of the estate.

In 1819, Peacock was appointed assistant to the examiner in the East India Office. The salary he derived from his position enabled him to marry Jane Gryffydh, a rector's daughter whom he had last seen in 1811, when he had been on a walking tour of Wales. The Peacock marriage was not a particularly happy one; the professional appointment proved rather more auspicious. In 1837, on the retirement of James Mill, Peacock became examiner at East India House. He capably held this important administrative post until his retirement in 1856.

The pleasures of Peacock's maturity were those he ascribes to various characters (most of them urbane clergymen) in his novels: good wine, good dinners, hours in the garden or in his study with the classics, rural walks from his house at Halliford in the Thames valley. One of the few new friends Peacock made during the latter half of his life was John Cam Hobhouse, Lord Broughton. Peacock's peaceful old age was saddened by the unhappiness of his favorite daughter, the talented Mary Ellen, who had imprudently married the novelist George Meredith, and by her death in 1861. Peacock died at Halliford in 1866.

Analysis · A writer with strong intelligence but weak invention is not likely to become a novelist. His talents would seem to be most serviceable elsewhere in the literary realm. Even so, the example of Peacock suggests that such a deficiency need not be fatal to a writer of fiction. True, his plots are often insignificant or implausible, and his characters tend to be sketches rather than rounded likenesses or, if three-dimensional, to have more opinions than emotions. His novels are nevertheless readable and re-readable, for he excels in anatomizing the follies, philosophies, and fashions that the age presents to his satirical eye. It is not enough for Peacock to make clear the inconsistencies and absurdities of pre-Reform Toryism, Byronic misanthropy, or the modern educational system: His talent for phrase-making ensures that even the bores and halfwits he creates spout golden epigrams.

Clear thinking and stylish writing are not the rarest of Peacock's gifts, though. Perhaps his distinctive excellence is his ability to embrace limitation without accepting diminution. He revels in ideas and delights in the good things of the world. A thoroughgoing classicist in his own views, he accurately understands most of the contemporary opinions and ideas he attacks (Samuel Taylor Coleridge's transcendentalism is a notable exception). He is opinionated without being ill humored. His erudition does not preclude strong practicality. The narrow range of emotions he articulates is the result of a positive rather than a negative quality, of brave stoicism rather than heartlessness. Although Peacock's novels are for the most part slender, they never seem the productions of a small mind.

Headlong Hall · *Headlong Hall,* Peacock's first novel, is far from being his finest piece, but it is a mature work in which the characteristic devices of Peacock's career are effectively, if not perfectly, deployed. One finds charming description of picturesque countryside, in this case Wales, where Peacock had happily traveled in 1809. One finds a rich rural lover of good conversation, Squire Headlong of the Hall, who, to gratify his taste, assembles a diverse set of wise and foolish talkers. Most important, one finds the talkers themselves.

In this novel, as in several of the later ones, Peacock's satire is general; his own perspective is not to be precisely identified with that of any one character. The principal way of grouping the speakers at Squire Headlong's symposium is to distinguish the philosophers, who genuinely seek to discover truth via Socratic dialogue, from the cranks, who find in conversation a chance to ride forth on their particular intellectual hobbyhorses, and who would rather lecture than learn. When Peacock wrote Headlong Hall in 1815, he was in daily contact with the Percy Bysshe Shelley circle, and the novel's three philosophers reason from stances Shelley, Peacock, and their friend Thomas Jefferson Hogg adopted in their intellectual discussions. Peacock's naming of the three characters indicates their respective positions. Foster the perfectabilian (φωστηρ, "one who guards a flame") articulates a position that Shelley sometimes took, that the human race is improving largely through technological advances. At the other pole is Escot the deteriorationist (εσ σκοτορ, "one looking on the dark side"), who takes the Rousseau-derived view that man has fallen from his pristine excellence largely because, as Shelley's friend J. F. Newton argued, he eats meat. Balancing these opposites is Jenkinson, the embracer of the status quo (αιερ εσ ιοωρ, "one who from equal measures can produce arguments on both sides"), who gives voice to Hogg's skepticism.

To fan the flames of intellectual discourse, Peacock provides an assortment of windy enthusiasts and eccentrics, none so finely drawn as later incarnations were to be, but none failing to amuse. The Reverend Mr. Gaster begins Peacock's series of gourmandizing clergymen; Panscope is his first and thinnest burlesque of Coleridge's transcendentalism. Marmaduke Milestone speaks for the Reptonian school of picturesque gardening, a taste Peacock deplored. The phrenologist Mr. Cranium leads off the series of freakish scientists that continues down through *Gryll Grange.* Representing literary enterprises, if not strictly speaking literature, are the poets Nightshade and Maclaurel, the reviewers Gall and Treacle, and Miss Philomela Poppyseed, a writer of feminine novels and one of the few stupid women in Peacock's gallery. Lest the fine arts be neglected, Peacock supplies Sir Patrick O'Prism, a painting dilettante, and Cornelius Chromatic, an amateur violinist.

The characters feast, drink, talk, sing. Having served their host's (and their author's) purposes, they are paired in the ordering dance of marriage, an inevitable conclusion according to the systems of both Foster and Escot, and an empirical state in which one suspects the two philosophers' theories will prove of precisely equal value.

Melincourt · Peacock's second and longest novel, *Melincourt*, is generally considered his weakest. At the time of its composition, Peacock's principal association was with Shelley, and in this novel Peacock drops the objectivity of the "laughing philosopher" and presents political views he shared with the poet, who was even then giving them poetic form in what was to be Shelley's *The Revolt of Islam* (1818). Melincourt sincerely satirizes the Tory government and, as Lord Byron's *The Vision of Judgment* (1822) would later do, former liberals such as the Lake Poets—Robert Southey, William Words-worth, and Coleridge (Feathernest, Paperstamp, and Mystic in the novel)—who had grown less critical of the establishment as their places in that order grew more comfortable. Certain episodes in *Melincourt* are memorable. The election at Onevote presents a marvelous empirical case for parliamentary reform, and the Anti-Saccha-rine Fête celebrates Peacock's belief that sugar, because its production permitted the West Indian slave trade to prosper, was a morally and politically abominable com-modity to be abjured by all true philanthropists "till it were sent them by freemen." For the most part, though, this sort of candor makes *Melincourt* shrill rather than forceful.

The romantic thread on which the beads of satiric incident are strung is likewise not among Peacock's strongest. The heroine of the piece and owner of its principal location is Anthelia Melincourt, "at the age of 21, mistress of herself and of ten thousand a year, and of a very ancient and venerable castle in one of the wildest valleys of Westmoreland." More than one critic has noticed that the assets mentioned and the rhetoric employed in this, *Melincourt's* opening passage, call to mind the famous first sentence of Jane Austen's *Emma*, published two years earlier in 1815. Unlike Austen's charming and self-deluded Miss Woodhouse, Miss Melincourt is an earnest and judicious lady, a fit match for Mr. Sylvan Forester, the second Peacock hero to embody Shelley's intellectual idealism.

These two young people, so obviously suited for each other, lose no time in discovering their mutual regard. The novel's complications and the lovers' tribula-tions must come from without: Anthelia is abducted to Alga Castle by the enamoured Lord Anophel Achthar. Having lost his bride-to-be, Forester, ostensibly seeking her, wanders about England's Lake District and calls on poets and reviewers at Main-chance Villa and Cimmerian Lodge. His dilatory pursuit gives Lord Anophel time to tire of waiting for Anthelia to yield to his repeated proposals. He threatens to compromise her, and, even though the lady is too strong-minded to think that his wickedness will be her disgrace, she is nevertheless grateful enough to be rescued from a test of her theory by Forester and his companion Sir Oran Hautton, who is barely prevented from administering "natural justice" by throwing Lord Anophel out the window.

The fierce, faithful, mute Sir Oran is, most readers agree, the book's chief delight, curious though it might seem for a speechless character to be the chief excellence in a book by a writer noted largely for his characters' conversations. In Sir Oran, who plays the flute, goes out in society, and gains a parliamentary seat, Peacock presents with only slight exaggerations a theory of the Scottish jurist Lord Monboddo that the orangutan is a "noble savage" distinguished from the rest of the human race only by its inability to speak. In the world of literature at least, Monboddo's argument may have more validity than readers might expect: A literary Darwin examining popular fiction might well be tempted to see in the still thriving breed of strong, silent, active heroes Sir Oran's not-too-distant descendants.

Nightmare Abbey · Peacock began writing his third novel, *Nightmare Abbey*, after Shelley and Mary Godwin departed England for Italy in March of 1818. The book is arguably his finest, certainly his best-focused and plotted, and easily his most controversial. In this novel, Peacock, one of the great English admirers of Aristophanes, lays himself open to the same sort of unfair criticisms that have been heaped on the Greek dramatist for his comedy *The Clouds* (423 B.C.E.). Just as Aristophanes was censured by various critics, from Plato on, for inaccurately and irresponsibly portraying Socrates, so Peacock has been condemned for faithlessness and poor taste by readers who consider *Nightmare Abbey* an unseemly depiction of one of the less commendable interludes in Shelley's life—his period of wanting to have Mary Godwin without giving up his wife Harriet.

There are indeed resemblances between Shelley and the novelist's protagonist Scythrop, part romantic idealist—part misanthrope, part would-be reformer. Marionetta O'Carroll, the sprightly coquettish cousin Scythrop professes to love, is like Harriet Shelley in spirit and appearance. Scythrop's other love, the heiress Celinda Toobad (known to him as Stella), is tall and raven-haired, the physical opposite of Mary Godwin, but very like Peacock's impression of that grave lady in her passion for philosophical speculation, political discussion, and transcendental romantic literature. Invention of detail was at no time Peacock's strong suit; he was obliged to borrow from real life.

Yet, despite having drawn certain details of his novel from Shelley's situation in 1814, Peacock was neither so tasteless nor so unkind as to write a book centering on his friend's romantic and domestic difficulties. The surest sign of Peacock's goodwill is Shelley's own admiration of the novel: "I am delighted with *Nightmare Abbey*," he wrote from Italy. "I think Scythrop a character admirably conceived and executed; and I know not how to praise sufficiently the lightness, chastity, and strength of the language of the whole." Rather than personalities, Peacock's targets were the dark gloom of modern literature, Byron's *Childe Harold's Pilgrimage* (1812-1818), and such other determinedly dismal works, and the black bile and blue devils introduced by this literature into the lives of its readers.

Nightmare Abbey is the only Peacock novel to take place at one scene only, namely the dreary and semidilapidated seat of Christopher Glowry, a gentleman "naturally of an atrabilarious temperament, and much troubled with those phantoms of indigestion which are commonly called *blue devils*." Disappointed in love and marriage, the gloomy squire of the Abbey surrounds himself with owls, ivy, water weeds, and servants with the most dismal names: Raven, Crow, Graves, Deathshead. His son Scythrop, a reader of gothic novels and transcendental philosophies, stalks the Abbey like a grand inquisitor. The young man is ruled by two passions: reforming the world by repairing the "crazy fabric of human nature" and drinking Madeira. These preoccupations alter materially when Mr. Glowry's sister and brother-in-law, their niece and ward Marionetta, and a host of other guests arrive for an extended taste of what hospitality the Abbey can afford. Among the houseguests are a particularly fine array of representative embodiments of morbid romanticism. The Honorable Mr. Listless, who spends whole days on a sofa, has perfected ennui. Mr. Flosky, who "plunged into the central opacity of Kantian metaphysics, and lay *perdu* several years in transcendental darkness, till the common daylight of common sense became intolerable to his eyes," is one of Peacock's more successful sketches of Coleridge. Mr. Toobad is a Manichaean Millenarian, the Byronic Mr. Cypress, a poet who, having quarreled with his wife, feels absolved from all duty and is about to set off on his travels.

Finely drawn though the gentlemen may be, as Marilyn Butler has noted in her treatment of *Nightmare Abbey*, Scythrop's two ladies divide the book between themselves. Scythrop's attraction to the volatile Marionetta, who playfully spurns him when he seems devoted and charms him when he seems distant, dominates the first half of the book, while his fascination for the mysterious and brilliant Stella, a creature of veils and conspiracies, overshadows lesser matters in the second half of the story. Scythrop can bring himself to dispense with neither lady: "I am doomed to be the victim of eternal disappointment," he laments in the tone of German high tragedy, "and I have no resource but a pistol." The two unrenounceable ladies, however, find it possible to renounce their suitor. Wishing Scythrop joy of Miss O'Carroll, Celinda/ Stella turns to the metaphysical Mr. Flosky. Wishing him all happiness with Miss Toobad, Marionetta engages herself to Mr. Listless. His disappointment validated, his misanthropy doubly confirmed, Scythrop thinks himself unlikely to make a figure in the world. His story ends not with a gunshot but with a sound more familiar in the Peacock world: "Bring some Madeira."

Peacock's next two novels, *Maid Marian* and *The Misfortunes of Elphin*, depart from the prevailing "country-house conversation" pattern. Both works are generally labeled "satirical romances," being set in the picturesque past but laying out oblique observations on present-day situations.

Maid Marian · The first of these romances is perhaps Peacock's most widely known story, primarily because it forms the basis for a popular operetta by J. R. Planché, *Maid Marian: Or, The Huntress of Arlingford* (1822). Peacock was sometimes considered to have borrowed portions of his novel from Sir Walter Scott's *Ivanhoe* (1819), but actually Scott and Peacock, who wrote most of his novel in 1818, shared their primary source: Joseph Ritson's *Robin Hood*, a collection of ancient poems, songs, and ballads about that hero. Like Scott's work, Peacock's novel is no plausible portrait of medieval life. Robin Hood is not a responsible steward of the wealth he commandeers; his superiority lies in being less hypocritical than his adversaries, the sheriff and Prince John. Friar Tuck is one in Peacock's long gallery of wine-loving clergymen; Maid Marian, whose swordsmanship and archery are commendable, and who decides in liberated fashion at the novel's end to retain her virginal title "though the appellation was then as much a misnomer as that of Little John," is one of Peacock's admirably independent heroines. The satiric object of the forest idyll? To mock the repressive and reactionary Holy Alliance, on which Byron, too, was then turning his sights in his *Don Juan* (1819-1824).

The Misfortunes of Elphin · As a perennial wandering woodsman, particularly in Windsor Forest, which had recently been enclosed, Peacock might have grown up with an interest in the Robin Hood material. His interest in the legendary past presented in *The Misfortunes of Elphin* dates to a more specific series of events. In 1820, Peacock married Jane Gryffydh, a young woman he had met on his travels in Wales ten years before, and her fluency in Welsh reawakened his interest in the Celtic legends of Elphin, Taliesin, and Arthur on which his story is based. Peacock's pastiche of Welsh myths is notable for its rousing songs and its depiction of the splendidly amoral inebriate Seithenyn. Its political satire is particularly effective. The crumbling of the ruinous seawall and castle administered by the drunken Seithenyn could be an apt allegory for any self-indulgent, backward-looking ruling class blind to imminent revolution and indifferent to public responsibility. The situation and the speeches of Seithenyn, however, superbly transmuted from those of the nineteenth century politican George Canning, are particularly relevant to an England on the brink of parliamentary reform.

Crotchet Castle · *Crotchet Castle*, written two years after *The Misfortunes of Elphin*, returns to the Pavonian mainstream. Here the mansion is a glorified villa; the owner, a rich and recently retired Scottish stockbroker; the target, progressive hypocrisy, represented in real life by Henry Brougham and in the novel by the "March of Mind." The novel divides into three parts. A house party at Crotchet Castle, carefully designed by its host to pit "the sentimental against the rational, the intuitive against the inductive, the ornamental against the useful, the intense against the tranquil, the romantic against the classical," is followed by a floating caravan proceeding up the Thames to the rural depths of Wales; the novel concludes with a Christmas gathering, more than a little Pickwickian, at the quasimedieval residence of Mr. Chainmail, a sturdy but sensitive anachronist patterned, as critic David Garnett has observed, after Sir Edward Strachey.

   This tale of past and present—that is, the past as it should have been and the future that the present shows all too much promise of becoming—sets Mr. Chainmail and the Reverend Dr. Folliot, one of Peacock's fiercer Tory clergymen, against the liberal utilitarians of the "March of Mind" school, preeminent among them one Mr. Mac-Quedy ("*Mac Q.E.D.*, son of a demonstration," as Peacock annotates his own pun). Two pairs of lovers require proper pairing as well. Mr. Chainmail, by story's end, overcomes his excessive regard for old names and blood and marries Susannah Touchandgo, a financier's daughter once engaged to the prospering speculator Crotchet, Jr. Having lost her fiancé when her father lost his fortune and decamped for America, Miss Touchandgo has withdrawn to a salubrious Welsh seclusion of music, country cream, fresh air, and exercise, in which charming situation Mr. Chainmail comes upon her.

   If old names must be foresworn, so must new money; in the romance dovetailed with the Chainmail-Touchandgo one, Lady Clarinda Bossnowl, generally acclaimed as the most delectable of Peacock's exceptionally pleasing heroines, breaks her engagement to young Crotchet and commits herself to the poor, pedigreed, and talented Captain Fitzchrome. Perhaps the best philosopher in the Crotchet Castle party, Lady Clarinda begins by playing at utilitarianism, intent on not giving her heart away when she can sell it. The journey from the stockbroker's villa to romantic Wales, however, gives her judgment time to concur with what her feelings long have suggested: that love in a cottage—and not even a *cottage ornée*—with the Captain is better than comfort at the Castle. Lady Clarinda's raillery, Folliot's prejudices, and Chainmail's enthusiasms make the novel's conversation particularly fine, and the climax, a spirited defense of Chainmail Hall against "Captain Swing" and that "coming race," the mob, is perhaps Peacock's most active.

Gryll Grange · Peacock, preoccupied with official duties and family concerns, did not write another novel for thirty years, but *Gryll Grange*, his last one, is of a vintage worth waiting for. Few readers would suspect that the author of this suave and mellow production was well acquainted with sorrow and disappointment. The satire here is less incisive and the development of character richer than in the earlier books—in part because the people portrayed have feelings as well as opinions, in part because Peacock's wit plays not on the characters but on the world outside Gryll Grange, the modern England of scientific advance, technological development, competitive examinations, and spiritualism—a society mocked by the Gryll Grange houseparty in their own satirical comedy "Aristophanes in London."

For the plot of *Gryll Grange,* Peacock harks back to the situation of *Melincourt.* Morgana, the niece and heiress of Gregory Gryll (the family, we learn, is descended from that Gryllus who alone among Ulysses' crewmen declined being released from the spell by which Circe has turned him into a pig), needs a fit husband who will take her name. Squire Gryll's friend the Reverend Dr. Opimian, a hearty man much like Peacock in his relish for "a good library, a good dinner, a pleasant garden, and rural walks," finds just such a suitor in Mr. Falconer, the new resident of a nearby tower significantly called the "Duke's Folly" by the neighborhood. Falconer, the last of Peacock's fictional projections of the young Shelley, is an idealistic recluse who lives a comfortable, scholarly life with seven beautiful sisters who manage his household and make his music. Once juxtaposed by the well-tried divine machine of a thunderstorm, Miss Gryll and Falconer are mutually attracted: The subsequent story in large measure centers on the hero's vacillations. Should he renounce his monastic retreat and the seven maidens who have been his companions since childhood, or should he forswear the social world so fetchingly represented by Gryll Grange and the one lady he loves?

Also staying at the Grange are Lord Curryfin, a lively, inventive, and engagingly ridiculous fellow, and the serenely beautiful Miss Niphet. Their presence further complicates the romantic dilemma. Lord Curryfin, at first drawn to Miss Gryll, finds himself increasingly enamoured of the other charmer and knows not where to offer his heart and title. Miss Niphet, a good friend to Morgana, loves the young lord but hesitates to bag a bird on whom she believes her friend's sights to be trained. Miss Gryll, who knows she loves Falconer but doubts whether she can get him, believes she can get Lord Curryfin but wonders whether she could truly love him. This tangled web of love, honor, and jealousy, so mild that it never becomes a vise, is straightened out by an event yet more providential than the convenient thunderstorm: the appearance and acceptance of seven stalwart rustics who want to marry the maidens of the tower and who thereby free Falconer from his reservations. The novel ends with all the lovers properly betrothed, a multiple wedding, and, as is fitting in the Peacock world, a vinuous salute. Addressing the wedding party, Dr. Opimian concludes, "Let all the corks, when I give the signal, be discharged simultaneously; and we will receive it as a peal of Bacchic ordnance, in honor of the Power of the Joyful Event, whom we may assume to be presiding on this auspicious occasion."

Peter W. Graham

Other major works

POETRY: *The Monks of St. Mark,* 1804; *Palmyra and Other Poems,* 1806; *The Genius of the Thames,* 1810; *The Philosophy of Melancholy,* 1812; *Sir Proteus: A Satirical Ballad,* 1814; *Rhododaphne,* 1818; *Paper Money Lyrics,* 1837.

NONFICTION: *The Four Ages of Poetry,* 1820; *Memoirs of Percy Bysshe Shelley,* 1858-1862.

Bibliography

Burns, Bryan. *The Novels of Thomas Love Peacock.* London: Croom Helm, 1985. Focuses on Peacock's novels, providing a close reading and analysis for each. The introduction traces his intellectual debts, especially to classical authors. The novels are read with a primarily textual approach, discussing language, characterization, syntax, and irony and suggesting that they are "dialectical" in nature. Burns does not offer much interpretation of Peacock's novels but does a good job of looking at their style, emphasizing their similarities but also insisting on their diversity. The bibliography is selective but includes important works, and the index is thorough.

Butler, Marilyn. *Peacock Displayed: A Satirist in His Context.* London: Routledge & Kegan Paul, 1979. A first-rate study of Peacock which focuses not only on him as an individual but also on the society in which he lived and worked. Discusses the relationship between Peacock and Percy Bysshe Shelley, contending that they derived mutual intellectual benefit from their friendship which is revealed in their work. Butler emphasizes Peacock's satiric abilities, attempting to explain that he does not debunk everything–a common charge against him–but instead is highly skeptical of systems. Includes a detailed reading of each of his major novels, plus an examination of Peacock as a critic. The introduction sets him in his literary, social, and biographical context.

Dawson, Carl. *His Fine Wit: A Study of Thomas Love Peacock.* Berkeley: University of California Press, 1970. Discusses most of Peacock's work in detail, including his poetry, essays, and music criticism. Does a very good job with his works and provides an alternative view, but is somewhat outdated. The chapter on Peacock's *The Four Ages of Poetry* provides illuminating background on the book and also on Percy Bysshe Shelley's response to it, which culminated in his famous *A Defense of Poetry.* Even so, Dawson does not treat Peacock as a minor writer or as a disciple of Shelley, as many critics do; in fact, he paints Shelley as something of a hypocrite. The index and chronology are not strong, and there is no bibliography; the book does include notes which could serve as a substitute.

McKay, Margaret. *Peacock's Progress: Aspects of Artistic Development in the Novels of Thomas Love Peacock.* Stockholm: Almqvist & Wiksell, 1992. Chapters on Peacock's poems and plays as well as on his novels. Peacock's major characters also receive considerable discussion. McKay provides good background information on the literary figures and movements Peacock satirized. Includes extensive bibliography.

Mulvihill, James. *Thomas Love Peacock.* Boston: Twayne, 1987. An excellent short sourcebook on Peacock, providing biographical background and sound context for each of his major works from his poetry to his novels (*Headlong Hall, Melincourt, Nightmare Abbey, Crotchet Castle, Gryll Grange, Maid Marian, The Misfortunes of Elphin*), as well as his essays and reviews. Attempts to place each work into its appropriate literary and historical background and provide a detailed, interesting, although fairly standard reading. A good starting place for work on Peacock because of its brevity. The bibliography and good chronology are helpful, as Peacock is such a little noticed author.

Prance, Claude A. *The Characters in the Novels of Thomas Love Peacock (1785-1866): With Bibliographical Lists.* Lewiston, N.Y.: E. Mellen Press, 1992. An excellent dictionary of characters in Peacock's works. Indispensable for the student of Peacock.

Tomkinson, Neil. *The Christian Faith and Practice of Samuel Johnson, Thomas De Quincey, and Thomas Love Peacock.* Lewiston, N.Y.: E. Mellen Press, 1992. Examines the religious literature of Peacock, Johnson, and De Quincey. Includes bibliographical references and an index.

Anthony Powell

Born: London, England; December 21, 1905
Died: Frome, Somerset, England; March 28, 2000

Principal long fiction · *Afternoon Men*, 1931; *Venusberg*, 1932; *From a View to a Death*, 1933; *Agents and Patients*, 1936; *What's Become of Waring*, 1939; *A Question of Upbringing*, 1951; *A Buyer's Market*, 1952; *The Acceptance World*, 1955; *At Lady Molly's*, 1957; *Casanova's Chinese Restaurant*, 1960; *The Kindly Ones*, 1962; *The Valley of Bones*, 1964; *The Soldier's Art*, 1966; *The Military Philosophers*, 1968; *Books Do Furnish a Room*, 1971; *Temporary Kings*, 1973; *Hearing Secret Harmonies*, 1975 (previous 12 titles known as *A Dance to the Music of Time*); *O, How the Wheel Becomes It!*, 1983; *The Fisher King*, 1986.

Other literary forms · Although Anthony Powell produced much writing other than his long fiction, he was primarily a novelist. Powell was an editor, an author of prefaces, a prolific book reviewer, and a screenwriter. While his miscellaneous writing includes light verse and fictional sketches, the stories, such as the ironic sequels to Charles Dickens's *A Christmas Carol* (1843) and D. H. Lawrence's *Lady Chatterley's Lover* (1928), are facile parodies, amusing but of limited interest. His skill in characterization and the fine art of gossip, basic to his major work, *A Dance to the Music of Time*, helps explain Powell's empathy with a seventeenth century expert in these matters, John Aubrey, author of *Brief Lives* (1813). Powell edited Aubrey's works and wrote a biographical study, *John Aubrey and His Friends* (1948, 1963).

Powell also wrote two plays, *The Garden God* and *The Rest I'll Whistle* (published together in 1971). These comedies of manners, while containing crisp dialogue and entertaining dramatic scenes, do not suggest that Powell is a dramatist *manqué*. Finally, he wrote his memoirs, in four volumes under the general title *To Keep the Ball Rolling* (1976, 1978, 1980, 1982). These books provide a valuable account of experiences that Powell transmuted into fiction; they also present vivid characterizations of many of Powell's contemporaries, including Constant Lambert, the Sitwells, Evelyn Waugh, Cyril Connolly, and George Orwell. In 1990, Powell published a substantial selection of his essays and reviews, *Miscellaneous Verdicts: Writings on Writers, 1946-1989*, followed in 1991 by a second collection, *Under Review: Further Writings on Writers 1946-1989*. Three volumes of Powell's journals were also published between 1995 and 1997.

Achievements · Anthony Powell's career as a novelist started with five novels published in the 1930's. These books had generally favorable reviews and reasonable sales; they established Powell's reputation as a skilled and successful, if perhaps minor, novelist. His reputation grew steadily with his twelve-volume sequence *A Dance to the Music of Time*, begun after World War II and completed in 1975, and by the 1980's he was generally recognized as one of the major English writers of the century. He is frequently compared to Marcel Proust, although, as Evelyn Waugh pointed out, Powell's *roman-fleuve* is more realistic and much funnier.

A Dance to the Music of Time is indeed funny. Becoming more somber in tone as it proceeds, incorporating numerous tragic events, never lacking a certain fundamental

seriousness, the series nevertheless remains comic, a comedy in more aspects than
Honoré de Balzac's meaning of a broad social portrait. The series does present a
picture of various segments of English society–essentially the privileged segments–
during the empire's decline since World War I. It has, thus, a certain limited value as
sociological documentation–as what W. D. Quesenbery termed an "anatomy of
decay"–but this is at best a secondary aspect. Primarily as excellent entertainment,
the novels are appreciated by a wide range of readers. One may enjoy, in each of the
individual novels, the wit, especially in dialogue, the characterization, and incident.
In the series as a whole, there is the additional pleasure of observing the complex
interactions of the characters as they appear, disappear, and reappear, forming
unexpected patterns in the "dance," the whole bound together, if somewhat loosely,
by theme.

From the first volume of the sequence, *A Question of Upbringing*, the work was
well-received, although it was, of course, only as subsequent volumes appeared that
readers, in increasing numbers, came to appreciate the complex interconnections of
the separate books. Powell's wit and style were commended, as was his characterization, expecially the creation, in Kenneth Widmerpool, of one of the great comic
villains in all of English literature. It was the narrative structure, however, that
eventually produced the most critical interest.

Although the series moves chronologically forward, through the half century from
1921 to 1971, it is presented through the memory of the narrator, Nicholas Jenkins,
who employs flashback and foreshadowing in a complex manner, recalling, for
example, in the sixth book, his childhood in 1914. Such a structure suggests Proust's
Á la recherche du temps perdu (1913-1927; *Remembrance of Things Past*, 1922-1931). The

comparison is relevant, and both
Powell and his protagonist, Nick
Jenkins, admire the French writer.
Powell's narrator is not similar to
Proust's, however; Nick's mind op-
erates differently. In addition, Henri
Bergson's theory of time, so im-
portant to Proust, has limited rele-
vance to Powell's work.

If Powell is not an English Proust,
comparisons with other novel sequences make even clearer the
unique quality of *A Dance to the
Music of Time*. In its focus upon the
individuality of character, it is dia-
metrically opposed, for example,
to "unanimism," the ideology of
collective experience which informs Jules Romains's *roman-fleuve
Les Hommes de bonne volonté* (1932-
1947). One of the few English
novel sequences of comparable
length, C. P. Snow's *Strangers and
Brothers* (1940-1970), employs a
structure quite different from Pow-

Courtesy D.C. Public Library

ell's. The eleven volumes of Snow's work shift between those that focus on the life of the central figure, Lewis Eliot, and those that do not, whereas Nick Jenkins remains in each book simultaneously a participant in, and an observer of, the "dance" that the series chronicles.

Powell's achievement, springing from an interest in character, expressed through matchless style, and distinctly structured, has then, as does any great work of art, a *sui generis* excellence. It won Powell a devoted and varied audience; the British Broadcasting Corporation produced the series; *A Dance to the Music of Time*'s translations include a Bulgarian version. A share of worldly honors, such as an honorary fellowship in the Modern Language Association of America and an honorary degree from Oxford, have come to Powell. Perhaps more significantly, he has earned the respect of fellow writers, those his own age and those younger, those who share his conservative beliefs and those who do not. In sincere flattery, at least one other writer, the major Canadian novelist Hugh Hood, is writing his own series of novels in admiring emulation of Powell's work.

Biography · Anthony Dymoke Powell (pronounced "Antony Diemoke Pole") was born December 21, 1905, in London, England. His mother was the daughter of a barrister; his father, himself the son of a colonel, was a lieutenant in the army who was to win decoration in World War I and retire as a lieutenant colonel. Powell, his parents' only child, spent his early years in a military environment. He was to have a continuing respect for the service; General Conyers, in *A Dance to the Music of Time*, is only one of a number of sympathetically portrayed army officers in Powell's fiction.

As a member of a well-to-do family, Powell had an upper-class education and acquired the values of his class. He entered Eton in 1918, where he made friends, such as Hubert Duggan, a source for Stringham, who were to contribute to his subsequent characterizations. When, in 1923, Powell matriculated at Balliol College, Oxford, he continued to collect the friends and the personal impressions that were to serve him well when he later described Nick Jenkins's experiences. Powell's memoirs, *To Keep the Ball Rolling*, written after *A Dance to the Music of Time*, are invaluable in dealing with the complex issue of the relation between fiction and "real life," but it may be said that Powell is not always entirely forthcoming, and that many of his fictional characters are based, often rather closely, upon particular prototypes.

While at Oxford, Powell made various vacation trips to the Continent; in 1924, he traveled to Finland, where his father was stationed. Later, he drew upon this travel in his early novel *Venusberg*. Powell graduated from Oxford in 1926 and went to work for the publishing firm of Duckworth, in London. There, Powell lived the quasi-bohemian life that is described in *A Buyer's Market* and subsequent volumes in *A Dance to the Music of Time*, and which is also reflected in his five prewar novels. He spent much time in the company of painters and musicians, meeting, among them, the composer Constant Lambert, who was to become a lifelong friend and the prototype for Hugh Moreland in Powell's series.

On December 3, 1934, Powell married Lady Violet Pakenham; they were to have two sons, Tristam and John. With his marriage, Powell acquired a large set of interesting in-laws; collectively, they were to contribute something to his fictional portrait of the Tollands; his brother-in-law Frank Pakenham, the seventh Earl of Longford, was to serve as a major source for the character Kenneth Widmerpool.

After his wedding, Powell left Duckworth's, and, in 1936, worked as a scriptwriter for Warner Bros. in London. There he met Thomas Phipps, the original of Chips

Lovell. In 1937, he went via the Panama Canal to Hollywood, California, in search of a scriptwriting job. Although the job did not work out, before returning, the Powells enjoyed an interesting interlude that included a meeting with F. Scott Fitzgerald. Upon his return to London, Powell engaged in journalism and wrote his fifth novel, *What's Become of Waring*. As World War II began, Powell, in 1939, was commissioned a lieutenant in the Welsh Regiment.

His war experiences are fairly accurately portrayed in the military trilogy, the third "movement" of the four in *A Dance to the Music of Time*. Powell, like Nick Jenkins, served first in a line regiment in Northern Ireland; he was transferred, in 1941, to Army Intelligence, worked as a liaison officer with Allied forces, served in France and Belgium, and gained the rank of major.

Just as Nick, after leaving the army at the end of the war, worked on a study of Robert Burton, so did Powell engage in historical research on John Aubrey, publishing his study in 1948, and an edited collection of Aubrey's work the next year. With Aubrey "finally out of the way," as Powell writes, he turned again to novel-writing, and began with *A Question of Upbringing*, his *roman-fleuve*. The novels in the series appeared at fairly regular intervals, averaging one every two years from 1951 until 1975. During these years, Powell continued his career in journalism, contributing sketches, articles, and reviews to *Punch*, the London *Daily Telegraph*, and other periodicals. In 1956, he was made a C.B.E; in 1961 he lectured in America at Dartmouth College, Amherst College, and Cornell University. He was appointed a trustee of the National Portrait Gallery in 1962. His plays, *The Garden God* and *The Rest I'll Whistle*, were published together in 1971, the same year in which the University of Sussex awarded him the honorary degree.

During his outwardly quiet postwar years, Powell continued to enjoy and expand his circle of friends, thereby finding some additional prototypes for the characters introduced in the later volumes of his series. The writer Julian Maclaren-Ross, the prototype of X. Trapnel, is a notable example.

Upon completing *A Dance to the Music of Time*, Powell began his memoirs, publishing *Infants of the Spring* in 1976, followed, at two-year intervals, by *Messengers of Day*, *Faces in My Time*, and *The Strangers All Are Gone*. In 1983, a year after the appearance of the final volume of his memoirs, Powell published a short novel or novella, *O, How the Wheel Becomes It!*, a satirical *jeu d'esprit*, his first work of fiction since the completion of *A Dance to the Music of Time*. This was followed in 1986 by *The Fisher King*, a full-length novel published to excellent reviews. During most of the period of his major work, Powell and his wife lived at Somerset. In the 1980's Powell continued to receive honors for writing, including a D.Litt. from Oxford in 1980.

Anthony Powell was one of the major figures of British letters after the 1920's and 1930's, and by the late 1990's he was the last surviving member of the so-called Brideshead generation, as described by Waugh. While he was a student at Eton, perhaps England's most prestigious public school, Powell's contemporaries included Harold Acton, Cyril Connolly, and George Orwell. At Oxford University he was a colleague of Waugh, Peter Quennell, and Maurice Bowra. He died in Somerset on March 28, 2000.

Analysis · Of the many pleasures and rewards offered by Anthony Powell's novels, none surpasses that to be found in coming to know, and continually being surprised by what happens to, a variety of fascinating characters. For Powell, an interest in character is primary. This can be seen in his absorption in the biographies sketched by John Aubrey, in the series of verbal portraits which dominate *To Keep the Ball Rolling*, and in his statement that a concern for character was central in his beginning *A Dance to the Music of Time*.

A Dance to the Music of Time · Successful fiction, though, involves more than the presentation of a series of characters, however intriguing. When characterization is conveyed with wit, in both dialogue and description, when the style becomes a pleasure in itself, as it does in Powell's work, one has enough ingredients to produce writing worth reading, but not enough for a novel, certainly not for a novel of the scope and stature of *A Dance to the Music of Time*. Such a novel, like any successful work of art, must satisfy the aesthetic requirement of unity—a sense of structure and order must be conveyed.

Although not the sole ingredient upon which a unified structure depends, character does help provide this sense of balance. For example, a degree of unity is achieved by having a single narrator, Nicholas Jenkins. Yet, *A Dance to the Music of Time* is not really the story of Nick Jenkins, just as it is not essentially the story of Kenneth Widmerpool, important as both these characters are. Although himself a participant in the "dance," Nick basically observes and reports; he does not give structure to the events that he relates. No persona, only Powell himself, can do this.

Many writers, certainly, achieve structure through plot, which may be the soul of fiction as Aristotle thought it was of drama. For Powell, however, the demands normally implied by "plot" run counter to his fundamental sense of time's complex mutability; to give his work a definite beginning, middle, and end, with action rising to and falling from a specific climax, would be justified neither by his sense of reality nor by his artistic intentions.

This is not to say that conscious arrangement of incident is not present in *A Dance to the Music of Time*. On the contrary, because the author has exercised intelligent concern for such arrangement, continual surprises are enjoyed in a first reading, and anticipation of the irony of coming events gives a special pleasure to rereading the series. It would be yielding too readily to the seductive appeal of paradox, however, to claim that it is a crafted sense of the random which gives basic structure to *A Dance to the Music of Time*—that its order lies in its apparent lack of order.

If not to be found primarily in character or plot, what is the key to the structure of the dance? Unwilling, with reason, to accept the idea that it *has* no clear structure, that it is, even if cut from a loaf made of remarkably milled flour, essentially "a slice of life," critics have proposed a variety of answers.

The title of the series, as Powell has explained, derives from an allegorical painting in the Wallace Collection in London, Nicholas Poussin's *A Dance to the Music of Time*. Comparisons between the painting and the novel may be ingeniously extended, but it seems improbable that they were extensively worked out by Powell as he began a series which, he writes in *Faces in My Time*, would consist of a number of volumes, "just how many could not be decided at the outset." It would appear more probable that the Poussin painting, expressing the French artist's sense of the permutations time produces in human life, while an important analogue to Powell's intention in the series, was only one of a number of sources of the work's pattern. Another source might have been Thomas Nashe's *Summer's Last Will and Testament* (1592), a masque organized around the four seasons, contrasting the arts and the utilitarian spirit, and involving a sophisticated, semidetached "presenter"; it was the basis of a musical composition by Powell's close friend Constant Lambert.

Other structural keys have been proposed, including the importance of mysticism (the Dr. Trelawney, Mrs. Erdleigh aspect) and the signs of the zodiac. There would seem to be some validity in most of these interpretations, but the attempt to see any one as a single key to the series appears reductionist, in the sense that a strict Freudian or Marxist reading of William Shakespeare is too limiting. Insofar as the pattern of the dance can be extrapolated from the work itself, most critics have agreed that it must be seen as a reflection of theme.

Of the many thematic strands, that which is central appears to be the conflict between power and art, or imagination and will. Jenkins himself suggests this at more than one point in the series. From the perspective of this conflict, in which Widmerpool, the extreme example of the self-centered power seeker, is thematically contrasted to Hugh Moreland the musician, and later to X. Trapnel the writer, the characters and their actions fall into a meaningful, if somewhat shadowy, pattern. The pattern is hardly simple, though; few characters are purely villainous or heroic; some artists seek power; some professional soldiers and businessmen are artistic and imaginative; both victories and defeats tend to be temporary.

Furthermore, the sexual designs woven in the "dance" complicate a bipolar view of theme. Sexual attraction, or love, in the novel usually involves both an imaginative appreciation of a perceived beauty in the desired partner, and some attempt to impose one's will upon another. Thus, with vagaries of desire, thematic antitheses and syntheses may fluctuate within individual characters. It is clear, however, that when Matilda Wilson goes from the artist Moreland to the industrialist Sir Magnus Donners, or Pamela Flitton leaves Widmerpool for the novelist X. Trapnel, a thematic point is made. (Indeed, the women in the series, generally less convincingly presented than the men, often seem to serve as scoring markers in the thematic game.)

That this thematic conflict, while it should not be simplistically defined, was essential to Powell's concept of the work's structure is shown additionally by the way prototypes were transmuted into fictional characters. Frank Pakenham, for example, unlike his fictional "counterpart" Widmerpool, not only would seem to have a number of virtues, but also has enjoyed a long and happy marriage, blessed by eight children. Clearly, the structure of the series requires that such satisfaction be denied its thematic villain.

A suggestion, then, may be made as to the probable way Powell proceeded in constructing his series. He apparently started with a novelist's interest in certain people that he knew, those he felt would be worth portraying. Then, to create order in his work, he fitted these people's fictional representatives into thematic patterns, changing reality as needed to accomplish this patterning. Using the thematically identified characters, he then, at a lower order of priority, considered and manipulated the plot, using plot itself to demonstrate another major theme, that of "mutability." The result was a uniquely constructed work of art.

Afternoon Men · Before beginning his major work, Powell wrote five novels; a case can be made for their being excellent works in their own right. Had Powell not gone on to write his *roman-fleuve*, they may have gained him a certain lasting recognition. As it is, inevitably they are regarded primarily as preparation for his masterpiece. The use of the "detached" narrator, coincidence in plot, ironic style, clipped dialogue, the theme of power, art, and love—all these attributes of *A Dance to the Music of Time* are anticipated in the early novels. *Afternoon Men*, picturing a London social scene the young Powell knew well, is the first of the five early novels. Powell has described it as "something of an urban pastoral . . . depicting the theme of unavailing love," with not much plot in the conventional sense. He sees the design of this first novel to be "not without resemblance to the initial framework" of the sequence. Although the protagonist, William Atwater, is not the narrator—the story is told mainly from his point of view, with the author occasionally intruding in his own voice—he may be compared, in his wit and detached forbearance, to Nicholas Jenkins. It is essentially in its ironic style, however, especially in the dialogue, that *Afternoon Men* anticipates the later series.

Venusberg and From a View to a Death · *Venusberg*, Powell's second novel, also has a protagonist, Lushington, who is comparable to Nick Jenkins. Flashback, a technique later significant to the series, is employed in this novel's construction, and the theme of love is extended to include adultery, while power and clairvoyance, topics prominent in *A Dance to the Music of Time*, are introduced. Powell's next novel, *From a View to a Death*, dealing with the interrelated themes of art, love, and power, emphasizes the latter. Arthur Zouch, a painter and womanizer, uses art and love in his search for the power he believes is his by right of his being an *Übermensch*. Fittingly, for one who not only debases the gift of imagination but is also a would-be social climber, he is defeated by a member of the country gentry. Technically, the book is interesting in that Powell experiments with a shifting point of view.

Agents and Patients · Art, sex, and power—specifically power derived from money—are the subjects that provide structure in *Agents and Patients*. In this novel, each of two confidence men, Maltravers and Chipchase, attempts to fleece a naïve young man, Blore Smith, Maltravers by playing upon Smith's sexual innocence, Chipchase by playing upon his artistic innocence. As the title, drawn from John Wesley, suggests, the issue of free will and determinism, significant in a less direct way in *A Dance to the Music of Time*, is an underlying theme. Excellent as it is as satiric comedy, *Agents and Patients* puts such an emphasis upon plot and theme that the characterization, usually Powell's strongest suit, tends somewhat toward caricature.

What's Become of Waring · *What's Become of Waring*, Powell's last novel before the war, is perhaps a less impressive achievement than the four that preceded it. It is, however, close to *A Dance to the Music of Time* in more than chronology. Although it has a carefully worked out, conventional plot, Powell still manages, as James Tucker observes, to "slip out of it and pursue his concern for people." In this work, a first-person narrator is employed. He is a publisher's reader; the work draws upon Powell's experience at Duckworth's. Never named, the narrator, in his overall attitude and as a partial alter ego for Powell, resembles Nicholas Jenkins. Again, the mystical element, later present in the series, is introduced through seances. Significantly, given the thematic center of *A Dance to the Music of Time*, *What's Become of Waring* ends with the narrator, as he drifts off to sleep, free-associating on the idea of power.

A Question of Upbringing · That Powell, after his lengthy hiatus from novel writing, returned to the idea of the quest for power is clear even from the first of the three volumes that constitute "Spring," the initial movement of his sequence. *A Question of Upbringing* introduces, at the very start, the series' most important character, Widmerpool, and it is clear that even as a schoolboy he is determined to dominate.

The early introduction of the major themes is an important aid to unity, for the start of a long series poses particular problems for its author. As Powell suggests in *Faces in My Time*, early volumes, in preparation for future ones, must introduce undeveloped characters and potential situations; additionally, some characters and situations, in view of their subsequent importance, must be overemphasized. These requirements may tend to confuse the reader, unless patterns are perceived.

A Question of Upbringing, which covers Nick's youth at public school and university, introduces an important pattern of repetition of related incidents by having Nick meet his Uncle Giles at both the beginning and the end of the volume. Another recurring structural device, the alternation of scenes described in dramatic detail with linking sections provided by Nick's subjective impressions, is present, as are the patterning devices of allusion and symbolism. The series begins with a scene of workmen gathered around a fire, repeated at the conclusion of the sequence, twelve volumes later, and mentions the Poussin painting which provides the title for the whole sequence. References to paintings are important throughout the series, including the Tiepolo ceiling in *Temporary Kings* and the oft-mentioned Modigliani drawing which is rescued in the final volume.

A Buyer's Market · Although the themes of love and art (which, along with the interrelated theme of power, dominate the series) are present in the first volume, they are more prominent in the second, *A Buyer's Market*. In this book, dominated by the social life of parties and dances which Nick, down from the university, enjoys, not only do sexual activities become important to Nick (a late bloomer as compared to his friends Templer and Stringham), but also the theme of the quest for power is extended to include politics. The radical young woman, Gypsy Jones (with whom Nick apparently loses his virginity), is utilized in one of Powell's recurring attacks upon the political Left, as well as to serve as an object of frustrated lust for Widmerpool, whose sex life is to be, throughout the series, eccentric and unsatisfactory.

The Acceptance World · *The Acceptance World*, the third volume in this movement, begins with another meeting between Nick and his Uncle Giles, who is now associated with Mrs. Erdleigh, a clairvoyant. She plays a major role in the dramatization of the subtheme of mysticism. Mysticism in the series, as seen later in Dr. Trelawney, and finally in Scorpio Murtlock, is related to an attempt to escape from what Mrs. Erdleigh calls the "puny fingers of Time" and gain power. Power in *The Acceptance World*, though, is considered more in political terms; there is an extension of the political satire against the Left, especially through Quiggin (whose character owes something to Cyril Connolly's), a university friend of Jenkins who moves in left-wing intellectual circles.

The volume's love interest involves Nick in a serious affair with Jean Templer, a school friend's sister. Much later in the series, in *The Military Philosophers*, Nick realizes that Jean, who breaks off the affair, really is attracted to money and power; she ultimately marries a Colonel Flores, who becomes a Latin American dictator. As Nick reflects in the first volume, "being in love is a complicated matter"; staying in love is even more so. The balance of thematic opposites, necessary to love, is seldom maintained. Nick is to be virtually unique in the series by virtue of his lasting, successful marriage, but the reader is given little direct insight into the secret of his success.

At Lady Molly's · Nick's courtship and engagement are described in the first volume of the second movement, "Summer." This volume is entitled *At Lady Molly's*; Lady

Molly Jeavons is a fictional amalgam of actual people including Rosa Lewis, the famous proprietor of the Cavendish Hotel, and Lady Astor, celebrated mistress of the magnificent country mansion, Cliveden, the prototype of the novel's Dogdene. Lady Molly, whose easygoing hospitality attracts a variety of guests, is the aunt of Chips Lovell (a character based on Thomas Phipps), who works with Nick as a scriptwriter for films. Powell here, as throughout the series, introduces new characters, thereby continually revivifying his novel, personifying its themes with variety, and causing the reader to wonder who, as well as what, is coming next. The actions of the two most permanent characters, Nick and Widmerpool, form the core of the volume; Nick's developing and successful love for Isobel Tolland is contrasted with the debacle that occurs when Widmerpool attempts a premarital seduction of his fiancé, Mildred Haycock.

Casanova's Chinese Restaurant · Love and marriage are even more central to the next book, *Casanova's Chinese Restaurant*, which introduces and focuses upon one of the series' most important and attractively realized characters, the composer Hugh Moreland, who becomes one of Nick's closest friends, just as Moreland's real-life prototype, Constant Lambert, became very important to Powell. Moreland is, thematically, *the* artist. As such, he is Widmerpool's antithesis, even though the two have too little in common to be antagonists other than thematically, the few occasions when they encounter each other are singularly, but not surprisingly, undramatic. One critic has suggested that even their names, Widmerpool's suggesting wetness, and Moreland's the opposite, indicate their antithesis. (Powell's names, as most readers will have noticed, are frequently suggestive and apt, as well as sometimes amusing—consider, for example, the name of the sexually experienced woman whom Widmerpool so decidedly fails to satisfy, Mrs. Haycock.)

A more significant difference between Moreland and Widmerpool is in their way of talking. Moreland produces very witty and pleasurable conversation; Widmerpool is given to pompous pronouncements that often entertain the reader by their unconscious self-satire. Like Widmerpool, however, although quite differently and for different reasons, Moreland has trouble with his love life; interconnections of art and love form much of the subject matter of the volumes in this movement.

The Kindly Ones · Other perspectives on love are introduced in *The Kindly Ones*, the last volume of "Summer," in which Widmerpool temporarily fades into the background, until the last chapter. The work begins with a flashback to Nick's childhood in 1914, thereby relating World War I to the approach of World War II in 1938, the time to which the book returns. The chronology is particularly complicated in this volume, and coincidence, always a feature of the series' plotting, is pushed to its limits when Nick, having gone to the seaside hotel where his Uncle Giles has died, meets, along with others from his past, Bob Duport, the former husband of Nick's past lover, Jean. The fact that for many readers, the complex structure of *The Kindly Ones* is unobtrusively successful, provides some measure of Powell's legerdemain.

At the end of *The Kindly Ones*, Nick has arranged for his commission in the army; the third movement, "Autumn," carries him though World War II. The reader learns from the autobiographical *Faces in My Time* that Nick's army experiences closely parallel Powell's own. Nick's service is distinguished, but the focus is more upon the tedium of war than its heroism.

In treating this often tedious, but different world of the service, Powell faced technical problems. He had to maintain the structure of his series within an entirely new environment. New characters, some from a social background that the novel had previously ignored, had to be used in a manner in accordance with the controlling themes. Furthermore, the style had to make some adaptation to the grim subject matter. Powell was not going to emphasize the comic elements of war, even though they are not ignored. The basic solution to these problems was to alternate the army scenes with those occurring when Nick is on leave. Thereby, the reader is able to experience the new, while still maintaining an interest in the old characters and themes.

The Valley of Bones · The first volume of the movement, *The Valley of Bones*, introduces, among many new characters, a particularly significant one, Captain Gwatkin. Gwatkin, while no artist–he had worked in a local Welsh bank–is a man of imagination, a sort of Miniver Cheevy actually in armor. He has romantic ambitions to be a perfect soldier, ambitions doomed to failure in his encounters with the men of power who are his superiors. Although he is eventually relieved of his command, Gwatkin finds some consolation in love, only to lose it when he learns of the infidelity of his beloved barmaid Maureen. Between these army scenes, Nick, while on leave, observes the continued amatory maneuvers of his friends and relations. The book ends with the dramatic appearance of Widmerpool as an influential major.

The Soldier's Art · In the next volume, *The Soldier's Art*, Nick is working as Widmerpool's junior assistant, in a position to observe his superior's continuing struggle for power, transferred from civilian to military life. Widmerpool hovers upon the verge of disaster, but at the end of the book his career is saved. Previously, he had failed to assist an old school fellow of his and Nick's, Stringham, now reduced to being an enlisted man working in the officers' mess, subsequently to die in a Japanese prisoner-of-war camp. Meanwhile, personal entanglements continue to form new patterns, while some of the characters, including Chips Lovell and Lady Molly, are killed in a bombing raid.

The Military Philosophers · The final volume of the movement, *The Military Philosophers*, finds Nick in the war office, working on liaison with Allied troops. This book, stylistically notable for its increased use of allusion, presents a number of the real personnel with whom Powell worked, little changed in their fictional guises. It is, however, an imagined character, or at least one for whom no prototype has been established, who reappears at this point, having been briefly introduced earlier as a young girl, subsequently to be a major figure. Pamela Flitton is, like Widmerpool, Stringham, Moreland, and Trapnel, one of the series' most memorable creations. She is a kind of ubiquitous nemesis, capable of bringing down the men of both art and power. Outstanding even in a cast of remarkably unusual and individual characters, she is made by Powell larger than life and yet believable, beautiful and yet repulsive, contemptible and yet capable of arousing the reader's sympathies. Although not all readers find her entirely convincing, she is certainly one of Powell's most fascinating characters. As the war ends, she is engaged to Widmerpool. No one could deserve her less, or more. With Pamela's entrance into the series, the tone, previously not essentially grim, even with the many deaths occurring during the war, changes.

Books Do Furnish a Room · In the final movement of the series, "Winter," the style also changes as Powell moves toward a concluding "wintery silence." While a sense of the comic is never abandoned, the mood becomes more somber, the action more direct. The first novel in this movement, *Books Do Furnish a Room*, is primarily the story of X. Trapnel, a novelist heavily based on Powell's friend, Julian Maclaren Ross. Trapnel, the artist, is juxtaposed with Widmerpool, the man of power, through the agency of Pamela Flitton, who leaves Widmerpool to live with Trapnel. The triumph of the artist is temporary, however, for not only is Pamela discovered to be both sexually insatiable and frigid, but she also destroys a manuscript of Trapnel's most recent novel by dumping it in the Maida Vale Canal and returns to Widmerpool.

Temporary Kings · In the next volume, *Temporary Kings*, which begins at an international literary conference in Venice, where the first half of the novel is set, Pamela is a dominant character. Her sexual debauchery continues, unsettling Widmerpool, but she encounters a man upon whom her charms fail, Professor Russell Gwinnett. Continuing his ability to rejuvenate the series by introducing new characters, Powell brings in this American scholar with necrophilic tastes, who is writing a book on Trapnel. Nick finds him "an altogether unfamiliar type," with "nothing simple" about his personality.

Thematically, Gwinnett, a curious variant of the *deus ex machina*, may embody a kind of resolution of the conflict between art and power. Having both an involvement with art and an exceptionally strong will, Gwinnett, whose superior psychic strength provokes Pamela's suicide, perhaps in a necrophilic ritual, may be thought to have avenged Trapnel, if not Widmerpool. Any resolution with Gwinnett is, however, a dark one, incorporating the cult rites with which he becomes involved before returning to America, and necessarily suggesting that to which he is most strongly related, death.

Hearing Secret Harmonies · The final volume of the sequence, *Hearing Secret Harmonies*, is focused on Widmerpool, who, with the exception of Nick himself, is the series' most enduring character. After becoming a kind of hero to rebellious youth, he joins a pagan religious cult and struggles with its leader, Scorpio Murtlock, for dominance. Finally, running at the end, just as he was in his first appearance in the sequence, he falls dead, exhausted by his effort to take the lead in a ritual run.

The ending of such a long work poses a particular problem. After twelve books, certainly some feeling of conclusion must be produced, yet the whole structure, the whole sense of the continually evolving dance of time, renders any strong sense of climax inappropriate. Powell, by having Nick learn at second hand of Widmerpool's death, and then returning to the initial image of the workmen's fire, quoting Robert Burton, and providing a carefully worded final image, skillfully solves this problem. The ending is a final reminder of the quality of literary skill and talent that is sustained through all the volumes of singularly satisfactory achievement.

The Fisher King · *The Fisher King* was Powell's second novel to be published after the completion of *A Dance to the Music of Time*. Most of the action involves a group of characters taking a summer cruise around the British Isles. Aboard the cruise ship *Alecto* is Saul Henchman, a famous photographer who received disabling and disfiguring injuries in World War II. He is traveling with his assistant and companion, a beautiful woman named Barberina Rookwood. Much of the story is narrated by another passenger, Valentine Beals, a writer of historical novels. As the cruise progresses, Henchman reveals himself as a thoroughly unpleasant individual, Beals is seen to be gossipy and pretentious, and Rookwood inspires the admiration of men and women alike. Three men on the cruise—Henchman, Gary Lamont, and Robin Jilson—vie for her attention.

The Fisher King provides numerous connections between its characters and mythological figures, generally commented on by Beals. Beals's interpretations and speculations are flawed in a number of ways, however, and Powell is perhaps suggesting that myth can still illuminate intriguing aspects of human behavior but cannot truly predict how humans will act. Throughout, Powell is less concerned with drawing precise mythological parallels than with providing an amusing and intellectually entertaining story of people and their foibles.

William B. Stone, updated by Eugene Larson and McCrea Adams

Other major works

PLAYS: *"The Garden God" and "The Rest I'll Whistle": The Text of Two Plays,* pb. 1971.
POETRY: *Caledonia: A Fragment,* 1934.
NONFICTION: *John Aubrey and His Friends,* 1948, 1963; *To Keep the Ball Rolling,* 1976-1982 (includes *Infants of the Spring,* 1976; *Messengers of Day,* 1978; *Faces in My Time,* 1980; *The Strangers All Are Gone,* 1982); *Miscellaneous Verdicts: Writings on Writers, 1946-1989,* 1990; *Under Review: Further Writings on Writers 1946-1989,* 1991; *Journals 1982-1986,* 1995; *Journals 1987-1989,* 1996; *Journals 1990-1992,* 1997; *A Writer's Notebook,* 2000.

Bibliography

Brennan, Neil. *Anthony Powell.* Boston: Twayne, 1974. Covers Powell's work up to 1973, when the eleventh volume of *A Dance to the Music of Time* was published. One-third of this study is devoted to *A Dance to the Music of Time,* Powell's tour de force; the rest is an analysis of his other works, including early novels such as *Afternoon Men* and *From a View to a Death.* Contains a chronology of Powell which includes his family ancestry.

Joyau, Isabelle. *Investigating Powell's "A Dance to the Music of Time."* New York: St. Martin's Press, 1994. An academic, Joyau writes an insightful and appreciative analysis of Powell's *A Dance to the Music of Time,* discussing structure, literary techniques, and characters.

Morris, Robert K. *The Novels of Anthony Powell.* Pittsburgh: University of Pittsburgh Press, 1968. The first book-length study of Powell's writing. Morris discusses all Powell's novels up to 1968 and focuses on what he discerns as Powell's central theme: the struggle between the power hungry and the sensualists. The second part of this study analyzes the first eight volumes of *A Dance to the Music of Time.*

Selig, Robert L. *Time and Anthony Powell.* Cranbury, N.J.: Associated University Presses, 1991. An analysis of Powell's use of time in *A Dance to the Music of Time,* both within the series and as the reader's sense of time is affected.

Spurling, Hilary. *Invitation to the Dance: A Guide to Anthony Powell's "Dance to the Music of Time."* Boston: Little, Brown, 1977. Spurling intends this as a reference cum "bedside companion for readers who want to refresh their memories." Whether or not it makes for bedside reading, this volume certainly is a useful guide to the complexities of Powell's opus. Contains a synopsis of each volume, by chapter and time sequence, and includes an extensive character index.

Taylor, D. J. "A Question of Upbringing." *The* [London] *Sunday Times Books,* January

29, 1995, p. 8. Taylor, a journalist and novelist, interviewed Powell about his career and recent life at the Powell country house in western England.

Tucker, James. *The Novels of Anthony Powell.* New York: Columbia University Press, 1976. An extensive appraisal of the twelve volumes of *A Dance to the Music of Time.* Includes a "who's who" of characters, themes, style, narrative, and method. A scholarly work, but quite readable. Also contains a bibliography.

J. B. Priestley

Born: Bradford, England; September 13, 1894
Died: Stratford-upon-Avon, England; August 14, 1984

Principal long fiction · *Adam in Moonshine,* 1927; *Benighted,* 1927; *Farthing Hall,* 1929 (with Hugh Walpole); *The Good Companions,* 1929; *Angel Pavement,* 1930; *Faraway,* 1932; *I'll Tell You Everything,* 1933 (with George Bullett); *Wonder Hero,* 1933; *They Walk in the City: The Lovers in the Stone Forest,* 1936; *The Doomsday Men: An Adventure,* 1938; *Let the People Sing,* 1939; *Blackout in Gretley: A Story of—and for—Wartime,* 1942; *Daylight on Saturday: A Novel About an Aircraft Factory,* 1943; *Three Men in New Suits,* 1945; *Bright Day,* 1946; *Jenny Villiers: A Story of the Theatre,* 1947; *Festival at Farbridge,* 1951 (pb. in U.S. as *Festival*); *Low Notes on a High Level: A Frolic,* 1954; *The Magicians,* 1954; *Saturn over the Water: An Account of His Adventures in London, South America, and Australia by Tim Bedford, Painter, Edited with Some Preliminary and Concluding Remarks by Henry Sulgrave and Here Presented to the Reading Public,* 1961; *The Thirty-first of June: A Tale of True Love, Enterprise, and Progress in the Arthurian and ad-Atomic Ages,* 1961; *The Shape of Sleep: A Topical Tale,* 1962; *Sir Michael and Sir George: A Tale of COMSA and DISCUS and the New Elizabethans,* 1964 (also known as *Sir Michael and Sir George: A Comedy of New Elizabethans*); *Lost Empires: Being Richard Herncastle's Account of His Life on the Variety Stage from November, 1913, to August, 1914, Together with a Prologue and Epilogue,* 1965; *Salt Is Leaving,* 1966; *It's an Old Country,* 1967; *The Image Men: Out of Town and London End,* 1968; *The Carfitt Crisis,* 1975; *Found, Lost, Found: Or, The English Way of Life,* 1976; *My Three Favorite Novels,* 1978.

Other literary forms · In addition to the nearly thirty novels that he published after *Adam in Moonshine* in 1927, J. B. Priestley wrote approximately fifty plays, upon which his future reputation will largely depend. These include such memorable works as *Dangerous Corner* (1932), *Eden End* (1934), *Time and the Conways* (1937), *An Inspector Calls* (1946), *The Linden Tree* (1947), and *The Scandalous Affair of Mr. Kettle and Mrs. Moon* (1955). He also collaborated with Iris Murdoch on the successful stage adaptation of her novel *A Severed Head* (1963).

There is, besides, a long list of impressive works which characterize Priestley as the twentieth century equivalent of an eighteenth century man of letters, a term he professed to despise. This list includes accounts of his travels both in England and abroad, the best of these being *English Journey* (1934), an account of English life during the Depression; *Russian Journey* (1946); and *Journey down a Rainbow* (1955), written in collaboration with Jacquetta Hawkes. Priestley produced several books of reminiscence and recollection, which include *Rain upon Godshill* (1939), *Margin Released* (1962), and *Instead of the Trees* (1977). His literary criticism includes studies of George Meredith, Charles Dickens, and Anton Chekhov; and his familiar essays, thought by many to be among his finest works, are represented in the volume entitled *Essays of Five Decades* (1968), and by *Postscripts* (1940), his broadcasts in support of England at war. Priestley created several picture books of social criticism such as *The Prince of Pleasure and His Regency, 1811-1820* (1969), *The Edwardians* (1970), and *Victoria's Heyday* (1972), and his far-reaching historical surveys detail an idiosyncratic view of people in time: *Literature and Western Man* (1960) and *Man and Time* (1964). Priestley's short-story collections include *Going Up* (1950) and *The Other Place and Other Stories of the Same Sort* (1953).

As this list indicates, no aspect of modern life escaped Priestley's scrutiny, and no genre was left untried. In a long and prestigious career, he earned for himself a secure place in the annals of literature.

Achievements · Although Priestley's accomplishments in the theater may prove more significant than his work in the novel, perhaps because of his experimentation within the dramatic genre, his fiction has nevertheless secured for him a high place in contemporary literature; it has been read and cherished by a large and very appreciative audience. *The Good Companions*, a runaway best-seller in 1929, allowed Priestley to turn his attention from journalism and the novel to the theater in the 1930's, but he kept returning to the novel form throughout his career.

Priestley produced no novel that equals James Joyce's *Ulysses* (1922) in scope or intellectual subtlety, no novel as prophetic as D. H. Lawrence's *The Rainbow* (1915), no novel illustrative of the intuitive faculty equal to Virginia Woolf's *To the Lighthouse* (1927), or of ethical concern equal to Joseph Conrad's *The Secret Agent* (1907) or William Faulkner's *Light in August* (1932). His place on the scale of literary achievement may be lower than theirs, but his audience has been, by and large, greater. Priestley aimed for and caught a popular audience that remained loyal to him through five decades of writing. His novels and plays have been widely translated and acted, most notably in the Soviet Union. His craft in the novel genre shows the influence of Charles Dickens, of the English Romantics, especially of William Wordsworth and William Hazlitt, and of the English music hall and its traditions. Priestley himself made no great claims for his fiction, beyond good-naturedly protesting once or twice that there is more to it than meets the top-speed reviewer's eye. His finest novel, *Bright Day*, however, earned general critical approval when it was published in 1946, and merited the praise of Carl Jung, who found its theme consonant with his notion of the oneness of all people.

Biography · John Boynton Priestley was born in Bradford, Yorkshire, on September 13, 1894. His mother died soon after his birth, and he was reared by a kind and loving stepmother. His father Jonathan was a schoolmaster whom Priestley has characterized in the autobiographical *Margin Released* as the man Socialists have in mind when they write about Socialists.

Bradford, in Priestley's early years, offered much to feed a romantic boy's imagination: theater, the music halls, a playgoer's society, an arts club, the concert stage, a busy market street, and a grand-scale arcade called the Swan. A tram ride away were the Yorkshire Dales and moors. As a young man, Priestley worked in a wool office, writing poetry and short stories into handmade notebooks in his spare time. An important early influence was Richard Pendlebury, his English master. Priestley later observed that Bradford and its environs did more for his education than did Cambridge University, which he attended years later.

In 1915, Priestley enlisted in the army. He was sent to France, invalided back to England after being wounded, and then sent back to France. Significantly, his experience of war does not figure explicitly in any fictional piece, with the single exception of a haunting short story entitled "The Town Major of Miraucourt" (1930). Priestley's entire creative output may, however, have been an attempt to put war and its ravages into a long-range context, a notion that pervades his *Postscripts* broadcasts for the British Broadcasting Corporation (BBC) during World War II. At the end of his army service, Priestley went to Cambridge, where he studied, between 1919 and 1922, literature, history, and political theory. His first book, *Brief Diversions* (1922), received good reviews but did not sell.

Leaving Cambridge for London and the precarious life of a journalist, Priestley worked for J. C. Squire and the *London Mercury*, for the *Daily News*, and for the Bodley Head Press. Meanwhile, he published critical books on George Meredith, Thomas Love Peacock, and modern literature. His first novel, *Adam in Moonshine*, appeared in 1927. Shortly thereafter, Hugh Walpole offered to collaborate with Priestley on a novel called *Farthing Hall* in order to give the younger writer a much-needed publisher's advance so that he could continue his work. In 1929, *The Good Companions* appeared, and Priestley was fully embarked on a long and distinguished career.

Priestley was married three times; his first marriage, to Pat Tempest, came in 1919. A year after her death, in 1925, he married Mary Holland Wyndham Lewis, from whom he was divorced in 1952. The two marriages produced four daughters and a son. In 1953, he married the distinguished anthropologist Jacquetta Hawkes. During his adult life, Priestley resided in London, on the Isle of Wight, and in Alveston, just outside Stratford-upon-Avon. He traveled widely, frequently using his journeys as background for his novels and plays. During World War II, he and his wife ran a hostel for evacuated children; after the war he campaigned vigorously for nuclear disarmament. He served as a UNESCO delegate and on the board of the National Theatre. He refused a knighthood and a life-peerage but did, in 1977, accept membership in the Order of Merit. In 1973, he happily accepted conferment of the Freedom of the City from his native Bradford.

Priestley did not retire from his writing work until well after he turned eighty. He died in 1984, one month shy of his ninetieth birthday.

Analysis · In his novels J. B. Priestley largely portrays a Romantic view of life. His focus is primarily England and the English national character, and on those aspects of people that ennoble and spiritualize them. Yet, there is a no-nonsense view of life portrayed in his fiction; hard work, dedication to ideals, and willingness to risk all in a good cause are themes which figure prominently. At times, the darker aspects of humanity becloud this gruff but kindly Yorkshireman's generally sunny attitudes. Ultimately, life in Priestley's fictional universe is good, provided the individual is permitted to discover his potential. In politics, this attitude reduces to what Priestley has called "Liberal Socialism." For Priestley, too much government is not good for the individual.

Romanticism largely dictated characterization in Priestley's novels, and his most valid psychological portraits are of individuals who are aware of themselves as enchanted and enchanting. These characters are usually portrayed as questers. It is Priestley's symbolic characters, however, who are the most forcefully portrayed, occasionally as god-figures, occasionally as devil-figures, but mostly as organizers—as stage-managers, impresarios, factory owners, butlers. Priestley's female characters fall generally into roles as ingenues or anima-figures. There are, however, noteworthy exceptions, specifically Freda Pinnel in *Daylight on Saturday*.

It is primarily through the presentation of his organizers that Priestley's chief plot device emerges: the common cause. A group of disparate characters is assembled and organized into a common endeavor; democratic action follows as a consequence.

"Liberal democracy. Expensive and elaborate, but best in the end," says a choric figure in *Festival at Farbridge,* echoing one of his author's deepest convictions.

A Romantic view of people in space and time also dictated the kind of novels that Priestley wrote. His fiction falls easily into three main categories. The first is the seriously conceived and carefully structured novel, in which symbolism and consistent imagery figure as aspects of craft. The best of this group are *Angel Pavement, Bright Day,* and *It's an Old Country.* The second category can be termed the frolic or escapade. This group includes *The Good Companions, Festival at Farbridge,* and the delightful *Sir Michael and Sir George.* The third category is the thriller or entertainment, which includes such science-fiction works as *The Doomsday Men* and *Saturn over the Water* as well as the detective story *Salt Is Leaving.* Priestley's favorite novel, and his longest, *The Image Men,* published in two volumes in 1968 and as one in 1969, incorporates these three categories within a controlled and incisive satirical mode.

In many of his works, but more so in his plays than in his fiction, Priestley dramatized a theory concerning the nature of time and experience which derived from his understanding of John William Dunne's *An Experiment with Time* (1927) and *The Serial Universe* (1934) and P. D. Ouspensky's *A New Model of the Universe* (1931). Briefly stated, this time theory, most explicit in *The Magicians,* a gothic tale which presents Priestley's characterizations of the Wandering Jew, and *Jenny Villiers,* originally written as a play for the Bristol Old Vic, proposes a means of transcendence. Priestley believed that Dunne's Serialism–"we observe something, and we are conscious of our observation . . . and we are conscious of the observation of the observation, and so forth"–permitted him to deal with character "creatively." For the ordinary individual, to "Observer One," the fourth dimension appears as time. The self within dreams becomes "Observer Two," to whom the fifth dimension appears as time. Unlike the three-dimensional outlook of Observer One, Observer Two's four-dimensional outlook enables him to receive images from coexisting past and future times. From Ouspensky, Priestley refined the notion that time, like space, has three dimensions; these three dimensions, however, can be regarded as a continuation of the dimensions of space. Wavelike and spiral, time provides for eternal recurrence, but a recurrence not to be confused with Friedrich Nietzsche's "eternal retour," with reincarnation, or with the Bergsonian *durée.* Ouspensky provided Priestley with the possibility of re-creation–that is, of intervention in space and time through an inner development of self. In other words, self-conscious awareness of self in past time can re-create the past in the present; sympathetic re-creation of self and others in what Priestley terms "time alive" can give new meaning to the present and shape the future. For Priestley, the seer–whether he be a painter or a musician, or the organizer of a festival or of a traveling group of entertainers, or even a butler in a country house–by looking creatively into the past, ameliorates the present and shapes a brighter future. Consequently, the organizer is Priestley's most forceful and symbolic character, and the thematic purpose of his novels depends upon an understanding of this character's motives.

The Good Companions · Priestley's first successful novel, *The Good Companions,* presents a cozy fairy tale against an essentially realistic background, the English music halls of the 1920's. A determined spinster, Elizabeth Trant, organizes a down-and-out group of entertainers who have called themselves the Dinky Doos into a successful group renamed the Good Companions. The adventures of these troupers on the road and on the boards provide the novel with its zest and comedy.

Angel Pavement · *Angel Pavement* is in some ways a departure from this earlier work inasmuch as its tone appears dark and ominous. In *Angel Pavement*, the organizer is not a cheerful woman of thirty-seven giving herself a holiday on the roads as an impresario, but a balding, middle-aged adventurer named Golspie. "A thick figure of a man but now slow and heavy," Golspie enters the London firm of Twigg and Dersingham, dealers in wood veneers, and breathes new life into the business in a period of economic depression. With his only commitment being his daughter Lena, Golspie seems at first the firm's savior, for he provides a supply of veneer from the Baltic at half the domestic price. Perhaps because he and his daughter are rejected by the more polite segments of London society, Golspie feels it unnecessary to play fair with his employers. Eventually, he ruins Twigg and Dersingham, putting the employees out of work. At the novel's end, he and Lena leave London for South America and new adventure.

What most distinguishes *Angel Pavement* is its portrayal of the city, London, in the midst of the Depression, and of those who people it. Lilian Matfield, the head secretary, is fascinated by Golspie but refuses to accept the life of adventure he offers her, and Henry Smeeth, the bookkeeper, accepts a raise in salary, only to discover that once Golspie has abandoned Twigg and Dersingham, the company is bankrupt and he is out of work. The streets, the offices, the pubs, the tobacco stands, the amusements, all combine to present a view of human enervation and despair. A confidence man but not exactly a charlatan, Golspie locks the novel to a seemingly pessimistic view. Despite the enervation and apathy portrayed, Golspie offers freedom. Through his sinister organizer, Priestley portrays the life of romance that lies beneath the ordinary. What *Angel Pavement* finally achieves is a startling view of the modern metropolis as a prison from which only the romantic can escape.

Bright Day · One of his own favorite works, Priestley's *Bright Day* has been justly admired by critics and readers alike. Its uniqueness lies not so much in its dexterous use of such novelistic techniques as the time-shift and memory digression as in the way it looks behind and beyond its immediate focus into that sense of race and identity all people share. Although the novel deals with time, Priestley here shows a greater indebtedness to Henri Bergson and Marcel Proust than he does to Ouspensky and Dunne.

Music, specifically a Franz Schubert trio, returns a middle-aged screenwriter, Gregory Dawson, the narrator, who has taken refuge from his unhappy life in a genteel hotel in Cornwall, to a memory of youth and joy. An old couple reminds him of the boy of eighteen he was when he fell in love with a family called Alington in Bruddersford, a wool-producing northern town. The Alingtons, charming and gracious, had sentimentally attached the young Gregory to themselves and had introduced the would-be writer to their world, which he had seen as one of grace and beauty. Ironically, the old couple who trigger the middle-aged Dawson's memories are in fact the Eleanor and Malcolm Nixey who had opportunistically intruded on his youthful idyll and brought an end to the prosperous wool business on which the Alingtons and their gracious world depended, and to Gregory's idealism as well.

In *Bright Day*, Priestley, concerned with a rite of passage, presents Gregory's initiation into a world of greed and suspicion, of appearance and falsehood; his is in fact an initiation into the modern world, and the novel symbolically spans the period of the two world wars. In the course of reconstructing the past, Gregory comes to terms with himself in the present, and it is his recognition of self in time that makes a commitment to the future possible for him. This liberation is confirmed by the stunning revelation made to him by Laura Bradshaw, who had also known the Alingtons, that Joan Alington in a jealous rage had pushed her sister Eva to her death from a cliff. The cancer of destruction had been in the Alingtons themselves; the Nixeys had merely served as catalysts.

Although Gregory Dawson is a quester for truth through self-knowledge, he is much more than a symbolic character. His psychological validity makes his growth in the course of the novel persuasive and compelling. The rediscovery of his romantic self in the present time of the novel is the rediscovery of a moment of beauty that had laid dormant in the rich soil of his memory. Many of Priestley's novels largely describe romance; *Bright Day* re-creates its essence, as does Evelyn Waugh's *Brideshead Revisited* (1945, 1959), with which it has much in common.

Lost Empires · Published in 1965 and representative of the novels Priestley produced in the later stages of his career, *Lost Empires* is in some ways a return to the world of *The Good Companions*, employing as it does the music hall as background. Unlike *The Good Companions*, however, whose chief interest was the high jinks of the troupers on the road, the theater serves here as a metaphor for the theme of appearance and reality and allows Priestley to allegorize loosely the politics of a world destined for war.

The protagonist, Dick Herncastle, one of Priestley's romantic questers here presented as an artist, is contrasted to his uncle, Nick Ollanton, the organizer, who is portrayed as a magician or mesmerizer. Ollanton and his "turn" allegorize the political activist and his propaganda techniques as he bends people to his will, much as does Thomas Mann's Cipolla in "Mario and the Magician." A time-perspective on Ollanton's influence on young Dick, who works as his assistant, is presented by means of a deftly presented prologue and epilogue, which encompass the action proper of the novel, set in the period of World War I. The main action ends with Dick succumbing to the illusion of a better world after the end of the war, and with Ollanton himself leaving the Old World for the United States, revealing his bag of tricks as a private escape from the "bloody mincing machine" of global war. There, he will manufacture machine-gun sights for warplanes. The novel proper, however, ends with the account in the prologue of Dick's return from the war and his successful career as a watercolorist, an illusionist of another sort.

The charm of *Lost Empires* goes well beyond its symbolic dimension; it lies chiefly in the presentations of the performers and the turns they perform on the boards. The juggler Ricardo, the comedian Beamish, the ballad singer Lily Farrish, and many others add to the plot and charm of the novel. That they are logically placed within the melodramatic and symbolic structure of the novel is simply another testimony to the skill of their author.

A. A. DeVitis

Other major works

SHORT FICTION: *The Town Major of Miraucourt*, 1930; *Going Up: Stories and Sketches*, 1950; *The Other Place and Other Stories of the Same Sort*, 1953; *The Carfitt Crisis and Two Other Stories*, 1975.

PLAYS: *The Good Companions*, pr. 1931 (adaptation of his novel; with Edward Knoblock); *Dangerous Corner*, pr., pb. 1932; *The Roundabout*, pr. 1932; *Laburnum Grove*, pr. 1933; *Eden End*, pr., pb. 1934; *Cornelius*, pr., pb. 1935; *Duet in Floodlight*, pr., pb.

1935; *Bees on the Boat Deck,* pr., pb. 1936; *Spring Tide,* pr., pb. 1936 (with George Billam); *People at Sea,* pr., pb. 1937; *Time and the Conways,* pr., pb. 1937; *I Have Been Here Before,* pr., pb. 1937; *Music at Night,* pr. 1938; *Mystery at Greenfingers,* pr., pb. 1938; *When We Are Married,* pr., pb. 1938; *Johnson over Jordan,* pr., pb. 1939; *The Long Mirror,* pr., pb. 1940; *Goodnight, Children,* pr., pb. 1942; *They Came to a City,* pr. 1943, pb. 1944; *Desert Highway,* pr., pb. 1944; *The Golden Fleece,* pr. 1944; *How Are They at Home?,* pr., pb. 1944; *An Inspector Calls,* pr. 1946; *Ever Since Paradise,* pr. 1946; *The Linden Tree,* pr. 1947; *The Rose and Crown,* pb. 1947 (one act); *The High Toby,* pb. 1948 (for puppet theater); *Home Is Tomorrow,* pr. 1948; *The Plays of J. B. Priestley,* pb. 1948-1950 (3 volumes); *Summer Day's Dream,* pr. 1949; *Bright Shadow,* pr., pb. 1950; *Seven Plays of J. B. Priestley,* pb. 1950; *Dragon's Mouth,* pr., pb. 1952 (with Jacquetta Hawkes); *Treasure on Pelican,* pr. 1952; *Mother's Day,* pb. 1953 (one act); *Private Rooms,* pb. 1953 (one act); *Try It Again,* pb. 1953 (one act); *A Glass of Bitter,* pb. 1954 (one act); *The White Countess,* pr. 1954 (with Hawkes); *The Scandalous Affair of Mr. Kettle and Mrs. Moon,* pr., pb. 1955; *These Our Actors,* pr. 1956; *The Glass Cage,* pr. 1957; *The Pavilion of Masks,* pr. 1963; *A Severed Head,* pr. 1963 (with Iris Murdoch; adaptation of Murdoch's novel).

SCREENPLAY: *Last Holiday,* 1950.

POETRY: *The Chapman of Rhymes,* 1918.

NONFICTION: *Brief Diversions: Being Tales, Travesties, and Epigrams,* 1922; *Papers from Lilliput,* 1922; *I for One,* 1923; *Figures in Modern Literature,* 1924; *Fools and Philosophers: A Gallery of Comic Figures from English Literature,* 1925 (pb. in U.S. as *The English Comic Characters*); *George Meredith,* 1926; *Talking: An Essay,* 1926; *The English Novel,* 1927, 1935, 1974; *Open House: A Book of Essays,* 1927; *Thomas Love Peacock,* 1927; *Too Many People and Other Reflections,* 1928; *Apes and Angels: A Book of Essays,* 1928; *The Balconinny and Other Essays,* 1929 (pb. in U.S. as *The Balconinny,* 1931); *English Humour,* 1929, 1976; *The Lost Generation: An Armistice Day Article,* 1932; *Self-Selected Essays,* 1932; *Albert Goes Through,* 1933; *English Journey: Being a Rambling but Truthful Account of What One Man Saw and Heard and Felt and Thought During a Journey Through England During the Autumn of the Year 1933,* 1934; *Four-in-Hand,* 1934; *Midnight on the Desert: A Chapter of Auto-biography,* 1937 (pb. in U.S. as *Midnight on the Desert: Being an Excursion into Autobiography During a Winter in America, 1935-1936,* 1937); *Rain upon Godshill: A Further Chapter of Autobiography,* 1939; *Britain Speaks,* 1940; *Postscripts,* 1940 (radio talks); *Out of the People,* 1941; *Britain at War,* 1942; *British Women Go to War,* 1943; *The Man-Power Story,* 1943; *Here Are Your Answers,* 1944; *The New Citizen,* 1944; *Letter to a Returning Serviceman,* 1945; *Russian Journey,* 1946; *The Secret Dream: An Essay on Britain, America, and Russia,* 1946; *The Arts Under Socialism: Being a Lecture Given to the Fabian Society, with a Postscript on What Government Should Do for the Arts Here and Now,* 1947; *Theatre Outlook,* 1947; *Delight,* 1949; *Journey down a Rainbow,* 1955 (with Jacquetta Hawkes); *All About Ourselves and Other Essays,* 1956; *The Writer in a Changing Society,* 1956; *The Art of the Dramatist: A Lecture Together with Appendices and Discursive Notes,* 1957; *The Bodley Head Leacock,* 1957; *Thoughts in the Wilderness,* 1957; *Topside: Or, The Future of England, a Dialogue,* 1958; *The Story of Theatre,* 1959; *Literature and Western Man,* 1960; *William Hazlitt,* 1960; *Charles Dickens: A Pictorial Biography,* 1962; *Margin Released: A Writer's Reminiscences and Reflections,* 1962; *The English Comic Characters,* 1963; *Man and Time,* 1964; *The Moments and Other Pieces,* 1966; *All England Listened: J. B. Priestley's Wartime Broadcasts,* 1968; *Essays of Five Decades,* 1968 (Susan Cooper, editor); *Trumpets over the Sea: Being a Rambling and Egotistical Account of the London Symphony Orchestra's Engagement at Daytona Beach, Florida, in July-August, 1967,* 1968; *The Prince of Pleasure and His Regency, 1811-1820,* 1969; *Anton Chekhov,* 1970; *The Edwardians,* 1970; *Over the*

Long High Wall: Some Reflections and Speculations on Life, Death, and Time, 1972; *Victoria's Heyday,* 1972; *The English,* 1973; *Outcries and Asides,* 1974; *A Visit to New Zealand, Particular Pleasures: Being a Personal Record of Some Varied Arts and Many Different Artists,* 1974; *The Happy Dream: An Essay,* 1976; *Instead of the Trees,* 1977 (autobiography).

CHILDREN'S LITERATURE: *Snoggle,* 1972.

EDITED TEXTS: *Essayist Past and Present: A Selection of English Essays,* 1925; *Tom Moore's Diary: A Selection,* 1925; *The Book of Bodley Head Verse,* 1926; *The Female Spectator: Selections from Mrs. Eliza Heywood's Periodical, 1744-1746,* 1929; *Our Nation's Heritage,* 1939; *Scenes of London Life, from "Sketches by Boz" by Charles Dickens,* 1947; *The Best of Leacock,* 1957; *Four English Novels,* 1960; *Four English Biographies,* 1961; *Adventures in English Literature,* 1963; *An Everyman Anthology,* 1966.

Bibliography

Atkins, John. *J. B. Priestley: The Last of the Sages.* London: John Calder, 1981. Cites Priestley as a major but neglected writer. A comprehensive look at his novels and plays as well as his career as a critic. Contains much valuable information.

Braine, John. *J. B. Priestley.* London: Weidenfeld & Nicolson, 1978. Not a critical analysis of Priestley's work, by Braine's admission, but a look at a selection of his writings. Braine, a fellow Bradfordian, offers a knowledgeable view of Priestley.

Brome, Vincent. *J. B. Priestley.* London: Hamish Hamilton, 1988. The first biography of Priestley. Brome, a seasoned biographer and prolific author, renders a lively portrait, doing justice to Priestley's many different careers as novelist, playwright, essayist, and public intellectual.

Cook, Judith. *Priestley.* London: Bloomsbury, 1997. An excellent biography of Priestley. Includes bibliographical references and an index.

Cooper, Susan. *J. B. Priestley: Portrait of an Author.* London: Redwood Press, 1970. A sympathetic account of Priestley written in an informal style. Cooper gives both criticism of his work and a look at the man himself: "warm hearted, generous."

DeVitis, A. A., and Albert E. Kalson. *J. B. Priestley.* Boston: Twayne, 1980. A good introduction to Priestley, which focuses on some eighty novels and plays, from the late 1920's to the 1960's. The authors note that Priestley's work has an "unerring ability to deal incisively with the idiosyncrasies of the English national character."

Evans, Gareth Lloyd. *J. B. Priestley: The Dramatist.* London: Heinemann, 1964. Analyzes the three collected volumes of Priestley's plays, which Evans has divided into "Time-plays," "Comedies," and "Sociological plays." An authoritative study that is primarily concerned with the dominant themes in Priestley's plays.

Barbara Pym

Mary Crampton

Born: Oswestry, England; June 2, 1913
Died: Oxford, England; January 11, 1980

Principal long fiction · *Some Tame Gazelle*, 1950; *Excellent Women*, 1952; *Jane and Prudence*, 1953; *Less than Angels*, 1955; *A Glass of Blessings*, 1958; *No Fond Return of Love*, 1961; *Quartet in Autumn*, 1977; *The Sweet Dove Died*, 1978; *A Few Green Leaves*, 1980; *An Unsuitable Attachment*, 1982; *Crampton Hodnet*, 1985; *An Academic Question*, 1986.

Other literary forms · In 1984, Hazel Holt and Hilary Pym published a one-volume edition of Barbara Pym's diaries and letters, entitled *A Very Private Eye: An Autobiography in Diaries and Letters*. In 1987, Holt edited a miscellany, *Civil to Strangers and Other Writings*, which contained mostly fiction but some nonfiction.

Achievements · Pym was a writer of distinctive qualities who, having suffered discouragement and neglect for fifteen years, was rediscovered toward the end of her life, to take her rightful place as a novelist of considerable originality and force. Often compared favorably with Jane Austen's novels, Pym's are essentially those of a private, solitary individual, employing precise social observation, understatement, and gentle irony in an oblique approach to such universal themes as the underlying loneliness and frustrations of life, culture as a force for corruption, love thwarted or satisfied, and the power of the ordinary to sustain and protect the men and women who shelter themselves under it. Also like Austen, Pym has no illusions about herself and very few about other people: "I like to think that what I write gives pleasure and makes my readers smile, even laugh. But my novels are by no means only comedies as I try to reflect life as I see it."

The story of Pym's early achievements, her long enforced silence, and her remarkable rediscovery perhaps says more about the publishing world than about either her books or her readers. Between 1949 and 1961, while working as an editorial assistant at the International African Institute, Pym wrote a novel every two years. As each manuscript was finished, she sent it off to Jonathan Cape. Her first six novels established her style, were well received by reviewers, and enjoyed a following among library borrowers. *Excellent Women*, her most popular novel, sold a little more than six thousand copies.

Then, in 1963, Pym put her seventh novel, *An Unsuitable Attachment*, in the mail. A short time later, it was returned: Times, she was told, had changed. The "swinging sixties" had no place for her gently ironic comedies about unconventional middle-class people leading outwardly uneventful lives. "Novels like *An Unsuitable Attachment*, despite their qualities, are getting increasingly difficult to sell," wrote another publisher, while a third regretted that the novel was unsuitable for its list.

Being a woman of determination with a certain modest confidence in herself, Pym went to work on an eighth novel, *The Sweet Dove Died*, and she sent it off to Cape; it too came back. She adopted a pseudonym–"Tom Crampton"–because "it had a swinging air to it," but twenty publishers turned down the novel. Humiliated and frustrated, she began to feel not only that her new books were no good, but also that nothing she had ever written had been good. *No Fond Return of Love* was serialized by the British Broadcasting Corporation (BBC) and Portway Reprints reissued five others; her books retained their popularity among library borrowers; and Robert Smith published an appreciation of her work in the October, 1971, issue of *Ariel*–but despite these signs of the continuing appeal of her work, Pym could not find a publisher, and by the mid-1970's, her name appeared to have been forgotten.

A renaissance in Pym's fortunes came with startling suddenness in 1977, when, to celebrate three-quarters of a century of existence, *The Times Literary Supplement* invited a number of well-known writers to name the most over- and underrated novelists of the century. Both Philip Larkin and Lord David Cecil–for years staunch admirers of hers–selected Pym as having been too long neglected, the only living writer to be so distinguished in the poll. Larkin praised her "unique eye and ear for the small poignancies and comedies of everyday life." Cecil called her early books "the finest example of high comedy to have appeared in England" in the twentieth century.

The publicity surrounding the article, not surprisingly, had positive effects on Pym's reputation. Macmillan published her new novel, *Quartet in Autumn*, near the end of 1977; later it was shortlisted for the Booker Prize. Cape began to reissue her earlier books; Penguin and Granada planned a series of paperbacks; she was widely interviewed; finally, she appeared on "Desert Island Discs" as well as in a television film called "Tea with Miss Pym." *The Sweet Dove Died* was published in 1978, followed by her last novel, the posthumously published *A Few Green Leaves* (1980). The manuscript of *An Unsuitable Attachment* was found among her papers after her death and published in 1982 with an introduction written by Philip Larkin. A book was prepared from her diaries and short stories.

Pym's novels are distinguished by an unobtrusive but perfectly controlled style, a concern with ordinary people and ordinary events, and a constant aim to be readable, to entertain in a world that is uniquely her own. They are also distinguished by a low-key but nevertheless cutting treatment of assumptions of masculine superiority and other sexist notions–all this well in advance of the women's movement, and without the rhetoric which mars so much feminist fiction. Although hers is a closed world, what Robert Smith called "an enchanted world of small felicities and small mishaps," it is also real and varied in theme and setting, with its own laws of human conduct and values, its peculiar humor and pathos. Middle-aged or elderly ladies, middle-aged or elderly gentlemen, civil servants, clergymen, anthropologists and other academics–these are the people about whom Pym develops her stories.

The world in which Pym's characters live, whether urban or provincial, is also a quiet world, evoked in such detail as to make the reader feel that the action could not possibly take place anywhere else. Taken together, her novels constitute that rare achievement: an independent fictional world, rooted in quotidian reality yet very much the creation of Barbara Pym. Central characters from one novel appear in passing or are briefly mentioned in another; delightful minor characters turn up in unexpected places. This pleasure of cross-references is characteristic of Pym's art, in which formal dexterity and a marvelous sense of humor harmonize with a modest but unembarrassed moral vision. "I prefer to write about the kind of things I have experienced," Pym said, "and to put into my novels the kind of details that amuse me in the hope that others will share in this."

Biography · Mary Crampton (Barbara Pym) was born on June 2, 1913, in Oswestry, Shropshire, a small English town on the border of Wales. Like many of her characters, she led a quiet but enjoyable life among middle-class people with an Anglican background. Her father, Frederick Crampton Pym, was a solicitor and sang in the choir; her mother, Irena (Thomas), was of half Welsh descent and played the organ. Pym was given a good education (Huyton College, a boarding school near Liverpool; and St. Hilda's College, Oxford, from which she received a B.A., 1934, in English language and literature); saw some wartime service (Postal and Telegraph Censorship in Bristol, 1939, and the Women's Royal Naval Service in England and Italy, 1943-1946); and lived in various sections of London: Pimlico, Barnes, and Kilburn. She wrote down everything she saw in a series of little notebooks, and later "bottled it all up and reduced it, like making chutney."

In 1948, Pym began working at the International African Institute, first as a research assistant and later as an assistant editor of the journal *Africa*. She was given the job of preparing the research for publication, and regretted that more of the anthropologists did not turn their talents to the writing of fiction. In their work, she found many of the qualities that make a novelist: "accurate observation, detachment, even sympathy." Needed was a little more imagination, as well as "the leavening of irony and humour." Several of her novels draw on her years at the Institute to study the behavior patterns and rituals of a group of anthropologists. In *Less than Angels*, for example, she portrays an anthropologist and his female co-workers, gently mocking the high seriousness with which they pursue their research among primitive African tribes and the shameless jargon in which they converse. No doubt the narrator is speaking for Pym herself when she concludes: "And how much more comfortable it sometimes was to observe [life] from a distance, to look down from an upper window, as it were, as the anthropologists did."

Although her first novel did not appear until 1950, Pym began writing when she was a schoolgirl, and even completed a novel when she was sixteen. After leaving Oxford, she started to write seriously and finished two more novels, but did not succeed in getting them published. By then, however, her literary tastes were well set. Above all, she was addicted to novels. Anthony Trollope and Jane Austen were her favorite novelists, and she knew their works intimately; but she read all the fiction she could, and listed among her favorites Ivy Compton-Burnett, Anthony Powell, and Iris Murdoch. She was less tolerant of contemporary novels, and viewed popular and sentimental fiction with the critical eye of the satirist. Nowhere in her own fiction does the reader find the sentimental excesses and sensational unrealities of current popular fiction.

In 1971, Pym had a serious operation, and in 1974, she retired to live with her sister near Oxford. She died on January 11, 1980, at the age of sixty-six.

Analysis · Like most novelists, Barbara Pym was interested above all in human nature, and for most of her life she trained both eye and ear upon the exploration of that subject in its many fascinating dimensions. Her first published novel, *Some Tame Gazelle*, sets the tone and subject for what is to come as she casts her specialist's eye on British lower-class and lower-middle-class life and focuses on the quiet domestic lives of a few people. At the center are two unmarried women who have decided that they will be happier living alone together. An all-pervasive influence of the Anglican church, numerous references to anthropology and English literature, the weakness of men, realism, and a sometimes devastatingly comic tone are among the many distinctive features of not only this early novel but the later ones as well. Much the same judgment may be made for two posthumously published novels: *Crampton Hodnet*, which she had written in the 1930's but never intended to publish, and *An Academic Question*, for which she had written two drafts (one in first person, another in third person) but abandoned to write *Quartet in Autumn*. In 1986, Hazel Holt published an amalgamation of the two drafts. In spite of their thin plots and shallow characterization, both novels contain Pym's characteristically sharp observations and lively dialogue among the minor characters, as well as her concern with the elderly. Considered together, in all twelve of her novels Pym communicates her vision in an engaging, entertaining, and readable way. Her wit, her sense of style, her devotion to language and its revelation of character, and the richness of her invention all compel respect and critical attention.

"In all of her writing," Philip Larkin has written of Pym, "I find a continual perceptive attention to detail which is a joy, and a steady background of rueful yet courageous acceptance of things." In this statement, Larkin points to perhaps the single most important technique—and theme—in Pym's work. *Excellent Women, A Glass of Blessings*, and *Quartet in Autumn* develop their effects, as indeed do all of Pym's twelve novels, by exploiting the comedy of contemporary manners. Like her anthropologists, whom she quietly mocks for their esoteric detachment, Pym scrupulously notes and records the frustrations, unfulfilled desires, boredom, and loneliness of "ordinary people, people who have no claim to fame whatsoever." The usual pattern for the heroine is either retrenchment into her own world or, as a result of interaction with others, self-realization. By representing intensively the small world most individuals inhabit, it is Pym's method to suggest the world as a whole as well.

Usually Pym appoints a heroine to comment on the intimate details of social behavior. In *Excellent Women*, the assignment falls to Mildred Lathbury, who, as an observer of life, expects "very little—nothing, almost." Typical of Pym's "excellent women," Mildred is preoccupied with order, stability, and routine, but her special interest centers on the lives and crises of those around her, including her new neighbors, Rockingham and Helena Napier; the vicar, Julian Malory; and the anthropologist, Everard Bone. Faced with Mildred's honesty, diffidence, and unpretentiousness, the crises are resolved happily.

In Pym's fifth novel, *A Glass of Blessings*, the heroine is Wilmet Forsyth, a young and leisured woman bored with her excessively sober civil-servant husband. Her near romances with a priest, her best friend's husband, and Piers Longridge (in whose friend Keith she discovers a rival) are only some of the pairings in this intricate drama of romantic errors. When the possibility of a love affair fails to materialize, Wilmet finds a different kind of consolation in religion.

Finally, Pym's antiheroic view of life is particularly obvious in her most somber work, *Quartet in Autumn*, the first of her novels to be published after fifteen years of silence. Whereas her earlier work was a small protest against everyday life, *Quartet in Autumn* offered a formal protest against the conditions both of life itself and of certain sad civilities. The comedy is cold and the outlook is austere in this story of four people in late middle age who suffer from the same problem: loneliness. In its manipulation of the narrative among Edwin, Norman, Letty, and Marcia, the novel also represents Pym's greatest technical achievement.

Excellent Women · *Excellent Women*, described by one critic as the most "felicitous" of all of Pym's novels, explores the complications of being a spinster (and a religious one, at that) in the England of the 1950's. The setting is a run-down part of London near Victoria Station, but the very high Anglican Church of St. Mary's also provides the background for some of the events described. In the quiet comfort of this world, where everything is within walking distance and a new face is an occasion for speculation, the pleasantness and security of everyday life dominate. Only small crises—such as an argument between Winifred and Alegra over how to decorate the church altar—form the counterpoint to comfort. As the narrator says, "life was like that for most of us—the small unpleasantnesses rather than the great tragedies; the little useless longings rather than the great renunciations and dramatic love affairs of history or fiction."

Mildred Lathbury, the narrator, is representative of one of Pym's favorite character types: the "excellent woman." She lives very much as she did growing up in a country rectory, working part-time for the aid of impoverished gentlewomen and devoting herself to the work of the parish. As one who tends to get involved in other people's lives, she knows herself, she says, "capable of dealing with most of the stock situations or even the great moments of life—birth, marriage, death, the successful jumble sale, the garden fête spoilt by bad weather."

In all of Pym's novels, says Philip Larkin, "a small incident serves to set off a chain of modest happenings among interrelated groups of characters." In this instance, it is the entry into Mildred's life of Rockingham Napier. A flag lieutenant to an admiral, Rockingham has just returned from Italy, where he served his country by being charming to dull Wren officers. His wife Helena, an anthropologist, does not welcome his return. Scornful of his easy charm and lack of serious purpose, she has become infatuated with another anthropologist, Everard Bone, her co-worker in Africa. As Helena pursues, however, Everard flees.

The reader depends upon Mildred for ironic commentary. Helena leaves her husband, who then departs for a cottage in the country. Excellent woman that she is, Mildred is invited by Rockingham to send him the Napier furniture, by Helena to get it back, by both to effect their reconciliation, and by Everard to read proof and make the index for his forthcoming book. Because the vicar, Julian Malory, needs to be protected from designing women and Everard needs her help with the book, it seems to Mildred that she may look forward to a "full life." Then she remembers Rockingham's smile and reads from Christina Rossetti: "Better by far you should forget and smile,/ Than that you should remember and be sad." "It was easy enough to read those lines and be glad at his smiling," she acknowledges, "but harder to tell myself there would never be any question of anything else." Still, Everard's affection is genuine, if undemonstrative—and not unmixed with a pragmatic desire to find a suitable typist, indexer, and all-around "helpmate"—and the reader is happy to learn, in a subsequent novel, that Mildred and Everard do indeed go on to wed.

A Glass of Blessings · Again set in the 1950's, town and country are contrasted in *A Glass of Blessings*, which Larkin regards as the "subtlest" of Pym's books. The novel opens in St. Luke's Church on the feast of its patron, the "beloved physician," as St. Paul called him. Celebrating the feast and her thirty-third birthday, Wilmet Forsyth, the narrator and heroine, is the well-to-do but aimless wife (subject to "useless little longings") of a typical Pym husband—hopelessly imperceptive, though well intentioned and reliable. Like Jane Austen's Emma, whom Pym has in mind throughout the novel, Wilmet is unused and spoiled. A beautiful woman, always exquisitely dressed, Wilmet is childless, idle, and snobbish. She is also utterly unknown to herself, unable to imagine another life, and afraid to risk herself, even on the London buses, certain that any disturbance will be disillusioning. Bored, without training for a career, despising routine, she plans "to take more part in the life of St. Luke's, to try to befriend Piers Longridge and perhaps even go to his classes."

Piers Longridge is a sour, moody homosexual, a fact Wilmet never quite seems to grasp until well into the novel. He has taken a seemingly useless degree and now teaches Portuguese in adult education classes. Believing that she might relieve his unhappiness, she forces herself on him, hoping for the grand passion of her life, another fact that she never really admits. Finally, in a scene of high comedy and bitter pain, exasperated by Wilmet's attentions and her naïveté, Piers confronts her with his secret lover, Keith, a male model, and accuses Wilmet of being incapable of affection. It is the first time anyone has told her anything near the truth, and in response, she says to Mary Beamish, "sometimes you discover that you aren't as nice as you thought you were—that you're in fact rather a horrid person, and that's humiliating somehow."

When she witnesses the courtship and marriage of Mary Beamish, an orphan and ex-Anglican nun, and Father Marius Lovejoy Ransome, Wilmet begins to perceive the possibilities of being useful in the parish and even of passion. After she finds out that Rodney has had an innocent flirtation with his secretary, Wilmet sees him differently, thinking, "I had always regarded Rodney as the kind of man who would never look at another woman. The fact that he could—and indeed had done so—ought to teach me something about myself, even if I was not quite sure what it was." The truth of it is that Wilmet has failed to recognize her society, including the parish of St. Luke's, for what it is, an erotic conclave of beauty and variety, both dangerous and enlivening. It is like George Herbert's "glass of blessings," full of the "world's riches"—"beautie . . . wisdome, honour, pleasure."

Quartet in Autumn · In her first six novels, Pym treats her characters with warm compassion and gentle irony. With *Quartet in Autumn*, however, her tone becomes harsher, more bitter, as she examines with bleak detachment the lonely rejection of the retired. Letty Crowe, another of Pym's excellent women, is sixty-five and faces retirement from the unspecified office job she has shared for many years with her colleagues, Marcia, Norman, and Edwin. For Letty, life in a rooming house is "a little sterile, perhaps even deprived." Retirement gives her a feeling of nothingness, as if she had never existed. During sleepless nights, her life unrolls before her, like that of a person drowning: forty years wasted looking for love. Images of dead leaves drifting to the pavement in autumn and being swept away recur throughout the novel. Indeed, Letty tries not to dwell on the image of herself lying among the autumnal leaves "to prepare for death when life became too much to be endured."

Her former colleagues are of no help to Letty. Norman is a scrawny, sardonic bachelor. Edwin is a widower preoccupied with "the soothing rhythms of the church's year." Marcia is gravely ill and at least slightly mad—collecting tins of food she never opens and milk bottles which she hoards in a shed. The only pleasures she knows are visits to the clinic for check-ups and bus trips to look at the mansion of her adored surgeon. Incapable of thought, she is far more pathetic than Letty.

Unlike her colleagues, Letty does try to act bravely, reading books on sociology, participating in church activities, still caring for her hair and her dress. "She told herself, dutifully assuming the suggested attitude toward retirement, that life was still full of possibilities." At the close of the novel, she is, like Mildred and Wilmet, where she was at the beginning. Yet, at the slightest change in the routine of her eventless days, she courageously assures herself, "at least it made one realize that life still held infinite possibilities for change."

In *Excellent Women, A Glass of Blessings*, and *Quartet in Autumn*, Pym relies neither on violence nor on the bizarre. Nothing outwardly momentous happens, but the frustrations of a half dozen or more characters emerge clearly and poignantly. Some critics have felt that the narrowness of her life inevitably imposed limitations on her work. Beneath the calm surface of her novels, however, the events of the day do make an imprint—to a degree appropriate to the lives of ordinary middle-class people. Each novel is a miniature work of art, distinguished by an air of assurance, an easy but firm control of the material, and the economy of means to achieve it.

Dale Salwak

Other major works
NONFICTION: *A Very Private Eye: An Autobiography in Diaries and Letters*, 1984.
MISCELLANEOUS: *Civil to Strangers and Other Writings*, 1987.

Bibliography
Allen, Orphia Jane. *Barbara Pym: Writing a Life*. Metuchen, N.J.: Scarecrow Press, 1994. Part 1 discusses Pym's life and work; part 2 analyzes her novels; part 3 examines different critical approaches to her work and provides a bibliographical essay; part 4 provides a comprehensive primary and secondary bibliography. An extremely useful volume for both beginning students and advanced scholars.

Benet, Diana. *Something to Love: Barbara Pym's Novels*. Columbia: University of Missouri Press, 1986. Benet's fresh and insightful study examines Pym as "a chronicler of universal problems" whose focus—the many guises of love—moves, shapes, or disfigures all of her major characters. Includes an index.

Burkhart, Charles. *The Pleasure of Miss Pym*. Austin: University of Texas Press, 1987. A very readable discussion of Pym's life and autobiographical writings, as well as her fiction through *An Academic Question*. Focuses on her worldview, the unique nature of her comedy, her religion, her place within the history of the novel, and her insights into male-female relationships. Includes photographs and an index.

Cotsell, Michael. *Barbara Pym*. New York: Macmillan, 1989. A cogent examination of all Pym's novels, paying particular attention to her characters' thoughts and feelings. Cotsell judges the novels to be "unabashedly romantic" and also considers Pym's sense of language, her unpublished writings, and her creative process. Includes an index.

Liddell, Robert. *A Mind at Ease: Barbara Pym and Her Novels*. London: Peter Owen, 1989. In this invaluable study, Liddell draws upon his fifty years of friendship with Pym to write a critical survey through *Crampton Hodnet*. Considers the attention she gave to her characters' domestic and emotional lives, examines the reasons for her revival in popularity, and guides the reader through her novels, explaining which ones are or are not successful and why. Also corrects errors by critics and dilutes the common misconception that Pym is a modern-day Jane Austen.

Long, Robert Emmet. *Barbara Pym*. New York: Frederick Ungar, 1986. A helpful treatment of Pym's first eleven novels, paying particular attention to her recurring themes and character types, her modes of social comedy and satire, and her pervasive concern with "unrealized" love and solitude. Finds that Jane Austen's dynamic English provincial world has reached a point of breakdown in Pym. Includes a chronology, notes, and an index.

Nardin, Jane. *Barbara Pym*. Boston: Twayne, 1985. An excellent introductory study of Pym's life and career, noting the origins and development of her themes, character types, and style. Contains a chronology, notes, a bibliography (listing primary and secondary sources), and an index.

Rossen, Janice, ed. *Independent Women: The Function of Gender in the Novels of Barbara Pym*. New York: St. Martin's Press, 1988. This collection of ten original essays seeks to test Pym's reputation by considering her craftsmanship, the literary influences on her work, and her special use of language. Includes biographical, historical, and feminist approaches to explore her unique creative process as it relates to events in her life. Notes and an index are provided.

_____. *The World of Barbara Pym*. New York: Macmillan, 1987. Focuses on twentieth century England as Pym saw, lived, satirized, and enjoyed it. Defines her significance within the framework of the modern British novel, traces her artistic development, explores interrelationships between her life and her fiction, and addresses broader themes regarding British culture in her work, such as spinsterhood, anthropology, English literature, the Anglican Church, and Oxford University. Notes and an index are provided.

Salwak, Dale, ed. *The Life and Work of Barbara Pym*. New York: Macmillan, 1987. Nineteen essays consider Pym's life and her novels, as well as her human and artistic achievements, from a variety of fresh perspectives. Includes notes and an index.

Snow, Lotus. *One Little Room an Everywhere: Barbara Pym's Novels*. Edited by Constance Hunting. Orono, Maine: Puckerbrush Press, 1987. In seven well-researched, clearly written chapters, Snow discusses Pym's interest in ordinary people and their mundane lives, her selection of character names, and her presentation of men and married women. Includes notes.

Weld, Annette. *Barbara Pym and the Novel of Manners*. New York: St. Martin's Press, 1992. Chapters on manners and comedy, poems, stories and radio scripts, the early novels, and her major fiction. Includes notes and bibliography.

Wyatt-Brown, Anne M. *Barbara Pym: A Critical Biography*. Columbia: University of Missouri Press, 1992. A fine narrative and analytical biography. See also the introduction: "Creativity and the Life Cycle." Includes notes and bibliography.

Ann Radcliffe

Born: London, England; July 9, 1764
Died: London, England; February 7, 1823

Principal long fiction · *The Castles of Athlin and Dunbayne*, 1789; *A Sicilian Romance*, 1790; *The Romance of the Forest*, 1791; *The Mysteries of Udolpho*, 1794; *The Italian: Or, The Confessional of the Black Penitents*, 1797; *Gaston de Blondeville*, 1826.

Other literary forms · In addition to her novels, Ann Radcliffe published *A Journey Made in the Summer of 1794 Through Holland and the Western Frontier of Germany* (1795). It recounts a continental journey made with her husband and includes copious observations of other tours to the English Lake District. The work became immediately popular, prompting a second edition that same year retitled *The Journeys of Mrs. Radcliffe*. Following a common practice of romance writers, Radcliffe interspersed the lengthy prose passages of her novels with her own verses or with those from famous poets. An anonymous compiler took the liberty of collecting and publishing her verses in an unauthorized edition entitled *The Poems of Ann Radcliffe* (1816). This slim volume was reissued in 1834 and 1845. Radcliffe's interest in versifying was increasingly evident when her husband, in arranging for the posthumous publication of *Gaston de Blondeville*, included with it a long metrical romance, *St. Alban's Abbey* (1826). Radcliffe also wrote an essay, "On the Supernatural in Poetry," which was published in *The New Monthly Magazine* (1826). The record of her literary achievement still remains available, as all of her novels and the poems are in print.

Achievements · Mrs. Radcliffe's fame as a novelist today in no way compares to the popularity she enjoyed in the 1790's. With the publication of her third novel, *The Romance of the Forest*, this relatively unknown woman established herself as the best-selling writer of the period, receiving rave reviews from the critics and increasing demand for her works from circulating libraries.

Radcliffe's five gothic romances, published between 1789 and 1797, owed a portion of their motivation to Horace Walpole's *The Castle of Otranto* (1765) and two earlier gothic writers, Sophia Lee and Clara Reeve. The gothic tale reached its full development with Radcliffe's ability to manipulate the emotions of love and fear in such a manner as to provoke terror in her characters and readers alike. Though managing an effective use of the little understood complexities of the imagination, she offered her readers stereotyped plots, characters, and settings. Her disguises of foreign characters and lands were as thin as the supernatural illusions which often seemed anticlimactic in their emotional appeal. These weaknesses did not deter Radcliffe's public, who remained fascinated by her distinctive brand of romanticism, which combined the gloomy darkening vale of the more somber poets of the graveyard school, the extremes of imaginative sensibility (as in Henry Mackenzie's *The Man of Feeling*, 1771), and the medieval extravagance of the Ossianic poems of James Macpherson, as well as the pseudoarchaic fabrications of Thomas Chatterton's Rowley poems (1777).

Radcliffe nurtured this cult of melancholy, primitivism, sentimentalism, exoticism, and medievalism in her novels, becoming the epitome of the gothic genre to her contemporaries. *The Mysteries of Udolpho*, her best-known work, was satirized by Jane Austen in *Northanger Abbey* (1818) as representative of the entire mode. Her later importance was seen in a number of major Romantic writers who read her romances in their childhood. Percy Bysshe Shelley's *Zastrozzi* (1810), an extravagant romance, was a youthful answer to the genre. Lord Byron's *Manfred* (1817) appears as a gothic villain committing spiritual murder in a landscape of "sublime solitudes." Matthew G. Lewis and Mary Wollstonecraft Shelley clearly benefited from Radcliffe's strengths as a novelist of suspense, mystery, and the picturesque. In America, Washington Irving's, Edgar Allan Poe's, and Nathaniel Hawthorne's tales of terror, along with Charles Brockden Brown's *Edgar Huntley* (1799), were suggested by Radcliffe's work.

As the most popular and perhaps most important novelist between the eighteenth century masters and Austen and Sir Walter Scott, Radcliffe continues to claim the attention of academicians. Psychological, feminist, folklorist, and the more traditional thematic studies have proved the strengths of her art. In 1980, Devendra P. Varma (*The Gothic Flame*, 1957) began serving as advisory editor for the Arno Press collection, *Gothic Studies and Dissertations*, which has published at least thirty-four texts dealing with Radcliffe's literary output; of those, fifteen discuss Radcliffe's novels at length. It is clear that there is at present a remarkable revival of interest in the gothic and in Radcliffe's work.

Biography · Mrs. Ann Radcliffe, *née* Ward, was born on July 9, 1764, in Holborn, a borough of central London, the only child of William Ward and Ann Oates Ward. Her father was a successful haberdasher who provided the family with a comfortable life, allowing Radcliffe access to a well-stocked library and the time to read the works of every important English author, as well as numerous popular romances.

This quiet, sheltered existence was enlivened by the visits of her wealthy and learned uncle, Thomas Bentley, who was the partner of Josiah Wedgwood, the potter. Bentley's London home was a center for the literati; there, among others, the pretty but shy girl met Mrs. Hester L. Thrale Piozzi, the friend and biographer of Samuel Johnson; Mrs. Elizabeth Montagu, "Queen of the Blue-Stocking Club"; and "Athenian" Stuart.

In 1772, Radcliffe joined her parents at Bath, where her father had opened a shop for the firm of Wedgwood and Bentley. She remained sequestered in this resort until her marriage to the young Oxford graduate, William Radcliffe, in 1788. William Radcliffe had first decided to become a law student at one of the Inns of Court but abandoned this for a career in journalism. The couple moved to London soon thereafter, where William subsequently became proprietor and editor of the *English Chronicle*. The marriage was happy but childless, and the couple's circle of friends were primarily literary, which added encouragement to William Radcliffe's argument that his wife should begin to write.

With her husband away on editorial business, Radcliffe spent the evenings writing without interruption. Her first book, *The Castles of Athlin and Dunbayne*, was unremarkable, but her next two novels established her reputation as a master of suspense and the supernatural. *A Sicilian Romance* and *The Romance of the Forest* attracted the public's voracious appetite for romances. Both works were translated into French and Italian, and numerous editions were published, as well as a dramatization of *The Romance of the Forest*, performed in 1794. Radcliffe's success culminated in the appearance of *The Mysteries of Udolpho*; her decision to rely less on external action and more on psychological conflict produced ecstatic reviews. The excitement created by the book threatened the relative solitude of the Radcliffes, but the publisher's unusually high offer of five hundred pounds freed them to travel extensively on the Continent.

In the summer of 1794, the Radcliffes journeyed through Holland and along the Rhine to the Swiss frontier. On returning to England, they proceeded north to the Lake District. While traveling, Radcliffe took complete notes concerning the picturesque landscape and included detailed political and economic accounts of the Low Countries and the Rhineland. These latter observations were probably contributed by her husband, though both Radcliffes found the devastation of the Napoleonic Wars appalling. In 1795, *A Journey Made in the Summer of 1794 Through Holland and the Western Frontier of Germany* appeared.

Radcliffe's interest in the human misery of these regions and the legends and superstitions of the great fortresses and Catholic churches of the Rhineland suggested her next work, *The Italian: Or, The Confessional of the Black Penitents.* As a romance of the Inquisition, it explored character motivation in great detail, while action became a method of dramatizing personalities and not a simple vehicle for movement from one adventure to another. *The Italian,* though not as popular as *The Mysteries of Udolpho,* was translated immediately into French and even badly dramatized at the Haymarket on August 15, 1797.

At the age of thirty-three, Radcliffe was at the height of her popularity; though she had never decided on writing as a potential source of income, her means by this time had become quite ample. With the deaths of her parents between 1798 and 1799, she found herself independently wealthy. Whether it was because of her secure financial condition or her displeasure with the cheap imitations of her novels, Radcliffe withdrew from the public domain and refrained from publishing any more works in her lifetime. Innumerable reports surfaced that she was suffering from a terminal illness, that the terrors of which she had written in her novels had driven her mad, or that she had mysteriously died. These reports were without substance; in fact, she wrote another novel, a metrical romance, and an extensive diary.

After her death, Radcliffe's husband found among her papers a novel, *Gaston de Blondeville,* which he arranged to have published. Written after Radcliffe's visit to the ruins of Kenilworth Castle in 1802, it came near to comparing with the historical romances of Scott but lost itself in a preoccupation with historical precision, leaving action and character to suffer from a lack of emphasis. The narrative poem, *St. Alban's Abbey,* appeared posthumously with this last novel; though Radcliffe had been offered an early opportunity for publication, she broke off negotiations with the publisher.

Content with retirement and relative obscurity, she wrote in her last years only diary entries concerning the places she and her husband had visited on their long journeys through the English countryside. From 1813 to 1816, she lived near Windsor and probably at this time began suffering from bouts of asthma. From all reports, she enjoyed the company of friends, maintained a ready wit and a sly humor, but insisted on delicacy and decorum in all things. Shortly before her final illness, she returned to London; she died there on February 7, 1823, in her sixtieth year. The "Udolpho woman" or "the Shakespeare of Romance Writers," as one contemporary reviewer called her, has achieved a secure place in the history of English literature.

Analysis · The novels of Ann Radcliffe serve as a transition between the major English novelists of the eighteenth century and the first accomplished novelists of the nineteenth century. In the years between 1789 and 1797, her five novels established a style which profoundly affected English fiction for the next twenty-five years and had a considerable impact in translation as well. From the negligible first novel, *The Castles of Athlin and Dunbayne,* to the sophisticated romances, *The Mysteries of Udolpho* and *The Italian,* Mrs. Radcliffe demonstrated an ability to enrich the motives, methods, and machineries of each succeeding work. Manipulating the conventions of the gothic while introducing new thematic concerns and experiments with narrative techniques, Radcliffe became a master of her craft.

Improved control over the complex atmosphere of the gothic romance proved an early factor in her success. Radcliffe went beyond the traditional gothic devices of lurking ghosts and malevolent noblemen torturing innocent girls to an interest in natural description. This delight with nature's sublime scenery gave tone and color to her settings while emphasizing the heightened emotions and imagination that were produced in reaction to the landscape. A skillful use of numerous atmospheric factors such as sunsets, storms, winds, thunderclaps, and moonlight intensified the romantic tendencies of her time.

A scene typifying the Radcliffe concept of landscape portraiture has a ruined castle in silhouette, arranged on a stern but majestic plain at nightfall. This view does not depend on precision of outline for effect but instead on an ominous vagueness, creating in the reader a queer mixture of pleasure and fear. Her delight in the architecture of massive proportions and in the picturesque derived in part from her reading of the nature poets and her study of the paintings of Claude Lorrain, Nicolas Poussin, and Salvator Rosa. She reflected a mid-eighteenth century English passion in cultivating an acute sensibility for discovering beauty where before it had not been perceived. While she made landscape in fiction a convention, it was her combining of beauty in horror and the horrible in the beautiful that reflected the Romantic shift away from order and reason toward emotion and imagination.

Radcliffe's novels rely not only on strategies of terror but also on the psychology of feelings. The novels of sensibility of the past generation offered her alternatives to the gothic trappings made familiar in Horace Walpole's *The Castle of Otranto*; those gothic aspects now became linked to various emotional elements in a total effect. By drawing on the poetry of Thomas Gray and Edward Young or the fiction of Oliver Goldsmith and Henry Mackenzie, Radcliffe created a minority of characters with complex natures who not only exhibited melancholy and doubt, love and joy, but also hate and evil intentions. She was one of the first English novelists to subject her characters to psychological analysis.

Of particular psychological interest are Radcliffe's villains. Cruel, calculating, domineering, relentless, and selfish, they are more compelling than her virtuous characters. Since their passions are alien to the ordinary person, she dramatically explores the mysteries of their sinister attitudes. Radcliffe's villains resemble those created by the Elizabethan dramatists, and their descendants can be found in the works of the great Romantics, Byron and Shelley.

At her best, Radcliffe manifested strengths not seen in her first two novels nor in her last. Her first novel, *The Castles of Athlin and Dunbayne,* exhibits the most obvious borrowings, from sources as well known as *The Castle of Otranto* to numerous other gothic-historical and sentimental novels. Though immature, the work offers her characteristic sense of atmosphere with the marvelous dangers and mysteries of feudal Scotland depicted to full advantage. Its weaknesses become evident all too soon, however, as stock characters populate strained, often confused incidents while mouthing rather obvious parables about morality. Didacticism seems the motivating principle of the work; as David Durant observes in *Ann Radcliffe's Novels* (1980), "The characters are so controlled by didactic interests as to be faceless and without personality." The rigid obligations of *The Castles of Athlin and Dunbayne* to the morality of sentimental novels, the uniformity of a neoclassical prose style, and the repetitious, predictable action of the romance plot trap Radcliffe into a mechanical performance.

A Sicilian Romance · Mrs. Radcliffe's second novel, *A Sicilian Romance*, has a new strategy, an emphasis on action and adventure while subordinating moral concerns. This approach, however, was not effective because of the obvious imbalance between the two methods, and characterization suffered before a mass of incident. The interest in fear was expanded throughout the tale as a long-suffering wife, imprisoned in the remote sections of a huge castle by a villainous nobleman (who has an attachment to a beautiful paramour), struggles helplessly until rescued, after much suspense, by her gentle daughter and the young girl's lover. The characters' shallowness is hidden by a chase sequence of overwhelming speed which prevents one from noticing their deficiencies. To dramatize the movement of plot, Radcliffe introduced numerous settings, offering the reader a complete vision of the Romantic landscape.

Though *A Sicilian Romance* lacks the sureness of technique of the later novels and remains a lesser product, it did establish Radcliffe's ingenuity and perseverance. It was followed by the three novels on which her reputation rests: *The Romance of the Forest*, *The Mysteries of Udolpho*, and *The Italian*. Radcliffe's last novel, the posthumous *Gaston de Blondeville*, which was probably never meant for publication, exhibits the worst faults of the two earliest romances. Lifeless characters abound in a narrative overloaded with tedious historical facts and devoid of any action. In reconstructing history, Radcliffe was influenced by Sir Walter Scott but clearly was out of her element in attempting to make history conform to her own preconceptions. The primary innovation was the introduction of a real ghost to the love story. This specter, the apparition of a murdered knight demanding justice, stalks the grounds of Kenilworth Castle at the time of the reign of Henry III. Radcliffe detracts from this imposing supernatural figure when she resorts to explanations of incidents better left mysterious.

The Romance of the Forest · With the publication of her third novel, *The Romance of the Forest*, Mrs. Radcliffe moved from apprenticeship to mastery. Her technique had advanced in at least two important elements: The chase with its multitude of settings is scaled down to an exacting series of dramas set among a few extended scenes, and characterization of the heroine is improved with the reduction of external action. Though suspense is extended rather illegitimately in order to produce a glorious final surprise, the novel is a genuine exploration of the realm of the unconscious. This remarkable advance into modern psychology gave life to the standard situations of Radcliffe's stories, allowing the reader to create his or her own private horrors.

Radcliffe's new emphasis on internal action makes her protagonist, Adeline, more credible than the stock romantic heroines whom she in many ways resembles. Adeline suffers from a nervous illness after mysteriously being thrust upon the LaMotte family, who themselves have only recently escaped, under curious circumstances, from Paris. Soon the group discovers a Gothic ruin, which contains the requisite underground room, rotten tapestries, blood stains, and a general aura of mystery.

Instead of the familiar chase scenes, a series of unified set-pieces portray the exploration of the ruin, the seduction of the heroine, and the execution of the hero.

The entire plot depends upon the actions of a vicious but dominating sadist, the Marquis Phillipe de Montalt, and his conspiratorial agent, Pierre de LaMotte, against the unprotected Adeline. Because of the uncertainty of her birth, the sexual implications of this situation involve the risk of incest. Among contemporary readers, *The Romance of the Forest* became an immediate success, owing to its well-constructed narrative, the charm of its description of Romantic landscape, and a consummate handling of the principle of suspense.

The Mysteries of Udolpho · Mrs. Radcliffe's next novel, *The Mysteries of Udolpho*, remains her best-known work. The sublimity of her landscapes and the control which she demonstrates in this novel mark an important change from her earlier novels; Radcliffe's handling of action and character also reached new levels of subtlety and success, moving the novel a step beyond the rather strict conventions of the sentimental mode to one of psychological inquiry.

The period of the novel is the end of the sixteenth century. The principal scenes are laid in the gloomy enclave of the Castle of Udolpho, in the Italian Apennines, but many glances are directed toward the south of France—Gascony, Provence, and Languedoc—and the brightness of Venice is contrasted with the dark horrors of the Apennines. Emily St. Aubert, the beautiful daughter of a Gascon family, is the heroine; she is intelligent and extraordinarily accomplished in the fine arts. Though revealing all the tender sensibilities of the characters associated with a hundred sentimental tales, Emily emerges as a credible figure who seems aware of the connections between the scenery around her and the characters who inhabit it. As a painter, she sees and thinks of life as a series of pictures. As David Durant explains in *Ann Radcliffe's Novels* (1980), "She does not merely feel fright, but conjures up imaginary scenes which elicit it . . . scenery inhabits the inner life of the heroine, as well as locating her actions." A further element of Emily's characterization that adds to her credibility is her internalizing of the suspense produced by the action in the narrative. Her heightened sensibility reacts to fear and terror in an all-inclusive way; this acuteness of sensibility makes her easy prey for the villain, Signor Montoni. This sinister figure marries Emily's aunt for her money, and then conveys Emily and her unhappy aunt to the "vast and dreary" confines of the castle.

This impossible castle becomes a superbly appointed stage for the playing of the melodrama. As the melodrama has hopes of communicating a real sense of mystery, its action and characters remain subordinate to the environment, which pervades the entire texture of the work. Description of landscape is a major part of the book's concept, and Radcliffe pays homage to Salvator Rosa and Claude Lorrain in emphasizing pictorial detail. The somber exterior of the castle prepares the reader for the ineffable horrors that lie within the walls and adumbrates the importance of landscape and massive architecture in the novel.

There are certain shortcomings in Radcliffe's method: Landscape description strangles action; the visual aspects of the novel have been internalized; and the device of the chase over great stretches of land has been subordinated by mental recapitulation of past scenes—action becomes tableaux. This internal action is slow-moving, tortuously so in a novel of 300,000 words. Critics have also objected to Radcliffe's penchant for a rational explanation of every apparent supernatural phenomenon she has introduced; others, however, point out that Radcliffe's readers enjoyed terror only if they were never forced into surrendering themselves.

The Mysteries of Udolpho brought new energy to the picturesque, the sentimental, and the gothic novel. Radcliffe alternated effectively between the picturesque vagueness of the landscape and the castle's hall of terrors. Her deft handling of sexual feeling, shown as antagonism between Montoni and Emily, is characteristic of her refusal to acknowledge sex overtly except as a frightening nameless power. The artificial terror, heightened sensibility, and the pervading air of mystery produced a powerful effect on her readers, yet many felt cheated by her failure to satisfy fully the intense imaginative visions awakened by the book. These readers would have to wait for *The Italian*, probably Radcliffe's finest work and the high-water mark of gothic fiction.

The Italian · The unity, control, and concentration of *The Italian* display a superb talent. Mrs. Radcliffe's narrative technique is more sophisticated than at any previous time, particularly in the subtle revelation of the unreliability of feelings based on first impressions rather than on rational judgment. The dramatic pacing remains rigorous throughout and relatively free from digressions. The story's impulse depends upon the Marchesa di Vivaldi's refusal to allow her young son, Vincentio, to marry the heroine, Ellena di Rosalba, whose origins are in doubt. The Marchesa relies on the sinister machinations of her monk-confessor, Schedoni, who decides to murder Ellena. Radcliffe's antipathy to Roman Catholicism is evident in her account of the horrors of the Carmelite abbey and its order, including the labyrinthine vaults and gloomy corridors. A strange blend of fascination and disgust is evoked here and in the scenes of the trial in the halls of the Inquisition, the ruins of the Paluzzi, and the prison of the Inquisition. Clearly, the gothic aspects of *The Italian* function as representations of a disordered and morally evil past.

The vividness continues through to the climax of the story, when Schedoni, dagger in hand, prepares to murder Ellena but hesitates when he recognizes the portrait miniature she wears. Believing the girl is his lost daughter, he tries to make amends for his crimes. Though the solution involves more complex developments, the excitement of the confrontation between these two figures remains exceptional. Ellena has been a paragon of virtue, displaying piety, sensibility, benevolence, constancy, and a love of nature. To this catalog, Radcliffe adds intelligence, courage, and ingenuity. As an idealized character, Ellena represents the strengths necessary to prevail in the Romantic conflict against external malign forces.

Schedoni, the devil/priest, is a figure of strong and dangerous sexual desire, associated, as is often the case in Radcliffe's work, with incest. Radcliffe counters the passivity and weakness of Ellena's virtues with this masculine version of desire, the lust of unregulated ambition. She describes him thus: "There was something terrible in his air, something almost superhuman. . . . His physiognomy . . . bore traces of many passions . . . his eyes were so piercing that they seemed to penetrate at a single glance into the hearts of men, and to read their most secret thoughts." His pride, greed, and loneliness combine to form a demonic figure vaguely suggesting John Milton's Satan.

Eino Railo, in *The Haunted Castle* (1964), believes *The Italian* and the central character, Father Schedoni, were created under the revivified Romantic impulse supplied by the tragic monastic figure in Matthew Gregory Lewis's *The Monk* (1796). According to Railo, the difference between Ambrosio and Schedoni is that the latter "is no longer a young and inexperienced saint preserved from temptations, but a person long hardened in the ways of crime and vice, alarmingly gifted and strenuous, hypocritical, unfeeling and merciless." Radcliffe was inspired by "Monk" Lewis to write a more impressive book than earlier conceived; her bias against sexual and sadistic impulses and toward heightened romantic effect win out in *The Italian.* While Ambrosio's passions remain tangled and confused by his need for immediate satisfaction and his lack of any lasting goal, Schedoni has well-defined goals for power, wealth, and status. His Machiavellian inclinations blend with pride, melancholy, mystery, and dignity, making him Radcliffe's most fully realized character. Her protest against *The Monk* created a story of tragic quality that goes beyond the conventional gothic paraphernalia and toward the psychological novel.

Mrs. Radcliffe remains the undisputed mistress of the gothic novel and a central figure in the gothic revival, beginning in the late 1950's, which has seen the resurrection of hordes of forgotten gothic novelists and their tales. The generous volume of Radcliffe criticism in recent decades has redefined her place in literary history, acknowledging the prodigious sweep of her influence. On first reading her works, one must remember to search behind the genteel exterior of the artistry to discover the special recesses of terror, subconscious conflict, and the psychology of feelings which played a major role in the evolution of dark Romanticism.

Paul J. deGategno

Other major works

POETRY: *The Poems of Ann Radcliffe,* 1816; *St. Alban's Abbey,* 1826.

NONFICTION: *A Journey Made in the Summer of 1794 Through Holland and the Western Frontier of Germany,* 1795.

Bibliography

Durant, David S. *Ann Radcliffe's Novels: Experiments in Setting.* Rev. ed. New York: Arno Press, 1980. Discovers a pattern of evolution in Radcliffe's novels from the sentimental *The Castles of Athlin and Dunbayne* to the historical *Gaston de Blondeville* that reflects the movement of eighteenth century British fiction and completes the transition between Fanny Burney's fiction and Sir Walter Scott's romances. This book still shows the shape of its original dissertation format, including footnotes; nevertheless, it is one of the few easily accessible books on Radcliffe. Devotes six chapters to detailed analyses of her six novels, putting them in the context of their time and genre and illustrating their experimental styles.

Kiely, Robert. *The Romantic Novel in England.* Cambridge, Mass.: Harvard University Press, 1972. An important book on Romantic fiction, including Radcliffe's gothic romances, which analyzes in depth twelve Romantic novels to define the intellectual context of the era. Notes that concepts of reality were tested and changed by Romantic novels and that Edmund Burke's ideas of the sublime modified aesthetic forms. Radcliffe is given a prominent place in this general thesis and *The Mysteries of Udolpho* is analyzed in detail as the focus of her chapter. Her novel is shown as a progressive revelation that nature weakens beneath the power of human imagination to project itself upon nature, as her heroine is deprived of consolation from natural order. Finds a common drift toward death in most novels of this genre. Includes a set of notes and an index.

McIntyre, Clara Frances. *Ann Radcliffe in Relation to Her Time.* New Haven, Conn.: Yale University Press, 1920. Reprint. New York: Archon Books, 1970. A dated, but still useful, 104-page study of Radcliffe which reviews the facts of her life and surveys her work. Presents contemporary estimates of her novels, considers their sources, and lists translations and dramatizations of them. Argues that Radcliffe's main contribution is in her improvement of Horace Walpole's method of dramatic structure, demonstrated by an analysis of her structures and their influences on the structures of Sir Walter Scott, Mary Shelley, and others. Contains a bibliography which includes a list of references to magazines.

Miles, Robert. *Ann Radcliffe: The Great Enchantress.* Manchester: Manchester University Press, 1995. Explores the historical and aesthetic context of Radcliffe's fiction, with separate chapters on her early works and mature novels. Miles also considers Radcliffe's role as a woman writer and her place in society. Includes notes and bibliography.

Murray, E. B. *Ann Radcliffe.* New York: Twayne, 1972. Surveys Radcliffe's life, drawing from her *A Journey Made in the Summer of 1794 Through Holland and the Western Frontier of Germany* to illustrate her novels' geography. Examines the background of the gothic, with its supernatural elements, sentiment and sensibility, and sense of the sublime and the picturesque. Looks at Radcliffe's modern romance of medieval experience, *The Castles of Athlin and Dunbayne*; concentrates on the heroine's sufferings in *A Sicilian Romance*; examines the strengths in plot and atmosphere of *The Romance of the Forest*; views *The Mysteries of Udolpho* as her first successful synthesis of modern and medieval; and argues that *The Italian* is Radcliffe's best novel because it sustains the reader's interest. Provides an overview of Radcliffe's literary accomplishments and influence. Includes notes, a selected annotated bibliography, and an index.

Rogers, Deborah D., ed. *The Critical Response to Ann Radcliffe.* Westport, Conn.: Greenwood Press, 1994. A good selection of critical essays on Radcliffe. Includes bibliographical references and an index.

Smith, Nelson C. *The Art of the Gothic: Ann Radcliffe's Major Novels.* New York: Arno Press, 1980. Contains a valuable introduction which reviews the scholarship on Radcliffe between 1967 and 1980. Analyzes the ways Radcliffe developed the sophistication of her fiction from *The Castles of Athlin and Dunbayne* to *The Mysteries of Udolpho* and *The Italian* in a six-year period. Examines the nature of the gothic in order to focus on Radcliffe's heroines of sensibility. Notes a decline of didacticism in Radcliffe's fiction by isolating her heroes and villains for study. Analyzes the narrative techniques used to craft the gothic tale and surveys the gothic writers who followed Radcliffe. Includes end notes for each chapter and a bibliography.

Mary Renault

Mary Challans

Born: London, England; September 4, 1905
Died: Cape Town, South Africa; December 13, 1983

Principal long fiction · *Purposes of Love*, 1939 (pb. in U.S. as *Promise of Love*, 1940); *Kind Are Her Answers*, 1940; *The Friendly Young Ladies*, 1944 (pb. in U.S. as *The Middle Mist*, 1945); *Return to Night*, 1947; *North Face*, 1948; *The Charioteer*, 1953; *The Last of the Wine*, 1956; *The King Must Die*, 1958; *The Bull from the Sea*, 1962; *The Mask of Apollo*, 1966; *Fire from Heaven*, 1969; *The Persian Boy*, 1972; *The Praise Singer*, 1978; *Funeral Games*, 1981; *The Alexander Trilogy*, 1984 (includes *Fire from Heaven, The Persian Boy*, and *Funeral Games*).

Other literary forms · All but two of Mary Renault's published works are novels. *The Lion in the Gateway: Heroic Battles of the Greeks and Persians at Marathon, Salamis, and Thermopylae* (1964) is a children's history of ancient Greek battles. *The Nature of Alexander* (1975) is a heavily documented biography placing the charismatic leader in the context of his time and customs, a book that also defines the two abiding preoccupations of Alexander's life and Renault's art. "Outward striving for honor," the Greek *to philotimo*, balances *arete*, the profound inward thirst for achievement knowingly made beautiful. Together, as Alexander himself wrote, they win immortality: "It is a lovely thing to live with courage,/ and die leaving an everlasting fame."

Achievements · Critics praised Renault's first five novels, written and set around World War II, for their realism, psychological depth, and literary technique. In 1946, one year prior to its publication, *Return to Night* won the MGM Award, $150,000, then the world's largest literary prize. Although this novel was never made into a motion picture, the award brought Renault American acclaim, augmented later by the success of her Greek novels, but her work has never gained the academic attention it deserves. She received the National Association of Independent Schools Award in 1963 and the Silver Pen Award in 1971, and she was a Fellow of the Royal Society of Literature.

Biography · Mary Renault (the pen name of Mary Challans), a physician's daughter, was born on September 4, 1905, in London. At eight, she decided to become a writer, and she read English at St. Hugh's College, Oxford, from 1924 to 1927, where she preferred to study the Middle Ages, the setting of an attempted historical novel she destroyed after several rejections. She had once thought of teaching, but after graduation she entered nurses' training at Radcliffe Infirmary, Oxford, where she received her nursing degree in 1937. She dated her literary career from 1939, though she continued as a neurosurgical nurse at Radcliffe Infirmary throughout the war, writing in her off-duty hours. Her first novels were widely popular, but she claimed that "if her early novels were destroyed irrevocably, she would feel absolutely no loss" (Bernard F. Dick, *The Hellenism of Mary Renault*, 1972).

Renault's postwar travels in the eastern Mediterranean provided the impetus for a new literary phase marked by her immigration to South Africa in 1948. After this move, her exhaustive self-taught knowledge of ancient Greek history and philosophy made her a mesmerizing novelist able to re-create a lost world. In the estimation of Bernard Dick, Renault was "the only bona fide Hellenist in twentieth century fiction."

Renault remained a resident of South Africa until her death on December 13, 1983.

Analysis · Mary Renault's novels celebrate and eulogize people's potential but transitory glory, a combination difficult for a world that has relinquished its acquaintance with the classics. Peter Wolfe regards Renault's first five novels as her literary apprenticeship, "1930's novels" marked by then-fashionable themes of political engagement and sexual liberation. Bernard F. Dick, her only other major commentator, believes her early fiction was influenced by the restrictive, pain-filled atmosphere of a World War II surgical hospital. Both are partly correct; Renault's early work deals with the individual's freedom from contemporary power structures and stifling social conventions.

Such topical concerns, however appealing to modern readers, are nevertheless peripheral to the core of Renault's art, the Platonism which she followed to the mythic depths in her later novels. When she began to write, Renault was already familiar with the Theory of Ideas developed in Plato's dialogues, wherein everything perceptible by human senses is imitative of changeless perfect Ideas beyond time and space. Each Idea corresponds to a class of earthly objects, all of which must inevitably change, leaving the Ideas the only objects of true knowledge in the universe. A transitory earthly object, however, may remind people of the Idea it represents. Plato theorized that before entering the body, the soul had encountered the infinite Ideas, and that once embodied, the soul might vaguely remember them. Renault often convincingly incorporates Plato's anamnesis, the doctrine that "learning is recollection," in her fiction. Plato also believed that hu-

Corbis

man recognition of such natural truths as the mathematically perfect circle could lead people stepwise to the contemplation of Absolute Truth, which he equated with Absolute Goodness and Absolute Beauty. He taught that the immortal human soul may be reborn through metempsychosis, or transmigration, another concept found throughout Renault's work.

Renault's novels are also informed by Plato's theory of love as defined by Socrates in *The Symposium* (c. 388-368 B.C.E.): love is the desire for immortality through possession of or union with the Beautiful. Love manifests itself on its lowest levels by human sexuality, proceeds upward through intellectual achievement, and culminates in a mystical union of the soul with the Idea of Beauty. That Renault's heroes aspire to such union is their glory; that being mortal they must fail is the fate she eulogizes.

Plato, like most classical Greeks, allowed heterosexual love only the lowest rung on his ladder of love, as the necessary element for reproduction. Only the homosexual relationship was considered capable of inspiring the lifelong friendships which offered each partner the ideal of *arete*. All of Renault's novels illustrate some aspect of Platonic love; in the first, *Promise of Love*, she shows Vivian, a nurse, and Mic, who loves her because she resembles her brother Jan, achieving self-knowledge not through sexual passion but by affection, the ultimate stage of Platonic love, which at the close of the novel "recalls the true lover of [Plato's dialogue] the *Phaedrus* who is willing to sleep like a servant at the side of his beloved."

Renault's other early novels also have strong Platonic elements. *Kind Are Her Answers* foreshadows her interest in theater as mimetic form, Plato's first literary love, which she realized more fully in *The Mask of Apollo*. Her third novel, *The Middle Mist*, concludes with references to Plato's *Lysis*, his dialogue on friendship which claims that erotic satisfaction destroys *philia*, the more permanent nonphysical union promised by Platonic love, a theme to which Renault returned more successfully in *The Last of the Wine*. Renault attempted unconvincingly in *Return to Night* and *North Face* to state the *amor vincit omnia* tradition of "women's fiction" in mythological metaphors, and found that she had to develop a new fictional mode capable of expressing her archetypal themes with Platonic concepts.

The Charioteer · Not published in the United States until 1959 because of its forthright treatment of homosexuality, *The Charioteer* is the only Renault novel to incorporate a systematic development of Platonic philosophy as the vehicle for commentary on contemporary life. In the *Phaedrus* (c. 388-368 B.C.E.), Plato depicted reason as a charioteer who must balance the thrust of the white horse of honor against the unruly black horse of passion. The image unifies Renault's tale of Laurie Odell, wounded at Dunkirk, who must come to terms with his homosexuality. After his friendship with the sexually naïve conscientious objector Andrew Raines dissolves, Laurie finds a lifelong partner in Ralph Lanyon, who brought him back wounded after they had fought at Dunkirk. Laurie attains an equilibrium between the two conflicting halves of his nature in a Platonic denial of sexual excess. As Renault comments in the epilogue, a Greek device she favors, "Now their [the horses'] heads droop side by side till their long manes mingle; and when the charioteer falls silent they are reconciled for a night in sleep."

In the ideal Platonic pattern, the older man assumes a compassionate responsibility for the honor of the younger, altogether transcending physical attraction and ce- mented by shared courage in battle. Renault's efforts at an entirely convincing presentation of such friendship are hindered by the intolerance with which homosex- ual relationships are usually viewed in modern society and the often pathetic insecu- rity it forces upon them. Despite these handicaps, Renault sympathetically portrays Laurie as "a modern Hephaestus, or maimed artist," as Wolfe notes, a character who wins admiration through striving to heal his injured life and nature and make of them something lasting and beautiful.

From roots far deeper than Plato's philosophy, Renault developed the vital im- pulse of her eight Greek novels, her major literary achievement. Central is the duality of Apollo and Dionysus, names the Greeks gave to the forces of the mind and of the heart, gods whose realms the mythologist Walter Otto described in *Dionysus, Myth and*

Cult (1965) as "sharply opposed" yet "in reality joined together by an eternal bond." In Greek myth, Zeus's archer son Apollo, wielder of the two-sided weapon of Truth, endowed people with the heavenly light called Art, by which he admonished humankind to self-knowledge and moderation through his oracle at Delphi. Paradoxically, Apollo shared his temple and the festival year at Delphi with his mysterious brother Dionysus, god of overwhelming ecstasy, born of mortal woman and all-powerful Zeus, torn apart each year to rise again, offering both wine's solace and its madness to humankind. Thought and emotion were the two faces of the Greek coin of life—in Otto's words, "the eternal contrast between a restless, whirling life and a still, far-seeing spirit."

Each of Renault's Greek novels focuses on a crucial nexus of physical and spiritual existence in Greek history. The age of legendary heroes such as Theseus of Athens, subject of *The King Must Die* and *The Bull from the Sea*, was followed by the Trojan War, 1200 B.C.E., the stuff of classical epic and tragedy and the harbinger of Greece's Dark Age, when only Athens stood against the Dorian invasion. By the sixth century B.C.E., the setting of *The Praise Singer*, Athens, under the benevolent tyrant Pisistratus, had become the model *polis* of the Greek peninsula, building a democracy that repelled imperial Persia and fostered the world's greatest tragedies in their Dionysian festivals. *The Last of the Wine* treats the fall of Athens to Sparta in the Peloponnesian Wars, 404 B.C.E., torn by internal strife and bled by foreign expansion. The restored Athenian democracy of a half-century later is the milieu of *The Mask of Apollo*. Shortly after Plato's death, his pupil Aristotle taught a prince in Macedon who dreams of Homeric deeds in *Fire from Heaven*, accomplishes them in *The Persian Boy*, and leaves an empire to be shattered by lesser men in *Funeral Games*–Alexander the Great.

The Last of the Wine · *The Last of the Wine*, like most of Renault's Greek fiction, is ostensibly a memoir, a form favored by classical authors. Its fictional narrator, a young and "beautiful" Athenian knight named Alexias, endures the agonizing aftermath of Athens' ill-fated Sicilian venture under Alkibiades, the magnetic but flawed former student of Sokrates. With Lysis, the historical figure on whom Plato modeled his dialogue on ideal friendship, Alexias begins the idealistic attachment they learned together from Sokrates, but physical passion, handled with sensitivity by Renault, overcomes them, and they ruefully must compromise their ideal. Sacrificing his honor for Lysis during the famine caused by the Spartan siege of Athens, Alexias models for sculptors, at least one lascivious, to feed his wounded friend, and in the battle to restore Athenian democracy, Lysis falls gloriously with Alexias's name upon his lips.

The novel's title, an allusion to the Greek custom in which the wine remaining in a cup is tossed to form the initial of a lover's name, metaphorically represents Athens's abandonment of the ideals of its Golden Age. Renault poignantly shows Lysis, a gentleman athlete in pursuit of *philotimo*, the hero's struggle for outward glory to emulate his ideal, beaten sadistically in the Isthmian Games by a monstrous professional wrestler, just as Athenian democracy is becoming warped by politicians such as the vicious Kritias and the cold-blooded Anytos, who will help condemn Sokrates. Alkibiades' personal disaster, abandoning Athens for its Spartan enemies, is an exemplary case of a leader who cannot resist abusing his charismatic gifts.

The Greek ideal of democracy learned at Sokrates' side and based on individual *arete*, inward pursuit of honor, still allows Lysis a moral victory often overlooked in this splendidly elegiac novel of the death of an era. "Men are not born equal in themselves," Lysis tells Alexias over wine one evening in Samos; "a man who thinks himself as good as everyone else will be at no pains to grow better." Lysis fights and dies for "a City where I can find my equals and respect my betters . . . and where no one can tell me to swallow a lie because it is expedient." At the end of the novel, as he listens to the distorted minds of bureaucrats, Alexias remembers the lamps of Samos, the wine-cup on a table of polished wood, and Lysis's voice: "Must we forsake the love of excellence, then, till every citizen feels it alike?"

The King Must Die and The Bull from the Sea · Renault analyzes the ideal of kingship in *The King Must Die* and *The Bull from the Sea*. In the earlier novel, she traces Theseus's early life from Troezen and Eleusis, where with the bard Orpheus he establishes the Sacred Mysteries, to the labyrinthine palace of Crete, where he destroys the brutal son of King Minos, who oppresses Athens. In the second, she pursues Theseus's progressive rule in Athens through his abandonment of Ariadne to Dionysus's bloody cult and his capture of the Amazon Hippolyta to the great tragedy of his life, his fatal curse on their son Hippolytus. Stylistically more evocative of Homer's mighty simplicity than the Attic cadences of *The Last of the Wine*, Renault's Theseus novels treat kingship as a manifestation of the divine inner voice that chooses the moment of willing consent when the monarch sacrifices himself for his people.

Both novels discuss a past so dim that its events have become the raw material of myth. Theseus's birth meshes the earthly with the supernatural, since it results from the divinely inspired compassion of the Athenian King Aigios for the stricken land of Troezen; the reader is left, as is customary in Renault's fiction, to decide where history ends and metaphysics begins. Until his son's death, Theseus practices the lesson learned from his grandfather's ritual sacrifice of the King Horse, one of the shocking joys hidden in pain that opens much of Renault's fiction: "The consenting . . . the readiness is all. It washes heart and mind . . . and leaves them open to the god."

By closing himself to the speaking god, however, obeying not his reason but his emotional reaction to his wife Phaedra's false accusations of Hippolytus, Theseus is lost. Only two bright moments remain to him, an anamnetic dream of Marathon where he fights beside the Athenians defending their City, his name their stirring war cry; and a glimpse before he dies of the boy Achilles, "as springy and as brisk as noonday, his arm round a dark-haired friend." Prescient, Theseus watches tragedy in the making: "The god who sent him that blazing pride should not have added love to be burned upon it," but—consoled that his own reputation has become Achilles' "touchstone for a man"—Theseus for the last time consents to the god of the sea.

The Mask of Apollo · By the mid-fourth century B.C.E., late in Plato's life, sophisticated Athenians had accepted the gods as metaphysical forces within the human personality. In *The Mask of Apollo*, Renault poses the primal duality of Apollo and Dionysus in Greek culture, the calm, far-seeing force of reason and art balanced against the irresistible force of ecstasy. An old mask of Apollo, reputedly from the workshop of the Parthenon's architect Phidias, accompanies Renault's narrator Nikeratos through his successful acting career, the fascinating backdrop to the political career of Dion of Syracuse, Plato's noble friend, who might have become the ideal philosopher-king Plato postulated in *The Republic*.

Though Dion is a model soldier and a principled statesman, circumstances force him to abandon his philosophical ideals to save Syracuse from devastation. Renault parallels his fall with Nikeratos's performance in Euripides' *The Bacchae* (405 B.C.E.), the enigmatic masterpiece named for the followers of Dionysus. As he meditates before Apollo's mask, Nikeratos hears his own voice: "With *The Bacchae* he [Euripides] digs down far below, to some deep rift in the soul where our griefs begin. Take that play anywhere, even to men unborn who worship other gods or none, and it will teach them to know themselves."

Plato's tragedy, acted out by Dion, was the "deep rift" that made people unable to follow him with united minds and hearts: "No one would fight for Dion, when he gave, as his own soul saw it, his very life for justice." By serving Apollo and Dionysus equally, however, Nikeratos the artist earns his gifts, one a Platonic dream of acting in a strange revenge drama, speaking lines beside an open grave to a clean skull in his hand. Through his love for his protégé Thettalos, whom he frees for achievements he knows will be greater than his own, Nikeratos plays Achilles in Aeschylus's *The Myrmidons* in a performance viewed by Alexander, a boy for whom men will fight and die, "whether he is right or wrong," a prince who "will wander through the world . . . never knowing . . . that while he was still a child the thing he seeks slipped from the world, worn out and spent." Had he encountered Plato's Ideals, which he instinctively sought, Renault proposes as the curtain falls on *The Mask of Apollo*, the Alexander of history might have made the philosopher-king Plato's Dion never could have been; but Nikeratos observes that "no one will ever make a tragedy—and that is well, for one could not bear it—whose grief is that the principals never met."

Fire from Heaven · Renault's Alexander grows from boy to king in *Fire from Heaven*, in which she abandons the memoir form for more objective narration, as though no single point of view could encompass Alexander's youthful ideals, fired by the blazing Homeric *philotimo* in Achilles' honor he learned at the epic-conscious Macedonian court. Modern archaeology supports Renault's conviction that Alexander deliberately patterned his actions, even his father Philip's funerary rites, upon the *Iliad* (c. 800 B.C.E.), which he read as though returning home, recognizing in his mutual love with Hephaistion the tragic bond of Achilles and Patroclus, the basis of the Western world's first, perhaps greatest, poem.

Arete, which cloaks the heavenly Idea of excellence in earthly beauty, came to Alexander less from Aristotle than through his instinctive attraction to Sokrates through Plato's works, which he read as a boy in Macedon. After defeating Thebes's Sacred Band at Cheironeia, where Philip's Macedonians secured the domination of all of Greece, Alexander stands "with surmise and regret" at Plato's tomb in Athens, listening to his disciple Xenokrates: "What he [Plato] had to teach could only be learned as fire is kindled, by the touch of the flame itself."

The Persian Boy · The novel in which Renault most precariously treats the question of homosexuality, *The Persian Boy*, is narrated by Bagoas, the handsome eunuch once King Darius's favorite and now the lover of Alexander. Renault's choice of Bagoas's point of view reflects her belief that Alexander was not corrupted by Persian luxury and imperial power, as many historians from classical times to the present have asserted, but that he sought to assimilate Eastern ways as a means of uniting his realm in spirit as well as military fact. Just as Alexander's "passionate capacity for affection" could allow him to accept affection wherever it was sincerely offered from the heart and yet remain wholly true to Bagoas's "victor now, forever," Hephaistion (who Renault feels is the most underrated man in history), Alexander felt "Macedon was my father's country. This is mine"—meaning the empire he had won for himself.

Renault believes that Alexander's eventual tragedy was that he was humanly unable to achieve equilibrium between his followers' personal devotion to him and their pragmatic selfish desires. Through Alexander's complex relationship with his dangerous mother Olympias, herself a devotee of Dionysus, Renault exemplifies the peril of neglecting the god of ecstasy basic to *The Bacchae*, in which Olympias herself had acted during Alexander's youth as a shocking challenge to Philip's authority. Toward the end of Alexander's own life, Dionysus's cruelty touches even him. Renault shows his purported deterioration as less his own fault than his men's when he must hold them by force as well as by love, even violating Macedon's dearest law, killing before their Assembly had condemned a man to death. The powerful god leads Alexander to excess; Bagoas sees that "his hunger grew by feeding." The Roman historian Arrian, following the memoir of Alexander's only faithful general Ptolemy, commented, "If there had been no other competition, he would have competed against himself."

Bagoas better than any also sees that "great anguish lies in wait for those who long too greatly." Alexander loses Hephaistion and with him nearly abandons his own senses, emerging only after his friend's funeral, in which he watches Thettalos, without Nikeratos for the first time, perform *The Myrmidons* one last time; "'perhaps,' Bagoas thought, 'the last of the madness had been seared out of him by so much burning.'"

At the close of *The Persian Boy*, Renault notes in her Afterword, "When his [Alexander's] faults (those his own times did not account as virtues) have been considered . . . no other human being has attracted in his lifetime, from so many men, so fervent a devotion. Their reasons are worth examining." In her two novels of Alexander's life, Renault not only has examined the reasons, but also has brilliantly probed to the heart of one of the greatest human mysteries: how one person can ask, as did Homer's Achilles, "now as things are, when the ministers of death stand by us/ In their thousands, which no man born to die can escape or even evade,/ Let us go."—and how other people, with all their hearts, can answer.

Such "true songs are still in the minds of men," according to the aged bard Simonides, narrator of *The Praise Singer*, recalling the "lyric years" when tragedy was being born of song and Athens was becoming the center of the earth. "We die twice when men forget," the ghosts of heroes seemed to tell him as a boy, and he has spent his life in "the bright and perilous gift of making others shine." In this novel, where Renault's heroic epitaph for *philotimo* and her noble elegy for people's hope of *arete* have given place to a gentler, less exalted nostalgia, she recognizes that "praising excellence, one serves the god within it." Renault also notes in her Afterword that "the blanket generalization 'absolute power corrupts absolutely' is a historical absurdity," and she demonstrates that the respected rule of Pisistratus, nominally a "tyrant," formed the solid foundation on which Pericles erected Athenian democracy, even presaging through a discredited seer "a lightning flash from Macedon."

In Alexander's time, Renault has remarked, "the issue was not whether, but how one made [war]." At his death, brought about at least in part by his self-destructive grief for Hephaistion, Alexander's generals embarked on a cannibalistic power struggle—only Ptolemy, his half-brother, emerging with any of the dignity Alexander had worn so easily in conquering his empire. Renault's *Funeral Games* is "the ancestral pattern of Macedonian tribal and familial struggles for his throne; except that Alexander had given them a world stage on which to do it."

Funeral Games · The most violent of Renault's Greek novels, *Funeral Games* contains a darkness that is alleviated only by flashes of Alexander reflected through the decency of the few who knew him best—Ptolemy; Bagoas; Queen Sisygambis, who looked upon Alexander, not Darius, as her son. In them, something of Alexander's flame lingers a little while, a heavenly light extinguished at last in the wreckage of his empire in human depravity which Alexander could not prevent nor Renault fail to record.

In her eight novels of ancient Greece, Renault far surpasses conventional historical fiction. She achieves a mythic dimension in her balance of Apollonian and Dionysian psychological forces and philosophical precision in her treatment of Platonic doctrines. Her style is adapted to the Greek literature of each period she delineates, Attic elegance for *The Last of the Wine* and *The Mask of Apollo*, Hellenic involution counterpoised against Alexander's Homeric simplicity of speech. Renault links all eight novels with a chain of works of art, a finely crafted touch the classical Greeks would have applauded: the great tragedies, *The Myrmidons* and *The Bacchae*, Polykleitos's sculpture of Hermes modeled on Alexias, and the bronze of the liberator Harmodios in Pisistratos's day all serve as shaping factors in the portrait of her ultimate hero, Alexander. Mastering time, space, and modern ignorance of the classical world, Renault captures the "sadness at the back of life" Virginia Woolf so aptly cited as the essence of Greek literature, the inevitable grieving awareness of people at the impassable gulf between their aspirations and their achievement. In the face of the eternal questions of existence, Renault's novels offer a direction in which to turn when, in Woolf's words, "we are sick of the vagueness, of the confusion, of the Christianity and its consolations, of our own age."

Mitzi M. Brunsdale

Other major works
NONFICTION: *The Nature of Alexander,* 1975.

CHILDREN'S LITERATURE: *The Lion in the Gateway: Heroic Battles of the Greeks and Persians at Marathon, Salamis, and Thermopylae,* 1964.

Bibliography

Burns, Landon C., Jr. "Men Are Only Men: The Novels of Mary Renault." *Critique: Studies in Modern Fiction* 4 (Winter, 1963): 102-121. A good, but limited, look at Renault's historical fiction. Burns examines character, theme, and use of classical myth in *The Last of the Wine, The King Must Die,* and *The Bull from the Sea.* Burns's careful study repeatedly stresses the high order of Renault's fiction.

Dick, Bernard F. *The Hellenism of Mary Renault.* Carbondale: Southern Illinois University Press, 1972. An excellent introduction to Renault's work, examining her entire literary output through *Fire from Heaven.* Places Renault in the mainstream of fiction and applauds her as one of the most creative historical novelists of the century.

Sweetman, David. *Mary Renault: A Biography.* New York: Harcourt Brace, 1993. The first part explores Renault's life in England, including her education at Oxford. The second part describes her years in South Africa. A fascinating study of Renault's sexuality as it relates to her historical novels. Includes a bibliography.

Wolfe, Peter. *Mary Renault.* New York: Twayne, 1969. The first full-length examination of the writer, but limited through *The Mask of Apollo.* Wolfe's study is both a plea for Renault's recognition by the critics as an important twentieth century writer and a critical analysis of her work. He has high praise for most of her novels but dislikes *North Face* and *The Bull from the Sea.*

Jean Rhys

Ella Gwendolen Rees Williams

Born: Roseau, Dominica Island, West Indies; August 24, 1894
Died: Exeter, England; May 14, 1979

Principal long fiction · *Postures*, 1928 (pb. in U.S. as *Quartet*, 1929); *After Leaving Mr. Mackenzie*, 1930; *Voyage in the Dark*, 1934; *Good Morning, Midnight*, 1939; *Wide Sargasso Sea*, 1966.

Other literary forms · Though Jean Rhys is now primarily remembered for her novels, her first published book was a collection of short stories, *The Left Bank and Other Stories* (1927). As Ford Madox Ford pointed out in the preface to the collection, Rhys's heroines are geographically, psychologically, and emotionally of "the Left Bank," not only of Paris–though Rhys captured the Paris of the 1920's as well as anyone–but also of all the cities of the world. They are underdogs, alone, betrayed, on the edge of poverty; they are women in a man's world.

Besides *The Left Bank*, Rhys published two other collections of stories: *Tigers Are Better-Looking* (1968) and *Sleep It Off, Lady* (1976). In 1987, *The Collected Short Stories* brought together her work in this genre. At her death, she left an essentially completed first section of an autobiography with Diana Athill, who had edited *Wide Sargasso Sea* and *Sleep It Off, Lady*. Athill published this section and a less complete second section as *Smile, Please: An Unfinished Autobiography* in 1979. A collection of letters was published in 1984.

Achievements · When *Wide Sargasso Sea*, her last novel, was published, Jean Rhys was described in *The New York Times* as the greatest living novelist. Such praise is overstated, but Rhys's fiction, long overlooked by academic critics, is undergoing a revival spurred by feminist studies. Rhys played a noteworthy role in the French Left Bank literary scene in the 1920's, and between 1927 and 1939, she published four substantial novels and a number of jewel-like short stories. Although she owes her current reputation in large measure to the rising interest in female writers and feminist themes, her work belongs more properly with the masters of literary impressionism: Joseph Conrad, Ford Madox Ford, Marcel Proust, and James Joyce. She began to publish her writing under the encouragement of her intimate friend Ford Madox Ford, and she continued to write in spite of falling out of favor with his circle. As prizes and honors came to her in her old age after the publication of *Wide Sargasso Sea*, it must have given her grim satisfaction to realize that she had attained entirely by her own efforts a position as a writer at least equal to that of her erstwhile friends.

Biography · Jean Rhys was born Ella Gwendolen Rees Williams in the West Indies on the island of Dominica in 1894, the daughter of a Welsh father and a part-Creole mother. English society classified her as "colored." Her child associates were often Creole, and she was surrounded by ideas peculiar to their culture, such as voodoo and witchcraft. At the same time, she attended a convent school and seriously considered the life of a nun. The colonial mentality was strong in Dominica, and the "proper" role for a well-bred young woman was sharply defined: passive, obedient, submissive.

In 1910, Rhys left Dominica and went to live in Cambridge, England, with her aunt, Clarice Rhys Williams. After a short term in a local school, she enrolled in the Royal Academy of Dramatic Art in London. Her father died soon after she arrived in England, and she found herself short of money. The transition from the West Indies to England must have been extremely painful for the sixteen-year-old girl: the climate harsh, the people cold, the social and economic situation threatening. Those who knew her as a young woman testified that she was strikingly beautiful. After a term at the Royal Academy of Dramatic Art, she toured as a minor actress or chorus girl with provincial theater troupes and did modeling. A young woman alone under these circumstances would have seen at first hand how male dominance and financial control in British society combined to exploit the female. Many of her stories and novels reflect scenes from her career on the stage, and most of them hinge on the theme of male exploitation of women through financial domination.

Near the end of World War I, Rhys married Jean Lenglet (alias Edouard de Neve), an adventurer who had served in the French Foreign Legion and who was probably employed by the French secret service during the war. The newlywed couple lived in Paris, constantly moving from one cheap hotel to another, although de Neve secured temporarily a position with the international mission administering Vienna. A son was born to them in 1919, but lived only three weeks. A daughter born in 1922 lived but required special medical care. Rhys tried to earn a living in Paris by modeling and writing. Pearl Adam, the wife of a correspondent for *The Times* of Paris, took an interest in some of her sketches and introduced her to Ford Madox Ford, then editor of *The Transatlantic Review*. Through him, she entered into the expatriate community of the early 1920's, meeting James Joyce, Ernest Hemingway, and other prominent writers. Shortly after Rhys met Ford in the autumn of 1924, her husband was sent to prison for illegal dealing in antiques. Ford was living at the time with the artist Stella Bowen. Rhys, penniless, moved in with them and soon formed an intimate relationship with Ford. A casual episode in Ford's generally messy life was something much more serious for the young woman; Rhys treats this affair in her first novel, *Quartet*. De Neve never forgave her for her involvement with Ford. After her divorce from de Neve, Rhys became closely involved with a literary agent, Leslie Tilden Smith. They were eventually married and lived together until his death in 1945. Subsequently, she married his cousin, Max Hamer, who later served time in prison for mismanagement of his firm's funds. Throughout the 1940's and 1950's, Rhys suffered greatly from poverty, poor health, and family problems. Her books were all out of print.

She was not, however, entirely forgotten. The actress Selma Vaz Diaz adapted a dramatic monologue from *Good Morning, Midnight* for stage use in 1949. Eight years later, the BBC's third program presented Selma Vaz Diaz's monologue, which received excellent notices. The publication of *Wide Sargasso Sea* in 1966 and the rapid growth of feminist studies led to a Rhys revival, and the reprinting of all her works followed.

Analysis · Jean Rhys's first novel, *Quartet*, reflects closely her misadventures with Ford Madox Ford. The heroine, Marya Zelli, whose husband is in prison, moves in with the rich and respectable Hugh and Lois Heidler. Hugh becomes Marya's lover, while Lois punishes her with petty cruelties. The central figure is a woman alone, penniless, exploited, and an outsider. In her next novel, *After Leaving Mr. Mackenzie*, the central figure, Julia Martin, breaks off with her rich lover, Mr. Mackenzie, and finds herself financially desperate. *Voyage in the Dark* tells the story of Anna Morgan, who arrives in England from the West Indies as an innocent young girl, has her first affair as a chorus girl, and descends through a series of shorter and shorter affairs to working for a masseuse. In *Good Morning, Midnight*, the alcoholic Sasha Jensen, penniless in Paris, remembers episodes from her past which have brought her to this sorry pass. All four of these novels show a female character subject to financial, sexual, and social domination by men and "respectable" society. In all cases, the heroine is passive, but "sentimental." The reader is interested in her feelings, rather than in her ideas and accomplishments. She is alienated economically from any opportunity to do meaningful and justly rewarding work. She is an alien socially, either from a foreign and despised colonial culture or from a marginally respectable social background. She is literally an alien or foreigner in Paris and London, which are cities of dreadful night for her. What the characters fear most is the final crushing alienation from their true identities, the reduction to some model or type imagined by a foreign man. They all face the choice of becoming someone's gamine, *garçonne*, or femme fatale, or of starving to death, and they all struggle against this loss of personal identity. After a silence of more than twenty years, Rhys returned to these same concerns in her masterpiece, *Wide Sargasso Sea*. While the four early novels are to a large degree autobiographical, *Wide Sargasso Sea* has a more literary origin, although it, too, reflects details from the author's personal life.

Wide Sargasso Sea · *Wide Sargasso Sea* requires a familiarity with Charlotte Brontë's *Jane Eyre* (1847). In Brontë's novel, Jane is prevented from marrying Rochester by the presence of a madwoman in the attic, his insane West Indian wife who finally perishes in the fire which she sets, burning Rochester's house and blinding him, but clearing the way for Jane to wed him. The madwoman in *Jane Eyre* is depicted entirely from the exterior. It is natural that the mad West Indian wife, when seen only through the eyes of her English rival and of Rochester, appears completely hideous and depraved. Indeed, when Jane first sees the madwoman in chapter 16 of the novel, she cannot tell whether it is a beast or a human being groveling on all fours. Like a hyena with bloated features, the madwoman attacks Rochester in this episode.

Wide Sargasso Sea is a sympathetic account of the life of Rochester's mad wife, ranging from her childhood in the West Indies, her Creole and Catholic background, and her courtship and married years with the deceitful Rochester, to her final descent into madness and captivity in England. Clearly, the predicament of the West Indian wife resembles that of Rhys herself in many ways. In order to present the alien wife's case, she has written a "counter-text," an extension of Brontë's novel filling in the "missing" testimony, the issues over which Brontë glosses.

Wide Sargasso Sea consists of two parts. Part 1 is narrated by the girl growing up in Jamaica who is destined to become Rochester's wife. The Emancipation Act has just been passed (the year of that imperial edict was 1833) and the blacks on the island are passing through a period of so-called apprenticeship which should lead to their complete freedom in 1837. This is a period of racial tension and anxiety for the privileged colonial community. Fear of black violence runs high, and no one knows exactly what will happen to the landholders once the blacks are emancipated. The girlish narrator lives in the interface between the privileged white colonists and the blacks. Although a child of landowners, she is impoverished, clinging to European notions of respectability, and in constant fear. She lives on the crumbling estate of her widowed mother. Her closest associate is Christophine, a Martinique *obeah* woman, or Voodoo witch. When her mother marries Mr. Mason, the family's lot improves temporarily, until the blacks revolt, burning their country home, Coulibri, and killing her half-witted brother. She then attends a repressive Catholic school in town, where her kindly colored "cousin" Sandi protects her from more hostile blacks.

Part 2 is narrated by the young Rochester on his honeymoon with his bride to her country home. Wherever appropriate, Rhys follows the details of Brontë's story. Rochester reveals that his marriage was merely a financial arrangement. After an uneasy period of passion, Rochester's feelings for his bride begin to cool. He receives a letter of denunciation accusing her of misbehavior with Sandi and revealing that madness runs in the family. To counter Rochester's growing hostility, the young bride goes to her former companion, the *obeah* woman Christophine, for a love potion. The nature of the potion is that it can work for one night only. Nevertheless, she administers it to her husband. His love now dead, she is torn from her native land, transported to a cruel and loveless England, and maddeningly confined. Finally, she takes candle in hand to fire Rochester's house in suicidal destruction.

In Brontë's novel, the character of the mad wife is strangely blank, a vacant slot in the story. Her presence is essential, and she must be fearfully hateful, so that Jane Eyre has no qualms about taking her place in Rochester's arms, but the novel tells the reader almost nothing else about her. Rhys fills in this blank, fleshing out the character, making her live on a par with Jane herself. After all, Brontë tells the reader a great deal about Jane's painful childhood and education; why should Rhys not supply the equivalent information about her dark rival?

It is not unprecedented for a writer to develop a fiction from another writer's work. For example, T. H. White's *Mistress Masham's Repose* (1946) imagines that some of Jonathan Swift's Lilliputians were transported to England, escaped captivity, and established a thriving colony in an abandoned English garden, where they are discovered by an English schoolgirl. Her intrusion into their world is a paradigm of British colonial paternalism, finally overcome by the intelligence and good feeling of the girl. This charming story depends on Swift's fiction, but the relationship of White's work to Swift's is completely different from the relationship of Rhys's work to Brontë's. Rhys's fiction permanently alters one's understanding of *Jane Eyre*. Approaching Brontë's work after Rhys's, one is compelled to ask such questions as, "Why is Jane so uncritical of Rochester?" and, "How is Jane herself like the madwoman in the attic?" Rhys's fiction reaches into the past and alters Brontë's novel.

Rhys's approach in *Wide Sargasso Sea* was also influenced by Ford Madox Ford and, through Ford, Joseph Conrad. In the autumn of 1924, when Rhys first met Ford, he was writing *Joseph Conrad: A Personal Remembrance*. Some thirty years earlier, when Joseph Conrad was just beginning his career as a writer, his agent had introduced him to Ford in hopes that they could work in collaboration, since Conrad wrote English (a language he had adopted only as an adult) with great labor. Ford and Conrad produced *The Inheritors* (1901) and *Romance* (1903) as coauthors. During their years of association, Ford had some hand in the production of several works usually considered Conrad's sole effort, although it has never been clear to what degree Ford participated in the creation of the fiction of Conrad's middle period. About 1909, after Ford's disreputable ways had become increasingly offensive to Conrad's wife, the two men parted ways. Immediately after Conrad's death in 1924, however, Ford rushed into print his memoir of the famous author. His memoir of Conrad is fictionalized and hardly to be trusted as an account of their association in the 1890's, but it sheds a great deal of light on what Ford thought about writing fiction in 1924, when he was beginning his powerful Tietjens tetralogy and working for the first time with Rhys. Ford claimed that he and Conrad invented literary impressionism in English. Impressionist fiction characteristically employs limited and unreliable narration, follows a flow of associated ideas leaping freely in time and space, aims to render the impression of a scene vividly so as to make the reader see it as if it were before his eyes, and artfully selects and juxtaposes seemingly unrelated scenes and episodes so that the reader must construct the connections and relationships that make the story intelligible. These are the stylistic features of Rhys's fiction, as well as of Ford's *The Good Soldier* (1915), Conrad's *Heart of Darkness* (1902), Henry James's *The Turn of the Screw* (1898), and Joyce's *Ulysses* (1922).

An "affair"–the mainspring of the plot in an impressionist novel–is some shocking or puzzling event which has already occurred when the story begins. The reader knows what has happened, but he does not understand fully why and how it happened. The story proceeds in concentric rings of growing complication as the reader finds something he thought clear-cut becoming more and more intricate. In Conrad's *Lord Jim* (1900), the affair is the scandalous abandonment of the pilgrim ship by the English sailor. In *The Good Soldier*, it is the breakup of the central foursome, whose full infidelity and betrayal are revealed only gradually. Brontë's *Jane Eyre* provided Rhys with an impressionist "affair" in the scene in which the mad West Indian wife burns Rochester's house, blinding him and killing herself. Like Conrad's Marlow, the storyteller who sits on the veranda mulling over Jim's curious behavior, or *The Good Soldier*'s narrator Dowell musing about the strange behavior of Edward Ashburnham, Rhys takes up the affair of Rochester and reworks it into ever richer complications, making the initial judgments in *Jane Eyre* seem childishly oversimplified. "How can Jane simply register relief that the madwoman is burned out of her way? There must be more to the affair than that," the secondary fiction suggests.

One of the most important features of literary impressionism is the highly constructive activity which it demands of the reader. In a pointillist painting, small dots of primary colors are set side by side. At a certain distance from the canvas, these merge on the retina of the eye of the viewer into colors and shapes which are not, in fact, drawn on the canvas at all. The painting is constructed in the eyes of each viewer with greater luminosity than it would have were it drawn explicitly. In order to create such a shimmering haze in fiction, Ford advises the use of a limited point of view which gives the reader dislocated fragments of remembered experience. The reader must struggle constantly to fit these fragments into a coherent pattern. The tools for creating such a verbal collage are limited, "unreliable" narration, psychological time-shifts, and juxtaposition. Ford observes that two apparently unrelated events can be set side by side so that the reader will perceive their connection with far greater impact than if the author had stated such a connection openly. Ford advises the impressionist author to create a verbal collage by unexpected selection and juxtaposition, and *Wide Sargasso Sea* makes such juxtapositions on several levels. On the largest scale, *Wide Sargasso Sea* is juxtaposed with *Jane Eyre*, so that the two novels read together mean much more than when they are read independently. This increase of significance is what Ford called the "unearned increment" in impressionist art. Within *Wide Sargasso Sea*, part 1 (narrated by the West Indian bride) and part 2 (narrated by Rochester) likewise mean more in juxtaposition than when considered separately. Throughout the text, the flow of consciousness of the storytellers cunningly shifts in time to juxtapose details which mean more together than they would in isolation.

Because *Wide Sargasso Sea* demands a highly constructive reader, it is, like *The Good Soldier* or *Heart of Darkness*, an open fiction. When the reader completes *Jane Eyre*, the mystery of Rochester's house has been revealed and purged, the madwoman in the attic has been burned out, and Jane will live, the reader imagines, happily ever after. *Jane Eyre* taken in isolation is a closed fiction. Reading *Wide Sargasso Sea* in juxtaposition to *Jane Eyre*, however, opens the latter and poses questions which are more difficult to resolve: Is Jane likely to be the next woman in the attic? Why is a cripple a gratifying mate for Jane? At what price is her felicity purchased?

The *Doppelgänger*, twin, or shadow-character runs throughout Rhys's fiction. All of her characters seem to be split personalities. There is a public role, that of the approved "good girl," which each is expected to play, and there is the repressed, rebellious "bad girl" lurking inside. If the bad girl can be hidden, the character is rewarded with money, love, and social position. Yet the bad girl will sometimes put in an appearance, when the character drinks too much or gets excited or angry. When the dark girl appears, punishment follows, swift and sure. This is the case with Marya Zelli in *Quartet*, Julia Martin in *After Leaving Mr. Mackenzie*, Anna Morgan in *Voyage in the Dark*, and Sasha Jensen in *Good Morning, Midnight*. It is also the case in Brontë's *Jane Eyre*. The education of Jane Eyre consists of repressing those dark, selfish impulses that Victorian society maintained "good little girls" should never feel. Jane succeeds in stamping out her "bad" self through a stiff British education, discipline, and self-control. She kills her repressed identity, conforms to society's expectations, and gets her reward—a crippled husband and a burned-out house. Rhys revives the dark twin, shut up in the attic, the naughty, wild, dark, selfish, bestial female. She suggests that the struggle between repressed politeness and unrepressed self-interest is an ongoing process in which total repression means the death of a woman's identity.

Todd K. Bender

Other major works

SHORT FICTION: *The Left Bank and Other Stories,* 1927; *Tigers Are Better-Looking,* 1968; *Sleep It Off, Lady,* 1976; *The Collected Short Stories,* 1987.

NONFICTION: *Smile Please: An Unfinished Autobiography,* 1979; *The Letters of Jean Rhys,* 1984 (also known as *Jean Rhys: Letters, 1931-1966*).

Bibliography
Angier, Carole. *Jean Rhys: Life and Work.* Boston: Little, Brown, 1990. This biography grew out of Angier's brief 1985 critical study of Rhys's work. As it expanded into an account of her life, Angier felt obliged to jettison her chapters devoted to Rhys's short stories. What survived is a book that is broken into four parts: "Life, 1890-1927," "Work, 1928-1939," "The Lost Years, 1939-1966," and "The Lost Years, 1966-1979." Angier's lengthy book is a good introduction to the life, but it is—of necessity—a less than complete account of the work.

Benstock, Shari. *Women of the Left Bank: Paris, 1900-1940.* Austin: University of Texas Press, 1986. Discusses Rhys's work in the context of the Left Bank literary community. Rhys knew the members of the community but stood outside it, and Benstock demonstrates that Rhys's position as an outsider in life influenced her fiction.

Harrison, Nancy R. *Jean Rhys and the Novel as Women's Text.* Chapel Hill: University of North Carolina Press, 1988. Harrison is a feminist critic who argues that women tend to write, and respond to writing, in a different fashion from men. Women write in a way that invites the reader to join in the creation of the work; the author's activity of writing is stressed, and the work is not offered as a finished product. Analyzes *Voyage in the Dark* and *Wide Sargasso Sea* along these lines.

Malcolm, Cheryl Alexander, and David Malcolm. *Jean Rhys: A Study of the Short Fiction.* New York: Twayne, 1996. This book makes up for what Angier's biography—and most critical assessments of Rhys—lacks. After a section devoted to their assessment of Rhys's short fiction, the Malcolms provide a chapter on Rhys's own views of herself, conveyed in excerpts from her letters and an interview, and conclude with a section that reprints a wide range of critical opinion about Rhys's fiction.

Staley, Thomas. *Jean Rhys: A Critical Study.* London: Macmillan, 1979. Probably most important for its first chapter, which gives an account of Rhys's life. Rhys has not been the subject of a full-length biography, and Staley's presentation of her life is the best available. Should be supplemented with Rhys's *Smile Please: An Unfinished Autobiography*, on which she was working at the time of her death in 1979.

Dorothy Richardson

Born: Berkshire, England; May 17, 1873
Died: Beckenham, England; June 17, 1957

Principal long fiction · *Pilgrimage*, 1938, 1967 (includes *Pointed Roofs*, 1915); *Backwater*, 1916; *Honeycomb*, 1917; *The Tunnel*, 1919; *Interim*, 1919; *Deadlock*, 1921; *Revolving Lights*, 1923; *The Trap*, 1925; *Oberland*, 1927; *Dawn's Left Hand*, 1931; *Clear Horizon*, 1935; *Dimple Hill*, 1938; *March Moonlight*, 1967.

Other literary forms · Dorothy Richardson's literary reputation rests on the single long novel *Pilgrimage*. She referred to the parts published under separate titles as "chapters," and they were the primary focus of her energy throughout her creative life. The first appeared in 1915; the last, unfinished and unrevised, was printed ten years after her death. Before 1915, she wrote some essays and reviews for obscure periodicals edited by friends and also two books growing out of her interest in the Quakers. She contributed descriptive sketches on Sussex life to the *Saturday Review* between 1908 and 1914. During the years writing *Pilgrimage*, Richardson did an enormous amount of miscellaneous writing to earn money—columns and essays in the *Dental Record* (1912-1922), film criticism, translations, and articles on various subjects for periodicals including *Vanity Fair, Adelphi, Little Review*, and *Fortnightly Review*. She also wrote a few short stories, chiefly during the 1940's. None of this material has been collected. A detailed bibliography is included in *Dorothy Richardson: A Biography* by Gloria G. Fromm (1977).

Achievements · The term "stream of consciousness," adapted from psychology, was first applied to literature in a 1918 review of Richardson's *Pointed Roofs, Backwater*, and *Honeycomb*. In the twentieth century, novels moved from outward experience to inner reality. The experiments that marked the change were made almost simultaneously by three writers unaware of one another's work: The first volume of Marcel Proust's *Remembrance of Things Past* appeared in 1913; James Joyce's *Portrait of the Artist as a Young Man* began serial publication in 1914; and the manuscript of *Pointed Roofs* was finished in 1913.

Richardson was the first novelist in England to restrict the point of view entirely to the protagonist's consciousness, to take for content the experience of life at the moment of perception, and to record the development of a single character's mind and emotions without imposing any plot or structural pattern. Her place in literature (as opposed to literary history) has been less certain; some critics feel that her work is interesting only because it dates the emergence of a new technique. The absence of story and explanation make heavy demands on the reader. Since the protagonist's own limited understanding controls every word of the narrative, readers must also do the work of evaluating the experience in order to create meaning.

Richardson wrote what Virginia Woolf called "the psychological sentence of the feminine gender," a sentence that expanded its limits and tampered with punctuation to convey the multiple nuances of a single moment. She deliberately rejected the description of events, which she thought was typical of male literature, in order to convey the subjective understanding that she believed was the reality of experience. The autobiographical basis of *Pilgrimage* was not known until 1963. Richardson, like her protagonist and like other women of her period, broke with the conventions of the past, sought to create her own being through self-awareness, and struggled to invent a form that would communicate a woman's expanding conscious life.

Biography · Dorothy Miller Richardson, born on May 17, 1873, was the third of four daughters. Her father, Charles Richardson, worked in the prosperous grocery business that his father had established, but he wanted to be a gentleman. He abandoned Nonconformity for the Church of England and, in 1874, sold the family business to live on investments. During Dorothy's childhood, periods of upper-middle-class luxury (a large house, servants, gardens, membership in a tennis club) alternated with moves arising from temporarily reduced circumstances.

Charles Richardson had hoped for a son, and he took Dorothy with him to lectures in Oxford and meetings of scientific associations. She was sent at age eleven to a private day school for the daughters of gentlemen. It was late enough in the century for the curriculum to emphasize academic subjects; her studies included logic and psychology. In 1890, realizing that her family's financial condition had become seriously straitened, Dorothy looked to the example of Charlotte Brontë and *Villette* (1853) and applied for a post as pupil-teacher in a German school. Six months in Hanover were followed by two years teaching in a North London private school and a brief spell as governess for a wealthy suburban family.

By the end of 1893, Charles Richardson was declared bankrupt; in 1895, two of Dorothy's sisters married. Her mother, Mary Richardson, was troubled by an unusually severe bout of the depression that had gripped her for several years. Dorothy took her mother to stay in lodgings near the sea and found that she required almost constant companionship and supervision. On November 30, 1895, while her daughter was out for a short walk in the fresh air, Mary Richardson committed suicide.

At the age of twenty-two, responsible for her own support and severely shaken by the past two years' events, Richardson moved to an attic room in a London lodging house and took a job as secretary and assistant to three Harley Street dentists. For young women at that time, such a step was unusual; by taking it Richardson evaded the restraint, protection, and religious supervision that made teaching an acceptable profession for young women of good family. The nineteenth century was drawing to a close and London was alive with new ideas. Richardson explored the city, made friends with women who worked in business offices, and lived on eggs and toast so that she could afford concert tickets.

Soon after moving to London, she was invited for a Saturday in the country by an old school friend, Amy Catherine Robbins, who had married her science instructor at London University—a man named H. G. Wells. He had just published *The Time Machine* (1895). Richardson was fascinated by Wells and by the people and ideas she encountered at his house but angered by his way of telling her what to do. She was aware that she stood outside the class system and between the Victorian and modern worlds. She was drawn both to picnics with cousins at Cambridge and to Anarchist and Fabian meetings. She sampled various churches, including Unitarian and Quaker, but refrained from committing herself to any group or cause.

In 1902, Richardson began contributing occasional articles and reviews to *Crank* and other magazines edited by a vegetarian friend. She refused a proposal from a respectable physician and broke her engagement to a Russian Jew, Benjamin Grad.

Her friendship with Wells passed at some point into physical intimacy, but she continued to struggle against being overwhelmed by his ideas and personality. In 1906, finding herself pregnant, she brought the affair to an end; she looked forward to rearing the child on her own and was distressed when she suffered a miscarriage.

Exhausted physically and mentally, Richardson left her dental job and went to Sussex to recover and think. In 1908, she began writing sketches for the *Saturday Review*. Then, as her fortieth year approached, she began deliberately searching for the form that would allow her to create what she called "a feminine equivalent of the current masculine realism."

Pointed Roofs was at first rejected by publishers. When it was published in 1915 it puzzled readers, distressed some reviewers, and failed to make money. Richardson persisted, however, on the course she had set, even while living an unsettled life in YWCA hostels and borrowed rooms and earning a minimal income by proofreading and by writing a monthly column for the *Dental Record*. In 1917, she married the artist Alan Odle, who was fifteen years younger than she and had been rejected for military service by a doctor who told him he had six months to live.

Richardson's books attracted some critical recognition in the years after World War I, but they never earned money; she was usually in debt to her publishers. She supported herself and Odle (who lived until 1948) and also coped with all the practical details of their life—housekeeping, paying taxes, writing checks, doing his business with publishers and exhibitors. The couple moved frequently, spending the off-season (when lodgings were less expensive) in Cornwall and going to rooms in London for the summer. During the early 1930's, Richardson took on the burden of five full-length translations from French and German. Returning to *Pilgrimage* and the state of mind in which it was begun became increasingly difficult for Richardson; the later volumes were weakened by extraliterary distractions and also by the psychological difficulty for the author in concluding the work that was based on her own life. The final segment, *March Moonlight*, was found unfinished among her papers after she died on June 17, 1957, at the age of eighty-four.

Analysis · *Pilgrimage* is a quest; the protagonist, Miriam Henderson, seeks her self and, rejecting the old guideposts, makes her own path through life. The book remains a problem for many readers, although since 1915 most of Dorothy Richardson's technical devices have become familiar: unannounced transitions from third-person narration to the first person for interior monologue, shifts between present and past as experience evokes memory, disconnected phrases and images and fragmentary impressions representing the continuous nonverbal operations of the mind. Looking back on the period when she was trying to find a way to embody Miriam Henderson's experience, Richardson described her breakthrough as the realization that no one was "*there* to *describe* her." Impressed by Henry James's control of viewpoint, she went one step further. The narrator and the protagonist merge; the narrator knows, perceives, and expresses only what comes to Miriam's consciousness. Furthermore, the narrator does not speak to any imagined reader and therefore does not provide helpful explanations. The scenes and people are presented as they impinge on Miriam's awareness—thus the most familiar circumstances are likely to be undescribed and the most important people identified only by name, without the phrases that would place them or reveal their relationship to Miriam. Many readers are discouraged by the attempt to follow the book and make meaning of it; some are tempted to use Richardson's biography to find out what "really" happened and others prefer to read isolated sections without regard to sequence, responding to the feeling and imagery as if it were poetry. Because there is no narrative guidance, meaning is continually modified by the reader's own consciousness and by the extent of identification.

The Miriam Henderson novels · The first three titles show Miriam Henderson in the last stages of her girlhood and form the prelude to her London life. *Pointed Roofs* covers her experience in Hanover; in *Backwater*, she is resident teacher in a North London school and still drawn to the possibility of romance with a young man from her suburban circle; in *Honeycomb*, she briefly holds a post as governess before her sisters' weddings and her mother's death complete the disintegration of her girlhood family. *The Tunnel* begins Miriam's years in London and introduces situations and characters that reappear in the next several volumes: the dental job, the room at Mrs. Bailey's lodging house, the new women Mag and Jan and the dependent woman Eleanor Dear, a visit to her school friend Alma who has married the writer Hypo Wilson. In *Interim*, Miriam perceives the difficulty of communicating her current thoughts and experiences to her sister and other old friends. *Deadlock* treats her acquaintance—growing into an engagement—with Michael Shatov. In *Revolving Lights*, she has decided not to marry Shatov and becomes increasingly involved with Hypo Wilson. *The Trap* shows her sharing a cramped flat with a spinster social worker and growing despondent about the isolation which, she realizes, she imposes on herself to avoid emotional entanglements. *Oberland* is a lyrical interlude about a holiday in Switzerland. In *Dawn's Left Hand*, Miriam has an affair with Hypo Wilson and an intense friendship with a young woman (Amabel) who becomes a radical suffragist. *Clear Horizon* concludes much of the practical and emotional business that has occupied Miriam for several years; she disentangles herself from Wilson, Shatov, and Amabel and prepares to leave London. In *Dimple Hill*, she lives on a farm owned by a Quaker family, absorbs their calm, and works at writing. *March Moonlight* rather hastily takes Miriam up to the point of meeting the artist who would become her husband and to the beginning of her work on a novel.

This summary of events is the barest framework. Life, for Miriam Henderson, exists not in events but in the responses that create her sense of awareness. The books are made up of relatively independent sections, each treating a single segment of experience or reflection. Because of the depth with which single moments are recorded, the overall narrative line is fragmentary. Despite *Pilgrimage*'s length, it embodies isolated spots of time. Frequently, neither narration nor the memories evoked by subsequent experience indicate what events may have taken place in the gaps between. Furthermore, the book concentrates on those moments important to Miriam's interior experience, and it leaves out the times when she acts without self-awareness— which may include significant actions that take place when Miriam is so engrossed by events that she does not engage in thought or reflection.

Richardson disliked the phrase "stream of consciousness" because it implies constant movement and change. She preferred the image of a pool—new impressions are added, and sometimes create ripples that spread over the previously accumulated consciousness. Thus, Miriam's interior monologue becomes steadily more complex as she grows older. Her consciousness widens and deepens; fragmentary phrases show her making connections with her earlier experiences and perceptions; her understanding of past events alters with later awareness. The earlier volumes have more sensory impression and direct emotion; later, as Miriam grows more self-aware, she has greater verbal skill and is more likely to analyze her responses. Because of her more sophisticated self-awareness, however, she also grows adept, in the later volumes, at suppressing impressions or fragments of self-knowledge that she does not want to admit to consciousness.

In many ways, Miriam is not likable—readers are sometimes put off by the need to share her mind for two thousand pages. In the early books, she is a self-preoccupied, narrow-minded adolescent, oppressively conscious of people's appearance and social class, annoyingly absorbed in wondering what they think about her, defensively judgmental. The wild swings in mood and the ebb and flow of her energies during the day appear to have little cause and to be unworthy of the attention she gives them. Most people, however, would appear unpleasantly selfish if their minds were open for inspection. Miriam creates her self by deliberate consciousness. The danger is that she tends to withdraw from experience in order to contemplate feeling.

Pilgrimage · The events of *Pilgrimage* span the decades at the turn of the century but, because of the interior focus, there is relatively little physical detail or explicit social history to create an objective picture of the era. Women's developing self-awareness, however, must be seen as one of the period's significant events. Miriam reflects the mental life of her times in her range of responses to religion, the books she reads, and the people, ideas, and movements she encounters.

A good deal of life's texture and even its choices take place at levels that are not verbalized. Richardson's first publisher described her work as "female imagism." Miriam responds particularly and constantly to the quality of light. Readers are also aware of her reaction to places, objects, and physical surroundings; ultimately, it is through mastering the emotional content of this response that she is able to discover what she needs to have in her life.

Another continuing thread is created by Miriam's thoughts about men, about men and women together, and about the roles of women in society. Her basic animosity toward men gives shape to a series of statements on their personal, emotional, social, and intellectual peculiarities that falls just short of a formal feminist analysis. Each possible romance, each rejected or forestalled proposal amounts to a choice of a way of life. The matter is, however, complicated by Miriam's sexual reticence. Even though she can talk about free love, she is not conscious—or perhaps will not permit herself to become conscious—of overt sexual urges or of physical attraction to men or to women. She struggles not to let her feeling for certain women lead her to be absorbed by their lives or roles. In *Backwater*, Miss Perne's religion is dangerously comfortable; Eleanor Dear's passive feminine helplessness forces Miriam to become her protector; Amabel's possessiveness is as stifling as Hypo Wilson's. At the end—in *March Moonlight*—there is a hint of emotional involvement with the unidentified "Jane." Struggling to know herself, Miriam is constantly faced with the problem of knowing other women.

Pointed Roofs · *Pointed Roofs* comes close to being a structural whole—it begins with Miriam Henderson's journey to Hanover and ends with her return home six months later. She is on her first trip away from home, looking at new scenes, anxious about her ability to do her job and earn her wages, having her first taste of independence. Since Miriam is seventeen—and, as a Victorian daughter, a relatively innocent and sheltered seventeen—the reader often understands more than Miriam does and can interpret the incidents that develop her sense of who she is and where she fits in the world. Some of Miriam's reactions are cast in the form of mental letters home or imaginary conversations with her sisters, which provide a structured way to verbalize mental processes. Miriam pays attention to the sights and sounds and smells of Hanover because they are new, giving readers a sense of the physical setting absent in many of the later books.

Miriam's moods are typically adolescent. An incident or object can set off a homesick reverie or a bout of self-recrimination; the sound of music or the sight of rain on paving stones can create an inexpressible transport of joy. She is alternately rebellious and anxious for approval; she is glad to learn that her French roommate is Protestant (because she could not bear living with a Catholic), proud of the skill in logic that allows her to criticize the premises of a sermon, moved by the sound of hymns in German. She worries about her plainness, her intellectual deficiencies, her inability to get close to people. Observing class and cultural differences lets her begin to understand that she has unthinkingly absorbed many of her tastes and ideas; she starts to grow more deliberate. This portrait of Miriam at seventeen—which forms the essential background for the rest of *Pilgrimage*—is also interesting for its own sake.

Because the narrative is limited to Miriam's consciousness, the reader is able to supply interpretation. In one key scene, the middle-aged Pastor Lahmann, chaplain to the school, quotes a verse describing his ambition for "A little land, well-tilled,/ A little wife, well-willed" and then asks Miriam to take off her glasses so that he can see how nearsighted her eyes really are. Miriam, who is both furious at being "regarded as one of a world of little tame things to be summoned by little men to be well-willed wives" and warmed by the personal attention that makes her forget, for a moment, that she is a governess, is oblivious to the sexual implications of Pastor Lahmann's behavior, and cannot understand why the headmistress is angry when she walks in upon the scene. Although Miriam's consciousness will develop in subsequent volumes, her combination of receptivity to male attention, anger at male assumptions, and blindness to sexual nuance will remain.

Deadlock · *Deadlock* contains a greater proportion of direct internal monologue than the earlier books. Miriam has grown more articulate; she interprets her emotional states and examines the premises underlying her conflicts. During her first years in London, she had cherished the city for the independence it gave her. By such acts as smoking, eating alone in restaurants, and dressing without regard to fashion, she deliberately rejected Victorian womanhood. In *Honeycomb*, she refused a marriage that would have satisfied her craving for luxuries because she could not accept a subordinate role. In *Deadlock*, Miriam is faced by the loneliness that seems inextricably linked to independence. Her work has become drudgery because she no longer has the sense of a social relationship with her employer. A Christmas visit to her married sister reveals the distance that has grown between them; Miriam had not even realized that Harriet's marriage was unhappy.

Deadlock is shaped by the course of Miriam's relationship with Michael Shatov. The romance forces her conflicts to the surface. Shatov is a young Jew recently arrived from Russia; a lodger at Mrs. Bailey's arranges for Miriam to tutor him in English. As she shows Shatov London, tired scenes recapture their original freshness. Miriam is excited by her ability to formulate ideas when she argues about philosophy or works on a translation. Yet, although Miriam is buoyed by the joy of sharing her thoughts with another person, Shatov's continual presence comes between her and the life that was her own. Her love has a maternal quality: Though Shatov is only three years younger than Miriam, he is a foreigner and also, Miriam finds, rather impractical; she feels protective. She is also sexually reticent: Because she has despised traditional femininity, she does not know how to behave as the object of a courtship. The romance ends when Miriam deliberately engages Shatov in an argument that reveals his views of woman's limited nature. (The final scene restates the problem more concretely when Miriam visits an Englishwoman married to a Jewish man.) Beneath these specific difficulties lies the friction between Miriam's individualism and Shatov's tendency to see problems in the abstract—she talks about herself, he dwells on the future of the race. For Richardson, the conflict reflects the irreconcilable difference between masculine objectivity (or materialism) and feminine subjectivity. The images of darkness accumulate as Miriam realizes the extent of her deadlock; unable to be a woman in the sense that men see women, she seems to have no path out of loneliness and alienation.

Dawn's Left Hand · *Dawn's Left Hand* is a prelude to the deliberate detachment and observation that would turn Miriam into a writer. *Oberland* (the preceding book) vibrates with the sensory detail of a two-week holiday in Switzerland that makes London complications seem far away; returning, Miriam sees people objectively even when she is with them. The transitions between third-person narrative and internal monologue are less noticeable; Miriam and the narrator have virtually merged. The visual content of scenes reveals their meaning. Miriam looks at pictorial relationships and examines gesture and tone for the nonverbal communications that, to women, are often more meaningful than words. (During the years that she worked on *Dawn's Left Hand*, Richardson wrote regularly about films—which were still silent—for the magazine *Close Up*.)

Images of light carry emotional and symbolic content throughout *Pilgrimage*. When Miriam visits Densley's medical office early in *Dawn's Left Hand*, the drawn shades are keeping out the light; she refuses his proposal—one last offer of conventional marriage—with a momentary wistfulness that is immediately replaced by a great sense of relief. She is increasingly aware of herself as an actor in the scenes of her life. Self-observation allows physical compositions to reveal power relationships: When Hypo Wilson comes into Miriam's room, she notices that he stands over her like a doctor, and when he embarks on a program of seduction to the music of Richard Wagner, she disputes his control by rearranging the chairs. On another occasion, in a hotel room, Miriam looks in the mirror to observe herself and Wilson. Her own position blocks the light and thus the scene is chilled even before she begins to see him as a pathetic naked male.

During the final stages of the Wilson affair, Miriam is increasingly preoccupied by a beautiful young woman—soon to be a radical suffragist—who pursues her ardently and pays homage to her as a woman in ways that bring home to Miriam the impossibility of real communion with men. Yet the deep commitment demanded by Amabel is frightening; her intense adoration forces Miriam into a role that threatens her independence more crucially than Hypo Wilson's overt attempts at domination. The advantage of being with people who interact only on superficial levels, Miriam realizes, is that she can retain her freedom.

March Moonlight · Although Richardson struggled to bring the events in *March Moonlight* up to 1912, the year that she began writing *Pilgrimage*, her form and subject virtually required the book to remain unconcluded. The narrative techniques of *March Moonlight* grow more deliberate; when Miriam begins to write, she thinks and sees differently and is aware of selecting and arranging details. Thus, the book's ending is only a middle: Miriam's sense of self would inevitably change as she reexamined and re-created her experiences in order to write novels. Once traditional formulas are rejected and *being* itself becomes the subject, there can be no ending; there is no epiphany, no coming of age, no final truth but rather a continuous process of self-making through self-awareness.

Sally Mitchell

Other major works
NONFICTION: *The Quakers Past and Present,* 1914; *Gleanings from the Works of George Fox,* 1914; *John Austen and the Inseparables,* 1930.

Bibliography

Bluemel, Kristin. *Experimenting on the Borders of Modernism: Dorothy Richardson's "Pilgrimage."* Athens: University of Georgia Press, 1997. The first chapter assesses Richardson and previous studies of her. Subsequent chapters explore Richardson's handling of gender, problems of the body, and science, and the author's quest for an ending to her long work. Includes notes and bibliography.

Fromm, Gloria G. *Dorothy Richardson: A Biography.* Champaign: University of Illinois Press, 1977. An objective biography, including previously inaccessible details, which could provide invaluable data to the literary analyst. Carefully draws distinctions between the events of Richardson's life and those of her fictional characters, but also identifies clear correlations between the two. Extensively researched and well written and supplemented by illustrations, chapter endnotes, a comprehensive bibliography, and an index.

Gevirtz, Susan. *Narrative's Journey: The Fiction and Film Writing of Dorothy Richardson.* New York: Peter Lang, 1996. A probing discussion of Richardson's aesthetic. This is a challenging study for advanced students. *Pilgrimage* receives detailed discussion throughout the book. Includes extensive bibliography not only on Richardson but also on feminist theory, literary and cultural theory, poetics and phenomenology, theology and spirituality, travel and travel theories, and narrative.

Radford, Jean. *Dorothy Richardson.* Bloomington: Indiana University Press, 1991. An excellent introductory study, with chapters on reading in *Pilgrimage,* the author's quest for form, London as a space for women, and Richardson as a feminist writer. Includes notes and bibliography.

Rosenberg, John. *Dorothy Richardson, the Genius They Forgot: A Critical Biography.* New York: Alfred A. Knopf, 1973. The strength of Rosenberg's biography lies in his scholarly credibility, as he aptly parallels events in *Pilgrimage* to Richardson's life. His concluding analysis of Richardson's pioneering impact upon the development of the novel, however, lacks the impact of his earlier writing. Contains both an index and an ample bibliography.

Samuel Richardson

Born: Derbyshire, England; July 31 (?), 1689
Died: London, England; July 4, 1761

Principal long fiction · *Pamela: Or, Virtue Rewarded,* 1740-1741; *Clarissa: Or, The History of a Young Lady,* 1747-1748; *Sir Charles Grandison,* 1753-1754.

Other literary forms · In addition to the three novels on which his fame and reputation rest, Samuel Richardson's best-known work is a collection of fictitious letters which constitutes a kind of eighteenth century book of etiquette, social behavior, manners, and mores: *Letters Written to and for Particular Friends, on the Most Important Occasions* (1741), customarily referred to as *Familiar Letters.* It had been preceded, in 1733, by a handbook of instruction concerning the relationship between apprentices and master printers, which grew out of a letter Richardson had written to a nephew in 1731, *The Apprentice's Vade Mecum: Or, Young Man's Pocket Companion* (1733). Throughout his life, Richardson, like so many of his contemporaries, was a prolific letter-writer; notable selections of his correspondence include six volumes edited by his contemporary and early biographer, Anna L. Barbauld, the first of which was published in 1804, and his correspondence with Johannes Stinstra, the Dutch translator of his novels to whom Richardson had sent a considerably important amount of autobiographical material. Of only minor interest is Richardson's *A Collection of the Moral and Instructive Sentiments, Maxims, Cautions, and Reflexions, Contained in the Histories of Pamela, Clarissa, and Sir Charles Grandison,* published anonymously in 1755, a series of excerpts emphasizing his conviction that "instruction was a more important obligation to the novelist than entertainment."

Achievements · Perhaps Richardson's most important contribution to the development of the novel was his concern for the nonexceptional problems of daily conduct, the relationships between men and women, and the specific class-and-caste distinctions of mid-eighteenth century England. He sought and found his material from life as he had observed and reflected upon it from childhood and youth as a member of the working class in a highly socially conscious society to his position as an increasingly successful and prosperous printer and publisher. He contemplated this material with passionate interest and recorded it with a kind of genius for verisimilitude that sets him apart from most of his predecessors. What one critic has called Richardson's "almost rabid concern for the details" of daily life and his continuing "enrichment and complication" of customary human relationship account in large measure for his enormous contemporary popularity: In *Pamela,* for example, the relationships between Pamela and Squire B. are so persistently grounded in the minutiae of ordinary life as to create a sense of reality seldom achieved in prose fiction prior to Richardson; at the same time, the outcome of the emotional and physical tugs-of-war between the two main characters and the happy outcome of all the intrigue, sensationalism, and hugger-mugger have about them the quality of conventional romantic love.

Richardson learned to *know* his characters, so intimately, so thoroughly, as to triumph over his prolixity, repetitiveness, moralizing, and sentimentality. Equally important was his development of the epistolary novel. Other writers had used letters as a storytelling device, but few if any of Richardson's predecessors had approximated his skill in recording the external events and incidents of a narrative along with the intimate and instant revelation of a character's thought and emotions in the process of their taking place, a method so flowing, so fluid, so flexible, as almost to anticipate the modern technique of stream of consciousness. Richardson's works, along with those of his three great contemporaries–Henry Fielding, Tobias Smollett, and Laurence Sterne–prepared the way for the great achievements of the nineteenth century English novel.

Biography · The exact date of Samuel Richardson's birth is uncertain, but he was born in Derbyshire, probably on July 31, 1689. His father was a joiner and, according to Richardson, a "good draughtsman" who "understood architecture" and whose ancestors had included several generations of small farmers in Surrey; of his mother, the second wife of Richardson *père*, little is known. The family returned to London, where Richardson may have attended the Merchant Taylor's School in 1701 and 1702, at which time his formal education ended. In 1706, he was apprenticed to the Stationers' Company, and in 1715, he became a "freeman" of the Company. He married his former employer's daughter, Martha Wilde, in November 23, 1721, set up his own business as a printer, was admitted to the Stationers' Company in 1722, and soon became what his major biographers–T. C. Duncan Eaves and Ben D. Kimpel–term a "prosperous and respected" tradesman. Six children, none of whom survived infancy or early childhood, preceded their mother's death in January, 1731. Two years later, on February 3, 1733, Richardson remarried, this time to Elizabeth Leake, also the daughter of a printer; four of their six children survived.

Richardson's career as an editor continued to prosper–among other distinctions, he was eventually awarded the lucrative contract to print the journals of the House of Commons–and by the mid-1730's, he had moved into a large house in Salisbury Court, where the family would live for the next two decades and where he would write the three novels on which his reputation rests.

For some time, two of Richardson's "particular friends," both of them London booksellers, had been urging him to compile a "little book . . . of familiar letters on the useful concerns of common life." An almost compulsive letter-writer since early childhood–before he was eleven he had written to an elderly widow, reprimanding her for her "uncharitable conduct"–Richardson began the undertaking, one letter of which was an actual account he had heard some years before, the story of a virtuous servant who eventually married her master. The recollection of the incident stimulated his imagination, and so, at the age of fifty, he temporarily abandoned the letters project. In two months, writing as much as three thousand words a day, he completed the novel that, on November 6, 1739, without the author's name on the title page, was to explode upon the English scene:

> *Pamela: Or, Virtue Rewarded. In a Series of Familiar Letters from a beautiful Young Damsel, to her Parents. Now first published in order to cultivate the Principles of Virtue and Religion in the Minds of the Youth of both Sexes. A Narrative which has its Foundation in Truth and Nature; and at the same time that it agreeably entertains, by a Variety of Curious and affecting Incidents, is entirely divested of all those Images, which, in too many Pieces calculated for Amusement only, tend to inflame the Minds they should instruct.*

Pamela was an instant success, going through five editions in less than a year and inspiring numerous burlesques, imitations, and parodies, including *An Apology for the*

Life of Mrs. Shamela Andrews (1741, probably the work of Henry Fielding and the only parody of interest today) and serving as the impetus for Fielding's *The History of the Adventures of Joseph Andrews, and of His Friend Mr. Abraham Adams* (1742). *Pamela* was also dramatized in several forms and translated into German, French, and Dutch; its success, for the worse rather than the better, led Richardson to write a sequel, centering on his heroine's life after her marriage.

Meanwhile, Richardson continued to combine the roles of successful and prosperous businessman and author. Exactly when he began the novel which was to be his

masterpiece is uncertain—one of his biographers thinks he was considering it as early as 1741—but he had the concept of *Clarissa* "well in mind" before 1744, began the actual writing in the spring or summer of that year, and by November was ready to send parts of the manuscript to his old friend Aaron Hill. Unlike *Pamela*, *Clarissa* did not have its origins in "real life"; Clarissa and Miss Howe, Richardson insisted, were "entirely creatures of his fantasy." The novel, almost a million words in length, was three years in the writing, including two "thorough" revisions, and published in seven volumes between December 1, 1747, and December 7, 1748; a subsequent eight-volume edition, "with Letters & passages restored from the original manuscript," was published between 1749 and 1751.

Though *Clarissa* was somewhat less controversial than *Pamela*, its reception was tumultuous; among other things, the author was accused of indecency because of the dramatic fire scene, and Richardson took the charges seriously enough to write an eleven-page pamphlet defending it. Sarah Fielding wrote what has been called an "ambitious defense" of the novel, and her brother Henry, whose masterpiece *The History of Tom Jones, a Foundling* was published soon after the last volumes of *Clarissa* in 1749, lavishly praised Richardson's work, although Richardson's dislike of what he considered Fielding's improprieties, along with the opening sections of *Joseph Andrews* and Fielding's possible authorship of *Shamela*, made any friendship between the two impossible (indeed, their relationship—or, more accurately, the lack of it—reflects little credit on Richardson).

One of Richardson's closest friends, Lady Bradshaigh, had written him soon after publication of the fourth volume of *Clarissa*, entreating him not to let his heroine die, and subsequently urged him to write a "novel about a Good Man." How much this influenced Richardson, if at all, is purely conjectural, but early in 1750, he had begun what was to be his last novel. Despite his stated intention not to publish this "new work," the first six volumes of *Sir Charles Grandison* were published late in 1753 (November 13 and December 11), and the concluding volume on March 14, 1754. As had been the case with *Pamela* and *Clarissa*, Dutch, German, and French translations soon followed.

In his preface to *Sir Charles Grandison*, Richardson, in his guise as the "editor" of the manuscript, announced that after this third novel he would write no more. He had, however, been in the process of compiling a series of selections from his novels which was published in March, 1755, as *A Collection of the Moral and Instructive Sentiments, Maxims, Cautions, and Reflexions, Contained in the Histories of Pamela, Clarissa, and Sir Charles Grandison*. He continued to be active as a printer and to make minor revisions in his novels, particularly *Pamela*, but his "dislike to the pen" continued. During his last years, he devoted more and more time to his correspondence—since the early 1740's, he had kept copies of all or most of his letters—apparently with the idea of eventual publication. On June 28, 1761, he suffered a stroke that resulted in his death a few days later on July 4, 1761.

Analysis · "Why, Sir, if you were to read Richardson for the story, your impatience would be so much fretted that you would hang yourself. But you must read him for the sentiment, and consider the story as only giving occasion to the sentiment." Samuel Johnson's comment is only partly relevant. As James E. Evans states in his introduction to Samuel Richardson's series of excerpts, the revival of Richardson's reputation in recent decades grows out of the assertion that he "remains a great writer in spite of his morality" and must be read "'for the story' (psychological realism and conscious artistry), because we no longer read 'for the sentiment.'"

Richardson himself stated quite clearly, in his prefaces to *Pamela* and *Clarissa,* and in his letters, that his purpose as an author was to depict "real life" and "in a manner probable, natural, and lively." At the same time, however, he wanted his books to be thought of as instruments of manners and morals intended to "teach great virtues." Fiction, he insisted, should be useful and instructive; it should edify readers of all ages, but particularly should be relevant and appealing to youth. Richardson observed with passionate interest and recorded with a genius for infinite detail the relationships between men and women, the concerns of daily life, and the particular class and caste distinctions of mid-eighteenth century England. This intense interest in the *usual* sets him apart from such predecessors as Daniel Defoe or the seventeenth century writers of prose romances. In all of his novels, and particularly, perhaps, in *Pamela,* the relationship between his main characters has about it the quality of traditional romantic love; at the same time, the novels are so realistically grounded in the accumulation of a mass of day-to-day realistic details as to create a remarkable sense of authenticity. Characteristic of this creation of the illusion of real life is the account, possibly apocryphal, of *Pamela*'s being read aloud by the local blacksmith to a small group of the village's inhabitants on the village green; finally, when Pamela's triumph by her marriage to Squire B. was assured, the villagers indulged in a spree of thanksgiving and merrymaking; it was *their* Pamela who had conquered.

Richardson, then, was both a conscious, self-avowed realist, and also an equally conscious, self-avowed teacher and moralist. This dualism permeates all three of his novels and is perhaps most apparent—and transparent—in *Pamela.* It is, indeed, Richardson's hallmark, and is the source both of his strength and weakness as a novelist.

Pamela · Reduced to its simplest terms, the "story" or "plot" of the first volume of *Pamela* is too well known to warrant more than the briefest summary. The heroine, a young servant girl, is pursued by her master, Squire B., but maintains her virginity in spite of his repeated and ingenious efforts, until the would-be seducer, driven to desperation, marries her. Thus is Pamela's virtue rewarded. The continuation of the novel in volume 2, a decided letdown, is virtually plotless, highly repetitive, and highlighted only by Squire B.'s excursion into infidelity. Volumes 3 and 4, written partly because of Richardson's indignation with the various parodies of the first volume of *Pamela,* have even less to recommend them. Labeled as "virtually unreadable" by one modern commentator, even Richardson's most understanding critic-biographers, T. C. Duncan Eaves and Ben D. Kimpel, have dismissed them as "Richardson at his worst, pompous, proper, proud of himself, and above all dull."

Despite his frequent excursions into bathos and sentimentality, when he is not indulging in sermonizings on ethics and morality, the Richardson of the first volume of *Pamela* writes vigorously, effectively, and with keen insight and intimate understanding of his characters. *Pamela* contains many powerful scenes that linger long in the reader's memory: the intended rape scene, the sequence in which Pamela considers suicide, even parts of the marriage scene (preceded by some prodigious feats of letter-writing to her parents on the day prior to the wedding, from six o'clock in the morning, half an hour past eight o'clock, near three o'clock [ten pages], eight o'clock at night, until eleven o'clock the same night and following the marriage) are the work of a powerful writer with a keen sense for the dramatic.

In the final analysis, however, the novel succeeds or fails because of its characters, particularly and inevitably that of Pamela herself. From the opening letter in which she informs her parents that her mistress has died and Squire B., her mistress's son, has appeared on the scene, to the long sequence of her journal entries, until her final victory when her would-be seducer, worn out and defeated in all his attempts to have her without marriage, capitulates and makes the "thrice-happy" Pamela his wife, she dominates the novel.

In effect, and seemingly quite beyond Richardson's conscious intent, Pamela is two quite different characters. On one hand, she is the attractive and convincing young girl who informs her parents that her recently deceased mistress had left her three pairs of shoes that fit her perfectly, adding that "my lady had a very little foot"; or having been transferred to Squire B.'s Lincolnshire estate, laments that she lacks "the courage to stay, neither can I think to go." On the other hand, she is at times a rather unconvincing puppet who thinks and talks in pious platitudes and values her "honesty" as a very valuable commodity, a character—in Joseph Wood Krutch's words—"so devoid of any delicacy of feeling as to be inevitably indecent."

Squire B. is less interesting than Pamela, and his efforts to seduce Pamela tend to become either boring or amusing. Her father, the Old Gaffer, who would disown his daughter "were she not honest," similarly frequently verges upon caricature, although one distinguished historian of the English novel finds him extremely convincing; and Lady Davers, Squire B.'s arrogant sister, tends to be more unbelievable than convincing, as do Pamela's captors, the odious Mrs. Jewkes and the equally repulsive Colbrand.

In spite of its shortcomings, *Pamela* cannot be dismissed, as one critic has commented, as "only a record of a peculiarly loathsome aspect of bourgeois morality." *Pamela* has great moments, scenes, and characters that pass the ultimate test of a work of fiction, that of *memorableness:* scenes that remain in the reader's consciousness long after many of the events have become blurred or dimmed. It is equally important historically: Among other things, its popularity helped prepare the way for better novelists and better novels, including what Arnold Bennett was to call the "greatest realistic novel in the world," Richardson's *Clarissa.*

Clarissa · Unlike *Pamela, Clarissa* did not have its origins in "real life"; his characters, Richardson insisted, were "entirely creatures of his fantasy." He commenced the novel in the spring or summer of 1744; it was three years in the making, two of which were primarily devoted to revision (it has been said that when his old friend Aaron Hill misread *Clarissa*, Richardson devoted a year to revising the text for publication). Almost a million words in length, the plot of *Clarissa* is relatively simple. Clarissa Harlowe, daughter of well-to-do, middle-class parents with social aspirations, is urged by her family to marry a man, Solmes, whom she finds repulsive. At the same time, her sister Arabella is being courted by an aristocrat, Robert Lovelace. Lovelace, attracted and fascinated by Clarissa, abandons his lukewarm courtship of Arabella and, after wounding the girl's brother in a duel, turns his attention to Clarissa, in spite of her family's objections. Clarissa lets herself be persuaded; she goes off with Lovelace, who imprisons her in a brothel, where he eventually drugs and rapes her; she finally escapes, refuses the contrite Lovelace's offers of marriage, and eventually dies. Lovelace, repentant and haunted by his evil act, is killed in a duel by Clarissa's cousin, Colonel Morden.

Counterpointing and contrasting with these two major characters are Anna Howe, Clarissa's closest friend and confidante, and John Belford, Lovelace's closest friend. Around these four are a number of contrasting minor characters, each of whom contributes to the minutely recorded series of events and climaxes, events which in their barest forms verge upon melodrama, and at times even farce. Even so, the novel in its totality is greater than the sum of its parts: It has about it the ultimate power of Greek tragedy, and Clarissa herself, like the major characters of Greek drama, rises above the occasionally melodramatic or improbable sequences to attain a stature not seen in English prose fiction before, and seldom surpassed since.

Much of the power and the drama of *Clarissa* grows out of the author's effective use of contrast—between Clarissa and Anna Howe; between Lovelace and Belford; and between the country life of the upper middle class and the dark, rank side of urban England. This and the richness and variety of incident redeem the sometimes improbable events and lapses into didacticism and give the novel a sense of reality larger than life itself.

In the final analysis, the great strength of the novel is the creation of its two main characters. Clarissa, with her pride and self-reliance, "so secure in her virtue," whose feelings of shame and self-hatred are such that she begs Lovelace "to send her to Bedlam or a private madhouse" (no less a master than Henry Fielding praised Clarissa's letter after the rape as "beyond anything I had ever read"), could have degenerated into bathos or caricature but instead attains a level of intensity and reality unique in the novel prior to 1740.

Though Clarissa dominates the novel, Richardson is almost as successful with Lovelace, despite the fact that in the early portions of the novel he seems for the most part like Squire B., just another Restoration rake. His transformation, following his violation of Clarissa, grows and deepens: "One day, I fancy," he reflects, "I shall hate myself on recollecting what I am about at this instant. But I must stay till then. We must all of us have something to repent of." Repent he does, after his terse letter announcing the consummation of the rape: "And now, Belford, I can go no further. The affair is over. Clarissa lives."

Belford, like the reader, is horror-stricken. By the rape, Lovelace has acted not as a man, but as an animal, and his expiation is, in its own way, much more terrible than that of Clarissa, who at times somewhat complacently contemplates her own innocence and eventual heavenly reward. Lovelace remains a haunted man ("sick of myself! sick of my remembrance of my vile act!") until his death in a duel with Colonel Morden, a death which is really a kind of suicide. The final scene of the novel, and Lovelace's last words, "Let this Expiate!," are among the most memorable of the entire novel, and Richardson's portrayal of a character soiled and tarnished, an eternally damaged soul, is unforgettable.

Sir Charles Grandison · As early as February, 1741, an anonymous correspondent had asked Richardson to write the "history of a Man, whose Life would be the path that we should follow." By the end of the decade, with *Pamela* and *Clarissa* behind him, and influenced by old friends, including Lady Bradshaigh, Richardson began thinking seriously about such a novel. Despite increasing ill health and the continuing demands of his business, he was soon immersed in the project, a novel designed to "present" the character of a "Good Man," and to show the influence such a character exerted "on society in general and his intimates in particular." Although he had at one time decided not to publish the novel during his lifetime, the first volumes of *Sir Charles Grandison* came out in 1753. Even before the seventh and last volume was in print the following year, some critics were stating their dissatisfaction with Sir Charles's "Unbelievable Perfection," a criticism Richardson repudiated in a concluding note to the last volume: "The Editor (that is, Richardson himself) thinks human nature has often, of late, been shown in a light too degrading; and he hopes from this series of letters it will be seen that characters may be good without being unnatural."

Subsequent critical opinion of the novel has varied widely, a few critics considering it Richardson's masterpiece, while many regard it as his least successful novel. *Sir Charles Grandison* differs dramatically from its predecessors in its concern with the English upper class and aristocracy, a world which Richardson freely acknowledged he had never known or understood: "How shall a man obscurely situated . . . pretend to describe and enter into characters in upper life?" In setting, too, the novel was a new departure, ranging as it does from England to Italy and including a large number of Italians, highlighted by Clementina, certainly the most memorable character in the novel. The conflict in Clementina's heart and soul, her subsequent refusal to marry Sir Charles because he is a Protestant, and her ensuing madness are as effective as anything Richardson ever wrote, and far more convincing than Sir Charles's rescue of Harriett Byron following her abduction by Sir Hargrove Pollexfen and their eventual marriage. Harriett, though not as interesting a character as either Pamela or Clarissa, shares with them one basic habit: She is an indefatigable letter writer, perhaps the most prolific in the history of English prose fiction, at times sleeping only two hours a night and, when not admiring Grandison from afar, writing letters to him (not uncharacteristic of her style is her appeal to the clergyman who is supposed to marry her to Sir Hargrove: "Worthy man . . . save a poor creature. I would not hurt a worm! I love everybody! Save me from violence!").

Sir Charles himself is similarly less interesting than either Squire B. or Lovelace, and it is difficult today for even the most sympathetic reader to find a great deal to admire in the man who is against masquerades, dresses neatly but not gaudily, is time and time again described as a "prince of the Almighty's creation," an "angel of a man," and "one of the finest dancers in England." Most of the other characters, including the Italians (with the notable exception of Clementina), are similarly either unconvincing or uninteresting, except for two small masterpieces of characterization: Aunt Nell, Grandison's maiden aunt; and Lord G., Charlotte Grandison's husband, a gentle and quiet man, in love with his temperamental wife, often hurt and bewildered by her sharp tongue and brusque actions.

Horace Walpole is said to have written off *Sir Charles Grandison* as a "romance as it would be spiritualized by a Methodist preacher"; and Lord Chesterfield also dismissed it, adding that whenever Richardson "goes, *ultra crepidem*, into high life, he grossly escapes the modes." On the other hand, Jane Austen specifically "singled . . . [it] out for special praise," and Richardson's major biographers believe that in *Sir Charles Grandison*, his "surface realism and his analysis of social situations are at their height."

Whatever his weaknesses, Richardson was one of the seminal influences in the development of the novel. His impact upon his contemporaries and their immediate successors was profound, not only in England but on the Continent as well, and eventually on the beginnings of the novel in the United States. He popularized the novel of manners as a major genre for several decades, and his use of the epistolary method added another dimension to the art of narrative. Though his novels have frequently suffered in comparison with those of his major contemporary, Henry Fielding, in recent years a renewed interest in and appraisal of Richardson and his work have placed him securely in the ranks of the major English novelists.

William Peden

Other major works

NONFICTION: *The Apprentice's Vade Mecum: Or, Young Man's Pocket Companion*, 1733; *Letters Written to and for Particular Friends, on the Most Important Occasions*, 1741; *A Collection of the Moral and Instructive Sentiments, Maxims, Cautions, and Reflections, Contained in the Histories of Pamela, Clarissa, and Sir Charles Grandison*, 1755; *The Correspondence of Samuel Richardson*, 1804 (Anna Barbauld, editor).

Bibliography

Bloom, Harold, ed. *Samuel Richardson*. New York: Chelsea House, 1987. This collection reprints in order of their appearance what Bloom judges to be the best of modern criticism of Richardson. In addition to Bloom's own introduction, there are six essays devoted to *Clarissa* and two each to *Pamela* and *Sir Charles Grandison*. The book also includes a chronology of Richardson's life and a brief bibliography.

Brophy, Elizabeth Bergen. *Samuel Richardson: The Triumph of Craft*. Knoxville: University of Tennessee Press, 1974. Rejecting the notion that Richardson's unconscious produced great novels in spite of the author–a view held by even his later biographers–Brophy examines Richardson's statements about fiction in his letters and his prefaces and postscripts to his novels. Having determined his theories about fiction, Brophy then compares these ideas with Richardson's practice. Two short appendices discuss the novelist's "nervous complaint" and conclude that he probably suffered from Parkinson's disease.

Bueler, Lois E. *Clarissa's Plots*. London: Associated University Presses, 1994. Examines the themes in Richardson's seminal work. Includes bibliographical references and an index.

Doody, Margaret Anne. *A Natural Passion: A Study of the Novels of Samuel Richardson*. Oxford, England: Clarendon Press, 1974. Seeks the antecedents of Richardson's fiction in seventeenth and eighteenth century drama, romance, religious writing, thought, and art. Doody shows how Richardson transformed these materials into fiction probing "man's relation to himself and his fate."

Eaves, T. C. Duncan, and Ben D. Kimpel. *Samuel Richardson: A Biography*. Oxford, England: Clarendon Press, 1971. The definitive biography, based on fifteen years of research. Devotes three chapters to each of the novels and concludes with four excellent chapters on Richardson's personality, thoughts, reading, and achievements.

Golden, Morris. *Richardson's Characters*. Ann Arbor: University of Michigan Press, 1963. A psychological study of Richardson that sees in his characters aspects of himself. Suggests that while ostensibly Richardson supported morality, at least unconsciously he favored passion.

Kinkead-Weakes, Mark. *Samuel Richardson: Dramatic Novelist*. Ithaca, N.Y.: Cornell University Press, 1973. Seeking to understand Richardson's achievement and his appeal to nineteenth century writers such as Jane Austen and George Eliot, this study demonstrates Richardson's dramatic use of immediacy and explores the implications of his "writing to the moment."

McKillop, Alan Dugald. *Samuel Richardson, Printer and Novelist*. Chapel Hill: University of North Carolina Press, 1936. Long the standard biography, this study remains a good treatment of Richardson's life, which McKillop discusses in a lengthy appendix. The text itself focuses "on the origins, publication, and reception of" the three novels.

Myer, Valerie Grosvenor, ed. *Samuel Richardson: Passion and Prudence*. London: Vision

Press, 1986. As in other collections of Richardson criticism, the majority of this volume's essays concern *Clarissa,* with one critical piece devoted to *Pamela* and one to *Sir Charles Grandison.* Myer also includes, in a section titled "The Sex's Champion," two essays on Richardson's influence. Unlike other collections of this type, Myer's book also contains a helpful index.

Watt, Ian. *The Rise of the Novel: Studies in Defoe, Richardson, and Fielding.* Berkeley: University of California Press, 1957. Contains excellent chapters on *Pamela* and *Clarissa,* praising the psychological depth of the characters. Analyzes Richardson's contribution to the development of English prose fiction and relates the novels to the social situation of their day.

Wolff, Cynthia Griffin. *Samuel Richardson and the Eighteenth-Century Puritan Character.* Hamden, Conn.: Archon Books, 1972. Examines Richardson's novels, especially *Clarissa,* as psychological and social studies, relating them to twentieth century psychology and eighteenth century Puritanism.

Susanna Rowson

Born: Portsmouth, England; 1762
Died: Boston, Massachusetts; March 2, 1824

Principal long fiction · *Victoria*, 1786; *The Inquisitor: Or, Invisible Rambler*, 1788; *Mary: Or, The Test of Honour*, 1789; *Charlotte: A Tale of Truth*, 1791 (pb. in U.S. as *Charlotte Temple*, 1797); *Mentoria: Or, The Young Lady's Friend*, 1791; *The Fille de Chambre*, 1792 (better known as *Rebecca: Or, The Fille de Chambre*, 1814); *Trials of the Human Heart*, 1795; *Reuben and Rachel: Or, Tales of Old Times*, 1798; *Sarah: Or, The Exemplary Wife*, 1813; *Charlotte's Daughter: Or, The Three Orphans*, 1828.

Other literary forms · Susanna Rowson was a prolific, well-rounded writer. Besides her ten works of long fiction, she produced three volumes of poetry: *Poems on Various Subjects* (1788), *A Trip to Parnassus* (1788), and *Miscellaneous Poems* (1804). Between 1794 and 1797, she wrote about seven dramatic works, most of which were probably performed but not published; the most popular of these was *Slaves in Algiers: Or, A Struggle for Freedom* (1794). She also composed the lyrics for numerous songs and contributed to the production of at least two periodicals: the *Boston Weekly Magazine*, for which she wrote articles on a wide range of subjects and apparently also served as editor between 1802 and 1805; and the *New England Galaxy*, which was founded in 1817 and for which Rowson wrote chiefly religious and devotional prose pieces. Finally, she wrote and had published six pedagogical works: *An Abridgement of Universal Geography* (1805), *A Spelling Dictionary* (1807), *A Present for Young Ladies* (1811), *Youth's First Step in Geography* (1818), *Exercises in History* (1822), and *Biblical Dialogues* (1822).

Achievements · Opinions of Rowson's achievements as a novelist have fluctuated widely since the nineteenth century. Earlier critics were high in their praises of the moral tendency of her work and her storytelling skills, while later estimates have tended to disparage both and to find her writing limited and ordinary.

As Dorothy Weil has shown, a well-developed system of aims and values emerges from all of Rowson's writings and gives her work notable unity and breadth. In particular, as Weil has demonstrated, Rowson's belief in the equality of the sexes and her concern with feminist issues and positive goals for women deserve wider recognition than they have received. In other respects, Rowson's novels are typical of the novelist's theory and practice in newly independent America and are interesting and revealing as a window on the nature of fiction in the late eighteenth century.

Biography · Susanna Haswell Rowson's remarkably full, active life began in Portsmouth, England, where she was born in 1762. Her mother died shortly after, and Rowson's first visit to America occurred when her father settled and married in Massachusetts and, in 1767, brought his daughter to join him, his new wife, and his three stepsons. Some of Rowson's experiences during this visit, including a shipwreck, appear later in *Rebecca*. By 1778, she was back in England, her father's apparently doubtful loyalty having led the fledgling American government first to confiscate his property and intern his family and him and then return them to England.

Library of Congress

Rowson's independence and initiative soon revealed themselves. By the time she was in her twenties, she had secured a position as governess in the family of the Duchess of Devonshire, beginning a life of service through teaching and writing; she also helped her father gain a pension, and she began publishing her fiction and poetry.

Rowson was twenty-four when her first novel, *Victoria*, appeared in London in 1786. The work's subtitle, a sign of her aims and interests as a novelist, declared that Victoria was "calculated to improve the morals of the female sex, by impressing them with a just sense of the merits of filial piety." Later in 1786, she married William Rowson, with whom she shared an interest in music and theater. The marriage lasted for thirty-eight years.

Between the time of her marriage and her immigration to America in 1793, she wrote prolifically, publishing five novels and two books of verse. In 1792, following the failure of her husband's hardware business, the couple, along with Rowson's sister-in-law Charlotte, decided to join a theater company and tour the British Isles. The decision was fateful, because in 1793 they were seen by Thomas Wignell, an American who was recruiting players for the theater he was about to open in Philadelphia. Wignell took them to America in 1793, and thus began Rowson's American period, during which she blossomed both as a performer and as an educator and moralist who attempted to serve others through many activities, including novel writing.

Rowson published her four-volume novel, *Trials of the Human Heart*, in 1795, and continued acting and writing in the theater until 1797. Then, once again, she turned her life and her career of service in a new direction. She opened a Young Ladies' Academy in Boston in 1797. Starting with only one pupil, she had one hundred and a waiting list within a year. She continued to instruct young women in her school until 1822, but she also continued to do so through her writing. She published the novels *Reuben and Rachel* and *Sarah* as well as another book of poetry, various songs and odes, and a theatrical piece. Her major works, however, were the six pedagogical books she wrote and published between 1805 and 1822 for use in her school.

All of this got done even as Rowson found time and energy for rearing several adopted children and for supporting church and charity, which included holding the presidency of Boston's Fatherless and Widow's Society. When she died on March 2, 1824, Rowson left in manuscript her final work, *Charlotte's Daughter*, the sequel to *Charlotte*; it was published posthumously in 1828.

Analysis · Benjamin Franklin certainly had neither women nor novelists foremost in his mind when he published his "Information for Those Who Would Remove to America" in 1782. Yet Susanna Rowson, who would remove to America a little more than a decade later, was exactly the sort of migrant Franklin would have wanted. America, he said, required useful members of society rather than persons "doing nothing of value, but living idly on the labour of others." Citizens of the new nation "do not inquire concerning a stranger, *what is he?* but *what can he do?* If he has any useful art, he is welcome; and if he exercises it and behaves well, he will be respected by all that know him."

Rowson understood the kind of labor Franklin meant, and the years she spent in America as a writer and educator show that she cared about becoming a useful, respected member of society. Doing this as a novelist was no easy task, for while fiction might be popular among young readers, the "common verdict with respect to novels," as Noah Webster expressed it in 1788, was that "some of them are useful, many of them pernicious, and most of them trifling."

Rowson responded by producing novels that consistently stress Franklin's service ideal, especially for the young women she saw herself addressing. "We are not sent into the world to pass through it in indolence," says one of Rowson's wise widows to the heroine of *Trials of the Human Heart*. "Life which is not serviceable to our fellow creatures is not acceptable to our Creator."

Such was the ideal that Rowson held up to the women for whom she wrote and that she herself sought to embody by writing novels that would be an honor to herself and a benefit to society. For many modern readers and writers of fiction, there may well be something objectionable about regarding novel writing as akin to useful arts of the kind Franklin mentions with approval in his prospectus—farming, carpentry, tanning, weaving, shoemaking, and the like—but Rowson and a few other scrupulous early American novelists were in effect trying to do just that: produce fiction that would be of direct, lasting benefit to its readers by helping them live happy, fulfilled lives.

Rowson's novels typically exhibit a clear moral purpose and an unmistakable connection between virtue and happiness. The strong didactic element which modern readers may find distasteful in Rowson and her contemporaries was in fact the essential finishing touch for many early American novelists. Of what use, these writers might have said, was an uncultivated field or undeveloped talent? Almost from the outset, Rowson stressed that the moral purpose of her fiction and the well-being of her readers were more important to her than financial or critical success.

Rowson realized, of course, that there were too many novels which were either trifling or pernicious, as Webster said, and did their readers no good. Her awareness was sharp enough that in *The Inquisitor* she offers a detailed summary of what she considered a typical "Modern Novel." To Rowson, the problem with such novels was that they were more likely to harm than improve the reader, mislead rather than enlighten. They tended to encourage vice and error by showing that they lead to happiness rather than suffering, thus making them attractive instead of repugnant to the unwary reader. Novels such as these, and writers such as Jean-Jacques Rousseau and Johann Wilhelm von Goethe, were said to misuse the power of fiction by ennobling errant behavior such as suicide or adultery and charming the reader into accepting and even living by untruths made too attractive.

For Rowson and her contemporaries, fiction was never to make error noble and vice fascinating, deluding the reader and ultimately causing her unhappiness; it should have exactly the opposite psychological effect. Rowson would have agreed with what Columbia College student Daniel Tompkins, in 1794, called fiction's "true design and intent." Novels, he wrote in his journal, "are representations of men and things qualified to excite to the love of virtue and the detestation of vice." Such novels used the power of narrative and the feelings and imaginations of readers to move the reader away from vicious behavior and toward that which was virtuous and rewarding. As Rowson describes this process in her preface to *Trials of the Human Heart*, she hopes to "awaken in the bosoms of . . . youthful readers a thorough detestation of vice, and a spirited emulation to embrace and follow the precepts of Piety, Truth, and Virtue."

At the heart of Rowson's novels, then, is her concern with what she likes to call the "true felicity" of her readers and her belief that virtue leads to happiness as surely as vice and error do not. In changing the reader for the better, the novels seek to be both moral and affective. They work through the feelings and imagination and end in well-rooted, satisfying behavior. A closer look at three representative novels of Rowson's will show how she tried to achieve these results.

Charlotte · As Dorothy Weil observes in her study of Rowson, *In Defense of Women* (1976), *Charlotte* (entitled *Charlotte Temple* in the American edition of 1797) is one of the wonders of American literature, primarily because of its immediate and long-lasting popularity. It was widely read upon its publication in America in 1797–about twenty-five thousand copies sold shortly after it appeared–and by the middle of the nineteenth century it had become the most frequently published popular novel in America. By 1905, it had gone through as many as two hundred editions, and in 1933, in his bibliographical study of Rowson, R. W. G. Vail claimed that more people had read *Charlotte* than any other work of fiction printed in America. Fueled by the novel's popularity, legends about the real-life identities of its main characters have flourished. In New York City's Trinity Churchyard, the grave of Charlotte Stanley, supposedly the model for the novel's heroine, now bears a slab with the inscription "Charlotte Temple."

The novel is also a revealing example of one kind of narrative by which Rowson tried to affect her readers as useful fiction was supposed to do. She does this by relating and having her readers imaginatively participate in one of the eighteenth century's favorite plots: the story of the causes and consequences of youthful error and delusion in which the heroine herself, and thus the reader, learns by bitter experience to love virtue and hate vice. Rowson also presents the heroine's learning process in a moral context of clearly stated values, thereby ensuring that the nature of virtue and vice is well defined throughout.

The main events of the novel are easily summarized. Charlotte Temple is a fifteen-year-old student at a boarding school in Chichester, England; the year is 1774. One day, she meets Lieutenant Montraville, who, finding Charlotte attractive and eventually deciding that he loves her, persuades her to see him and then to accompany him to America. Although she doubts herself the moment she decides to go, Charlotte nevertheless leaves her friends and her parents behind and, in the company of her lover, his deceitful friend Belcour, and her evil teacher Mademoiselle La Rue, sails to America. Once there, Montraville falls in love with another woman even as Belcour deceives him into believing that Charlotte has been unfaithful; Montraville abandons her, though she is now pregnant with his child. Virtually alone and friendless, Charlotte has her baby and dies just after her distracted father has finally located her. Montraville kills Belcour in a duel and lives out his days married to the woman he loves but still sad and remorseful over his part in Charlotte's ruin. La Rue later dies in misery brought on by her life of dissipation.

This is the grisly narrative that Rowson attempts to make useful and instructive to the "young and thoughtless of the fair sex." She does this first by anchoring the events of the story in a context of contrasting values. In a novel designed to make virtue lovely and vice and error detestable, the reader should be very certain just what virtue and its opposites are. Among the important good people offered as attractive examples of the life of virtue are Charlotte's parents and Mrs. Beauchamp, her only real friend in America. These characters are distinguished by that active service to others that Rowson valued so highly. Each possesses a feeling heart and a generous hand, and each knows the exquisite satisfaction of comforting less fortunate fellow creatures. Moreover, these characters have given up fast-paced city life in favor of the simple, contented rural existence that befits men and women of feeling.

In contrast to such characters are the novel's bad people, especially La Rue and Belcour, who represent the false pleasures and values of selfishness. These clear contrasts between virtue and vice are established early in the novel and are regularly reinforced by a narrator who both relates and freely comments on the story. "Oh, my dear girls, for to such only am I writing," she says at one point in a typical utterance, "listen not to the voice of love unless sanctioned by parental approbation . . . pray for fortitude to resist the impulse of inclination when it runs counter to the precepts of religion and virtue."

The secret of fiction's power to further the happiness of readers lay not in static commentary and contrast, however, as much as in *process*–the learning process which the feeling reader would go through by participating imaginatively in the experience of the novel's heroine, Charlotte Temple. She is a poor deluded child who must learn by adversity that virtue leads to happiness, vice to misery. The novel is thus a psychological history of the causes and effects of error and vice, with Charlotte starting the novel as "an innocent artless girl" and ending "a poor forsaken wanderer" suffering "extreme agitation of mind" and "total deprivation of reason" as a result of her mistakes.

Rowson tries to show that Charlotte's basic problem is her inability to resist an impulse when it runs counter to the precepts of religion and virtue. Despite the fact that she was reared by exemplary parents, Charlotte falls, and she does so, Rowson shows, because she allows herself to come under the influence of bad people who disable her power to resist dangerous, delusive inclinations in herself–just what was said to happen to weak, unwary readers of pernicious novels. Charlotte thus ends as "the hapless victim of imprudence and evil counsellors," the "poor girl by thoughtless passion led astray."

Like bad novels, the evil counsellors who overwhelm Charlotte's discretion and good sense are capable of using appearances–particularly the power of language and dress–to disable and deceive. A sorceress possessed of the "art of Circe," La Rue convinces Charlotte to meet, and later to continue seeing, Montraville against her own better judgment. Thus does Charlotte "forsake the paths of virtue, for those of vice and folly." Eloping to America with Montraville, becoming pregnant and then left abandoned "to die with want and misery in a strange land," the very opposite of a useful and respectable member of society, Charlotte is "held up as an object of terror, to prevent us from falling into guilty errors." The reader, Rowson would hope, sees and feels that deviation from virtue is "an object of detestation," and vice and error themselves as detestable as their opposites, embodied in happy characters, are desirable. The ideal reader is the "reader of sensibility" who will "acutely feel the woes of Charlotte" and therefore behave so as to avoid them.

Mentoria · Implicit in *Charlotte* is a pattern for a second type of useful novel which Rowson employed in *Mentoria*. As noted, the third-person narrator of *Charlotte* both relates and comments on the tale, making sure her readers understand its moral import and learn from it. In *Mentoria*, the nameless, wholly reliable preceptress of *Charlotte* becomes the story's main character. Her name is Helena Askham, and, in a series of letters to Lady Winworth's three daughters for whom she earlier was governess, Helena dispenses stories and lessons based on her own experience, which are designed to instruct young women on subjects of concern to them.

Like Charlotte, Helena combines humble origins with a good education. Unlike Charlotte, she is strong enough to resist impulses which run counter to the precepts of religion and virtue. She is able to do so because, sensitive and feeling though she is, she is also "endowed with discernment and sense far superior to the generality of young women of her age."

She shows her mettle early on when, placed in a situation very much like Charlotte's with Montraville, she is courted by Lady Winworth's son. Unlike Charlotte, who allowed the rhetoric and appearance of La Rue and Montraville to disable her judgment and excite errant, delusive hopes, Helena displays the control of feeling and pleasing inclination that is the mark of Rowson's strong women, and that enables her to stifle her rising passion for her suitor and reject him. Later, he does in fact marry someone closer to him in rank and fortune, and so does Helena, until her husband's death leaves her free to become governess and then mentor to the three Winworth children.

As this wise widow, a woman who, like the narrator of *Charlotte*, combines sensibility with strong good sense, Helena becomes the central character of *Mentoria*. The several stories she relates, therefore, are meant to do what the single story of Charlotte did: Use the power of narrative as a memorable, striking means of instruction for young women, a way of making "a lasting impression on the minds of fair readers" and thereby of advancing their happiness.

For example, the life of Helena's friend Louisa Railton is offered as "a model by which every young woman who wishes to promote her own felicity, will regulate her conduct." The beauty of the virtue of filial piety is illustrated by Louisa's choosing, after her mother's death, "a low roofed mansion, scanty meals, and attendance on a sick peevish father, to the lofty apartments, plenteous table, and variety of amusements she might have enjoyed with Lady Mary," her rich relative. She thereby gains, however, "a contented happy mind, [and] serenity dwelt in her heart and cheerfulness beamed in her eyes. . . . She lived beloved by all and died universally regretted." Made desirable and attractive, and distinguished as in *Charlotte* from its selfish opposite, the virtue of filial devotion should impress the reader and prompt her to imitation. As Helena writes her pupils, "Be wise, my dear children, follow Louisa's example, so shall your lives be happy and your last moments peace." Helena continues to deal similarly with such topics as friendship, reputation, love, pleasure, and marriage, using the force of the striking instance to impress readers with the felicity of the virtuous life and the miseries of vice and error.

Trials of the Human Heart · In *Trials of the Human Heart*, Rowson demonstrates a third type of "useful fiction." Her aim is to achieve the same effect as before—"to awaken in the bosoms of my youthful readers," as she says in the novel's preface, "a thorough detestation of vice, and a spirited emulation, to embrace and follow the precepts of Piety, Truth and Virtue." Like *Charlotte, Trials of the Human Heart* is a story of adolescent initiation, but rather than involving the reader in the misfortunes of a heroine such as Charlotte whose imprudence is her undoing, Rowson offers the character of Meriel Howard, who is the undeserving victim of the cruelty or caprice of others and as a result suffers through what one character calls "some of the heaviest trials to which the human heart is incident"–four volumes' worth, in fact, related through letters exchanged among the characters.

Like other Rowson heroines, Meriel is artless and innocent at the start, having indeed spent much of her childhood in a convent, and she possesses a generous heart as well. As she writes her convent friend Celia, "I am weak as an infant, whenever a scene of distress or happiness meets my eye; I have a tear of sympathy for the one, and a smile of gratulation for the other." Thus endowed, Meriel leaves the convent and enters a world that ends up causing her far more distress than happiness.

The first incidents of the novel, when Meriel is about sixteen, are typical of the pattern of disappointed expectation that repeats itself in Meriel's life and occasions her learning and uttering many lessons about life. On her way home to Bristol, she thinks about the coming reunion with her parents, whom she has not seen for most of her childhood. "I pictured them to myself, as very amiable old people–and, in fancy, felt their embraces and kissed off the tears of joy I saw falling from their eyes." What she finds instead is a "suffering saint" of a mother, her settled melancholy the result of living with a husband who is cruel and unfeeling and a son notable for "frigid coldness." Meriel soon discovers that her father–who much later in the novel turns out *not* to be her father–is a freethinker and a hypocritical villain, concealing under the "mask of integrity and honour every vice which can disgrace human nature." Indeed, it was because of her father's vitiated morals that Meriel was originally placed in a convent. She now finds him ardently pursuing an adulterous affair; after she succeeds in breaking that up, she herself becomes the object of his amorous attention, an event one character describes as "too dreadful, too shocking to human nature, to wear even the face of probability."

Soon after, Meriel reflects that she no doubt has many more trials yet to endure, and she is absolutely right. In one episode after another, she–like her counterpart Rebecca, the heroine of the novel of the same name–attracts the compromising notice rather than the solicitude of married men and the venom rather than the pity of other women. As Meriel remarks later, looking back over her life, "how hard is my fate. Possessed as I am of a heart moulded to compassion, glowing with universal affection toward my fellow creatures, I am constantly thrown among people, whose every feeling is absorbed in self."

For Meriel as for the reader of this and virtually every other Rowson novel, the purpose of the heroine's experiences is to teach about truth and error, what Meriel calls the "useful lessons taught me in the school of adversity." Born to be the sport of fortune, Meriel learns that "this is a sad–very sad world to live in.–For if we love anything we are sure to lose it." The truly important lesson, however, follows on this. Having so painfully discovered the error of her innocent belief that "every heart glowed with humanity, friendship and sincerity toward each other," Meriel periodically entertains the opposite error. "What a world this is," she writes to her enviably placid convent friend. "Were it not impious, I could wish I had never entered it."

Despair is indeed impious, and the heroine, like the reader, learns that such feelings run counter to the precepts of religion and virtue. Unlike Charlotte, however, Meriel is capable of pulling back from harmful vice and error. The proper response to misfortune is, first, to bear up under it; one's duty, as Meriel says, is "to submit without repining, to the will of Him, who never lays on his creatures the rod of affliction but for some wise purpose." Second, one must serve, not retreat: "We are not sent into the world to pass through it in indolence," Meriel is told. "Remember, that life which is not in some measure serviceable to our fellow creatures, is not acceptable to our Creator." As Meriel and the reader learn, the suicidal response in any form is never appropriate. At the end of the novel, Meriel anticipates a happy marriage and hopes both to deserve and preserve her good fortune "by exerting the abilities with which I am amply endowed to chear the desponding heart, sooth the afflicted spirits and soften the bed of pain."

Like other Rowson heroines, Meriel has found the secret of happiness. For her readers, Rowson wanted nothing less. Living happily in the real world of human folly and disappointment is the ideal which her many novels and her own varied life embody. To have found so many ways to demonstrate that ideal is surely a tribute to her strength and her inventiveness.

Michael Lowenstein

Other major works

PLAYS: *Slaves in Algiers: Or, A Struggle for Freedom,* pr., pb. 1794; *The Female Patriot,* pr. 1795; *The Volunteers,* pr., pb. 1795; *Americans in England,* pb. 1796, pr. 1979 (revised as *The Columbian Daughter*).

POETRY: *Poems on Various Subjects,* 1788; *A Trip to Parnassus,* 1788; *Miscellaneous Poems,* 1804.

NONFICTION: *An Abridgement of Universal Geography,* 1805; *A Spelling Dictionary,* 1807; *A Present for Young Ladies,* 1811; *Youth's First Step in Geography,* 1818; *Exercises in History,* 1822; *Biblical Dialogues,* 1822.

Bibliography

Davidson, Cathy N. *Revolution and the Word: The Rise of the Novel in America.* New York: Oxford University Press, 1986. Davidson's superb interdisciplinary study of the eighteenth century "reading revolution" highlights commonplace responses to *Charlotte Temple* and analyzes Rowson's complex characterization of the villain Montraville. Argues that Rowson's plots of "sexual crime and feminine punishment" expose society's double standard of justice.

Fiedler, Leslie A. *Love and Death in the American Novel.* Rev. ed. New York: Stein & Day, 1966. Although a classic study of the novel, Fiedler defines sentimentalism and specifically *Charlotte Temple* as "not literature" and "completely a woman's book"; he is equally mean-spirited in his denigration of Rowson's literary skills. The study has minor use for placing Rowson in the literary context of "Prototypes and Early Adaptations."

Loshe, Lillie Deming. *The Early American Novel.* New York: Columbia University Press, 1907. Significant biographical details support Loshe's contention that Rowson relied upon personal experience for many of her themes. This study is of most value, however, for placing Rowson's work in the context of the early sentimental novel: Unlike most authors of "domestic melodrama," Rowson developed realistic rather than romantic plots.

Spengemann, William C. *The Adventurous Muse: The Poets of American Fiction, 1789-1900.* New Haven, Conn.: Yale University Press, 1977. Spengemann argues that *Charlotte Temple* is a "pure" example of "the spirit of domesticity." Although he criticizes the emotionalism of Rowson's characterizations and her extravagant style, Spengemann acknowledges the value Rowson placed on factuality. Most useful for its discussion of the distinguishing features of American "domestic romances."

Stern, Julia A. *The Plight of Feeling: Sympathy and Dissent in the Early American Novel.* Chicago: University of Chicago Press, 1997. Studies *Charlotte Temple*, Hannah Webster Foster's *Coquette*, and Charles Brockden Brown's *Ormond.*

Vail, R. W. G. *Susanna Haswell Rowson, the Author of "Charlotte Temple": A Bibliographical Study.* Worcester, Mass.: American Antiquarian Society, 1933. Vail's comprehensive bibliography of Rowson's writings includes not only standard lists of editions of her various novels but also such delightfully unusual features as the parts Rowson portrayed as an actress and auction records that attest to her continuing popularity among collectors. Brief biographical essays are also included.

Weil, Dorothy. *In Defense of Women: Susanna Rowson (1762-1824).* University Park: Pennsylvania State University Press, 1976. An astute analysis of Rowson's literary aspirations and accomplishments and of her extensive concern for the religious, moral, and intellectual education of young women. Weil's text incorporates extensive excerpts from rarely published works by Rowson and includes an excellent bibliography of primary and secondary sources.

Dorothy L. Sayers

Born: Oxford, England; June 13, 1893
Died: Witham, England; December 17, 1957

Principal long fiction · *Whose Body?*, 1923; *Clouds of Witness*, 1926; *Unnatural Death,* 1927 (also as *The Dawson Pedigree*); *Lord Peter Views the Body*, 1928; *The Unpleasantness at the Bellona Club*, 1928; *The Documents in the Case*, 1930 (with Robert Eustace); *Strong Poison,* 1930; *The Five Red Herrings*, 1931 (also known as *Suspicious Characters*); *The Floating Admiral,* 1931 (with others); *Have His Carcase*, 1932; *Ask a Policeman*, 1933 (with others); *Murder Must Advertise*, 1933; *The Nine Tailors*, 1934; *Gaudy Night*, 1935; *Six Against the Yard, 1936* (with others; also known as *Six Against Scotland Yard*); *Busman's Honeymoon*, 1937; *Double Death: A Murder Story*, 1939 (with others); *The Scoop, and Behind the Scenes*, 1983 (with others); *Crime on the Coast, and No Flowers by Request*, 1984 (with others).

Other literary forms · In addition to the twelve detective novels that brought her fame, Dorothy L. Sayers wrote short stories, poetry, essays, and plays, and distinguished herself as a translator and scholar of medieval French and Italian literature. Although she began her career as a poet, with Basil Blackwell bringing out collections of her verse in 1916 and 1918, Sayers primarily wrote fiction from 1920 until the late 1930's, after which she focused on radio and stage plays and a verse translation of Dante. She also edited a landmark anthology of detective fiction, *Great Short Stories of Detection, Mystery, and Horror* (1928-1934; also known as *The Omnibus of Crime*).

Outside of her fiction, the essence of Sayers's mind and art can be found in *The Mind of the Maker* (1941), a treatise on aesthetics that is one of the most illuminating inquiries into the creative process ever written; in her essays on Dante; and in two religious dramas, *The Zeal of Thy House* (1937), a verse play written for the Canterbury Festival that dramatizes Sayers's attitude toward work, and *The Man Born to Be King,* a monumental series of radio plays first broadcast amidst controversy in 1941-1942, which takes up what Sayers regarded as the most exciting of mysteries: the drama of Christ's life and death, the drama in which God is both victim and hero. Of her many essays, the 1946 collection *Unpopular Opinions* and the 1947 *Creed or Chaos?* provide a good sampling of the acumen, wit, and originality with which Sayers attacked a variety of subjects, including religion, feminism, and learning.

In 1972, James Sandoe edited *Lord Peter*, a collection of all the Wimsey stories. Two other collections, both published during Sayers's lifetime (*Hangman's Holiday*, 1933, and *In the Teeth of the Evidence and Other Stories*, 1939), include non-Wimsey stories. At her death, Sayers left unfinished her translation of Dante's *Cantica III: Paradise*, which was completed by her friend and colleague Barbara Reynolds and published posthumously in 1962 as the final volume in the Penguin Classics edition of Dante that Sayers had begun in 1944. An unpublished fragment of an additional novel, called *Thrones, Dominations* and apparently abandoned by Sayers in the 1940's, was also left unfinished, as was her projected critical/biographical study of Wilkie Collins. This last fragment was published in 1977. From 1973 to 1977, the British Broadcasting Corporation (BBC) produced excellent adaptations of five of the Wimsey novels for television, thus creating a new audience for Sayers's work.

Achievements · One of the chief pleasures for readers of Dorothy Sayers is the companionship of one of fiction's great creations, Lord Peter Wimsey, that extraordinarily English gentleman, cosmopolite, detective/scholar. Although the Wimsey novels were created primarily to make money, his characterization demonstrates that his creator was a serious, skillful writer. As the novels follow Wimsey elegantly through murder, mayhem, and madness, he grows from an enchanting caricature into a fully realized human being. The solver of mysteries thus becomes increasingly enigmatic himself. Wimsey's growth parallels Sayers's artistic development, which is appropriate, since she announced that her books were to be more like mainstream novels than the cardboard world of ordinary detective fiction.

Lord Peter is something of a descendant of P. G. Wodehouse's Bertie Wooster, and at times he emulates Arthur Conan Doyle's Sherlock Holmes, but in Wimsey, Sayers essentially created an original. Sayers's novels integrate elements of earlier detective fiction, especially the grasp of psychological torment typified by Joseph Sheridan Le Fanu and the fine delineation of manners exemplified in Wilkie Collins—with subjects one would expect from a medieval scholar: virtue, corruption, justice, punishment, suffering, redemption, time, and death. The hallmarks of her art—erudition, wit, precision, and moral passion—provoke admiration in some readers and dislike in others.

Sayers's novels are filled with wordplay that irritates those who cannot decipher it and delights those who can. Her names are wonderful puns (Wimsey, Vane, Freke, de Vine, Snoot, Venables); her dialogue is embedded with literary allusions and double entendres in English, French, and Latin; and her plots are spun from biblical texts and English poetry. Reading a Sayers novel, then, is both a formidable challenge and an endless reward. Hers are among the few detective novels that not only bear rereading, but actually demand it, and Sayers enjoys a readership spanning several generations. To know Sayers's novels is to know her time and place as well as this brilliant, eccentric, and ebullient artist could make them known. Because of her exquisite language, her skill at delineating character, and her fundamentally serious mind, Sayers's detective fiction also largely transcends the limits of its time and genre. Certainly this is true of novels such as *Strong Poison, The Nine Tailors, Gaudy Night,* and *Busman's Honeymoon,* books which did much toward making the detective novel part of serious English fiction.

Biography · Dorothy Leigh Sayers was born on June 13, 1893, in the Choir House of Christ Church College, Oxford, where her father, the Reverend Henry Sayers, was headmaster. Mr. Sayers's family came from County Tipperary, Ireland; his wife, the former Helen Mary Leigh, was a member of the old landed English family that also produced Percival Leigh, a noted contributor to the humor magazine *Punch.* Sayers's biographer, James Brabazon, postulates that her preference for the Leigh side of the family caused her to insist upon including her middle initial in her name; whatever the reason, the writer wished to be known as Dorothy L. Sayers.

When Sayers was four, her father left Oxford to accept the living of Bluntisham-cum-Earith in Huntingdonshire, on the southern edge of the Fens, those bleak expanses of drained marshland in eastern England. The contrast between Oxford and the rectory at Bluntisham was great, especially as the new home isolated the family and its only child. Sayers's fine education in Latin, English, French, history, and mathematics was conducted at the rectory until she was almost sixteen, when she was sent to study at the Godolphin School, Salisbury, where she seems to have been quite

Library of Congress

unhappy. Several of her happiest years followed this experience, however, when she won the Gilchrist Scholarship in Modern Languages and went up to Somerville College, Oxford, in 1912. At Somerville, Sayers enjoyed the congenial company of other extraordinary women and men and made some lasting friends, including Muriel St. Clare Byrne. Although women were not granted Oxford degrees during Sayers's time at Somerville, the university's statutes were changed in 1920, and Sayers was among the first group of women to receive Oxford degrees in that year (she had taken first honors in her examination in 1915).

Following her undergraduate days, Sayers did various kinds of work for several years: first, as poetry editor for Blackwell's in Oxford from 1916 to 1918, then as a schoolmistress in France in 1919, and finally in London, where she worked as a freelance editor and as an advertising copywriter for Benson's, England's largest advertising agency. At Benson's, Sayers helped create "The Mustard Club," a phenomenally successful campaign for Colman's mustard. Around 1920, when Sayers's mind was focused not only upon finding suitable employment but also upon surviving economically, the character of Lord Peter Wimsey was miraculously born, and Sayers's first novel, *Whose Body?*, introduced him to the world in 1923.

These early years in London were scarred by two bitterly disappointing love affairs, one of which left Sayers with a child, born in 1924. The novelist married Oswald Atherton Fleming, a Scottish journalist, in 1926, and shortly thereafter assumed financial responsibility for him as he became ill and ceased working several years after their marriage. Perhaps these pressures encouraged Sayers to keep turning out the increasingly successful Wimsey novels.

By the end of the 1930's, however, Sayers was in a position to "finish Lord Peter off" by marrying him to Harriet Vane, the detective novelist who first appeared in *Strong Poison* and who, like Wimsey, reflected part of Sayers's personality. After the Wimsey novels, Sayers was free to do the kind of writing she had always wanted to do: manifestly serious work such as religious dramas and a translation of Dante that would occupy most of her time from 1944 to 1957. While working on these demanding projects and writing incisive essays on a wide range of issues, Sayers also became something of a public figure, playing the role of social critic and Christian apologist with great brilliance and panache.

On December 17, 1957, Sayers died of an apparent stroke while alone in the house that she had shared with Fleming from 1928 until his death in 1950. Although she left an unpublished autobiographical fragment, "My Edwardian Childhood," much of

Sayers's life is reflected in her novels, which depict the Oxford of her college days (*Gaudy Night*), the Fen wastes of her girlhood (*The Nine Tailors*), and the excitement and confusion of the London she knew as a young writer (*Murder Must Advertise*). Excellent though much of her other work is, Sayers will probably be remembered primarily for her novels.

Analysis · If one should wish to know England as it was between the two world wars—how it was in its customs, among its different classes, and in its different regions, how it regarded itself and the world, what weaknesses festered, what strengths endured—there is no better place to learn its soul or to revel in its singular delights and peccadilloes than in the novels of Dorothy L. Sayers. When Harriet Vane marries Peter Wimsey in *Busman's Honeymoon*, she happily realizes that she has "married England," revealing that Sayers herself recognized the symbolic import of her hero. As a survivor of World War I, a war that decimated a generation of young Englishmen and left their society reeling, Wimsey represents England's fragile link with a glorious past and its tenuous hold on the difficult present. His bouts of "nerves" and persistent nightmares dramatize the lasting effects of this "War to End All Wars," while his noble attempts at making a meaningful life represent the difficult task of re-creating life from the rubble.

Sayers's England encompasses tiny villages unchanged for centuries (*Busman's Honeymoon*), the golden-spired colleges of Oxford (*Gaudy Night*), the "gloom and gleam" of London (*Murder Must Advertise*), the deceptive calm of the southern seacoast (*Have His Carcase*), the brooding Fens (*The Nine Tailors*), and the primitive north counties (*Clouds of Witness*). The novelist ranges throughout this varied landscape with some constants: Accompanied by his indefatigable "man," Bunter (who is Jeeves transformed), Lord Peter reasons his way through all but one mystery (he is absent from *The Documents in the Case*). Through Wimsey's well-wrought consciousness, Sayers maintains a certain *Weltanschauung* that seems a peculiar blend of mathematical rigor and lush, witty, insightful language.

Carolyn Heilbrun's praise for Sayers's special blend of "murder and manners" points out to an understanding of both the novelist's appeal and her place in English fiction: Sayers is an inheritor not only of the more literary branch of detective fiction, but also of the older comedy-of-manners tradition. She can reveal a character, time, or place in a bit of dialogue or one remark. From a brief sentence, for example, the reader knows the Duchess of Denver: "She was a long-necked, long-backed woman, who disciplined herself and her children." A short speech summarizes all *The Unpleasantness at the Bellona Club*, revealing not only a character but also the values and condition of his world:

> Look at all the disturbance there has been lately. Police and reporters—and then Penberthy blowing his brains out in the library. And the coal's all slate. . . . These things never happened before the War—and great heavens! William! Look at this wine! . . . Corked? Yes, I should think it *was* corked! My God! I don't know what's come to this club!

The character upon whom Sayers lavishes most of her considerable talent is Lord Peter. Although it is possible, as some of her critics have said, that Sayers created Wimsey, the perfect mate for an intellectual woman, because actual men had disappointed her, the psychobiographical approach can explain only part of her novels' motivation or meaning. In Wimsey, Sayers dramatizes some significant human problems, including the predicament of the "Lost Generation," the necessity of every person's having a "proper job," and the imperative synthesis of forces that are often perceived as opposites, but which are really complementary: intellect and emotion, good and evil, male and female. When viewed in these terms, Sayers's fictional world fits naturally into the entire cosmos of her creation, because it deals with some of the very subjects she addressed in other, more patently serious forms.

It is appropriate to speak of all Sayers's work as one, for, as she concludes in *The Mind of the Maker*, "the sum of all the work is related to the mind [of the artist] itself, which made it, controls it, and relates it to its own creative personality." From beginning to end, Sayers's work investigates the possibility of creative action; for her the creative act consists of establishing equilibrium among competing powers, of drawing together disparate, even warring elements. Of course, since she wrote detective novels, Sayers focused upon the opposite of creative action in the crimes of her villains, crimes that destroy life, property, sanity, peace. Wimsey, who solves the mysteries and thereby makes a life from destruction, is the creative actor.

The Mind of the Maker argues that there is a discoverable moral law, higher than any other, that governs the universe. In a way, Sayers's novels attempt to discover or reveal this universal moral law, which in its most superficial form is reflected in civil codes. This process of moral discovery, however, becomes increasingly complex and ambiguous; if Sayers's subjects are constant, her understanding of them deepens as her art matures. Since Sayers's artistic maturation parallels her hero's development, a comparison of how Wimsey functions in the early and late novels will elucidate both the consistency and the change that mark Sayers's fiction.

Whose Body? · The most striking quality of *Whose Body?* as a first novel is the deftness with which it presents Sayers's hero and his world. In its opening pages, the reader gets to know Lord Peter Wimsey, the dashing man-about-town and collector of rare books (which, amazingly, he seems to read). Keen of mind and quick of tongue, like an exotic bird chirping in a formal English garden that, perhaps, conceals a jolly corpse or two, he is a remarkable personage at birth. Wimsey is also quite marvelously a wealthy man who knows how to spend both his time and his money; his elegant apartment's only acknowledged lack is a harpsichord for his accomplished renditions of Domenico Scarlatti. The product of an older England marked by civility, restraint, and order, Wimsey is accompanied in his first tale by two challengers to his wits and position: his valet, Bunter, and the middle-class Inspector Parker of Scotland Yard, who will make sure that Wimsey never nods during fourteen years of fictional sleuthing. Even his mother, the delightfully balmy duchess of Denver, is introduced here, and the reader quickly guesses from their relationship that Sayers is interested in how men and women coexist in this world. The Dowager Duchess and her son are as different in appearance as they are similar in character, the narrator remarks, thus signaling that the superficial differences between men and women often conceal more important similarities. Wimsey and his entourage enter the world nearly complete, and their creator has a firm grasp of character, dialogue, and the mystery plot from the beginning of her career.

The theme of *Whose Body?* plants the seeds of one of Sayers's ever-flourishing ideas. Her first and perhaps most horrid villain, Sir Julian Freke, suffers from one of the great problems facing modern people: the disassociation from mind and heart that often renders "civilized" people incapable of moral behavior. The great surgeon Freke, who is aptly named because he is a freakish half-human, denies the importance of intangibles such as the conscience, which he considers akin to the vermiform appendix. With this perfectly criminal attitude, Freke coolly kills and dissects an old competitor, ironically from one of the oldest, least rational of motives, jealousy and revenge. Freke therefore demonstrates Sayers's point: that people, as creatures of both intellect and passion, must struggle to understand and balance both if moral action is to be possible. Freke, the dissector of life, destroys; the destruction he causes awaits the truly healing powers of a creative mind.

The somewhat surprising link between moral action and detective work is suggested by Wimsey, who observes that anyone can get away with murder by keeping people from "associatin' their ideas," adding that people usually do not connect the parts of their experience. The good detective, however, must study the fragments of human life and synthesize the relevant data. This synthesis, the product of imagination and feeling as well as reason, reveals not only "who did it," but how, and why. Thus, according to Sayers's own definitions, her detective pursues moral action in his very sleuthing, not only in its final effects of punishment for the criminal and retribution for society. Wimsey's detective method typifies this creative synthesis by incorporating different aspects of a rich experience: poetry, science, history, psychology, haberdashery, weather reports. When Wimsey finally realizes that Freke is the murderer, he remembers "not one thing, nor another thing, nor a logical succession of things, but everything, the whole thing, perfect and complete . . . as if he stood outside the world and saw it suspended in infinitely dimensional space." In this moment, Wimsey is not merely a successful detective, he is a creator, his mind flashing with godlike insight into human life. The story has moved, therefore, from destruction to creation because disparate aspects of life have been drawn together.

Freke's failure as a human being is exemplified in his failure as a physician, just as Wimsey's successful life is instanced in the skillful performance of his "job," his compulsive "hobby of sleuthing." More than a hobby, detection is actually Wimsey's "proper job." In a crucial discussion with Inspector Parker, Wimsey admits to feeling guilty about doing detective work for fun, but the perceptive Parker warns him that, as a basically responsible person for whom life is really more than a game, he will eventually have to come to terms with the seriousness of his actions. What is clear to the reader at this point is that Wimsey, an English aristocrat displaced by social change and scarred by World War I, is at least carving out a life that is socially useful while it is personally gratifying. He is not simply feeding the Duke of Denver's peacocks.

The Nine Tailors · If Wimsey seems almost too perfect in the early novels, Sayers redeems him from that state by slowly revealing the finite, flawed, and very human man within the sparkling exterior. To make this revelation, she has to create a woman capable of challenging him, which she does in the character of Harriet Vane. By the time he appears in *The Nine Tailors*, Wimsey is less of a god and more of a human being. After all, the great lover has been humiliatingly unsuccessful in wooing Harriet Vane, whom he saved from the hangman four years earlier in *Strong Poison*. The beginning of *The Nine Tailors* finds Wimsey, the super-sleuth, wandering about the Fens, that bleak terrain of Sayers's childhood, muttering about the misery of having one's car break down on a wintery evening and dreaming of hot muffins. When offered shelter at the rectory of Fenchurch St. Paul, the great connoisseur of haute cuisine is delighted with tea and oxtail stew. The greatest change in Wimsey's character and in Sayers's fiction, however, is evidenced in the novel's richer, more subtle structure, and in its newly complex view of crime and punishment, of good and evil.

Indicative of Sayers's increasing subtlety, *The Nine Tailors* is as much a metaphysical meditation on time and change as it is a murder mystery; there is not even a corpse until Part 2. In place of Lord Peter's jolly but rather macabre singing of "We insist upon a [dead] body in a bath" (in *Whose Body?*), *The Nine Tailors* resonates with the sound of church bells and an explication of campanology (bell or change-ringing). The bells at Fenchurch St. Paul, which are rung for both weddings and funerals, seem ambiguously to stand for both life and death, good and evil. The whole question of good versus evil is quite complicated here, for unlike the wholly innocent victim of the cold-blooded murder in *Whose Body?*, the man killed here is probably the worst person in the book, and he is accidentally killed by the ringing of holy bells. Locked in the church's bell chamber as a precaution by someone who knows of his criminal past, Geoffrey Deacon is killed by the intense sound of the bells, and ultimately by the hands of every man who unwittingly pulls a bell rope that New Year's Eve. This group includes Wimsey, who just happens to be there because of several coincidences.

Although Deacon perhaps deserves to die, not only for his jewel robbery but also because of a generally dishonorable life, his death forces Wimsey to reexamine himself and his motives. In ringing the changes, Wimsey thought he was simply following a set of mathematical permutations to a neat conclusion; in reality, he was taking a man's life. This greatly sobers the old puzzle-solver, who has always had some qualms about attacking life as a game. Indeed, Wimsey's role in Deacon's death is but an exaggerated version of the detective's role in any mystery: He causes the villain or criminal to come to justice, which usually means death. Wimsey cannot ignore the consequences of his actions in *The Nine Tailors*, because they are direct, obvious, and significant in human terms. He voices his concern about the morality of all his "meddling" to the rector, who assures him that everyone must "follow the truth," on the assumption that this path will lead invariably if somewhat indirectly to God, who has "all the facts" in the great case of life. Thus, it is impossible to be too curious, to probe too far, to ask too many questions, even though some answers or consequences may be painful.

In this great novel, Wimsey actually experiences the central Christian paradox, that of good coming from evil or of the two being inextricably linked. The mystery is over when he realizes, in a grisly pun, that Deacon's killers are already hanged, since they are the very bells in the church's tower. As one of the inscriptions on this ancient church says, the nine tailors, or the nine peals, "make a man," suggesting that the bells not only signify a man when they toll his passing, but also stand as timeless, disinterested judges of human behavior. The dead man, Deacon, mocked honorable work in his thievery, and thus began the cycle of destruction that ends in his own death, a death which ironically leads to Wimsey's discovery or creative act. From evil thus confronted and comprehended, good may grow. Mr. Venables, the rector, wittily pricks Wimsey with the irony that "there's always something that lies behind a mystery . . . a solution of some kind." For Wimsey, as for Sayers, even the solution to a mystery leads to further mysteries; the answer to the mystery of Deacon's death leads to a more subtle inquiry into one of the essential mysteries of life: how to determine responsibility or meaning for human action. In this paradoxical world, victims may be villains and right action is often based in error, chance, or even transgression.

Gaudy Night · Wimsey leaves this complex novel with greater insight into himself and the ambiguous nature of life; he is, therefore, finally ready to come to terms with the greatest mystery of his life, Harriet Vane, who is also about ready to accept his inquiry. In *Gaudy Night,* Wimsey reaches his fulfillment, a fulfillment that is expressed in terms of resolving the conflict between man and woman, between intellect and emotion, and between good and evil. In fact, Wimsey's fulfillment represents the culmination of Sayers's search for a resolution of these forces. The novel's subject is also one of Sayers's oldest: the moral imperative for every person to do good work that is well done, and the terrible consequences of not doing so. All these ideas come into play in this subtle novel, which is on one level the mystery of the "Shrewsbury Poison Pen" and on another, more important one, an unusual and profound love story. Reflecting the subtlety and delicacy with which Sayers spins her tale, there is not even a death in this book; the psychological violence caused by the Poison Pen is alarming, but here evil is banal, and all the more powerful for being so.

Gaudy Night takes place at Oxford, which held happy memories for Sayers as the place of her birth and formal education, and the entire novel is a paean to that golden-spired city. Harriet Vane goes to Oxford to attend the Shrewsbury Gaudy, an annual spring homecoming celebration, where she has the opportunity to judge her old classmates and teachers in terms of how well they, as women, have been able to live meaningful lives. Shrewsbury is obviously a fictional version of Somerville, Sayers's college, and just as clearly Vane, a famous detective novelist who is wrestling with the question of "woman's work" and with the problem of rendering reality in fiction, is to some extent Sayers, the self-conscious artist. Having been pursued by Wimsey for five frustrating years, Vane finally accepts him at the end of *Gaudy Night.* She accepts him because the experiences in this book teach her three interrelated things: that Wimsey, as an extraordinary man, will not prevent her from doing her "proper job," a consequence she feared from any relationship with a man; that men and women can live together and not destroy each other, but create a good life; and therefore, that there can be an alliance between the "intellect and the flesh." Vane's discoveries in this novel thus signal the solution of problems that had preoccupied Sayers throughout her career.

Vane learns all these things through Wimsey's unraveling of the mystery of the Poison Pen, who is a woman frightfully flawed because she has never been able to strike a balance between the intellect and the flesh, and therefore has never done her proper job. Annie Wilson, the Poison Pen who creates so much confusion and instills so much fear in the intellectual women of Shrewsbury, is the victim of sentimentality and a radically disassociated sensibility; she hates all learning because her dead husband was punished long ago for academic dishonesty. Ironically, Harriet Vane suffers from the same problem, but in its other manifestation; she begins the novel capable of trusting only the intellect, and fears any bonds of the flesh or heart. When she finally sees that neither the sentimentality of Annie nor the hyperintellectualism of Shrewsbury can solve the "problem of life," Harriet realizes that it is only through balancing intellect and passion that creative or truly human action is possible.

Wimsey, who solves the mystery because he is able to bring these forces into equilibrium and to acknowledge the potency of both, is rendered acceptable to Vane because of this ability. Her new willingness to admit her feelings reveals to her what Sayers's readers had known for a long time: She loves Wimsey. The man she loves has changed, too. He is no longer an unattainable paragon who sees good and evil as discrete and life as a game, but a middle-aged man who fears rejection and death, who is idiotically vain about his hands, and who, to Harriet's surprise, looks as vulnerable as anyone else when he falls asleep: the man behind the monocle. All of this does not argue that Wimsey is less extraordinary than he was; in fact, perhaps what is most extraordinary about him now is that he seems a real person—flawed, finite, vulnerable—who is yet capable of that rare thing, creative action. Indeed, his very life seems a work of art.

Busman's Honeymoon · Wimsey and Vane finally embark upon marriage, that most mundane and mysterious of journeys, in *Busman's Honeymoon*, the final novel that Sayers aptly called a "love story with detective interruptions": The detective novelist had moved that far from the formula. In the closing scene of this last novel, Wimsey admits that his new wife is "his corner," the place where he can hide from a hostile, confusing world and shed tears for the murderer whose execution he caused. This is not the Wimsey who blithely dashed about in the early novels, treating criminals as fair game in an intellectual hunting expedition, but it is the man he could have become after fourteen years of living, suffering, and reflecting. Indeed, it was a masterful stroke for Sayers to create Harriet Vane, a woman who could match Wimsey's wits and passions, because through her and through his loving her, the reader can learn the most intimate facts of this once-distant hero. If a man is to cry in front of anyone, that witness should most likely be his wife, especially if she is an extraordinary person who understands his tears. The early Wimsey may have been the kind of man that an intellectual woman would imagine for a mate, but the mature Wimsey is one with whom she could actually live. The fragment of a later novel called *Thrones, Dominations* indicates that the Wimsey-Vane marriage was just this workable.

Finally, the marriage of Wimsey and Vane symbolizes the paradoxical and joyful truth of good coming out of evil, for if Harriet had not been falsely accused of murder, they would never have met. She quiets Wimsey in one of his familiar periods of painful self-scrutiny about his "meddling" by reminding him that, if he had never meddled, she would probably be dead. The point seems clear: that human action has consequences, many of which are unforeseen and some painful, but all necessary for life. It is not difficult to imagine a novelist with this vision moving on shortly to the drama of Christ's crucifixion and resurrection, nor even the next step, her study and translation of that great narrative of good and evil, desire and fulfillment, mortality and eternity, Dante's *The Divine Comedy* (c. 1320). Indeed, all of Sayers's work is of a piece, creating that massive unity in diversity by which she defined true art.

Catherine Kenney

Other major works

SHORT FICTION: *Hangman's Holiday*, 1933; *In the Teeth of the Evidence and Other Stories*, 1939; *Lord Peter*, 1972 (James Sandoe, editor); *Striding Folly*, 1972.

PLAYS: *Busman's Honeymoon*, pr. 1937 (with Muriel St. Clare Byrne); *The Zeal of Thy House*, pr., pb. 1937; *The Devil to Pay, Being the Famous Play of John Faustus*, pr., pb. 1939; *Love All*, pr. 1940; *The Just Vengeance*, pr., pb. 1946; *The Emperor Constantine*, pr. 1951 (revised as *Christ's Emperor*, 1952).

RADIO PLAY: *The Man Born to Be King: A Play-Cycle on the Life of Our Lord and Saviour Jesus Christ*, pr. 1941-1942.

POETRY: *Op 1*, 1916; *Catholic Tales and Christian Songs*, 1918; *Lord, I Thank Thee—*, 1943; *The Story of Adam and Christ*, 1955.

NONFICTION: *The Greatest Drama Ever Staged*, 1938; *Strong Meat*, 1939; *Begin Here: A War-Time Essay*, 1940; *Creed or Chaos?*, 1940; *The Mysterious English*, 1941; *The Mind of the Maker*, 1941; *Why Work?*, 1942; *The Other Six Deadly Sins*, 1943; *Unpopular Opinions*, 1946; *Making Sense of the Universe*, 1946; *Creed or Chaos? and Other Essays in Popular Theology*, 1947; *The Lost Tools of Learning*, 1948; *The Days of Christ's Coming*, 1953, rev. 1960; *The Story of Easter*, 1955; *The Story of Noah's Ark*, 1955; *Introductory Papers on Dante*, 1957; *Further Papers on Dante*, 1957; *The Poetry of Search and the Poetry of Statement, and Other Posthumous Essays on Literature, Religion, and Language*, 1963; *Christian Letters to a Post-Christian World*, 1969; *Are Women Human?*, 1971; *A Matter of Eternity*, 1973; *Wilkie Collins: A Critical and Biographical Study*, 1977 (E. R. Gregory, editor).

CHILDREN'S LITERATURE: *Even the Parrot: Exemplary Conversations for Enlightened Children*, 1944.

TRANSLATIONS: *Tristan in Brittany*, 1929 (Thomas the Troubadour); *The Heart of Stone, Being the Four Canzoni of the "Pietra" Group*, 1946 (Dante); *The Comedy of Dante Alighieri the Florentine*, 1949-1962 (Cantica III with Barbara Reynolds); *The Song of Roland*, 1957.

EDITED TEXTS: *Oxford Poetry 1917*, 1918 (with Wilfred R. Childe and Thomas W. Earp); *Oxford Poetry 1918*, 1918 (with Earp and E. F. A. Geach); *Oxford Poetry 1919*, 1919 (with Earp and Siegfried Sassoon); *Great Short Stories of Detection, Mystery, and Horror*, 1928-1934 (also known as *The Omnibus of Crime*); *Tales of Detection*, 1936.

Bibliography

Brabazon, James. *Dorothy L. Sayers: A Biography*. New York: Charles Scribner's Sons, 1981. The "authorized" biography based upon Sayers's private papers, containing an introduction by her only son, Anthony Fleming. Brabazon shows that Sayers's real desire was to be remembered as an author of poetry and religious dramas and as a translator of Dante.

Coomes, David. *Dorothy L. Sayers: A Careless Rage for Life*. New York: Lion Publishing, 1992. Coomes concentrates on reconciling the author of religious tracts with the detective novelist, thereby providing a portrayal of a more "complex Sayers." He draws heavily on her papers at Wheaton College. Brief notes, no bibliography.

Dale, Alzina, ed. *Dorothy L. Sayers: The Centenary Celebration*. New York: Walker, 1993. Memoirs and essays situating Sayers in the history of detective fiction. Includes a brief biography and annotated bibliography.

Gaillard, Dawson. *Dorothy L. Sayers*. New York: Frederick Ungar, 1981. In a brief 123 pages, Dawson tries to establish a link between Sayers's detective fiction and her other literary works. One chapter is devoted to her short stories, four to her mystery novels, and a sixth to a summary of Sayers's literary virtues.

Hall, Trevor H. *Dorothy L. Sayers: Nine Literary Studies*. Hamden, Conn.: Archon Books, 1980. In nine critical essays, Hall discusses the connection between Sayers's creation, Lord Peter Wimsey, and Arthur Conan Doyle's creation, Sherlock Holmes. Hall also speculates in some detail on the influence of Sayers's husband, Atherton Fleming, on her writing.

Scott-Giles, Charles Wilfrid. *The Wimsey Family: A Fragmentary History from Correspondence with Dorothy Sayers*. New York: Harper & Row, 1977. Scott-Giles, an expert on heraldry, creates a family history and biography for Sayers's most memorable creation, Lord Peter Wimsey. Illustrations include the Wimsey family coat of arms, designed by Sayers.

Youngberg, Ruth Tanis. *Dorothy L. Sayers: A Reference Guide*. Boston: G. K. Hall, 1982.

An extensive guide to 942 English-language reviews, articles, books, introductions, and addresses published between 1917 and 1981. The annotations are designed to provide information, rather than criticism, to allow the reader to evaluate the particular item's usefulness.

Sir Walter Scott

Born: Edinburgh, Scotland; August 15, 1771
Died: Abbotsford, Scotland; September 21, 1832

Principal long fiction · *Waverley: Or, 'Tis Sixty Years Since*, 1814; *Guy Mannering*, 1815; *The Antiquary*, 1816; *The Black Dwarf*, 1816; *Old Mortality*, 1816; *Rob Roy*, 1817; *The Heart of Midlothian*, 1818; *The Bride of Lammermoor*, 1819; *A Legend of Montrose*, 1819; *Ivanhoe*, 1819; *The Monastery*, 1820; *The Abbot*, 1820; *Kenilworth*, 1821; *The Pirate*, 1821; *The Fortunes of Nigel*, 1822; *Peveril of the Peak*, 1823; *Quentin Durward*, 1823; *St. Ronan's Well*, 1823; *Redgauntlet*, 1824; *The Betrothed*, 1825; *The Talisman*, 1825; *Woodstock*, 1826; *The Fair Maid of Perth*, 1828; *Anne of Geierstein*, 1829; *Count Robert of Paris*, 1831; *Castle Dangerous*, 1831; *The Siege of Malta*, 1976.

Other literary forms · Sir Walter Scott's first published work was a translation of two ballads by Gottfried August Bürger, which appeared anonymously in 1796. In 1799, he published a translation of Johann Wolfgang von Goethe's 1773 drama *Götz von Berlichingen with the Iron Hand*. In 1802, the first two volumes of *Minstrelsy of the Scottish Border* appeared, followed by the third volume in 1803. This was a collection of popular ballads, annotated and often emended and "improved" with a freedom no modern editor woud allow himself. A fascination with his country's past, formed in his early years and lasting all his life, led him to preserve these ballads, the products of a folk culture that was disappearing. In 1805 came *The Lay of the Last Minstrel*, the first of the series of long narrative poems that made Scott the most widely read poet of the day. It was followed by *Marmion: A Tale of Flodden Field* (1808). *The Lady of the Lake* (1810) brought him to the height of his popularity as a poet. The later poems were less successful and he was gradually eclipsed by Lord Byron. In 1813, he completed the manuscript of a novel he had laid aside in 1805. This was *Waverley*, which appeared anonymously in 1814. (Scott did not publicly admit authorship of his novels until 1827.) It created a sensation and launched him on the series that remained his chief occupation until the end of his life. Other important works were his editions of Dryden (1808) and of Swift (1814), a series of lives of the English novelists completed in 1824, and *The Life of Napoleon Buonaparte*, begun in 1825 and published in nine volumes in 1827. *Chronicles of the Canongate* (1827) is composed of three short stories: "The Highland Widow," "The Two Drovers," and "The Surgeon's Daughter."

Achievements · The central achievement of Scott's busy career is the series of novels that is conventionally designated by the title of the first of them. The sheer bulk of the Waverley novels is in itself impressive, as is the range of the settings they present. For example, *Ivanhoe* is set in twelfth century England, *The Talisman* in the Holy Land of the Third Crusade, *Quentin Durward* in fifteenth century France, *The Abbot* in the Scotland of Queen Mary, *Kenilworth* in the reign of Elizabeth, and *The Fortunes of Nigel* in that of James I. In spite of his wide reading, tenacious memory, and active imagination, Scott was not able to deal convincingly with so many different periods. Moreover, he worked rapidly and sometimes carelessly, under the pressures of financial necessity and, in later years, failing health. Some of the novels are tedious and wooden, mechanical in their plots and stilted in their dialogue. Scott himself was aware of their flaws and he sometimes spoke and wrote slightingly of them.

Yet most readers find that even the weaker novels have good things in them, and the best of them have a narrative sweep and a dramatic vividness that render their flaws unimportant. The best of them, by common consent, are those set in Scotland as far back as the latter part of the reign of Charles II. When he attempted to go further back, he was less successful, but in such novels as the four discussed below—*Waverley, Old Mortality, Rob Roy,* and *The Heart of Midlothian*—Scott's sense of history is strong. They are among the most impressive treatments of his great theme, the conflict between the old and the new, between Jacobite and Hanoverian, between the heroic, traditional, feudal values of the Tory Highlands and the progressive commercial interests of the Whig Lowlands, between stability and change. Though some of the other novels offer historical conflict of a comparable kind (*Ivanhoe* and *Quentin Durward,* for example), the Scottish novels present the conflict with particular insight and force and convey a strong sense of the good on both sides of it. Scott values the dying heroic tradition even as he recognizes the benefits that change brings. Earlier writers had mined the past to satisfy a market for the exotic, the strange, or the merely quaint. Scott saw the past in significant relation to the present and created characters clearly shaped by the social, economic, religious, and political forces of their time, thus providing his readers with the first fictions that can properly be called historical novels.

Biography · An important factor in the vividness of the Scottish novels was the strong oral tradition to which Sir Walter Scott had access from his early childhood. After a bout with polio in his second year, he was sent away from Edinburgh to his paternal

grandfather's house at Sandyknowe in the Border country, in the hope that the climate would improve his health. It did, and though he remained lame for the rest of his life, his boyhood was an active one. In this region from which his ancestors had sprung, he heard stories of Border raids, Jacobite risings, and religious struggles from people for whom the past survived in a living tradition. Throughout his life he added to his fund of anecdotes, and his notes to the novels show how very often incidents in them are founded on actual events which he had learned about from the participants themselves or from their more immediate descendants.

Scott's father was a lawyer, and in 1786, having attended Edinburgh High School and Edinburgh

Library of Congress University, Scott became an apprentice in his father's office. In 1792, he was admitted to the bar, and all his life he combined legal and literary activities. After losing his first love, Williamina Belsches, to a banker, he married Charlotte Carpenter in 1798. In 1805, he entered into a secret partnership with the printer James Ballantyne, and four years later they formed a publishing firm. This firm ran into financial difficulties, and in 1813, Scott escaped ruin only through the intervention of another publisher, Archibald Constable. Scott continued to overextend himself. In 1811, he had bought a farm on the Tweed at a place he named Abbotsford, and in the years that followed he wrote furiously to provide funds for building a splendid house and buying additional land. His ambition was to live the life of a laird. In 1826, the financial collapse of Constable and Ballantyne ruined Scott. In his last years, he worked tirelessly to pay his creditors. The effort told on his health, and he died in 1832, at the age of sixty-one. The debts were finally cleared after his death by the sale of his copyrights.

Analysis · *Waverley* displays, at the start of Sir Walter Scott's career as a novelist, many of the features that were to prove typical of his best work. In the Jacobite rebellion of 1745, he saw an instance of the conflict between the older feudal and chivalric order, strongly colored with heroic and "romantic" elements, and the newer order of more practical and realistic concerns which had already begun to supplant it. His focus is not on the great public figures whose fates are at stake, and this too is typical. The Pretender, Prince Charles Edward, is not introduced until the novel is more than half over, and most of the major events of this phase of his career are only alluded to, not presented directly. He is shown almost exclusively in his dealings with the fictional character for whom the novel is named, and largely through his eyes.

Waverley · Edward Waverley, like so many of Scott's heroes, is a predominantly passive character who finds himself caught between opposing forces and "wavering" between his loyalty to the House of Hanover and the attractions of the Stuart cause. Though his father occupies a post in the Whig ministry, he has been reared by his uncle Sir Everard, a Tory who had supported the earlier Jacobite rebellion of 1715, though not so actively as to incur reprisals when it was put down. His father's connections procure Edward a commission in King George's army, and he is posted to Scotland. Shortly after arriving, he makes an extended visit to his uncle's Jacobite friend, the Baron of Bradwardine, and his daughter Rose. When a Highland raider, Donald Bean Lean, steals several of the Baron's cows, Waverley goes into the Highlands in the company of a follower of Fergus MacIvor, a chieftain who has the influence to secure the return of the cows. Waverley is impressed by Fergus and infatuated with his sister Flora. They are both confirmed Jacobites preparing to declare for the Pretender upon his arrival in Scotland.

As a result of Waverley's protracted absence and of a mutiny among the small band of men from his family estate who had followed him into the army, Waverley is declared absent without leave and superseded in his office. By coincidence, his father also loses his government position. Waverley's resentment at this twofold insult to his family by the Hanoverian government is heightened when, on a journey to Edinburgh to clear himself, he is arrested. Rescued by Donald Bean Lean, he is later brought to Edinburgh (now in the hands of the Jacobites), meets the Pretender, and is won over to his cause. He takes part in the Jacobite victory at Preston but is separated from Fergus's troop in a skirmish at Clifton, in which Fergus is captured. After a period in hiding, Waverley is pardoned, through the good offices of Colonel Talbot, whom he had saved from death and taken prisoner at Preston. Fergus is executed for treason.

Objections to *Waverley* usually center on the character of the hero, whom Scott himself called "a sneaking piece of imbecility." Certainly it is possible to be impatient with his lack of self-awareness, and the frequency with which he is acted upon rather than acting puts him often in a less than heroic light. Waverley, however, is not intended to be a romantic hero, and his susceptibility to external influence is necessary to enable Scott to show within a single character the conflict between the two forces that compose the novel's theme. For most of the book, Scott's view of the hero is ironic, emphasizing his failings. There is, for example, his vanity. One of the things that reconciles his Jacobite Aunt Rachel to his serving in the Hanoverian army is the fact that he is becoming infatuated with a local girl. Scott mocks Waverley's feelings, first by giving their object the inelegant name of Cecilia Stubbs, and then by telling the reader that on Waverley's last Sunday at the parish church he is too preoccupied with his own dashing appearance in his new uniform to notice the care with which Miss Stubbs has arrayed herself. The complement of this detail occurs later in the novel when Waverley, having joined the Jacobites, puts on Highland dress for the first time, and one of Fergus's followers remarks that he is "majoring yonder afore the muckle pier-glass." More seriously, the memory of "the inferior figure which he had made among the officers of his regiment," resulting from his inability to keep his mind on detail and routine, contributes to his decision to change sides.

In addition to exposing his vanity, Scott often undercuts Waverley's Romantic view of experience. On finding himself for the first time in the Highlands, he muses over "the full romance of his situation." It occurs to him that "the only circumstance which assorted ill with the rest, was the cause of his journey—the Baron's milk cows! this degrading incident he kept in the background." If, instead of deploring Waverley's inadequacy as a romantic hero, one attends to the irony with which Scott undercuts his fascination with romance and heroism, one will be better prepared for the author's reluctant dismissal of heroic virtues at the end of the novel. Waverley's character is perfectly appropriate to one who will survive into the new age, an age in which the dashing but destructive energies of Fergus have no place.

The real problem with the character is not his passivity or his ordinariness, but Scott's occasional failure to dramatize certain features of his personality, as opposed to merely making assertions about them. On two occasions he is credited with remarkable conversational powers, but no sample of them is given. During Waverley's period in hiding, Scott declares, "he acquired a more complete mastery of a spirit tamed by adversity, than his former experience had given him," but there is no demonstration of this "mastery." These flaws, however, hardly justify dismissing the characterization as a failure. The eagerness of Waverley's response to the new scenes and experiences he encounters, the growth of his resentment against the established government and his conversion to Jacobitism, his delayed recognition of his love for Rose, the cooling of his regard for Fergus as he comes to see the chieftain's selfishness and then the reawakening of that regard when Fergus is in danger—all these phases of his development are convincingly presented. Moreover, there are a few scenes where he shows real firmness (for example, his confrontation with Fergus when he has been shot at by one of Fergus's men), and several where he displays active generosity.

This said, one may concede that Waverley remains a rather slender figure to carry the weight of a novel of this length. He does not have to, however, for Scott surrounds him with a number of vivid characters from a wide range of classes and backgrounds. It is chiefly through their speech that he makes his characters live. The dialogue is not consistently successful: The bright small talk between Fergus and Flora can be downright dreadful, and some of the language of the other upper-class characters is stiff. The speech of most of the secondary characters, however, is convincing, and the dialect writing is particularly effective. Scott's most important contribution here is the achievement of a wide variety of tones in dialect speech. Before Scott, dialect was almost exclusively a comic device, but he was able to write dialect in different keys all the way up to the tragic. The best evidence of this is the scene in which Fergus and his follower Evan Dhu Maccombich are condemned to death. When Evan Dhu offers his life and the lives of five others in exchange for his chieftain's freedom, volunteering to go and fetch the five others himself, laughter breaks out in the courtroom. In a speech that loses nothing in dignity by being couched in dialect, Evan Dhu rebukes the audience and then proudly rejects the judge's invitation to plead for grace, preferring to share his chieftain's fate.

Fergus is perhaps the most interesting of the major characters. He possesses throughout the capacity to surprise the reader. Scott prepares the reader carefully for his first appearance. Waverley first hears of him in chapter 15 as an extorter of blackmail or protection money and is surprised to learn that he is nevertheless considered a gentleman. When he is introduced several chapters later, the reader discovers that this feudal leader of a troop of half-savage Highlandmen is a polished and literate individual with a very good French education. He is clearly fond of his sister, and yet quite prepared to exploit her as bait to draw Waverley into the Jacobite ranks. In the early part of the novel, the emphasis is on his courage, his hospitality, and his ability to inspire loyalty, and he is for the most part an attractive figure.

Gradually, however, both Waverley and the reader come to view him more critically. It grows increasingly clear that his commitment to the Jacobite cause is founded on self-interest. On learning that Prince Charles Edward is encouraging Bradwardine to leave his estate to Rose instead of to a distant male relative, he attempts to make the Prince promote his marriage to Rose. When the Prince refuses, he is furious, later saying that he could at that moment have sold himself to the devil or King George, "whichever offered the dearest revenge" (chap. 53). Yet as the Jacobite fortunes ebb, his generosity returns, and for the first time he attempts to use his influence over Waverley for the latter's good, telling him there is no dishonor in his extricating himself from the now certain wreck of their cause and urging him to marry Rose: "She loves you, and I believe you love her, though, perhaps, you have not found it out, for you are not celebrated for knowing your own mind very pointedly." He refuses to allow Waverley to witness his execution, and, by a generous deception regarding the hour at which it is to take place, he spares his sister the pain of a final interview. As he strides out of his cell, it is he who is supporting Waverley.

Throughout the novel, the portrait of Fergus is sharpened by a number of contrasts, explicit and implicit, between him and other characters. The contrast with Waverley is obviously central. There is also a contrast between him and his sister. While Fergus's Jacobitism is tinged with self-interest and he sometimes resorts to duplicity to advance the cause, Flora's devotion to the Stuarts is absolutely pure. She cannot reconcile herself to her brother's dealing with a thief of Donald Bean Lean's stripe even in the interest of the cause, and she resists his wish that she encourage Waverley's infatuation with her in order to win him to their side. Fergus's preoccupation with the more practical aspects of the campaign is set against Bradwardine's comically pedantic concern with form and ceremony in the question of whether and how to exercise his hereditary privilege of drawing off the king's boots. Yet Bradwardine's old-fashioned loyalty lacks all taint of self-interest, and, though he has been largely a comic figure, he behaves after the failure of the rebellion with a gallant fortitude comparable to that of Fergus. In the latter part of the novel, a new character enters to serve as Fergus's complete antithesis. Colonel Talbot, who supplants him in guiding Waverley's fate, differs from Fergus on practically every count—political affiliation, disinterested generosity, attitude toward women, and even age.

Several other characters are paired in contrast. Flora's strength of character, heroic bent, intellectual accomplishments, and striking beauty are repeatedly contrasted with the less remarkable gifts of the placid and domestic Rose. Sir Everard Waverley and his brother Richard are opposite numbers in all respects. When Waverley is arrested on his way to Edinburgh, Melville and Morton, the magistrate and the clergyman who hear his defense, take differing views of his case. One of Fergus's henchmen, Callum Beg, commits a crime for his master when he attempts to shoot Waverley, while Humphry Houghton, one of Waverley's followers, involves himself in a conspiracy and mutiny. Both are carrying out what they mistakenly believe to be their masters' wishes, and they receive differing treatment for their actions.

This network of contrasts contributes much to the unity of a novel that is sometimes criticized as loosely structured. Scott's general preface to the 1829 edition of the whole series lends credence to this charge: "The tale of Waverley was put together with so little care, that I cannot boast of having sketched any distinct plan of the work. The whole adventures of Waverley, in his movements up and down the country with the Highland cateran Bean Lean, are managed without much skill." Whatever Scott meant by this, it cannot really be said that the book is loosely plotted. A glance at the retrospective explanations contained in chapters 31 and 65 will remind any reader of the great number of details that at first looked unimportant but that turn out to be essential to the mechanics of the plot. Such after-the-fact explanations may be technically awkward, and they may lay Scott open to the charge of unnecessary mystification in the episodes leading up to them, but they certainly evidence some careful planning.

It is rather for excessive reliance on coincidence that the plot can be criticized. The retrospective explanations just mentioned make some of these appear less unreasonable and incredible, but there are still a great many of them, and this is true of all Scott's novels. Also, the pace of the narrative is at times uncertain. Although the opening chapters describing Waverley's education are important to an understanding of the character, they make an undeniably slow beginning, and some of the set pieces retard the narrative flow.

In spite of its flaws, however, the novel is sustained by its central theme of the process of historical change and by Scott's ability to do justice to both sides in the conflict. Part of him responded strongly to the gallant romance of the Jacobite and to the love of tradition behind it. At the same time, he realized that the world had passed all that by. As Waverley himself points out, there have been four monarchs since James II was deposed, and the divine right absolutism for which the Stuarts stood would have sorted ill with the political and economic realities of the mid-eighteenth century. So Fergus is executed, his head is stuck up over the Scotch gate, and the Edinburgh youth whom Waverley has engaged as a valet comments, "It's a great pity of Evan Dhu, who was a very weel-meaning, good-natured man, to be a Hielandman; and indeed so was [Fergus MacIvor] too, for that matter, when he wasna in ane o' his tirrivies [tantrums]." In a snatch of dialogue, the heroic perspective is replaced by one more down-to-earth and commonplace. The threat to the prevailing order that the rebellion represented is already diminishing in importance in the popular view. To the common man secure in the established order, the energies that burned in Fergus amount to no more than "tirrivies."

Old Mortality · *Old Mortality* deals with an earlier rebellion, one in which the issue is religious. Charles II had won the support of the Scottish Presbyterians by subscribing to the Solemn League and Covenant, which provided for the establishment of Presbyterianism as the state religion in Scotland and in England and Ireland as well. After the Restoration, however, Charles sought to impose episcopacy on Scotland, and the Covenanters were persecuted for their resistance to the bishops. In 1679, the assassination of the Archbishop of St. Andrews by a small party of Covenanters led by John Balfour of Burley sparked a gathering of insurgents who managed at Drumclog to defeat the Cavalier forces, under John Graham of Claverhouse, that were sent against them. A few weeks later, however, the Covenanters, divided by moderate and extremist factions, were routed at Bothwell Bridge by an army commanded by the Duke of Monmouth. The novel's title is the nickname of an old man who travels through Scotland refurbishing the markers on the graves of the martyred Covenanters.

Out of these events, Scott built one of his starkest and swiftest plots. Once again he portrays a hero caught between conflicting forces. Just after the Archbishop's murder, Henry Morton gives shelter to Burley because Burley and his father had been comrades-in-arms and Burley had saved the elder Morton's life. Henry Morton's moderate principles lead him to condemn the murder, but he also deplores the oppression that provoked it, and Burley hopes that he will eventually take up arms with the Covenanters. Morton is, however, drawn to the Cavalier side by his love for Edith Bellenden (one of Scott's more pallid heroines) and by his friendship for her granduncle.

Morton receives some firsthand experience of the oppressive measures of the Cavaliers when he is arrested for harboring the fugitive Burley and is brought before Claverhouse. This figure is Burley's opposite number, rather as Talbot is Fergus MacIvor's in *Waverley*, except that Talbot is wholly admirable while Claverhouse is a more complex character. Like Burley, Claverhouse sees in Morton qualities of courage and leadership that could be valuable to the rebels. He is about to have him executed when one of his subordinates, Lord Evandale, intervenes. Evandale is a suitor of Edith, and at her request he generously asks Claverhouse to spare his rival's life. Morton is carried along as a prisoner with Claverhouse's troops, and when they are defeated by the Covenanters at Drumclog, he is set free. Under Burley's auspices, he is given a high post in the rebel army.

In this phase of the novel, Morton shows himself a much more active hero than Waverley. He quickly repays his debt to Evandale by saving his life in the rout of the loyalist forces, and he does so again in a later chapter, when Evandale has become Burley's prisoner. He plays a prominent part in the Covenanters' attempts to take Glasgow. He draws up a statement of the rebels' grievances and presents it to Monmouth just before the battle of Bothwell Bridge, and even though the Covenanters obstinately refuse the terms he secures, he does not defect, but instead fights heroically in the battle that ensues.

In spite of the vigor with which Morton fulfills his commitment to the Presbyterians, they distrust him, and Scott sharply dramatizes their ignorance, factiousness, bigotry, and cruelty. He also exposes the unscrupulous streak in Burley's enthusiasm.

This zealot is convinced that the most barbaric cruelties and the rankest deceptions are justified by his cause. He is surrounded by a gallery of fanatics, of whom the most horrifying is the insane preacher Habbakuk Mucklewrath. In flight after the defeat at Bothwell Bridge, Morton and his servant Cuddie stumble upon a group of Covenanting leaders in an isolated farmhouse at Drumshinnel. They have been praying for guidance, and the arrival of Morton, whom they irrationally regard as the cause of their defeat, convinces them that God has sent him to them as a sacrifice. They conduct a kind of trial, though the verdict of death is never in doubt. It is the Sabbath, however, and they are unwilling to execute him before midnight. Eventually, Mucklewrath jumps up to put the clock ahead, crying, "As the sun went back on the dial ten degrees for intimating the recovery of holy Hezekiah, so shall it now go forward, that the wicked may be taken away from among the people, and the Covenant established in its purity."

This display of the Covenanters' fanaticism is the complement of the earlier trial before Claverhouse, in which Morton was threatened with the arbitrary cruelty of the Cavalier side. Ironically, it is Claverhouse who now arrives to save Morton. (He has been led to the farmhouse by Cuddie, who had been allowed to escape.) Most of the Covenanters are slaughtered. Riding back to Edinburgh in the custody of his rescuers, Morton is divided between horror at Claverhouse's habitual cold indifference to bloodshed and admiration for his urbanity and his valor. Claverhouse admits that he is as much a fanatic as Burley but adds, "There is a difference, I trust, between the blood of learned and reverend prelates and scholars, of gallant soldiers and noble gentlemen, and the red puddle that stagnates in the veins of psalm-singing mechanics, crack-brained demagogues, and sullen boors." Scott counters this assessment in the very next chapter by showing the fortitude of one of the Covenanting leaders, Ephraim MacBriar, as he is brutally tortured and then condemned to death. The reader may also recall that it was prolonged imprisonment by the Cavaliers that drove Mucklewrath insane. As in *Waverley*, Scott sees both sides objectively.

Morton is sentenced to exile, and there is a gap of ten years in the narrative. In 1689, when the Glorious Revolution has put William and Mary on the throne, Morton is free to return to Scotland. Edith is on the point, finally, of accepting marriage to Evandale. Claverhouse, loyal to the Stuarts, is now ironically a rebel in his turn. He is killed in the battle of Killecrankie, but his army is victorious. He had once said to Morton, "When I think of death . . . as a thing worth thinking of, it is in the hope of pressing one day some well-fought and hard-won field of battle, and dying with the shout of victory in my ear—*that* would be worth dying for, and more, it would be worth having lived for!" The rather too crowded closing pages describe the deaths of Burley and Lord Evandale.

The novel displays Scott's dramatic gifts at their best. Though the language of Morton, Edith, and Evandale is sometimes stiff, the dialogue of the rest of the characters is vigorous and precisely adjusted to their various stations and backgrounds, and the language of the Covenanters, loaded with scriptural allusions, idioms, and rhythms, constitutes a particularly remarkable achievement. In addition to the characters already discussed, three others stand out. One is Sergeant Bothwell, who is descended from an illegitimate son of James VI and resents his failure to attain preferment. He is one of the novel's chief embodiments of the bullying oppression and extortion to which the Covenanters are subjected, but he is also capable of the courtesy and bravery that he regards as incumbent on one of his blood. Another is Mause Headrigg, whose compulsive declarations of her extreme Presbyterian principles are always ill-timed, to the chagrin of her pragmatic son Cuddie, who has no ambition to become a martyred Covenanter. The third is Jenny Dennison, Edith's maid. Like her mistress, Jenny has a suitor on each side of the conflict, and Scott thus creates a comic parallel to the Morton-Edith-Evandale triangle. She chooses Morton's servant Cuddie over her other suitor, a soldier in the Cavalier army, and this match foreshadows the eventual union of Edith and Morton. Jenny, however, has more vitality, resourcefulness, and charm than her mistress. She has been criticized for trying to promote Edith's marriage to the wealthy Evandale with a view to securing the future of herself, her husband, and their children. One can admit this fault and go on to point out that it is related to the success of the characterization. The most convincing characters in *Old Mortality* are those in whom Scott reveals a mixture of motivations or a blending of admirable with deplorable traits.

Rob Roy · *Rob Roy* is probably the least successful of the four novels considered here. It resembles *Waverley* in that it takes a young Englishman into the Highlands during a Jacobite rising, this time that of 1715. Like Edward Waverley, Frank Osbaldistone has a romantic and poetical turn and responds eagerly to the unfamiliar world of the Highlands. Like Waverley, he has a touch of vanity and of obstinacy in his temper. Like Waverley, he is slow to understand his feelings for the heroine. That he is not as slow as Waverley was to realize that he loved Rose may be attributed to two factors: There is only one possible object for Frank's affections, not two; and that object, Diana Vernon, bears a much closer similarity to Flora, who captivated Waverley immediately, than to Rose.

Frank Osbaldistone, however, is a less interesting hero than Waverley, largely because he does not experience any serious internal conflict. In spite of his love for Diana, a committed Jacobite, he never considers supporting the Pretender. His conflicts are all external. Having angered his father by refusing to follow him into trade, Frank is sent to stay with his uncle's family in Northumberland, to be replaced in the firm by one of his cousins. Though it is understandable that his father should turn to a nephew when his son has disappointed him, it is not clear what point he has in sending Frank to Osbaldistone Hall. Frank's uncle and five of his cousins are boors with no interests beyond hunting and drinking. The sixth son, Rashleigh, is clever, villainous, ugly, and lame. He is the one chosen to take Frank's place in the firm. He had been tutor to Diana, who is his cousin on his mother's side, but had attempted to seduce her, and she has since kept him at a distance. Nevertheless, their common Jacobite sympathies remain a bond between them. Rashleigh, resenting Diana's obvious liking for Frank and smarting under an insult from him, forms a plan that will ruin the Osbaldistone firm and at the same time hasten the rising of the clans in support of the Pretender. The financial details of this scheme are not clear, and it therefore lacks credibility. This flaw in the plot is fairly serious because in *Rob Roy* commercial activity has considerable thematic importance.

Once in London, Rashleigh wins his uncle's confidence and then absconds with certain crucial documents. Frank's task is to follow him to Glasgow and then into the Highlands to recover them. It is in fact not Frank but Diana Vernon's father (whose identity is a mystery to Frank and the reader until the end of the book) who gets the documents back, and this in spite of the fact that he is also a Jacobite and might thus be expected to further rather than thwart Rashleigh's plot. Punishment comes to Rashleigh not from Frank but from the Highland chieftain Rob Roy. Rashleigh turns traitor to the Jacobites, and, after the failure of the rebellion, he arranges the arrest of

Diana and her father. In the process of rescuing them, Rob Roy kills Rashleigh.

Thus, though Frank is a party to his fair share of adventures, he is too often merely a party rather than the chief actor, even though he is clearly meant to be the hero. Although Rob Roy appears at practically every crisis of the story, those appearances are intermittent, and the crises mark stages in the experience of Frank. Everything, down to the use of Frank as first-person narrator, points to him as the central character. (Everything, that is, except the title, but a writer with Scott's sense of what sells would hardly call a book *Osbaldistone*.) At too many crucial points, however, Rob Roy displaces Frank as the focus of the reader's interest. Though their relationship may appear to resemble that of Waverley and Fergus or of Morton and Burley, Morton and even Waverley are more active characters than Frank and thus are never eclipsed by Burley and Fergus to the extent that Frank is by Rob Roy. This seems to be largely a result of the bonds that unite Fergus with Waverley and Morton with Burley in a common enterprise for much of their respective stories. The cause shared by each pair of characters makes it possible for each pair to share the spotlight, so to speak, against a common background without compromising the novel's unity. Rob Roy and Frank, by contrast, do not act together in a public cause, since Frank is not a Jacobite. Furthermore, the distance between them is emphasized in the early part of the novel by the fact that, though he takes action several times in Frank's behalf, Rob Roy's identity is unknown to Frank until the novel is half over. In short, the plot keeps these characters separate as Waverley is not kept separate from Fergus nor Morton from Burley, and as a result the novel seems marred by a divided focus.

There is also a failure to unify the public and the private themes as convincingly as in the other two novels. The vagueness of the link between the ruin of the Osbaldistone firm and the rising of the clans has already been noted. A related problem is the absence of specificity about Diana Vernon's Jacobite activities. A wary reader will recognize Scott's irony in having Frank respond to an early warning about Diana with the words, "Pshaw, a Jacobite?–is that all?" There is, however, a lack of concrete detail about her role in the conspiracy. This is perhaps inevitable, given the first-person point of view and the fact that Diana keeps Frank out of the secret of the conspiracy, but it weakens the characterization of the heroine. In contrast, Flora MacIvor's political obsession is fully convincing. Diana is perhaps not meant to seem as much a fanatic as Flora, yet she too has sacrificed all personal inclination to the cause—or to her father's will. At the end of the novel, the reader learns that her father has been a central figure in the conspiracy and has often stayed at Osbaldistone Hall in the disguise of a priest, and that Rashleigh's hold over Diana resulted from his having penetrated her father's disguise. This is a fairly dramatic situation, but the reader is, so to speak, asked to do the dramatizing for himself in retrospect. The specifics about Diana's part in the conspiracy are too little too late.

Since Sir Frederick Vernon has no identity for the reader until the closing pages, he can never be more than a minor figure. Yet to him, Scott assigns the account of the actual rebellion. In the penultimate chapter, the rebellion and its collapse are perfunctorily described by Sir Frederick in less than two pages. This is a signal failure to unify the personal and historical dimensions. Instead of the climax that it should have been, the 1715 rising seems almost an afterthought.

There is, however, a good deal of effective characterization in the novel. Diana Vernon is probably the most attractive and interesting of Scott's heroines. She is well educated, strong-minded, outspoken, aggressive, and witty. She may not quite hold her own in the company to which critical opinion sometimes promotes her, the company of William Shakespeare's Beatrice and Jane Austen's Elizabeth Bennett, but the dialogue Scott gives her does indeed amply express intelligence and vitality. If there is one false note, it is Scott's finally allowing her to marry Frank, but one's reservations may be qualified by the consideration that Frank seems politically almost neutral. If he does not support the Stuarts, he is not in the debt of Hanover either. It is not quite as if Flora MacIvor had married Edward Waverley.

Diana first appears before Frank on horseback wearing "what was then somewhat unusual, a coat, vest, and hat, resembling those of a man, which fashion has since called a riding-habit." Scott several times underlines her firm and forthright behavior by comparing it to a man's. There is a much stronger masculine streak in the only other important female character in this book which has just four speaking roles for women. Rob Roy's wife Helen is a virago capable of ambushing a British troop with only a small band and of cold-bloodedly ordering the drowning of a hostage. She should have been a powerful figure, but the language she speaks is impossibly bookish and rhetorical, an objection which is not sufficiently answered by Scott's later remarking that her "wild, elevated, and poetical" style is caused by the fact that she is translating from Gaelic into English, "which she had acquired as we do learned tongues."

The characterization of Rob Roy himself is on the whole successful, despite a certain lack of impact in his first few appearances, during which a reader who has skipped Scott's unusually cumbersome prefatory material may not even realize that this is the titular character. He gains added weight by being the chief embodiment of one side of the novel's main thematic conflict. The focus of the novel is not on the Jacobite-Hanoverian struggle but on the related but distinguishable conflict between the half-barbaric feudal life of the Highland clans and the modern commercial world of trade. Rob Roy is an outlaw relying on blackmail to support himself and his followers, who acknowledge no leader but him. Their way of life breeds narrow loyalties (a point emphasized also by the judge in the trial of Fergus MacIvor). Helen MacGregor cannot "bide the sight o' a kindly Scot, if he come frae the Lowlands, far less of an Inglisher." The clansmen are a threat to peace and order because rebellion and disorder are conditions far more likely to improve their lot. As Rob Roy says of the expected uprising, "Let it come . . . and if the world is turned upside down, why, honest men have the better chance to cut bread out of it."

Rob Roy is contrasted with the Glasgow weaver and magistrate Bailie Nichol Jarvie. A business associate of the Osbaldistone firm, he accompanies Frank in his pursuit of Rashleigh. Scott makes Rob Roy and Jarvie kinsmen in order to point out the contrasts between them more sharply. These contrasts are most clearly drawn in two fine scenes, one in the Glasgow jail midway through the novel and the other near the end. In the latter scene, when Bailie Nichol Jarvie deplores the ignorance of Rob Roy's sons, the Highlander boasts, "Hamish can bring down a black-cock when he's on the wing wi' a single bullet, and Rob can drive a dirk through a twa-inch board." Jarvie retorts, "Sae muckle the waur for them baith! . . . An they ken naething better than that, they had better no ken that neither." Rob Roy scorns his kinsman's offer to take his sons as apprentices: "My sons weavers! . . . I wad see every loom in Glasgow, beam, traddles, and shuttles, burnt in hell-fire sooner!" Shortly afterward, however, he admits to Frank that he is troubled at the thought of his sons "living their father's life." That kind of life in fact remained possible for only about three more decades, for after the rising of 1745, the rule of law was extended into the Highlands and the power of the clans was permanently broken.

That defeat in effect completed the Union of England and Scotland that had been established in 1707. In chapter 27, when Andrew Fairservice, Frank's servant, speaks disparagingly of the Union, Jarvie sternly rebukes him:

> Whisht, sir—whisht! it's ill-scraped tongues like yours, that make mischief atween neighbourhoods and nations. . . . I say, Let Glasgow flourish! . . . judiciously and elegantly putten round the town's arms, by way of by-word—Now, since St. Mungo catched herrings in the Clyde, what was ever like to gar [make] us flourish like the sugar and tobacco trade? Will ony body tell me that, and grumble at the treaty that opened us a road westawa' yonder?

Jarvie expresses Scott's own sense of the benefits that the growing commercial activity of the eighteenth century had brought to Scotland. Emotionally, he admired the romantic and adventurous character of Rob Roy's way of life, but his reason put him finally on the Bailie's side. Jarvie states the theme in terms of honor versus credit: "I maun hear naething about honour—we ken naething here but about credit. Honour is a homicide and a bloodspiller, that gangs about making frays in the street; but Credit is a decent honest man, that sits at hame and makes the pat play [pot boil]" (chap. 26).

The Heart of Midlothian · *The Heart of Midlothian* is regarded by many as Scott's best work. In addition to the familiar virtues of a fully realized specific historical milieu and a large cast of characters from a variety of social levels who create themselves through the dialogue, the novel has for its heroine one of the common people, with whom Scott's powers of characterization were at their surest, and it has a truly serious ethical theme in the heroine's refusal to lie to save the life of her younger sister. Jeanie Dean's dilemma enables Scott to examine the relation of the law to justice and to mercy.

The novel opens with an extended presentation of an actual historical event, the Porteous riots in Edinburgh in 1736. Immediately after the execution of a smuggler named Wilson, John Porteous, Captain of the City Guard, reacts to a minor disturbance among the spectators by needlessly ordering his troop to fire upon the crowd. Several people are killed, and Porteous is sentenced to be hanged. On the very day set for his execution, he is reprieved by Queen Caroline. That night a mob storms the prison, the Tolbooth (to which the novel's title is a reference). Porteous is dragged out and hanged.

In Scott's version, the mob is led by George Robertson, an accomplice of Wilson, who would have died along with him had Wilson not generously made possible his escape. Robertson has another reason besides revenge on Porteous for breaking into the Tolbooth. In the prison is Effie Deans, who has been seduced by him and has borne his child. She is to stand trial under a statute which stipulates that if a woman conceals her pregnancy and then can neither produce the infant nor prove that it died a natural death, she shall be presumed to have murdered it and shall suffer the death penalty. Once inside the prison, Robertson seeks her out and urges her to make her escape in the confusion, but she refuses. (One wonders why he did not remove her forcibly, but evidently he has his hands full directing Porteous's fate.) The next night, Robertson summons Effie's sister Jeanie to a remote spot and tells her that the case can be removed from under the statute if Effie is found to have communicated her condition to anyone. Jeanie refuses to lie about her sister's having done this, and she repeats her refusal in an affecting interview with Effie just before the trial. When Effie is condemned to death, Jeanie travels on foot all the way from Edinburgh to London, wins the support of the Duke of Argyle, and persuades Queen Caroline to pardon her sister. A few days after Effie is released, she elopes with Robertson.

At this point the novel is in effect finished, or nearly so, but Scott added a fourth volume to stretch the book to the length for which he had contracted. In it, the Duke of Argyle arranges for Jeanie, her new husband Reuben Butler (a clergyman), and her father to remove to a remote part of Scotland under his protection. This pastoral coda contrasts too strongly with the tone of the rest of the novel, and there is an unfortunate emphasis on the material blessings showered on Jeanie that rather qualifies one's sense of the disinterested heroism of her achievement. The closing chapters are, to be sure, tied to the main plot by the reappearance of Effie and her husband and by the discovery of their son, now a member of a small gang of bandits. Robertson is killed in an encounter with this gang, probably by his own son. There is an interesting variation on the novel's central situation, for the son, probably actually guilty of unnatural murder as his mother Effie was not, escapes when Jeanie goes to the room where he is confined and in her compassion loosens his painfully tight bonds. If this repetition of the novel's central event, Jeanie's saving a prisoner from execution, is aesthetically interesting, it is nevertheless ethically problematic, for the youth is a lawless individual who shows no compunction at what he has done and who does not hesitate, once Jeanie has loosened his bonds, to endanger her life by setting a fire in order to effect his escape. Jeanie's mercy seems in this case ill-judged.

It is the first three volumes that contain the most effective probing of the relation of the law to justice and to mercy. Scott contrasts a number of characters, each of whom stands in a different relation to the law. Wilson is a criminal justly condemned for smuggling, but his last offense is the generous one of saving a life by enabling his young accomplice to escape, and it wins him the sympathy of the populace and sets him in sharp contrast to the enforcer of the law, the Captain of the City Guard. Porteous's excessive zeal in the performance of his office leads to the loss of life and earns him the hatred of the populace when he gives the order to fire upon the crowd. His callousness is also shown by his earlier refusal to loosen Wilson's painfully tight handcuffs on the way to the execution, pointing out that all his pain will soon be at an end.

Among the mob that punishes Porteous, Robertson is concerned to preserve order because he wishes to stress the justice of their action, yet in his own person he has much to fear from justice. He is, moreover, clearly moved more by a desire for revenge than by a true concern for justice, and also, as has already been noted, he has in Effie Deans an ulterior motive for storming the Tolbooth.

Of all the prisoners the novel describes, Effie is in the worst plight, since she is entirely innocent of the crime she is charged with and since the statute does not even require that a crime be proved to have occurred. Moreover, she is in a sense to suffer for the guilt of others, for the government wishes to make an example of her because of the increasing frequency of child murder. Also, the Queen's anger at the response to the pardon of Porteous makes a royal pardon for Effie unlikely. Her situation is rendered more hopeless by these two factors that in strict justice have no bearing on her case.

Effie is linked with Wilson in that he and she have both sacrificed themselves for Robertson. Effie staunchly refuses to reveal her seducer's identity, even when she is "offered a commutation and alleviation of her punishment, and even a free pardon, if she would confess what she knew of her lover." In her desire to protect Robertson, she goes so far as to withhold all information concerning Meg Murdockson, the woman to whom Robertson had sent her when her child was due.

Robertson clearly does not deserve her generosity (nor Wilson's, for that matter). He is completely selfish. Effie is not the first girl he has abused. Meg Murdockson had long been a servant in his family, and he had seduced her daughter Madge. When her mother put Madge's infant out of the way so it would not pose an obstacle to Madge's finding a husband, Madge lost her wits. She is one of a number of pathetic simpletons who wander through Scott's novels, a company that includes David Gellatley in *Waverley* and Goose Gibbie in *Old Mortality*. Robertson's guilt in Madge's case has far-reaching consequences, for it is anger at the prospect of Effie taking her daughter's place that moves Meg Murdockson to spirit away Effie's infant and later to attempt to waylay Jeanie on her journey to London.

Robertson's real name is Staunton. He has been among other things an actor, and this is appropriate, for, besides being selfish, he is the rankest hypocrite. In the scene where he confronts Jeanie to explain how she can save her sister, he heaps blame on himself liberally, but it is all empty gesture and rhetoric. He expects someone else to solve the problem. Jeanie is to save Effie by telling a lie when he could do it by surrendering himself and telling the truth. When Effie has finally been sentenced, then indeed he leaps on his horse with the intention of securing her reprieve by giving himself up as the leader of the Porteous mob, but his horse loses its footing and Staunton is thrown and severly injured. Jeanie learns of this on her journey to London when, by a remarkable coincidence, she meets him in his father's house, where he is recuperating. He authorizes her to trade his life for that of her sister, but only if her own unsupported plea is refused.

When Effie is reprieved and Staunton marries her, he becomes an actor in good earnest, and so does she. Sir George and Lady Staunton live for years in fear that their past will be discovered, and his unhappiness is much aggravated by the fact that they are childless. A series of coincidences reveals that their son is not dead, but is part of a small gang of bandits in the very vicinity where Jeanie and her family now live. When Staunton arrives in search of him and is killed, Jeanie prepares the body for burial. She discovers "from the crucifix, the beads, and the shirt of hair which he wore next his person, that his sense of guilt had induced him to receive the dogmata of a religion, which pretends, by the maceration of the body, to expiate the crimes of the soul" (chap. 52). The verb *pretends* conveys Scott's view of the appropriateness of Staunton's conversion to Roman Catholicism.

Jeanie Deans, in contrast, is firmly anchored in her father's rigid Presbyterianism and has a horror of every kind of pretense or falsehood. Her principles prevent her from lying to save Effie, but her generosity enables her to accomplish what all of Staunton's empty heroics are powerless to achieve. It is interesting to consider a misunderstanding that arises between Jeanie and her father, David Deans, regarding her testifying at Effie's trial. Deans is a Cameronian, the strictest kind of Scottish Presbyterian, and his memory goes back to the battle of Bothwell Bridge and the persecutions that followed it. He is doubtful of the propriety of even appearing in court, since doing so might seem to constitute an acknowledgment of a government that has abandoned the Solemn League and Covenant and that exercises what he regards as undue influence over the Kirk. Though Deans has never before hesitated to tell anyone what to do, in the present case he says to himself, "My daughter Jean may have a light in this subject that is hid frae my auld een—it is laid on her conscience, and not on mine—If she hath freedom to gang before this judicatory, and hold up her hand for this poor cast-away, surely I will not say she steppeth over her bounds" (chap. 18). The inconsistency is too touching and too clearly rooted in his love for Effie to be called hypocrisy. It is another instance of the conflict between principles of conduct and emotional claims, and it enriches the character and under-lines his relation to the central theme.

When he attempts to convey to Jeanie his resolution of his scruples, she, who has no thought of refusing to appear in court, takes it that he is encouraging her to give false testimony. The misunderstanding increases her sense of isolation and lack of support and thus makes her behavior all the more heroic.

The heroic impact of the journey itself is marred somewhat by the melodramatic events with which Scott seeks to enliven it. The lurid coloring is overdone in the scene of Jeanie's captivity at the hands of Meg, Madge, and two underworld cronies of theirs (to whom the old woman is known as Mother Blood). Scott is more successful when he modulates into comedy in the scene in which the demented Madge, in the absence of Meg and the others, leads Jeanie to a nearby village and then into church, where Madge's fantastic behavior causes her captive considerable embarrassment. The tension between the comic elements here and the very real danger of Jeanie's situation makes a strong effect. Shortly afterward, however, the tone shifts back to melodrama with the coincidental meeting with the convalescent Staunton, and the dramatic temperature drops during one of those retrospective narratives which Scott's complex plotting often forced on him.

The climactic confrontation with the Queen is very well done. Oddly enough, although Scott often had trouble finding a convincingly natural mode of utterance for his invented characters of the upper class, for actual historical figures he often succeeded in writing dialogue that is elevated without being stilted, polished without being wooden. Such is the language of Prince Charles Edward in *Waverley*, of Claver-house in *Old Mortality*, and of Queen Caroline here.

The psychology of the Queen and her language are noteworthy. Jeanie's simple plea is effective, but it is not, or not only, emotional considerations that cause the Queen to grant the pardon. Even her response to Jeanie's main speech–"This is eloquence"–suggests objective evaluation of the speech more than emotional assent, and Scott keeps the scene well clear of sentimentality by a persistent emphasis on the political factors in the Queen's decision. She is divided between resentment of the Scots for their response to her pardoning of Porteous and her inclination to remain on good terms with Jeanie's sponsor, the Duke of Argyle. Even though he is at present out of favor, her policy is based on the principle that political allies may become opponents and opponents may again become allies. Another element in the scene is her complex attitude toward Lady Suffolk, also present at the interview. The Queen has so arranged matters that Suffolk is both her chief confidante and the King's mistress. After inadvertently making a remark that the Queen construes as a reflection on herself, Jeanie rights herself with a chance reference to "the stool of repentance," the punishment in Scotland "for light life and conversation, and for breaking the seventh command." The Queen is amused at the obvious embarrassment of "her good Suffolk."

The novel as a whole indicates that although the law is an absolute necessity, it can never do more than approximate justice because it is made and administered by human beings. It is ironically the generous instincts of Effie (in protecting Staunton) and the uncompromising honesty of Jeanie that make Effie the victim of a law which, it is repeatedly suggested, is a bad law because it exacts punishment in cases where there may have been no crime. It seems unjust too that the strict enforcement in the present instance is caused by factors external to Effie's case, the rise in child murder and the royal anger over the Porteous affair. Moreover, the author tends to place the human agents who enforce the law in an unflattering light. Porteous abuses the authority vested in him. The Doomster, or executioner, is a kind of untouchable who inspires horror in everyone when he makes his ritual appearance at Effie's sentencing. Ratcliffe, a thief four times condemned to the gallows, is the only prisoner besides Effie who rejects the opportunity to escape when the mob breaks into the Tolbooth. His reason is that he wants the post of underturnkey. The authorities actually grant this audacious request after considering how valuable his knowledge of the underworld is likely to prove. Scott provides a striking emblem of the amount of practical compromise involved in the enforcing of the law when he shows Ratcliffe and Sharpitlaw, the superintendent of police, at the start of the interview in which they bargain over Ratcliffe's request: "They sate for five minutes silent, on opposite sides of a small table, and looked fixedly at each other, with a sharp, knowing, and alert cast of countenance, not unmingled with an inclination to laugh."

The scene with the Queen indicates that the prerogative of mercy that is intended to mitigate the sternness of the law or correct miscarriages of justice is likewise governed by considerations of policy and expediency. The outcome of that scene, however, shows that the gap between ideal justice on one hand, and policy or expediency on the other, can be bridged by the selfless exertions of someone motivated simply by love.

Although the four novels discussed here are likely to appear on anyone's list of the best of Scott, they are by no means the only ones worthy of a modern reader's attention. *The Antiquary, The Bride of Lammermoor, A Legend of Montrose,* and *Woodstock* have all found advocates among modern critics. There is also a very successful third panel in what might be called the Jacobite triptych that includes *Waverley* and *Rob Roy: Redgauntlet,* set in the 1760's, describes the last throes of the Jacobite movement. In addition to a plot full of intrigue, it is noteworthy for its combination of letters and journals with third-person narration and for autobiographical elements in the main characters of Alan Fairford and Darsie Latimer. Obviously Scott will never again have the huge audience he enjoyed throughout the nineteenth century, but he is more than merely a chapter in literary history. In addition to establishing the genre of the historical novel and influencing nineteenth century historiography, he wrote several novels that can be judged major achievements by any but the most narrow and rigid criteria.

John Michael Walsh

Other major works

SHORT FICTION: *Chronicles of the Canongate,* 1827.

PLAYS: *Halidon Hill,* pb. 1822; *Macduff's Cross,* pb. 1823; *The Doom of Devorgoil,* pb. 1830; *Auchindrane: Or, The Ayrshire Tragedy,* pr., pb. 1830.

POETRY: *The Eve of Saint John: A Border Ballad,* 1800; *The Lay of the Last Minstrel,* 1805; *Ballads and Lyrical Pieces,* 1806; *Marmion: A Tale of Flodden Field,* 1808; *The Lady of the Lake,* 1810; *The Vision of Don Roderick,* 1811; *Rokeby,* 1813; *The Bridal of Triermain: Or, The Vale of St. John, in Three Cantos,* 1813; *The Lord of the Isles,* 1815; *The Field of Waterloo,* 1815; *The Ettrick Garland: Being Two Excellent New Songs,* 1815 (with James Hogg); *Harold the Dauntless,* 1817.

NONFICTION: *The Life and Works of John Dryden,* 1808; *The Life of Jonathan Swift,* 1814; *Lives of the Novelists,* 1825; *The Life of Napoleon Buonaparte: Emperor of the French, with a Preliminary View of the French Revolution,* 1827.

TRANSLATIONS: *The Chase, and William and Helen: Two Ballads from the German of Gottfried Augustus Bürger*, 1796; *Goetz von Berlichingen*, 1799 (Johann Wolfgang von Goethe).

EDITED TEXTS: *Minstrelsy of the Scottish Border*, 1802-1803 (3 volumes); *A Collection of Scarce and Valuable Tracts*, 1809-1815 (13 volumes); *Chronological Notes of Scottish Affairs from the Diary of Lord Fountainhall*, 1822.

Bibliography

Crawford, Thomas. *Scott*. Rev. ed. Edinburgh: Scottish Academic Press, 1982. A revision and elaboration of Crawford's widely acclaimed study of Scott. Examines Scott's work as a poet, balladist, and novelist in a compact style.

Daiches, David. *Sir Walter Scott and His World*. London: Thames and Hudson, 1971. A well-written account of Scott, generously illustrated. Contains much valuable information in a readable style by an eminent scholar of Scott.

deGategno, Paul J. *Ivanhoe: The Mask of Chivalry*. New York: Twayne, 1994. This volume of the Twayne Masterwork Series follows the series format, placing the novel in literary and historical context before it is given a particular reading. DeGategno's reading emphasizes the novel's pertinence to its own time and its importance as a reflection of Scott's society. But then, interestingly, deGategno concludes his book with a selection of his students' responses to *Ivanhoe*. This book provides a good general introduction to one of Scott's most compelling and long-lived works.

Hart, Francis R. *Scott's Novels: The Plotting of Historical Survival*. Charlottesville: University of Virginia Press, 1966. A survey of Scott's novels, generally favorable and emphasizing the author's diversity.

Humphrey, Richard. *Waverley*. Cambridge, England: Cambridge University Press, 1993. This short volume also provides a useful introduction to a seminal Scott novel. Humphrey divides his analysis of the novel into four parts: "Scott's changing world and the making of *Waverley*," "*Waverley* as story," "*Waverley* as history," and "*Waverley* as initiator"—by which he means that the novel provided a model not only for subsequent Scott works but also for novels written by many other writers. An interesting appendix contains contemporary accounts of the Battle of Prestonpans.

Johnson, Edgar. *Sir Walter Scott: The Great Unknown*. 2 vols. New York: Macmillan, 1970. Now considered the definitive biography of Scott, replacing John Gibson Lockhart's. Johnson has used the many sources and information available on Scott to present an accurate portrayal of the author. A must for the serious Scott scholar.

Lauber, John. *Sir Walter Scott*. Rev. ed. Boston: Twayne, 1989. A good introduction to Scott, ideal for the beginning student or new reader of Scott. Rather than concentrating on the *Waverley* novels, takes a "sampling" of Scott's finest works. Contains a useful bibliography.

Mary Wollstonecraft Shelley

Born: London, England; August 30, 1797
Died: London, England; February 1, 1851

Principal long fiction · *Frankenstein*, 1818; *Valperga: Or, The Life of Castruccio, Prince of Lucca*, 1823; *The Last Man*, 1826; *The Fortunes of Perkin Warbeck*, 1830; *Lodore*, 1835; *Falkner*, 1837.

Other literary forms · Mary Shelley was a prolific writer, forced into copiousness by economic necessity. Punished by Sir Timothy Shelley, her husband Percy Bysshe Shelley's father, for her violation of his moral codes with his son, Mary Shelley was denied access to the Shelley estate for a long time after her husband's death. Her own father, William Godwin, was eternally in debt himself and spared her none of his troubles. Far from helping her, Godwin threw his own financial woes in her lap. It fell to Mary to support her son by writing, in addition to her novels, a plethora of short stories and some scholarly materials. The stories were mainly available to the public in a popular annual publication called the *Keepsake*, a book intended for gift-giving. Her stories were firmly entrenched in the popular gothic tradition, bearing such titles as "A Tale of Passion," "Ferdinand Eboli," "The Evil Eye," and "The Bride of Modern Italy." Her scholarly work included contributions to *The Lives of the Most Eminent Literary and Scientific Men* in *Lardner's Cabinet Encyclopedia* (1838). She attempted to write about the lives of both her father and her husband, although her efforts were never completed. She wrote magazine articles of literary criticism and reviews of operas, an art form that filled her with delight. She wrote two travel books, *History of a Six Weeks' Tour Through a Part of France, Switzerland, Germany, and Holland* (1817) and *Rambles in Germany and Italy* (1844). Shelley edited two posthumous editions of her husband's poetry (1824 and 1839), and she wrote several poetic dramas: *Manfred*, now lost, *Proserpine* (1922), and *Midas* (1922). She wrote a handful of poems, most of which were published in *Keepsake*.

Achievements · Shelley's literary reputation rests solely on her first novel, *Frankenstein*. Her six other novels, which are of uneven quality, are very difficult indeed to find, even in the largest libraries. Nevertheless, Mary Shelley lays claim to a dazzling array of accomplishments. First, she is credited with the creation of modern science fiction. All subsequent tales of the brilliant but doomed scientist, the sympathetic but horrible monster, both in high and mass culture, owe their lives to her. Even Hollywood's dream factory owes her an imaginative and economic debt it can never repay.

Second, the English tradition is indebted to her for a reconsideration of the Romantic movement by one of its central participants. In her brilliant *Frankenstein* fantasy, Mary Shelley questions many of the basic tenets of the Romantic rebellion: the Romantic faith in people's blissful relationship to nature, the belief that evil resides only in the dead hand of social tradition, and the Romantic delight in death as a lover and restorer.

Finally, she created one of the great literary fictions of the dialogue with the self.

The troubled relationship between Dr. Frankenstein and his monster is one of the foundations of the literary tradition of "the double," doubtless the mother of all the doubles in Charles Dickens, in Robert Louis Stevenson, and even in Arthur Conan Doyle and Joseph Conrad.

Library of Congress

Biography · Mary Shelley, born Mary Wollstonecraft Godwin, lived the life of a great romantic heroine at the heart of the Romantic movement. She was the daughter of the brilliant feminist Mary Wollstonecraft and the equally distinguished man of letters William Godwin. Born of two parents who vociferously opposed marriage, she was the occasion of their nuptials. Her mother died ten days after she was born, and her father had to marry for the second time in four years to provide a mother for his infant daughter. He chose a rather conventional widow, Mary Jane Clairmont, who had two children of her own, Jane and Charles.

In her childhood, Mary Shelley suffered the torments of being reared by a somewhat unsympathetic stepmother; later, she led the daughter of this extremely middle-class woman into a life of notoriety. The separation traumas in her early years indelibly marked Mary Shelley's imagination: Almost all of her protagonists are either orphaned or abandoned by their parents.

Mary Shelley's stormy early years led, in 1812 and until 1814, to her removal to sympathetic "foster parents," the Baxters of Dundee. There, on May 5, 1814, when she was seventeen years old, she met Percy Bysshe Shelley, who was then married to his first wife, Harriet. By March 6, 1815, Mary had eloped with Shelley, given birth to a daughter by him, and suffered the death of the baby. By December 29, 1816, the couple had been to Switzerland and back, had another child, William, and had been married, Harriet having committed suicide. Mary Shelley was then nineteen years old.

By the next year, Mary's stepsister, Jane Clairmont, who called herself Claire Clairmont, had had a baby daughter by Lord Byron, while Mary was working on *Frankenstein*, and Mary herself had given birth to another child, Clara.

The network of intimates among the Shelley circle rapidly increased to include many literati and artists. These included, among others, Leigh and Marrianne Hunt, Thomas Love Peacock, Thomas Jefferson Hogg, and John Polidori. The letters and diaries of the Shelleys from this period offer a view of life speeded up and intensified, life at the nerve's edge.

While the Shelleys were touring Switzerland and Italy, they sent frantic communications to their friends, asking for financial help. Mary issued frequent requests for purchases of clothing and household items such as thread. There were also legal matters to be taken care of concerning publishing, Shelley's estate, and the custody of his children from his previous marriage.

The leaves of the letters and diaries are filled with urgent fears for the safety of the Shelley children and the difficulties of what was in effect an exile necessitated by the Shelleys' unorthodox style of life. In 1818, Clara Shelley died, barely a year old, and in 1819, William Shelley died at the age of three. Five months later, a son, Percy Florence, was born, the only child of the Shelleys to grow to maturity.

In 1822, Mary Shelley's flamboyant life reached its point of desolation. Percy Shelley, while sailing with his close friend Edward Williams, in his boat *Ariel*, drowned in the Gulf of Spezia. Mary's letters and diaries of the time clearly reveal her anguish, her exhaustion, and her despair. Her speeding merry-go-round suddenly and violently stopped.

Literary historians find themselves in debate over this point in Mary Shelley's life. Her letters and diaries record unambiguous desolation, and yet many scholars have found indications that Percy Shelley was about to leave her for Jane Williams, the wife of the friend with whom he drowned. There is also some suspicion that Mary's stepsister had recently given birth to a baby by Percy Shelley, a rumor that Mary Shelley denied. Because of Percy Shelley's mercurial nature, such speculations are at least conceivable. Against them stands Mary's diary, a purely private diary, which suggests that she would have no reason to whitewash her marriage among its confidential pages.

Mary's tragedy did not prompt warmth and help from her estranged father-in-law. He refused to support his grandson, Percy Florence, unless Mary gave the child to a guardian to be chosen by him. This she would not do, and she was rewarded for her persistence. Her son became heir to the Shelley estate when Harriet Shelley's son died in 1826. After the death, Mary's son became Lord Shelley. Just as important, however, was the warm relationship that he maintained with Mary until her death. Mary Shelley's life ended in the tranquil sunshine of family affection. Her son married happily and had healthy children. Mary seems to have befriended her daughter-in-law, and, at the last, believed herself to be a truly fortunate woman.

Analysis · Mary Shelley's six novels are written in the gothic tradition. They deal with extreme emotions, exalted speech, the hideous plight of virgins, the awful abuses of charismatic villains, and picturesque ruins. The sins of the past weigh heavily on their plot structures, and often include previously unsuspected relationships.

Shelley does not find much use for the anti-Catholicism of much gothic fiction. Her nuns and priests, while sometimes troublesome, are not evil, and tend to appear in the short stories rather than in the novels. She avoids references to the supernatural so common in the genre and tends instead toward a modern kind of psychological gothic and futuristic fantasy. Like many gothic writers, she dwells on morbid imagery, particularly in *Frankenstein* and *The Last Man*. Graphic descriptions of the plague in the latter novel revolted the reading public which had avidly digested the grotesqueries of Matthew Gregory Lewis's *The Monk* (1796).

With the exception of *Frankenstein*, Shelley's novels were written and published after the death of her husband; with the exception of *Frankenstein*, they appear to be attempting to work out the sense of desolation and abandonment that she felt after his death. In most of her novels, Shelley creates men and particularly women who resign themselves to the pain and anguish of deep loss through the eternal hope of love in its widest and most encompassing sense. Reconciliation became Shelley's preponderant literary theme.

Frankenstein · *Frankenstein* is Shelley's greatest literary achievement in every way. In it, she not only calls into the world one of the most powerful literary images in the English tradition, the idealistic scientist Victor Frankenstein and his ironically abominable creation, but also, for the one and only time, she employs a narrative structure of daring complexity and originality.

The structure of *Frankenstein* is similar to a set of Chinese boxes, of narratives within narratives. The narrative frame is composed of the letters of an arctic explorer, Robert Walton, to his sister, Mrs. Saville, in England. Within the letters is the narrative of Victor Frankenstein, and within his narrative, at first, and then at the end within Walton's narrative, is the firsthand account of the monster himself. Walton communicates to England thirdhand then secondhand accounts of the monster's thoroughly unbelievable existence. Here, it would seem, is the seminal point of Joseph Conrad's much later fiction, *Heart of Darkness* (1902): the communication to England of the denied undercurrents of reality and England's ambiguous reception of that intelligence. In *Frankenstein* as in *Heart of Darkness*, the suggestion is rather strong that England cannot or will not absorb this stunning new perception of reality. Just as Kurtz's fiancé almost a century later cannot imagine Kurtz's "horror," so Mrs. Saville's silence, the absence of her replies, suggests that Walton's stunning discovery has fallen on deaf ears.

The novel begins with Walton, isolated from his society at the North Pole, attempt-ing to achieve glory. He prowls the frozen north "to accomplish some great purpose"; instead, he finds an almost dead Victor Frankenstein, who tells him a story which, in this setting, becomes a parable for Walton. Frankenstein, too, has isolated himself from society to fulfill his great expectations, and he has reaped the whirlwind.

Frankenstein tells Walton of his perfect early family life, one of complete kindness and solicitude. It is a scene across which never a shadow falls. Out of this perfection, Victor rises to find a way of conquering death and ridding himself and humankind of the ultimate shadow, the only shadow in his perfect middle-class life. Like a man possessed, Frankenstein forges ahead, fabricating a full, male, human body from the choicest corpse parts he can gather. He animates the creature and suddenly is overwhelmed by the wrongness of what he has done. In his success, he finds utter defeat. The reanimated corpse evokes only disgust in him. He abandons it in its vulnerable, newborn state and refuses to take any responsibility for it.

From that day, his life is dogged by tragedy. One by one, all his loved ones are destroyed by the monster, who at last explains that he wanted only to love his creator but that his adoration turned to murderous hate in his creator's rejection of him. Ultimately, Frankenstein feels that he must destroy the monster or, at the very least, die trying. He succeeds at both. After Frankenstein's death in the presence of Walton—the only man other than Frankenstein to witness the monster and live—the monster mourns the greatness that could have been and leaves Walton with the intention of hurling himself onto Frankenstein's funeral pyre.

The critical task regarding this fascinating work has been to identify what it is that Frankenstein has done that has merited the punishment which followed. Is the monster a kind of retribution for people's arrogant attempt to possess the secrets of life and death, as in the expulsion from Eden? Is it the wrath of the gods visited on people for stealing the celestial fire, as in the Prometheus legend, a favorite fiction of Percy Shelley? Or is this a rather modern vision of the self-destructiveness involved in the idealistic denial of the dark side of human reality? Is this a criticism of Romantic optimism, of the denial of the reality of evil except as the utterly disposable dead hand of tradition? The mystery endures because critics have suggested all these possibilities; critics have even suggested a biographical reading of the work. Some have suggested that Victor Frankenstein is Shelley's shrewd insight into her husband's self-deceived, uncritical belief in the power of his own intelligence and in his destined greatness.

Valperga · *Valperga*, Shelley's second novel, has a fairy-tale aura of witches, princes, maidens in distress, castles, and prophecies. The author uses all these fantasy appara-tuses, but actually deflates them as being part of the fantasy lives of the characters which they impose on a fully logical and pragmatic reality. The novel pits Castruccio, the Prince of Lucca, a worldly, Napoleonic conquerer, against the lost love of his youth, the beautiful and spiritual Euthanasia. Castruccio's one goal is power and military dominion, and since he is enormously capable and charismatic, not to mention lucky, he is successful. Nevertheless, that he gains the world at the price of his soul is clearly the central point of the novel.

To gain worldly sway, he must destroy Valperga, the ancestral home of his love, Euthanasia. He must also turn Italy into an armed camp which teems with death and in which the soft virtues of love and family cannot endure. His lust for power raises to predominance the most deceitful and treacherous human beings because it is they who function best in the context of raw, morally unjustified power.

In the midst of all this, Castruccio, unwilling to recognize his limits, endeavors to control all. He wants to continue his aggrandizing ways and have the love of Euthanasia. Indeed, he wants to marry her. She reveals her undying love for him but will yield to it only if he yields his worldly goals, which he will not do. As his actions become more threatening to her concept of a moral universe, Euthanasia finds that she must join the conspirators against him. She and her cohorts are betrayed, and all are put to death, with the exception of Euthanasia. Instead, Castruccio exiles her to Sicily. En route, her ship sinks, and she perishes with all aboard. Castruccio dies some years later, fighting one of his endless wars for power. The vision of the novel is that only pain and suffering can come from a world obsessed with power.

Surely the name Euthanasia is a remarkable choice for the novel's heroine. Its meaning in Shelley's time was "an easy death"; it did not refer to the policy of purposefully terminating suffering as it does today. Euthanasia's death is the best one in the story because she dies with a pure heart, never having soiled herself with hurtful actions for the purpose of self-gain. Possibly, the import of Shelley's choice is that all that one can hope for in the flawed, Hobbesian world of *Valperga* is the best death possible, as no good life can be imagined. It is probable that this bleak vision is at least obliquely connected with the comparatively recent trauma of Percy Shelley's death and Mary Shelley's grief and desolation.

The Last Man · The degenerating spiral of human history is the central vision of *The Last Man*. Set in the radically distant future of the twenty-first century, this novel begins with a flourishing civilization and ends with the entire population of the world, save one man, decimated by the plague. Lionel Verney, the last man of the title, has nothing to anticipate except an endless journey from one desolate city to another. All the treasures of man are his and his alone; all the great libraries and coffers open only to him. All that is denied to him—forever, it seems—is human companionship.

The novel begins before Lionel Verney's birth. It is a flashback narrated by Lionel himself, the only first-person narrator possible in this novel. Lionel describes his father as his father had been described to him, as a man of imagination and charm but lacking in judgment. He was a favorite of the king, but was forced out of the king's life by the king's new wife, a Marie Antoinette figure. The new queen, depicted as an arrogant snob, disapproves of Verney's father and effects his estrangement from the king by working on her husband's gullible nature.

Verney's father, in ostracized shame, seeks refuge in the country, where he marries a simple, innocent cottage girl and thus begets Lionel and his sister Perdita. Verney's father can never, however, reconcile himself to his loss of status and dies a broken man. His wife soon follows, and Lionel and Perdita live like wild creatures until chance brings the king's son, Adrian, into their path. Their friendship succeeds where the aborted friendship of their fathers failed, despite the continued disapproval of the queen.

What is remarkable to the modern reader is that Shelley, having set her story two hundred years in the future, does not project a technologically changed environment. She projects instead the same rural, agrarian, hand and animal-driven society in which she lived. What does change, however, is the political system. The political system of *The Last Man* is a republican monarchy. Kings are elected, but not at regular intervals. The bulk of the novel concerns the power plays by which various factions intend to capture the throne by election rather than by war.

Adrian and Lionel are endlessly involved with a dashing, Byronic figure named

Lord Raymond, who cannot decide whether he wants life in a cottage with Perdita, or life at the top. Ultimately, Raymond, like the protagonist of *Valperga*, wants to have both. He marries Perdita and gives up all pretensions to power, but then returns with her to rule the land. Power does not make him or his wife happy.

Despite the sublimation of the power process into an electoral system, the rage for power remains destructive, degenerating finally into war. The plague which appears and irrevocably destroys humankind is merely an extension of the plague of people's will to power. Not only Raymond and Perdita, but also their innocent children, Lionel's wife, Iris, and Adrian's sister, who stayed home to eschew worldly aspirations, are destroyed. No one is immune.

Lionel's survival carries with it a suggestion of his responsibility in the tragedy of humankind. His final exile in a sea of books and pictures suggests that those who commit themselves solely to knowledge and art have failed to deal with the central issues of life. In simply abdicating the marketplace to such as Lord Raymond, the cultivators of the mind have abandoned humanity. Through Lionel, they reap a bitter reward, but perhaps the implication is that it is a just reward for their failure to connect with their fellow human beings.

A number of critics consider *The Last Man* to be Mary Shelley's best work after *Frankenstein*. Like *Frankenstein*, this novel rather grimly deals with the relationship between knowledge and evil. Its greatest drawback for modern audiences, however, is its unfortunate tendency to inflated dialogue. Every sentence uttered is a florid and theatrical speech. The bloated characterizations obscure the line of Shelley's inventive satire of people's lemminglike rush to the sea of power.

The Fortunes of Perkin Warbeck · *The Fortunes of Perkin Warbeck* attempts to chronicle the last, futile struggles of the House of York in the Wars of the Roses. Perkin Warbeck was a historical character who claimed to be Richard, the son of Edward IV of England. Most scholars believe that Richard died in the tower with his brother Edward; Perkin Warbeck claimed to be that child. Warbeck said that he had survived the tower, assumed another identity, and intended to reclaim the usurped throne held by Henry VII.

Shelley's novel assumes that Perkin was indeed Richard and documents his cheerless history from his childhood to his execution in manhood by Henry VII. The novel attempts to explore once more man's fruitless quest for power and glory. Richard is an intelligent, virtuous young man who finds true companionship even in his outcast state, and the love of a number of women, each different, utterly committed, and true. He is unable, however, to forsake the dream of conquest and live simply. As he presses onward to claim the throne, he suffers a series of crushing losses, not one of which will he yield to as a revelation of the wrongheadedness of his quest. His rush toward the throne achieves only the death of innocent persons. When he is executed at the end of the novel, his wife Katherine is given the last words. She needs to find a way of continuing to live without him. She is urged by his adherents to forsake the world, and for his sake to live a reclusive life. Although Katherine appears only briefly in the interminable scenes of war and the grandiose verbiage through which the reader must trudge, her appearance at the end of the novel and her refusal to forsake the world in her grief are the most impressive moments in the work.

In refusing to retreat from the world, Katherine commits herself to the only true value in the novel, love, a value which all the senseless suffering of Richard's quest could not destroy. Katherine, as the widow of the gentle but misguided warrior, becomes a metaphor for the endurance of love in a world that has its heart set on everything but love. Her final, gracious words are a relaxing change from the glory-seeking bombast of the action, "Permit this to be, unblamed–permit a heart whose sufferings have been and are, so many and so bitter, to reap what joy it can from the strong necessity it feels to be sympathized with–to love." Once again, Shelley's basic idea is an enthralling one, but her execution of her plan includes a grandiose superfluity of expression and incident.

Lodore · *Lodore* and Shelley's last novel, *Falkner,* form a kind of reconciliation couplet to end her exploration of loss and desolation. Reward for persistence in loving through the trials of death and social obliquity is her final vision. In *Lodore,* an extremely long parade of fatal misunderstandings, the central image is the recovery of a lost mother. The novel begins veiled in mystery. Lord Lodore has exiled himself and his fairylike, delicate daughter, Ethel, to the forests of Illinois in far-off America. Lord Lodore is without his wife, who has done something unnamed and perhaps unnameable to provoke this unusual separation. Reunion with her is the central action of the plot.

Lord Lodore is a perfect gentleman amid the cloddish but honest American settlers. His one goal is to produce the perfect maiden in his daughter, Ethel. Father and daughter are entirely devoted to each other. A series of flashback chapters reveal that Lady Lodore, very much the junior of Lord Lodore, had been overly influenced by her mother, who had insinuated herself between husband and wife and alienated her daughter's affections from Lord Lodore. Lord and Lady Lodore lived what life they had together always on the brink of rapprochement, but utterly confounded by the wiles of the mother-in-law, who managed to distort communicated sentiments to turn husband and wife away from each other, finally effecting a radical separation that neither Lord nor Lady Lodore wanted.

The American idyll ends for Ethel and her father when Ethel is about fifteen years old. The unwanted attentions of a suitor threaten Ethel's perfect life, and her father moves his household once more. Lodore thinks of reestablishing the bond with his estranged wife but is killed in a duel hours before departing for England. His last thoughts of reconciliation are buried with him, because the only extant will is one recorded years ago when he vindictively made Lady Lodore's inheritance dependent on her never seeing Ethel again. Ethel returns to England shaken and abandoned, but not to her mother. Instead, she lives with Lodore's maiden sister.

Ethel is wooed and won by a gentleman, Edward Villiers, coincidentally one of the few witnesses to her father's death and many years older than herself. The marriage of this truly loving couple is threatened because Edward, reared in luxury, is in reduced financial circumstances owing to the irresponsibility of his father, one of the few truly despicable characters in the novel.

Much suffering ensues, during which Edward and Ethel endeavor to straighten out priorities: Which is more important, love or money? Should they part to give Ethel a chance at a more comfortable life, or should they endure poverty for love? They choose love, but Edward is taken to debtor's prison, Ethel standing by for the conjugal visits that the prison system permits.

Through a series of chance encounters, Lady Lodore, now a seemingly shallow woman of fashion, becomes aware of Ethel's needs and of her need to be a mother to the young woman. Telling no one but her lawyer what she intends, she impoverishes herself to release Edward from prison and to set the couple up appropriately. She then removes herself to a humble country existence, anticipating the blessings of martyrdom. She is, however, discovered, the mother and daughter are reunited, and Lady Lodore is even offered an advantageous marriage to a rich former suitor who originally was kept from her by the machinations of his sisters.

Lodore includes many particulars that are close to the biographical details of the author's life: the penury and social trials of her marriage to Shelley, the financial irresponsibility of her father, and the loss of her mother. Shelley's familiarity with her material appears to have dissolved the grandiose pretensions of the previous novels, which may have sprung from her distance from their exotic settings and situations. *Lodore* has the force of life despite its melodramatic plot. If it were more widely available, it would be a rich source of interest for historians and literary scholars. It contains an interesting image of America as envisioned by the early nineteenth century European. It also contains a wealth of interest for students of women's literature.

Falkner · If *Lodore* offers a happy ending with the return of a long-lost mother, then *Falkner* finds contentment in the restoration of an estranged father. Here, the father is not the biological parent, but a father figure, Rupert Falkner. The plot is a characteristic tangle of gothic convolutions involving old secrets and sins, obdurate Catholic families, and the pure love of a young girl.

The delightful Elizabeth Raby is orphaned at the age of six under severe circumstances. Because her fragile, lovely parents were complete strangers to the little town in Cornwall to which they had come, their death left Elizabeth at the mercy of their landlady. The landlady is poor, and Elizabeth is a financial burden. The landlady keeps her only because she suspects that the now decimated, strange little family has noble connections. Thus begins a typical Shelley fiction—with abandonment, innocence, and loss of love.

The plot is set in motion by a mysterious stranger who identifies himself as "John Falkner." Falkner undertakes the guardianship of Elizabeth, not only because of her charm, but also because of an unfinished letter found in the family cottage. This letter connects Elizabeth's mother to one "Alithea." The reader comes to learn that Falkner was Alithea's lover, that he carries the guilt of her ruin and death since Alithea was a married woman, and that her husband continues to bear his wife's seducer a vindictive grudge. Happily, for the moment, Alithea's husband believes that the seducer was surnamed Rupert. Alithea's husband was and is an unsuitable mate for a sensitive woman, and the marriage was one from which any woman would have wanted to flee. Alithea's infraction was only against the letter of the marriage bond, not its spirit.

The vindictive husband has conceived a hatred for Alithea's son, Gerard, on account of Alithea's connection with "Rupert." Elizabeth, Falkner's ward, coincidentally meets and forms an attachment to Gerard. Falkner repeatedly attempts to separate them because of his guilty feelings. Their attachment blooms into a love which cannot be denied, and Falkner is forced to confess all to Gerard after the boy saves Falkner's life. He is the infamous Rupert, Rupert Falkner.

With the revelation comes the separation of Elizabeth and Gerard, she to stand loyally with Falkner, he to defend his father's honor. For the first time in his life, Gerard finds himself on his father's side, but familiarity breeds contempt. Gerard wants to fight a manly duel for honor, while his father wants to crush Falkner for economic gain in the legal system. Gerard finds this an inexcusable pettiness on his father's part. He then joins Elizabeth to defend Falkner in court. To do this, they will need to go to America to bring back a crucial witness, but the witness arrives and saves them the voyage: Falkner is acquitted. The legal acquittal is also metaphorical: In comparison with the ugly sins of greed, the sins of passion are pardonable.

Elizabeth, the reader knows, is also the product of an elopement in defiance of family, a sin of passion. The proud Catholic family which once spurned her decides to acknowledge Elizabeth. Gerard and Elizabeth, both wealthy and in their proper social position, marry. Falkner will have a home with them in perpetuity.

Once again, Shelley's fictional involvement in the domestic sphere tones down her customary floridity and affords the reader fascinating insights into the thinking of the daughter of an early feminist, who was indeed an independent woman herself. It can only clarify history to know that such a woman as Mary Shelley can write in her final novel that her heroine's studies included not only the "masculine" pursuits of abstract knowledge, but also needlework and "the careful inculcation of habits and order . . . without which every woman must be unhappy—and, to a certain degree, unsexed."

Martha Nochimson

Other major works

SHORT FICTION: *Mary Shelley: Collected Tales and Stories*, 1976.

PLAYS: *Proserpine*, pb. 1922; *Midas*, pb. 1922.

NONFICTION: *History of a Six Weeks' Tour Through a Part of France, Switzerland, Germany, and Holland*, 1817; *Lardner's Cabinet Cyclopaedia*, 1838 (Numbers 63, 71, 96); *Rambles in Germany and Italy*, 1844; *The Letters of Mary Shelley*, 1980 (2 volumes; Betty T. Bennett, editor).

Bibliography

Baldick, Chris. *In "Frankenstein"'s Shadow: Myth, Monstrosity, and Nineteenth-Century Writing*. Oxford, England: Clarendon Press, 1987. Baldick analyzes the structure of modern myth as it has adapted and misread Shelley's novel until the film version of 1931. Focuses on Shelley's novel as itself a monster, which is assembled, speaks, and escapes like its protagonist. Also examines transformations in E. T. A. Hoffmann, Nathaniel Hawthorne, Herman Melville, and Elizabeth Gaskell; links *Frankenstein* to Thomas Carlyle, Charles Dickens, and Karl Marx; and traces the novel's influence on late Victorian stories of mad scientists, H. G. Wells, Joseph Conrad, and D. H. Lawrence. The last chapter argues that literary realism is itself a result of *Frankenstein*'s shadow. Includes footnotes, five illustrations, an appendix summarizing the novel's plot, and an index.

Forry, Steven Earl. *Hideous Progenies: Dramatizations of "Frankenstein" from Mary Shelley to the Present*. Philadelphia: University of Pennsylvania Press, 1990. Examines the influence of Shelley's novel on the history of theater and cinema from 1832 to 1930, discussing in great detail the popularization of the story until it became an enduring myth. After an introduction to the prevailing theater in London from 1823 to 1832, Forry studies the various Victorian adaptations of the novel from 1832 to 1900 and its revivals in twentieth century drama and cinema from 1900 to 1930. Provides the texts of seven dramatic adaptations of *Frankenstein*, from Richard Brinsley Peake's 1823 *Presumption* to John Lloyd Balderston's 1930 *Frankenstein*. Contains thirty-one illustrations, a list of ninety-six dramatizations from 1821 to 1986, an appendix with the music from *Vampire's Victim* (1887), a bibliography, and an index.

Kiely, Robert. *The Romantic Novel in England.* Cambridge, Mass.: Harvard University Press, 1972. An important book on Romantic prose fiction, including Shelley's gothic romances, which analyzes in depth twelve Romantic novels to define the intellectual context of the era. Notes that concepts of reality were tested and changed by Romantic novels and Edmund Burke's ideas of the sublime modified aesthetic forms. Shelley makes a significant contribution to this general thesis, and *Frankenstein* is analyzed in detail. Examines the story as a tragedy of suffering and superiority, in which a nightmarish experience carries moral themes. Finds a common drift toward death in most novels of this genre. Includes a set of notes and an index.

Mellor, Anne K. *Mary Shelley: Her Life, Her Fiction, Her Monsters.* London: Methuen, 1988. An important book which argues against trends of analysis which subordinate Shelley to her husband Percy Bysshe Shelley. Extends feminist and psychoanalytic criticism of *Frankenstein* to include all of Shelley's life and work, arguing that her stories are creations of the family she never enjoyed. The strength of her stories is their expression of her ambivalent desire for and criticism of the bourgeois family as an exploitation of property and women by a patriarchal ideology. Establishes Shelley's need for family, her feminist critique of science, and her analysis of the relationship between fathers and daughters. Includes eight illustrative plates, a chronology, ample notes, a bibliography, and an index.

Nitchie, Elizabeth. *Mary Shelley: Author of "Frankenstein."* New Brunswick, N.J.: Rutgers University Press, 1953. This critical biography evaluates Shelley in her own right in the milieu of people and places she knew. Assesses Shelley's temperament and talent, discussing her faults and strengths. Follows her life and career, from her earliest appearance as a self-conscious girl with a critical mind to her widowhood when she wrote largely forgotten works. Although primarily a biography, contains valuable comments on her writings, seen as art and as expressions of her life. A bibliography, an index, and six appendices, including a chronology, a list of works, a note on the unpublished novella *Mathilda*, the stage history of *Frankenstein*, and some unpublished poems, are provided.

Smith, Johanna M. *Mary Shelley.* New York: Twayne, 1996. This good introductory volume on Mary Shelley opens with a chapter devoted to her biography, then divides Shelley's works into categories. Separate chapters consider science fiction (including *Frankenstein*), historical fiction, domestic-sentimental fiction, literary biography and criticism, and travel narratives. More descriptive than analytical, this overview of Shelley's career is most accessible. A selected bibliography includes both primary and secondary sources.

Spark, Muriel. *Mary Shelley.* London: Constable, 1988. A revision of Spark's *Child of Light* (Essex, England: Tower Bridge, 1951) which reassesses the view that Shelley craved respectability after her husband's death. Spark skillfully narrates Shelley's life and then analyzes her writings. Argues that Shelley's pessimism was the consequence of her rationalist upbringing by William Godwin, but that she possessed an inner tranquility with which she created her novels. Concentrates on *Frankenstein* as the end of gothic fiction for its rational exposé of gothic mystery, on *The Last Man* as an expression of Shelley's feeling of solitude, and on *The Fortunes of Perkin Warbeck* as her challenge to learn from Sir Walter Scott's Waverley novels. Contains eight pages of illustrations, a selected bibliography, and an index.

Tobias Smollett

Born: Dalquhurn, Scotland; March 19, 1721 (baptized)
Died: Antignano, Italy; September 17, 1771

Principal long fiction · *The Adventures of Roderick Random*, 1748; *The Adventures of Peregrine Pickle: In Which Are Included Memoirs of a Lady of Quality*, 1751; *The Adventures of Ferdinand, Count Fathom*, 1753; *The Adventures of Sir Launcelot Greaves*, 1760-1761; *The Expedition of Humphry Clinker*, 1771.

Other literary forms · Tobias Smollett combined his medical practice with an active and varied career as a man of letters. His earliest, though unsuccessful, effort was as a playwright with *The Regicide: Or, James the First of Scotland, a Tragedy* (1749), published by subscription a full ten years after fruitless attempts at having it staged in London. Two other disappointments followed with his inability to secure a production for *Alceste* (1748-1749), a combination of opera, tragedy, and masque, and with the rejection of his first comedy, *The Absent Man* (1751), which was never produced or published. Both of these works have now been lost. His only success on the stage came finally with *The Reprisal: Or, The Tars of Old England* (1757), a comedy; this farce was produced by David Garrick at the Theatre Royal, Drury Lane.

Smollett's deep moral energy surfaced in two early verse satires, "Advice: A Satire" (1746) and its sequel, "Reproof: A Satire" (1747); these rather weak poems were printed together in 1748. Smollett's poetry includes a number of odes and lyrics, but his best poem remains "The Tears of Scotland." Written in 1746, it celebrates the unwavering independence of the Scots, who had been crushed by English troops at the Battle of Culloden.

As Smollett's literary career grew, his hackwork for publishers increased with translations. His most popular work among these projects was *A Complete History of England* (1757-1758) and its sequel, *Continuation of the Complete History of England* (1760-1765). He took great pride in his achievements as a historian and as a historical editor of *A Compendium of Authentic and Entertaining Voyages* (1756). A diversity of interests from medicine to politics prompted the writing of numerous pamphlets and essays. *An Essay on the External Use of Water* (1752) was a farsighted proposal for the improvement of public hygiene at Bath that caused a furor among the resort's staff and patrons.

Though his health was rapidly deteriorating from overwork, Smollett completed a thirty-five-volume edition of *The Works of M. de Voltaire* (1761-1774). In the hope that a warm climate would improve his health, he traveled to France and Italy, and on returning to England he published *Travels Through France and Italy* (1766). His didactic observations instructed his readers to accept England, for all its faults, as the best nation for securing happiness on earth. His last nonfiction works were *The Present State of All Nations* (1768-1769) and the political satire *The History and Adventures of an Atom* (1749, 1769). Lewis M. Knapp offers the best modern edition of the *Letters of Tobias Smollett* (1970).

Achievements · Smollett cannot be said to have added dignity to the art of the novel in the manner of Henry Fielding's imitation of the epic, nor can it be argued that he gave form to the genre as did Samuel Richardson, yet the eighteenth century novel cannot be discussed without giving full attention to Smollett's stylistic virtuosity and satiric intent.

Smollett successfully challenged Richardson's and Fielding's substantial popular reputation by providing "familiar scenes in an uncommon and amusing point of view." In *The Adventures of Roderick Random* (commonly known as *Roderick Random*), his first novel, he displayed a thorough understanding of the distinction between the novel and the romance, of which Samuel Johnson would speak in *The Rambler* essays (1750-1752). Borrowing from Latin comedy and Elizabethan drama, Smollett created caricatures of human beings with the dexterity of William Hogarth and Thomas Rowlandson. Though his characters lack the psychological depth of Richardson's, they possess breathtaking energy and evocative power.

Only in the late twentieth century did Smollett's role in the development of the English novel become fully appreciated. Criticism of that time emphasized the wrongheadedness of viewing Smollett's satiric energy as a deviation from Fielding's epic ambitions for the novel. Instead, Smollett is seen at the beginning of another tradition. Sir Walter Scott and Charles Dickens both valued Smollett's work; Dickens acknowledged his debt to Smollett's picaresque realism and comic characterization in *Pickwick Papers* (1836-1837). Among modern novelists, the savage comedy of writers as various as Evelyn Waugh and Joseph Heller is in Smollett's tradition rather than that of Fielding or Richardson.

Smollett's works continue to provoke critical inquiry. Several books and numerous dissertations have appeared, as well as many articles. The Oxford English Novels series has published all five of his novels, and the University of Delaware has begun to publish its *Bicentennial Edition of the Works of Tobias Smollett*, under the editorship of O. M. Brack, with *The Expedition of Humphry Clinker* (commonly known as *Humphry Clinker*) appearing in 1979.

Biography · Tobias George Smollett was born at Dalquhurn, Dumbartonshire, in western Scotland, and baptized on March 19, 1721. He was the son of Archibald Smollett, a lawyer, who suffered from ill health, and Barbara Cunningham Smollett, a woman of taste and elegance but no fortune. Smollett's grandfather, of whom the boy was especially proud, had been knighted by King William in 1698 and had become an influential member of the landed gentry as a local Whig statesman. When Smollett's father died only two years after his son's birth, the family suffered from lack of money.

Smollett's education, for all of his family's financial deterioration, was of superior quality though erratic. He entered Dumbarton Grammar School in 1728, remaining for five years, and received the traditional grounding in the classics. His matriculation to Glasgow University (though officially unrecorded) was interrupted when he be-came a Glasgow surgeon's apprentice while still attending university medical lectures. In the fall of 1739, Smollett was released from his apprenticeship to go to London; now eighteen, he had some reputation as a writer of earthy satires and doggerel. While traveling to London, Smollett carried the manuscript of a tragedy, *The Regicide*, which, he soon realized, would provide no entrée for him with the London theater managers. He is described at this time as "attractive, entertaining as a *raconteur*, and blessed with self-assurance." His future as a London man of letters uncertain, Smollett received advice from a number of Scottish physicians suggesting he continue practicing medicine. On March 10, 1740, he received a medical warrant from the Navy Board and embarked on the HMS *Chichester* as a surgeon's second mate.

The author's naval experience, material used later for *Roderick Random*, began during the outbreak of war with Spain and continued through the bloody Carthagena, West Indies, expedition of 1741. Smollett returned to England in 1742 but was drawn back to Jamaica, where he resided until 1744. While living on the island, he met the daughter of an established family of planters, the Lassellses; he married Anne Lassells in 1743. She is described as an affectionate and beautiful woman, in her early twenties, of considerable fortune.

Smollett, on the advice of her family, returned to London alone, where he set up a practice as a surgeon on Downing Street in May, 1744. Having never lost hope of a literary career, he worked on improving his fluency in Spanish and then began his translation of Miguel de Cervantes's *Don Quixote de la Mancha* (1605, 1615), which was published in 1755. The years from 1747 to 1750 were marked by considerable literary activity, numerous changes in residence, various trips abroad, a widening circle of acquaintances, and the birth of his only child, Elizabeth, in 1747.

In January, 1748, *Roderick Random* was published; this was followed by the impressive translations of Alain Le Sage and Cervantes, and in 1749, *The Regicide* was printed. The success of *Roderick Random* was instantaneous and prolonged, with sixty-five hundred copies sold in twenty-two months; it was to rival the popularity of Fielding's *Joseph Andrews* (1742). The success of *Roderick Random*, which was written in less than six months, became a kind of revenge on the theater managers of London. During this period, Smollett made plans to produce *Alceste*, his opera (George Frideric Handel was contracted for the music), but this effort was to fail; only a lyric from this work survives. His comedy *The Absent Man* was submitted to David Garrick but not accepted; Smollett's failure at drama was a continuing source of frustration throughout his career.

In June, 1750, Smollett purchased his medical degree from Marischal College, Aberdeen, and in the same month moved his family to Chelsea, a fashionable London suburb. It became an ideal home for him, where both his medical practice and his writing flourished; he remained there for thirteen years until forced abroad by his health in 1763. It was in Chelsea that he wrote *The Adventures of Peregrine Pickle* (commonly known as *Peregrine Pickle*), a work of nearly 330,000 words composed at top speed in anticipation of a trip to Paris. On February 25, 1751, his second novel was published to laudatory reviews and wide popularity.

Smollett's involvement with various periodicals began during the 1750's, first as a book reviewer for the *Monthly Review* and later as editor and proprietor of the *Critical Review*. Smollett joined Oliver Goldsmith in launching the *British Magazine* (the *Monthly Repository* beginning in 1760), remaining as coeditor until 1763. With a final venture, Smollett gained public notoriety and untold enemies by agreeing to write the *Briton*, a political effort in support of Lord Bute's ministry. Of Smollett's various journalistic efforts, only the work in the *Critical Review* is exceptional; as a literary periodical, it remains one of the most significant of the last half of the eighteenth century.

In the early 1750's, Smollett was driving himself in order to escape debt. Publishing a medical paper, *An Essay on the External Use of Water*, brought him little money, and in February, 1753, his third novel, *The Adventures of Ferdinand, Count Fathom* (commonly known as *Ferdinand, Count Fathom*), was published with poor financial results. The book attracted few readers, and Smollett was forced to borrow money and to supplement his medical fees with further hackwork. The years of hack writing began in earnest with *A Complete History of England*, a translation of Voltaire's writings, a geographical reference work, and several digests of travel. The period from 1756 to 1763 destroyed Smollett's health, but his reputation as a critic and a successful writer became unquestioned. Unfortunately, this frantic production hardly kept him from debtor's prison. Returning to the novel in the *British Magazine*, Smollett published "the first considerable English novel ever to be published serially"—*The Adventures of Sir Launcelot Greaves* (commonly known as *Sir Launcelot Greaves*). In monthly installments from January, 1760, to December, 1761, the novel gave the six-penny periodical substantial popularity.

In the midst of this literary hard labor, Smollett was imprisoned for three months, having been convicted of libeling an Admiral Knowles in an article in the *Critical Review*. On his release in early 1761, Smollett continued fulfilling his contracts with certain booksellers but also traveled extensively, possibly to Dublin, even though troubled by asthma and tuberculosis. In addition to these difficulties, his spirit was nearly broken by the illness and death of his daughter in April, 1763. This final shock caused him to cut all his London ties and move his family to the Continent, hoping to calm his wife and cure his ailments in the mild climate of the south of France and Italy. He spent two years abroad, returning to England in July, 1765; the literary result of his tour was *Travels Through France and Italy*. Though ill health plagued him, he sought for the third time a consulship but was rejected; in 1768 he left England for the last time.

Arriving in Pisa, Italy, Smollett visited with friends at the university, finally settling at his country villa in Antignano, near Leghorn, in the spring of 1770, where he completed his masterpiece, *Humphry Clinker*. Immediately following its publication, he received the rave notices of friends and critics concerning the novel, but he had little time to enjoy the praise. On September 17, 1771, he died from an acute intestinal infection and was buried at the English cemetery at Leghorn.

Analysis · Tobias Smollett is not only a great comic novelist; he is also a morally exhilarating one—a serious satirist of the brutality, squalor, and hideous corruption of humankind. His definite moral purposes are firmly grounded in the archetypal topic of all novelists—people's unceasing battle for survival in the war between the forces of good and evil. Smollett insists that people defy "the selfishness, envy, malice, and base indifference of mankind"; in such a struggle, the hero will ultimately prevail and will be rewarded for his or her fortitude.

Roderick Random · The principal theme of Smollett's first novel, *Roderick Random*, is the arbitrariness of success and failure in a world dominated by injustice and dishonesty. Smollett's decision to use realistic detail as a guise for his satire produces a lively and inventive work; moreover, the hero, Roderick, is not a mere picaro nor a passive fool but an intent satiric observer "who recognizes, reacts, and rebukes." The novel is organized in a three-part structure. The initial stage reveals Roderick's numerous trials as a young man; he loses his innocence during the years of poverty in Scotland, of failure in London, and of brutal experience in the Navy. The middle of the narrative embodies "the lessons of adversity" as the hero declines into near collapse. In a final brief section, Roderick recovers his physical and moral equilibrium and promotes the simple human values of friendship, love, and trust as the only viable bases for a satisfying existence.

Roderick's problem is both to gain knowledge of the world and to assimilate that knowledge. M. A. Goldberg, in *Smollett and the Scottish School* (1959), finds that "at first his responses are dictated by his indignation, by passions . . . eventually, he learns . . . to govern the emotions with reason." The struggle between these two forces is central to an understanding of eighteenth century England and its literature. In Smollett's first novel, good sense seems a sufficient defense against the sordid viciousness of the world. Good sense, however, can only be achieved, or learned, when the hero can control his pride and passionate nature, which are inextricably linked. Equilibrium, an orderly existence, arises paradoxically from the ashes of his random adventures. This understanding develops as the hero pursues the happiness he thinks he deserves but can never fully attain; as a good empiricist, Roderick gathers knowledge from each reversal, finally achieving a "tranquility of love" with the prudent Narcissa.

In *Roderick Random*, the hero's search for happiness differs significantly from the quest of the traditional picaro. While gaining an education and suffering the rebukes of others, Roderick remains good and effectual, unlike Don Quixote, who is powerless against cruelty. Roderick's youthful ferocity contributes to the practicality of the satire. Smollett's approach to correcting the ills of society is to allow no attack or insult to go unavenged. A thorough whipping of a bully or the verbal punishment of a pedant lifts the book beyond the picaresque and advances it past the formal verse satire. The center of the satiric discussion implicates the surroundings and not the hero, thus permitting Smollett to offer a long list of evil, self-centered figures who provide an excellent contrast to the goodness and charity of the ill-served protagonist. Only his faithful servant, Strap; his uncle, Tom Bowling; and the maid, Narcissa, join him in opposing his neglectful grandfather, the scoundrel Vicar Shuffle, the tyrannical Captain Oakum, the dandiacal Captain Whiffle, and the rapacious Lord Strutwell.

The last section of the novel provides the hero with the riches of his long quest: family, wealth, and love. The moral of the adventures follows as Roderick's recently discovered father "blesses God for the adversity I had undergone," affirming that his son's intellectual, moral, and physical abilities had been improved "for all the duties and enjoyments of life, much better than any education which affluence could bestow." The felicity of this final chapter provides a conventional ending, but the crucial point is that Roderick, having completed a rigorous education in the distinctions between appearance and reality, is now deserving of these rewards.

Peregrine Pickle · The protagonist of Smollett's long second novel, *Peregrine Pickle*, reminds one of Roderick in every aspect, except that Peregrine is an Englishman, not a Scot. The supporting players are improved; among the novel's outstanding comic creations are Commodore Hawser Trunnion and the spinster, Grizzle Pickle. Often described as the best picaresque novel in English, *Peregrine Pickle* satirizes the upper classes of mid-eighteenth century England. Rufus Putney argues in "The Plan of *Peregrine Pickle*" (1945) that Smollett "meant to write a satire on the affectations and meannesses, the follies and vices that flourished among the upper classes in order that his readers might learn with Peregrine the emptiness of titles, the sordidness of avarice, the triviality of wealth and honors, and the folly of misguided ambition."

The novel begins by sketching Peregrine's social and emotional background and introducing other principal characters. Following this introductory section, Smollett's protagonist describes his adolescence and education at Winchester and Oxford, where he becomes addicted to coarse practical jokes and to satisfying his overbearing pride. Here the hero meets Emilia, a beautiful orphan with whom he falls in love; because of his capricious nature, however, he cannot remain long with her. Having become alienated from his parents, Peregrine departs on the Grand Tour with the best wishes of his guardian, Trunnion.

Peregrine returns from France an unprincipled, arrogant rogue whose every action supports his vanity. After numerous incidents including the death of Trunnion and his replacement with the eccentric Cadwallader Crabtree as Peregrine's mentor, the hero tests the virtue of Emilia and is rebuffed. The remainder of the novel observes the long distress, the eventual imprisonment, and the final rehabilitation of the protagonist, who by now is convinced of the fraud and folly of the world. As Putney mentions, only after matriculating to the "school of adversity," which reduces his pride and vanity, can Peregrine hope to achieve wealth, marry his true love, triumph over his enemies, and retire to the country. Adversity teaches him to distinguish between the complex vices of the urban sophisticates and the simpler but more substantial pleasures of generosity and love in a rural retreat. Despite its picaresque vigor and satisfactory resolution, the novel suffers from a confusion of purposes: Peregrine's arrogance undermines the credibility of his role as a satirist of high society. Thus, Smollett's satiric intentions are blunted by his aspirations to a novel of character.

Ferdinand, Count Fathom · *Ferdinand, Count Fathom* is remembered today for its dedication, in which Smollett gives his famous definition of the novel, and for its place as the first important eighteenth century work to propose terror as a subject for a novel. In *The Novels of Tobias Smollett* (1971), Paul-Gabriel Boucé finds that the major defect of the novel is the author's "mixture of genres, without any transition brought about by unfolding of the story or the evolution of the characters." Fathom's dark cynicism informs the majority of the work, with the last ten chapters unraveling into a weak melodrama; nevertheless, Smollett's satire remains effective as a bitter denunciation of the hypocrisy and violence of elegant society. As an early contribution to the literature of terror, the novel probes the emotions of a young, virtuous girl who undergoes isolation, deprivation, and sadistic brutality at the hands of a rapacious creature. The figure of Fathom is used to undercut sentimental conventions and show their uselessness when civilized norms are forgotten.

Sir Launcelot Greaves · *Sir Launcelot Greaves* completed serialization in December, 1761, and was published as a book in March, 1762. Because of its serial publication, the novel's structure suffers from the frequent contrivance of artificial suspense. Recent criticism, however, has pointed to an underlying thematic unity based upon a series of variations on the theme of madness, with minute investigation into the physical, psychological, and moral aspects of the disorder. Greaves, the quixotic hero, launches a noble crusade for reform. His hopeless demand that a corrupted world listen to reason embraces Smollett's social idealism. If moral intention were the only measure of a novel's worth, then the didactic power of *Sir Launcelot Greaves* would guarantee its success; unfortunately, the delicate balance of the genre remains disordered by the force of an overobvious moral preoccupation.

Humphry Clinker · Smollett's last novel, *Humphry Clinker*, appeared in the bookstalls on June 15, 1771; Smollett had written the three volumes over a five-year period. It is his masterpiece, and it remains among the great English novels. The work was inspired by the epistles of Christopher Anstey's witty and popular *New Bath Guide* (1766). Using the epistolary method instead of the travel narrative of the early novels, Smollett characterizes his correspondents by means of their wonderfully individual letter-writing styles. Old Matthew Bramble of Brambleton Hall, Wales, travels with his household through Gloucester, Bath, London, Scarborough, Edinburgh, Cameron (Smollett country), Glasgow, and Manchester, and home again. Squire Bramble suffers various physical complaints, and his ill health makes him sensitive to the social ills surrounding him on his journey. Bramble searches for a recovery but finds himself becoming worse, not better, yet his compassionate nature remains undiminished. The journey was begun so that Bramble might distract his young niece, Lydia Melford, from a strolling actor named Wilson. The party also includes Tabitha, his aging, narrow-minded, old-maid sister; her malapropic maid, Winifred Jenkins, the classic example of the illiterate servant; and the modishly cynical nephew, Jery. En route, they adopt, much to Tabitha's delight, a Scottish veteran of American Indian warfare, Obadiah Lismahago. Soon, they add Humphry Clinker to the party as a new footman; he turns out to be the natural son of Matthew.

There are three major plots to develop, and numerous minor episodes, all of which hinge upon the characteristic picaresque device of the journey; Smollett exchanged the rogue hero for a group of picaros—Bramble and nephew Jery—who analyze and observe society. Through careful stages in letter after letter, Matthew's character is revealed to the reader, who learns to trust him as a reliable observer of society's foibles; in this respect *Humphry Clinker* is much stronger than *Peregrine Pickle*, where the satire was blunted by the protagonist's unreliability.

Smollett's satire strikes not individuals but categories of people and assorted social institutions; in particular *Humphry Clinker* is an exposé of the false attitudes and disordered life of the eighteenth century *nouveaux riches*. His conservative political views are displayed in Bramble's rages against an unrestricted press, politically biased juries, and the ignorance of the mob, and, as in *Peregrine Pickle*, he contrasts the folly and depravity of urban life with idealized pictures of the country.

Smollett's achievement in *Humphry Clinker* depends on his skillful use of the picaresque and epistolary traditions. His last novel is also distinguished by a warmth and tolerance not found to such a degree in his earlier works. Bramble's cynicism never becomes obnoxious to the reader; the brutality of Roderick is muted here. Smollett allows his hero to accept human society, despite "the racket and dissipation." Finally, for all his burlesque of Samuel Richardson's epistolary method, Smollett's characterization of Lydia has a depth and intensity that raises her above mere romantic convention.

In contrast to many critical reports, *Humphry Clinker* ends on a buoyant note of pure happiness, a happiness which fulfills the eighteenth century dictum of conformity to the universal order. Smollett's novels embrace moral and virtuous methods for pursuing one's goals. Passions and reason must remain in balance, and within this harmony, nature and art can moderate the demands of vice and folly.

Paul J. deGategno

Other major works

PLAYS: *The Regicide: Or, James the First of Scotland, a Tragedy*, pb. 1749; *The Reprisal: Or, The Tars of Old England*, pr. 1757.

NONFICTION: *The History and Adventures of an Atom*, 1749, 1769; *An Essay on the External Use of Water*, 1752; *A Compendium of Authentic and Entertaining Voyages*, 1756; *A Complete History of England*, 1757-1758; *Continuation of the Complete History of England*, 1760-1765; *Travels Through France and Italy*, 1766; *The Present State of All Nations*, 1768-1769; *Letters of Tobias Smollett*, 1970 (Lewis M. Knapp, editor).

TRANSLATIONS: *The Adventures of Gil Blas of Santillane,* 1748 (Alain René Le Sage); *The History and Adventures of the Renowned Don Quixote,* 1755 (Miguel de Cervantes); *The Works of M. de Voltaire,* 1761-1774 (35 volumes); *The Adventures of Telemachus, the Son of Ulysses,* 1776 (François de Salignac de La Mothe-Fénelon).

Bibliography

Bold, Alan, ed. *Smollett: Author of the First Distinction.* New York: Barnes & Noble Books, 1982. Contains four essays dealing with general issues and five concentrating on each of Smollett's major novels. Indexed.

Boucé, Paul-Gabriel. *The Novels of Tobias Smollett.* Translated by Antonia White. London: Longman, 1976. A slightly abridged version of the 1971 French study. Includes a biographical sketch, chapters on the major novels, and good discussions of Smollett's realism and comic devices. Contains a chronologically arranged bibliography of secondary works from 1928 to 1975.

Bulckaen, Denise. *A Dictionary of Characters in Tobias Smollett.* Nancy, France: Presses Universitaires de Nancy, 1993. An extremely useful way of keeping track of the plethora of characters in Smollett's fiction. Each character is identified; chapter and page number of the character's first appearance are also cited. There is also an index of the main categories of characters.

Grant, Damian. *Tobias Smollett: A Study in Style.* Totowa, N.J.: Rowman & Littlefield, 1977. As the title suggests, Grant ignores questions of realism and moral purpose to concentrate on what he regards as Smollett's three styles: comic, passionate, and, to a lesser extent, lyrical.

Knapp, Lewis Mansfield. *Tobias Smollett: Doctor of Men and Manners.* Princeton, N.J.: Princeton University Press, 1949. The standard life, sympathetic and detailed, but with little critical analysis of the works.

Rousseau, G. S. *Tobias Smollett: Essays of Two Decades.* Edinburgh: T. & T. Clark, 1982. Collects fifteen previously published essays and reviews on such topics as Smollett as letter writer and his role in various medical controversies of his day. Makes a good case, *inter alia,* for not regarding Smollett's novels as picaresques.

Rousseau, G. S., and Paul-Gabriel Boucé, eds. *Tobias Smollett: Bicentennial Essays Presented to Lewis M. Knapp.* New York: Oxford University Press, 1971. Includes ten essays that examine all aspects of Smollett's writings, including his voluminous, oft-neglected histories. The index allows for cross-references.

Spector, Robert D. *Smollett's Women: A Study in an Eighteenth-Century Masculine Sensibility.* Westport, Conn.: Greenwood Press, 1994. Organized differently from most books on Smollett, with chapters on society, personality, and literary tradition; heroines, fallen women, and women as victims; and the comic and the grotesque. Includes notes and bibliography.

_____. *Tobias George Smollett.* 1968. Rev. ed. Boston: Twayne, 1989. The first chapter of the book quickly surveys Smollett's minor works and the rest consider his novels. Contains a useful annotated bibliography of secondary criticism.

Wagoner, Mary. *Tobias Smollett.* New York: Garland, 1984. Provides an extensive list of editions of Smollett's works as well as an annotated bibliography of secondary material. Arranged by subject (for example, "Biographies and Biographical Material" and "The Expedition of Humphry Clinker") and therefore easy to use for locating criticism on a specific topic.

C. P. Snow

Born: Leicester, England; October 15, 1905
Died: London, England; July 1, 1980

Principal long fiction · *Death Under Sail*, 1932, 1959; *New Lives for Old*, 1933; *The Search*, 1934, 1958; *Strangers and Brothers* series (includes *Strangers and Brothers*, 1940 [reissued as *George Passant*, 1972]; *The Light and the Dark*, 1947; *Time of Hope*, 1949; *The Masters*, 1951; *The New Men*, 1954; *Homecomings*, 1956 [pb. in U.S. as *Homecoming*]; *The Conscience of the Rich*, 1958; *The Affair*, 1960; *Corridors of Power*, 1964; *The Sleep of Reason*, 1968; *Last Things*, 1970); *The Malcontents*, 1972; *In Their Wisdom*, 1974; *A Coat of Varnish*, 1979.

Other literary forms · Reflecting his various careers and interests, C. P. Snow published, in addition to his novels, a number of books, including the literary biographies *Trollope: His Life and Art* (1975) and *The Realists* (1978), as well as many reviews and articles. He had some interest in the drama, encouraging the staging of his novels *The Affair, The New Men,* and *The Masters*; writing a full-length play, *A View over the Bridge*, produced in London in 1950; and collaborating with his wife, Pamela Hansford Johnson, on six one-act plays published in 1951: *Spare the Rod, The Pigeon with the Silver Foot, Her Best Foot Forward, The Supper Dance, To Murder Mrs. Mortimer,* and *Family Party.*

Achievements · As a man, Snow's accomplishments were many and varied; as a novelist his achievement was more limited, and yet probably more long lasting. Snow the scientist and Snow the public figure cannot, however, be divorced from Snow the writer. Just as his novels drew upon his experiences in his nonliterary careers, so were his sociopolitical ideas presented in his novels. Yet, there is less of the details of "doing" science, less of the specificity of the public life than one might have expected from Snow's background had he been more of a naturalistic novelist, and there is less ideological content than might have been anticipated from one with Snow's strong views had he been more of a propagandist.

Snow was, rather, a realistic novelist, using his particular knowledge, background, and political ideology not primarily for their own sake, but in the service of his art. This art was conventional, relatively old-fashioned. Snow had limited patience with James Joyce and the literary avant-garde. As a *roman-fleuve, Strangers and Brothers* has a few interesting features, but it certainly lacks the subtlety that Snow admired in Marcel Proust. Snow did little to advance novelistic techniques; his own craftsmanship shows scant development over the course of a long writing career. His style has frequently been described as dull or pedestrian; Edmund Wilson found his novels "unreadable."

Snow implicitly defended his own style in discussing Anthony Trollope's, praising his predecessor for using language that was often intentionally made flat in order to be clear. Snow's style is certainly more serviceable than inspired. His imagery is limited and repetitious. Unity and impact are achieved through the recurrence of a limited number of images, such as those of lighted windows and rivers, but the impact is gained at the expense of a degree of monotony.

If Snow's style and imagery are little more than adequate, his plot construction is only somewhat more skillful. Unlike Trollope, whom Snow admired and to whom he has frequently been compared, Snow uses plots that are usually suspenseful; one reads his books partly to see how they will come out. This element of suspense, going back to his first published novel, a "whodunit," no doubt helps explain his having attracted a fairly wide and loyal audience, many of whom were not regular readers of novels. Snow's plots, however, are seldom particularly ingenious or original; essentially, they are a means to the revelation of character.

It is in characterization that Snow's prime virtue as a novelist lies; yet his characterizations excel only within certain limits. These limits arise from his subject matter. As has been frequently noted, Snow is particularly effective in dealing with "man in committee." This focus, related to the election, by thirteen Fellows, of a new head of their college, is central to Snow's most highly praised novel, *The Masters*. A similar focus is present in a number of his other novels, most strongly in *The Affair*. The men operate in committees because of the nature of their work—they are professionals involved in their careers, as academics, businessmen, scientists, civil servants. This *work*—not the physical labor described in a "proletarian novel" but the work of "The New Men," the professional, bureaucratic, technological, managerial classes—is presented with knowledgeable detail to be found in hardly any other novelist. Snow's work, in effect, filled a vacuum.

Snow filled another vacuum in his treatment of love and sex. While these topics have hardly been ignored by novelists, Snow's consideration of the social dimensions of a love affair or a marriage—the effect, for example, of a particular passion upon a man's career, such as Jago's protective love, in *The Masters*, for his wife—is rare, if not unique, among modern novelists, especially as, in Snow, the passion per se, however important, is never (not even in *Time of Hope*) the central concern.

This concern is character; the conditions of work, the politicking in committee, the impact of love—all these are used to reveal character in action. Thus, Snow is fundamentally a very traditional novelist, even though his distinctive reputation rests upon his having been a kind of contemporary social psychologist, carefully observing particular segments of modern society. While he is likely to continue to be read for some time for the picture of parts of society that his special experience allowed him to present, he may well still be read when this picture, encrusted by time, is of only historical interest. If, as seems likely, his novels do so survive, it will be because, while dealing with the time-bound particulars of their age, they were able to rise to an understanding of fundamental human motivation and thus to enjoy the longevity of true art.

Biography · Charles Percy Snow was born on October 15, 1905, in the Midland city of Leicester, the second of four sons. His background was similar to that of his fictional persona, Lewis Eliot. Snow's family had risen to the lower levels of the middle class; his father worked as a clerk in a shoe factory. Like Eliot's father, who led a choir, Snow's father played the organ in church; when he was no longer able to do so, he died soon after, at the age of eighty-four.

In school, Snow specialized in science; after graduation he worked as a laboratory assistant while he prepared for the examination which won him a scholarship, in 1925, at the University College of Leicester. He was graduated, in 1927, with First Class Honors in chemistry and received a grant that allowed him to proceed to a Master of Science degree in physics in 1928. Subsequently, he gained a scholarship to Cambridge, where he entered Christ's College as a research student in physics, published a paper on the infrared investigation of molecular structure, and, in 1930, received a Ph.D. and was elected a Fellow of Christ's College, a post he held until 1950, serving as Tutor from 1935 until 1945.

Like the fictional Lewis Eliot, whose law career hinged upon doing well in examinations and receiving scholarships, Snow must have worked hard (as did the hero of *The Search*) and must have been driven by ambition. His lifelong friend William Cooper (H. S. Hoff) has written novels about the life of the young people in Leicester in which the young Snow appears in fictional form; this work helps confirm the autobiographical quality of Snow's *Time of Hope*. Snow himself suggests the autobiographical aspect of *The Conscience of the Rich*, writing that when he was "very poor and very young," he "was taken up by one of the rich patrician Anglo-Jewish families."

Just as Lewis Eliot changes careers, and as the narrator of *The Search* turns from science to writing, Snow also did not rest in the comfort of being a rising young scientific don. He later wrote that since eighteen or so he knew that he wanted to be a writer, and while an undergraduate he wrote a novel, never published, called *Youth Searching*. He had gone into science because it offered a practical possibility for a poor boy. Although he did good scientific work at Cambridge and published some significant papers, according to William Cooper in *C. P. Snow* (1959), when some of Snow's scientific research went wrong through oversight, he abandoned scientific experimentation and turned more to his writing.

Snow had already published his first novel, *Death Under Sail*, a detective story, in 1932; he looked on it as practice for his later, more serious fiction. The next year he published *New Lives for Old*, combining his interest in science and politics in a work of science fiction. Worried that it would hurt his scientific career, he published this novel anonymously; it has never been reprinted. The first of his "serious" novels, *The Search*, appeared in 1934; like the Lewis Eliot series, it had a significant autobiographical element.

Snow did not move away from science to a complete commitment to literature at this time; rather, he became involved in administration, starting at his college. In 1939, he was appointed to a committee of the Royal Society that was organizing scientists for the war effort. This position led to a career in civil service; during World War II, he worked with the Ministry of Labour, being responsible for scientific personnel; after the war, he recruited scientists for government service. Beginning in 1944, he was associated with the English Electric Company, becoming a member of its Board of Directors in 1947. He was a Civil Service Commissioner from 1945 until 1960.

Snow's public life led to public honors; in 1943 he was made a Commander of the British Empire; in 1957 he was knighted. In 1964, when the Labour Party resumed power, Snow, making a decision different from Lewis Eliot's, was made a life peer, Baron Snow, of the City of Leicester and served for two years as parliamentary secretary of the Ministry of Technology.

During these years of public service, Snow was, of course, also living a personal life. He married the novelist Pamela Hansford Johnson in 1950. Like Margaret Davidson in the *Strangers and Brothers* series, she had been previously married, and like Lewis Eliot, Snow became a stepfather before having a son of his own, Philip Hansford Snow, born in 1952. Lady Snow has written autobiographically; her accounts are especially interesting in suggesting the similarities and differences between her children and the fictional children presented, especially in *Last Things*, by Snow.

Both the public and the personal sides of Snow's life were reflected in the *Strangers and Brothers* series, the idea for which occurred to him, he wrote, on January 1, 1935, while he was in France. It is difficult to determine the degree to which the whole series was worked out in advance. It would seem that Snow developed early certain controlling themes, such as "possessive love" and the idea of the "resonance" of experience upon the narrator, Lewis Eliot, while remaining flexible regarding the number and nature of the volumes that would make up the series. The first volume, *Strangers and Brothers*, which was to give the title to the whole series, appeared in 1940. It was followed in 1947 by *The Light and the Dark*. The subsequent nine volumes of the series appeared at roughly two-year intervals. They continued to draw directly upon his own life, including his eye operations, his cardiac arrest, his interest in the Moors murder case, and his experience in Parliament.

The course of Snow's simultaneous literary and public careers brought him increased recognition and honors, including numerous honorary degrees, and appointment as rector of the University of St. Andrews, Scotland. (Like Lewis Eliot, he postponed the first of his eye operations in order to attend this academic installation.) They also involved him in notable controversy, the most famous resulting from his Cambridge lectures in 1959, later published as *The Two Cultures and the Scientific Revolution*. Snow's position, which included a criticism of intellectuals' general lack of understanding of modern science, provoked much discussion and a strong attack, renewed in 1961 by the noted Cambridge literary critic, F. R. Leavis. In 1960, Snow, while on one of his trips to the United States, stirred up another controversy by his lectures at Harvard. In those lectures, he criticized some of the military-scientific decisions made by Winston Churchill's government during World War II.

In his later years, Snow continued to speak out on public policies. He remained a controversial figure, but he gradually acquired the image of an elderly, liberal sage, even if his sagacity was frequently questioned by both the political Left and Right. Following the completion of the *Strangers and Brothers* series, he revised it for an "Omnibus Edition" and continued his writing, publishing *The Malcontents*, *In Their Wisdom*, and, ending his career as he began it, with a detective story (of sorts), *A Coat of Varnish*. His remarkably full life ended on July 1, 1980.

Analysis · Characterization is the foundation of Snow's fiction. While theme and idea, as one might expect from a writer as political and *engagé* as was C. P. Snow, are important to his work, and while plot is nearly always a major source of interest, character is fundamental. It was his special approach to characterization, at once limited and complex, that allowed him to employ theme and plot, as well as style and imagery, in its service and which made certain subject matter particularly appropriate. Consequently, his works have their own distinctive and satisfying unity.

In his study of Anthony Trollope, a writer whom he valued highly and with whom he identified in a number of ways, Snow speaks interestingly of characterization. He defines character as persona, distinguishes it from inherent, individual nature, and considers personality to be a fusion of nature and character. These distinctions are certainly relevant to Snow's own work. His starting interest is in "characters," that is, an individual's personal qualities that are conditioned by, and expressed in, social experience. Yet, recognizing that this "character" interacts with "nature," Snow, in attempting to represent a rounded picture of "personality," must demonstrate the interaction. His fiction, then, is simultaneously concerned with showing people their "character" in social situations, indicating their "nature" or personal psychology, and presenting the interplay of the two, the social character and the private nature. All people have, in differing proportions, both a private and a social side to their personalities; all are both strangers and brothers.

Given this approach, it is not difficult to understand why Snow dealt frequently with "man in committee," or why he balanced this social material with presentation of individual passions, such as Lewis Eliot's for Sheila. Work and careers, seen in relation to individual "nature" and love and sex, were the two poles to which his subject matter flowed. As the social side of personality developed, Snow was able to suggest its changing formation. One observes, for example, Walter Luke's evolution from a brash young scientist to Lord Luke of Salcombe; his persona, but not his basic nature, changes with the years. Because an individual's "nature" is inherent (like his or her physiology), it is taken as a *donnée*, and its effects are dealt with. It is, for example, a given fact that Roy Calvert is a kind of "manic-depressive"; the reader discovers what the results of this nature will be, both for Calvert himself and for those with whom he interacts.

It was convenient for Snow that this approach to character was quite appropriate to the type of plotting that he apparently preferred. Most of his novels pose a question: "What will Martin decide?" "Who will be elected master?" "Will Roger Quaife succeed?" The reader, in attempting to anticipate the answer, and Snow, in providing and justifying it, must consider the personalities involved. This consideration requires some understanding of the characters' public personae, their social interactions, and their private passions. Plot, a strong element in its own right, is based on character.

Imagery also consistently reinforces Snow's binocular view of personality. The light of brotherhood wages a never-ending Manichaean conflict with the dark of private estrangement. Windows may be lit, inviting people to "come home" to social involvement, but they often walk the dark streets, locked out in their lonely individuality.

Much of Snow's style also reflects his view of personality. E. A. Levenston, in a careful study of Snow's sentence structure (*ES*, 1974), has noticed the prevalence of qualifying "interrupters." Many of these are a result of Snow's comparing the particular to the general, one person's qualities to many people's. Expressions such as "very few men, George least of all" or "Roy was not a snob, no man was less so," run throughout his work.

Thus, Snow was consistent in his craft. If this consistency imposed some limitations on his achievements, it also provided a valuable unity to his whole literary corpus.

Death Under Sail · For reasons that he later described as "obscure," Snow "signalled" that he intended to abandon his scientific career by writing "a stylised, artificial detective story very much in the manner of the day." *Death Under Sail* is a competent example of this form; it remains quite readable and in some ways foreshadows his more significant work. Told in the first person (curiously, for a book by a twenty-six-year-old, the narrator is sixty-three), it employs light and dark and also water imagery; it includes a political discussion regarding class society being justified through the ranks of the elite being open to talent; and it is concerned with friendship and the "generation gap." More important, the plot hinges on character. While the novel's characterization is relatively superficial, it involves both social character, as seen in the interaction of a small group (the narrator, the detective, and the suspects), and the individual psychology of concealed motives. It is thus typical of Snow's novels, most of which have the element of a suspense story based on the two sides, public and private, of personality.

New Lives for Old · Snow's second published novel, *New Lives for Old*, is the weakest of his whole canon, but it is not without its virtues. The story involves the discovery of a rejuvenating process and the subsequent questions of whether the process will be suppressed, its effects on the love lives of some of the characters, and the political implications of the discovery. These three questions are not well unified; instead of integrating the love interest and the politics, in this one instance Snow treats them as essentially separate stories, at the expense of both. The love story in the middle section becomes tedious; in the last section of the book Snow, atypically, lets a political interest stifle the story. The first part of the book, however, is fairly successful. Here, the plot is related to character, social interactions, private motivations, and moral decisions. Snow is doing what he does best. The falling-off of the work after its relatively effective beginning, however, justifies his decision not to have it reprinted; it is now a difficult book to obtain.

The Search · His third published novel, *The Search*, was slightly revised and reprinted twenty-four years after its first appearance. It is generally superior to the first two novels and more easily related to the *Strangers and Brothers* series, especially *Time of Hope* and *Homecoming*. Although Snow warns the reader, in his preface to the 1958 edition, that the book's narrator and protagonist, Arthur Miles, is "not much like" Snow himself, clearly there is an autobiographical element in the story of a poor boy's using his talent, determination, and scholarships to make a career in science, later to abandon it to turn to writing. The book was praised for its accurate picture of what it is like to be a scientist; in fact, very little scientific activity per se is present. Rather, professional concerns, ambitions, the relation between love and career, and the decisions made by men in committees constitute the basic material of the book. The protagonist might just as easily be a barrister as a scientist. Indeed, *The Search*, while a worthwhile book in its own right, can be seen as a trying out of the material that Snow was to go on to develop in his series. The defects of *The Search* result primarily from attempting to try out too much at once; the book's construction becomes somewhat confused. The virtues arise from Snow's basing his work on personal experience; he employed, more thoroughly than in his first two published novels, his skill in showing the interconnections of the personal and public aspects of personality.

The favorable reception given to *The Search* certainly encouraged Snow to continue his career as a novelist; within a year of its publication, he conceived of the series on which his reputation rests. He must have made various plans for the series as a whole; the first volume, however, did not appear until 1940, six years after *The Search*. Writing a *roman-fleuve*, as opposed to a series of individual novels, presents an author with certain problems and various opportunities. While Snow avoided some of the pitfalls, such as narrative inconsistency, he failed to take advantage of some of the potentialities of the form. The overall pattern of this series is more blurred than it need have been. This is indicated by the order in which the books were published; it is not the essentially chronological order of the "Omnibus Edition," published after the series was concluded. While this authorial rearrangement must be accepted, the fact that Snow did not originally insist on it suggests a certain random quality to the series' organization as first conceived of and executed. Furthermore, proposed systems of classification of the books within the series—as, for example, novels of "observed experience" and of "direct experience," or novels dealing with individuals, groups, or a mixture of both—while useful, fail to make clear a compelling pattern.

Indeed, the individual volumes of the series, with the possible exception of the final *Last Things*, stand on their own and easily can be enjoyed separately. That is not to say that nothing is gained by reading them all in the order that they appear in the "Omnibus Edition." As compared, however, to a work such as Anthony Powell's *roman-fleuve, A Dance to the Music of Time* (1951-1975), *Strangers and Brothers* fails to develop the potential cumulative effect of a series.

The series form does allow the overlapping of incident and the "resonance" between events as seen and felt by the narrator, Lewis Eliot. Snow has an interesting concept here but he does too little with it. The reader does not, as in some of the novels of Joyce Cary, see the same events through different eyes; rather, one is given different accounts by a relatively consistent Eliot. The result is that events described for the second time sometimes bore the reader; at other times the reader feels cheated by the inadequacy of the first account. Only occasionally does the technique work well, as, for example, in the two accounts, in *The Light and the Dark* and *The Masters*, of Roy Calvert's giving of a self-damning paper to Winslow. The first account omits material in order to focus on Calvert; subsequently, as one learns of the larger implications of the act, it takes on new meaning.

The Strangers and Brothers series · More obvious benefits of a series novel are present in *Strangers and Brothers*; the reader observes more characters, over a longer period of time, than would normally be possible in a single volume. Snow, however, possibly in the interest of verisimilitude, does relatively little with his opportunity. Roy Calvert is killed off, George Passant's change is not traced; one does see more of Martin Eliot and Francis Getliffe, but their developments, such as they are, have little drama. There is little in Snow corresponding to the surprises that Powell gives the reader when, for example, his villain, Widmerpool, makes one of his sudden appearances. Only quite rarely does Snow make effective use of surprise, as when the elderly Hector Rose is found to have acquired a younger, sexy wife.

The time span of the series does, however, allow Snow to present the succession of generations, and he does a fine job of suggesting how childhood experiences affect parents as they react to their own children and their friends' children. The parents' point of view is an important part of human experience, infrequently treated in fiction; here again, in presenting parental love, Snow effectively filled a vacuum.

A more fundamental aspect of the *roman-fleuve* is the development of the narrator. Lewis Eliot does change, both in his attitudes and in his style, becoming more ironic in the later volumes. Looking back on earlier events, such as his support of Jago in *The Masters*, he recognizes his errors. While Eliot's development adds interest to the whole series, it would be difficult to maintain that this interest is central.

There are two final aspects of a series novel that make *Strangers and Brothers* something other than eleven separate books—repetition and thematic development. The former is a two-edged device. Any reader of the whole series will be struck by the frequent repetition of certain phrases, sententious remarks, images, and tricks of style, and can readily assemble a list. Are the values of the repetition—interesting variations on a theme and a sense of continuity—greater than the drawback of monotony? In Snow's case, it is something of a toss-up. On balance, although many readers may be inclined to say "Oh no! Not another lighted window," the recurring images of light and darkness do form a pattern that unifies the series and reinforces its themes.

Finally, there is theme. Snow himself, in a note preceding *The Conscience of the Rich*, indicated the importance of recurring themes, including "possessive love" and love of, and renunciation of, power. The list could be easily expanded; as has been indicated, the title of the series itself points to a fundamental thematic concern. By seeing these various themes dramatized through different characters in differing circumstances, and learning Lewis Eliot's reactions, the reader certainly gains a perspective that would be impossible in a single volume. Thematic perspective, then, provides the most convincing justification for Snow's series. It is a sufficient justification; the whole is greater than the sum of the parts. That Snow's strength lay more in characterization than thematic presentation may account for the occasional failures of the series.

A brief discussion of three of the eleven novels of the series may serve to suggest aspects of the volumes considered as individual works. *Time of Hope* is both an early novel and one that focuses upon Lewis Eliot; *The Masters*, generally the most highly regarded of the series, is from the middle period and has a "collective hero"; *Corridors of Power*, a later novel, centers on a protagonist other than Eliot.

Time of Hope · *Time of Hope* was the third volume in the series; in terms of internal chronology, however, it comes first, dealing with the years 1914 to 1933, during which Lewis Eliot matures from a boy of nine to an established barrister, involved in an "impossible" marriage. Strongly unified by its plot, it is perhaps the most emotionally moving volume of the whole series, and one of the more successful.

Indicative of Snow's central concern for the interconnections of the public and private aspects of character, the title refers both to the hope for a better society that Lewis Eliot shares with George Passant's group and to the hero's private ambitions. Asked what he wants from life, Eliot, in a phrase he returns to much later in the series, replies that he wants to see a better world, spend his life not unknown, and gain love.

The suspense in the novel is based on the question of whether Eliot will succeed, whether he will at least be started on the road to realizing these hopes. The conflict and tension behind this question provide the angst that contrasts to the hope. The book begins with a "homecoming," dreaded by the young Eliot. (In a clear parallel with Marcel Proust, Snow picks this up at the start of the very last volume of the series.) Just as he had reason to fear this first homecoming, Eliot later dreads subsequent returns to the woman he manages to marry. Eliot's success is mingled with failure. Through a combination of his "nature," which gives him the drive to struggle, and his social "character," which wins him the help of George Passant, Eliot's "personality" wins through on the public level: He succeeds in becoming a barrister. On the personal level, however, while he "succeeds" in marrying Sheila, his possessive love evokes no response; his marriage is personally disastrous and a handicap to his career.

Snow in *Time of Hope* thus successfully utilizes his approach to character and his recurring themes in a self-contained story, but one which also prepares for subsequent volumes. His techniques in this volume are typical of the series: The imagery of light and darkness prevails; secondary characters, such as Herbert Getliffe, the barrister under whom Eliot trains, are well drawn; the "nature" of a major character is presented as a *donneé*. Not being shown what makes her the strange person she is, one must take Sheila's problems as given. Fortunately for the story, it is easier to do so than to accept Roy Calvert's inherent depression in *The Light and the Dark*. As a *Bildungsroman*, *Time of Hope* is more conventional than the majority of the volumes in the series. Consequently, it is both one of the more satisfactory of Snow's novels and one of the less distinctively interesting.

The Masters · While *Time of Hope* has a clear protagonist, *The Masters*, the first volume in the revised series, has no one hero. Snow is particularly good at dealing with interactions within a group, and *The Masters* has been the most highly regarded of his novels. The title refers to two "masters" or heads of a college; after the first one dies, a new one must be elected. It is on this election, involving the votes of thirteen Fellows of the college, that the plot centers. The election comes down to two candidates, Jago and Crawford. While Lewis Eliot, now one of the Fellows, supports Jago, and while the reader's sympathies are involved on this side, Snow is careful to avoid making the choice one between good and evil. There are very few outright villains in Snow's novels, and Crawford is certainly not one. Politically on the left, but personally not so well suited for the mastership, he is contrasted to Jago, whom Eliot finds less appealing politically but much more appealing as a man. Thus, the issue is essentially between personal "nature" and public "character." The different Fellows line up on this basis, thereby reflecting their own natures and characters; their ultimate votes demonstrate the balance of these two aspects of "personality."

Interestingly, given Snow's famous dispute, following the publication of the *The Masters*, over "the two cultures," the literary and the scientific, one might see Jago, a scholar of English literature, as the humanists' candidate, and Crawford, a member of the Royal Society, as the scientists'. Snow, opposed to the split between the "cultures," does not have the Fellows vote on the basis of this split. Walter Luke, a scientist, judges by nature and sticks with Jago. Francis Getliffe, also a scientist, although recognizing Jago's virtues, is motivated by "public" principle and supports Crawford. Eustace Pilbrow, a literary scholar, agrees with Getliffe. Nightingale, another scientist, jealous of Crawford's professional success, initially supports Jago. Paradoxically, Despard-Smith, because he identifies with Jago, supports Crawford.

Having established the initial lineup of votes, Snow skillfully shows the interactions of motives that cause some of them to shift. One particularly important consideration is the question of Jago's wife; her character, thought to be unsuitable for that of a Master's spouse, becomes an issue in the election. The personal issue here involves another form of "possessive love" and sets up a "resonance" for Eliot, who is ambivalently trapped in his marriage to Sheila. Snow handles the development of the plot and the suspense leading to the election quite effectively. In bringing so many insightful changes on the interactions of the personalities within a small group, Snow wrote what may be his own masterpiece.

In the later volumes of the series, Eliot moves from college to national and interna-tional political maneuvers; the implications are that there is not that much difference. Nevertheless, the "Tolstoyan" view of history—that individuals are secondary to the larger forces of history, which is explicitly mentioned more than once in the series—is more pronounced in the later volumes. Snow suggests that with other people, probably the same policies would be carried out, the same forces would operate. Thus, the *mechanisms* of politics are of primary interest, but to understand them, one must understand the people who work and are worked by them. As Snow once said, one must understand how the world "ticks" if one is to change it for the better.

Corridors of Power · *Corridors of Power*, the ninth volume in the series, gives the reader a picture of how the high-level decision making that he also described in *The New Men* and questioned in *Science and Government* (1961) does operate. However deterministic its underlying historical philosophy, the novel supports the statement of one of its characters that what is important is how something is done, who it is done by, and when it is done.

The story centers on Roger Quaife, a politician committed to an "enlightened" view of the use of atomic weapons. Once again, one sees both the public and private side of a protagonist, the "nature" and "character" that interact to form Quaife's "personality"; again, however, the nature is essentially a *donneé*–Quaife is to be taken as found. Ostensibly happy in his marriage, Quaife has a mistress; she is a factor, although not a decisive one, in his political career. Snow is quite good at showing the interactions of career considerations and more personal feelings within the triangle composed of Quaife; his wife, Caro; and his mistress, Ellen. Sex is seen as a *relationship*, social as well as emotional and physical. In order to present this relationship, however, verisimilitude must be stretched a bit, because Lewis Eliot, the narrator, has to be in places and hear confidences from which one would expect him to be barred. Not only does Eliot learn much about private lives, but also he is rather surprisingly ubiquitous at political councils. Here, in describing some of the behind-the-scenes maneuvers, Snow is quite effective, as he is with the presentation of secondary characters, such as the member of Parliament, "Sammikins," and the important civil servant, Hector Rose.

After the completion and revision of the *Strangers and Brothers* series, Snow not only worked on biographical studies–*Trollope* (1975), *The Realists* (1978), *The Physicists* (1981)–but also continued his novel writing. Although the final volume in the series, *Last Things*, was diffuse in plotting, he returned, in his final novels, to the use of a strong plot line. Both *The Malcontents* and *A Coat of Varnish* are forms of the "whodunit," and *In Their Wisdom*, like *The Sleep of Reason*, maintains the reader's interest in the outcome of a law case.

The Malcontents · *The Malcontents* received generally poor reviews. It does have obvious weaknesses; the dialogue, usually one of Snow's stronger points, is somewhat unconvincing. Well attuned to the talk of his cohorts, Snow's ear for the speech of contemporary youth was less acute. A more serious defect is related to the mystery-story requirement of providing a goodly number of suspects. Too many characters are introduced at the beginning; the reader has an initial problem in differentiating them, and the book gets off to a slow start. Once the story is underway, however, the narrative interest is strong. It involves the interaction of a group of seven young people, planning to take action against the establishment. One of them is known to be an informer. Typically for a Snow novel, to appreciate the narrative fully one must consider the formative aspects of each individual's personality. Class background, family relations, ideological positions, and love interests all enter in. Diffused through seven characters, however, Snow's analysis of these factors is somewhat superficial, with the exception of Stephen Freer, whose relationship to the older generation is presented with sensitivity. An underlying sympathy for the ends, if not the means, of the young radicals informs much of the book. This sympathy, while somewhat Olympian, avoids being patronizing and becomes one of the novel's virtues.

In Their Wisdom · *In Their Wisdom* is a more successful work. Again, to develop narrative interest, a problem is posed. In this instance, it involves an argument over a will and the results of a trial over the disputed legacy. Just as the reader's sympathy is involved, in *The Masters*, on Jago's side, here there is no question of whom to support in the contest. Julian, a selfish and opportunistic young man, is Snow's closest approach to a clear villain. By simplifying some of the characters, Snow is able to devote more attention to the others. Jenny is particularly interesting, different from characters in Snow's earlier books. In showing her life of genteel poverty and the effect upon her of the trial and its outcome, Snow once again effectively intertwines the personal and the public. Although it devotes an excessive amount of space to the House of Lords, *In Their Wisdom* is one of Snow's more successful novels.

A Coat of Varnish · His last novel, *A Coat of Varnish*, was a return to the detective-story genre of his first book. A less pure example of this genre than *Death Under Sail*, however, it is somewhat unsatisfactorily considered simply as a mystery. The title refers to a line within the book, to the effect that civilization is a thin coat of varnish over barbarism, a notion relevant also to *The Sleep of Reason*. A fairly interesting cast of characters is introduced, but none of them is treated with the depth of analysis of which Snow was capable. Here, character is secondary to plot, and plot itself is used to comment on society. To try to work out who is guilty, one must understand motives: money, sex, and power. In understanding these motives, one gains, Snow expects, an understanding of society. Although this is one of Snow's weaker novels, certainly not ending his career triumphantly, it does manage a degree of fulfillment of the Horatian formula, to delight and to instruct.

Perhaps one should ask for no more. Throughout his career as a novelist, Snow, although with varying degrees of success, never failed to provide a number of intelligent readers with these twin satisfactions. This may not put him in the ranks of a Leo Tolstoy or a Proust; it is, nevertheless, no small accomplishment.

William B. Stone

Other major works

PLAYS: *A View over the Bridge*, pr. 1950; *The Supper Dance*, pb. 1951 (with Pamela Hansford Johnson); *Family Party*, pb. 1951 (with Johnson); *Spare the Rod*, pb. 1951 (with Johnson); *To Murder Mrs. Mortimer*, pb. 1951 (with Johnson); *The Pigeon with the Silver Foot*, pb. 1951 (with Johnson); *Her Best Foot Forward*, pb. 1951 (with Johnson); *The Public Prosecutor*, pr. 1967 (with Johnson; adaptation).

NONFICTION: *Richard Aldington: An Appreciation*, 1938; *Writers and Readers of the Soviet Union*, 1943; *The Two Cultures and the Scientific Revolution*, 1959 (revised as *Two Cultures and a Second Look*, 1964); *The Moral Un-Neutrality of Science*, 1961; *Science and Government*, 1961; *A Postscript to Science and Government*, 1962; *Magnanimity*, 1962; *C. P. Snow: A Spectrum, Science, Criticism, Fiction*, 1963; *Variety of Men*, 1967; *The State of Siege*, 1969; *Public Affairs*, 1971; *Trollope: His Life and Art*, 1975; *The Realists*, 1978; *The Physicists*, 1981.

Bibliography

De la Mothe, John. *C. P. Snow and the Struggle of Modernity*. Austin: University of Texas Press, 1992. Chapters on Snow's view of literature, science, and the modern mind and his career as writer and public intellectual. Includes extensive notes and bibliography.

Karl, Frederick S. *C. P. Snow: The Politics of Conscience*. Carbondale: Southern Illinois University Press, 1963. A generally useful study of Snow that analyzes his novels up to and including *The Affair*. Some of the statements about him are misleading, however, and should be read with caution.

Ramanathan, Suguna. *The Novels of C. P. Snow: A Critical Introduction*. London: Macmillan, 1978. A fresh, sympathetic assessment of Snow that discusses all of his novels save his two earliest works, *Death Under Sail* and *New Lives for Old*. Notes Snow's "imaginative impulse," his understanding of the changing social scene in England over a span of fifty years, and the gradual change in his outlook from hopefulness to doom. Upholds Snow as being free from fanaticism. A recommended reading.

Shusterman, David. *C. P. Snow*. Rev. ed. Boston: Twayne, 1991. A competent, compact study of Snow, including his early life, the controversies surrounding his nonfiction, and his literary output. Contains an in-depth analysis of the *Strangers and Brothers* series of novels, noting their interest apart from their literary value. Includes a chronology and a select bibliography.

Snow, C. P. *C. P. Snow: A Spectrum, Science, Criticism, Fiction*. Edited by Stanley Weintraub. New York: Charles Scribner's Sons, 1963. A useful introduction to Snow's life and works. The commentary covers many aspects of his fiction, criticism, and writings on science.

Thale, Jerome. *C. P. Snow*. New York: Charles Scribner's Sons, 1965. Considered an excellent secondary source on Snow that is both readable and informative. Presents Snow's work up to and including 1964. Discusses his nonfiction writings, among which are his two controversial works *The Two Cultures and the Scientific Revolution* and *Science and Government*.

Muriel Spark

Born: Edinburgh, Scotland; February 1, 1918

Principal long fiction · *The Comforters*, 1957; *Robinson*, 1958; *Memento Mori*, 1959; *The Ballad of Peckham Rye*, 1960; *The Bachelors*, 1960; *The Prime of Miss Jean Brodie*, 1961; *The Girls of Slender Means*, 1963; *The Mandelbaum Gate*, 1965; *The Public Image*, 1968; *The Driver's Seat*, 1970; *Not to Disturb*, 1971; *The Hothouse by the East River*, 1973; *The Abbess of Crewe: A Modern Morality Tale*, 1974; *The Takeover*, 1976; *Territorial Rights*, 1979; *Loitering with Intent*, 1981; *The Only Problem*, 1984; *A Far Cry from Kensington*, 1988; *Symposium*, 1990; *The Novels of Muriel Spark*, 1995; *Reality and Dreams*, 1996; *Aiding and Abetting*, 2000.

Other literary forms · In addition to her novels, Muriel Spark produced a sizable amount of work in the genres of poetry, the short story, drama, biography, and criticism. Her volumes of poetry include *The Fanfarlo and Other Verse* (1952) and *Collected Poems I* (1967). Her first collection of short stories, entitled *The Go-Away Bird and Other Stories*, appeared in 1958, followed by *Collected Stories I* (1967) and *The Stories of Muriel Spark* (1985). *Voices at Play*, a collection of short stories and radio plays, appeared in 1961, and a play, *Doctors of Philosophy*, was first performed in London in 1962. Spark's literary partnership with Derek Stanford resulted in their editing *Tribute to Wordsworth* (1950), a collection of essays on the centenary of the poet's death, and *My Best Mary: The Selected Letters of Mary Shelley* (1953). Spark and Stanford also edited *Letters of John Henry Newman* (1957). Spark produced a study of Mary Shelley, *Child of Light: A Reassessment of Mary Wollstonecraft Shelley* (1951, revised as *Mary Shelley*, 1987), and of *John Masefield* (1953). Spark also edited *The Brontë Letters* (1954; pb. in U.S. as *The Letters of the Brontës: A Selection*, 1954).

Achievements · Critical opinion about Spark's status as a novelist is sharply divided. In general, her work is less highly valued by American critics; Frederick Karl, for example, dismissed her work as being "light to the point of froth" and said that it has "virtually no content." English critics such as Frank Kermode, Malcolm Bradbury, and David Lodge, on the other hand, would consider Spark a major contemporary novelist. Kermode complimented her on being "obsessed" with novelistic form, called *The Mandelbaum Gate* a work of "profound virtuosity," and considered her to be a "difficult and important artist." Bradbury, who regarded Spark as an "interesting, and a very amusing, novelist" from the beginning of her career, later added his assessment that she is also a "very high stylist" whose work in the novella shows a precision and economy of form and style. In a reassessment of *The Prime of Miss Jean Brodie*, Lodge commented on the complex structure of the novel and Spark's successful experimentation with authorial omniscience.

Spark is known for being able to combine popular success with critical acclaim. In 1951, she received her first literary award, the *Observer* Story Prize for the Christmas story "The Seraph and the Zambesi." A radio drama based on *The Ballad of Peckham Rye* won the Italia Prize in 1962, and in the same year she was named Fellow of the Royal Society of Literature. In 1965, Spark received the prestigious James Tait Black

Memorial Prize for Fiction for the *The Mandelbaum Gate*. Spark earned the Order of the British Empire in 1967.

Biography · Muriel Sarah Spark was born in Edinburgh, Scotland, on February 1, 1918, of a Jewish father, Bernard Camberg, and an English mother, Sarah Uezzell Camberg. She attended James Gillespie's School for Girls in Edinburgh, an experience that later formed the background for *The Prime of Miss Jean Brodie*. She lived in Edinburgh until 1937, when she married S. O. Spark and moved to Africa. During the next two years she gave birth to her son, Robin, and divorced Spark, who had become abusive and was showing signs of mental illness. She moved into an apartment with a young widow and her child and wrote poems and plays while waiting for the long process of her divorce to conclude. Her life in Rhodesia and South Africa provided background material for some of her earliest successful short stories, such as "The Portobello Road" and "The Seraph and the Zambesi." The onset of World War II interfered with her plans to return to Scotland, and she worked at a number of jobs before managing to book a passage home in 1944; because there were travel restrictions for children, her son was unable to join her for a year and a half.

During her sojourn as young divorcee awaiting the arrival of her child, she moved to London to find work, and she lived at the Helena Club, which had been endowed by Princess Helena, the daughter of Queen Victoria, for "ladies from good families of modest means who are obliged to pursue an occupation in London." Spark's experiences at the Helena Club with other young women earning a living in a big city became the background for her novel *The Girls of Slender Means*.

From 1944 to 1946, she worked in the Political Intelligence Department of the British Foreign Office, an experience she later drew upon when writing *The Hothouse by the East River*. Her interest in poetry led to her serving as General Secretary of the Poetry Society in London from 1947 to 1949 and as editor of the *Poetry Review*; in 1949, she introduced a short-lived journal entitled *Forum Stories and Poems*. In the 1950's, she began a successful career as a critic and editor which included books on William Wordsworth, Mary Shelley, Emily Brontë, John Masefield, and John Henry Newman, publishing several of these works with her literary partner and friend Derek Stanford.

The major turning point in Spark's career as a writer occurred in 1954, when she converted to Roman Catholicism. Brought up in the Presbyterian religion, she said that she had "no clear beliefs at all" until 1952, when she became "an Anglican intellectually speaking," although she did not formally join the Anglican Church until late in 1953. The Church of England was, however, a halfway house for Spark, who was an Anglo-Catholic for only nine months before her conversion to Roman Catholicism. She believed that the writings of John Henry Newman were an important factor in her move to the Catholic Church. Her conversion initially caused her a great deal of emotional suffering, and she said that her mind was, for a period of time, "far too crowded with ideas, all teeming in disorder." This feeling of mental chaos gave way later to what she called "a complete reorganization" of her mind that enabled her to begin writing fiction. Several persons encouraged her to produce a novel, among them Graham Greene and Macmillan and Company, which was looking for new writers at the time; the result was *The Comforters*.

In 1961, Spark traveled to Jerusalem to research the background for *The Mandelbaum Gate*, and in 1964 she moved from her home in London to New York. She lived for less than a year in an apartment close to the United Nations Building, a location that later became the setting for *The Hothouse by the East River.* In 1967, she was awarded the Order of the British Empire and left England to settle in Italy. In 1982, after fifteen years in Rome, she moved to Tuscany.

Analysis · Muriel Spark frequently used the word "minor" to describe her achievement as a novelist, a term which, in her vocabulary, is not as derogatory as it may at first appear. Believing that the artist is by definition a "minor public servant," Spark claimed that she chose to write "minor novels deliberately." This characterization of the artist and of her own intentions as a writer reflects her concerns about the novel as a form and the creative process in general, issues which are present throughout her work. She admitted that while writing her first novel, *The Comforters,* she had difficulty resigning herself to the fact that she was writing a novel, a genre which, in her opinion, was a "lazy way of writing poetry." For Spark at that time, poetry was the only true literature, while the novel was an "inferior way of writing" whose "aesthetic validity" was very much in doubt. Although she apparently revised her earlier low estimation of the novel, she said that she always considered herself a poet rather than a novelist and believed that her novels are "the novels of a poet."

Spark's distrust of the novel form also results from her suspicions about fiction's relationship to truth; she said that she was interested in "absolute truth" and that fiction is a "kind of parable" from which a "kind of truth" emerges which should not be confused with fact. The truth that the novel can embody is similar to her definition of "legend" in *Emily Brontë: Her Life and Work.* Speaking of the literary legends that surround a writer such as Emily Brontë, she said that these stories, though not literally true, are "the repository of a vital aspect of truth" which should be accorded respect in their own right. It remains imperative, however, for writers and readers to discriminate among types of truth and between life and art, a discrimination that Charmian Colston, the aged novelist in *Memento Mori,* is capable of making. She tells another character that "the art of fiction is very like the practice of deception," and, when asked if the practice of deception in life is also an art, replies, "In life . . . everything is different. Everything is in the Providence of God." Spark, who was careful to maintain this distinction in her statements about her work, described her own novels as a "pack of lies."

Caroline Rose in *The Comforters,* who shares this distrust of fiction, struggles against being a character in a novel because she resents being manipulated by the novelist. At one point, she describes the author

Jerry Bauer

of the fiction as an "unknown, possibly sinister being." The writer's "sinister" nature results from his or her ability to create fictions that are imaginative versions and extensions of the truth rather than the truth itself; perhaps more important, the novelist deprives his or her characters of their free will and independence. As Patricia Stubbs observed, Spark perceives a parallel between God and the novelist, and the act of creating fiction is, in a sense, "dabbling in the devil's work."

As a result, Spark's novels are filled with would-be artists and artist-figures, people who attempt to create fictions in real life and consequently bring about discord and mischief. In *The Prime of Miss Jean Brodie*, Miss Brodie begins to view the people around her as characters in a story she is creating and attempts to bring about sexual pairings and heroic deeds in her self-made "plot" with disastrous results. Both Alec Warner in *Memento Mori* and Dougal Douglas in *The Ballad of Peckham Rye* are involved in "research" into the lives of the people around them; Douglas carries his curiosity about others a step further, fictionalizing an autobiography for an actress and later becoming the author of "a lot of cock-eyed books." In two later novels, *The Public Image* and *Territorial Rights*, fictions are devised even more consciously—and are potentially more dangerous. In *The Public Image*, film actress Annabel Christopher is, for the most part, merely the product of a clever publicity campaign with its accompanying lies, distortions, and omissions. After her husband's suicide, she becomes the victim of his well-planned attempt to destroy her career, for he has left behind a group of letters that would impugn her sexual morality and destroy her carefully devised "public image." In *Territorial Rights*, Robert Leaver stages his own kidnapping and sends threatening letters filled with truth and lies to his family and friends. In addition, he leaves fragments of a "novel" he is supposedly writing that contain a sensational mixture of fact and fiction which could hurt many of the people around him. Just as these characters are guilty of trying to manipulate reality by inserting carefully constructed "fictions" into the lives of real people, Sir Quentin Oliver in *Loitering with Intent* overtly plagiarizes a fictional model to accomplish his ends. After reading Fleur Talbot's novel *Warrender Chase*, he begins to orchestrate the lives of the members of the Autobiographical Association according to its plot, an action which causes Fleur to complain that "He's trying to live out my story."

The ubiquitous "listening devices" and spying present in Spark's fiction are another aspect of her fascination with the process of creating fictions. Dougal Douglas, the artist-to-be, sells tape recorders to African witch doctors; the Abbey in *The Abbess of Crewe* is bugged; and Curran in *Territorial Rights* has a sudden moment of paranoia in a restaurant when he wonders if his fellow diners are all spies armed with "eavesdropping devices." As the servants in *Not to Disturb* realize, recording and preserving experience allows the person doing the recording to alter, and, in a sense, to create reality. Armed with tape recorders and cameras, they are busy creating their own version of the events of an evening that culminates in the deaths of the Baron and Baroness Klopstock and their secretary; the servants are artist-figures, manipulating the plot of the story which they will soon sell to the public media. Spark sees the novelist, like the "typing ghost" who plagues Caroline Rose in *The Comforters*, as an eavesdropper who spies upon his characters and then manipulates their actions in order to create a fiction; and she peoples her novels with characters who are also engaged in this process.

Because Spark is so intent upon acknowledging her fiction as fiction, most of her novels are consciously artificial in both form and content. She never had a desire to be a realistic novelist or to write the "long novel"; she said she grew bored writing her only lengthy novel, *The Mandelbaum Gate*, because of its length. Rather, she claimed to speak in a "kind of shorthand" in which the narrative voice is curiously impersonal. Not surprisingly, in several novels, among them *Not to Disturb* and *The Driver's Seat*, she experimented with her own version of the New Novel. In Spark's fiction, however, unlike that of many of the antinovelists, all details, no matter how arbitrary they at first appear, are ultimately significant. In fact, a word that appears throughout her statements about fiction and in her novels is "economy." In *The Takeover*, the narrator mentions the "intuitive artistic sense of economy" that characterizes the creative person, and Spark emphasized her belief that the artist should carefully select only the most appropriate details in order to create meaning.

At the same time, holding the belief that it is "bad manners to inflict emotional involvement on the reader," in her novels the narrator's witty detachment from the subject matter signifies Spark's goal of creating art that remains distanced from the human suffering it presents. Literature, according to her, should not continue to sympathize with the victims of violence and tyranny; art should instead abandon sentimental depictions of the human condition so that it can "ruthlessly mock" the forces which cause the individual to suffer. It is Spark's belief that art needs "less emotion and more intelligence" and should aspire to become an art of satire and ridicule. The world, for Spark, is essentially absurd, and "the rhetoric of our time should persuade us to contemplate the ridiculous nature of the reality before us, and teach us to mock it."

The Comforters · Spark's first novel, *The Comforters*, reflects the two pivotal experiences of her life: her conversion to Roman Catholicism and her change as a writer from poet to novelist. Spark said that in order to overcome her aesthetic skepticism about the novel form, it was necessary for her "to write a novel about somebody writing a novel." In addition, she believed that *The Comforters* is a result of the "complete reorganization" of her mind that followed her conversion and that its theme is "a convert and a kind of psychic upheaval." Caroline Rose, the novel's central character, is in the process of coming to terms with both these issues. A recent convert to Catholicism who dislikes many of her fellow Catholics, Caroline is writing a book called *Form in the Modern Novel* and trying to understand why she has begun to overhear a disembodied "novelist," complete with typewriter, who is writing a novel about her and her friends.

The Comforters is about the battle between the author and her characters, a battle in which Caroline struggles to preserve her free will in the face of the novelist's desire to control the events of the story. Caroline finds the experience of being "written into" someone else's narrative painful, just as her friend Laurence Manders protests that "I dislike being a character in your novel" when he discovers that Caroline is writing fiction that includes the story of their relationship. Caroline believes that it is her "duty" to "hold up the action" of the novel, to "spoil" it, and she asserts her right to make her own decisions, finding, however, that this is usually impossible; the predetermined "plot" of the novelist prevails.

Caroline remains unaware, however, that she in turn is capable of affecting the novel as it is being written. The narrator admits that Caroline's "remarks" continue to interfere with the book and that she does not realize her "constant influence" on the story's development. From Caroline's perspective, she has only partial knowledge of the plot, and she complains that the voices she overhears only give her "small crazy fragments" of a novel in which there may be other characters whom she does not know. In this sense, Caroline is a surrogate for Spark the novelist, a character who "discovers" the plot, as does its creator, while it is being written. As a result, *The Comforters* concludes with Caroline leaving London to write a novel which apparently will be *The Comforters*.

Spark would appear to be working out both the technique and the morality of writing fiction in her first novel. Caroline's fascination with "form in the modern novel" is also Spark's fascination, and Spark writes a story about the problems involved in writing a story: *The Comforters* is about the struggle between the novelist's will to impose form and the continued growth and development of the characters, who begin to become independent entities in the narrative, insisting upon the right to break free of the restraints of plot and situation. One of the reasons Caroline Rose gives for opposing the novelist is that Caroline "happens to be a Christian"; Spark, as a Catholic, is uneasy with the idea of the novelist "playing God" and depriving her characters of choice.

The Comforters is also about Catholicism and the recent convert's attempts to find an identity as a Catholic. Georgina Hogg, the Catholic in the novel whom Caroline particularly despises, symbolizes Caroline's (and Spark's) reservations about individual Catholics. These reservations are not, it should be emphasized, about Catholicism as a religion. Rather, Mrs. Hogg represents a Catholicism which, in the hands of a certain type of individual, becomes simply dogma. Mrs. Hogg, who lacks insight or any true feeling about her religion, uses her sense of self-righteousness to impinge upon the people around her. In the novel, she is called a "sneak," a "subtle tyrant," and a "moral blackmailer," and she is indeed guilty of all these accusations. At one point in the story, Caroline decides that Mrs. Hogg is "not a real-life character . . . merely a gargoyle"; she is so lacking in identity that she literally "disappears" when there are no other people around to perceive her existence. As several characters observe, Georgina Hogg "has no private life," a phrase which ironically underscores her lack of substance as a character and a Catholic.

Mrs. Hogg's lack of identity is a major theme of the novel, and a problem which several other characters share. Helena Manders, when she has a sudden sense of how "exhilarating" it is to be herself, actually perceives her personality as belonging to someone else. Eleanor Hogarth, as Caroline realizes, has completely lost contact with her true personality because she has for so long been satisfied with mimicking others, adopting other roles to play. Caroline's auditory hallucinations are another aspect of this problem, for she feels that her free will as an individual is being taken from her: Is she Caroline Rose, or simply a character in someone else's novel? At the same time, she is obsessed with the identity of what she calls the "typing ghost," at one point making a list entitled *"Possible identity"* which speculates about who the typist-novelist may be—Satan, a hermaphrodite, a woman, or a Holy Soul in Purgatory.

The characters' lack of identity is related to their isolation and inability to communicate with one another. "Is the world," asks Caroline, "a lunatic asylum then? Are we all courteous maniacs discreetly making allowances for everyone else's derangement?" Although she rejects this idea, *The Comforters* certainly depicts a world in which individuals search for an identity while remaining locked into a very subjective set of preconceptions about everything external to them. The way out of this trap, at least for Caroline, is to write a novel, the novel which Spark has actually written. *The Comforters* represents Spark's successful confrontation with and resolution of the issues of Catholicism, creativity, and the novel as a genre. Her interest in the novel as a form and the process of creating fictions has continued throughout her career as a novelist.

The Prime of Miss Jean Brodie · In an interview, Spark said that the eponymous protagonist of *The Prime of Miss Jean Brodie* represents "completely unrealised potentialities," a descriptive phrase which reflects the same ambiguity with which she is treated in the novel. The story of an Edinburgh schoolmistress and her effects on the lives of six of her pupils, *The Prime of Miss Jean Brodie* concentrates on the relationship between Jean Brodie and Sandy Stranger, the student who eventually "betrays" her. Like many other characters in Spark's fiction, Miss Brodie begins to confuse fact and fiction, and it is when Sandy perceives that her teacher has decided that Rose Stanley must begin an affair with art teacher Teddy Lloyd that Sandy realizes that Jean Brodie is no longer playing a game or advancing a theory: "Miss Brodie meant it." As David Lodge notes in his article on the novel in *The Novelist at the Crossroads* (1971), Sandy and Jenny intuitively understand when their fiction, a made-up correspondence between Miss Brodie and music teacher Gordon Lowther, should be buried and forgotten; unlike her students, Jean Brodie does not know when fantasies should be discarded.

In addition to seeing herself as an artist-figure who can manipulate the lives of her students and lovers, Jean Brodie is also guilty, in Sandy's eyes, of serious religious and political errors. Although she has not turned to religion at the time, a very young Sandy is frightened by her vision of all the "Brodie set" in a line headed by their teacher "in unified compliance to the destiny of Miss Brodie, as if God had willed them to birth for that purpose." Later, Sandy is horrified to discover that her former teacher "thinks she is Providence" and that she can see the beginning and the end of all "stories." Jean Brodie's lack of guilt over any of her actions results from her assurance that "God was on her side"; she elects herself to grace with an "exotic suicidal enchantment" which drives her to the excesses that eventually result in her forced retirement. Jean Brodie's view of herself as "above the common moral code," a phrase she applies to Rose, her chosen surrogate for an affair with Teddy Lloyd, is related to her political views as well. An early admirer of Italian Premier Benito Mussolini and German Chancellor Adolf Hitler whom Sandy later characterizes as a "born fascist," she sees herself as duty-bound to shape the personalities and the destinies of the young girls around her. "You are mine," she says to her "set," whom she has chosen to receive what she calls the "fruits of her prime," which will remain with the girls "always," a prophecy which is partially true.

The complexity of *The Prime of Miss Jean Brodie* lies in the fact that Jean Brodie is not simply a villainous character who oversteps her bounds as a teacher and begins to exert a potentially corruptive force on the young people entrusted to her. Although she flirts with fascism (after the war she calls Hitler "rather naughty"), she at the same time encourages a fierce individualism in her chosen students, who, as the headmistress of the Marcia Blaine School for Girls sadly learns, are totally lacking in "team spirit." She makes good her promise to "put old heads on young shoulders" and creates the "capacity for enthusiasm" for knowledge that remains with several of her students for life. The lecture to her girls on her theory of education—"It means a leading out. To me education is a leading out of what is already there in the pupil's soul. . . . Never let it be said that I put ideas into your heads"—is, like the portrait of Jean Brodie that Spark presents in the novel, open to several interpretations. Although in the later years of her prime, Miss Brodie *does* attempt to put "ideas" into the girls' heads, at the same time she bequeaths to her students a knowledge of and sensitivity to art, culture, and ideas that would have been impossible in a more conventional educational situation.

862 Notable British Novelists

Just as *The Prime of Miss Jean Brodie* is about "unrealised potentialities," Miss Brodie also communicates to her students a knowledge of the unlimited potential inherent in all experience. In her late thirties, Jenny Gray has an experience that reawakens a memory of her "sense of the hidden possibility in all things" that she felt as an eleven-year-old student under the tutelage of Jean Brodie. More important, however, is the teacher's influence on Sandy Stranger. In his book on Spark, Derek Stanford said that "Truth, for Muriel Spark, implies rejection," and Sandy laments in the novel that she has had nothing, particularly in the religious realm, to react against or reject. Jean Brodie finally provides this catalyst, and Sandy's decision to "put a stop" to her results from a variety of reasons: her moral indignation over Miss Brodie's "plans" for Rose and Joyce Emily, sexual jealousy of Teddy Lloyd's continued infatuation with her teacher, and her awakening sense of Christian morals.

As an adult, however, Sandy acknowledges that Jean Brodie was her most important formative influence and in a sense responsible for the course her life has taken. Her conversion to Catholicism and taking of the veil are the result of her affair with Teddy Lloyd, an affair she instigates in order to subvert Jean Brodie's plans. Although Spark does not indicate the exact subject of the psychological treatise that has made Sandy famous, other than the fact that it concerns the nature of "moral perception," its title, "The Transfiguration of the Commonplace," reveals that it in some way deals with the mind's ability to alter everyday reality. Clearly, this topic owes a debt to Jean Brodie's communication to her students of the endless "possibilities" that surrounded them and is a reflection of Jean Brodie's constantly changing nature in the novel. The narrator observes that, unlike her colleagues, Miss Brodie is in a "state of fluctuating development"; like her students, her "nature was growing under their eyes, as the girls themselves were under formation." One element of Jean Brodie's "prime" is her nonstatic personality, and the problem, of course, is the direction in which the changes take place. As the narrator notes, "the principles governing the end of her prime would have astonished herself at the beginning of it."

In *The Prime of Miss Jean Brodie*, Spark is at the height of her powers as a novelist, and nowhere else in her fiction is she more in control of her subject. The "flash-forwards" which occur throughout the novel cause the reader to concentrate on the characters' motivations and interrelationships rather than on any intricacies of the plot, and Spark makes use of the principle of "economy" that she so values on almost every page, providing only the most telling details of the story while refraining, for the most part, from any authorial interpretation. In fact, the idea of economy is an important thematic element in the book. Sandy is first fascinated by the economy of Jean Brodie's fusing her tales of her dead lover, Hugh, with her current associations with Gordon Lowther and Teddy Lloyd, and later she is angered and intrigued by the economy of the art teacher's paintings, which make Jean Brodie's students resemble their teacher. When Sandy betrays Miss Brodie to the headmistress, she uses this principle after concluding that "where there was a choice of various courses the most economical was the best." Both in form and style, *The Prime of Miss Jean Brodie* shows Spark utilizing her own "intuitive artistic sense of economy."

The Driver's Seat · In *The Driver's Seat*, Spark writes her revisionist version of the New Novel. She said that she disagreed with the philosophical tenets of the antinovel, and she adopted many of its techniques to prove the invalidity of its philosophy. Although *The Driver's Seat* initially appears to be filled with randomly chosen, objectively described phenomena, ultimately the novel denies the entire concept of contingency.

As Frank Kermode states in *The Sense of an Ending* (1966), Spark's fiction is not about any kind of "brutal chaos" but rather presents a "radically non-contingent reality to be dealt with in purely novelistic terms." Every event, every description becomes, in the light of the ending of *The Driver's Seat*, significant.

The novel concerns a young woman named Lise who leaves her home in northern Europe to travel south. Spark carefully fails to specify which cities are involved in order to create the same impersonal, anonymous air in the novel that characterizes Lise's world in general. The purpose of her journey is to find a man to murder her, and in this story Spark inverts the typical thriller: The "victim" relentlessly stalks her murderer and finally "forces" him to act. Lise, who has abandoned the sterile loneliness of her former existence symbolized by her apartment, which "looks as if it were uninhabited," takes control of her life for the first time and decides to take the most dramatic final step possible. In the opening scene, she shouts at a salesgirl who attempts to sell her a dress made of nonstaining fabric because, having already decided that she is to be stabbed to death, she wishes for clothing that will provide the more lurid touch of bloodstains. At the conclusion of the scene, Lise again shouts at the salesgirl "with a look of satisfaction at her own dominance over the situation," and the remainder of the novel is about Lise's carefully planned murder and the trail of information and clues she leaves for Interpol all across Europe.

Unlike Caroline Rose in *The Comforters*, whose response to being a character in a novel is to write a novel about characters in a novel, Lise actually wrests control of the plot from the narrator, who is forced to admit ignorance of her thoughts and intentions. "Who knows her thoughts? Who can tell?" asks the narrator, who is even unsure as to whether or not Lise tints her hair or the reason she attracts so much attention. As a result, the narrator is forced to give only external information, but this information is, as the reader begins to realize, all pertinent to the outcome of the novel. Only at the conclusion, after Lise's death, does the narrator seem privy to the interior knowledge accessible to the omniscient author.

One of the most important themes in *The Driver's Seat* is, as in many other Spark novels, the inability of people to communicate with one another. In the majority of the conversations, no logical connections are made between the participants, who remain isolated in their own worlds of obsessional concerns. It would even appear that the more sane the individual, the less likely it is that any communication can take place. Instead, it is the more psychotic characters who are capable of nonverbal, intuitive understanding. Lise realizes immediately, as does Richard, that he is the man who is capable of murdering her, and he initially avoids any conversation with her. The three men who do converse with her, Bill, Carlos, and the sickly looking man on the plane, are not, as she phrases it, "her type"; this is because they attempt to communicate verbally with her. As Lise says of the salesman in the department store, "Not my man at all. He tried to get familiar with me. . . . The one I'm looking for will recognize me right away for the woman I am, have no fear of that." The verb "sense," which is used several times in the novel, signifies the subterranean, psychotic apprehension of other people that is the only perception taking place in *The Driver's Seat*.

Although most of Mrs. Friedke's conversations with Lise have the same illogical, uncommunicative structure that characterizes the other dialogues, she does momentarily enter Lise's realm of supernatural perception. She buys a paper knife for her nephew Richard similar to the one Lise decides against purchasing at the beginning of her journey, and this gift becomes the weapon Richard uses to murder Lise. She also prophetically insists that "you and my nephew are meant for each other . . . my dear, you are the person for my nephew." It is at this point that Lise reveals how she will recognize the man for whom she is searching.

In a phrase that tells a great deal about her past life, she says that she will know him not as a feeling of "presence" but as a "lack of absence." Malcolm Bradbury, in his essay on Spark in *Possibilities: Essays on the State of the Novel* (1973), says that Spark's fiction "conveys significant absences, a feeling of omission, and so has considerable resemblances to a good deal of contemporary art, including the *nouveau roman*." Lise's search for a "lack of absence" is a statement about the emptiness and lack of meaning in her own existence and the type of novel Spark has chosen to write about her: The form of the antinovel is used to comment both on the psychosis of the main character and on the failure of the New Novel to deal with the ultimate significance of phenomena. In the New Novel, the present tense frequently signifies the meaningless-ness and ephemerality of events; in *The Driver's Seat*, the present tense is used to create a world of terrifying inevitability in which the smallest details become integral elements in Lise's carefully plotted death.

Spark called *The Driver's Seat* "a study, in a way, of self-destruction" but also admitted that the novel was impossible for her to describe. She said that she became so frightened while writing the story that she was forced to enter a hospital in order to complete it. The fear the novel inspired in her—and many readers—cannot be explained simply by Lise's self-destructiveness; Lise's decision to assert herself, to play god with her life independent of any control by the novelist or a higher power, also contributes to the frightening dimension of the novel. Spark, who expressed a belief that "events are providentially ordered," creates a character who decides to *become* providence and the author of her own story; unlike Jean Brodie, who mistak-enly thinks she can see the "beginning and the end" of all stories, Lise successfully orchestrates the novel's conclusion.

Loitering with Intent · In *Loitering with Intent*, Spark's heroine, novelist Fleur Talbot, frequently quotes from Benvenuto Cellini's *The Autobiography of Benvenuto Cellini* (wr. 1558-1562): "All men . . . who have done anything of merit, or which verily has a semblance of merit . . . should write the tale of their life with their own hand." *Loitering with Intent* is the fictional autobiography of its "author," Fleur Talbot, and a meditation by Spark on her own career as a novelist; it is, in addition, a meditation on the creative process and the relationship between fiction and autobiography. Spark shows that she has come a long way from her early distrust of the novel: *Loitering with Intent* is a paean to the artistic, fiction-making sensibility. Although the habitual tension between life and art and the danger of confusing the two are still present in this novel, Spark firmly comes down on the side of art, defending it against individuals who would seek to "steal" its myth and pervert its truth.

Fleur Talbot frequently comments on "how wonderful it is to be an artist and a woman in the twentieth century." At the conclusion, she admits that she has been "loitering with intent"; that is, she has used her observations about the people and events around her as fictional material, taking joy in both the comic and tragic occurrences in the lives of the individuals who become characters in her own "autobiography." "I rejoiced in seeing people as they were," she says, and the word "rejoice" occurs many times in the novel as Fleur repeatedly uses Cellini's phrase, saying that she "went on her way rejoicing." In her later life she is accused by her friend Dottie of "wriggling out of real life," but Fleur makes no apologies for the way in which she handles the relationship between her life and her creativity; instead,

Loitering with Intent calls into question the use "real" people make of the fictions of others.

Fleur becomes the secretary of Sir Quentin Oliver, head of the spurious Autobiographical Association he has formed in order to bring people together to compose their memoirs. Like the character of Warrender Chase in the novel Fleur is in the process of completing, Sir Quentin begins to exert a devastating influence on the Association's members, psychologically manipulating them not for blackmailing purposes but for the enjoyment of pure power. Instead of encouraging them to fictionalize their autobiographies, as Fleur attempts to do, Sir Quentin begins to fictionalize their lives with tragic results. Fleur says that

> I was sure . . . that Sir Quentin was pumping something artificial into their real lives instead of on paper. Presented fictionally, one could have done something authentic with that poor material. But the inducing them to express themselves in life resulted in falsity.

Fiction, when acknowledged as fiction, can help the individual to comprehend reality more clearly, as Fleur notes when she tells a friend that she will have to write several more chapters of *Warrender Chase* before she will be able to understand the events of the Autobiographical Association. In the same way, she says that one can better know one's friends if they are imaginatively pictured in various situations. Sir Quentin, however, inserts "fictions," frequently stories and events taken from Fleur's novel, into the lives of the Association's members.

The relationship between Sir Quentin and Fleur symbolizes the battle between life and art that is waged in *Loitering with Intent,* for Fleur accuses him of "using, stealing" her myth, "appropriating the spirit" of her legend, and trying to "live out the story" she creates in *Warrender Chase*. Although she believes that it is wrong for Sir Quentin to take her "creation" from her, she in turn believes that he may well be a creation of hers, particularly when he begins to resemble her character Warrender Chase as the story progresses. She takes pride in saying that she could almost "have invented" Sir Quentin and that at times she feels as if she *has* invented him; in fact, this feeling so persists that she begins to wonder if it is Warrender Chase who is the "real man" on whom she has partly based the fictional character of Sir Quentin. From Fleur's point of view, this kind of inversion of life and art is necessary and productive for the artistic process and is not dangerous because it results in a bona fide fiction that acknowledges itself as fiction; Sir Quentin's appropriation of her "myth," however, is dangerous because he refuses to acknowledge the fictiveness of his creation. One irony of this situation is editor Revisson Doe's refusal to publish *Warrender Chase* because it too closely resembles the activities of the Autobiographical Association: Sir Quentin's literal and figurative theft of Fleur's novel almost results in its never becoming a work of art available to the public.

The relationship between life and art has another dimension in *Loitering with Intent.* In this novel, Spark is also concerned with the psychic potential of the artist, the ability of the creative imagination to foresee the future in the process of creating fictions. Just as Fleur remarks that writing a novel or imagining her friends in fictional situations helps her to understand them better, so does the artist often predict the future while constructing a work of art. At the end of the novel, Dottie admits that Fleur had "foreseen it all" in *Warrender Chase*, and the events of *Loitering with Intent* do bear an eerie resemblance to the plot of Fleur's first novel. In her book on Emily Brontë, Spark said that "Poetic experience is . . . such that it may be prophetic." In *Loitering with Intent*, Fleur uses reality as raw material for her novel, while Sir Quentin attempts to use art to tamper with the lives of real people; at another level, however, Fleur's poetic imagination perceives and creates future events.

Loitering with Intent also permits Spark to look back on her life as a novelist and defend many of her fictional techniques. Fleur's philosophy of art is, to a great degree, Spark's philosophy, and Fleur's descriptions and explanations of her craft could easily be addressed by Spark directly to her readers. Like Spark, Fleur is a believer in economy in art, observing "how little one needs . . . to convey the lot, and how a lot of words . . . can convey so little." Fleur does not believe in authorial statements about the motives of her characters, or in being "completely frank" with the reader; in fact, "complete frankness is not a quality that favours art." She defends herself against the charge of writing novels that are called "exaggerated" by critics and states that her fiction presents "aspects of realism." The novel, she believes, is not a documentary transcription of reality but should always seek to transform its subject. "I'm an artist, not a reporter," she informs her readers.

Fleur also answers the critics who in the past have accused Spark of treating her material in a flippantly detached manner. She says that she treats the story of Warrender Chase with a "light and heartless hand" which is her method when giving a "perfectly serious account of things" because to act differently would be hypocritical: "It seems to me a sort of hypocrisy for a writer to pretend to be undergoing tragic experiences when obviously one is sitting in relative comfort with a pen and paper or before a typewriter." At one point in the novel, Spark even challenges the "quality" of her readers, having her narrator remark that she hopes the readers of her novels are of "good quality" because "I wouldn't like to think of anyone cheap reading my books."

The most significant theme of *Loitering with Intent*, however, is joy: the joy the artist takes in the everyday reality that contributes to the imaginative act, and the euphoria the artist feels in the act of creation. Spark has indeed traveled a great distance from her early suspicions of the fiction-making process and of the novel as form.

The Only Problem · In her three novels after *Loitering with Intent*– *The Only Problem*, *A Far Cry from Kensington*, and *Symposium*–Spark continued to play variations of her characteristic themes. *The Only Problem* centers on the problem of evil: How can a just God "condone the unspeakable sufferings of the world"? Spark's protagonist, Harvey Gotham, an eccentric Canadian millionaire, wrestles with this question in a treatise on the Book of Job. Harvey's study is repeatedly interrupted as a consequence of the escapades of his young wife, Effie, who joins a terrorist group, kills a French policeman, and is herself eventually shot and killed by the police during a raid on a terrorist hideout. The intrusion of these events helps Harvey to appreciate the ultimate inscrutability of the human condition. Here again Spark celebrates the fiction-making process: In contrast to scholars who attempt to rationalize Job's story or abstract the philosophical issues from it, Harvey recognizes the unique power to the story itself. Spark's novel is thus a "commentary" on Job that remains true to the spirit of the original.

A Far Cry from Kensington · *A Far Cry from Kensington*, like *Loitering with Intent*, draws on Spark's experiences in postwar London. *A Far Cry from Kensington* is a retrospective first-person narrative; from the vantage point of the 1980's, the narrator recalls events that took place in 1954 and 1955. She was then in her late twenties, a war widow who had married at age eighteen a man whom she had met only a month before. Throughout the narrative other characters address her as Mrs. Hawkins (her married name), rather than by her given name, and she is regarded as a reliable confidante, in part, she suggests, because she was then rather fat. As Mrs. Hawkins loses weight, she acquires a first name, Nancy, and gradually becomes Nancy in her own eyes and those of others. Some of her neighbors and office peers worry that she is ill and wasting away, especially the superstitious war refugee Wanda, who believes there is a curse on her. The medical student, William, who lives in the flat next to Nancy, begins to see her as a woman, not merely as a confidante and a doer of good works. Nancy and William begin an affair and ultimately get married.

As Mrs. Hawkins loses weight and gains a personal life of her own, she is less willing to fill the needs of others. She says to the reader,

> My advice to any woman who earns the reputation of being capable, is not to demonstrate her ability too much. You give advice; you say, do this, do that, I think I've got you a job, don't worry, leave it to me. All that, and in the end you feel spooky, empty, haunted. And if you then want to wriggle out of so much responsibility, the people around you are outraged. You have stepped out of your role. It makes them furious.

Spark shows how the transformation of Mrs. Nancy Hawkins evokes resentment from those around her for services not rendered, services others never should have expected.

The backdrop of the story is the London publishing scene, especially its dubious fringe. The narrator's encounters with a variety of publishers and literary hangers-on are deftly sketched; also figuring in the plot are devotees of "radionics," a pseudo-science employing a device similar to Wilhelm Reich's orgone box. In particular, Mrs. Hawkins jousts with a hack writer and an adept of radionics, Hector Bartlett, whom she dubs a *pisseur de copie*. Initially, this conflict might seem to be merely a matter of aesthetics, and Bartlett—with his absurd pretensions and truly awful writing—merely a figure of comedy, yet he is shown to be an agent of evil, responsible for the death of a troubled woman. Unsettled by this mixture of nostalgia and satire, light comedy and metaphysical probing, the reader is never allowed to become comfortable. Evidently, this is Spark's intention.

Symposium · *Symposium*, focusing on a dinner party in Islington, offers a similarly unsettling mixture, for which the reader is duly prepared by an epigraph from Plato's *Symposium* that suggests the interdependence of comedy and tragedy. *Symposium* features an omniscient narrator who tells of the robbery of two of the dinner guests prior to the beginning of the main story, then injects flashbacks and parallel happenings, as the dinner, which constitutes the body of the story, progresses. Spark's technique owes something to that used by Virginia Woolf in *Mrs. Dalloway* (1925); her juxtaposition of a gala dinner party and a murder that is occurring simultaneously also remind the reader of W. H. Auden's 1939 poem, "Musée des Beaux Arts."

At the beginning of the novel, many characters are introduced and described; some prove to be unimportant and are never mentioned again. Spark seems to be deliberately confusing the reader by obscuring the main focus of the novel, perhaps in imitation of real-life events, in which often the most important elements are initially obscure and only become clear with time. Neither the guests nor those who serve them are what they seem. The butler and his attractive young assistant, an American graduate student who has been employed by several of the guests and is admired for working his way through school, are in a burglary ring that observes houses and files away conversations spoken at society parties about valuable possessions. Among the guests are a newly married young couple; the bride is a fresh, appealing Scottish girl who is so innocent and kind she appears to be too good for this world. In time the reader will come to see this young lady in a different light.

As *Symposium* progresses, the plot grows denser and darker, although an overlay of superficial dinner conversation pervades the novel. There is talk of the "evil eye" (reminiscent of the occult machinations of Hector Bartlett in *A Far Cry from Kensington*). The concept is absurd, and yet as the narrative develops there is evidence that one of the women present at the party genuinely possesses this maleficent power. In this novel, more than ever, Spark manipulates her characters with detachment: The reader is always aware that this is a performance. Yet if Spark's novels are coolly ironic entertainments, they are also oblique parables that explore with obsessive persistence the nature of evil.

Angela Hague,
updated by Isabel Bonnyman Stanley

Other major works

SHORT FICTION: *The Go-Away Bird and Other Stories*, 1958; *Voices at Play*, 1961 (with radio plays); *Collected Stories I*, 1967; *The Stories of Muriel Spark*, 1985; *Open to the Public: New and Collected Stories*, 1997.

PLAY: *Doctors of Philosophy*, pr. 1962.

POETRY: *The Fanfarlo and Other Verse*, 1952; *Collected Poems I*, 1967.

NONFICTION: *Child of Light: A Reassessment of Mary Wollstonecraft Shelley*, 1951 (rev. as *Mary Shelley*, 1987); *Emily Brontë: Her Life and Work*, 1953 (with Derek Stanford); *John Masefield*, 1953; *Curriculum Vitae*, 1992 (autobiography).

CHILDREN'S LITERATURE: *The Very Fine Clock*, 1968.

EDITED TEXTS: *Tribute to Wordsworth*, 1950 (with Derek Stanford); *My Best Mary: The Selected Letters of Mary Shelley*, 1953 (with Stanford); *The Brontë Letters*, 1954 (pb. in U.S. as *The Letters of the Brontës: A Selection*, 1954); *Letters of John Henry Newman*, 1957 (with Stanford).

Bibliography

Montgomery, Benilde. "Spark and Newman: Jean Brodie Reconsidered." *Twentieth Century Literature* 43 (Spring, 1997): 94-106. An insightful study of the influence of John Henry Newman on the tension between Jean Brodie and Sandy Stranger in *The Prime of Miss Jean Brodie*, arguably Spark's most enduring novel.

Page, Norman. *Muriel Spark*. New York: St. Martin's Press, 1990. Part of the Modern Novelists series, this book contains biographical information, criticism, and interpretation of Spark and her works. Includes bibliography and index.

Randisi, Jennifer Lynn. *On Her Way Rejoicing: The Fiction of Muriel Spark*. Washington, D.C.: Catholic University of America Press, 1991. A good view of Spark's fiction that both updates and complements earlier studies.

Richmond, Velma Bourgeois. *Muriel Spark*. New York: Frederick Ungar, 1984. A valuable resource on Spark that includes commentary on her plays. Chapter 8, "The Darkening Vision," gives sound interpretations of *The Driver's Seat*, *The Public Image*, and *Not to Disturb*.

Walker, Dorothea. *Muriel Spark.* Boston: Twayne, 1988. An informative study on the main themes of Spark's work, with emphasis given to the wit and humor of her characters. The extensive bibliography is particularly helpful.

Whittaker, Ruth. *The Faith and Fiction of Muriel Spark.* New York: St. Martin's Press, 1982. A definitive look at Spark and the relationship between the secular and the divine in her work. This scholarly study, with its extensive bibliography, is a fine source for reference and critical material on Spark.

Laurence Sterne

Born: Clonmel, Ireland; November 24, 1713
Died: London, England; March 18, 1768

Principal long fiction · *The Life and Opinions of Tristram Shandy, Gent.*, 1759-1767; *A Sentimental Journey Through France and Italy*, 1768.

Other literary forms · Laurence Sterne began his literary career with political pieces in the *York-Courant* in 1741. Two years later, he published a poem, "The Unknown World," in *The Gentleman's Magazine* (July, 1743). His song, "How Imperfect the Joys of the Soul," written for Kitty Fourmantel, appeared in Joseph Baildon's *Collection of New Songs Sung at Ranelagh* (1765), and a four-line epigram, "On a Lady's Sporting a Somerset," was attributed to Sterne in *Muse's Mirror* (1778). His sermons were published in three installments: two volumes in 1760, another two in 1766, and a final three volumes in 1769. A political satire entitled *A Political Romance* was published in 1759 but quickly suppressed. After Sterne's death, *Letters from Yorick to Eliza* appeared in 1773, and his daughter arranged for the publication of *Letters of the Late Rev. Mr. L. Sterne to His Most Intimate Friends* (1775, three volumes). These volumes include an autobiographical *Memoir* and the *Fragment in the Manner of Rabelais*. In 1935, Oxford University Press published the definitive edition of Sterne's letters, edited by Lewis Perry Curtis. The *Journal to Eliza*, composed in 1767, was not published until 1904.

Achievements · When Sterne went to London in March, 1760, he was an obscure provincial parson. He rode as a guest in Stephen Croft's cart, and he brought with him little more than his "best breeches." Two months later, he returned to York in his own carriage. Robert Dodsley, who the year before had refused the copyright of *The Life and Opinions of Tristram Shandy, Gent.* (commonly called *Tristram Shandy*) for 50 pounds, now gladly offered Sterne 250 pounds for the first two volumes, 380 pounds for the next two, as yet unwritten, and another 200 pounds for two volumes of sermons. The famous artist William Hogarth agreed to provide a frontispiece to the second edition of volume 1 and another for volume 3; Joshua Reynolds painted Sterne's portrait. Like Lord Byron, Sterne could have said that he awoke to find himself famous. As Sterne did say, in a letter to Catherine Fourmantel, "I assure you my Kitty, that Tristram is the Fashion." Despite the carpings of a few—Horace Walpole thought *Tristram Shandy* "a very insipid and tedious performance," and Samuel Richardson thought it immoral—the novel was the rage of London, inspiring so many continuations and imitations that Sterne had to sign the later volumes to guarantee their authenticity.

After the novel's initial popularity, sales did drop off. In book 8, Tristram complains that he has "ten cart-loads" of volumes 5 and 6 "still unsold." Dodsley abandoned publication of the work after volume 4, and Sterne's new publisher, Thomas Becket, complained in April, 1763, that he had 991 copies of volumes 5 and 6 unsold (from a printing of 4,000). Samuel Johnson's famous comment, though ultimately incorrect, probably reflected the opinion of the day: "Nothing odd will do long. *Tristram Shandy* did not last." Even Sterne may have tired of the work; the

volumes grew slimmer, and volume 9 appeared without its mate, volume 10 having, in Sterne's apt words for an obstetrical novel, "miscarried."

Yet *Tristram Shandy* has lasted. It retains its readership, even if it has continued to justify Sterne's complaint of being "more read than understood." Twentieth century readers have made great, perhaps exaggerated, claims for the novel, seeing it as the harbinger of the works of Marcel Proust, James Joyce, and Albert Camus, who, it is said, derived from Sterne the concept of relative time, the stream of consciousness, and a sense of the absurd. Even if one discounts such assertions, there can be no question of the work's importance in the development of the novel or of *Tristram Shandy*'s place in the first rank of eighteenth century fiction.

Less has been claimed for *A Sentimental Journey Through France and Italy* (commonly called *A Sentimental Journey*), yet this work, apparently so different from and so much simpler than *Tristram Shandy*, greatly influenced Continental, especially German, literature of the Romantic period. Though critics debate the sincerity of the emotions in the work, eighteenth century readers generally did not question Yorick's sentimentality, which contributed to the rise of the cult of sensibility exemplified by such works as Henry Mackenzie's *The Man of Feeling* (1771) and Sarah Morton's *The Power of Sympathy* (1789). Because of its brevity, its benevolence, and its accessibility, *A Sentimental Journey* has enjoyed continued popularity since its first appearance. Though lacking the stature of *Tristram Shandy*, it remains a classic.

Biography · Laurence Sterne was born in Clonmel, Tipperary, Ireland, on November 24, 1713. On his father's side, he could claim some distinction. His great-grandfather, Richard Sterne, had been Archbishop of York, and his grandfather, Simon Sterne, was a rich Yorkshire country squire. Roger Sterne, Laurence's father, was less distinguished. Sterne describes his father as "a little smart man—active to the last degree, in all exercises—most patient of fatigue and disappointments, of which it pleased God to give him full measure." Sterne added that his father was "of a kindly, sweet disposition, void of all design." Many have seen Roger Sterne as the model for Uncle Toby Shandy. At the age of sixteen, Roger joined the Cumberland Regiment of Foot, and on September 25, 1711, he married Agnes Nuttall. Agnes, according to her son, was the daughter of "a noted sutler in Flanders, in Queen Ann's wars," whom Roger married because he was in debt to her father. Actually, she may have been the daughter of a poor but respectable family in Lancashire.

From his birth to the age of ten, Sterne led a nomadic life, wandering from barracks to barracks across Great Britain. During these years, he may have acquired some of the military knowledge that appears throughout *Tristram Shandy*, or at least that fondness for the military which marks the work.

When Sterne was ten, his uncle Richard sent him to school near Halifax, in Yorkshire, and in 1733, Sterne's cousin sent him to Jesus College, Cambridge, where his great-grandfather had been a master and where both his uncle Jaques and his cousin had gone. At Cambridge, Sterne met John Hall, who later renamed himself John Hall-Stevenson. Hall-Stevenson was to be one of Sterne's closest friends throughout his life; his library at "Crazy Castle" would furnish much of the abstruse learning in *Tristram Shandy*, and he would himself appear in both that novel and *A Sentimental Journey* as "Eugenius," the sober adviser. While at Cambridge, Sterne suffered his first tubercular hemorrhage.

After receiving his bachelor's degree in January, 1737, Sterne had to choose a profession. Because his great-grandfather and uncle had both gone into the Church, Sterne followed their path. After Sterne served briefly in St. Ives and Catton, his uncle Jaques, by then Archdeacon of Cleveland and Canon and Precentor of the York Cathedral, secured for him the living of Sutton on the Forest, a few miles north of York. A second post soon followed; Sterne received the prebend of Givendale, making him part of the York Cathedral chapter and so allowing him to preach his turn there.

At York, Sterne met Elizabeth Lumley, a woman with a comfortable fortune. Their courtship had a strong sentimental tinge to it. Indeed, if Sterne actually wrote to Elizabeth the letters that his daughter published after his death, his is the first recorded use of the word *sentimental*, and the emotions expressed in these letters foreshadow both *A Sentimental Journey* and the *Journal to Eliza*. Even if these letters are spurious, Sterne's description of his courtship in the *Memoirs* is sufficiently lachrymose to rival the death of Le Fever in *Tristram Shandy*. Unfortunately for Sterne, he, unlike Tristram, did go on; on March 30, 1741, he married Elizabeth. The unfavorable portrait of Mrs. Shandy owes much to Sterne's less than sentimental feelings toward his wife, whom he called in March, 1760, the "one Obstacle to my Happiness."

The year 1741 was also important for Sterne because it marked his first appearance in print. His uncle Jaques was a strong Whig, and he recruited his nephew to write in support of the Whig candidate for York in that year's election. Sterne wrote, the Whig won, and Sterne received the prebend of North Newbold as a reward. The Whig success was, however, short-lived. When the Walpole government fell in 1742, Sterne wrote a recantation and apology for his part in "the late contested Election," and thereby earned the enmity of his uncle, an enmity that ended only with Jaques's death in 1759.

For the next eighteen years, Sterne lived as a typical provincial clergyman, attending to the needs of his parishioners and publishing two sermons. One of these, "For We Trust We Have a Good Conscience," Sterne reprints in its entirety in the second volume of *Tristram Shandy*. In 1751, he received the commissaryship of Pickering and Pocklington, despite his uncle's efforts to secure this position for Dr. Francis Topham. Sterne and Topham collided again in 1758, when Topham intended to include his son in a patent and thus secure for him a post after his own death. When the dean of York Cathedral blocked the inclusion, a pamphlet war ensued. Sterne fired the final shot; his *A Political Romance* so squashed Topham that he agreed to abandon the fray if Sterne would withdraw his pamphlet. Sterne did withdraw *A Political Romance*, but he was not finished with Topham, who was to appear in *Tristram Shandy* as Phutatorius and Didius.

A Political Romance is little more than a satirical squib, but it shows that Sterne was familiar with the works of Jonathan Swift. In its use of clothes symbolism as well as in its severity it recalls *A Tale of a Tub* (1704), and it shows that Swift's work was running in Sterne's head between 1758 and 1759. He was making other use of Swift, too. On May 23, 1759, Sterne wrote to Robert Dodsley, "With this You will receive the Life & Opinions of *Tristram Shandy*, which I choose to offer to You first." By this time, the first volume of the novel was finished. Although Dodsley refused the copyright for the fifty pounds Sterne requested, Sterne continued to write, completing a second volume and revising the first to remove "all locality" and make "the whole . . . more saleable," as he wrote to Dodsley several months later.

Salable it was. The York edition sold two hundred copies in two days when it appeared in December, 1759, and when Sterne went up to London, he was told that the book was not "to be had in London either for Love or money." Dodsley, who had been unwilling to risk 50 pounds on the copyright, now purchased it for 250 pounds, gave another 380 pounds to publish the still unwritten volumes 3 and 4, and yet another 200 pounds for two volumes of Sterne's sermons. Sterne was honored by the great. Thomas Gray wrote to Thomas Wharton, "Tristram Shandy is still a greater object of admiration, the Man as well as the Book. One is invited to dinner, where he dines, a fortnight beforehand."

In March, 1760, Sterne also succeeded to the curacy of Coxwold, a better position than his earlier one at Sutton. In May, 1760, he therefore settled at Coxwold, renting Shandy Hall from Earl Fauconberg. Here he worked on the next two volumes of *Tristram Shandy*, which he brought to London at the end of the year. In 1761, he repeated this pattern, but he did not return to Yorkshire after delivering the manuscript of volumes 5 and 6. Having suffered a tubercular hemorrhage, he set off for the warmer, milder air of France.

There he repeated his earlier triumph in London, and he incidentally acquired materials for book 7 of *Tristram Shandy* and *A Sentimental Journey*. Sterne remained in France for almost two years; when he returned to England, he hastily wrote the next two volumes of *Tristram Shandy*, which appeared in January, 1765. In October of that year, he brought twelve sermons to London rather than more of his novel. After leaving the manuscript with his publisher, he again set off for the Continent; he would combine the adventures of this trip with those of his earlier one in writing *A Sentimental Journey*.

In June, 1766, Sterne was back in Coxwold, where he wrote what proved to be the last installment of *Tristram Shandy*. This he brought with him to London in late December; shortly after his arrival, he met Eliza Draper, the wife of an East India Company clerk twenty years her senior. Though initially unimpressed with her, Sterne was soon madly in love. When Sterne met her, she had already been in England some two years, and she was to return to India less than three months later, yet she was to color Sterne's last year of life. Before she sailed on the *Earl of Chatham* on April 3, 1767, Sterne visited her daily, wrote letters to her, drove with her, and exchanged pictures with her. After their separation, Sterne continued his letters; those he wrote between April 13 and the beginning of August, 1767, constitute the *Journal to Eliza*. When he broke off this journal with the words "I am thine—& thine only, & for ever" to begin *A Sentimental Journey*, her spirit haunted that work, too, as the Eliza upon whom Yorick calls.

By December, Sterne had finished the first half of *A Sentimental Journey* and again set off for London and his publisher. On February 27, 1768, *A Sentimental Journey*, volumes 1 and 2, appeared. Less than a month later, on March 18, Sterne died. He was buried in London on March 22; on June 8, 1769, he was reinterred in the Coxwold churchyard in Yorkshire.

Analysis · Readers may be tempted to see Laurence Sterne's works either as *sui generis* or as eighteenth century sports that had no mate until Marcel Proust and James Joyce. In fact, Sterne was very much a product of his age. His humor owes much to such earlier writers as François Rabelais, Miguel de Cervantes, Michel de Montaigne, Sir Thomas Browne, and Jonathan Swift, all of whom influenced his experimentation with the form of the newly emerged novel. Even this experimentation is typical of the age. Thomas Amory's *The Life and Opinions of John Buncle Esquire* (1756-1766) may have suggested to Sterne his complete title *The Life and Opinions of Tristram Shandy, Gent.* Like *Tristram Shandy*, Amory's book is full of digressions, and its narrator is conceited.

Sterne's experimentation did go beyond the traditional. One need look no farther than the typography, the varying length of the chapters in *Tristram Shandy*, from four lines to sixty pages, or the unusual location of certain conventional elements—for example, the placing of *Tristram Shandy*'s preface after the twentieth chapter of book 3 or Yorick's writing the preface to *A Sentimental Journey* after chapter 6. At the same time, Sterne relied on the conventions of the novel. He is meticulous in his descriptions of clothing, furniture, and gesture. His characters are fully developed: They walk, sometimes with a limp, they cough, they bleed, they dance. From Swift, Daniel Defoe, and Samuel Richardson, Sterne took the first-person narrator. From Richardson, he adopted the technique of writing to the moment; from Henry Fielding, he got the idea of the novel as a comic epic in prose. From numerous sources—Rabelais, Cervantes, and Swift, to name but three—he learned of the satiric potential of the genre.

A Political Romance reveals Sterne's powerful satiric abilities, but this work has little in common with the novels. True, the personal satire of the pamphlet does persist. Sterne lampoons Dr. Burton (Dr. Slop), Dr. Richard Meade (Dr. Kunastrokius), and Francis Topham (Phutatorius, Didius) in *Tristram Shandy*; Tobias Smollett (Smeldungus) and Samuel Sharp (Mundungus) in *A Sentimental Journey*. For the most part, though, Sterne is after bigger game. As he wrote to Robert Dodsley, the satire is general; and, as he wrote to Robert Foley some years later, it is "a laughing good tempered Satyr," another distinction between the novels and the pamphlet.

The objects of this general satire are several: system-makers of all types, pedants, lawyers, doctors, conceited authors, prudes, and self-deceivers. A common thread uniting all these satiric butts is folly, the folly of believing that life should conform to some preconceived notion, of trying to force facts to fit theories rather than the other way around.

Sterne's insistence on common sense and reason is consistent with the Augustan tradition, which itself is rooted in Anglican beliefs that Sterne emphasized in his sermons as well as in his fiction. Although Sterne's satire is good-tempered, it attacks people's tendency to evil, a tendency noted in Article IX of the Thirty-nine Articles of the Anglican Church. Like his fellow Augustans, Sterne saw this tendency to evil in many spheres. Like them, therefore, he attacked these deviations from the norm as established by religion and reason (which for Sterne are the same), by nature, by tradition, and by authority. The characters in *Tristram Shandy* and Yorick in *A Sentimental Journey* (who is the only sustained character in that work) are laughable because they deviate from the norm and because they refuse to accept their limitations.

Sterne repeatedly reminds the reader of people's finiteness. Thus, death haunts the novels: In *Tristram Shandy*, Toby, Walter, Mrs. Shandy, Yorick, Trim, and Bobby are all dead, and Tristram is dying. In *A Sentimental Journey*, a resurrected Yorick sees death all around him—a dead monk, dead children, a dead ass, dead lovers. Another, less dramatic symbol of the characters' limitation is their inability to complete what they begin. *Tristram Shandy* and *A Sentimental Journey* remain fragments. Trim never finishes his tale of the King of Bohemia and his seven castles. Walter never finishes the *Tristrapaedia*. Obadiah never goes for yeast. Yorick never finishes the story of the notary. Nor can characters communicate effectively with one another: Walter's wife never appreciates his theories, Toby's hobbyhorse causes him to understand all words in a military sense, Dr. Slop falls asleep in the middle of Trim's reading, and Yorick in *A Sentimental Journey* never pauses long enough to develop a lasting friendship.

Death, the prison of the self, the petty and great disappointments of life—these are the stuff of tragedy, yet in Sterne's novels they form the basis of comedy, for the emphasis in these novels is not on the tragic event itself but rather on the cause or the reaction. Bobby's death, for example, is nothing to the reader, not only because one never meets Bobby alive but also because one quickly becomes involved in Walter's oration and Trim's hat. In *A Sentimental Journey*, Sterne focuses on Yorick's reaction to Maria rather than on her poignant tale: Consequently, one laughs at Yorick instead of crying with Maria. The prison of words that traps the characters is not the result of people's inherent isolation but rather of a comic perversity in refusing to accept the plain meaning of a statement. The tragic is further mitigated by its remoteness. Though Tristram writes to the moment, that moment is long past; Tristram's account is being composed some fifty years after the events he describes, and Yorick, too, is recollecting emotions in tranquillity. The curious order of *Tristram Shandy* and the rapid pace of *A Sentimental Journey* further dilute the tragic. Yorick dies in book 1 but cracks the last joke in book 9. Yorick has barely begun a sentimental attachment with a *fille de chambre* in Paris when he must set off for Versailles to seek a passport. Though the disappointments, interruptions, failures, and deaths recur, individually they quickly vanish from view. What remains are the characters, who are comic because they refuse to learn from their failures.

Sterne's world is therefore not tragic; neither is it absurd. In the world of the absurd, helpless characters confront a meaningless and chaotic world. For Sterne, the world is reasonable; he shares the Augustan worldview expressed so well by Alexander Pope: "All Nature is but Art, unknown to thee,/ All Chance Direction which thou canst not see." The reasonableness of the world is not, however, to be found in the systematizing of Walter Shandy or the sentimentalism of Yorick. People can live in harmony with the world, Sterne says, only if they use common sense. The comedy of these novels derives in large part from people's failure or laziness to be sensible.

Tristram Shandy · In *Aspects of the Novel* (1927), E. M. Forster writes: "Obviously a god is hidden in *Tristram Shandy* and his name is Muddle." There is no question that the muddle is present in the novel. Chapters 18 and 19 of book 9 appear as part of chapter 25. The preface does not appear until the third volume. There are black, marbled, and white pages. In book 4, a chapter is torn out and ten pages dropped. Uncle Toby begins knocking the ashes out of his pipe in book 1, chapter 21, and finishes this simple action in book 2, chapter 6. The novel begins in 1718 and ends, if it may be said to end, in 1713. Although called *The Life and Opinions of Tristram Shandy, Gent.*, the novel recounts the life of Uncle Toby and the opinions of Walter Shandy.

One must distinguish, though, between the muddle that the narrator, Tristram, creates, and the ordered universe that Sterne offers. Theodore Baird has demonstrated that one can construct an orderly sequence of events from the information in *Tristram Shandy*, beginning with the reign of Henry VIII (III,xxxiii) through the wounding of Trim in 1693 (VIII,xix; II,v), the siege of Namur at which Toby is wounded in 1695 (I,xxv), the conception and birth of Tristram Shandy in 1718 (I-III), the death of Bobby (1719; IV,xxxii and v,ii), the episode of Toby and the fly (1728; II,xii), the death of Yorick (1748; I,xii), and the composition of the novel (1759-1766). Tristram does attempt to impose some order upon these events; the first five and a half books trace his life from his conception to his accident with the window sash and his being put into breeches. He then breaks off to recount the amours of Uncle Toby, which again appear essentially in sequence, with the major exception of book 7, Tristram's flight into France.

Although Tristram attempts to order these events, he fails. He fails not because life is inherently random or absurd, but because he is a bad artist. He pointedly rejects the advice of Horace, whose *The Art of Poetry* (c. 17 B.C.E.) was highly respected among eighteenth century writers. He will not pause to check facts and even refuses to look back in his own book to see whether he has already mentioned something; this is writing to the moment with a vengeance. He refuses to impose any order at all upon his material, allowing his pen to govern him instead of acting the part of the good writer who governs his pen.

In governing his pen, the good writer carefully selects his material. Many a person has told a plain, unvarnished tale in less space than Tristram, but Tristram cannot decide what is important. Must one know what Mrs. Shandy said to Walter on the night of Tristram's begetting, which, incidentally, may not be the night of Tristram's begetting at all, since the night described is only eight months before Tristram's birth rather than nine—does Tristram realize this fact? Does one need so vivid an account of how Walter falls across the bed upon learning of Tristram's crushed nose? Is it true that one cannot understand Toby's statement, "I think it would not be amiss brother, if we rung the bell," without being dragged halfway across Europe and twenty-three years back in time? Such details serve the purpose of Tristram's creator by highlighting the follies of a bad writer, but they hardly help Tristram proceed with his story.

Tristram's failure to select his material derives in part from laziness. "I have a strong propensity in me to begin this chapter very nonsensically, and I will not balk my fancy," he writes (I,xxiii), for it requires intellectual effort to balk a fancy. In part, too, this failure to select reflects Tristram's belief that everything concerning himself is important. His is a solipsistic rendering of the humanist's credo, *Homo sum, humani nihil a me alienum puto*—"I am a man, and nothing that relates to man can be foreign to me." He is confident that the more the reader associates with him, the fonder he (the reader) will become. Hence, the reader will want to know about his failure with Jenny, about his aunt Dinah's affair with the coachman, about his attire as he writes, about his casting a fair instead of a foul copy of his manuscript into the fire. Tristram sets out to write a traditional biography, beginning with a genealogy and proceeding to birth, education, youthful deeds that foreshadow later achievements, marriage, children, accomplishments, death, and burial. He becomes so bogged down in details, however, that he cannot get beyond his fifth year. The episode of Toby and the fly must substitute for a volume on education, and the setting up of his top replaces an account of his youthful deeds.

Although Tristram refuses to impose any system on his writing, he is a true son of Walter Shandy in his willingness to impose systems on other aspects of his world. He devises a scale for measuring pleasure and pain, so that if the death of Bobby rates a five and Walter's pleasure at delivering an oration on the occasion rates a ten, Walter proves the gainer by this catastrophe. Tristram has another scale for measuring his own writing; he awards himself a nineteen out of twenty for the design of the novel. Tristram attaches much significance to the way he is conceived, believing that one's conception determines his entire life. His declared method of describing character is similarly reductive, focusing strictly on the individual's hobbyhorse. He has a theory on knots, on window sashes, and on the effect of diet on writing. Tristram thus serves as a satire on systematizers as well as on bad writers.

The more obvious butt of Sterne's satire on system-makers is Walter Shandy. The Augustan Age has also been called the Age of Reason, and Sterne recognizes the importance of reason. At the same time, the Augustans recognized that a person's reason alone is often an insufficient guide because it can be corrupted by a ruling passion, as Yorick's sermon in *Tristram Shandy* reveals. Tristram fails as an author because he trusts exclusively to his own logic instead of following conventional guidelines. Walter Shandy is another example of one who becomes foolish because of his reliance on his own reason. Like Pope's dunces, Walter is well read, and like Pope's dunces, he fails to benefit from his learning because he does not use common sense. He will look in the Institutes of Justinian instead of the more obvious, and more reliable, catechism—part of Sterne's joke here is that the source Walter cites does not contain what he wants. Walter will consult Rubenius rather than a tailor to determine of what cloth Tristram's breeches should be made. From his reading and reasoning he develops a host of theories: that cesarean birth is the best way of bringing a child into the world, that Christian names determine one's life, that auxiliary verbs provide a key to knowledge. Each of these theories rests on a certain logic. Walter is correct that no one would name his child Judas. From this true observation, though, he erects a most absurd theory, proving Tristram's statement that "when a man gives himself up to the government of a ruling passion,—or, in other words, when his Hobby-Horse grows headstrong,—farewell cool reason and fair discretion" (II,v). Neither Walter nor his son will rein in his hobbyhorse, and, as a result, they become ridiculous.

They may also become dangerous. While Walter is busily engaged in composing his *Tristrapaedia* that will codify his theories of child rearing, Tristram grows up without any guidance at all. Walter is willing, indeed eager, to have his wife undergo a cesarean operation because he believes that such an operation will be less harmful to the infant than natural childbirth. That such an operation will cause the death of Mrs. Shandy is a fact that apparently escapes him.

Even the benign and lovable Uncle Toby makes himself ridiculous by yielding to his hobbyhorse. Not only does this hobbyhorse lead him into excessive expense and so deprive him of money he might put to better use, but also it keeps his mind from more worthwhile occupations. Repeatedly, Sterne, through Tristram, likens Toby's garden battlefield to a mistress with whom Toby dallies; the Elizabethan sense of hobbyhorse is precisely this—a woman of easy virtue. As Tristram notes early in the novel, when "one . . . whose principles and conduct are as generous and noble as his blood" is carried off by his hobbyhorse, it is better that "the Hobby-Horse, with all his fraternity, (were) at the Devil" (I,viii). Deluding himself that he is somehow contributing to the defense of England, Toby blinds himself to the real horrors of war. Wrapped up in his military jargon, he isolates himself verbally from those around him; a bridge or a train has only one meaning for him. No less than Tristram, he is betrayed by words, but in his case as in Tristram's the fault lies not with the words but with the individual betrayed.

Nor is Toby's hobbyhorse dangerous to himself alone. It keeps him away from the Widow Wadman and so prevents his fulfilling his legitimate social responsibilities of marrying and begetting children; his hobbyhorse renders him sterile even if his wound has not. This hobbyhorse also comes close to rendering Tristram sterile, for Trim removes the weights from the window sash to make cannon for Toby's campaigns.

Each of the major characters is trapped in a cell of his own making. Tristram can never finish his book because his theory of composition raises insurmountable obstacles. The more he writes, the more he has to write. Walter's and Toby's hobby-horses blind them to reality and prevent their communicating with each other or anyone else. The Shandy family is well named; "shandy" in Yorkshire means crack-brained. Significantly, the novel begins with an interrupted act of procreation and ends with sterility. As in Pope's *The Dunciad* (1728-1743), the uncreating word triumphs because of human folly.

Sterne's vision is not quite as dark as Pope's, though; the novel ends not with universal darkness but with a joke. Yorick, the voice of reason and moderation, remains to pull the reader back to reality. Yorick is a jester, and the role of the jester is to remind his audience of the just proportion of things as well as to make them laugh. Yorick does not put a fancy saddle on a horse that does not deserve one. He will destroy a sermon because it is too bad (unlike Tristram, who destroys a chapter because it is too good). He makes only modest claims for his sermons and is embarrassed even by these (unlike Tristram, who repeatedly proclaims himself a genius). Yorick thus offers in word and deed an example of living reasonably and happily.

Sterne offers a second consolation as well. Even though characters isolate themselves with their hobbyhorses, even though they cannot or will not understand one another's words, they can and do appreciate one another's feelings. These emotional unions are short-lived, but they are intense and sincere. Walter will continue to make fun of Toby even after promising not to, but at the moment the promise is made, the two are united spiritually and physically. Tristram and Jenny quarrel, but they also have their tender moments. Trim looks for a carriage in a book by shaking the leaves, and he mistakes fiction for reality in a sermon, but he allows his parents three halfpence a day out of his pay when they grow old. The benevolence that Sterne urged in his sermons is capable of bridging self-imposed isolation. Although one laughs at the characters in *Tristram Shandy*, one therefore sympathizes with them as well, seeing their weaknesses but also their underlying virtue. Though they have corrupted that virtue by yielding to a natural tendency to evil, they redeem themselves through their equally natural tendency to kindness.

Tristram Shandy offended many contemporary readers because of its bawdy tales; reviewers much preferred such seemingly sentimental episodes as the death of Le Fever and urged Sterne to refine his humor. *A Sentimental Journey* superficially appears to have been written to satisfy these demands. It is full of touching scenes, of tears, of charity, of little acts of kindness. Moreover, in a letter to Mrs. William James in November, 1767, Sterne describes the novel as dealing with "the gentle passions and affections" and says his intention is "to teach us to love the world and our fellow creatures better than we do." Sterne's letters, and especially his *Journal to Eliza*, reveal him as a man of feeling, and *Tristram Shandy* satirizes all aspects of human life except for benevolence. Sterne's sermons reinforce his image as a believer in the importance of charity. As a Latitudinarian, he believed that the Golden Rule constitutes the essence of religion, that ritual and church doctrine, while important, are less significant than kindness. Because Yorick in *Tristram Shandy* is Sterne's spokesman, it is tempting to see Yorick in *A Sentimental Journey* as having the same normative function. Though the narrator of *Tristram Shandy* is a dunce and a satiric butt, can one not still trust the narrator of *A Sentimental Journey*?

No. In a famous letter to Dr. John Eustace, Sterne thanks Eustace for the gift of a curious walking stick: "Your walking stick is in no sense more shandaic than in that of its having *more handles than one*." Readers could regard *Tristram Shandy* as total nonsense, as a collection of bawdy stories, as a realistic novel, as a satire on the realistic novel, or as a satire on the follies of humankind. Sterne's second novel, too, is "shandaic." The reader can see it as a tribute to the popular spirit of sentimentality or can view it as a satire of that spirit, yet a careful reading of the book will demonstrate why Sterne wrote to the mysterious "Hannah" that this novel "shall make you cry as much as ever it made me laugh." In other words, Sterne is sporting with rather than adopting the sentimental mode.

A Sentimental Journey · The object of Sterne's laughter is Yorick. The Yorick who recounts his travels is not the same normative parson as appears in *Tristram Shandy*. He is by now twice dead—dead in William Shakespeare's *Hamlet* (1600-1601) and dead again in *Tristram Shandy* some fifteen years prior to the events of *A Sentimental Journey*. This second resurrection may itself be a joke on the reader, who should recall Yorick's death in book 1 of the earlier novel.

This revived Yorick bears a great similarity to Tristram. He is, for one thing, a systematizer. He establishes three degrees of curses; he discovers "three epochas in the empire of a French woman" ("Paris"), he is able to create dialogues out of silence, and he derives national character not from "important matters of state" but rather from "nonsensical minutiae" ("The Wig–Paris"). Like Tristram, too, Yorick is vain. He gives a sou to a beggar who calls him "My Lord *Anglois*" and another sou for *"Mon cher et très charitable Monsieur."* He does not worry about being unkind to a monk but is concerned that as a result a pretty woman will think ill of him.

Even his style, though less difficult to follow than Tristram's, bears some similarities to that of Sterne's earlier narrator. In the midst of the account of his adventures in Versailles, Yorick introduces the irrelevant anecdote of Bevoriskius and the mating sparrows, thus combining Tristram's habit of digressing with Walter's love of abstruse learning. Yorick later interpolates an account of the Marquis d'E****, and while telling about Paris he presents a "Fragment" that does nothing to advance the story. Like Tristram, too, Yorick cannot finish his account, breaking off in mid-sentence. Apparently, he is more governed by his pen than governing.

Yorick also reminds the reader of the narrator in Swift's *A Tale of a Tub*, who believes that happiness is the state of being well deceived. Yorick is disappointed to learn that his small present to Le Fleur has been sufficient only to allow his servant to buy used clothes: "I would rather have imposed upon my fancy with thinking I had bought them new for the fellow, than that they had come out of the *Rue de friperie*" ("Le Dimanche–Paris"). Instead of inquiring about the history of the lady at Calais, he invents a pleasant account of her until he gets "ground enough for the situation which pleased me" ("In the Street–Calais"). He deceives himself into believing that he is accompanying a pretty *fille de chambre* as far as possible to protect her when actually he wants her company. Even his benevolence is self-deception. He conjures up images to weep over—a swain with a dying lamb, a man in the Bastille, an imaginary recipient of charity. When in this last instance he confronts the reality, his behavior is hardly benevolent, though.

Sterne is not satirizing benevolence as such. In his sermons "The Vindication of Human Nature" and "Philanthropy Recommended" he rejects the notion that people are inherently selfish and stresses his belief in humankind's natural benevolence. Yet he had to look no farther than his own nose to discover that benevolence can become a hobbyhorse that can carry a person away from the path of reason. Yorick's hobbyhorse of benevolence is no less dangerous than Uncle Toby's or Walter Shandy's. Yorick will weep over a carriage, over a dead ass, or over a caged starling. He admits that he does not even need an object for his sympathy: "Was I in a desert, I would find out wherewith in it to call forth my affection" ("In the Street–Calais"). Real human misery, however, he cannot understand. He can weep over his imagined prisoner in the Bastille, but he cannot imagine the real suffering there. He can be callous to the poor, but never to a pretty young woman.

Yorick's benevolence is thus a compound of self-deception and lust. He will give no money to the poor monk until he wants to impress a pretty woman. He gives a sou to a beggar with a dislocated hip, but he gives an unsolicited crown to a pretty *fille de chambre*, and he gives three *louis d'or* to a pretty grisette. He imagines that in offering to share his chaise with another pretty young lady, he is fighting off "every dirty passion" such as avarice, pride, meanness, and hypocrisy. Actually, he is yielding to desire.

True benevolence is guided by reason, and it is not a thing of the moment only, as

Sterne points out in his sermon on the Good Samaritan. Yorick's benevolence is impulsive and short-lived. The cry of a caged starling moves him greatly: "I never had my affections more tenderly awakened," he says ("The Passport–The Hotel at Paris"). The hyperbole of the language is itself a warning of Yorick's inability to temper emotion with reason. After such a reaction, his attitude changes abruptly; Yorick buys the starling but never frees it. After tiring of it, he gives it away to another as callous as himself. At Namport, he mourns for a dead ass and praises its owner for his kindness, adding, "Shame on the world! . . . Did we love each other, as this poor soul but loved his ass–'twould be something" ("Namport–The Dead Ass"). By the next page, Yorick is sending his postillion to the devil. Yorick goes out of his way to find the mad Maria, whom Sterne had introduced in book 7 of *Tristram Shandy*. He weeps with Maria at Moulines; she makes such an impression on him that her image follows him almost to Lyon–an entire chapter.

Yorick is humorous because, like Tristram, Walter, and Toby, he is the victim of his hobbyhorse. He gallops away from reason, failing to examine his motivation or to temper his sudden fanciful flights. In "Temporal Advantages of Religion," Sterne provides a picture of the ideal Christian traveler. "We may surely be allowed to amuse ourselves with the natural or artificial beauties of the country we are passing through," Sterne notes, but he warns against being drawn aside, as Yorick is, "by the variety of prospects, edifices, and ruins which solicit us." More important, Yorick forgets the chief end of people's earthly sojourn: "Various as our excursions are–that we have still set our faces towards Jerusalem . . . and that the way to get there is not so much to please our hearts, as to improve them in virtue." Yorick has come to France for knowledge, but he learns nothing. His benevolence is much closer to wantonness than to virtue; it is fitting that he ends his account in the dark, grasping the *fille de chambre*.

In *A Sentimental Journey*, as in *Tristram Shandy*, Sterne mocks excess. He shows the folly that results from the abdication of reason. Though he introduces norms such as Yorick in *Tristram Shandy* or the old soldier in *A Sentimental Journey*, the ideal emerges most clearly from a depiction of its opposite–perverted learning, bad writing, and unexamined motives. When Sterne came to London in 1760, Lord Bathurst correctly embraced him as the heir to the Augustan satirists.

Joseph Rosenblum

Other major works

NONFICTION: *A Political Romance*, 1759; *The Sermons of Mr. Yorick*, 1760 (vols. 1-2), 1766 (vols. 3-4); *Sermons by the Late Rev. Mr. Sterne*, 1769 (vols. 5-7); *Letters from Yorick to Eliza*, 1773; *Sterne's Letters to His Friends on Various Occasions, to Which Is Added His History of a Watch Coat*, 1775; *Letters of the Late Rev. Mr. L. Sterne to His Most Intimate Friends*, 1775 (3 volumes); *In Elegant Epistles*, 1790; *Journal to Eliza*, 1904.

Bibliography

Cash, Arthur Hill. *Laurence Sterne*. 2 vols. London: Methuen, 1975-1986. The definitive biography. The first volume follows Sterne's life to early 1760 and offers many details about his role in the religious and political affairs of York. The second volume treats Sterne the author. Presents a realistic picture freed from Victorian strictures and romantic glosses. The appendices provide a series of portraits and of letters never before published.

_____. *Sterne's Comedy of Moral Sentiments: The Ethical Dimension of the Journey*.

Pittsburgh: Duquesne University Press, 1966. Comparing Sterne's sermons with *A Sentimental Journey Through France and Italy*, Cash finds a moral stance in the novel, one that condemns Yorick for excessive sentimentality. Sterne laughs at Yorick, at himself, and at humankind for abandoning reason.

Cash, Arthur Hill, and John M. Stedmond, eds. *The Winged Skull: Papers from the Laurence Sterne Bicentenary Conference.* Kent, Ohio: Kent State University Press, 1971. A collection of essays on a range of subjects, including Sterne's style, his reputation outside England, and his fictional devices. Includes some helpful illustrations.

Hartley, Lodwick. *This Is Lorence: A Narrative of the Reverend Laurence Sterne.* Chapel Hill: University of North Carolina Press, 1943. Still the best general introduction to the man and his work. In a sprightly biography for the general reader, Hartley quotes generously from Sterne and sets him clearly in his age.

Kraft, Elizabeth. *Laurence Sterne Revisited.* New York: Twayne, 1996. Kraft begins her short book with two chapters about Sterne's early writings, then devotes one chapter each to *Tristram Shandy* and *A Sentimental Journey*. The first chapter is primarily biographical, giving readers an overview of Sterne's life as a cleric before he became a literary celebrity. The second chapter concerns the fruit of Sterne's years as a clergyman, *The Sermons of Mr. Yorick.* Kraft also includes a final chapter on Sterne's changing critical reputation as well as a selected bibliography.

Myer, Valerie Grosvenor, ed. *Laurence Sterne: Riddles and Mysteries.* New York: Barnes & Noble Books, 1984. Contains eleven essays on *The Life and Opinions of Tristram Shandy, Gent.*, covering such matters as the nature of Sterne's comedy, the intellectual background of the novel, and Sterne's influence on the work of Jane Austen. Includes a brief annotated bibliography.

New, Melvin. *"Tristram Shandy": A Book for Free Spirits.* New York: Twayne, 1994. After providing a literary and historical milieu for Sterne's most famous work, New explores five different methods of approaching *Tristram Shandy*: "Satire," "Heads" (that is, intellectually), "Hearts" (that is, emotionally), "Joy," and "Tartuffery" (as a humorous attack on hypocrisy). New's approach is somewhat too schematic and too dependent on Friedrich Nietzsche's writings about *Tristram*, but it could act as a helpful guide for students attempting to come to terms with this shifting and slippery text.

Putney, Rufus D. "The Evolution of *A Sentimental Journey.*" *Philological Quarterly* 19 (1940): 349-369. Treats the novel as a hoax in which readers could find the sentimentality they were seeking, while Sterne could create the humorous fiction he wanted to write.

Stedmond, John M. *The Comic Art of Laurence Sterne: Convention and Innovation in "Tristram Shandy" and "A Sentimental Journey."* Toronto: University of Toronto Press, 1967. Sterne's novels highlight the comic distance between aspiration and attainment that is endemic in human existence. Provides helpful readings of the novels and an appendix recording Sterne's direct borrowings.

Robert Louis Stevenson

Born: Edinburgh, Scotland; November 13, 1850
Died: Vailima, near Apia, Samoa; December 3, 1894

Principal long fiction · *Treasure Island,* 1881-1882 (serial), 1883 (book); *Prince Otto,* 1885; *The Strange Case of Dr. Jekyll and Mr. Hyde,* 1886; *Kidnapped,* 1886; *The Black Arrow,* 1888; *The Master of Ballantrae,* 1889; *The Wrong Box,* 1889; *The Wrecker,* 1892 (with Lloyd Osbourne); *Catriona,* 1893; *The Ebb-Tide,* 1894 (with Osbourne); *Weir of Hermiston,* 1896 (unfinished); *St. Ives,* 1897 (completed by Arthur Quiller-Couch).

Other literary forms · In addition to his novels, Robert Louis Stevenson published a large number of essays, poems, and short stories, most of which have been collected under various titles. The best edition of Stevenson's works is the South Seas Edition (32 volumes) published by Scribner's in 1925.

Achievements · A man thoroughly devoted to his art, Stevenson was highly regarded during his lifetime as a writer of Romantic fiction. Indeed, few, if any, have surpassed him in that genre. Combining a strong intellect and a wide-ranging imagination with his ability to tell a story, he produced novels that transport the reader to the realms of adventure and intrigue. After his death, his literary reputation diminished considerably, until he was regarded primarily as a writer of juvenile fiction, unworthy of serious critical attention. With the growth of scholarly interest in popular literature, however, Stevenson is sure to enjoy a reevaluation. Certainly his narrative skill speaks for itself, and it is on that base that his literary reputation should ultimately rest. Anyone who has vicariously sailed with Jim Hawkins in quest of buried treasure or sipped a potion that reduces intellect to instinct with Henry Jekyll can vouch for the success of Stevenson as a writer and agree with what he wrote in "A Gossip of Romance" (1882): "In anything fit to be called reading, the process itself should be absorbing and voluptuous; we should gloat over a book, be rapt clean out of ourselves, and rise from the perusal, our mind filled with the busiest kaleidoscopic dance of images, incapable of sleep or of continuous thought."

Biography · The only child of Thomas and Margaret (Balfour) Stevenson, Robert Louis Stevenson was born on November 13, 1850, in Edinburgh, Scotland. He was in poor health even as a child, and he suffered throughout his life from a tubercular condition. Thomas, a civil engineer and lighthouse keeper, had hopes that Stevenson would eventually follow in his footsteps, and the youngster was sent to Anstruther and then to Edinburgh University. His fragile health, however, precluded a career in engineering, and he shifted his efforts to the study of law, passing the bar in Edinburgh in 1875.

Even during his preparation for law, Stevenson was more interested in literature, and, reading widely in the essays of Michel de Montaigne, Charles Lamb, and William Hazlitt, he began imitating their styles. Their influence can be seen in the style that Stevenson ultimately developed–a personal, conversational style, marked by an easy familiarity.

Library of Congress

Between 1875 and 1879, Stevenson wandered through France, Germany, and Scotland in search of a healthier climate. In 1876, at Fontainebleau, France, he met Fanny Osbourne, an American with whom he fell in love. She returned to California in 1878, and in that same year became seriously ill. Stevenson set out immediately to follow her. Traveling by steerage, he faced considerable hardships on his journey, hardships that proved detrimental to his already poor health. In 1880, he married Fanny and settled for a few months in a desolate mining camp in California. After a return to Scotland, the couple journeyed to Davos, Switzerland, for the winter.

Again returning to Scotland in the spring, Stevenson worked on his novel *Treasure Island*. Moving back and forth between Scotland and Switzerland was not conducive to improved health, and Stevenson decided to stay permanently in the south of France. Another attack of illness, however, sent him to Bournemouth, England, a health resort, until 1887, during which time he worked assiduously on his writing. In August of that year he sailed for America, settling at Saranac Lake in New York's Adirondacks. There he wrote *The Master of Ballantrae* in 1889. He finally settled in the islands of Samoa in the South Seas, a setting that he used for *The Wrecker* and *The Ebb-Tide*. He died there on December 3, 1894, ending a short but productive life.

Analysis · By the time that Robert Louis Stevenson published his first novel, *Treasure Island*, the golden age of Victorianism in England was over. The empire was far-flung and great, but the masses of England had more immediate concerns. The glory of the Union Jack gave small comfort to a working class barely able to keep its head above water. If earlier novelists wrote for the middle-class reader, those of the last twenty years of the century revolted against the cultural domination of that class. Turning to realism, they dealt with the repression caused by a crushing environment. Stevenson, however, disdained moral and intellectual topics, preferring the thin, brisk, sunny atmosphere of romance. Consequently, he stands apart from such figures as Thomas Hardy, Arnold Bennett, and George Gissing.

In "A Humble Remonstrance," Stevenson spoke of the function of a writer of romance as being "bound to be occupied, not so much in making stories true as in making them typical; not so much in capturing the lineament of each fact, as in marshalling all of them to a common end." Perhaps, then, Stevenson should be seen not simply as an antirealistic writer of romance, but as a writer whose conception of realism was different from that of his contemporaries.

In his study of Stevenson, Edwin Eigner points out that the novelist's heroes are drawn from real life and are usually failures. Moreover, says Eigner, "very few of the characters, whether good *or* evil, manage even to fail greatly." Stevenson himself wrote in his essay "Reflection and Remarks on Human Life" that "our business in this world is not to succeed, but to continue to fail, in good spirits." His own ill health may have caused him to see life in terms of conflict, and in his case a conflict that he could not win. This element of failure adds a somber dimension to Stevenson's romances—a note of reality, as it were, to what otherwise might have been simply adventure fiction. It is the element of adventure superimposed on reality that gives Stevenson's writing its peculiar character. A writer's stories, he remarked, "may be nourished with the realities of life, but their true mark is to satisfy the nameless longings of the reader, and to obey the ideal laws of the daydream." In doing this, the writer's greatest challenge, according to Stevenson, is to give "body and blood" to his stories. Setting, circumstance, and character must all fall into place to give a story the power to make an impression on the mind of the reader, "to put the last mark of truth upon a story and fill up at one blow our capacity for sympathetic pleasure." In this way a story becomes more than merely literature; it becomes art.

Stevenson regarded the tales of the *Arabian Nights* as perfect examples of the storyteller's art: tales that could captivate the reader in his childhood and delight him in his old age. Such was the goal that he sought in his own works: to bring the reader to the story as an involved spectator who does not shy away from the unpleasantries or the villainy, but finds in witnessing them the same pleasure he does in witnessing the more optimistic and uplifting aspects of the piece. Perhaps this is Stevenson's greatest achievement: He illustrates with his stories a sometimes forgotten truth—"Fiction is to the grown man what play is to the child."

Treasure Island · "If this don't fetch the kids, why, they have gone rotten since my day," Stevenson wrote in a letter to Sidney Colvin on August 25, 1881. He was speaking of *Treasure Island,* the novel on which he was then at work. He need not have worried, for since its publication it has been a favorite of children everywhere—and, indeed, of many adults. Stevenson wrote the book, according to his own account, in two bursts of creative activity of about fifteen days each. "My quickest piece of work," he said. The novel was begun as an amusement for his stepson Lloyd Osbourne, then twelve years old. Upon its completion in November of 1881, the novel was serialized in the magazine *Young Folks*; since it did not raise circulation to any degree, it was not considered particularly successful. The book was an altogether different story.

As a tale of adventure, *Treasure Island* stands as one of the best. Buried treasure has always had an aura of mystery and intrigue about it, and this case is no exception. Young Jim Hawkins is the hero of the novel; the adventure starts when Bill Bones, an old seaman, comes to Jim's father's inn, the Admiral Benbow, to wait for a one-legged seaman, who does not arrive. Bones does have two other visitors: a seaman named Black Dog, whom he chases away after a fight, and a deformed blind man named Pew, who gives him the black spot, the pirates' death notice. Bones is so frightened that he dies of a stroke. In the meantime, Jim's father has also died, leaving Jim and his mother alone. Opening Bones's locker, they find an oilskin packet that Jim gives to Squire Trelawney and Dr. Livesey.

Finding in the packet a treasure map, Trelawney and Livesey decide to outfit a ship and seek the treasure. Jim is invited to come along as cabin boy. Just before they sight the island where the treasure is supposed to be, Jim overhears the ship's cook, the one-legged Long John Silver, and some of the crew plotting a mutiny. When Silver and a party are sent ashore, Jim smuggles himself along to spy on them.

When Trelawney and Livesey learn of Silver's duplicity, they decide to take the loyal crew members and occupy a stockade they have discovered on the island, leaving the ship to the pirates. Unable to take the stockade, Silver offers a safe passage home to its defenders in return for the treasure map. The offer is refused, and, after another attack, the party in the stockade is reduced to Trelawney, Livesey, Captain Smollett, and Jim. Jim rows to the ship, shoots the only pirate on board, and then beaches the ship. Returning to the stockade, he finds his friends gone and Silver and the pirates in control. Silver saves Jim's life from the other pirates and reveals the treasure map, which Dr. Livesey had given him secretly when the former had come to treat some of the wounded pirates. What Silver does not know is that Ben Gunn, the lone resident of the island, has already found the treasure and moved it to his own quarters. When the pirates find no treasure, they turn on Jim and Silver, but Gunn and Jim's friends arrive in time to rescue them. The ship is floated by the tide, and Jim, his friends, and Silver leave the island. Silver jumps ship with only a bag of coins for his efforts, but the rest of the group divide the treasure. "Drink and the devil had done for the rest."

Though Jim may be the hero of the novel, it is Long John Silver who dominates the book. He is an ambiguous character, capable of murder, greed, and double-dealing on one hand and magnanimity on the other. He was Stevenson's favorite character—and the one who ultimately raises the book from a pedestrian adventure story to a timeless, mythically resonant tale which has absorbed generations of readers. The unifying theme of *Treasure Island* is people's desire for wealth. Trelawney and Livesey may be more moral in society's eyes than Silver, but their motivation is certainly no higher. As for Jim, he cannot, like Silver, give a belly laugh in the face of such a world and go off seeking another adventure. One such adventure is enough for Jim, and that one he would rather forget.

The Black Arrow · Serialized in *Young Folks* in 1883, *The Black Arrow* was labeled by Stevenson as "tushery," a term he and William Henley used for romantic adventures written for the market. In a letter to Henley in May, 1883, he said, "Ay, friend, a whole tale of tushery. And every tusher tushes me so free, that may I be tushed if the whole thing is worth a tush." Stevenson had hopes, however, that *The Black Arrow* would strike a more receptive note in *Young Folks* than did *Treasure Island,* and in this respect, his hopes were realized.

Though it lacks the depth of *Treasure Island, The Black Arrow* was enormously popular in its time and does not deserve its critical neglect. Set in the fifteenth century against the background of a minor battle of the Wars of the Roses and the appearance of the infamous Richard, Duke of Gloucester, the story recounts the adventures of Dick Shelton as he attempts to outwit his scheming guardian, Sir Daniel Brackley. An unscrupulous man, Sir Daniel has fought first on one side of the war and then on the other, adding to his own lands by securing the wardships of children orphaned by the war.

Planning to marry Dick to Joanna Sedley, an orphaned heiress, Sir Daniel has ridden away to take charge of the girl. In his absence, Moat House, his estate, is attacked by a group of outlaws led by a man with the mysterious name of John Amend-All, who pins a message to the church door of Moat House swearing vengeance on Sir Daniel and others for killing Dick's father, Henry Shelton.

Dick, deciding to remain quiet until he can learn more of the matter, sets out to inform Sir Daniel of the attack. In the meantime, Joanna, dressed as a boy, has eluded Sir Daniel. On his way back to Moat House, Dick meets Joanna in the guise of "John Matcham." Unaware that Sir Daniel has planned the marriage and unaware that John is Joanna, Dick offers to help his companion reach the abbey at Holywood. They eventually arrive at Moat House, where Dick learns that John is really Joanna and that his own life is in danger. He escapes and, after a lengthy series of intrigues and adventures, saves the life of Richard of York, Duke of Gloucester, and rescues Joanna from Sir Daniel, who is killed by Ellis Duckworth (John Amend-All). Dick then marries Joanna and settles at Moat House.

As an adventure story, *The Black Arrow* is thoroughly successful. The movement from episode to episode is swift, and the reader has little opportunity to lose interest. The love story between Dick and Joanna is deftly handled, with Joanna herself a delightfully drawn character. Still, the novel does not venture beyond the realm of pure adventure. Like many adventure stories, it is often contrived and trivial, but this fact does not detract from its readability.

The Strange Case of Dr. Jekyll and Mr. Hyde · Stories and theories abound regarding the writing of *The Strange Case of Dr. Jekyll and Mr. Hyde*. In "A Chapter of Dreams" (1888), Stevenson himself gave an account of the composition of the novel, explaining that "for two days I went about racking my brain for a plot of any sort; and on the second night I dreamed the scene at the window; and a scene afterwards split in two, in which Hyde, pursued for some crime, took the powder and underwent the change in the presence of his pursuers. All the rest was made awake, and consciously." The whole, according to Stevenson, was written and revised within a ten-week period.

The novel is based on the idea of the double personality in every person, an idea with which Stevenson had long been concerned. Referring to Jekyll, he said to Will H. Low, a painter, that "I believe you will find he is quite willing to answer to the name of Low or Stevenson." Not the first to use the idea in literature, Stevenson does give it a different twist. Hyde is not the double of the sinner, a conscience as it were, but, as one reviewer put it, Hyde is a personality of "hideous caprices, and appalling vitality, a terrible power of growth and increase."

As the story opens, Richard Enfield and Mr. Utterson, a lawyer, are discussing the activities of a Mr. Hyde, who has recently trampled down a small child. Both friends of Dr. Henry Jekyll, they are perturbed that the latter has named Hyde as heir in his will. A year later, Hyde is wanted for a murder, but he escapes. Soon after, Dr. Jekyll's servant Poole tells Utterson of strange goings-on in his employer's laboratory. He is concerned that possibly Jekyll has been slain. Poole and Utterson break into the laboratory and find a man dead from poison. The man is Edward Hyde. A note in the laboratory contains Jekyll's confession of his double identity.

Early in life, he had begun leading a double existence: a public life of convention and gentility and a private life of unrestrained vice. Finally, he discovered a potion that transformed him physically into Edward Hyde, his evil self. Though Jekyll wanted desperately to be rid of Hyde, he was not strong enough to overcome his evil side. He finally closed himself in his laboratory, seeking a drug that would eliminate Hyde. Failing in his search, he committed suicide.

As an exploration into the darkest recesses of the human mind, *The Strange Case of Dr. Jekyll and Mr. Hyde* is skillfully constructed. Not only are Jekyll and Hyde presented in a haunting fashion, but Utterson also is a character brought clearly to life. The plot, sensational though it is, does not rely on the standard gothic claptrap to hold the reader. On the contrary, the story is subtly undertold, and the reader is drawn into the horror of it by Stevenson's penetrating imagination and his easy mastery of language and style. The reader, said one reviewer, "feels that the same material might have been spun out to cover double the space and still have struck him as condensed and close knit workmanship. It is one of those rare fictions which make one understand the value of temperance in art."

Kidnapped · Stevenson completed *Kidnapped* in the spring of 1886, intending it originally as a potboiler, and it surely has all the ingredients of high adventure: a stolen inheritance, a kidnapping, a battle at sea, and several murders. Having gained an interest in Scottish history from his travels through the Highlands, Stevenson used as his principal source of historical information *Trial of James Stewart* (1753), a factual account of the 1752 Appin murder trial.

Kidnapped is the story of David Balfour, whose only inheritance from his father is a letter to Ebenezer Balfour of Shaws, David's uncle. On the way to see Mr. Rankeillor, the family lawyer, to get the true story of the inheritance, David is tricked and sent off on a ship for slavery in the American colonies. He meets Alan Breck, an enemy of the monarch because of his part in a rebellion against King George, and, though David is loyal to the king, the two become fast and true friends. Escaping from the ship, they have numerous adventures, finally returning to Scotland, where David learns the truth of the inheritance. His father and uncle had both loved the same woman; when David's father married the woman (David's mother), he generously gave up his inheritance to his brother Ebenezer. Ebenezer knew that such an arrangement would not hold up legally, and thus he tried to kill David. David accepts Ebenezer's offer of two-thirds of the income from the inheritance, and, with the money, he helps Alan reach safety from the king's soldiers who are pursuing him.

Kidnapped is rich in its depiction of the Scottish Highlands, and the novel's dialogue is particularly effective. The contrast between David, a Lowlander and a Whig, and Alan, a Highlander and a Jacobite, for example, is well drawn. Ignoring their differences, the two, like Huck and Jim in Mark Twain's *Adventures of Huckleberry Finn* (1884), prove that their friendship is more important than geographical and political differences.

Whatever Stevenson thought of *Kidnapped,* his friend Edmund Gosse thought it the "best piece of fiction that you have done." Many would argue with Gosse's statement. While it perhaps has more human interest than does *Treasure Island,* it lacks the sharpness and force of Stevenson's masterpiece.

The Master of Ballantrae · Although not as well known as *Treasure Island* and *Kidnapped, The Master of Ballantrae* is considered by many to be Stevenson's best novel. Stevenson himself saw it as a "most seizing tale," a "human tragedy." Despite his preoccupation with character delineation in the story, he still regales the reader with a plethora of adventurous incidents. Set in eighteenth century Scotland, *The Master of Ballantrae* recounts the story of two brothers as they compete for title and love. When Stuart the Pretender returns to Scotland in 1745 to claim the English throne, Lord Durrisdeer decides to send one son to fight with Stuart and to keep one at home, hoping that way to make his estate secure regardless of the outcome of the struggle. James, Master of Ballantrae and his father's heir, joins Stuart, and Henry remains behind. When news of Stuart's defeat and James's death comes, Henry becomes

Master of Ballantrae. He marries Alison Graeme, who had been betrothed to James.

James, however, is not dead, and, after adventures in America and France, returns to Scotland. Goading Henry and pressing his attentions on Alison, James soon angers his brother to the point of a midnight duel. Henry thinks that he has killed James, but again the latter escapes death—this time going to India. He surprises Henry once more by showing up alive at Durrisdeer. Taking his family, Henry secretly leaves for America, but James, with his Indian servant Secundra Dass, follows. Searching for treasure that he buried on his previous trip to America, James falls sick and dies, but Henry, thinking his brother able to return at will from death, goes to the grave one night and sees Secundra Dass performing strange ministrations over James's exhumed body. Although the servant is unable to revive James, Henry believes that he sees his brother's eyes flutter and dies from heart failure. Thus, both Masters of Ballantrae are united in death.

The Master of Ballantrae, perhaps more than any other of Stevenson's novels, goes beyond the bounds of a mere adventure story. Adventure is a key element in the book, but the characters of James and Henry Durie are drawn with such subtlety and insight that the novel takes on dimensions not usually found in Stevenson's works. Like Long John Silver in *Treasure Island*, James Durie is not an ordinary villain. Henry, who moves from a kind of pathetic passivity in the first part of the novel to a villainy of his own, is unable to assume the true role of Master of Ballantrae. Overmatched and possessed by James, he lacks the dash and charm and strength of personality that makes the latter the real Master of Ballantrae. "In James Durie," wrote one reviewer, "Mr. Stevenson has invented a new villain, and has drawn him with a distinction of touch and tone worthy of Vandyke." With all the attributes of a hateful fiend, James nevertheless has a wit and a courage that are captivating.

Perhaps the novel does, as Stevenson himself feared, leave the reader with an impression of unreality. Still, whatever its shortcomings, *The Master of Ballantrae* has all the trademarks of Stevenson's fiction: an intricately and imaginatively designed plot, power of style, clear evocation of scene, and lifelike characters. G. K. Chesterton felt that Stevenson was the "first writer to treat seriously and poetically the aesthetic instincts of the boy." In his own way, Stevenson contributed a fair number of readable and memorable works to the English literary heritage, and that heritage is the richer for it.

Wilton Eckley

Other major works

SHORT FICTION: *The New Arabian Nights*, 1882; *More New Arabian Nights*, 1885; *The Merry Men and Other Tales and Fables*, 1887; *Island Nights' Entertainments*, 1893.

PLAYS: *Deacon Brodie*, pb. 1880 (with William Ernest Henley); *Macaire*, pb. 1885 (with Henley); *The Hanging Judge*, pb. 1887 (with Fanny Van de Grift Stevenson).

POETRY: *Moral Emblems*, 1882; *A Child's Garden of Verses*, 1885; *Underwoods*, 1887; *Ballads*, 1890; *Songs of Travel and Other Verses*, 1896.

NONFICTION: *An Inland Voyage*, 1878; *Edinburgh: Picturesque Notes*, 1878; *Travels with a Donkey in the Cévennes*, 1879; *Virginibus Puerisque*, 1881; *Familiar Studies of Men and Books*, 1882; *The Silverado Squatters: Sketches from a Californian Mountain*, 1883; *Memories and Portraits*, 1887; *The South Seas: A Record of Three Cruises*, 1890; *Across the Plains*, 1892; *A Footnote to History*, 1892; *Amateur Emigrant*, 1895; *In the South Seas*, 1896; *The Lantern-Bearers and Other Essays*, 1988.

Bibliography

Bell, Ian. *Dreams of Exile: Robert Louis Stevenson: A Biography*. New York: Henry Holt, 1992. Bell, a journalist rather than an academic, writes evocatively of Stevenson the dreamer and exile. This brief study of Stevenson's brief but dramatic life does a fine job of evoking the man and the places he inhabited. It is less accomplished in its approach to the work.

Calder, Jenni, ed. *The Robert Louis Stevenson Companion*. Edinburgh: Paul Harris, 1980. Forty-one illustrations accompany eight articles by different authors on the life and work of Stevenson. Some of the authors knew Stevenson personally. These topical articles were written between 1901 and 1979.

Daiches, David. *Robert Louis Stevenson and His World*. London: Thames and Hudson, 1973. A standard popular biography written in chronological and narrative style. Complete with 116 illustrations and a chronological page of events pertinent to Stevenson.

Hammond, J. R. *A Robert Louis Stevenson Companion: A Guide to the Novels, Essays, and Short Stories*. London: Macmillan, 1984. The first three sections cover the life and literary achievements of Stevenson and contain a brief dictionary which lists and describes his short stories, essays, and smaller works. The fourth section critiques his novels and romances, and the fifth is a key to the people and places of Stevenson's novels and stories.

Knight, Alanna. *The Robert Louis Stevenson Treasury*. London: Shepherd-Walwyn, 1985. An extremely useful compendium, arranged in eight parts with twenty-eight illustrations. Contains four maps: of Scotland, France, the South Seas, and the United States, as they pertained to Stevenson's life. Includes an alphabetized index of his works, letters, and characters, as well as works published about him in text, film, and radio. Also covers people and places that factored in his life.

McLynn, Frank. *Robert Louis Stevenson: A Biography*. New York: Random House, 1993. Published on the eve of Stevenson's centenary (1994), McLynn's biography seeks to rehabilitate Stevenson's literary reputation. For McLynn, Stevenson is Scotland's greatest writer of English prose. This an accomplished, serious reappraisal of a writer long relegated to the shelves of "boy's books." A final epilogue helps to explain how Stevenson's family squandered his legacy.

Swearingen, Roger G. *The Prose Writings of Robert Louis Stevenson*. Hamden, Conn.: Archon Books, 1980. A complete (350-entry) chronological list of Stevenson's prose writings–from his earliest childhood until his death in 1894–which is concerned with his literary activity as his career progressed. The data include the first appearance of each work, with its particular history of development, and actual locations of the works today.

Jonathan Swift

Born: Dublin, Ireland; November 30, 1667
Died: Dublin, Ireland; October 19, 1745

Principal long fiction · *A Tale of a Tub*, 1704; *Gulliver's Travels*, 1726 (originally entitled *Travels into Several Remote Nations of the World, in Four Parts, by Lemuel Gulliver, First a Surgeon, and Then a Captain of Several Ships*).

Other literary forms · Jonathan Swift's oeuvre includes a large and important body of verse, best assembled in *The Poems of Jonathan Swift* (1937, 1958), edited by Harold Williams. His letters may be found in *The Correspondence of Jonathan Swift* (1963-1965), also edited by Williams. Outstanding among a variety of political writings are Swift's contributions to *The Examiner* (1710-1711), the treatise called *The Conduct of the Allies and of the Late Ministry, in Beginning and Carrying on the Present War* (1711), and the important *The Drapier's Letters to the People of Ireland* (1735). His prose, collected in *The Prose Works of Jonathan Swift* (1939-1968), is a fourteen-volume collection edited by Herbert Davis.

Achievements · It is generally conceded that Swift is the greatest English satirist, possibly the most brilliant ironist and acerb wit in any language. Yet the force of his satiric barbs has rendered him controversial, and many critics have retaliated against his potent quill by claiming that Swift is reckless, uncontrolled, spiteful, insensate, heathenish, and insane. Such rash responses merely demonstrate the powerful effect his writing instigates.

Swift is not an overt lampooner, diatribe-monger, or name-caller. Curiously, he never utilizes the direct approach: he almost always speaks through a defective mouthpiece, a flawed, self-incriminating persona who forges a case against himself. Indeed, Swift is to be remembered as a grand satiric mimic, finely shaping and generating the voices of knaves and fools alike (the "modern" hack writer in *A Tale of a Tub*, the ignorant serving-woman Frances Harris, the idiot astrologer Isaac Bickerstaff, the callous and mathematical Modest Proposer, the proud but demented simpleton Lemuel Gulliver).

Swift's ear for clichés and inflections of dullness is almost perfect, and an author such as Herbert Read (in *English Prose Style*, 1928) hails Swift as the inevitable and clear master of "pure prose" style. Swift is, without doubt, the major satirist in prose, yet he is also a first-rate light poet (in the manner of Horace and the coarser Samuel "Hudibras" Butler), and, if anything, his reputation as a poet is rising. Furthermore, Swift wrote political pamphlets with ruthless force, and his prose in sermons, letters, and treatises is virile and direct. Finally, Swift should not be forgotten as wit and jester. He invented a child-language when corresponding with Stella, wrote mock-Latin sayings, devised wicked epigrams, created paraphrases of Vergil and Ovid, and could even toy with versifying when devising invitations to dinner. In a word, Swift is the all-around English expert in straightforward exposition—especially when it is bent to provoke savage mockery and the *jeu d'esprit*.

Biography · Jonathan Swift was born in Dublin on November 30, 1667, after the death of his father, a lower-middle class Anglo-Irishman. His grandfather, the Reverend Thomas Swift, had been a vicar in Herefordshire. His father, Jonathan, had settled in Ireland to work as a steward of the King's Inns in Dublin. His mother was Abigail Erick, the daughter of a Leicestershire clergyman. Swift's mother had entrusted her young son to a nurse; the nurse had spirited the infant Swift away from Ireland for several years, and although he was eventually returned, Jonathan was peculiarly linked with Ireland throughout his life. In any case, it was his fancy to picture himself a lonely outcast amid barbarians. He attended Kilkenny School in his youth and Trinity College, Dublin, obtaining a Bachelor's degree in 1686. He spent most of the following decade at Moor Park, Surrey, in the household of Sir William Temple, the distinguished Whig statesman. It was at Moor Park that Swift met, in 1689, the child of Esther Johnson (whom Swift later immortalized as "Stella"), the daughter of Temple's widowed housekeeper. Swift helped in supervising her education and inaugurated a lifelong (and little understood) relationship, for Stella later immigrated to Dublin and spent her life near the Anglican Dean Swift. Naturally, under Temple's aegis, Swift hoped for introductions and advancement, but little came of promises and possibilities; and in 1694, he returned to Dublin long enough to be ordained an Anglican priest (in 1695). He subsequently was reunited with Temple until the latter's death in 1699. Thereafter, he returned to Ireland as chaplain to the Earl of Berkeley. His reputation for talent and wit was rapidly growing.

Swift's great political period took place in London from 1708 to 1714. He became the chief spokesman, apologist, and pamphleteer for the powerful Tory leaders then in power, Robert Harley and Henry St. John Bolingbroke. Their fall and disgrace ushered in a lengthy era of Whig dominance that permanently drove Swift back to what he must have considered exile in Ireland. Swift had been finally rewarded (although he would have perceived it as a paltry recognition) with the Deanery of St. Patrick's Cathedral in Dublin, where he served for the remainder of his life. His powerful satires had earned him powerful enemies, and significant advancement in the Church or in England was never permitted to him.

In any event, Swift served with precision, justness, and rectitude as a clergyman, and continued throughout his career to be an admirable satirist and wit. He even elected to champion the rights of the maltreated Irish, and he came to be admired as their avatar and protector, a "Hibernian Patriot." In his last years, Swift suffered increasingly from deafness and vertigo (the results of a lifelong affliction by Ménière's Syndrome, a disease of the inner ear), which resulted in senility, and most likely a stroke. Guardians were appointed in his last years, and he died in 1745, shortly before his seventy-eighth birthday.

Swift's last ironic jest was played upon humankind in his will, which committed the bulk of his estate to the founding of a "hospital" for fools and madmen, just as he had pronounced the plan in his *Verses on the Death of Dr. Swift* (1731):

> He gave the little Wealth he had,
> To build a House for Fools and Mad;
> And shew'd by one satyric Touch,
> No Nation wanted it so much

Analysis · Initially, it must be noted that Jonathan Swift's "fictions" are nothing like conventional novels. They seldom detail the "adventures" of a hero or even a protagonist and never conclude with his Romantic achievement of goals or fulfillment of desires. Indeed, Swift is the great master of fictionalizing nonfiction. His satires always purport to be something factual, humdrum, diurnal, unimaginative: a treatise, a travel diary, an annotated edition, a laborious oration, a tendentious allegory, a puffed-out "letter-to-a-friend." Extremist Protestant sects condemned fiction, and "projectors" and would-be investigators in the dawning Age of Science extolled the prosaic, the plodding, the scholarly, the methodical, and the factual. At the same time, urban population growth and the rise of the middle class created a growing new audience, and printing presses multiplied in accordance with demand. Many "popular" and best-seller art forms flourished: sermons, true

Library of Congress

confessions, retellings (and Second Parts) of hot-selling tales and political harangues, news items, hearsay gossip, and science all became jumbled together for public consumption, much of which led to spates of yellow journalism. Throughout his life Swift rebelled against such indelicacies and depravities, and his satiric procedure included the extremist parody of tasteless forms—*reductio ad absurdum*. It was by such means that Swift secured his fame as an author.

A Tale of a Tub · Doubtless his most dazzling prose performance of this kind was his earliest, *A Tale of a Tub*, which appeared anonymously in 1704. (Swift, in fact, published most of his satires anonymously, although his work was usually instantly recognized and acclaimed.) *A Tale of a Tub* is actually a "medley" of pieces imitating the penchant for an author's combining fiction, essays, letters, verse, fragments, or anything to enable him to amass a book-length manuscript. It contained "The Battle of the Books," a wooden allegorical piece in the manner of Aesop's Fables, detailing the "quarrel of ancients versus moderns," and a fragmentary treatise upon "The Mechanical Operation of the Spirit," trussed up in the inept form of a casual letter to a friend.

The treatise mocked the new "scientific" trend of reducing all things to some species of Cartesian (or Newtonian) materialism. Rather comically, it deploys in a blasé manner the language of ancient Greek and Roman atomists—Democritus and Epicurus—as if they were contemporary modernists. Indeed, one pervasive theme throughout this volume is the ridiculousness of the modernist position of "independence"—although they might be ignorant of the past, the ideas and genres of classical antiquity keep recurring in their works, a fact which belies the Moderns' supposed originality (even while demonstrating that, as a result of solipsism, their form and control disintegrate into chaos).

Clearly, the titular piece, "A Tale of a Tub," is Swift's early masterpiece, and one of the great (and most difficult) satires in any language. In its pages, an avowed fanatic "modern" aspires to "get off" an edition, to tout and sell himself, to make money, to demonstrate his uniqueness and, however evanescently, tyrannically to be "the latest modern." He seeks to reedit an old tale of three brothers and their adventures. Naturally, he decorates and updates such a version to give it the latest cut and fashion, the style and wit and jargon of the moment. (It is perhaps an accident that this tale of the dissensions of Peter, Martin, and Jack parallels the vicissitudes of the history of Christianity, as it splinters into differing and quarreling religious sects. The Modern appears ignorant of historical sense.)

The new version of the old story, however, is fragmented: Every time the Modern's imagination or his fancy supplies him with a spark, he promptly follows his rather meandering Muse and travels into an elaboration, an annotation, or a digression. In fact, the opening fifty pages of the work are cluttered with the paraphernalia of "modern" publishing: dedications, publisher's comments, introductions, apologies, gratulations, notes to the second edition, acknowledgments, prefaces, and forewords. Thereafter, when such a cloud of ephemeral formalities would seem to have been dispensed with, the author still manages to interject a plethora of digressions—afterthoughts, asides, cute remarks apropos nothing, commentary, snipings at critics, obsequious snivelings for the reader, canting pseudophilosophy for the learned, and pity and adoration for himself. In no time at all, the entire tale is awash in detours, perambulations, and divagations.

This modern storyteller is nothing if not effervescent, boorish, and chronically self-indulgent. He claims that his pipe dreams and diversions are in essence planned excursions and in fact deliberately philosophic meditations, rich with allegorical meanings. The opposite is also true, and the Modern's Tub is like an empty cart—rattling around most furiously in its vacuity, making the most noise. Furthermore, the digressions become unwieldy. The tale is disrupted more and more frequently and the digressions become longer and longer. The Modern is his most penetrating in the trenchant Section IX—a digression in praise of madness—as he coyly confesses that his reason has been overturned, his intellectuals rattled, and that he has been but recently confined. The continued multiplication of digressions (until they subvert sections of the tale) and the finale when the Modern loses his notes and his ramblings give out entirely are easily understood as the wanderings of a madman—a Modern who suppresses the past, memory, reason, and self-control.

If Swift's warning about the growing taste for newness, modernity, and things-of-the-moment appears madcap and farcical, it is nevertheless a painfully close nightmare preview of future fashions, fantasms, and fallacies that subsequently came to be real.

A Tale of a Tub clearly demonstrates several of Swift's most common fictional ploys and motifs. Some representative of the depraved "moderns" is usually present, always crass, irreligious, ignorant, arrogant, proud, self-adulatory, concerned with the events of the moment. Indeed, Swift was fond of scrupulously celebrating every April 1 as All Fool's Day, but he also recognized April 2: All Knave's Day. He doubtless felt that both halves of humankind deserved some token of official recognition. Yet Swift also favored mixing the two: He frequently shows readers that a man who is manipulator, con man, and knave in one set of circumstances is himself conned, befooled, and gulled in another. As such, the Modern reveals an unexpected complexity in his makeup; he also illustrates the era (as Swift imagines it) that he inhabits, a period overfull of bad taste and poor writing which are the broad marks of cultural decadence.

In the work of a satirist, the world is regularly depicted as cyclic in historic periods, and usually in decline. Swift and Sir William Temple both stressed some trend toward decay in the modern era, and spoke often of barbarians and invasions; it was a type of satiric myth suitable to the disruptive fictions that the satirist envisions. In Section IX of *A Tale of a Tub*, the Modern vacillates between viewing all humankind as being "curious" or "credulous," as busy probers, analysts, and excavators, and the superficial and the inert: knaves versus fools. As is typical of Swift, the fool and knave personas are infused with enough familiar traits to suggest that all people partake of either. Further, Swift entraps his reader by implying that there are no other categories: One is either fool or knave or both. His irony is corrosive and inclusive, capturing the reader in its toils. In that sense, Swift is deliberately disruptive; he seeks to startle and to embroil the reader in his fictions about stupidity and depravity. To such an end, he tampers with logic to make his case appear substantial and manipulates paradox to keep his readers off balance. Such techniques lend Swift his volatile force.

These strategies are to be found in Swift's best verse; the same may be said for his two great, ironic short-prose pieces: *An Argument to Prove That the Abolishing of Christianity in England May, as Things Now Stand, Be Attended with Some Inconveniences, and Perhaps Not Produce Those Many Good Effects Proposed Thereby* (1708) and *A Modest Proposal for Preventing the Children of Poor People of Ireland from Being a Burden to Their Parents or the Country, and for Making Them Beneficial to the Public* (1729). Both of these works seek to shock the reader and to propose the discomforting, the alarming, the untenable.

Gulliver's Travels · Swift's undisputed masterpiece is *Gulliver's Travels*, originally entitled *Travels into Several Remote Nations of the World, in Four Parts, by Lemuel Gulliver, First a Surgeon, and Then a Captain of Several Ships*. This fictional work accommodates all of Swift's perennial themes and does so effectually. First, the work is perhaps the definitive study of new middle-class values, specifically the preoccupation with slang, cash, smug self-righteousness, self-assertion, and self-gratulation. Second, it might not be considered a "novel" in the conventional sense of the term, but it is a delightfully fact-filled simulation of adventure fiction, and it stems assuredly from the satiric picaresque tradition (in Spain and France) that greatly contributed to the formulation of modern novelistic techniques and themes.

Swift's Lemuel Gulliver (a mulish gull) is a model representative of the fool and the knave: He aspires to befool others but nevertheless befuddles himself. His medium is the very popular literary genre of the travelogue or record of a "voyage of discovery." The genre grew popular through its Cartesian emphasis upon an inductive observer-self and the Romantic subject of adventures in far-off lands. Such a travelogue format allows the narrator to take his readers on a vicarious journey of adventure and concludes by suggesting that the traveler has fulfilled the pattern of the *Bildungsroman* and has attained education, growth, experience, and Aristotelian *cognitio* (insight, maturation, the acquisition of new knowledge). As might be expected in an exemplary case manipulated by Swift, Gulliver is anything but the apt learner. He is a crass materialist for whom experiences consist of precise measurements of objects observed; a tedious cataloging of dress, diet, and customs; and an infinite variety of pains in note-taking, recording, transcribing, and translating. He is superficiality and rank objectivity incarnate. Naturally, therefore, his everyday mean density prevents his acquisition of any true understanding.

Gulliver is a minor physician, the mediocre little man, eager, like Daniel Defoe's Robinson Crusoe, to make sight-seeing tours and to acquire cash. His first of four voyages carries him to the land of six-inch mites, the Lilliputians, and his Second Voyage to the land of gargantuan giants, the Brobdingnagians. Gulliver remains myopic in either location, for he can hardly consider that little midgets can (and do) perpetuate monstrous deeds; and, once he perceives that the giants are rather tame, he leaps to the conclusion that they are infinitely superior to other human types (even though their political and social institutions are no better than they should be, given the quirks and flaws of human nature).

In sum, the tour from very small to very large merely stimulates in Gulliver a sense of wondrous contrast: He expects in these different worlds wondrous differences. Amusingly, what the reader finds is much the same, that is the uneven and imperfect human nature. Equally amusing, Gulliver behaves much the same himself in his attempts to ingratiate himself with his "superiors": He aspires to become a successful competitor in all worlds as a "titled" nobleman, a Nardac, a "courtier" with "connec- tions" at court. Like many middle-class people, he is a man in the middle, aspiring above all for upward mobility, mouthing the commonplaces of the day, utterly incapable of judging people and events. He is also the worst sort of traveler; he is a man who sees no farther than his own predilections and preconceptions and who imitates all the manners that he sees around him. Actually, the realms of big and little are merely distortions of the real world. Here, one of the work's central ironies is found in the fact that Gulliver could have learned as much, or as little, if he had stayed at home.

The world of sizes is replaced in the Third Voyage by the world of concepts: The muddled peoples he visits are victims of mathomania and abstraction-worship. At the same time, it is revealed that the world of the past, like the world of the present, has been tainted and corrupt. Even the potentially ideal Struldbruggs—immortals who live forever—are exposed as being far from lucky. They are, rather, especially accursed by the afflictions of impotence, depression, and senility. Swift has, with cartoon facility, carted Gulliver all around the world, showing him the corrosive face of fallen humanity, even among the various robbers, cowards, pirates, and mutineers that had beset him as he traveled in European ships; but Gulliver does not see.

The stage is properly set for the Fourth Voyage. Utilizing his favorite ploys of reversal and entrapment, Swift puts Gulliver into a land of learned and rational horses (the Houyhnhnms) and debauched hairy monkeylike beasts (the Yahoos). Once again, there is no middle ground: All in this world is rational horse or wolfish (and oafish) bestiality. Obviously, Gulliver chooses the equestrian gentlemen as his leaders and masters. (Indeed, throughout all the voyages, Gulliver the conformist has been in quest of a staid position and "masters" who will tell him what to do and grant him praise and sustenance for his slavish adulation.)

Slowly it is revealed, however, the Yahoos are men: Gulliver *is* a debased, gross, and deformed member of the Yahoo tribe; as Swift sweetly and confoundingly phrases it, Gulliver is a "perfect yahoo." The horses themselves rebuff this upstart, and Gulliver, who has undergone every other sort of ignominy in the course of his travels, is finally evicted as an undersirable alien from the horsey paradise. At last, Gulliver thinks he has learned a lesson; he aspires to be a horse, and, back in Europe, he shuns the human species and favors the environs of straw and stables. He has hardly acquired the rationality of his leaders and appears quite mad. Swift's ultimate paradox seems to imply that people can "know" about reason and ideals but can never master or practice them. Yet, even here, Swift cruelly twists the knife at the last moment, for the fond Gulliver, several years later, is revealed as slowly forgetting his intense (and irrational) devotion to the Houyhnhnms and is slowly beginning to be able to tolerate and accept the lowly human race that he had earlier so intransigently spurned. Gulliver cannot even stick to a lesson painfully and rudely learned during many years; he has neither the brains, drive, ambition, nor consistency to keep him on any course. Gulliver's travels eventually get him nowhere.

In sum, *Gulliver's Travels* makes a huge tragicomical case for the absurdity of pretentious man. Gulliver is fool enough to believe that he is progressing and knave enough to boast about it, and to hope to gain some position and affluence from the event. Yet, at his proudest moments, he is little more than a driveller, a gibbering idiot who is raveningly insane. Gulliver's painful experiences and the brute instruction his readers acquire are a caustic finale to much of the heady and bold idealism of the Renaissance, and a cautionary plea for restraint in an era launched on celebrating reason, science, optimism, and enlightenment. Time has shown that Swift was largely right; blithe superconfidence in people, their sciences, and their so-called "progress" is very likely to come enormously to grief. *Gulliver's Travels* speaks to everyone because it addresses crucial issues about the human condition itself.

John R. Clark

Other major works

POETRY: *Cadenus and Vanessa*, 1726; *Verses on the Death of Dr. Swift*, 1731; *On Poetry: A Rapsody*, 1733; *The Poems of Jonathan Swift*, 1937, 1958 (3 volumes; Harold Williams, editor).

NONFICTION: *A Discourse of the Contests and Dissensions Between the Nobles and the Commons in Athens and Rome*, 1701; *The Battle of the Books*, 1704; *An Argument to Prove That the Abolishing of Christianity in England May, as Things Now Stand, Be Attended with Some Inconveniences, and Perhaps Not Produce Those Many Good Effects Proposed Thereby*, 1708; *A Project for the Advancement of Religion, and the Reformation of Manners By a Person of Quality*, 1709; *The Conduct of the Allies and of the Late Ministry, in Beginning and Carrying on the Present War*, 1711; *A Proposal for Correcting, Improving and Ascertaining the English Tongue, in a Letter to the Most Honourable Robert Earl of Oxford and Mortimer, Lord High Treasurer of Great Britain*, 1712; *The Public Spirit of the Whigs, Set Forth in Their Generous Encouragement of the Author of the Crisis*, 1714; *A Letter from a Lay-Patron to a Gentleman, Designing for Holy Orders*, 1720; *A Modest Proposal for Preventing the Children of Poor People of Ireland from Being a Burden to Their Parents or the Country, and for Making Them Beneficial to the Public*, 1729; *The Drapier's Letters to the People of Ireland*, 1735; *A Complete Collection of Genteel and Ingenious Conversation, According to the Most Polite Mode and Method Now Used at Court, and in the Best Companies of England, in Three Dialogues, by Simon Wagstaff Esq.*, 1738; *Directions to Servants in General . . .* , 1745; *The History of the Four Last Years of the Queen, by the Late Jonathan Swift DD, DSPD*, 1758; *Journal to Stella*, 1766, 1768; *Letter to a Very Young Lady on Her Marriage*, 1797; *The Correspondence of Jonathan Swift*, 1963-1965 (5 volumes; Harold Williams, editor).

MISCELLANEOUS: *Miscellanies in Prose and Verse*, 1711; *Miscellanies*, 1727-1733 (4 volumes; with Alexander Pope and other members of the Scriblerus Club); *The Prose Works of Jonathan Swift*, 1939-1968 (14 volumes; Herbert Davis, editor).

Bibliography

Ehrenpreis, Irvin. *Swift: The Man, His Works, and the Age.* 3 vols. Cambridge, Mass.: Harvard University Press, 1962-1983. A monumental biography that rejects long-held myths, provides much new information about Swift and his works, and relates him to the intellectual and political currents of his age.

Fox, Christopher, and Brenda Tooley, eds. *Walking Naboth's Vineyard: New Studies of Swift.* Notre Dame: University of Notre Dame Press, 1995. The introduction discusses Swift and Irish studies, and the subsequent essays all consider aspects of Swift as an Irish writer. Individual essays have notes, but there is no bibliography.

Hunting, Robert. *Jonathan Swift.* Rev. ed. Boston: Twayne, 1989. In this revision of his earlier book on Swift, Hunting incorporates recent scholarship to provide an overview of Swift's life and his major works. Includes a chronology and a selective, annotated secondary bibliography.

Nokes, David. *Jonathan Swift, a Hypocrite Reversed: A Critical Biography.* Oxford, England: Oxford University Press, 1985. Draws heavily on Swift's own writings, offering a good introduction for the general reader seeking information about his life and works. Nokes views Swift as a conservative humanist.

Palmieri, Frank, ed. *Critical Essays on Jonathan Swift.* New York: G. K. Hall, 1993. Divided into sections on Swift's life and writings, *Gulliver's Travels*, *A Tale of a Tub* and eighteenth century literature, and his poetry and nonfiction prose. Includes index but no bibliography.

Quintana, Ricardo. *The Mind and Art of Jonathan Swift.* 1936. Reprint. London: Oxford University Press, 1953. One of the standards of Swift criticism, concentrating on the public Swift. Examines his political activities and writings, tracing the intellectual sources of his thought. Includes synopses of his major works and provides a useful historical background. The 1953 edition contains additional notes and an updated bibliography.

Rawson, Claude. *The Character of Swift's Satire: A Revised Focus.* Newark: University of Delaware Press, 1983. Presents eleven essays by Swift scholars, including John Traugatt's excellent reading of *A Tale of a Tub*, Irvin Ehrenpreis on Swift as a letter writer, and F. P. Lock on Swift's role in the political affairs of Queen Anne's reign.

Real, Hermann J., and Heinz J. Vienken, eds. *Proceedings of the First Münster Symposium on Jonathan Swift.* Munich: Wilhelm Fink, 1985. Includes twenty-four essays on all aspects of Swift's work, each preceded by an abstract. Indexed for cross-referencing.

William Makepeace Thackeray

Born: Calcutta, India; July 18, 1811
Died: London, England; December 24, 1863

Principal long fiction · *Catherine: A Story*, 1839-1840 (as Ikey Solomons, Jr.); *The History of Samuel Titmarsh and the Great Hoggarty Diamond*, 1841 (later as *The Great Hoggarty Diamond*, 1848); *The Luck of Barry Lyndon: A Romance of the Last Century*, 1844; *Vanity Fair: A Novel Without a Hero*, 1847-1848; *The History of Pendennis: His Fortunes and Misfortunes, His Friends and His Greatest Enemy*, 1848-1850; *Rebecca and Rowena: A Romance upon Romance*, 1850 (as M. A. Titmarsh); *The History of Henry Esmond, Esquire, a Colonel in the Service of Her Majesty Q. Anne*, 1852 (3 volumes); *The Newcomes: Memoirs of a Most Respectable Family*, 1853-1855; *The Virginians: A Tale of the Last Century*, 1857-1859; *Lovel the Widower*, 1860; *The Adventures of Philip on His Way Through the World, Shewing Who Robbed Him, Who Helped Him, and Who Passed Him By*, 1861-1862; *Denis Duval*, 1864.

Other literary forms · William Makepeace Thackeray's career as a satirist and journalist contributed to his novelistic style. His works appeared in a number of periodicals, including *The National Standard*, which he owned, *The Constitutional*, for which he was Paris correspondent, and *The New Monthly Magazine*. More important, however, the bulk of his writing appeared in *Fraser's Magazine* and in *Punch*, until, in 1860, he became editor of the *Cornhill Magazine*. In many of his reviews, short stories, burlesques, and travel writings, he adopts facetious pen names that reveal the snobbish preconceptions of his personae. "The Yellowplush Correspondence" appeared in *Fraser's Magazine* in 1837-1838 as the supposed diary of Charles James Yellowplush, an illiterate footman who betrays all the social prejudices of his employers. The story was later published as *Memoirs of Mr. Charles J. Yellowplush* in 1856. Thackeray assumed two pseudonyms for some of his comic pieces. As Michael Angelo Titmarsh, Thackeray published *A Legend of the Rhine* (1845), *Mrs. Perkin's Ball* (1847), and *The Rose and the Ring: Or, The History of Prince Giglio and Prince Bulbo* (1855) among others, in addition to some nonfiction works such as *The Paris Sketch Book* (1840), *The Irish Sketch Book* (1843), and *Notes of a Journey from Cornhill to Grand Cairo . . .* (1846); as George Savage Fitz-Boodle, an aging and susceptible bachelor, Thackeray wrote *The Confessions of George Fitz-Boodle, and Some Passages in the Life of Major Gahagan* (1841-1842) and *Men's Wives* (1843). "Punch's Prize Novelists," which appeared in *Punch* magazine, was a series of parodies of popular novelists of the day, such as Benjamin Disraeli and James Fenimore Cooper, and was perhaps even more effective than the burlesque *Catherine* (which he wrote as Ikey Solomons, Jr.). Thackeray's other achievements include *The English Humourists of the Eighteenth Century* (1853) and *The Four Georges: Sketches of Manners, Morals, Court and Town Life* (1860); a number of tales and short stories, including *A Shabby Genteel Story and Other Tales* (1852), and a series of ballads and verses, such as the nostalgic "The Ballad of Bouillabaisse" (1849).

Achievements · Long remembered as a social satirist *par excellence*, Thackeray wrote more in the manner of Henry Fielding than of Samuel Richardson and more in the

Library of Congress

realistic vein than in the style of the "novel of sensibility," that production of the early nineteenth century that sought to achieve heightened emotional effects at the expense of believable plot and characterization. Both in his miscellaneous writings and in his first great novel, *Vanity Fair*, Thackeray sought to counter the kind of melodramatic and pretentious entertainment provided by such authors as Edward Bulwer-Lytton, William Harrison Ainsworth, and even the early Charles Dickens. He attempted, instead, to make his readers see through the social and literary hypocrisy that, as he believed, characterized the age. To this end, he adopted a number of pseudonyms in his early essay writing, pseudonyms that can be said to foreshadow the personae he used in his fiction.

In reviewing both art and literature for such magazines as *Fraser's Magazine* and *The New Monthly Magazine*, Thackeray adopted the Yellowplush and Titmarsh signatures; he was thus able to ridicule in a lively way what he found false. His reviews were no less devastating to the current trend of idolizing criminals and rogues, as seen in the series of popular "Newgate Novels." As Ikey Solomons, Jr., he produced *Catherine*, the tale of a murderess, but even here, his attempt to deglamorize the account was mitigated by his growing sympathy for his created characters. Again, *A Shabby Genteel Story* attempted to deal with the middle class in unvarnished terms. His first sustained narrative, *The Luck of Barry Lyndon*, features an Irish adventurer recounting his own life; the novel follows the rise and fall of its picaresque hero to illustrate the specious nature of worldly success. Perhaps most telling in his ten-year preparation for fiction writing were two series that appeared in *Punch*. "The Snobs of England" was a series of verbal portraits of social types, most drawn for their pretension; "Punch's Prize Novelists" was a collection of parodic rewritings of popular novelists' works.

In his sustained works, however, Thackeray leaves his readers not with a collection of isolated vignettes but with a panoramic study of humankind under the guidance of a witty persona whose satirical bent is tempered by the realization that he himself partakes of the foibles of his own characters. Thackeray's characteristic persona derives not only from Fielding and his prefaces to the various books of *The History of Tom Jones, a Foundling* (1749), but also from Samuel Johnson, who ends *Rasselas, Prince of Abyssinia* (1759) by suggesting that since an ideal world is impossible, a wise individual will stoically accept the one that exists. Certainly, Thackeray's experimentations with the persona in *The History of Henry Esmond, Esquire*, for example, a novel written in the memoir form, laid the groundwork for such masters of psychological realism and irony as Henry James and James Joyce. In addition, Thackeray's experimentations with the generational form, in which several novels are melded together through the familial relationships of their characters, look forward to such productions as John Galsworthy's *The Forsyte Saga* (1922). In presenting the affairs of Henry Esmond's grandsons and the development of the beautiful Beatrix Esmond into a worldly old woman in *The Virginians*, he was also implicitly exploring the kind of genetic and environmental influence that the naturalists defined as determinism.

While many modern readers are perhaps not as comfortable as their nineteenth century forebears with the conception of the authorial voice as a constant, even necessary factor in the plot, Thackeray nevertheless remains noteworthy, especially in his early novels, both for the realistic renderings of individuals in all social walks and for his moral standpoint, best expressed in the preface to *Vanity Fair* as a charitable outlook on human foibles.

Biography · William Makepeace Thackeray was born on July 18, 1811, in Calcutta, India. His father, Richmond Thackeray, pursued a family career in the East India Company; his mother, Anne Becher, traced her ancestry back to a sixteenth century sheriff of London. The senior William Makepeace Thackeray and John Harman Becher had extensive interests in India. After his father's death in 1815, Thackeray's mother married Major Henry Carmichael-Smith, a former suitor. As was the custom, Thackeray was sent to England at the age of five for reasons of health and education. His unhappy, early experiences at the Arthurs' school and at Chiswick were later rendered in "Dr. Birch and his Young Friends" (1849). At Cambridge, as a member of a privileged class, he was trained in the standards and preconceptions that he later pilloried in his *The Book of Snobs* (1848, 1852) and in many other works. He was left with a distaste for bullying and with a distrust of his own intellectual abilities. After two years at Cambridge, Thackeray abandoned the pursuit of academic honors. Although he believed that his education had, on the whole, served him ill, it nevertheless had given him a background in history and culture, a double appreciation that is well evidenced in *The History of Henry Esmond, Esquire*; it also convinced him of his social status, although his expensive aristocratic habits were to prove difficult to control.

The gentle satire evident in *Vanity Fair*'s Pumpernickel chapters reflect Thackeray's happy six-month tour of Germany before he undertook to study law in London. While the discipline soon proved not to his taste, his life as a gentleman of fashion (a life that included large gambling debts) was congenial, at least until the collapse of many of the Indian commercial houses reversed his inheritance prospects. Almost relieved to be forced to make his own way, Thackeray decided to develop his talent for drawing, making friends with Daniel Maclise and being tutored by George Cruikshank. While in Paris studying art, he met and married Isabella Shawe, the daughter of a colonel in the Indian army. He endeavored to support his family through journalistic activities, even offering to illustrate Charles Dickens's *Pickwick Papers* (1836-1837). His friendship with Daniel Maginn made his "Yellowplush Papers" welcome in the columns of *Fraser's Magazine*, whose readers were regaled with the malapropisms of a rascally footman. In addition, he wrote for the London *Times* and for a number of obscure journals. His first long attempt at fiction was *Catherine*, a parody of the "Newgate Novel"; in quick succession he produced *A Shabby Genteel Story* and *The Paris Sketch Book*.

In 1840, Thackeray was visited by domestic calamity; upon the birth of their third daughter, his wife, Isabella, went insane and required institutionalization. The child-rearing was assumed by Thackeray's parents, leaving him to recoup his writing career, initially with *The History of Samuel Titmarsh and the Great Hoggarty Diamond* and soon with contributions to *Punch* and the *Morning Chronicle*. During these middle years, Thackeray solaced himself for the want of domestic connections with a series of friendships with old Cambridge acquaintances such as Alfred, Lord Tennyson and W. H. Brookfield, as well as with journalistic brethren such as Francis Sylvester Mahoney (the "Father Prout" of *Fraser's Magazine* fame) and with Dickens himself, whom Thackeray could, however, never accept as a "gentleman." His travel literature was published at this time. His connection with *Punch*, begun in 1842, was an important one. From contributing fillers, he went on to write a number of series; moreover, Thackeray's rivalry with the other principal writer, Douglass Jerrold, was to affect the course of *Punch*'s publishing history, turning the tide from radicalism and democracy to a Whiggish conservatism of which Dickens himself much disapproved.

The year 1847 was crucial for Thackeray. He began to parody novels for *Punch* in the "Punch's Prize Novelists" series, he began a long platonic affair with Jane Brookfield, and he published *Vanity Fair*, the novel that has achieved abiding interest for its panoramic social view and its narrator's satirical viewpoint. His four-year relationship with Jane Brookfield certainly affected his writing; much of the nostalgia and agonizing provoked by the affair are reproduced in *The History of Henry Esmond, Esquire.* Just as important was his entreé into aristocratic circles, for he, along with his daughters Anny and Minnie, with whom he had set up an establishment in Kensington, were welcome not only at Holland House but also in the demirep world of Lady Blessington. Leaving his daughters was the only blight on his first American tour in 1852, when he lectured about "English Humorists of the Eighteenth Century" and marveled at the way in which the *nouveaux riches* mingled with the best society.

Upon his return, Thackeray entered the height of the London social season and visited his daughters in Paris. He began *The Newcomes*, a novel much interrupted by illness but, even as its title suggests, much influenced by his social experiences. His work on the "Four Georges," an indictment of the House of Hanover as well as of the monarchy and the upper classes, indicated his changed attitudes. After his second American tour (undertaken, like the first, to provide stipends for his daughters), Thackeray not only published *The Virginians* but also became editor of *Cornhill Magazine*, a project that allowed him to move "out of novel-spinning back into the world" of the essay. The periodical was an immediate success, publishing such authors as Anthony Trollope and George Henry Lewes. Although Thackeray retired as editor in 1862, he continued to publish his "Roundabout Papers" there until the year after. Indeed, his last unfinished novel, *Denis Duval*, appeared in *Cornhill Magazine* posthumously in 1864, after Thackeray had died on December 24, 1863, in London.

Analysis · While William Makepeace Thackeray may indeed be best known as the author of *Vanity Fair*, to examine all of his novels is to understand why his contribution to the history of the novel is singular. His use of the intrusive narrator, although presaged by Henry Fielding, was developed so carefully that it became a new form of fiction, a "genuine creation of narrative experiment," as critic Alexander Welsh calls it. In addition, his panoramic realism—although creating that anathema of Henry James, the novel that is "a loose and baggy monster"—explored, both seriously and satirically, a number of topics from which other Victorian writers shied away, such as married life and the development of the middle-class gentleman.

Quite aside from the interest generated by the story line, many of Thackeray's novels offer explanations of the art of creating fiction as well as criticism of some of his contemporaries' inadequacies. When Amelia in *Vanity Fair*, for example, tries to visualize George's barracks, the doors are closed to her, for the romantic imagination is in all respects inadequate to the exigencies of real life. In *The Newcomes*, Thackeray compares his method of character-building to the work of the paleontologist who discovers a series of bones and who must construct the habits, behavior, and appearance of his subject from a mere skeleton. He thereby suggests that any such "reality" is merely an illusion, for like the paleontologist, the author must work with probabilities. Insofar as his characters follow a probable course of events, they are true to life and, in a sense, interact without the help of the author. That Thackeray meant his novels to be something more than believable illusionary worlds is clear when his conclusions are examined. In *The Newcomes*, for example, Thackeray retreats at the end from Pendennis's narrative to suggest that the sentimental world he has created has no basis in fact, although the reader may believe so if he wishes to delude himself, and in the well-known ending to *Vanity Fair*, Thackeray puts his "puppets"—his characters—back into their box.

Rather than following Samuel Taylor Coleridge's idea of "willing suspension of disbelief," Thackeray is philosophical, inviting the reader into a reconsideration of his own or of conventional beliefs and preconceptions. Certainly, Thackeray's satire is operative here, particularly in his *Punch* series, in *Catherine*, and in *The Luck of Barry Lyndon*, in which he deliberately spoofed popular historical, crime, and romantic novels, respectively. The reader is asked to look at more than literary conventions, however; he is asked to examine his own degree of hypocrisy and snobbery. In so doing, the reader is reminded again and again that if he laughs at his neighbors, he condemns himself. Thackeray's work is thus truly homiletic, both in a literary and in an extraliterary sense. Unlike many of his predecessors, he examined in detail the difficulties occasioned not only by marriage but also by other personal relationships; rather than assuming that a novel should end with marriage, he makes it his subject. Certainly, his personally tragic domestic situation and his affair with Jane Brookfield are reflected in Rachel Esmond's trials with her reckless husband in Henry Esmond's growing love for her. In the family chronicle *The Newcomes*, Thackeray looks at the misery occasioned by parental marriage choices; Mrs. Mackenzie (known as the "Campaigner"), a strong-minded virago who runs her daughter's life, is modeled on Mrs. Shawe, Isabella's termagant mother. Finally, in *The Virginians*, he traces the development of family characteristics and family ties.

Another one of the many senses in which Thackeray's novels are educative is the way in which he redefines the word "gentleman" to apply not to a member of a particular social class, but rather to one who possesses a set of personal characteristics, such as clear-sightedness, delicacy, generosity, and humanitarianism. His upper-class upbringing in India as well as his Cambridge education coupled with his love of the high life would seem to mitigate against such a redefinition, but, in fact, it is the greengrocer's son, Dobbin, in *Vanity Fair* who is the gentleman, rather than the pompous, vain George Osborne, and it is Colonel Newcome who, despite his misguided attempts to settle his son Clive's happiness, emerges as the paradigmatical enemy to snobbery and to greed.

Vanity Fair · *Vanity Fair*, whose title is taken from John Bunyan's *The Pilgrim's Progress* (1678, 1684), proved to be Thackeray's most successful novel. Indeed, its attention to realistic detail and its panoramic sweep, to say nothing of the constant presence of the author-cum-narrator, caused many reviewers to label Thackeray "the Fielding of the nineteenth century." While neither the initial reviews nor the sales were immediately promising, interest in the serial grew steadily until the publication of the volume guaranteed the author a financial as well as a critical success. Rivaling Thackeray at the time was Charles Dickens, whose *Dombey and Son* (1846-1848) appealed to a wide audience; even Thackeray himself, upon reading the passage describing little Paul's death, despaired about writing "against such power." Thackeray, however, had his own power, that of the saritist who created "A Novel Without a Hero" and thus ran counter to his readership's expectations, and that of the moralist who included his reader and himself in his reflective view of society.

The hero that *Vanity Fair* must do without is the typically romantic hero. George Osborne (whose first name conjures up the dandified Regency court) is handsome, dashing, and well loved, but he is also vain, shallow, and pompous. After Joseph Sedley has gone bankrupt, George marries the pining Amelia Sedley only at the urging of his friend William Dobbin; during their honeymoon, he engages in a flirtation with Becky Sharp, herself newly married to Rawdon Crawley. Killed at the battle of Waterloo, George is cherished as a hero only by Amelia. Dobbin is at the other extreme: Gangly, awkward, and low in social standing, he is nevertheless possessed of compassion and understanding, yet he is so blinded by his selfless love for Amelia that he does not see until the end of the novel on how slight a character he has set his affection. Even Rawdon, who develops from a typical "heavy dragoon" who lives by his gambling into an affectionate father for his neglected son, lacks intellectual acumen, and, after his separation from Becky, accepts the post that her prostitution to Lord Steyne earned him.

As A. E. Dyson suggests, Thackeray is indeed writing "an irony against heroes"—and against heroines as well. Amelia and Becky are as different as George and Dobbin. Initally, Amelia seems to be a conventional heroine, but the reader who views her in that light will be shocked to discover that he is idealizing the passivity, self-sacrifice, and hero-worship that are the earmarks of neuroticism, the three characteristics well seen in her treatment of her son Georgy, who is absurdly spoiled despite Amelia's and her parents' penury. No wonder, then, that readers preferred "the famous little Becky puppet" for her wit and ambition. From the moment she rides away from Miss Pinkerton's finishing school, leaving Dr. Johnson's dictionary lying in the mud, her energy in making a place for herself in society is impressive. Failing to entangle Amelia's brother Jos, she eventually marries Rawdon, the favorite of his wealthy aunt, and only repines when Lord Crawley himself proposes—too late. She turns her very bohemianism into an asset as she gains entry into the best society, and while she claims that she too could be a "good woman on £5000 a year," her energy in luring dupes to Rawdon's card table, wheedling jewels from Lord Steyne, being presented to the king, and playing charades at a social affair belies her claim. As John Loofbourow shows, as Becky comes into social ascendancy, Amelia declines into obscurity. Amelia lacks Becky's energy, while Becky lacks Amelia's morality. In the end, when Dobbin has won his prize, Becky has devolved into a female picaresque rogue, traveling across the Continent from disreputable gaming table to questionable boarding house. Neither she nor Amelia qualifies as a heroine.

It is Thackeray's preface that reveals the moral purpose behind his satire. Posing as the "Manager of the Performance," Thackeray reminds his readers that they are embarked on a fictional journey through an emblematic Vanity Fair, an evocation related only partly to the original in Bunyan's work. Vanity Fair, for Thackeray, is a representation of the human condition; it is not for the reader, like Bunyan's Christian, to pass through and eschew its lures, but rather to experience it "in a sober, contemplative, not uncharitable frame of mind," for the reader and author alike are part of the fair. Thackeray's comments throughout serve the purpose of distancing the reader from the characters and forcing him to judge not only the created "puppets" but also his own preconceptions. If everyone is indeed part of the fair, to condemn the booth-owners' hypocrisy, or social climbing, or snobbery, or mendacity, is to condemn one's own failings. To be possessed of "charity"–to be able to pity others with the same care one has for oneself–this, Thackeray suggests, is the best that can be expected when the puppets are put back in the box.

The History of Pendennis · The subtitle of *The History of Pendennis–His Fortunes and Misfortunes, His Friends and His Greatest Enemy*–gives ample indication that the novel is a *Bildungsroman*. As Juliet McMaster points out, however, it is also a *Künstlerroman*; that is, a tale about the development of an artist. It is perforce autobiographical, detailing as it does the way in which a young man learns enough about the world and himself to become a writer of "good books." The novel is important in a study of Thackeray's technique, presenting, as it does, the background for the persona who was to narrate *The Newcomes* and showing Thackeray's struggles with Victorian prudery. Indeed, in his preface he complains that his readers, unlike those of Fielding, are unwilling to accept a truthful portrayal of human beings unless they are given "a conventional simper." Thackeray's reviewers, however, welcomed the novel, their only complaint being the cynicism with which he endowed Pen. Such cynicism refutes Henry James, Sr.'s remark that Thackeray "had no ideas," for Thackeray's wryness results from a consideration of political and religious turmoil, from the "skepticism" brought about by the 1848 French Revolution, and from the controversy occasioned by the Oxford movement and Cardinal John Henry Newman's conversion from Anglicanism to Catholicism. Clearly, one reason for Thackeray's contemporary appeal was that he reflected the very doubts of his own readers, for whom belief was an exercise in paradox.

The tension between the heart and the world that animates *The History of Pendennis* is well represented by the frontispiece to the first volume, in which a youthful figure is clasped on one side by a woman representing marital duty and on the other by a mermaid representing the siren lure of worldly temptations. Within the dictates of the plot, the same tension is demonstrated by the demands of Pen's sentimental mother, Helen Pendennis, who urges her son to marry the domestic Laura, her ward, and those of his uncle, Major Pendennis, who is willing to blackmail his acquaintance, Sir Francis Clavering, so that Pen can have a seat in Parliament and the hand of Clavering's wealthy but artificial daughter Blanche. Between the two, Pen must, as McMaster points out, find his own reality; he must acquire "his uncle's keen perception without the withering selfishness" and participate in his mother's world of emotions without engaging in "romantic illusion." Pen's education progresses primarily through his amours, but also through his choice of career, for to be a writer, he must determine the relationship between fact and fiction.

Pen's abiding interest in the nature of experience makes his involvement with an actress allegorical in nature. His first affair is with Emily Costigan (known as "the Fotheringay"), an Irish actress older than he and one who plays her parts serenely unconscious of their philosophical implications; her ignorance Pen passes off as "adorable simplicity." Extricated by his uncle, who "lends" Emily's father a small sum in return for Pen's love letters, Pen next enters Oxbridge, and then, influenced by his roommate, George Warrington, determines to study law and to become a writer. His affair with Fanny Bolton, the daughter of his landlady, is again one of an attraction to "adorable simplicity," and his consequent illness a kind of purgation. His attachment to Blanche Clavering is more serious and more dangerous, for Blanche is a social "actress" with whom Pen plays the role of world-weary lover. With her he believes he has matured because he is willing to compromise with disillusionment. His real moment of maturity comes, however, when he finds that he cannot put up with his uncle's worldliness, for in discovering that Clavering's second marriage is bigamous and that the Baronet is paying blackmail money to his wife's first husband, the Major in turn blackmails Clavering to give up his seat in Parliament to Pen and to cede his estate to Blanche.

Pen's responsible decision to honor his proposal to Blanche despite the resultant scandal is, in fact, unnecessary, for she jilts him for a more suitable match, freeing him to marry Laura, whose steadfast, honest devotion represents the alternative to Blanche's sham affection. Laura, in fact, is Pen's muse, his living "laurel wreath"; she has insight and a critical faculty that force Pen to come face to face with himself. With her, Pen finally frees himself from both romantic illusion and worldly disillusionment.

Henry Esmond · Like Dickens, who turned from the largely unplotted "loose and baggy monsters" of his novelistic apprenticeship to produce the tightly controlled *Dombey and Son*, Thackeray moved from the looseness occasioned by serial publication to the careful construction of *The History of Henry Esmond, Esquire, a Colonel in the Service of Her Majesty Q. Anne*, more commonly known as *Henry Esmond*. While the novelist Anthony Trollope agreed with Thackeray that the book was his "*very* best," initial critical reaction was mixed, ranging from high praise for Thackeray's realism to a scandalized outcry against what Gordon Ray calls the "emotional pattern" of the work—Esmond's marriage to Lady Castlewood, his cousin and senior by eight years. All agreed, however, that the novel was profoundly moving. Much of its power is owing to its genesis: Written when Thackeray was recovering from his alienation from Jane Brookfield, the novel reflects his own emotional current, his nostalgia, his suffering, and his wish-fulfillment. In addition, *Henry Esmond* may be read on many levels—as historical fiction, as novel of manners, and as romance.

Superficially, Thackeray might seem an unlikely figure to write a historical novel, inasmuch as he composed a series of parodies of "costume dramas" (as he called them) for *Punch* and inasmuch as the historical novel was going out of fashion by 1852. Nevertheless, because Thackeray was steeped in seventeenth century history, the work has a verisimilitude that, in the view of some critics, allowed him to outstrip even Sir Walter Scott. The point of view he adopts, that of the first-person narrator, adds to the illusion. This tour de force is accomplished with a success that even Henry James, the master of psychological realism, might envy. The entire story is presented from the limited point of view of Esmond, the cheated heir of the Castlewood estate, who is adopted by his cousins, falls in love with the beautiful but irresponsible Beatrix Esmond, and for her sake joins the Jacobite cause; then, when Beatrix becomes the Pretender's mistress, he realigns himself on the side of the Stuarts, marries Beatrix's mother, and immigrates to America.

That Thackeray could, through a limited narrator, represent the complexity of Lady Castlewood's growing love for the innocent and unconscious Henry is remarkable in its own right. Thackeray's own memories of his boyhood helped him to re-create Henry's loneliness; his relationship with Jane Brookfield shaped his characterization of Lady Castlewood. As John Tilford points out, Thackeray prepares carefully for the marriage, doubtless aware that it challenged many readers' expectations and moral assumptions. Through nuances of dialogue, Rachel Castlewood's awareness of her feelings and of Henry's is revealed. A number of crucial scenes prepare for the denouement: Rachel's hysterical reaction to Henry's early affair with the blacksmith's daughter, an affair that brings smallpox to the family; her vituperation of Henry as he lies in prison for his involvement in a duel that killed Lord Castlewood, whose drinking, gambling, and hunting had contributed to a loveless marriage; and, finally, her overwhelming joy when she sees Henry after his long period of military service.

One early criticism of the novel was recorded by William Harrison Ainsworth, with whom Thomas Carlyle joined in objecting to the exultation of "sentiment above duty" in the novel; other critics found the comparison between the excitement of romantic love and marital unhappiness to be dangerous. The more sophisticated analysis of McMaster registers an "ironic tension" between "Rachel's moral rectitude and . . . the psychological damage" it can cause.

Like Henry James's Mme de Mauves, Rachel is possessed of a cool virtue based on a conviction of moral and intellectual superiority; as McMaster suggests, she may indeed welcome evidence of her husband's coarseness as a way of rationalizing her affection for Henry and may therefore be responsible for exacerbating her husband's untoward behavior. Thackeray does give both sides: While Castlewood, like Fielding's Squire Western, is rough and careless, pursuing a prodigal, adulterous life once his wife has lost her beauty to smallpox, he accuses her of pride and of a blighting coldness, and pleads for "the virtue that can forgive." Even Beatrix complains that her mother's saintliness provided so impossible a model that she was driven to ambitious selfishness. Such complaints themselves sound like rationalizations, however, for at the end of the novel, Rachel has undergone a long period of repentance. Having sent her temptation–Henry–away, she lives with the renunciation of happiness while he matures. Upon his return, then, she is no longer an angel, but, as he says, "more fondly cherished as woman perhaps than ever she had been adored as divinity."

The Newcomes · Subtitled *Memoirs of a Most Respectable Family, The Newcomes* is a novel of manners that explores the way in which four generations of a nouveau riche family acquire social respectability. The novel, the first third of which is densely packed with background material and consequently slow-moving, is a deliberate return to the serial format that Thackeray had abandoned in *Henry Esmond.* While some modern critics object to the pace of this "monster," nineteenth century reviewers believed that, with this novel, Thackeray had outstripped even Dickens, whose antiutilitarian manifesto, *Hard Times* (1854), was running concurrently. To be sure, a number of reviewers noted some repetition in theme and characters, a charge against which Thackeray defended himself in the "Overture" but admitted to in private, acknowledging a failure of invention because of sheer exhaustion. One such "repetition," which is, in fact, a way of extending the scope of the novel, is that Pendennis is the "editor" of the Newcome memoirs. This device allows Thackeray not only to assume an objective stance from which his satire is more telling, but also to criticize the very social punctiliousness that Pendennis reveals, thereby achieving an advanced form of psychological analysis.

What provides the novel's "unifying structural principle," as McMaster notes, is "the repetition of the mercenary marriage and its outcome between various couples." This theme, however, is a manifestation of the larger examination of the nature of "respectability," as the subtitle implies. For Barnes Newcome, the banker, for the aristocratic Lady Kew, and even for her granddaughter, Ethel Newcome, affection and generosity are weighed against wealth and social position and found wanting. The touchstone figure is Colonel Thomas Newcome, Barnes's half brother; unworldly, honest, and loving, he is seen by Gordon Ray as a model of Christian humility. The underlying cynicism of the novel is underscored by the inability of the characters to gain happiness, whether they satisfy their acquisitiveness or rebel against such a value, for Thackeray reminds his readers that real fulfillment only exists in "Fable-land."

To pursue the marriage theme is to understand that in Thackeray's world even the best intentions go awry. Certainly, the unhappiness that accrues in some relationships seems self-created: While the joining of money and class in Barnes's marriage to Lady Clara Pulleyn satisfies the dictates of the marriage market, Barnes's brutality drives his wife to elope with a former suitor. In contrast, Clive Newcome, the Colonel's son, is forbidden by Lady Kew to marry Ethel because his profession as an artist is unacceptable. Even Clive himself is infected by the view, for he neglects his modest muse to devote himself to society. For his part, the Colonel, seeing Clive's unhappiness, schemes to marry him to the sweet but shallow Rosey Mackenzie, the niece of his old friend James Binnie. The loveless though well-intentioned match is unhappy, for Clive longs for Ethel's companionship and the couple is tormented by the dictatorial Mrs. Mackenzie after the Colonel's bankruptcy.

Ethel, like Becky Sharp and Beatrix Esmond, is a complex heroine, one who, through much trial and error, weans herself from the respectable avarice she was reared to accept. In love with Clive despite her relations' objections, she nevertheless admits that she delights in admiration, fine clothes, and jewelry, and, although she despises herself for it, that she enjoys being a coquette. Her fine sense of irony about the marriage market, however, prompts her to wear a "sold" ticket pinned to her dress, much to the annoyance of her respectable relatives. At first affianced to Lord Frank Kew, she breaks the engagement; then, capitulating to social pressure, pursues the feeble-minded Lord Farintosh, only to repent at the last moment when the devastation of Barnes's marriage, on which her own is to be patterned, is borne in upon her. In revulsion from her family's values, she devotes herself to Barnes's children and manages to divert some of the Newcome fortune to the impoverished Colonel and his son.

Ethel's "conversion" and Rosey's death do not, however, lead necessarily to a happy ending, for in the years of following Ethel hopelessly, of neglecting his painting, and, finally, of engaging in a loveless marriage, Clive has become less resilient, more demoralized. Indeed, a conventional ending to *The Newcomes* would be as unwieldy as the happy denouement that Dickens was persuaded to tack on to *Great Expectations* (1860-1861). All Thackeray does promise is that in "Fable-land . . . Ethel and Clive are living most comfortably together." As McMaster points out, "poetic justice does not operate in life, however it operates in romance and fairytale." In the end, Thackeray refuses to cater to weak sentimentality.

The Virginians · Written while Thackeray was fighting a lingering illness, *The Virginians* is a long, formless novel, many of whose characters appear in earlier works. The weight of critical opinion, both contemporary and twentieth century, implies that Thackeray, as he well suspected, was at the end of his fictional powers. To Walter

Bagehot, the novelist merely presented an "annotated picture," and, indeed, many complained about the plethora of details that substituted for imaginative creation. Thackeray's habit of digressing grew more pronounced, aided by his failure to preserve a distance between himself and his persona for the second half of the novel, the sardonic George Warrington. Connected with such digressions was Thackeray's increasing propensity to justify himself in the eyes of his critics; such justification introduced in a work of fiction was as gratuitous, many felt, as the air of mordant rumination that colored the novel.

On the other hand, Thackeray's supporters cited his adept portraiture of character and his classical style. Geoffrey Tillotson's suggestion that all of Thackeray's works are like one long novel well represents this point of view. In reviving earlier characters and in introducing their descendants, Thackeray studies the development of character traits as well as repetitive familial situations. Beatrix Esmond, for example, having been mistress to the Pretender and the King and having buried two husbands, one a bishop, reappears as a fleshy old woman with a caustic tongue and piercing black eyes. The enigmatic George Washington in *The History of Pendennis* reappears in the person of his namesake; George and Henry Warrington are twin sons of Rachel, Henry Esmond's daughter.

Unfortunately, Thackeray was unable to pursue his original plan, which was to place the brothers on opposite sides in the Revolutionary War and to insert real-life sketches of such figures as Oliver Goldsmith and Dr. Samuel Johnson. The American section was foreshortened, although Thackeray's prodigious reading in American history lends it a remarkably realistic air—so realistic that some American readers were initially incensed that George Washington should be portrayed in so commonplace a light. The book falls into halves, the first reserved for the English adventures of the innocent, gullible Henry. As Gordon Ray points out, the theme, although difficult to discern, is "the contrast between American innocence and Old World corruption."

Henry becomes involved with his cousins at Castlewood, who welcome him as the heir of the Virginia estates, on the supposition that George has died in the battle of Fort Duquesne. Enticed into a proposal by the elderly Maria and encouraged to dissipate his fortune by his infamous cousins, Henry is rescued from debt by his twin, who had not died but was taken prisoner by the French. Deceived by his fortune-seeking relatives, Henry returns to Virginia to marry the housekeeper's daughter. The second half, narrated by George, details his adventures in London. Kept on short funds by his mother, he marries Theo Lambert, the daughter of the gentlemanly General Lambert, a figure much like Colonel Newcome.

Even a brief plot outline of *The Virginians* reveals a number of Thackeray's recurring themes. The attraction of young men to older women is one: Just as Henry Esmond married Rachel, many years his senior, so his grandson becomes attached to Maria, and, conversely, so his mother, Mrs. Esmond Warrington, becomes attached to a much younger suitor. The dogmatic and clinging nature of the parent-child relationship is another, much-explored theme: Hetty Lambert gives up her love for Harry to nurture the General, who is loathe to let either of his daughters leave; Mrs. Esmond Warrington throws impediments in the way of George's marriage to Theo; even George himself meditates on his fear that his own daughters will eventually marry. In the final analysis, while *The Virginians* is justly faulted for its digressiveness, Thackeray's treatment of character and his mellow, pure style grant to this work what Gordon Ray calls "a modest vitality."

Overshadowed in modern assessments by his great contemporaries, Dickens and George Eliot, Thackeray is an essential figure in the history of the English novel, and his masterpiece, *Vanity Fair*, is among the great novels in the language. It is with this work that Thackeray is assured a place among the great authors in British literature.

Patricia Marks

Other major works

SHORT FICTION: *The Yellowplush Papers*, 1837-1838; *Some Passages in the Life of Major Gahagan*, 1838-1839; *Stubb's Calendar: Or, The Fatal Boots*, 1839; *Barber Cox and the Cutting of His Comb*, 1840; *The Bedford-Row Conspiracy*, 1840; *Comic Tales and Sketches*, 1841 (2 volumes); *The Confessions of George Fitz-Boodle, and Some Passages in the Life of Major Gahagan*, 1841-1842 (as George Savage Fitz-Boodle); *Men's Wives*, 1843 (as Fitz-Boodle); *A Legend of the Rhine*, 1845 (as M. A. Titmarsh); *Jeames's Diary: Or, Sudden Wealth*, 1846; *The Snobs of England, by One of Themselves*, 1846-1847 (later as *The Book of Snobs*, 1848, 1852); *Mrs. Perkin's Ball*, 1847 (as Titmarsh); *'Our Street,'* 1848 (as Titmarsh); *A Little Dinner at Timmins's*, 1848; *Doctor Birch and His Young Friends*, 1849 (as Titmarsh); *The Kickleburys on the Rhine*, 1850 (as Titmarsh); *A Shabby Genteel Story and Other Tales*, 1852; *The Rose and the Ring: Or, The History of Prince Giglio and Prince Bulbo*, 1855 (as Titmarsh); *Memoirs of Mr. Charles J. Yellowplush [with] The Diary of C. Jeames De La Pluche, Esqr.*, 1856.

POETRY: *The Chronicle of the Drum*, 1841.

NONFICTION: *The Paris Sketch Book*, 1840 (2 volumes; as M. A. Titmarsh); *The Irish Sketch Book*, 1843 (2 volumes; as Titmarsh); *Notes of a Journey from Cornhill to Grand Cairo, by Way of Lisbon, Athens, Constantinople and Jerusalem, Performed in the Steamers of the Penninsular and Oriental Company*, 1846 (as Titmarsh); *The English Humourists of the Eighteenth Century*, 1853; *Sketches and Travels in London*, 1856; *The Four Georges: Sketches of Manners, Morals, Court and Town Life*, 1860.

Bibliography

Bloom, Harold, ed. *William Makepeace Thackeray*. New York: Chelsea House, 1987. This critical anthology brings together major essays on Thackeray's main novels. Includes a chronology and a bibliography.

_____, ed. *William Makepeace Thackeray's "Vanity Fair."* New York: Chelsea House, 1987. In addition to Bloom's original introductory essay, the volume reprints, in the order in which they appeared, seven important previously published critical essays on the novel. Subjects range from Dorothy Van Ghent's evaluation of Becky Sharp to H. M. Daleski's consideration of the form of Thackeray's most important work.

Carey, John. *Thackeray: Prodigal Genius*. London: Faber & Faber, 1977. Takes a thematic approach, concentrating on his earlier writings and the shaping of Thackeray's imagination, especially its obsessive quality. The last two chapters relate this theme to the later fiction, *Vanity Fair* in particular. Indexed.

Clarke, Micael M. *Thackeray and Women*. De Kalb: Northern Illinois University Press, 1995. Examines Thackeray's treatment of female characters. Includes bibliographical references and an index.

Colby, Robert A. *Thackeray's Canvass of Humanity: An Author and His Public*. Columbus: Ohio State University Press, 1979. Colby seeks to capture Thackeray's "Protean" personality as expressed in his fiction. A very full text which contains a chronology.

Harden, Edgar F. *Thackeray the Writer: From Journalism to "Vanity Fair."* New York: St. Martin's Press, 1998. A thorough study of Thackeray's literary career.

_____. *"Vanity Fair": A Novel Without a Hero.* New York: Twayne, 1995. A clear, understandable review of the seminal novel. Excellent for any student of *Vanity Fair*.

Hardy, Barbara. *The Exposure of Luxury: Radical Themes in Thackeray.* London: Peter Owen, 1972. Takes a thematic approach to Thackeray's fiction, seeking to demonstrate the satiric and revolutionary feeling behind it. The themes covered include love, feasting, art and nature, and the exploitation of art.

Peters, Catherine. *Thackeray's Universe: Shifting Worlds of Imagination and Reality.* Boston: Faber & Faber, 1987. Relates Thackeray's fiction to his life, stressing particularly Thackeray's challenge to his society. A selected bibliography is provided.

J. R. R. Tolkien

Born: Bloemfontein, South Africa; January 3, 1892
Died: Bournemouth, England; September 2, 1973

Principal long fiction · *The Hobbit*, 1937; *The Lord of the Rings*, 1955 (includes *The Fellowship of the Ring*, 1954; *The Two Towers*, 1954; *The Return of the King*, 1955); *The Silmarillion*, 1977; *The Book of Lost Tales I*, 1983; *The Book of Lost Tales II*, 1984; *The Lays of Beleriand*, 1985; *The Shaping of Middle-Earth*, 1986; *The Lost Road and Other Writings*, 1987; *The Return of the Shadow: The History of "The Lord of the Rings,"* Part One, 1988; *The Treason of Isengard: The History of "The Lord of the Rings,"* Part Two, 1989; *The War of the Ring: The History of "The Lord of the Rings,"* Part Three, 1990; *Sauron Defeated, the End of the Third Age: The History of "The Lord of the Rings,"* Part Four, 1992; *Morgoth's Ring*, 1993; *The War of the Jewels*, 1994; *The Peoples of Middle-Earth*, 1996 (previous 12 novels collectively known as The History of Middle-Earth).

Other literary forms · J. R. R. Tolkien's novels represent only a small part of the complicated matrix from which they evolved. During his lifetime, he published three volumes of novellas and short stories, *Farmer Giles of Ham* (1949), *Tree and Leaf* (1964), and *Smith of Wootton Major* (1967). Some of these tales had originally been bedtime stories for his own children, such as the posthumous *The Father Christmas Letters* (1976) or *Roverandom* (1998). *The Silmarillion* and *Unfinished Tales of Numenor and Middle-Earth* (1980) both contain stories Tolkien composed early in his life, material that sets the stage for the events in his novels. His poetry collections, *Songs for the Philologists* (1936), *The Adventures of Tom Bombadil* (1962), and *The Road Goes Ever On: A Song Cycle* (1967), link Tolkien's poetic formulations of Middle-Earth's themes with the historical and linguistic themes of which both his professional work and much of his dreams were made, "the nameless North of Sigurd of the Völsungs, and the prince of all dragons." Tolkien's academic publications dealt with the history of the English language and Middle English literature: *A Middle English Vocabulary* (1922) and editions of *Sir Gawain and the Green Knight* (1925) with E. V. Gordon and the *Ancrene Wisse* (1962). His seminal essay "Beowulf: The Monsters and the Critics" (1936) and his only play, *The Homecoming of Beorhtnoth Beorhthelm's Son* (1953), offer fresh interpretations of ancient English epic poems.

Tolkien's novels have been adapted for cinema and television, and many, though not all, of his fragmentary stories, articles, and letters have been published since his death. His histories of Middle-Earth, a remarkable invented mythology comprising chronicles, tales, maps, and poems, were edited as a series by his son, Christopher Tolkien. Volumes include *The Book of Lost Tales*, *The Lays of Beleriand*, *The Shaping of Middle-Earth*, and *The Lost Road and Other Writings*.

Achievements · Tolkien's fiction dismayed most of his fellow scholars at the University of Oxford as much as it delighted most of his general readers. Such reactions sprang from their recognition of his vast linguistic talent, which underlay both his professional achievements and his mythical universe. Tolkien led two lives at once, quietly working as an Oxford tutor, examiner, editor, and lecturer, while concurrently Middle-Earth and its mythology were taking shape within his imagination.

Houghton Mifflin Company

For twenty years after he took First Class Honours in English Language and Literature at Oxford, Tolkien's teaching and linguistic studies buttressed his scholarly reputation. Editing the fourteenth century text of *Sir Gawain and the Green Knight* with E. V. Gordon helped bring Tolkien the Rawlinson and Bosworth Professorship of Anglo-Saxon at Oxford in 1925. His lecture "Beowulf: The Monsters and the Critics" approached the Anglo-Saxon epic poem from an entirely new perspective and is considered a landmark in criticism of Western Germanic literature. As he was shaping his linguistic career, however, Tolkien was also formulating an imaginary language, which as early as 1917 had led him to explore its antecedents, its mythology, and its history, all of which he molded into the tales of *The Silmarillion*. Over the years, he shared them with friends, but he never finished putting them into a unified structure.

His preoccupation with Middle-Earth and the practical demands of his teaching distracted Tolkien from scholarship, and between his celebrated essay *On Fairy Stories* in 1939 and his edition of the Middle English *Ancrene Wisse* in 1962, Tolkien published only fiction, a circumstance acknowledged with polite forbearance by most of Oxford's scholarly community, although his novels eventually met with astonishing popular success. *The Hobbit*, originally a children's story, was published in 1937 after a six-year gestation, and by 1949, *The Lord of the Rings* was complete. Its sales, though steadily increasing after its publication in 1954 1955, did not soar until 1965, when an unauthorized American printing proved a disguised blessing, resulting in a campus cult responsible for the sale of three million copies by 1968.

Most critics of *The Lord of the Rings* have not achieved moderation. As W. H. Auden observed, "People find it a masterpiece of its genre, or they cannot abide it." Auden himself and C. S. Lewis, Tolkien's Oxford friend, headed the "masterpiece" faction, while Edwin Muir in England and Edmund Wilson in America deplored Tolkien's style and aims.

Honorary fellowships, an honorary Doctorate of Letters from Oxford and a C.B.E. from Queen Elizabeth all descended upon Tolkien with the unexpected wealth of his last years, which were nevertheless darkened by his reluctance to complete *The Silmarillion*. His reputation rests not on his academic talent or scholarly production, nor even on his brilliant linguistically oriented "mythology for England," but upon the novels that began as tales for his children and blossomed into a splendid imaginative tree of fiction whose roots feed upon the archetypes of northern European civilization and whose leaves shelter its finest aspirations.

Biography · John Ronald Reuel Tolkien was born in Bloemfontein, South Africa, on January 3, 1892. The piano-manufacturing firm of his father's family, originally descended from German aristocracy, had gone bankrupt, and the elder Tolkien had taken a South African bank position in hopes of improving his shaky finances. Tolkien's mother, Mabel Suffield, joined her husband at Bloemfontein, but when the climate strained J. R. R.'s health, she took their two sons home to England in 1895. Less than a year later, Arthur Tolkien died in South Africa, leaving his widow and children nearly penniless.

In the summer of 1896, Mabel Tolkien rented a rural cottage at Sarehole Mill, close to Birmingham, and for the next four years she taught her boys French, Latin, drawing, and botany, to save school expenses. Much later, Tolkien called these "the longest-seeming and most formative part" of his life. Mabel Tolkien's attraction to Roman Catholicism led to her conversion in 1900, and she moved to a Birmingham suburb from which Tolkien attended one of England's then leading grammar schools, King Edward's, on a scholarship. Already, he was demonstrating the fascination with ancient languages which was to determine his career. He was involved in learning such northern European languages as Norse, Gothic, Finnish, and Welsh, as well as the Old and Middle English in which he achieved his academic reputation. He claimed this philological bent dated from the time he was five or six years old.

In 1904, his mother died at thirty-four, leaving her children in the care of Father Francis Morgan, her friend and pastor. Tolkien's devotion to his mother was inextricably intertwined with his own Catholic faith, and both played vital roles in the development of his fiction. Thus at sixteen, Tolkien looked back upon a series of grievous losses: his father, whom he considered as "belonging to an almost legendary past"; the Sarehole countryside he loved; his mother, whom he considered a martyr to her faith. Not surprisingly for a lonely boy, Tolkien fell in love early when he met Edith Bratt, another orphan, in his Birmingham boarding house. She was three years older than he, and she had just enough inheritance to support herself modestly while she dreamed of becoming a musician. Recognizing the boy's scholarly talent and fearing for his future, Father Morgan finally stopped all communication between Tolkien and Edith until Tolkien was twenty-one. Tolkien himself commented thirty years later, "Probably nothing else would have hardened the will enough to give such an affair (however genuine a case of true love) permanence." When he and Edith were reunited in 1913, they seemed to have little in common, but on the eve of his military departure to France in 1916, they were married.

By this time Tolkien had won a scholarship to Oxford University and graduated with first-class honors in 1913. He enlisted in the Lancashire Fusiliers in 1915, embarking for France in 1916. He survived the Battle of the Somme but was invalided back to England suffering from trench fever. While in a military hospital in 1917, Tolkien began *The Book of Lost Tales*, the genesis of *The Silmarillion*, although he dated the original ideas for the complete oeuvre from as early as 1910 and the original story of Beren and Tinuviel back to 1913. By 1918 he had read a version of "The Fall of Gondolin" to a college group.

After demobilization, Tolkien gained employment on the new *Oxford English Dictionary*, until in 1921 he was appointed to the University of Leeds in Yorkshire to lecture in Old English. While there he began to establish an academic reputation with his *Middle English Vocabulary* and an edition of *Sir Gawain and the Green Knight* done with Professor E. V. Gordon. On the strength of these and his connections back at Oxford, he was appointed the Rawlinson and Bosworth Professor of Anglo-Saxon Studies at Oxford in 1925, a post he held until 1945, when he was appointed Merton Professor of English Language and Literature at the same university. He held this post until his belated retirement in 1959. Various honorary degrees were bestowed upon him, and in 1938 he was Andrew Lang Lecturer at the University of St. Andrews, where he gave his famous lectures on fairy stories.

However, the central part of his life lay in his secret creation of the mythology of Middle-Earth. It was initially the demands of his growing family (three boys and a girl) that brought any of this to light, particularly in *The Hobbit*, which was first drafted, according to his close friend and science-fiction novelist C. S. Lewis, by the beginning of 1930. Then it was through the influence of the Inklings, a club or group of like-minded university friends, that *The Hobbit* was reformulated and sent for eventual publication in 1937. The importance of the Inklings cannot be stressed enough, especially the friendship of C. S. Lewis, who encouraged Tolkien with *The Lord of the Rings* during World War II and immediately after, and who reviewed it in glowing terms. In a sense, Lewis was repaying the enormous debt he owed Tolkien for his conversion to Christianity. The Inklings continued till Lewis's death in 1963, though the two men had drifted apart somewhat by then.

Even so, the vast bulk of Middle-Earth mythology lay in a constant state of revision, expansion, and rearrangement, and despite the best efforts of friends and publishers, it was unpublished at his death. In fact, after the publication of *The Lord of the Rings* in 1955, he concentrated again on his academic work, and only after retirement did he make any serious inroads again into the mythology. In the end, it was left to his third son, Christopher, also an academic, to order the material and have it published, as he did with a number of incomplete academic studies. Tolkien's death in 1973 had been preceded by his wife's in 1971. They were both buried outside Oxford, their graves suitably inscribed with the names Beren and Lúthien. The year before his death he had been made Companion of the Order of the British Empire (C.B.E.) by Queen Elizabeth II.

Analysis · Looking back around 1951 upon his Middle-Earth, J. R. R. Tolkien commented, "I do not remember a time when I was not building it . . . always I had the sense of recording what was already 'there,' somewhere: not of inventing." He conceived of fantasy as a profound and powerful form of literature with intense philosophical and spiritual meaning, serious purposes, and eternal appeal. He believed the imagination, the mental power of making images, could be linked by art to "sub-creation," the successful result of imagemaking, and so he regarded the genuine artist as partaking in the Creator's divine nature.

Three major factors of Tolkien's personality and environment combined to shape the theory of fantasy underlying his novels, as first enunciated in the essay "On Fairy-Stories" (1938). His love of language for its singular rewards, his delight in the English countryside, and his shattering experience of trench warfare during World War I all provided the seeds for his three longest pieces of fiction. They also contributed to the points of view, astonishingly nonhuman and yet startlingly convincing, of *The Silmarillion, The Hobbit,* and *The Lord of the Rings,* where Elves and Hobbits illuminate the world of Men.

Even as a boy, Tolkien had been enchanted by Welsh names on railway coal cars, a sign of his unusual linguistic sensitivity, and as a mature scholar, he devoted himself to the mystery of the word in its northern manifestations. In "On Fairy-Stories," he wrote that "*spell* means both a story told, and a formula of power over living men." Tolkien cast his spells in the building blocks of words drawn from the imaginary languages he had been constructing as long as he could remember. The two languages he formulated for his Elves, the Elder Race, both derived from a common linguistic ancestor as human languages do, and this "nexus of languages" supplied the proper names for his fiction, so that despite their considerable length and complication they possess "cohesion, consistency of linguistic style, and the illusion of historicity." The last was possibly the greatest achievement of Tolkien's mastery of language in his novels, fostering vital credence in his imaginary world. He felt that the finest fairy stories "open a door on Other Time, and if we pass through . . . we stand outside our own time, outside Time itself, maybe." In his own childhood, a "troublous" one Tolkien said, he had "had no special 'wish to believe' "; he instead "wanted to know," as, perhaps, do his readers, aided by the resonance of his masterful use of words.

The memory of his years at Sarehole, the happiest of his boyhood, gave Tolkien an abiding love of nature, "above all trees," which formed the basis for one of his principal concepts, "the inter-relations between the 'noble' and the 'simple.'" He found "specially moving" the "ennoblement of the ignoble," a theme which recurs throughout his fiction. Tolkien's Elves practice love and respect toward nature, as do his Hobbits, "small people" connected closely to "the soil and other living things" who display both human pettiness and unexpected heroism "in a pinch." The Elves, Hobbits, and good Men are countered in Tolkien's Middle-Earth by the threat of the machine, by which he meant "all use of external plans or devices," as opposed to "the development of inner powers or talents." The evil of the machine in Tolkien's eyes (he did not own a car after World War II) derived from the misguided human desire for power, itself a rebellion against the Creator's laws, a Fall from Paradise, another recurring theme in his fiction.

The horrors of World War I must have struck Tolkien as evil incarnate, with new military technology that devastated the countryside, struck down the innocent, and left no place for chivalry, heroism, or even common decency. Unlike Andrew Lang, an early Scottish collector of fairy tales, who felt children most often ask, "Is it true?," Tolkien declared that children far more often asked him of a character, "Was he good? Was he wicked?" Tolkien shared G. K. Chesterton's conviction that children "are innocent and love justice; while most of us are wicked and naturally prefer mercy." The child's stern perception of right and wrong, as opposed to the "mercy untempered by justice" which leads to "falsification of values," confirmed Tolkien's long-held inclination toward the steely world of the northern sagas, where human heroism faces inevitable defeat by the forces of evil, and the hero, according to Edith Hamilton, "can prove what he is only by dying." From his basic distrust of the machine and his firsthand memories of the Somme, Tolkien drew one of the major lessons of his fiction: "that on callow, lumpish and selfish youth peril, sorrow, and the shadow of death can bestow dignity, and even sometimes wisdom."

Reconciling this harsh northern *Weltbild* with his Roman Catholic faith did not seem to be difficult for Tolkien. An indispensable element of his theory of fantasy is the "sudden joyous 'turn'" of a "eucatastrophic" story, a moment in fiction accompanied by "a catch of the breath, a beat and lifting of the heart, near to (or indeed accompanied by) tears." By inserting the "turn" convincingly into his tale, the sub-creator "denies universal final defeat" and gives "a fleeting glimpse of Joy, Joy beyond the walls of the world, poignant as grief." Hence, Tolkien believed that such a joy was the "mark of the true fairy story," the revelation of truth in the fictional world the sub-creator built. It might even be greater, "a far-off gleam or echo of *evangelium* in the real world." Tolkien was able to see the Christian Gospels as "the greatest and most complete conceivable eucatastrophe," believing that in fantasy the human sub-creator might "actually assist in the effoliation and multiple enrichment of creation."

Tolkien's *The Silmarillion, The Hobbit,* and *The Lord of the Rings* form, as he always hoped, one coherent and archetypal whole. His "creative fantasy" effectively shows the three dissimilar faces his theory demanded: "the Mystical towards the Supernatural; the Magical towards Nature; and the Mirror of scorn and pity toward Man." Humanity's "oldest and deepest desire," the "Great Escape" from death, is satisfied in Tolkien's major fiction, not by denying Mortality but by accepting it gracefully as a gift from the Creator, a benefit to humankind that Tolkien's immortal Elves envied. The Elves' own magic is actually art, whose true object is "sub-creation" under God, not domination of lesser beings whose world they respectfully share. Scorn for fallen people (and fallen Elves and Hobbits as well) abounds in Middle-Earth, but pity, too, for guiltless creatures trapped in the most frightful evil Tolkien could envision, evil that he believed arises "from an apparently good root, the desire to benefit the world and others—speedily—and according to the benefactor's own plans." Middle-Earth lives forever in Tolkien's novels, and with it an affirmation of what is best, most true, and most beautiful in human nature.

For almost fifty years, mostly in the quiet academic atmosphere of Oxford, Tolkien built his resounding tales of "a body of more or less connected legend, ranging from the large and cosmogonic, to the level of romantic fairy-story." He consciously dedicated it simply "to England; to my country." The intellectual absorption with language he had always enjoyed gave him the starting place for his mythology, which he implemented in *The Silmarillion,* whose unifying theme is the Fall of Elves and Men. His happiness in the English countryside seems to have provided him the landscape from which *The Hobbit* grew, perhaps his most approachable "fairy-story" for both children and adults, illustrating the happiness to be gained from simplicity and the acceptance of the gift of mortality. The chivalric dreams of noble sacrifice shattered for Tolkien's generation by World War I were redeemed for him by his realization that the humble may effectively struggle against domination by the misguided technological values of modern civilization. The heroic legend of *The Lord of the Rings* best illustrates Tolkien's resolution of the conflict between the northern values he had admired from youth and the Roman Catholic religion of hope and consolation to which he was devoted. Tolkien wanted to illuminate the simplest and the highest values of human existence, found in a human love that accepts and transcends mortality. Tolkien's "mythology for England," a unique gift of literature and language, has earned its immense popular success by appealing to humanity's eternal desire to understand its mortal lot. As Hilda Ellis Davidson commented of the great northern myths, so like Tolkien's own, "In reaching out to explore the distant hills where the gods dwell and the deeps where the monsters are lurking, we are perhaps discovering the way home."

The Silmarillion · Both in Tolkien's life and in the chronology of Middle-Earth, the tales of *The Silmarillion* came first, but the book was not published until four years after his death. The volume called *The Silmarillion* contains four shorter narratives as well as the "Quenta Silmarillion," arranged as ordered chronicles of the Three Ages of Tolkien's Middle-Earth by his son Christopher, following his father's explicit intention.

Tolkien began parts of *The Silmarillion* in 1917 after he had been invalided home from France. The work steadily evolved after more than forty years, and, according to Christopher Tolkien, "incompatibilities of tone" inevitably arose from his father's increasing preoccupation with theology and philosophy over the mythology and poetry he had originally favored. Tolkien himself never abandoned his work on *The Silmarillion*, even though he found himself unable to complete it. As Christopher Wiseman had suggested to Tolkien, "Why these creatures live to you is because you are still creating them," and so Tolkien painstakingly revised, recast, and polished these stories, unwilling to banish their characters from his imagination.

The Silmarillion opens with "Ainulindalë," a cosmogonical myth revealing the creation of Middle-Earth by God ("Iluvatar") in the presence of the Valar, whom Tolkien described as angelic powers. He wanted "to provide beings of the same order . . . as the 'gods' of higher mythology" acceptable to "a mind that believes in the Blessed Trinity." The universe to which Middle-Earth belonged was set in living motion by music, "beheld as a light in the darkness."

The short "Valaquenta" enumerates the individual Valar, whose personal responsibilities covered all created things of Middle-Earth, stopping short of the act of creation itself. One of the Valar, Melkor, rebelled in the First Age; Tolkien believed that "there cannot be any 'story' without a fall." Melkor "began with the desire of Light, but when he could not possess it for himself alone, he descended . . . into a great burning." One of Melkor's servants was Sauron, who later embodied evil in the Third Age of Middle-Earth.

The twenty-four chapters of the "Quenta Silmarillion" recount the legendary history of the immortal Elves, the First-Born of Iluvatar, whom Tolkien elsewhere called "rational incarnate creatures of more or less comparable stature with our own." After writing *The Lord of the Rings*, Tolkien clearly indicated that the Elves were "only a representation of an apprehension of a part of human nature" from which art and poetry spring, but, he said, "that is not the legendary mode of talking." The Elves originally share the Paradise of the Valar, Valinor, but the Elves suffer a fall from that grace in the "Quenta Silmarillion," the rebellion and exile to Middle-Earth of one of the great families of Elves, led by their chief, the artificer Fëanor, who has captured the primal light of Iluvatar in the three Silmarils. Tolkien described these great jewels as aglow with the "light of art undivorced from reason, that sees things both scientifically (or philosophically) and imaginatively (or subcreatively) and 'says that they are good'—as beautiful." Fëanor's lust to possess the Silmarils for himself leads to their capture by Melkor, and in the struggle to redeem them, splendid deeds are performed by Beren, a Man of Middle-Earth beloved of the Elvish princess Lúthien. Tolkien called this "the first example of the motive (to become dominant in Hobbits) that the great policies of world history . . . are often turned . . . by the seemingly unknown and weak." The union of Beren and Lúthien is the first between mortal Man and immortal Elf; they win Paradise together, and eventually Earendil the Elven Mariner closes the "Quenta Silmarillion" by bringing the gem Beren painfully rescued from Melkor to the land of the Valar. His Silmaril was set into the sky as its brightest star, while the others were lost in the depths of the earth and sea, and the First Age of Middle-Earth came to its end.

Tolkien saw the Second Age of Middle-Earth as dark, and he believed "not very much of its history is (or need be) told." The Valar continued to dwell at Valinor with the faithful Elves, but the exiled Elves with Fëanor were commanded to leave Middle-Earth and live in the lonely Isle of Eressëa in the West. Some of them, however, ignored the order and remained in Middle-Earth. Those Men of Middle-Earth who had aided the Elves to redeem the Silmarils were given the Atlantis-like realm of Númenor as their reward, as well as lifespans three times the normal age of Men. Though Melkor was chained, his servant Sauron remained free to roam Middle-Earth, and through his evil influence, both Men of Númenor and the Delaying Elves came to grief.

The decay of Númenor is told in the *Akallabeth*, a much briefer illustration of Tolkien's belief that the inevitable theme of human stories is "a Ban, or Prohibition." The long-lived Númenoreans were prohibited by the Valar from setting foot on "immortal" lands in the West. Their wrongful desire to escape death, their gift from Iluvatar, causes them to rebel and bring about their own watery destruction through the worship of Sauron, Melkor's servant. At the same time, the Elves who delayed in Middle-Earth suffered the painful consequences of their flawed choice. Tolkien said they "wanted to have their cake without eating it," enjoying the perfection of the West while remaining on ordinary earth, revered as superior beings by the other, lesser races. Some of them cast their lot with Sauron, who enticed them to create three Rings of Power, in the misguided hopes of making Middle-Earth another Valinor. Sauron secretly made another ring himself, one with the power to enslave all the others. The ensuing war between Sauron and the Elves devastated Middle-Earth, but in the Last Alliance of Elves and Men against Sauron, the One Ring was lost. Tolkien calls this the "catastrophic end, not only of the Second Age, but of the Old World, the primeval age of Legend."

The posthumous collection called *The Silmarillion* ends with Tolkien's résumé "Of the Rings of Power and the Third Age," which introduces the motives, themes, and chief actors in the next inevitable war between Sauron and the Free Peoples of Middle-Earth. Although *The Hobbit* and *The Lord of the Rings* have proved vastly more popular, and both can be enjoyed without the complicated and generally loftily pitched history of *The Silmarillion*, its information is essential to a thorough understanding of the forces Tolkien set at work in the later novels. Even more important, *The Silmarillion* was for Tolkien, as his son Christopher has said, "the vehicle and depository of his profoundest reflections," and as such, it holds the bejewelled key to the autobiography Tolkien felt was embedded in his fiction.

The Hobbit · Around 1930, Tolkien jotted a few enigmatic words about "a hobbit" on the back of an examination paper he was grading. "Names always generate a story in my mind," he observed, and eventually he found out "what hobbits were like." The Hobbits, whom he subsequently described as "a branch of the specifically *human* race (not Elves or Dwarves)," became the vital link between Tolkien's mythology as constructed in *The Silmarillion* and the heroic legend that dominates *The Lord of the Rings*. Humphrey Carpenter, Tolkien's official biographer, believes that Bilbo Baggins, hero of *The Hobbit*, "embodied everything he [Tolkien] loved about the West Midlands." Tolkien himself once wrote, "I am in fact a hobbit, in all but size," and beyond personal affinities, he saw the Hobbits as "rustic English people," small in size to reflect "the generally small reach of their imagination—not the small reach of their courage or latent power."

Tolkien's Hobbits appear in the Third Age of Middle-Earth, in an ominously quiet lull before a fearful storm. Sauron had been overthrown by the Elflord Gil-galad and the Númenorean King Elendil, but since evil is never completely vanquished, Sauron's creatures lurk in the margins of Middle-Earth, in the mountain-enclosed region of Mordor, while a few Elves keep watch on its borders. Descendants of a few Númenoreans were saved from their land's disaster (Atlantean destruction was a recurrent nightmare for both Tolkien and his son Christopher), and they rule in the Kingdoms of Arnor in the North of Middle-Earth and Gondor of the South. The former Númenoreans are allies of the Homeric Riders of Rohan, whose human forefathers had remained in Middle-Earth when Númenor came to be. The three Elven Rings of Power secretly guard Rivendell and Lothlórien, which Tolkien called "enchanted enclaves of peace where Time seems to stand still and decay is restrained, a semblance of the bliss of the True West."

The Hobbits live in The Shire, in "an ordered, civilised, if simple rural life." One day, the Hobbit Bilbo Baggins receives an odd visitor, Gandalf the Wizard, who sends Bilbo off with traveling dwarves, as a professional burglar, in search of Dragon's Gold, the major theme of the novel. In the process, Tolkien uses the humble Hobbit to illustrate one of his chief preoccupations, the process by which "small imagination" combines with "great courage." As he recalled from his months in the trenches, "I've always been impressed that we are here, surviving, because of the indomitable courage of quite small people against impossible odds."

Starting from the idyllic rural world of The Shire, *The Hobbit*, ostensibly a children's book, traces the typical quest of the northern hero about whom Tolkien himself had loved to read in his youth. Gandalf shares certain characteristics with the Scandinavian god Odin, said to wander among people as an "old man of great height," with a long grey cloak, a white beard, and supernatural powers. Gandalf, like Odin, understands the speech of birds, being especially fond of eagles and ravens, and his strange savage friend Beorn, who rescues the Hobbits at one critical point, recalls the berserkers, bearskin-clad warriors consecrated to Odin who fought with superhuman strength in the intoxication of battle. The Dwarves of Middle-Earth distinctly resemble their Old Norse forebears, skilled craftsmen who made treasures for the gods. Smaug the Dragon, eventually slain by the human hero Bard, is surely related to "the prince of all dragons" who had captured Tolkien's boyish imagination and who would reappear in *Farmer Giles of Ham*. The Germanic code of the *comitatus*, the warrior's fidelity unto death, celebrated in the tenth century Anglo-Saxon poem "The Battle of Maldon," inspired Tolkien's only play and applies to *The Hobbit*, too, since Bilbo's outward perils are overshadowed by the worst threat of all to the northern hero, the inward danger of proving a coward.

Bilbo's hard-won self-knowledge allows him to demonstrate the "indomitable courage of small people against great odds" when he saves Dwarves, Men, and Elves from suicidal war against one another, after the Dragon has been slain and its treasure freed. *The Hobbit* far exceeded its beginnings as a bedtime story for Tolkien's small sons, since it is also a fable about the child at the heart of every person, perceiving right and wrong as sternly as did the heroes of the North.

In late 1937, at the suggestion of his British publisher, Stanley Unwin, Tolkien began a sequel to *The Hobbit.* To the East, a malignant force was gathering strength in the Europe that even the mammoth sacrifices of World War I had not redeemed from oppression, and while Tolkien often cautions against interpreting his works allegorically, the apprehensive atmosphere of prewar England must have affected his own peace of mind. He described his intention in *The Lord of the Rings* as "an attempt to . . . wind up all the elements and motives of what has preceded." He wanted "to include the colloquialism and vulgarity of Hobbits, poetry and the highest style of prose." The moral of this novel, not a "trilogy" but, he stressed, "conceived and written as a whole," was "obvious": "that without the high and noble the simple and vulgar is utterly mean; and without the simple and ordinary the noble and heroic is meaningless."

The Lord of the Rings · *The Lord of the Rings* is a vast panoramic contest between good and evil, played out against the backdrop of Tolkien's mythology as presented in *The Silmarillion.* The One Ring of Sauron, long lost, was found by little Bilbo Baggins, and from him it passed to his kinsman Frodo, who becomes the central figure of the quest-in-reverse: Having found the Ring, the allied Men, Elves, Dwarves, and Hobbits must destroy it where it was forged, so that its power can never again dominate Middle-Earth. Another quest takes place simultaneously in the novel, as the mysterious Strider who greets the Hobbits at Bree on the first stage of their perilous journey is gradually revealed as Aragorn, son of Arathorn and heir to Arnor in the North, descendant of Elendil who kept faith with the Valar; he is the human King of Middle-Earth who must reclaim his realm. Sauron's minions rise to threaten the Ringbearer and his companions, and after many adventures, a great hopeless battle is fought before the Gates of Mordor. As Tolkien stated in "Of the Rings of Power and the Third Age," "There at the last they looked upon death and defeat, and all their valour was in vain; for Sauron was too strong." This is the paradoxical defeat-and-victory of the northern hero, whose glory is won in the manner of his death. As a practicing Christian, though, Tolkien had to see hope clearly in the ultimate struggle between right and wrong, "and help came from the hands of the weak when the Wise faltered." Frodo the Hobbit at last managed to carry the Ring to Mount Doom in spite of Sauron, and there it was destroyed, and "a new Spring opened up on Earth." Even then, Frodo's mission is not completed. With his three Hobbit companions, he has to return to the shire and undo the evil that has corrupted the hearts, minds, and landscape of that quiet region. Only after that may Frodo, with the Elves, depart for the far west.

In retrospect, Tolkien acknowledged that another central issue of *The Lord of the Rings* was "love in different modes," which had been "wholly absent from *The Hobbit.*" Tolkien considered the "simple 'rustic' love" between Sam, Frodo's faithful batman, and his Rosie was *"absolutely essential"* both to the study of the main hero of the novel and "to the theme of the relation of ordinary life . . . to quests, to sacrifice, causes, and the 'longing for Elves,' and sheer beauty." The evidence of Tolkien's own life indicates the depth of his ability to love, like Beren, always faithful to his Lúthien. Such love that made all sacrifice possible forms the indestructible core of *The Lord of the Rings*, which moved C. S. Lewis to speak of "beauties which pierce like swords or burn like cold iron . . . a book that will break your heart."

Love exemplified in two important romances softens the necromancy and the battles of *The Lord of the Rings*: the poignant "mistaken love" of Eowyn for Aragorn, as Tolkien described it, and the novel's "highest love-story," the tale of Aragorn and Arwen, daughter of Elrond, leader of the Elves of Middle-Earth. Eowyn is niece to Theoden, King of Rohan, the land of the horsemen Tolkien patterned after ancient Anglo-Saxon tribes he had first encountered through William Morris's *House of the Wolfings* (1889). In Theoden's decline, the shield-maiden Eowyn gives her first love to the royalty-in-exile she senses in Aragorn, and though he in no sense encourages her, Eowyn's tragedy is one only he can heal once he is restored as King. In contrast, Tolkien merely alludes to the love of Aragorn and Arwen in *The Lord of the Rings*, since it seems almost too deep for tears. Arwen must forsake her Elven immortality and join Aragorn in human death, paralleling the earlier story of Beren and Lúthien. Like Tolkien's own love for Edith, Aragorn's for Arwen is temporarily prevented from fruition until he can return to her in full possession of his birthright. The shadow of her possible loss lends stature to the characterization of Aragorn, the hero of *The Lord of the Rings*.

In 1955, Tolkien observed that "certain features . . . and especially certain places" of *The Lord of the Rings* "still move me very powerfully." The passages he cited sum up the major means by which the novel so strongly conveys love, redemption, and heroism achieved in the face of overwhelming odds. "The heart remains in the description of Cerin Amroth," he wrote, the spot where Aragorn and Arwen first pledged their love and where, many years later at the beginning of his fearful quest, "the grim years were removed from the face of Aragorn, and he seemed clothed in white, a young lord tall and fair." Tolkien magnifies this small epiphany of love through the eyes of the Hobbit Frodo. Another key episode, the wretched Gollum's failure to repent because Sam interrupts him, grieved Tolkien deeply, he said, for it resembled "the *real* world in which the instruments of just retribution are seldom themselves just or holy." In his favorite passage, however, Tolkien was "most stirred by the sound of the horns of the Rohirrim at cockcrow," the great "turn" of *The Lord of the Rings*, a flash of salvation in the face of all odds that comes beyond hope, beyond prayer, like a stroke of unexpected bliss from the hand of the Creator.

The "turn" that makes *The Lord of the Rings* a "true fairy-story" in Tolkien's definition links fidelity to a vow, a Germanic value, to the Christian loyalty that animated many of the great Anglo-Saxon works Tolkien had spent his scholarly life studying. By weaving the immensely complex threads of Elves, Hobbits, Men, and Dwarves into his heroic legend of the last great age of Middle-Earth, he achieved a valid subcreation, sharing in the nature of what for him was most divine.

The History of Middle-Earth · Tolkien's son Christopher undertook the massive task of editing and commenting on the many drafts and manuscripts Tolkien left unpublished. These volumes, grouped under the generic title of *The History of Middle-Earth*, became commentary of a painstaking, scholarly kind, such as Tolkien himself would have enjoyed, no doubt, though it leaves the average reader rather befuddled. Each volume reprints, compares, and comments on original draft material in chronological order. One interesting feature is the emergence of the *Annals*, running alongside the stories; another is the evolution of the Elvish languages and etymologies. Tolkien's original attempt to make this a mythology of England through the character of Aelfwine, an Anglo-Saxon who had somehow reached Middle-Earth and then translated some of its material into Old English, can also be seen. *The Lost Road* (1937) emerges as a fragment produced as part of an agreement with C. S. Lewis for a science-fiction story on time travel that would complement a story by Lewis on space. The latter produced *Out of the Silent Planet* (1938), but Tolkien gave up on his, though the attempt to connect it to the *Akallabeth* can be seen clearly.

Christopher also edited the childhood stories and poetry; others have dealt with Tolkien's drawings, illustrations, and mapmaking predelictions. The production of such Tolkiana is perhaps in some danger of overshadowing the myth that gave it life. Tolkien saw all of his work as unfinished and imperfect. As C. S. Lewis saw too in his *Chronicles of Narnia* (1950-1956), our myths can only ever be the first page of the Great Myth that goes on forever.

Mitzi M. Brunsdale,
updated by David Barratt

Other major works

SHORT FICTION: *Tree and Leaf,* 1964, revised 1988; *Unfinished Tales of Numenor and Middle-Earth,* 1980 (Christopher Tolkien, editor); *The Book of Lost Tales,* 1983-1984.

PLAY: *The Homecoming of Beorhtnoth Beorhthelm's Son,* pb. 1953.

POETRY: *Songs for the Philologists,* 1936 (with E. V. Gordon et al.); *The Adventures of Tom Bombadil,* 1962; *The Road Goes Ever On: A Song Cycle,* 1967 (music by Donald Swann); *Poems and Stories,* 1980; *The Lays of Beleriand,* 1985.

NONFICTION: *A Middle English Vocabulary,* 1922; *The Letters from J. R. R. Tolkien: Selection,* 1981 (Humphrey Carpenter, editor); *The Monsters and the Critics, and Other Essays,* 1983.

CHILDREN'S LITERATURE: *Farmer Giles of Ham,* 1949; *Smith of Wootton Major,* 1967; *The Father Christmas Letters,* 1976; *Roverandom,* 1998.

TRANSLATIONS: *Sir Gawain and the Green Knight, Pearl, and Sir Orfeo,* 1975; *Finn and Hengest: The Fragment and the Episode,* 1982.

EDITED TEXTS: *Sir Gawain and the Green Knight,* 1925 (with E. V. Gordon); *Ancrene Wisse: The English Text of the Ancrene Riwle,* 1962; *The Old English Exodus: Text, Translation, and Commentary by J. R. R. Tolkien,* 1981.

MISCELLANEOUS: *The Tolkien Reader,* 1966.

Bibliography

Carpenter, Humphrey. *Tolkien: A Biography.* London: Allen & Unwin, 1977. Written with access to Tolkien's unpublished letters and diaries, this mostly chronological narrative traces the development of the world of Middle-Earth from Tolkien's philological work. Balances the details of his rather pedestrian life with the publishing history of Tolkien's writings. An extensive section of black-and-white photographs, a detailed bibliography, a family genealogy, and an index add to the value of this standard biography.

Crabbe, Katharyn W. *J. R. R. Tolkien.* Rev. ed. New York: Continuum, 1988. A study of Tolkien's writings (including a chapter on *The Silmarillion* and another on the posthumous History of Middle-Earth series) unified by a vision of "the quest." After a brief biographical chapter, Crabbe considers Tolkien's use of languages to delineate character in his major works. Argues that his quest was for a suitable pre-Christian mythology which could ground the imaginative works of the future in a great mythic past for his beloved Britain.

Curry, Patrick. *Defending Middle-Earth: Tolkien–Myth and Modernity*. London: Harper-Collins, 1997. Curry examines the relevance of Tolkien's mythological creation, especially in terms of its depiction of struggle of community, nature, and spirit against state. There are chapters on politics, ecology, and spirituality.

Foster, Robert. *The Complete Guide to Middle-Earth: From "The Hobbit" to "The Silmaril-lion."* Rev. ed. New York: Ballantine, 1978. An alphabetical annotated compendium of each of the proper names in Tolkien's major works, including persons, places, and things, with page references to standard editions of each work. An invaluable reference, written from a perspective within the world created by Tolkien. The guide provides translations of Middle-Earth tongues, chronologies as appropriate, and masterful summaries of complex events.

Hammond, Wayne, and Christina Scull. *J. R. R. Tolkien: Artist and Illustrator*. London: HarperCollins, 1995. A full commentary on Tolkien's illustrations for his major, minor, and unfinished stories. It brings out Tolkien's own skills as an artist and the quality of his visual imagination.

Isaacs, Neil D., and Rose A. Zimbardo, eds. *Tolkien and the Critics: Essays on J. R. R. Tolkien's "The Lord of the Rings."* Notre Dame, Ind.: University of Notre Dame Press, 1968. A collection of fifteen original and reprinted critical articles dealing with *The Lord of the Rings* as literature. Among the contributors, C. S. Lewis offers a paean to the author, critic Edmund Fuller allows that Tolkien's work lifts one's spirits, and translator Burton Raffel calls most of Tolkien's poetry "embarrassingly bad." An index of Middle-Earth references completes a lively and accessible volume.

Reynolds, Patricia, and Glen GoodKnight, eds. *Proceedings of the J. R. R. Tolkien Centenary Conference, 1992*. Altadena, Calif.: Mythopoeic Press, 1995. As the title suggests, this is a collection of papers given at the Tolkien conference held at Keble College, Oxford, in 1992 and represents a significant collection of views on Tolkien.

Anthony Trollope

Born: London, England; April 24, 1815
Died: London, England; December 6, 1882

Principal long fiction · *The Macdermots of Ballycloran*, 1847; *The Kellys and the O'Kellys*, 1848; *The Warden*, 1855; *Barchester Towers*, 1857; *The Three Clerks*, 1858; *Doctor Thorne*, 1858; *The Bertrams*, 1859; *Castle Richmond*, 1860; *Framley Parsonage*, 1860-1861; *Orley Farm*, 1861-1862; *The Small House at Allington*, 1862-1864; *Rachel Ray*, 1863; *Can You Forgive Her?*, 1864-1865; *Miss Mackenzie*, 1865; *The Belton Estate*, 1865-1866; *The Claverings*, 1866-1867; *The Last Chronicle of Barset*, 1867; *Phineas Finn, the Irish Member*, 1867-1969; *He Knew He Was Right*, 1868-1869; *The Vicar of Bulhampton*, 1869-1870; *The Eustace Diamonds*, 1871-1873; *Phineas Redux*, 1873-1874; *The Way We Live Now*, 1874-1875; *The Prime Minister*, 1875-1876; *The American Senator*, 1876-1877; *Is He Popenjoy?*, 1877-1878; *John Caldigate*, 1878-1879; *The Duke's Children*, 1879-1880; *Dr. Wortle's School*, 1880; *Ayala's Angel*, 1881; *The Fixed Period*, 1881-1882; *The Landleaguers*, 1882-1883; *Mr. Scarborough's Family*, 1882-1883.

Other literary forms · Anthony Trollope's novels were frequently serialized in various periodicals such as *Cornhill Magazine* and *The Fortnightly Review*. They appeared subsequently in a two- or three-volume format. Trollope wrote several books of cultural reportage which were more than mere travelogues: *The West Indies* (1859), *North America* (1862), *Australia and New Zealand* (1873), and *South Africa* (1878), along with the more impressionistic *Travelling Sketches* (1865-1866). Three volumes of short stories appeared: *Lotta Schmidt and Other Stories* (1867), *An Editor's Tales* (1870), and *Why Frau Frohmann Raised Her Prices and Other Stories* (1882). He wrote sketches of clerical men in *Clergymen of the Church of England* (1865-1866) and detailed biographies of William Makepeace Thackeray, a longtime friend (1879), and Lord Palmerston, the prominent politician (1882). His own *Autobiography* appeared posthumously in 1883. He tried his hand at classical translation in an edition of *The Commentaries of Caesar* (1870). Trollope's letters were edited by Bradford A. Booth (1951), but 205 complete and three fragmentary letters remain unpublished at Princeton University.

Achievements · Trollope was acknowledged during his lifetime as a prominent though not necessarily a weighty or enduring writer. He wished to entertain and he did so, at least until the late 1860's when *He Knew He Was Right* turned out to be a failure. His posthumous reputation was harmed by his *Autobiography*, which claimed that he wrote automatically, that his characters were imitations of commonly observed types, that he transcribed reality without much aesthetic control, and that he forced his production by his methodical habits of composition whatever the circumstances. These admissions brought upon him the wrath of the next generation of writers in the 1880's and 1890's who were imbued with more aesthetic doctrines of carefully contrived and consistent viewpoints, detailed representation of interior states, a conscious interplay of ideas, and a complex style to suit a more complex method of storytelling.

Later, Trollope suffered from those who deemed him a pedestrian realist padding his work with creaking plots, flat characters, prosaic situations, and dull prose. He was, and still is for much of the public, the novelist of a single work, *Barchester Towers*, but other writers and critics have not forgiven him for writing more than thirty novels and setting himself a goal to exceed in quantity if not in quality. Despite what seems to be a simple theory of fiction—the writer tries as closely as possible to make the reader's experience approximate his own, to make his characters and events appear to parallel actual life—Trollope was more sophisticated than he allows.

Walter Kendrick finds that before Trollope's *He Knew He Was Right*, his inner thought is not distinguished from outer events, consciousness is presented chronologically, and characters, at least by implication, appear without authorial intervention. Afterward, character becomes "a zone of space on a canvas" with changes of age, feeling, and appearance even while outside the narrative. Various linear plots create a spatial unity for the reader, and they become a mosaic on which the character exists. Fiction writing becomes a subject in the novel, and the characters are a warning against efforts to define their existence with the narrative. This view sees the characters as a complex interplay between narrative and reader. Nathaniel Hawthorne had a very different view of Trollope, equating him to a giant hewing a great lump out of the earth as the earth's inhabitants go about the business of putting it under a glass case. This comment leads, unfortunately, in the direction of Henry James's evaluation after Trollope's death that he had "a great deliberate apprehension of the real" but that his "great fecundity is gross and importunate."

Trollope is a mixture of several kinds of writer, sometimes realistic in the sociological way of Honoré de Balzac, analyzing class and caste, sometimes a comedian of manners and mores like Henry Fielding, at times a sentimental melodramatist like Charles Dickens, fairly often an ironist deliberately breaking fictional illusions like Thackeray, often introspective if not as equally learned as George Eliot, and periodically a brilliant chronicler of dementia like Joseph Conrad. This mixture is what creates havoc with critical response. Trollope is a master of convincing and accurate dialogue, good at retrospective interior analysis, and gifted with varieties of ironic voices. The building of his reputation, aided by Michael Sadleir's biography in the 1920's, was materially assisted by *The Trollopian* (now *Nineteenth Century Studies*), a journal devoted to studies of his novels; further work by scholars, such as Ruth apRoberts, Robert M. Polhemus, and James R. Kincaid; and new critical techniques, which have given Trollope his present reputation as a leading English novelist.

Biography · Anthony Trollope, born on April 24, 1815, in London, seems to have owed his boisterous energy, booming voice, quarrelsome touchiness, and reticent sensitivity to a childhood of off-handed upbringing. C. P. Snow refers to him as "weighed down by 20 years of neglect and humiliation." His father was a tactless and impractical barrister who had pretensions about being a landowner in Harrow. There, he established his family in an elegant though quickly declining farm, Julians, later the model for the experimental Orley Farm in the novel of that name. Trollope's mother, Frances, was the driving force of the family; she was closer to Trollope's oldest brother, Tom, than to Anthony: Anthony received neither much encouragement nor much regular affection from her. After starting his education at Sunbury School, with a brief stint at Harrow, Anthony was sent to Winchester, his father's old school, for three years. In 1827, the family was forced to move into a smaller house in Harrow for financial reasons.

Meanwhile, his mother made the acquaintance of a zealous utopian reformer,

Fanny Wright, and went with her and three of her children—Henry, Cecilia, and Emily—to America. Their experiences there border on black comedy. Among other misfortunes, Frances, without past experience or common sense, started a fancy emporium or bazaar in Cincinnati; the building evolved into a grand structure modeled upon an Egyptian temple. The enterprise only succeeded in making the family penniless. Through the efforts of a painter friend, her husband, and son Tom, they managed to piecemeal their way home to England.

Library of Congress

In 1830 Anthony was removed from Winchester, which deprived him of the chance to enter Oxford University, from which he might have entered into the clergy, the usual course at that time. He returned as a day student to Harrow School, where the intense and entrenched snobbery made the shabby boy the butt of ridicule and persecution, and perhaps began his lifelong pattern of irritability. Also at that time, Trollope's father sank into petty miserliness and self-pitying moroseness, becoming more obsessively preoccupied with his scholarly work, an ecclesiastical encyclopedia.

The success of Frances's *The Domestic Manners of the Americans* (1832), a book adversely critical of American society, temporarily kept the family from bankruptcy, but her husband's financial mismanagement created more debts. To prevent his arrest for bankruptcy in 1834, the family, without Anthony, went to Bruges, Belgium. Any possible happiness they might have found was destroyed by tuberculosis, which killed Anthony's father, brother Henry, and sister Emily between 1834 and 1836. Frances Trollope was obviously too occupied with nursing to pay much attention to Anthony, but she did get him a tutoring position in Belgium for a short time. He returned to England where he survived in squalid lodgings in Marylebone, London, at a clerk's job in the main post office for seven years. At age twenty-six, he got the chance which changed his life, obtaining the post of deputy surveyor, the overseer of mail service, in western Ireland.

At Banaghar, he found a comfortable social milieu for the first time, though his manner with carriers and postmasters was brusque and his temper was at times violent. Trollope became a man jovial with companions, truculent with superiors, bullying with inferiors, and tender with close friends and family. In 1842, he married Rose Heseltine, an Anglo-Irish woman. Her bank-manager father, like one of Trollope's own shady characters, was an embezzler. A trusted partner, Rose handled Trollope's financial affairs, edited his manuscripts, and accompanied him on his journeys around the world. The portraits of solid, sensible, and compassionate wives and mothers found throughout his work, such as Lady Staveley in *Orley Farm*, suggest the type of woman Trollope had found in Rose.

Irish scenery and politics, and the models of his mother and his brother, Tom, led Trollope to his own fiction writing. Thus, not coincidentally, his first two novels have an Irish theme. In these years, Trollope also began rearing a family, two sons. Henceforth, Trollope's career ran on a dual path, pursuing his duties for the postal service and his writing.

Posted to southwest England in 1851 to correct faults in rural delivery, Trollope and his family led a roving existence for three years until he became his own boss as full surveyor in Belfast, at age thirty-nine. The experience of sleepy country towns and a current topic—the Anglican Church's misuse of endowed charity funds to create sizable incomes for administrators—resulted in the writing of *The Warden*, finished in Belfast and published in 1855; it was his first major success. When Trollope moved his family to Dublin, he established a daily routine of writing. The successor to *The Warden, Barchester Towers*, his best-known novel, is a social comedy in the eighteenth century mock-heroic vein of Henry Fielding or Oliver Goldsmith.

During a visit to see his mother and brother in Italy, Trollope met a young American woman, Kate Field, and began a long and close friendship, mostly carried out by correspondence. C. P. Snow thinks that Trollope was impressed by the independent and self-assertive woman, who was rather unlike English women. Intrigued by Kate's advocacy of feminine freedom, in *Orley Farm* Trollope presents a woman who affronts social and moral conventions by an act of forgery to save the inheritance of her infant son. The motivation is a bit slick, but the fact that the resolute heroine succeeds against a determined male antagonist suggests that Kate's independence was sympathetically perceived.

Trollope went to North America during the early Civil War (1861-1862), a trip which resulted in a travel book. Like his mother's work, the book took a negative stance toward American institutions. He then published, among others, *Rachel Ray, The Last Chronicle of Barset*, and *The Claverings*, which gained Trollope his biggest sales price ever. His works were also being serialized in various periodicals, such as *The Fortnightly Review*. It became obvious, however, that Trollope's continued output led him to repeat themes and recycle characters.

Immersed as he was in writing and somewhat resentful of his position at the post office, Trollope resigned in October, 1867, after the offer of the editorship of a new journal, *St. Paul's Magazine*. He continued to do some work on behalf of the post office, however, since he went to Washington to negotiate a postal treaty in 1868. Trollope ran *St. Paul's Magazine* for three years before it went under financially. He was not temperamentally suited to deal with authors.

In his own writing, Trollope tended, as Walter Kendrick sees it, to turn toward more sensational materials, which other authors had discarded, but he was also experimenting in the psychological novel. In *He Knew He Was Right*, Trollope treats the subject of insanity and he presents a fascinating study of psychosis. Ruth apRoberts praises the novel for its economy and the supporting relationships of closely knit characters. Yet, Trollope's work began to command less popular attention, and he increasingly turned to the political world. He created Phineas Finn, an Anglo-Irish politician, who appears in the novel of that name in 1869 and reappears in *Phineas Redux*, part of the loose series sometimes referred to as the Palliser novels. Trollope, however, did not give up what is really his chief subject: conflict between the sexes.

In 1871, having sold Waltham House and given up his editorship, Trollope and his wife embarked on an eighteen-month visit to New Zealand and a stay with their son,

Fred, a relatively unprosperous sheep-farmer in Australia. Trollope continued to write during their stay in the primitive sheep-station. A travel commentary and materials for *John Caldigate* were the result of the voyage, as well as further work on the novel *The Eustace Diamonds*. The Trollopes then settled in London where he wrote on the current topic of "the condition of England" in *The Way We Live Now* and *The Prime Minister*. Trollope presented his skeptical views about the ability of a democratic society to govern itself effectively.

The final stage of Trollope's life was a restless one in his sixties. He took another trip to Australia for eight months in 1875, returning through the United States and meeting with Kate Field. Then, he immediately went to South Africa to inspect the Boer territory with the encroaching British settlement based on gold and diamond exploitation. The Trollopes again returned to the land by moving into a refined farmhouse at Hartung, near Hastings, where Trollope worked on his autobiography. Along with other fiction, he wrote a mystery novel, *Mr. Scarborough's Family*, which was serialized before his death but published posthumously in 1883. Farm living aggravated Trollope's asthma which drained his energy, thus causing him to return to London. He was enjoying club life, dinners, and letters to his son, Henry, who was also a writer, when Trollope suffered a sudden stroke in the fall of 1882 that left him paralyzed, and a month later, on December 6, 1882, he died, at the age of sixty-seven.

Analysis · Twentieth century criticism of Anthony Trollope acknowledged his affinity with comic satirists of the eighteenth century, and this affinity is reflected in his best-known work, *Barchester Towers*. There are two distinct worlds in the novel: that of London vanity, represented by Mr. Slope, the London preacher who comes to Barchester as the protégé of Mrs. Proudie; and that of the smaller, conservative rural world, represented by Archdeacon Grantly of Barchester Cathedral, who opposes Mr. Slope with "high and dry" Anglicanism. At the end, Slope is rejected but so is the siren of the comic interlude, Signora Madeleine Vesey Neroni, daughter of the gentlemanly but parasitic, self-indulgent Dr. Vesey Stanhope, canon of the Cathedral.

Barchester Towers · The novel is concerned with the pursuit of Eleanor Bold, a young prosperous widow and daughter of Mr. Harding, by Obadiah Slope, a brash and unctuous social climber. The newly vacant position of warden provokes a struggle between the Grantly forces and the Proudie forces (including Mr. Slope), with Mrs. Proudie at the head. In this strand of the plot, the mock-heroic or mock-epic combat parodies the Miltonic epic tradition, with Grantly and his supporters as the rebel angels struggling against the tyrant Mrs. Proudie, with Slope as a kind of fallen angel. Slope is first supported by Mrs. Proudie in his efforts to prevent the return of the vacant post to Harding, but Slope, in his effort to attain favor with Eleanor Bold, eventually gets the position for Harding.

Slope is emasculated by Signora Neroni, who transfixes him with her bright eyes and silvery laughter during rural games and festivities at Ullathorne, the ancient seat of the Thornes and center of a static pastoral world. Seduced by her witchery, he is humiliated by this demoniac Eve and defeated by the godlike rebuff of Eleanor, who slaps his face as he presses his suit upon her. Further, he incurs the wrath of his patroness, Mrs. Proudie, with his attentiveness to Signora Neroni, who, although crippled, rules from a couch where she resides in state like Cleopatra. In this world of sham battles, Grantly celebrates his triumph, including a dean's position for Mr.

Harding in a solemn conclave of the clergy.

The disputants in these mock-exercises practice their feints around innocent third parties: Bishop Proudie between Slope and Mrs. Proudie; Quiverful, the other candidate for the wardenship, a pathetically comic father of numerous children, between his determined wife and Slope; and Harding between Slope and Grantly. In this formally ordered structure, it is appropriate that Eleanor and Frances Arabin, the naïve Oxford academician, be matched by Miss Thorne, reaffirming the power of the old order, yet still contending with Proudies. The marriage of Eleanor and Arabin asserts the two worlds, old and new, country and city, innocent and corrupt.

The novel has a rich galaxy of minor characters. For example, there is Bertie Stanhope, the dilettante sculptor, who is pressed into proposing to Eleanor, but he undermines his own courtship by the candid admission of his motives; Mr. Harding, the unwilling tool of both Slope and Grantly, who takes such delight in the cathedral music that he mechanically saws an imaginary cello during moments of partisan plots and counterplots; and Mrs. Quiverful, who functions like a wailing chorus in a Greek tragedy, piteously reminding the world and Mrs. Proudie of the cruel difficulties of pinched means and a large family. Although Trollope did write important novels on more serious themes, *Barchester Towers* remains his best known, with its effective comic scenes, the balletlike entrances and exits, the lively irony, and the mock-heroic bathos. The orchestration of speaking styles ranging from the pomposity of the Archdeacon to the vacuity of Bertie Stanhope is another example of the buoyancy and playful wit that Trollope achieved only intermittently thereafter.

Orley Farm · *Orley Farm* was written during Trollope's middle period. Its central situation revolves around the plight of Lady Mason, the second wife of a rich man, who, twenty years earlier, forged a codicil to her dying husband's will so that it leaves Orley Farm, her sole economic support, to her and her young child, Lucius. The possession of the farm has become a matter of regret, as the suspicions of the legitimate heir, Joseph Mason, otherwise the inheritor of considerable wealth, eventuate in a trial to break the will. The effort fails only because Lady Mason commits perjury. Using the omniscient viewpoint, Trollope shows both her guilt and her anguish in trying to provide security for her infant son. Lucius, as the novel opens, is a proud, priggish young man given to notions of scientifically reforming agricultural practice; he is well educated, theoretical, and self-righteous.

The novel's unusual perspective poses two main themes: first, how justice can be accomplished, and second, whether justice can actually be achieved. In setting human rights against legal rights, Trollope portrays Lady Mason's crime in the light of vested interests and the selfish motives of various people. Like C. P. Snow in a novel such as *The Masters* (1951), Trollope displays in *Orley Farm* an abstract ideal distorted and transformed by human emotions, calculations, and egotism. Joseph Mason is more concerned with defeating Lady Mason than enjoying the actual property; Sir Peregrine Orme, a highly respected landowner, proposes marriage to Lady Mason in order to extend the protection of his name, but even he is forced to realize the stain upon his honor if the truth should come out, and after Lady Mason refuses his offer, he, having been told the damning truth, keeps his promise to support her in her new trial. Another perspective is provided through Mr. Dockwrath, the country lawyer who discovers the evidence which necessitates the new trial, and hopes it will prove lucrative and will enhance his legal reputation. Lady Mason's solicitor, Mr. Furnival, carefully avoids definite knowledge of her guilt, though he suspects it, while also wishing she were proven guilty so that he might forgive her with pleasure. A less selfish attitude is seen in Edith Orme, Sir Peregrine's widowed daughter-in-law, who recognizes with compassion the necessity for Lady Mason's crime and the suffering it has entailed for her.

Trollope reveals some of his other typical thematic concerns in the subplots of *Orley Farm*. He explores various attitudes toward marriage and money in the romances of Peregrine, Jr., Lucius Mason, and Felix Graham, a poor barrister, with a variety of modern young women. The women's responses to the gentlemen's advances run from prudent calculation of worldly advantages to prudent reticence in acknowledging love until family wisdom approves it. Also, Trollope's impulses toward indulgence of children are exemplified in Lord and Lady Staveley, who, having made their way without worldly advantages, are willing to offer the same chance to their children by permitting the engagement of a daughter to Felix Graham, whose success has been impeded by his honesty. Trollope's conservatism is revealed through the reluctance of these young people to avow their love until they have consent from the Staveleys.

With regard to the central theme of moral and legal justice, purely through the oratorical skills of the trial lawyer, Lady Mason is found innocent of perjury, a finding wholly incorrect. The trial frees the guilty, turns the truthful into villains, makes the innocent bear the burden of deceit, challenges the loyalty of lawyers, and implicates the idealists' posturings. The system has turned Lady Mason's desperate chicanery into heroism. It is somewhat anticlimactic that Trollope has the pure Edith Orme take Lady Mason to her heart and, from a sense of Christian charity, refuse to render judgment against her.

Meanwhile, Lady Mason's greatest trial has been alienation from Lucius who, unaware of her guilt, has attempted vigorous countermeasures to defend her honor rather than respecting her dignified silence. His discovery of the truth cuts deeply into his priggish pride, destroys his dreams of becoming a gentleman-farmer, and makes him restore the farm to Joseph Mason before departing abroad with his mother. Again, Trollope makes an ambivalent statement through this conclusion. Although forgiveness implies repentance and restitution, Lady Mason has not been, at least in public, repentant, and the restitution is as much a matter of pride as of justice. The effect is a tacit denial of Lady Mason's innocence and thus the aborting of the whole effort to save her reputation.

Can You Forgive Her? · If the power of money, or the distortions of human choice and desire which money brings, is Trollope's major concern, the warfare of the sexes and the frustrations which that warfare brings are secondary themes in his novels. *Can You Forgive Her?*, the first of the Palliser series—which includes *Phineas Finn, Phineas Redux*, and *The Prime Minister*, each grounded in politics—raises the issue of what sort of love a woman wishes in marriage or indeed whether marriage is a suitable institution. The novel presents the case of Alice Vavasour, a "new woman" who does not know what she wants in life but resents the demands of social propriety. She especially resents the expectation that she accept the marriage proposal of John Grey, whom she really does love, merely because everyone knows him to be a suitable partner. Her cousin, the heiress Lady Glencora McCluskie, has married Plantagenet Palliser, the dull younger son of a ducal family, to support his Liberal political career with her money; but she has fallen in love with the handsome Burgo Fitzgerald, an unconventional, ruinous, yet passionate charmer. Alice reinstitutes her former affection for her cousin George Vavasour, another charmingly irresponsible man who needs her money to campaign to keep his seat in Parliament. For Alice, the masculine excitement of politics makes George attractive, although she honestly admits his desire for her money.

The novel has low-comedy relief in Alice's aunt, Arabella Greenow, and her two suitors, a grocer with money and a retired military officer without it. Arabella means to have her own way, giving her lovers only as much liberty as she desires, choosing the officer because of "a sniff of the rocks and the valleys" about him. The comedy underscores the desire of Alice and Glencora, who, if they had a choice, would put themselves at the mercy of weak men.

In a melodramatic turn of the main plot, George knocks down his sister, Kate, for refusing to assist him in overturning their grandfather's will, which had left all the family property to her. This turn of the plot demonstrates, through George's furious masculine rage, the falsity of the normal economic subjugation of women, which has been reversed in Kate's case. Arabella Greenow, for her part, is also financially independent and can bargain her way into a satisfactorily romantic liaison balancing "rocks and valleys" against "bread and cheese."

Glencora, aware of being sold into matrimony, almost runs off with Burgo but is dissuaded at the last minute by the vigilance of Alice, who makes clear to Plantagenet the temptation he has given to his wife by his conduct. In an improbable reversal that displays Trollope's own romanticism, Plantagenet sacrifices his political hopes for a cabinet appointment in order to take her away from the scenes of her misery after she has confessed her infatuation. Indeed, he is even willing to provide Burgo, who becomes a frequenter of gambling tables, with an allowance at her behest when they encounter him abroad.

Plantagenet can make a sacrifice for Glencora because he has money and social position; George Vavasour, by contrast, is defeated in politics and exiled for lack of money. John Grey, meanwhile, has interposed himself in Alice's arrangement with George so that her fortune is not at stake. This conduct, chivalrous in one sense, paternalistic in another, results in George's challenging him to a duel. The Victorian world is not that of Regency rakes, however, and George's blustering challenge is physically rebuffed, and he is sent away degraded. Alice finally accepts John Grey in a contrite mood. Although Grey has kindly intentions, Alice's undefined longings for autonomy anticipate those Henrik Ibsen made memorable through Nora Helmer in *A Doll's House* (1879), where Nora sacrifices love in the effort to mould her own destiny.

If the future of his heroines seems to lie within conventional marital arrangements or respectable spinsterhood secured by inherited money, Trollope's questioning title for the novel seems to turn the issue of feminine aspiration somewhat ambivalently to the reader. He has shown women challenging the decorum of prudent emotions and affections based on money, but only the ungenteel Mrs. Greenow succeeds in mastering her destiny through financial manipulation.

The Eustace Diamonds · In *The Eustace Diamonds*, Trollope shows the psychologically damaging effects of survival in an upper-class and aristocratic hierarchy, a society that channels affections and loyalties in terms of property and money, where people struggle for ascendancy, domination, and power, while subscribing to Romantic illusions of unfettered expression and creative self-development. The narrator ironically undercuts the Romantic pretensions as the novel delineates the unrealistic strategies of men and women coping with the moral corruption of social ambition. They seek security, status, prestige, and elegance while evincing pretentiousness, snobbery, envy, and parasitism. Trollope takes an anarchic pleasure in those egotistical characters who subvert institutions by undermining the rules of conduct, stretching them to the point of fatuity.

In the novel, Lizzie Eustace appropriates the diamonds without specific authority from her late husband, Sir Florian, and uses them as weapons against the respectable family lawyer, Mr. Camperdown, and the man she intends as her second husband, the morally honorable Lord Fawn. The diamonds become a symbol of Lizzie's inner rage against the world, a rage arising from self-doubt prompted by the excessive demands of her own idealized views of herself. While denying that ownership of the necklace gives her any pleasure, Lizzie simultaneously insists that she will throw the diamonds away while guarding them zealously. When the box in which she ostentatiously houses them is stolen, Lizzie claims that the necklace has been stolen as well. The lie is psychologically predictable. The diamonds exemplify her attitudes toward herself, toward Lord Fawn, whom she despises for his complete disdain of the diamonds, and toward Frank Greystock, her champion before the world, whom she has lured away from his serious attentions to Lucy Morris. The supposed theft is Lizzie's symbolic punishment for a guilt which will be lessened if the diamonds are believed stolen, but it is also an aggrandizement of her own self-esteem since secretly she knows they are still in her possession. The diamonds, however, are stolen in a second robbery, which ends Lizzie's control of the situation.

Lizzie's desire for social domination gains dimension through the narrator's ironic moral judgment and through the close-ups of the omniscient viewpoint that reveal her own rationalizations and fears. Seeking support, Lizzie confesses to Lord George, hoping that he will be cynically brutal, but instead she receives his weak acknowledgment of her supposed cunning. When the police discover the truth, Lizzie prefers the illusion of submitting to the police administrator to the reality of confronting her own self-destructive behavior. Lizzie then tries desperately to reestablish control by triumphing over someone: She reproaches Mrs. Carbuncle, her friend; breaks her engagement with Lord Fawn, ignoring his earlier efforts to end the relationship and pretending to be heartlessly jilted; offers herself to Lord George, who also refuses her; and finally bids for the attentions of Frank Greystock through his need for money, yet Frank is simply provoked into promising he will abandon her utterly if she persists.

Yielding to a fantasy logic, Lizzie entertains a marriage proposal from Mr. Emilius, an impudent and sanctimonious popular preacher whom she had once refused. She deliberately accepts him knowing that he is a fraud and admitting that his bogus qualities attract her. Lizzie's limited knowledge of how the world operates is supported by Emilius's brazen effrontery, which will offer her a new chance for social domination.

The secondary characters are drawn with an equal sense of psychological aberration. For example, there is the cynical honesty of Lord George, which conceals a fearful vacillation that abhors responsibility yet is resolute in pushing his companion, Sir Griffin Tewett, into marriage with Lucinda Roanoke. Alternately submissive and aggressive, he turns vindictive in denouncing Lizzie for the damage she has caused his reputation by creating suspicions of his complicity in her concealment of the necklace. He is also forgiving, on the other hand, of Mrs. Barnacle, his former mistress, for her good intentions in encouraging her niece, Lucinda, to marry for money. Lord George appears cognizant of obligations assumed by others though irresolute in taking them upon himself. Further, he shows the unreality of Lizzie's dreams; but his own conduct is the model of a romantic neurosis. Other examples of psychologically crippled characters are Lucinda, who suffers from strong sexual repression and emotional sterility, and Sir Griffin, cool, vindictive, and arrogant, who is repelled by anyone who would love him.

These characters are set up in contrast to the more conventional ones, such as Mrs. Hittaway, who reflect the pathological tendencies that a materialistic society encourages. The baffled efforts of Lizzie, Lord George, Sir Griffin, and Lucinda to deal with destructive self-deception reflect the results of social forces inhibiting real creative growth in understanding. V. S. Pritchett has criticized Trollope for being "a detailed, rather cynical observor of a satisfied world," and said that "we recognize that he [Trollope] has drawn life as people say it is when they are not speaking about themselves." C. P. Snow commented that an exploratory psychological writer such as Trollope "has to live on close terms with the blacker—including the worse—side of his own nature." *The Eustace Diamonds* is the record of Trollope's endurance of a mental nature that was divided. Pritchett has accused Trollope of not capturing or presenting the depth of moral experience. This may reflect a demand for a more complex style, a more intensive depiction of the intricacies of moral struggle, and a more insistent emphasis on values. Snow, however, perceived the simple, direct style as cutting out everything except the truth. Trollope was not temperamental or self-advertising, but as a novelist he covers a wide range of social, institutional, and religious issues and controversies constituting the fabric of Victorian society. He dramatizes the moral and intellectual dilemmas often arising from them and has considerable insight as well as the ability to present the sheer flux of mental life, which anticipates later developments in the work of James Joyce, Virginia Woolf, and Dorothy Richardson.

Roger E. Wiehe

Other major works

SHORT FICTION: *Tales of All Countries*, 1861, 1863; *Lotta Schmidt and Other Stories*, 1867; *An Editor's Tales*, 1870; *Why Frau Frohmann Raised Her Prices and Other Stories*, 1882.

NONFICTION: *The West Indies*, 1859; *North America*, 1862; *Clergymen of the Church of England*, 1865-1866; *Travelling Sketches*, 1865-1866; *The Commentaries of Caesar*, 1870 (translation); *Australia and New Zealand*, 1873; *South Africa*, 1878; *Thackeray*, 1879; *Lord Palmerston*, 1882; *Autobiography*, 1883; *The Letters of Anthony Trollope*, 1951 (Bradford A. Booth, editor).

Bibliography

Felber, Lynette. *Gender and Genre in Novels Without End: The British Roman-fleuve*. Gainesville: University Press of Florida, 1995. Discusses Trollope's Palliser novels, Dorothy Richardson's *Pilgrimage*, and Anthony Powell's *Dance to the Music of Time*. An excellent study.

Hall, N. John. *Trollope: A Biography*. Oxford, England: Clarendon Press, 1991. One of several biographies of Trollope that have appeared since the mid-1980's, Hall's book draws heavily on the great Victorian's own words—not surprising, as Hall also edited the two-volume edition of Trollope's *Letters* (1983)—and pays particular attention to Trollope's travel writing and his final decade.

_____, ed. *The Trollope Critics*. Basingstoke, England: Macmillan, 1981. Of a number of critical anthologies, this is probably the best for introductory purposes. Includes twenty leading Trollope critics and covers a wide range of topics. An excellent bibliography is provided.

Halperin, John. *Trollope and Politics.* New York: Macmillan, 1977. This study focuses on each of the six Palliser novels and includes several more general chapters. Contains a select bibliography and indexes.

Mullen, Richard, and James Munson. *The Penguin Companion to Trollope.* New York: Penguin, 1996. A thorough guide to Trollope's life and works. With an index and Trollope bibliography.

Pollard, Arthur. *Anthony Trollope.* Boston: Routledge & Kegan Paul, 1978. Pollard seeks to put all of Trollope's novels and a variety of miscellaneous works within the context of his life and time. Stresses Trollope's evocation of his age and his guiding moral purpose. Includes an index.

Terry, R. C., ed. *Trollope: Interviews and Recollections.* New York: St. Martin's Press, 1987. This invaluable collection is a useful adjunct to the numerous biographies of Trollope. Terry collects forty-six memories of Trollope by a host of individuals who knew him at various points in his life. These selections are arranged in roughly chronological order, starting with his granddaughter Muriel's reminiscences about Anthony's mother and ending–again with Muriel–with images of Anthony as an old man. Terry also includes critical evaluations of Trollope's work.

Wright, Andrew. *Anthony Trollope: Dream and Art.* Basingstoke, England: Macmillan, 1983. This brief study of fifteen of Trollope's novels sees them as contemporary fictions, transfiguring life in a certain way. Contains a bibliography and an index.

John Wain

Born: Stoke-on-Trent, Staffordshire, England; March 14, 1925
Died: Oxford, England; May 24, 1994

Principal long fiction · *Hurry on Down*, 1953 (pb. in U.S. as *Born in Captivity*); *Living in the Present*, 1955; *The Contenders*, 1958; *A Travelling Woman*, 1959; *Strike the Father Dead*, 1962; *The Young Visitors*, 1965; *The Smaller Sky*, 1967; *A Winter in the Hills*, 1970; *The Pardoner's Tale*, 1978; *Young Shoulders*, 1982 (pb. in U.S. as *The Free Zone Starts Here*); *Where the Rivers Meet*, 1988; *Comedies*, 1990; *Hungry Generations*, 1994.

Other literary forms · A complete man of letters, John Wain published short stories, poetry, drama, many scholarly essays, and a highly respected biography in addition to his novels. Wain's writing reflects his determination to speak to a wider range of readers than that addressed by many of his modernist predecessors; it reflects his faith in the common reader to recognize and respond to abiding philosophical concerns. These concerns include his sense of the dignity of human beings in the midst of an oftentimes cruel, indifferent, and cynical world. His concern is with a world caught up in time, desire, and disappointment.

Most significant among Wain's writings other than novels are several collections of short stories—including *Nuncle and Other Stories* (1960), *Death of the Hind Legs and Other Stories* (1966), *The Life Guard* (1971), and *King Caliban and Other Stories* (1978)—and volumes of poetry, such as *Mixed Feelings* (1951), *A Word Carved on a Sill* (1956), *Weep Before God: Poems* (1961), *Wildtrack: A Poem* (1965), *Letters to Five Artists* (1969), *The Shape of Feng* (1972), *Feng: A Poem* (1975), and *Open Country* (1987). Wain also published criticism that communicates a sensitive and scholarly appreciation of good books. Readers should pay particular attention to *Preliminary Essays* (1957), *Essays on Literature and Ideas* (1963), *A House for the Truth: Critical Essays* (1972), *Professing Poetry* (1977), and his autobiography, *Sprightly Running: Part of an Autobiography* (1962). Most readers believe that *Samuel Johnson* (1974) is the best and most lasting of all Wain's nonfiction. In this monumental biography, many of the commitments reflected in Wain's other writings come through clearly and forcefully.

Achievements · John Wain is noted for his observance of and compassion for human sorrow. *Young Shoulders*, an examination of the ramifications of a fatal accident on the people left behind, won the 1982 Whitbread Best Novel Award.

Biography · Although his world was that of the twentieth century, John Wain was very much an eighteenth century man. He delighted in pointing out that he and eighteenth century writer Samuel Johnson were born in the same district ("The Potteries") and in much the same social milieu; that he attended the same university as Johnson (Oxford, where he served from 1973 to 1978 as Professor of Poetry); and that he knew, like Johnson, the Grub Street experiences and "the unremitting struggle to write enduring books against the background of an unstable existence." What chiefly interests the critic in surveying Wain's formative years are the reasons for his increasingly sober outlook. Wain's autobiography, *Sprightly Running*, remains the best account of his formative years as well as offering engaging statements of many of his opinions. In it, the reader finds some of the profound and lasting effects on Wain's writing of his childhood, his adolescence, and his years at Oxford.

John Barrington Wain was born on March 14, 1925, in Stoke-on-Trent, Staffordshire, an industrial city given over to pottery and coal mining. Here, as in other English cities, a move upward in social status is signaled by a move up in geographical terms. Therefore, the Wain family's move three years later to Penkhull–a manufacturing complex of kilns and factories and, incidentally, the setting for Wain's third novel, *The Contenders*–marked a step up into the middle-class district.

From infancy, Wain had a genuine fondness for the countryside. He immersed himself in the sights and sounds and colors of rural nature, all of which made an impression on him that was distinctive as well as deep. This impression developed into an "unargued reverence for all created life, almost a pantheism." On holidays, he and his family traveled to the coast and hills of North Wales, an association which carried over into his adult years, when, at thirty-four, he married a Welsh woman. His feeling for Wales–for the independent life of the people, the landscape and mountains, the sea, the special light of the sun–is recorded in *A Winter in the Hills*. Here and elsewhere is the idea that nature is the embodiment of order, permanence, and life. Indeed, the tension between the nightmare of repression in society and the dream of liberation in the natural world is an important unifying theme throughout Wain's work.

The experience of living in an industrial town also left an indelible imprint upon Wain's mind and art. His exposure to the lives of the working class and to the advance of industrialism gave him a profound knowledge of working people and their problems, which he depicts with sympathy and humanity in his fiction. Moreover, Wain's experiences at Froebel's Preparatory School and at Newcastle-under-Lyme High School impressed on him the idea that life was competitive and "a perpetual effort to survive." He found himself surrounded and outnumbered by people who resented him for being different from themselves. His contact with older children, schoolboy bullies, and authoritative schoolmasters taught Wain that the world is a dangerous place. These "lessons of life" were carried into his work. The reader finds in Wain's fiction a sense of the difficulty of survival in an intrusive and demanding world. The worst of characters is always the bully, and the worst of societies is always totalitarian. Beginning with *Hurry on Down*, each of Wain's published novels and stories is concerned in some way with the power and control that some people seek to exercise over others:

To cope with these injustices as well as with his own fears and inadequacies during his early years, Wain turned to humor, debate, and music. For Wain, the humorist is above all a moralist, in whose hands the ultimate weapon of laughter might conceivably become the means of liberating humankind from its enslavement to false ideals. Thus, his mimicry of both authorities and students was used as the quickest way to illustrate that something was horrible or boring or absurd. In both *Hurry on Down* and *The Contenders*, the heroes use mockery and ridicule to cope with their unjust world.

Wain's interest in jazz also influenced his personal and literary development. He spoke and wrote often of his lifelong enthusiasm for the trumpet playing of Bill Coleman, and he admitted that Percy Brett, the black jazz musician in *Strike the Father Dead*, was created with Coleman in mind. Accompanying this interest was a growing interest in serious writing and reading. Unlike many youths, Wain did not have to endure the agonizing doubt and indecision of trying to decide what he wanted to do in life. By the age of nine, he knew: he wanted to be an author. He began as a critically conscious writer who delighted in "pastiche and parody for their own sake," though he had problems maintaining a steady plotline. Wain matched his writing with voracious reading. His early interest in the novels of Charles Dickens, Tobias Smollett, Daniel Defoe, and others in the tradition of the English novel influenced his later literary style. Like these predecessors, Wain approached his characters through the conventional narration of the realist, and his concerns were social and moral.

The second major period in Wain's life occurred between 1943, when he entered St. John's College, Oxford, and 1955, when he resigned his post as lecturer in English at Reading University to become a full-time writer. Two friends made in his Oxford period especially influenced his writing. One was Philip Larkin, whose "rock-like determination" provided an inspiring example for Wain. The other friend was Kingsley Amis, whose work on a first novel inspired Wain to attempt writing a novel in his spare time. Wain wrote his first novel, not particularly because he wished to be a novelist, but to see if he could write one that would get into print. In 1953, Frederick Warburg accepted *Hurry on Down*, and its unexpected success quickly established Wain as one of Britain's promising new writers.

Wain's exhilarating experience with his first book was, however, poor preparation for the sobering slump that followed. Ill health, divorce proceedings, and the drudgery of a scholar's life pushed him into a crisis of depression and discouragement. He tried to climb out of this crisis by leaving the university for a year and retreating to the Swiss Alps. There, he let his imagination loose on his own problems. The result was *Living in the Present*, a depressing book of manifest despair and disgust. Out of this period in his life, Wain developed a profound awareness of love and loneliness, union and estrangement. The essential loneliness of human beings, and their more or less successful attempts to overcome their loneliness by love, became major themes in his later fiction.

Although Wain was never sanguine about the human condition or the times in which he lived, his life was to be more fulfilling than he anticipated at this time. As a result of his year of self-assessment, in 1955 Wain did not return to the junior position he had held at the University of Reading but instead began working full-time at his writing. Little more than a decade later, his reputation had become so well established that he could reenter the academic world as a visiting professor. Eventually Wain was appointed Professor of Poetry at Oxford University, a post he held from 1973 to 1978.

Sprightly Running, published in 1962, was evidence that Wain was much more contented than he had been seven years before. He was now happily married to Eirian James, an intelligent, insightful woman who provided him with companionship and sometimes help with his work (she coedited *The New Wessex Selection of Thomas Hardy's Poetry* in 1978). They had three sons. Their life together ended only with Eirian's death in 1987. The following year, Wain married Patricia Dunn.

Despite ill health and diminished vision, Wain labored on courageously at what proved to be his final project, three novels that together constitute the Oxford Trilogy. On May 24, 1994, Wain died of a stroke at the John Radcliffe Hospital in Oxford.

Analysis · As a novelist, John Wain has been described as a "painfully honest" writer who always, to an unusual degree, wrote autobiography. His own fortunes and his emotional reactions to these fortunes are, of course, transformed in various ways. His purpose is artistic, not confessional, and he shaped his material accordingly. As Wain himself stated, this intention is both pure and simple: to express his own feelings honestly and to tell the truth about the world he knew. At his best–in *Hurry on Down, Strike the Father Dead, A Winter in the Hills,* and *The Pardoner's Tale*–Wain finds a great many ways to convey the message that life is ultimately tragic. Human beings suffer, life is difficult, and the comic mask conceals anguish. Only occasionally is this grim picture relieved by some sort of idealism, some unexpected attitude of unselfishness or tenderness. What is more, in all his writings Wain is a thoughtful, literate man coming to terms with these truths in a sincere and forthright manner.

To understand something of Wain's uniqueness as a novelist, the reader must look back at least to the end of World War II. For about ten years after the war, established writers continued to produce successfully. English novelists such as Aldous Huxley, Graham Greene, Evelyn Waugh, C. P. Snow, and Anthony Powell had made their reputations before the war and continued to be the major literary voices. Most of them had been educated in "public" schools, then at Oxford or Cambridge, and were from upper or upper-middle-class origins. Their novels were likely to center around fashionable London or some country estate. Often they confined their satire to the intellectual life and the cultural as well as social predicaments of the upper-middle class.

A combination of events in postwar England led to the appearance of another group of writers, soon referred to by literary journalists as the "Angry Young Men." Among these writers was John Wain, who, along with Kingsley Amis, John Braine, John Osborne, Angus Wilson, Alan Sillitoe, and others, turned away from technical innovations, complexity, and the sensitive, introspective protagonist to concentrate on concrete problems of current society. Thus, in the tradition of the eighteenth century novel, Wain fulfills most effectively the novelist's basic task of telling a good story. His novels move along at an even pace; he relies upon a simple, tightly constructed, and straightforward plot; clarity; good and bad characters; and a controlled point of view. The reader need only think of James Joyce and Franz Kafka, and the contrast is clear. What most of Wain's novels ask from the reader is not some feat of analysis, but a considered fullness of response, a readiness to acknowledge, even in disagreement, his vision of defeat.

Wain's typical protagonist is essentially an "antihero," a man at the mercy of life. Although sometimes capable of aspiration and thought, he is not strong enough to carve out his destiny in the way he wishes. Frequently, he is something of a dreamer, tossed about by life, and also pushed about, or at least overshadowed, by the threats in his life. Wain's Charles Lumley (*Hurry on Down*) and Edgar Banks (*Living in the Present*) bear the marks of this type. Often there is discernible in his characters a modern malaise, a vague discontent, and a yearning for some person or set of circumstances beyond their reach. Sometimes, this sense of disenchantment with life as it is becomes so great that the individual expresses a desire not to live at all, as Edgar Banks asserts in *Living in the Present* and as Gus Howkins declares in *The Pardoner's Tale*.

Wain is also accomplished in his creation of place and atmosphere. In *Strike the Father Dead*, he fully captures the grayness of a London day, the grayness of lives spent under its pall, the grayness of the people who wander its streets. When Wain describes an afternoon in which Giles Hermitage (*The Pardoner's Tale*) forces himself to work in the subdued light at home, when Arthur Geary (*The Smaller Sky*) walks the platforms at Paddington Station, when Charles Lumley walks in on a literary gathering, or when Roger Furnivall (*A Winter in the Hills*) makes his way home through the Welsh countryside–at such moments the reader encounters Wain's mastery of setting and atmosphere.

The themes communicated through Wain's novels are, like his method, consistent. It is clear that he sees the eighteenth century as a time of dignity, pride, and self-sufficiency—qualities lacking in the twentieth century. Like Samuel Johnson, Wain defends the value of reason, moderation, common sense, moral courage, and intellectual self-respect. Moreover, his fictional themes of the dignity of the human being, the difficulty of survival in the modern world, and the perils of success have established him principally as a moralist concerned with ethical issues. In later works, the value of tradition, the notion of human understanding, and the ability to love and suffer become the chief moral values. In all his novels, he is primarily concerned with the problem of defining the moral worth of the individual. For all these reasons, Wain is recognized as a penetrating observer of the human scene.

One final point should be noted about Wain's capacities as a novelist. Clearly, the spiritual dimension is missing in the world he describes, yet there is frequently the hint or at least the possibility of renewal, which is the closest Wain comes to any sort of recognized affirmation. Charles Lumley, Joe Shaw, Jeremy Coleman, and Roger Furnivall are all characters who seem to be, by the end of their respective stories, on the verge of rebirth of a sort, on the threshold of reintegration and consequent regeneration. In each case, this renewal depends on the ability of the individual to come to terms with himself and his situation; to confront and accept at a stroke past, present, and future; and to accept and tolerate the contradictions inherent in all three. Wain's sensitive response to the tragic aspects of life is hardly novel, but his deep compassion for human suffering and his tenderness for the unfortunate are more needed than ever in an age when violence, brutality, and cynicism are all too prevalent.

Hurry on Down · In his first novel, *Hurry on Down*, Wain comically perceives the difficulties of surviving in a demanding, sometimes fearful world. Detached from political causes and progress of his own life, the hero is a drifter, seeking to compromise with or to escape from such "evils" as class lines, boredom, hypocrisy, and the conventional perils of success. Although the novel carries a serious moral interest, Wain's wit, sharp observations, and inventiveness keep the plot moving. His comedy exaggerates, reforms, and criticizes to advocate the reasonable in social behavior and to promote the value and dignity of the individual.

Hurry on Down has the characteristic features of the picaresque novel: a series of short and often comic adventures loosely strung together; an opportunistic and pragmatic hero who seeks to make a living through his wits; and satirical characterization of stock figures rather than individualized portraits. Unlike the eighteenth century picaro, however, who is often hard-hearted, cruel, and selfish, Wain's central character is a well-intentioned drifter who compromises enough to live comfortably. His standby and salvation is a strong sense of humor that enables him to make light of much distress and disaster. Lumley's character is revealed against the shifting setting of the picaresque world and in his characteristic response to repeated assaults on his fundamental decency and sympathy for others. He remains substantially the same throughout the novel; his many roles—as window cleaner, delivery driver, chauffeur, and the like—place him firmly in the picaresque tradition. Lumley's versatility and adaptability permit Wain to show his character under a variety of circumstances and in a multiplicity of situations.

Lumley's character is established almost immediately with the description of his conflict with the landlady in the first chapter. The reader sees him as the adaptable antihero who tries to control his own fate, as a jack of all trades, a skilled manipulator, an adept deceiver, an artist of disguises. Wain stresses Lumley's ingenuity rather than his mere struggle for survival; at the same time, he develops Lumley's individual personality, emphasizing the man and his adventures. The role that Lumley plays in the very first scene is one in which he will be cast throughout the story—that of a put-upon young man engaged in an attempt to cope with and outwit the workaday world.

The satire is developed through the characterization. Those who commit themselves to class, who judge others and define themselves by the class structure, are satirized throughout the novel. Surrounding the hero is a host of lightly sketched, "flat," stock figures, all of whom play their predictable roles. These characters include the proletarian girl, the American, the landlady, the entrepreneur, the middle-class couple, and the artist. In this first novel, Wain's resources in characterization are limited primarily to caricature. The comedy functions to instruct and entertain. Beneath the horseplay and high spirits, Wain rhetorically manipulates the reader's moral judgment so that he sympathizes with the hero. In the tradition of Tobias Smollett and Charles Dickens, Wain gives life to the grotesque by emphasizing details of his eccentric characters and by indicating his attitude toward them through the selection of specific bodily and facial characteristics.

Wain has also adopted another convention of eighteenth century fiction: the intrusive author. The active role of this authorial impresario accounts for the distance between the reader and the events of the novel; his exaggerations, his jokes, and his philosophizing prevent the reader from taking Lumley's fate too seriously. In later novels, Wain's authorial stance changes as his vision deepens.

Any discussion of comic technique in *Hurry on Down* leads inevitably to the novel's resolution. Ordinarily, readers do not like to encounter "perfect" endings to novels; nevertheless, they are not put off by the unrealistic ending to this novel because they know from the beginning that they are reading a comic novel which depends upon unrealistic exaggeration of various kinds. Elgin W. Mellown was correct when he called the novel "a pastiche: Walter Mitty's desire expressed through the actions of the Three Stooges—wish fulfillment carried out through outrageous actions and uncharacteristic behavior." The reader feels secure in the rightness of the ending as a conclusion to all the comic wrongness that has gone on before.

Strike the Father Dead · In *Strike the Father Dead*, Wain further extended himself with a work more penetrating than anything he had written before. Not only is it, as Walter Allen said, a "deeply pondered novel," but it is also a culmination of the promises inherent in Wain's earlier works. Plot, theme, character, and setting are integrated to tell the story of a son who breaks parental ties, thereby freeing himself to make his own way in life as a jazz pianist. Pointing to the foibles of his fellowman and probing the motives of an indignant parent, Wain's wit and sarcastic humor lighten this uncompromising study of the nonconformist's right to assert his nonconformity.

Two later Wain novels—*A Winter in the Hills* and *The Pardoner's Tale*—continue and elaborate upon many of the central themes of his fiction, but they surpass the earlier novels in richness and complexity. Both novels exhibit, far more than do his earlier writings, an interest in the tragic implications of romantic love; a greater complexity in character development allows Wain to portray convincingly men whose loneliness borders on self-destruction. Each novel is not simply another story of isolation or spiritual desolation, although it is that. Each hero is cast into a wasteland, and the novel in a sense is the story of his attempts to find the river of life again, or possibly for the first time. One of the themes that develops from this period in Wain's career is that personal relationships are the most important and yet most elusive forces in society.

The plot of *Strike the Father Dead* is arranged in an elaborate, seven-part time-scheme. Parts 1 and 6 occur sometime late in 1957 or early in 1958; part 2 takes place in the immediate prewar years; and the other divisions follow chronologically up to the last, which is set in 1958. The scene shifts back and forth between a provincial university town and the darker, black-market-and-jazz side of London, with a side trip to Paris.

Wain narrates the story from the points of view of four characters. The central figure, Jeremy Coleman, revolts against his father and the academic establishment in search of self-expression as a jazz pianist. Alfred Coleman, Jeremy's father and a professor of classics, is an atheist devoted to duty and hard work. Eleanor, Alfred's sister and foster mother to Jeremy, is devoted to Jeremy and finds comfort in innocent religiosity. Percy Brett, a black American jazz musician, offers Jeremy his first real parental leadership. Like Ernest Pontifex, in Samuel Butler's *The Way of All Flesh* (1903), Jeremy escapes from an oppressive existence; he has a passion for music, and once he has the opportunity to develop, his shrinking personality changes.

Strike the Father Dead marks a considerable advance over *Hurry on Down* in the thorough rendering of each character and each scene. By employing a succession of first-person narrators, Wain focuses attention more evenly on each of the figures. The result is that the reader comes away knowing Jeremy even better, because what is learned about him comes not only from his own narration but from other sources as well. Inasmuch as there are three central characters, *Strike the Father Dead* represents a larger range for Wain. Each interior monologue is a revelation; the language is personal, distinctive, and descriptive of character.

In the manner of a *Bildungsroman, Strike the Father Dead* is also a novel which recounts the youth and young manhood of a sensitive protagonist who is attempting to learn the nature of the world, discover its meaning and pattern, and acquire a philosophy of life. Setting plays a vital role in this odyssey. The provincial and London backgrounds and the accurate rendering of the language make the novel come alive. *Strike the Father Dead* moves between two contemporary worlds—a world of rigidity and repression, represented by Alfred, and a world of creativity, international and free, represented by London and Paris. The first world oppresses Jeremy; the second attracts and draws him. He dreams about it and invents fictions about it. Central to this new world is Jeremy's love of jazz. For him, the experience of jazz means beauty, love, life, growth, freedom, ecstasy—the very qualities he finds missing in the routine, disciplined life of Alfred.

Although *Strike the Father Dead* tells the story of a British young man who becomes successful, the success is to a certain extent bittersweet. In his triumphs over his home circumstances, Jeremy loses something as well. There are various names given to it: innocence; boyhood; nature; the secure, predictable life at home. The world beyond the academic life waits for Jeremy, and he, unknowingly, does his best to bring it onstage. With such a life comes a developing sense of injustice, deprivation, and suffering. These concerns become focal points in Wain's subsequent novels, as he turns toward the impulse to define character and dilemma much more objectively and with greater moral responsibility.

A Winter in the Hills · With its setting in Wales, *A Winter in the Hills* marked a departure from Wain's first seven novels, all of which were centered in England. The story expresses, perhaps more comprehensively than any other, Wain's feelings for the provincial world, its cohesion and deep loyalties, and its resistance to innovation from outside. Here the reader finds Wain's sympathy for the underdog, his respect for decency and the dignity of humanity, and his affirmation of life; here, too, is expressed Wain's deep interest in the causes and effects of loneliness and alienation.

The reader's first inclination is to approach the novel as primarily a novel of character, the major interest and emphasis of which is the constantly developing character of Roger Furnivall himself. Using third-person narration, Wain keeps the focus on his main character as he progresses straight through several months that constitute a time of crisis in his life. Through most of the novel, Roger struggles doggedly against a combination of adverse circumstances, always in search of a purpose. Outwardly, he forces himself on Gareth, for example, as a way of improving his idiomatic Welsh. Inwardly, he "needed involvement, needed a human reason for being in the district." The guilt he carries because of his brother's suffering and death helps to propel him into a more active engagement with contemporary life. His conflict with Dic Sharp draws him out of his own private grief because he is helping not only Gareth, but also an entire community of people.

The reader learns about Roger in another way, too: Wain uses setting to reveal and reflect the protagonist's emotions and mental states. Roger's walk in the rain down the country roads, as he attempts to resolve his bitterness and disappointment at Beverley's rejection of him, is vividly depicted. It carries conviction because Roger's anxiety has been built up gradually and artistically. The pastoral world is a perpetually shifting landscape, and Wain depicts its shifts and contrasts with an acute eye for telling detail. Especially striking are the sketches of evening coming on in the Welsh hills, with their rocks and timber and vast expanses of green. Such descriptions help to convey Roger's yearning for happiness in a world which seems bent on denying it to him.

One major theme of the book is the invasion of the peaceful, conservative world of Wales by outsiders who have no roots in the region, and therefore no real concern for its inhabitants. These invaders are characterized by a sophisticated corruption that contrasts sharply with the unspoiled simplicity and honesty of the best of the natives. A related theme is the decline of the town: its economic insecurity, its struggle to resist the progressive and materialistic "cruelty, greed, tyranny, the power of the rich to drive the poor to the wall." Through Roger's point of view, Wain expresses his opposition to the pressures–economic, political, cultural–that seek to destroy the Welsh and, by implication, all minority enclaves. Thus, *A Winter in the Hills* is more than a novel about the growth of one human being from loneliness and alienation to mature and selfless love; it is also a powerful study of the quality of life in the contemporary world, threatened by the encroachments of bureaucracy, greed, and materialism.

The Pardoner's Tale · The somewhat optimistic resolution of *A Winter in the Hills* stands in stark contrast to that of *The Pardoner's Tale*, Wain's most somber novel. In no other work by Wain are the characters so lonely, so frustrated, or so obsessed with thoughts of mutability, lost opportunities, and death. The novel is really two stories: a first-person tale about Gus Howkins, an aging Londoner contemplating divorce, and a third-person narrative (the framing narrative) about Giles Hermitage, an established novelist and bachelor living in an unnamed cathedral town, who gets involved with the Chichester-Redferns, a woman and daughter, while he is working out the story of Howkins. It is the interplay between these two stories which constitutes the plot of *The Pardoner's Tale.*

Giles Hermitage is obviously the figure with whom Wain is the most intimately involved. He is a highly idiosyncratic figure with very recognizable weaknesses; he is easily discouraged (there is an early thought of suicide), and he resorts to excessive drinking. The root cause of his death wish and of his drinking is loneliness. Like Wain's earlier heroes, he is very much a modern man: vague in his religious and humanitarian aspirations, rootless and alienated from the social life of the community in which he lives, and initially weak and confused in his relationships with women. Plagued by anxiety, depression, vague discontent, and a sense of inner emptiness, he seeks peace of mind under conditions that increasingly militate against it. Add to his problems the ever-growing urge toward self-destruction, and the reader begins to recognize in this novel a truly contemporary pulsebeat. Hermitage is a stranger in a world that does not make sense.

Unlike Wain's earlier heroes, however, Hermitage tries to make sense of the world through the medium of his writing by stepping back into what he calls "the protecting circle of art." His approach to writing is autobiographical, personal, even subjective. The hero of his novel is a mask for himself. The author is creating a character who is in his own predicament, and the agonies he endures enable him to express his deepest feelings about life. In Hermitage, Wain presents a character who tries to create, as artists do, a new existence out of the chaos of his life.

The remaining major characters in *The Pardoner's Tale* bear family resemblances to those in other of Wain's novels. If the part of the lonely, alienated hero so effectively carried in *A Winter in the Hills* by Roger Furnivall is here assigned to Giles Hermitage, then the role of the manipulator is assigned in this novel to Mrs. Chichester-Redfern. Although a good deal less ruthless than Dic Sharp, she nevertheless seeks to exploit the hero.

The process by which Mrs. Chichester-Redfern is gradually revealed through the eyes of Hermitage is subtle and delicate. At first merely a stranger, she comes to seem in time a calculating and educated woman, the innocent victim of a man who deserted her, a seventy-year-old woman grasping for answers to some vital questions about her own life. She summons Hermitage under the pretense of wanting to gain insight into her life. From these conversations, the reader learns that she, like Hermitage, is confronted and dislocated by external reality in the form of a personal loss. Also like the hero, she desires to come to some understanding of her unhappy life through the medium of art. Her true motive is revenge, however, and she wants Hermitage to write a novel with her husband in it as a character who suffers pain. Then, she says, "there will be that much justice done in the world."

In addition to the alienated, lonely hero and the manipulator, most of Wain's fiction portrays a comforter. In his latest novel, the comforter is embodied in Diana Chichester-Redfern, but the happiness Diana offers is only temporary. In this novel, love is reduced to a meaningless mechanical act: Diana, also, is living in a wasteland.

The basic tension of this novel is a simple and classic one—the life-force confronting the death-force. As surely as Mrs. Chichester-Redfern is the death-force in the novel, Diana is the active and life-giving presence. She is depicted as an abrasive, liberated, sensual, innately selfish modern young woman who stands in positive contrast to the deathlike grayness of her mother. She is earthy and fulfilled, accepting and content with her music (playing the guitar satisfies her need for proficiency), her faith (which takes care of "all the moral issues") and her sexuality (which she enjoys because she has no choice). Diana goes from one affair to another, not in search of love (she claims she "can't love anybody") but out of a need for repetition. Diana defines love and meaning as the fulfillment of a man or woman's emotional requirements. To her, love does not mean self-sacrifice; rather, love is synonymous with need.

The world of *The Pardoner's Tale* is thus the archetypal world of all Wain's fiction: random, fragmented, lonely, contradictory. It is a world in which wasted lives, debased sexual encounters, and destroyed moral intelligences yield a tragic vision of futility and sterility, isolation from the community, estrangement from those who used to be closest to one, and loneliness in the midst of the universe itself.

Young Shoulders · Amid all this, Wain's unflinching honesty and his capacity for compassion make his definition of the human condition bearable. Both characteristics are evident in *Young Shoulders*. Again, Wain focuses on senseless waste. A plane of English schoolchildren crashes in Lisbon, Portugal, killing everyone aboard. Seventeen-year-old Paul Waterford, whose twelve-year-old sister Clare was one of the victims, describes his journey to Lisbon with his parents, their encounters with other grief-stricken relatives, the memorial service they attend, and their return to England. Because he is still untainted by convention, Paul feels free to see the other characters as they are, often even to find them funny; however, he has to admit that he can be wrong about people. The seemingly calm Mrs. Richardson, a teacher's widow, collapses during the memorial service; the restrained Janet Finlayson howls in the hotel lobby that God is punishing them all; Mr. Smithson, whom Paul assessed as a man on his way up, goes crazy on the tarmac; and everyone depends upon Paul's parents: the mother Paul saw only as a drunk and the father Paul dismissed as hopelessly withdrawn.

Because Wain has the eighteenth century writer's hunger for universals, we may assume that the real subject of *Young Shoulders* is not how individuals behave in the face of tragedy but what the young protagonist and, by extension, the reader has learned by the end of the novel. Paul comes to see that human beings avoid acknowledging their emotions in so many ways that an outsider's judgment is likely to be inaccurate. He also recognizes the extent to which he deludes himself, whether by imagining a utopian society he will govern or by addressing "reports" to Clare, thus denying that she is dead. By losing his innocence, Paul gains in compassion.

The Oxford Trilogy · With its single plotline, its compressed time scheme, and its limited cast, *Young Shoulders* is much like a neoclassical play. By contrast, the three novels composing the Oxford Trilogy have an epic quality, as indeed they must if they are to "describe and dramatize the Oxford that has been sinking out of sight, and fading from memory, for over thirty years," as Wain states in his preface to the final volume. The series does indeed cover three decades. *Where the Rivers Meet* introduces the protagonist Peter Leonard and takes him through his undergraduate years at Oxford; *Comedies* begins in 1933, with Leonard's appointment as a fellow, and ends after World War II; and *Hungry Generations* covers Leonard's life from 1947 to 1956. There is a multitude of characters, ranging from Oxford intellectuals to the patrons of the pub that Leonard's parents run, each with definite ideas about local politics, world news, and the progress of society. Wain's honesty is reflected in the way he permits all the characters to speak their minds; his compassion is revealed in his attempt to understand even the least appealing of them. These qualities, along with his creative genius and his consummate artistry, should ensure for John Wain a permanent place in twentieth century literary history.

Dale Salwak,
updated by Rosemary M. Canfield Reisman

Other major works

SHORT FICTION: *Nuncle and Other Stories,* 1960; *Death of the Hind Legs and Other Stories,* 1966; *The Life Guard,* 1971; *King Caliban and Other Stories,* 1978.

PLAYS: *Harry in the Night: An Optimistic Comedy,* pr. 1975; *Johnson Is Leaving: A Monodrama,* pb. 1994.

TELEPLAY: *Young Shoulders,* 1984 (with Robert Smith).

RADIO PLAYS: *You Wouldn't Remember,* 1978; *A Winter in the Hills,* 1981; *Frank,* 1982.

POETRY: *Mixed Feelings,* 1951; *A Word Carved on a Sill,* 1956; *A Song About Major Eatherly,* 1961; *Weep Before God: Poems,* 1961; *Wildtrack: A Poem,* 1965; *Letters to Five Artists,* 1969; *The Shape of Feng,* 1972; *Feng: A Poem,* 1975; *Poems for the Zodiac,* 1980; *Thinking About Mr. Person,* 1980; *Poems, 1949-1979,* 1981; *Twofold,* 1981; *Open Country,* 1987.

NONFICTION: *Preliminary Essays,* 1957; *Gerard Manley Hopkins: An Idiom of Desperation,* 1959; *Sprightly Running: Part of an Autobiography,* 1962; *Essays on Literature and Ideas,* 1963; *The Living World of Shakespeare: A Playgoer's Guide,* 1964; *Arnold Bennett,* 1967; *A House for the Truth: Critical Essays,* 1972; *Samuel Johnson,* 1974; *Professing Poetry,* 1977; *Samuel Johnson 1709-1784,* 1984 (with Kai Kin Yung); *Dear Shadows: Portraits from Memory,* 1986.

CHILDREN'S LITERATURE: *Lizzie's Floating Shop,* 1981.

EDITED TEXTS: *Contemporary Reviews of Romantic Poetry,* 1953; *Interpretations: Essays on Twelve English Poems,* 1955; *International Literary Annual,* 1959, 1960; *Fanny Burney's Diary,* 1960; *Anthology of Modern Poetry,* 1963; *Selected Shorter Poems of Thomas Hardy,* 1966; *Selected Shorter Stories of Thomas Hardy,* 1966; *Thomas Hardy's "The Dynasts,"* 1966; *Shakespeare: Macbeth, a Casebook,* 1968; *Shakespeare: Othello, a Casebook,* 1971; *Johnson as Critic,* 1973; *The New Wessex Selection of Thomas Hardy's Poetry,* 1978 (with Eirian James).

Bibliography

Gerard, David. *John Wain: A Bibliography.* London: Mansell, 1987. Contains a critical introduction to Wain's writings and a comprehensive list of his books and contributions to books and periodicals. Also includes other critical and biographical references and reviews of works by Wain.

Gindin, James. "The Moral Center of John Wain's Fiction." In *Postwar British Fiction: New Accents and Attitudes.* Berkeley: University of California Press, 1962. Gindin contends that Wain creates characters who always exhibit dignity and moral commitment. Considers Wain's first four novels and his stories in the volume *Nuncle and Other Stories.* In an introductory essay, Gindin evaluates Wain in the context of other authors from the 1950's.

Hague, Angela. "Picaresque Structure and the Angry Young Novel." *Twentieth Century Literature* 32 (Summer, 1986): 209-220. Hague views Wain's *Hurry On Down* as erroneously grouped with the "Angry Young Men" novels of the 1950's. She compares Wain's heroes with those in the novels of Kingsley Amis and Iris Murdoch; all are essentially loners who, like the picaresques of the eighteenth century, respond to tensions between traditional values and societal change.

Heptonstall, Geoffrey. "Remembering John Wain." *Contemporary Review* 266 (March, 1995): 144-147. An appreciation of the author and a thoughtful assessment of his place in the literary tradition. Though Wain has fallen out of favor with critics, it is argued that his works will continue to appeal to the public and that his worth will be recognized by future generations. An excellent overview.

Rabinovitz, Rubin. "The Novelists of the 1950's: A General Survey." In *The Reaction Against Experiment in the English Novel, 1950-1960.* New York: Columbia University Press, 1967. Rabinovitz places Wain in the context of novelists who embraced traditional values rather than those who experimented with unconventional ideas or forms, aligning Wain's novels with those of Arnold Bennett and eighteenth century picaresque novelists.

Salwak, Dale. *Interviews with Britain's Angry Young Men.* San Bernardino, Calif.: Borgo Press, 1984. This useful resource characterizes Wain as an "eighteenth century man." Engages Wain in a discussion of the role of criticism in the author's life, his goals as a writer, his response to the phenomenon of the Angry Young Men, and the sources and themes in several of his novels.

_____. *John Wain.* Boston: Twayne, 1981. After a chapter introducing Wain's life and art, the text contains four chapters on his novels, focusing on his early works, *Hurry on Down* and *Strike the Father Dead,* and two of his late works, *A Winter in the Hills* and *The Pardoner's Tale.* "Other Fiction, Other Prose" covers Wain's stories, poems, and biographical works. A selected bibliography completes the text.

Taylor, D. J. *After the War: The Novel and English Society Since 1945.* London: Chatto & Windus, 1993. An attempt to define the nature of postwar writing. Wain is grouped with William Cooper and Kingsley Amis as being antimodernist, or opposed to the psychological emphasis and stylistic complexity of James Joyce and Virginia Woolf, and antiromantic.

Evelyn Waugh

Born: London, England; October 28, 1903
Died: Combe Florey, England; April 10, 1966

Principal long fiction · *Decline and Fall*, 1928; *Vile Bodies*, 1930; *Black Mischief*, 1932; *A Handful of Dust*, 1934; *Scoop*, 1938; *Put Out More Flags*, 1942; *Brideshead Revisited*, 1945, 1959; *Scott-King's Modern Europe*, 1947; *The Loved One*, 1948; *Helena*, 1950; *Men at Arms*, 1952; *Love Among the Ruins: A Romance of the Near Future*, 1953; *Officers and Gentlemen*, 1955; *The Ordeal of Gilbert Pinfold*, 1957; *The End of the Battle*, 1961 (also known as *Unconditional Surrender*); *Basil Seal Rides Again: Or, The Rake's Regress*, 1963; *Sword of Honour*, 1965 (includes *Men at Arms*, *Officers and Gentlemen*, and *The End of the Battle*).

Other literary forms · Evelyn Waugh wrote seven travel books, three biographies, an autobiography, and numerous articles and reviews. The only completed section of Waugh's planned three-volume autobiography, *A Little Learning* (1964), discusses his life at Oxford and his employment as a schoolmaster in Wales—subjects fictionalized in *Brideshead Revisited* and *Decline and Fall*. The autobiographical background for virtually all of Waugh's novels is evident in his travel books, his diaries, and his letters. His articles and reviews for English and American periodicals include a wide range of topics—politics, religion, and art—and contribute to his reputation as a literary snob, an attitude Waugh himself affected, especially in the 1940's and 1950's.

Achievements · Waugh was esteemed primarily as a satirist, especially for his satires on the absurdly chaotic world of the 1920's and 1930's. His ability to make darkly humorous the activities of the British upper class, his comic distance, and his vivid, at times brutal, satire made his early novels very popular among British and American literary circles. His shift to a more sentimental theme in *Brideshead Revisited* gave Waugh his first real taste of broad popular approval—especially in the United States—to which he reacted with sometimes real, sometime exaggerated, snobbishness. Waugh's conservative bias after the war, his preoccupation with religious themes, and his expressed distaste for the "age of the common man" suggested to a number of critics that he had lost his satiric touch. Although his postwar novels lack the anarchic spirit of his earliest works, he is still regarded, even by those who reject his political attitudes, as a first-rate craftsman of the comic novel.

Biography · Evelyn Arthur St. John Waugh was born in Hampstead, a suburb of London, in 1903 to Arthur and Catherine Waugh. He attended Lancing College from 1917 to 1924 and Hertford College, Oxford, from 1921 to 1924, from which he left without taking a degree. Although Waugh turned to writing novels only after aborted careers as a draftsman, a schoolmaster, and a journalist, his family background was literary; his father directed Chapman and Hall publishers until 1929, and his older brother Alec published his first novel, *The Loom of Youth*, in 1917.

Waugh's years at Oxford and his restless search for employment during the 1920's brought him experiences which were later fictionalized in several of his novels. After leaving Oxford in 1924, he enrolled in the Heatherley School of Fine Art, where he aspired to be a draftsman; later in that year, he was apprenticed to a printer for a brief period. His employment as a schoolmaster in Wales in 1925 and in Buckinghamshire in 1926 formed the background for his first novel, *Decline and Fall.* His struggle to establish himself as a writer and his participation in the endless parties of London's aristocratic youth during the last years of the 1920's are fictionalized in his second novel, *Vile Bodies.*

In 1927, Waugh was engaged to Evelyn Gardner and, despite the objections of her family, married her in 1928 when his financial prospects seemed more secure after the publication of his life of Dante Gabriel Rossetti and his first novel. In 1929, while Waugh was working

Library of Congress

in seclusion on *Vile Bodies,* his wife announced that she was having an affair; the couple, temperamentally unsuited to each other, were divorced that year.

The next seven years of Waugh's life were a period of activity and travel. Two trips to Africa in 1930 and 1931 resulted in a travel book and provided Waugh with the background of *Black Mischief.* A journey through Brazil and British Guiana in 1932 resulted in another travel book and his fourth novel, *A Handful of Dust.* In addition, Waugh traveled to the Arctic and once more to Africa; he was a correspondent for the London *Times,* reviewed books for *The Spectator,* and wrote a biography of Edmund Campion, a British-Catholic martyr. During this unsettled period, Waugh converted to Roman Catholicism in 1930, an event which provided much of the stability of his later life. In 1933, he met Laura Herbert, a Catholic, whom he married in 1937, after securing an annulment of his previous marriage from the Catholic Church.

Waugh's experiences during World War II are fictionalized in *Put Out More Flags* and the *Sword of Honour* trilogy. After several months unsuccessfully seeking military employment, Waugh joined the Royal Marines in 1939 and was part of an ineffectual assault on Dakar in 1940. Later in 1940, Waugh joined a commando unit with which he served in the Middle East, taking part in the battle of Crete in 1942. In 1943, after an injury in parachute training, Waugh was forced to resign from the commandos, and, in 1944, he was granted military leave to write *Brideshead Revisited.* In the last year of the war, he served as a liaison officer with the British Military Mission in Yugoslavia, where he struggled against the persecution of Roman Catholics by the partisan government.

Waugh's life from 1945 to 1954 was relatively stable. The success of *Brideshead Revisited,* a Book-of-the-Month Club selection in America, brought him moderate financial security and several offers from filmmakers. Although none of these film offers materialized, they resulted in the trip to Hollywood in 1947 that inspired *The Loved One*, and in several commissioned articles for *Life*. During this nine-year period, Waugh published four short novels and the first volume of the World War II trilogy. In the first three months of 1954, on a voyage to Ceylon, Waugh suffered the mental breakdown that he later fictionalized in *The Ordeal of Gilbert Pinfold*.

Waugh led a relatively reclusive life during the last ten years, avoiding the public contact that had made him notorious earlier. In this period, he finished the war trilogy and published a biography of Ronald Knox, another travel book on Africa, the first volume of his autobiography, a revision of *Brideshead Revisited*, and the recension of the war trilogy into a single volume; he also began several other projects which were never completed. Waugh died on Easter Day in 1966.

Analysis · Evelyn Waugh's novels are distinguished by the narrative detachment with which they survey the madness and chaos of the modern age. His characters partici- pate in a hopeless, often brutal, struggle for stability which hardens them to the absurdities of civilization and leads them, ultimately, to an unheroic retreat from the battle of life. Ironic detachment, thus, is Waugh's principal comic technique and his principal theme as well.

Because each of Waugh's novels reflects actual experiences, the nature of this detachment changes through the course of his career. In his early works, which satirize the havoc and instability of the 1920's and 1930's, he achieves comic detachment by splicing together the savage and the settled, the careless and the care-ridden, the comic and the tragic. Victims and victimizers alike are caught in the whirlwind of madness. Waugh's satiric method changes in his postwar novels: Comically ineffectual characters still wage battle against the absurdities of life, but one is more aware of their struggle to maintain or recapture spiritual and moral values amid the absurdity. Waugh maintains comic distance in these novels by recommending a quiet sort of spiritual heroism as the only source of people's happiness in the uncertain postwar world.

Decline and Fall · Waugh's first novel, *Decline and Fall*, traces the misadventures of Paul Pennyfeather, a temperate, unassuming student of theology at Scone College, Oxford. He is "sent down" for indecent behavior when drunken members of the university's most riotous (and, ironically, most aristocratic) club assault him, forcing him to run the length of the quadrangle without his trousers. Like Voltaire's Candide, Pennyfeather is an innocent victim temperamentally ill suited for the world into which he is thrust. Indeed, *Decline and Fall* owes much to *Candide* (1759): its Menippean satire, its cyclical "resurrection" of secondary characters, and the hero's ultimate resignation from life.

The action itself provides a thin framework for Waugh's satire on modern life. Pennyfeather finds employment, as Waugh himself did, as a schoolmaster in Wales— the only occupation, Pennyfeather is told, for a young man dismissed from the university for indecent behavior. At Llanabba Castle, he meets three characters with whose stories his own is interlaced: Grimes, a pederast and bigamist who pulls himself out of the continual "soup" he gets into by feigning suicide; Prendergast, a doubting cleric who becomes a "modern churchman" and is eventually murdered by a religious fanatic; and Philbrick, the school butler, a professed imposter, jewel thief, and arsonist who manages to secure a continual life of luxury by his preposterous stories about his criminal life. At Llanabba, Pennyfeather also meets Margot Beste-Chetwynde, a rich socialite to whom he becomes engaged; he is arrested the afternoon of their wedding for unknowingly transporting girls to France for her international prostitution ring. His innocent association with Margot thus leads to his conviction for another act of "indecent behavior," this time leading to a prison sentence in Blackstone Gaol—a "modern" penal institution.

What strikes one about the novel is not the injustices served Pennyfeather, but the very madness of the world with which his innocence contrasts. Characters with criminal designs—Margot, Philbrick, and Grimes—are unaffected by changes in fortune; those in charge of social institutions—Dr. Fagan of Llanabba Castle and Sir Lucas-Dockery of the experimental prison—are eccentrically out of touch with reality. Their absurdity, when contrasted with Pennyfeather's naïve struggle, defines Waugh's theme: The only sanity is to become cautiously indifferent to the chaos of modernism. At the end of the novel, when Pennyfeather returns to Oxford under a new identity and continues his study of the Early Church, he assumes the role of a spectator, not a participant, in the madness of life.

Although *Decline and Fall*'s narrative structure is more derivative and its characters less fully rounded than those of Waugh's later novels, it displays techniques typical of his fiction at its best. The callous descriptions of the tragic—little Lord Tangent's death from Grimes's racing pistol or Prendergast's decapitation at Blackstone Gaol—and their fragmented interlacement into the plot are hallmarks of Waugh's comic detachment. Tangent's slow death from gangrene is presented through a series of casual offstage reports; the report of Prendergast's murder is incongruously worked into verses of a hymn sung in the prison chapel, "O God, our Help in Ages Past." The tragic and the savage are always sifted through an ironic filter in Waugh's novels, creating a brutal sort of pathos.

A Handful of Dust · Waugh's fourth novel, *A Handful of Dust*, was his first to present a dynamically sympathetic protagonist. Pennyfeather, from *Decline and Fall*, and Adam Symes, from *Vile Bodies*, attract one's interest largely because they provide a detached perspective from which one can observe the chaos of modern civilization. Basil Seal in *Black Mischief*, although a participating rogue, is amiable largely because of his comic disregard for the mischief he makes. Tony Last of *A Handful of Dust*, however, is a fully sympathetic character as well as a pathetic victim of the modern wasteland to which the title alludes. Unlike Paul Pennyfeather, Tony is not simply an observer of social chaos: His internal turmoil is set against the absurdity of external events, and in that respect, his quest for lost values anticipates that of Charles Ryder in *Brideshead Revisited* and of Guy Crouchback in *Sword of Honour*.

Waugh's theme is the decadence of tradition, emblematized, as it is in many of Waugh's novels, by the crumbling estates of the aristocracy. Tony's futile effort to maintain his Victorian Gothic estate, Hetton Abbey, thus symbolizes his struggle throughout the plot. He is wedded to the outmoded tradition of Victorian country gentlemen, while his wife, Brenda, embraces the social life of London. She eventually cuckolds Tony by having an affair with the parasitic John Beaver, whose mother, an interior decorator, sees in her son's affair an opportunity to "modernize" Hetton with chromium plating and sheepskin carpeting.

The pathos one feels for Tony is ultimately controlled by the absurd contexts into which Waugh sets the pathetic scenes. When his son, John Andrew, dies in a riding accident, Tony is left emotionally desolate, yet the cause of the accident is ironic; John

Andrew's horse is startled by a backfiring motorcycle, a modern "horse." Later, one is made brutally aware of the irony of Tony's grief when one learns of Brenda's initial reaction to the news of her son's death: She assumes it was John Beaver, her lover, not John Andrew, her son, who died. In the same way, Tony's later divorce from Brenda empties him of values he traditionally respected. He consents to the legal convention that he should give evidence of his infidelity, even if his wife has been the unfaithful partner. His evidence incongruously turns into an uncomfortable weekend with a prostitute and her daughter at Brighton, and the absurdity of this forced and inconsummate infidelity further defines Tony's loneliness. Ironically, it provides him with a means to deny an exorbitant divorce settlement that would force him to sell Hetton Abbey.

In the end, Tony searches for his Victorian Gothic city in the jungles of South America and suffers a delirium in which his civilized life at Hetton Abbey is distorted; these scenes are made comically pathetic by interlaced scenes of Brenda in London trying to regain the civilized life she lost in her estrangement from Tony. Ultimately, she does not find in London the city she sought, nor does Tony in South America. Tony does find, instead, an aberration of his vision; he is held captive by an illiterate who forces him to read aloud from Charles Dickens's novels in perpetuity.

Perhaps Waugh's emotional reaction to his own divorce from Evelyn Gardner prior to the publication of the novel accounts for the increase of pathos in *A Handful of Dust.* Perhaps Waugh realized that thinness of characterization in his earlier novels could lead only to stylistic repetition without stylistic development. Whatever the reason, this novel depicts characters struggling for moral equilibrium in a way that no previous Waugh novel had done.

Brideshead Revisited · *Brideshead Revisited* is different from Waugh's earlier novels in two important ways. First, it is the only novel Waugh finished which employs the first-person point of view. (He had attempted the first person in *Work Suspended* in 1942, but either the story itself faltered, or Waugh could not achieve a sufficient narrative detachment to complete it.) Second, *Brideshead Revisited* was the first novel in which Waugh explicitly addressed a Roman Catholic theme: the mysterious workings of divine grace in a small aristocratic Catholic family. As a result, it is Waugh's most sentimental and least funny novel. Although it departed radically from his earlier satires, it was Waugh's most popular and financially successful work.

The narrative frame creates much of what is sentimental in the novel but also provides a built-in detachment. Charles Ryder's love for Sebastian Flyte during his years at Oxford in the 1920's and for Julia Mottram, Sebastian's sister, a decade later, live vividly in Ryder's memories when he revisits the Brideshead estate during a wartime bivouac. His memories tell the story of Sebastian's and Julia's search for happiness, but because they are remembered by an emotionally desolate Ryder, the novel is a study of his spiritual change as well.

Before he meets Sebastian, Ryder is a serious-minded Oxford undergraduate, not unlike Paul Pennyfeather at the end of *Decline and Fall.* Like Pennyfeather, he is drawn into a world for which he is unprepared, yet unlike Waugh's earlier protagonist, Ryder is enthralled by a make-believe world of beauty and art. The Arcadian summer Ryder spends with Sebastian at Brideshead and in Venice are the most sumptuously written passages in any of Waugh's novels, reflecting—as Waugh admitted in his 1959 revision of the novel—the dearth of sensual pleasures available at the time of its composition. The change in style also reflects a change in theme. Sebastian's eccentricities about his stuffed bear, his coterie of homosexual "aesthetes," and his refusal to take anything seriously would have been the object of satire in Waugh's earlier novels. In *Brideshead Revisited*, however, the absurdities are sifted through the perspective of a narrator aware of his own desperate search for love. When Sebastian's make-believe turns to alcoholism, the narrator himself becomes cynically indifferent.

Ryder's love for Julia ten years after he has left Brideshead is an attempt to rediscover the happiness he lost with Sebastian. One is more aware, in this second half of the narration, of Ryder's cynicism and of the discontentment which that cynicism hides. When he and Julia fall in love on a transatlantic voyage back to England, they are both escaping marriages to spouses whose worldly ambitions offer no nourishment for the spiritual emptiness each feels. Julia's return to the Church after the deathbed repentance of her father causes Ryder to realize that he has fathomed as little about Julia's faith as he had about Sebastian's. The narration itself thus ends on a note of unhappiness which recalls the separation of Ryder and Sebastian. In the epilogue following Ryder's memories, however, Waugh makes it clear that the narrator himself has converted to Catholicism in the intervening years. Ryder sees in the sanctuary light of the chapel at Brideshead the permanence he sought with Sebastian and Julia and finds contentment, if not hope for the future.

It is easy to overstress the religious implications of the novel. Indeed, many critics find Julia's hysteria about sin, Lord Marchmain's return to the Church, and Ryder's conversion strained. Some, such as Edmund Wilson, see the novel as an adulation of the British upper classes. *Brideshead Revisited*, however, is less a Roman Catholic novel than it is a lament for the past and a study in spiritual and artistic awakening. It was a turning point in Waugh's fiction: His novels after *Brideshead Revisited* dealt less with the absurdity of life and more with the spiritual values that have disappeared as a result of the war.

The Loved One · Perhaps the grimmest of Waugh's satires, *The Loved One* presents a sardonic vision of American culture. Its principal satiric target is Forest Lawn Memorial Park—a place that in many ways served for Waugh as the epitome of American pretensions to civilization. In "Half in Love with Easeful Death," an essay Waugh wrote for *Life* in 1947 after his visit to Hollywood, Waugh describes Forest Lawn as it would appear to archaeologists in the next millennium: a burlesque necropolis, like the tombs of the pharaohs in its aspirations, but, in fact, the product of a borrowed, devalued culture. His version of Forest Lawn, Whispering Glades, is a distorted wonderland in which the cosmetic and the artificial substitute for beauty and in which banality is glorified and substitutes for the poetic vision.

It is fitting that the protagonist, Dennis Barlow, be a poet—even though an unproductive one who has been seduced to Hollywood by a consultantship with Megalo Studios. Like many of Waugh's other protagonists, he is the filter through which one sees absurdities satirized. Like Basil Seal in *Black Mischief* and *Put Out More Flags*, he is an opportunist, flexible enough to engineer a profit for himself out of the chaotic world into which he is thrust. His vision is grimly sardonic, however, in a way that even Seal's is not.

When he first enters Whispering Glades, he is intrigued, as Seal would be, by its absurd glamour and by the potential of using that glamour to improve his own position at The Happier Hunting Grounds, a pet mortuary where he is employed. Whispering Glades, however, has a far deeper attraction; it would be the kind of place, if it were real, that would appeal to any poet, but Barlow is enchanted by its very fraudulence. At the human-made Lake Isle of Innisfree (complete with mechanized humming bees), Barlow falls in love with a mortuary cosmetician and enchants her by the very fact that he is a poet. The enchantment is false, just as everything is at Whispering Glades; he sends her plagiarized verses from *The Oxford Book of English Verse* and pledges his troth to her by reciting a stanza from Robert Burns's "A Red, Red Rose" at The Lover's Nook near the Wee Kirk o' Auld Lang Syne.

If plagiarism lies at the heart of Barlow's involvement at Whispering Glades, it also lies at the heart of Whispering Glades itself and the characters who work there—even though the place and the people are possessed by the utmost seriousness. The girl with whom Barlow falls in love is named Aimee Thanatogenos. Although she professes to be named after Aimee McPherson—the American huckster of religion whom Waugh satirized in *Vile Bodies*—her given name and her surname both translate into the euphemism that embodies all of Whispering Glades's false coating: "The loved one." Her enchantment with Barlow eventually takes the form of a burlesque tragedy. She is torn between Barlow and the head mortician, Mr. Joyboy, a poet of a different sort, whose special art is preparing infant corpses.

Aimee's tragedy results from a bizarre sequence of events, comic in its effects. When she discovers Joyboy's mother fixation and Barlow's fraudulence, she seeks advice from her oracle, the Guru Brahmin, an advice columnist. When the Guru, Mr. Slump—fired from his job and in an alcoholic funk—advises Aimee to jump off a roof, she kills herself in the more poetic environment of Whispering Glades. Her suicide by drinking embalming fluid gives a doubly ironic force to her name and to the title of the novel. The tragedy ends with a darkly humorous catharsis. Joyboy, fearful that Aimee's death on his table might mar his lofty position at Whispering Glades, consents to Barlow's extortion and to Barlow's plan to cremate their beloved Aimee at The Happier Hunting Grounds. The novel's conclusion, thus, strikes the grimmest note of all: Barlow sits idly by, reading a cheap novel, while the heroine—a burlesque Dido—burns in the furnace.

In some ways, *The Loved One* is atypical of Waugh's postwar novels. In *Scott-King's Modern Europe* and the *Sword of Honour* trilogy, Waugh turns his satiric eye to political issues. *The Loved One*, however much it satirizes American values, transcends topical satire. Barlow lacks the spiritual potential of Charles Ryder in *Brideshead Revisited*, even though he displays Ryder's callousness. Barlow is an artist in search of beauty, but he leaves California, ironically, with an artist's load far different from what he expected. It is the view of an ironist, like Waugh himself, who could hardly make a better travesty of Whispering Glades than it makes of itself.

Sword of Honour · The *Sword of Honour* trilogy, like *Brideshead Revisited*, is infused with a predominantly religious theme; it traces Guy Crouchback's awakening to spiritual honor—a more active form of spiritual growth than Charles Ryder experienced. Like *Brideshead Revisited, Sword of Honour* is more somber and more deliberately paced than Waugh's satires in the 1920's and 1930's, but it shares with his early works a detached satiric framework. Each volume is composed at a distance of ten or more years from its historical occurrence and, as a result, reflects a greater consciousness of the long-range implications of the absurdities presented.

Men at Arms · *Men at Arms* concerns the chaos of Britain's first entry into the war, much like Waugh's wartime satire *Put Out More Flags*. One is immediately aware, however, of the difference in Waugh's detachment. *Put Out More Flags* was the product of a writer in his mid-thirties looking wryly at the days of peace from the middle of the war. Its protagonist, Basil Seal, is a mischief-making opportunist for whom greater chaos means greater fun and profit; the novel satirizes the madness of a world which leaves the characters trapped in the ever-changing insanity of war. *Men at Arms*, however, and, indeed, the entire trilogy, looks back from the perspective of the author's later middle age, with a sense of disappointment at the final results of the war. Appropriately enough, Guy is an innocent at the outset of the war, not a mischief maker like Basil Seal. He is a middle-aged victim who is literally and figuratively cast into a battle for which he is ill prepared.

Guy's heroic illusions are shattered in three successive stages through the separate volumes of the trilogy. *Men at Arms* concerns Guy's search for the self-esteem he lost eight years earlier after his divorce from his wife. As an officer-trainee in the Royal Corps of Halberdiers, Guy temporarily finds self-respect, but the elaborate traditions of the Halberdiers and his traineeship at commandeered preparatory schools cause Guy to revert to adolescence. His physical awkwardness, his jealousy of fellow trainees, his vanity about growing a mustache, his ineffectual attempt to seduce his former wife on Saint Valentine's Day, and the blot he receives on his military record at the end of the novel all seem more appropriate for a schoolboy than for an officer preparing to lead men into battle.

As in Waugh's earlier novels, the comedy of *Men at Arms* depends not on the protagonist, but on the events and characters that he encounters. Apthorpe, a middle-aged *miles gloriosus*, and Ben Ritchie-Hook, Guy's brigadier, represent two forms of the military insanity for which Guy trains. Apthorpe's preoccupation with boots, salutes, and his portable field latrine, the "Box," makes him an unlikely candidate for leading men into battle; Ritchie-Hook, whose only notion of military strategy is to attack, makes an elaborate game out of officer training by booby-trapping Apthorpe's "Box"—a prank that causes Apthorpe to sink deeper into his madness. The confrontation between Apthorpe and Ritchie-Hook defines an absurd pattern which recurs later in the trilogy. Seeming madmen control the positions of power, and the protagonist is unwittingly drawn into their absurd worlds.

Officers and Gentlemen · *Officers and Gentlemen* further trains Guy in the illogic of military life, this time focusing on the efforts of gentlemen soldiers to re-create the comforts of their London clubs during the war. The novel ends on a more somber note, however, than did *Men at Arms*. Guy finds temporary solace in the commando unit to which he is transferred after his disgrace as a Halberdier and believes again that he will find some honorable role to play in the war, but the British defeat at Crete at the end of this volume negates whatever notions of honor he entertained.

Even more than *Men at Arms, Officers and Gentlemen* relentlessly travesties *esprit de corps* and pretentions to heroism. Ian Kilbannock's gentlemanly service as a military journalist, for example, is to transform the ineffectual Trimmer into a propaganda hero for the common person. Julia Stitch's yacht, the *Cleopatra*, brings the comforts of the English social world to the Mediterranean war. The burrowing Grace-Groundling-Marchpole absurdly continues the secret file he began in *Men at Arms* about Guy's supposed counterintelligence activities. All these events occur while England is suffering the first effects of German bombing and while the British disgrace at Crete looms ahead.

For a time, Guy imagines that the commandos are the "flower of England"; he even sees Ivor Claire as the ideal soldier, the kind of Englishman whom Hitler had not taken into account. The flower withers, however, in the chaotic retreat of British forces from Crete. Although Guy himself manages to maintain an even keel through most of the ordeal, the officers with whom he serves prove unheroic. His commander, "Fido" Hound, suffers a complete mental collapse in the face of the retreating troops; Ivor Claire, unable to face the prospect of surrendering, deserts his men and flees to India, where he is protected by his genteel birth. Eventually, Guy unheroically joins a boat escaping from the island and, exhausted, suffers a mental collapse. Guy initially resists Julia Stitch's efforts to cover up Claire's disgrace, but eventually destroys his own diary recording the orders to surrender when he learns that nothing will be done about Claire's desertion and when he learns of England's alliance with Russia. Unlike the first volume, the second volume ends with Guy's realization that he is an ineffectual player in a war that has lost a sense of honor.

It is curious to note that Waugh announced in the dust-jacket blurb for *Officers and Gentlemen* that, although he had planned the series for three volumes, he wanted his readers to regard it as finished with this second volume. The grimness of Guy's disillusionment thus sheds a somber light on Waugh's personal dilemma during the mid-1950's. After completing about a third of the draft of this second volume, Waugh suffered the mental collapse fictionalized in *The Ordeal of Gilbert Pinfold.* Guy's hallucination at the end of *Officers and Gentlemen* probably owes some of its vividness to the madness Waugh himself endured in 1954, and perhaps the numbness that affects Guy at the end of the novel reflects Waugh's own consciousness of his failing physical and mental powers.

The End of the Battle · *Men at Arms* and *Officers and Gentlemen* each deflate Guy's illusions about honor. *The End of the Battle* follows the same pattern in terms of wartime politics and in terms of Guy's military life, but in personal terms, Guy achieves a kind of unheroic, unselfish honor by the end of the novel. As a soldier, Guy accomplishes nothing heroic; even his efforts to liberate the Jewish refugees from partisan Yugoslavia is unsatisfying. Although most of the refugees are liberated, the leaders of the group—the Kanyis—are imprisoned and presumably executed. Guy's struggle with the Yugoslavian partisans and his disgust at Britain's alliance with the Communist-bloc countries further define the dishonorable end that Guy and Waugh see in the war.

Unlike the two previous volumes, however, *The End of the Battle* ends on a note of tentative personal hopefulness, effected by Guy's renewed Roman Catholic faith. In the first two novels of the trilogy, Guy's religion lay dormant—a part of his life made purposeless since his divorce from Virginia. In *The End of the Battle*, the death of Guy's piously religious father causes Guy to realize that honor lies not in the "quantitative judgments" of military strategy, but in the spiritual salvation of individual souls. Guy's efforts to rescue the Yugoslavian Jews is selflessly honorable, even if ultimately futile. His remarriage to Virginia, who is pregnant with Trimmer's baby, is directed by the same sense of honor. Guy has little to gain emotionally from his remarriage; he does it for the preservation of the child's life and, implicitly, for the salvation of its soul. It is a different sort of heroism than he sought at the beginning of the war, possible only because Virginia has died.

Sword of Honour is, in many ways, a fitting climax to Waugh's literary career. It poignantly expresses his reverence for religious values yet recognizes the anomalous existence of those values in the modern world. It burlesques the eccentric and the absurd, yet moves beyond superficial satire to a more deeply rooted criticism of postwar politics. It displays Waugh's masterful ability to capture minor characters in brisk, economical strokes while working them thematically into the emotional composition of the protagonist. Waugh's importance as a novelist lay in his ability to achieve this kind of economy in a traditional form. He kept alive, in short, a tradition of the comic novel that reaches back to the eighteenth century.

James J. Lynch

Other major works

SHORT FICTION: *Mr. Loveday's Little Outing*, 1936; *Tactical Exercise*, 1954; *Charles Ryder's Schooldays and Other Stories*, 1982.

NONFICTION: *Rossetti: His Life and Works*, 1928; *Labels*, 1930; *Remote People*, 1931; *Ninety-two Days*, 1934; *Edmund Campion: Jesuit and Martyr*, 1935; *Waugh in Abyssinia*, 1936; *Robbery Under the Law*, 1939; *The Holy Places*, 1952; *The Life of the Right Reverend Ronald Knox*, 1959; *Tourist in Africa*, 1960; *A Little Learning*, 1964; *The Diaries of Evelyn Waugh*, 1976 (Christopher Sykes, editor); *The Letters of Evelyn Waugh*, 1980 (Mark Amory, editor).

Bibliography

Carens, James F., ed. *Critical Essays on Evelyn Waugh.* Boston: G. K. Hall, 1987. Contains twenty-six essays divided into three sections: general essays, essays on specific novels, and essays on Waugh's life and works. In his lengthy introduction, Carens provides a chronological overview of Waugh's literary work and a discussion of Waugh criticism. This well-indexed book also contains a bibliography of Waugh's writings and a selective list of secondary sources.

Cook, William J., Jr. *Masks, Modes, and Morals: The Art of Evelyn Waugh.* Rutherford, N.J.: Fairleigh Dickinson University Press, 1971. Considers Waugh's novels squarely in the ironic mode, tracing Waugh's development from satiric denunciation to comic realism to romantic optimism to ironic realism. Cook provides lengthy analyses of the novels, which he suggests move from fantasy to reality and from satire to resignation. Well indexed and contains an excellent bibliography, which also lists articles.

Crabbe, Katharyn. *Evelyn Waugh.* New York: Continuum, 1988. Crabbe's book is most helpful: She provides a chronology of Waugh's life, a short biography, and five chapters of detailed criticism on Waugh's major novels. Crabbe reads *The Ordeal of Gilbert Pinfold* as an autobiographical novel. A concluding chapter on style is followed by a bibliography and a thorough index.

Davis, Robert Murray. *Evelyn Waugh: Writer.* Norman, Okla.: Pilgrim Books, 1981. Drawing from previously unavailable manuscript materials, Davis examines Waugh's fiction in terms of his artistic technique, his extensive revisions, and his reworking of his novels. After an opening chapter on Waugh's biography of Dante Gabriel Rossetti, Davis focuses exclusively on the novels, *Brideshead Revisited* and *Sword of Honour* in particular. Well documented and well indexed.

Hastings, Selina. *Evelyn Waugh: A Biography.* Boston: Houghton Mifflin, 1994. An excellent one-volume biography. Hastings notes that hers is not an academic biography such as Stannard has written, but a lively attempt to recapture Waugh's personality as it seemed to him and to his friends.

Lane, Calvin W. *Evelyn Waugh.* Boston: Twayne, 1981. Indispensable for Waugh scholars, Lane's relatively short volume contains a detailed chronology, a biography stressing the factors influencing his literary career, and lengthy treatments of

Waugh's novels. Stresses Waugh's irony, satire, and conversion to Catholicism, which greatly influenced his fiction after 1930. Lane's selected bibliography contains articles, annotated book-length studies, and four interviews with Waugh.

Stannard, Martin. *Evelyn Waugh.* New York: W. W. Norton, 1987. A scholarly, well-documented account of Waugh's early literary career, Stannard's biography provides valuable publication details about the novels and utilizes Waugh's diaries and letters. Also contains many photographs and illustrations, a genealogical chart of Waugh's ancestry, a selected bibliography, and an excellent index.

_____. *Evelyn Waugh: No Abiding City, 1939-1966.* London: Dent, 1992. The second volume of a meticulous, scholarly biography. Includes notes, bibliography, illustrations, and two indexes: a general index and one of Waugh's work.

Fay Weldon

Born: Alvechurch, England; September 22, 1931

Principal long fiction · *The Fat Woman's Joke*, 1967 (pb. in U.S. as . . . *And the Wife Ran Away*, 1968); *Down Among the Women*, 1971; *Female Friends*, 1974; *Remember Me*, 1976; *Words of Advice*, 1977 (pb. in England as *Little Sisters*, 1978); *Praxis*, 1978; *Puffball*, 1980; *The President's Child*, 1982; *The Life and Loves of a She-Devil*, 1983; *The Shrapnel Academy*, 1986; *The Rules of Life*, 1987; *The Hearts and Lives of Men*, 1987; *The Heart of the Country*, 1987; *Leader of the Band*, 1988; *The Cloning of Joanna May*, 1989; *Darcy's Utopia*, 1990; *Growing Rich*, 1992; *Life Force*, 1992; *Affliction*, 1993 (pb. in U.S. as *Trouble*, 1993); *Splitting*, 1995; *Worst Fears*, 1996; *Big Women*, 1997 (pb. in U.S. as *Big Girls Don't Cry*, 1997); *Rhode Island Blues*, 2000.

Other literary forms · Fay Weldon began her writing career with plays for radio, television, and theater, but she soon transferred her efforts to novels, for which she is best known. She has also published short stories, a biography of Rebecca West, and an introduction to the work of Jane Austen in fictional form, *Letters to Alice on First Reading Jane Austen* (1984).

Achievements · In addition to a successful career as an advertising copywriter, Fay Weldon has enjoyed a long career as a television scriptwriter, a playwright (for television, radio, and theater), and a novelist. Her radio play *Spider* (1972) won the Writers' Guild Award for Best Radio Play in 1973, and *Polaris* (1978) won the Giles Cooper Award for Best Radio Play in 1978. Weldon has earned growing acclaim for her humorous fictional explorations of women's lives and her biting satires that expose social injustice, and her novel *Praxis* was nominated for the Booker Prize, a prestigious literary award in England. In 1983, Weldon became the first woman chair of judges for the Booker Prize. She was again recognized for her many achievements in 1997, when she received the Women in Publishing Pandora Award. Although her works often focus primarily on the lives of women, Weldon comments on a wide-ranging number of issues with relevance to all. Her work reveals a deep yet unsentimental compassion for all human beings, an understanding of their weaknesses and foibles, and a celebration of their continued survival and ability to love one another in the face of adversity.

Biography · Fay Weldon was born into a literary family in the village of Alvechurch, England, in 1931. Her mother, her maternal grandfather, and her uncle were all published novelists. While still a child, Weldon emigrated with her family to New Zealand, where she grew up. When she was six years old, her parents (Frank Thornton Birkinshaw, a doctor, and Margaret Jepson Birkinshaw) were divorced; Weldon continued to live with her mother and sister. This experience of being reared by a single mother in an era that did not easily accommodate single-parent families gave Weldon early insight into the lot of women who flouted social norms. When she was fourteen, Weldon, her mother, and her sister joined her grandmother in London. These were years of hardship in postwar England, but the strong and independent women of the family set a good example. Weldon was able to observe, at first hand, both the trials women faced and the importance of family and of humor in overcoming these difficulties.

In 1949, Weldon earned a scholarship to St. Andrews University in Scotland, and in 1952 she was graduated with an M.A. in economics and psychology. In 1955, she had her first son, Nicholas, whom she supported as a single mother. Weldon's literary ambitions had not yet crystallized—though she had begun writing—so she drifted into a series of writing jobs: propaganda for the Foreign Office; answering problem letters for a newspaper; and, finally, composing advertising copy. In this last career she was quite successful, producing many jingles and slogans that would become household sayings and honing her talent for concision, wit, and catchy, memorable phrasing.

In 1960, she married Ronald Weldon, a London antiques dealer, and together they settled in a North London suburb, where they had three children: Daniel (born 1963), Thomas (born 1970), and Samuel (born 1977). Beginning in the mid-1960's, Weldon combined professional and family responsibilities with a burgeoning career as a writer. Her efforts were at first directed toward writing plays. Her one-act play "Permanence" was produced in London in 1969 and was followed by many successes. For British television networks, Weldon has written more than fifty plays, as well as other scripts, including an award-winning episode of *Upstairs, Downstairs.*

Writing for television led to fiction: Weldon's first novel, *The Fat Woman's Joke,* in 1967, had begun as a television play. Her third novel, *Female Friends,* solidified her reputation. In the 1970's, Weldon left her job in advertising. She was able to devote more of her time to writing, earning further acclaim for *Praxis* in 1978. *The President's Child,* in 1982, was an even bigger best-seller, thanks to its "thriller" quality, while *The Life and Loves of a She-Devil,* in 1983, introduced Weldon's work to a mass audience when it was made into a motion picture, *She-Devil* (1990), starring Meryl Streep and Roseanne Barr.

In addition to her novels, in the 1980's and 1990's Weldon also published collections of her short fiction, including *Moon over Minneapolis: Or, Why She Couldn't Stay* (1991) and *Wicked Women: A Collection of Short Stories* (1995). She also put her comic gifts to work in three books for children, *Wolf the Mechanical Dog* (1988), *Party Puddle* (1989), and *Nobody Likes Me* (1997). Meanwhile, after the author and her husband of thirty-four years were divorced in 1994, she married Nicholas Fox and settled down in London. There she continued to write and to crusade for writers' rights and to attack the two great enemies of her profession, censorship and exploitation by unscrupulous publishers.

Analysis · In her fiction, Fay Weldon explores women's lives with wit and humor. She is caustic in her implicit condemnation of injustice but avoids preaching by satirizing both sides of every issue and by revealing the gulf between what characters say and what they do. Despite their realistic settings, her novels blend fable, myth, and the fantastic with satire, farce, and outlandish coincidence to produce tragicomedies of manners.

Weldon's admiration for writers such as Jane Austen (whose work she has adapted for television) is expressed openly in *Letters to Alice on First Reading Jane Austen,* but it is also evident from the parallels in Weldon's own work. In a typical Weldon novel, a limited cast of characters interacts in a well-defined setting. A series of misunderstandings or trivial coincidences initiates the action, which then takes on a momentum of its own, carrying all along with it until an equally trivial series of explanations or coincidences brings closure and a resolution that restores all to their proper place. The theme is often a minor domestic drama, such as a marital crisis, rather than an epic upheaval, but such personal interactions are seen to represent in microcosm society as a whole and therefore have a universal appeal.

. . . And the Wife Ran Away

. . . And the Wife Ran Away · This structure is present even in Weldon's early work, no doubt because it is a formula that works well for television. In her first novel, originally entitled *The Fat Woman's Joke* but renamed *. . . And the Wife Ran Away* for its American publication in 1968, Weldon takes as her subject the crisis in the marriage of a middle-aged, middle-class couple, Esther and Alan Wells, when Alan decides to have an affair with his young and attractive secretary, Susan. The beginning of Alan's affair coincides with Esther and Alan's decision to go on a diet, a symbolic attempt, Weldon suggests, to recapture not only their lost youthful figures, but also their youthful love, ambition, and optimism. Infidelity, the novel therefore subtly suggests, is related to aging and to a more deep-seated identity crisis. Weldon frequently uses hunger or the satisfaction of food as a metaphor for other, more metaphysical and intangible, needs, and this theme recurs in a number of her works (for example, in the short story "Polaris," 1985).

The influence of Weldon's background as a scriptwriter (and the novel's origin as a play) is also evident in its form. Esther, who has left her husband at the opening of the novel, recounts her version of events to her friend Phyllis, as she gorges herself on food to compensate for the self-denial she has suffered during the diet. Esther's narrative is intercut with scenes of Susan telling her version to her friend Brenda. The novel is thus almost entirely conveyed through dialogue describing flashbacks seen from the perspective of the female characters. This technique is evident elsewhere in Weldon's early work—for example, in *Female Friends*, where parts of the novel are presented in the form of a script.

The Life and Loves of a She-Devil

The Life and Loves of a She-Devil · *The Life and Loves of a She-Devil* stands as one of Weldon's most accomplished works. It represents the themes that are the hallmark of Weldon's fiction (a concern with women's lives and the significance of human relationships such as marriage) while encompassing her use of fantasy in one of her most carefully constructed and formally satisfying novels. The plot tells the story of a middle-class, suburban housewife, Ruth, whose accountant husband leaves her for a rich and attractive writer of romance novels. Unlike the typical wife, however, Ruth does not simply bow to the inevitable. When her husband calls her a "she-devil" in a moment of anger, this becomes her new identity, and she musters a formidable array of resources to live up to it. Through a series of picaresque adventures, she makes the life of her husband Bobbo and his new love Mary Fisher impossible, has Bobbo framed and then imprisoned for embezzlement, destroys Mary's ability and will to write, and finally undergoes massive plastic surgery so that she looks just like the now-dead rival Mary and can assume her place in Bobbo's broken life. The configuration at the end of the novel thus mirrors the beginning, but with the variation that the power dynamics of the relationship have been inverted: Ruth is now in command, while Bobbo has been humiliated and accepts his fate like a downtrodden wife.

The tale not only presents a certain kind of symmetry reminiscent of fairy stories but also evokes a poetic magic in the telling of it. Many of the chapters begin with a variation on the opening line of the novel: "Mary Fisher lives in a High Tower, on the edge of the sea." These incantations, repeated with variations, have the hypnotic quality of a witch's spell, reinforcing both Ruth's supernatural power and her obsession with Mary Fisher (whose residence in a tower evokes a fairy-tale princess). This poetic refrain also unifies the narrative and gives a cyclical structure to the plot.

The Shrapnel Academy · At first glance, *The Shrapnel Academy* appears to be a variation on the theme of the "country house weekend" plot, a staple of British literature. A group of characters, most of them unknown to one another, are seen arriving at the Shrapnel Academy, a military institute, for a weekend. Bad weather will ensure that they remain confined to the academy, cut off from the outside world and forced to confront one another and the problems that arise.

While many novelists fail to acknowledge the presence of the host of servants who make such country weekends possible, Weldon's novel takes the reader below stairs and into the lives of the hundreds of illegal immigrant servants and their extended families and camp followers. The Shrapnel Academy could thus be subtitled "Upstairs, Downstairs," like the television series about an upper-class Edwardian family and its servants (to which Weldon contributed an award-winning episode). *The Shrapnel Academy* strays far beyond the realist conventions of the television series, however, and by presenting the clash between shortsighted, class-based militarism and the struggle for survival and dignity in the microcosm of the academy, Weldon succeeds in painting an apocalyptic allegory.

The Shrapnel Academy illustrates how Weldon avoids assigning blame by showing how character flaws and opportunity combine to create problems. Despite the black humor of this novel, Weldon's moral universe is not one of black and white. The reader is made to sympathize with the choices of the militarists and is shown the complicity of the victims so that simplistic judgments become impossible. As in most of Weldon's novels, no one villain is responsible for the misfortunes that befall the characters; instead, everyone bears some degree of responsibility for the accumulation of trivial choices and decisions that combine to make up the "frightful tidal wave of destiny." The theme of destiny increasingly preoccupies Weldon; it is one of the major themes in *The Cloning of Joanna May*, for example, in which the role of coincidence is the subject of mystical and metaphysical speculation.

Many thematic and stylistic elements of Weldon's work also recur in *The Shrapnel Academy*, such as the revenge fantasy theme, food symbolism, and the revision of mythology and fable. Since war affects everyone—increasingly, Weldon argues, women and children—the militaristic theme of *The Shrapnel Academy* should not be construed as belying a male-oriented narrative. Weldon uses the female characters in this novel to offer characteristic insight into the position of the various women above stairs—Joan Lumb, the officious administrator, the General's mistress Bella, Shirley the unquestioning and dutiful wife, Muffin the fluff-brained assistant—as well as the often anonymous women who are raped, die in childbirth, or become prostitutes in the "third world" below stairs.

Formally, too, the novel displays typical characteristics of Weldon's work (short narrative passages with aphoristic asides, the use of dialogue), as well as innovative and experimental qualities. Weldon interrupts the narrative at frequent intervals, sometimes to offer a satirical summary of military history, highlighting advances in warfare or giving accounts of famous battles. Weldon brings out the absurdity of celebrating such "progress" and uses her fine wit to draw the reader's attention to the Orwellian doublespeak and the underlying assumptions of military thinking. At other times, Weldon interpellates the reader directly, apologizing for the delay in getting on with the story or inviting readers to put themselves in the place of one of the characters—invitations that pointedly drive home the lesson that the reader is no better than the characters he or she is inclined to judge. Weldon even interrupts the story to offer a recipe for cooking pumpkin, only one of the ways Weldon breaks with the conventional codes of narrative (elsewhere she offers lists, timetables, and even a seating plan and a menu).

Life Force · Weldon also breaks with her readers' expectations, as in *Life Force*, which, instead of being an indictment of male callousness and infidelity, is a lusty tribute to male sexuality. The central figure in the book is Leslie Beck, a man with no virtues except his power to please women through the skillful use of his huge genitalia and his equally outsized imagination. Structurally, *Life Force* follows the pattern established in Weldon's earlier novels: It begins with a seemingly unimportant incident that stimulates the narrator to relive and reassess complex relationships. That incident eventually becomes a crucial element in a dramatic resolution, in which a woman avenges herself upon a man who has wronged her.

When Leslie Beck turns up at the Marion Loos Gallery, carrying a large painting by his late wife Anita, it does not seem possible that this unappealing, sixty-year-old man could for so long have been the Lothario of upper-middle-class London. However, the owner of the gallery, who at this point is the first-person narrator, explains to the reader why she is so shocked when she sees the unimpressive painting that her former lover expects her to sell on his behalf. Its subject is the bedroom and the bed in which Leslie once gave Marion so much pleasure. Naturally, the painting prompts Marion to recall her involvement with Leslie and to wonder how much Anita knew about the affair.

However, nothing in this novel is as straightforward as it seems. In the second chapter, not only does Weldon change narrators, now telling the story through the eyes of Nora, another of Beck's former lovers, but also she has Nora admit that it was she, not Marion, who actually wrote the first chapter, simply imagining herself as Marion. Although the two narrators continue to alternate as the book progresses, from time to time the author reminds us that Marion's narrative is Nora's fiction, based as much on gossip and guesses as on fact. Thus, Weldon suggests that since the only approach to truth is through what human beings see and say, what we call reality will always include as much fiction as fact.

Trouble · After *Life Force*, in which she showed both genders as being controlled by their own animal instincts, Weldon again turned her attention to a society that permits men to victimize women. The protagonist of *Trouble*, which was published in England under the title *Affliction*, is Annette Horrocks, a woman who, after ten years of trying, has finally become pregnant, only to find that her once-devoted husband Spicer has become monstrous. Not only does he now seem to loathe Annette, but also none of his tastes, opinions, and prejudices are what they were just a few months before.

Eventually, Annette discovers the source of the problem: Spicer has been seduced by a pair of unscrupulous, sadistic New Age psychiatrists. Before she is finally cured of what she comes to recognize as her addiction to Spicer, Annette loses her home, her baby, and very nearly her mind. If in *Life Force* Weldon shows the battle of the sexes as essentially comic, in *Trouble* Weldon tells a story with tragic overtones. Again she points out how vulnerable women are in a society that believes men have a monopoly on the truth, but in this case she shows what can happen when the male version of reality is reinforced by the self-seeking therapy industry, the primary target of satire in this novel.

Weldon's fiction has developed from dialogue-based, scriptlike narratives to a style that resembles more conventional forms of the novel, although still with a characteristic lack of reverence for the conventions of storytelling. Her themes have expanded from domestic dramas and personal relationships to topical questions of national and international import, but without abandoning the belief that the personal remains the minimal unit of significance at the base of even the largest human networks. Humor has remained a constant feature of her work, her delicious wit and sharp irony the armor that protects her from charges of overseriousness, preaching, or doctrinaire political stances.

Melanie Hawthorne,
updated by Rosemary M. Canfield Reisman

Other major works

SHORT FICTION: *Watching Me, Watching You,* 1981; *Polaris and Other Stories,* 1985; *Moon over Minneapolis: Or, Why She Couldn't Stay,* 1991; *Wicked Women: A Collection of Short Stories,* 1995; *A Hard Time to Be a Father,* 1999.

PLAYS: *Permanence,* pr. 1969; *Time Hurries On,* pb. 1972; *Words of Advice,* pr., pb. 1974; *Friends,* pr. 1975; *Moving House,* pr. 1976; *Mr. Director,* pr. 1978; *Action Replay,* pr. 1979 (also known as *Love Among the Women*); *I Love My Love,* pr. 1981; *After the Prize,* pr. 1981 (also known as *Wordworm*).

TELEPLAYS: *Wife in a Blonde Wig,* 1966; *The Fat Woman's Tale,* 1966; *What About Me,* 1967; *Dr. De Waldon's Therapy,* 1967; *Goodnight Mrs. Dill,* 1967; *The Forty-fifth Unmarried Mother,* 1967; *Fall of the Goat,* 1967; *Ruined Houses,* 1968; *Venus Rising,* 1968; *The Three Wives of Felix Hull,* 1968; *Hippy Hippy Who Cares,* 1968; *£13083,* 1968; *The Loophole,* 1969; *Smokescreen,* 1969; *Poor Mother,* 1970; *Office Party,* 1970; *On Trial,* 1971 (in *Upstairs, Downstairs* series); *Old Man's Hat,* 1972; *A Splinter of Ice,* 1972; *Hands,* 1972; *The Lament of an Unmarried Father,* 1972; *A Nice Rest,* 1972; *Comfortable Words,* 1973; *Desirous of Change,* 1973; *In Memoriam,* 1974; *Poor Baby,* 1975; *The Terrible Tale of Timothy Bagshott,* 1975; *Aunt Tatty,* 1975 (adaptation of Elizabeth Bowen's story); *Act of Rape,* 1977; *Married Love,* 1977 (in *Six Women* series); *Pride and Prejudice,* 1980 (adaptation of Jane Austen's novel); *Honey Ann,* 1980; *Watching Me, Watching You,* 1980 (in *Leap in the Dark* series); *Life for Christine,* 1980; *Little Miss Perkins,* 1982; *Loving Women,* 1983; *Redundant! Or, The Wife's Revenge,* 1983.

RADIO PLAYS: *Spider,* 1972; *Housebreaker,* 1973; *Mr. Fox and Mr. First,* 1974; *The Doctor's Wife,* 1975; *Polaris,* 1978; *Weekend,* 1979 (in *Just Before Midnight* series); *All the Bells of Paradise,* 1979; *I Love My Love,* 1981.

NONFICTION: *Letters to Alice on First Reading Jane Austen,* 1984; *Rebecca West,* 1985.

CHILDREN'S LITERATURE: *Wolf the Mechanical Dog,* 1988; *Party Puddle,* 1989; *Nobody Likes Me,* 1997.

EDITED TEXT: *New Stories Four: An Arts Council Anthology,* 1979 (with Elaine Feinstein).

Bibliography

Barreca, Regina, ed. *Fay Weldon's Wicked Fictions.* Hanover, N.H.: University Press of New England, 1994. This important volume contains thirteen essays by various writers, in addition to five by Weldon. The editor's introduction provides a useful overview of Weldon criticism. Indexed.

Cane, Aleta F. "Demythifying Motherhood in Three Novels by Fay Weldon." In *Family Matters in the British and American Novel,* edited by Andrea O'Reilly Herrera, Elizabeth Mahn Nollen, and Sheila Reitzel Foor. Bowling Green, Ohio: Bowling Green State University Popular Press, 1997. Cane points out that in *Puffball, The Life and Loves of a She-Devil,* and *Life Force,* dysfunctional mothers produce daughters who are also dysfunctional mothers. Obviously, it is argued, Weldon agrees with the feminist position about mothering, that it cannot be improved until women cease to be marginalized.

Mitchell, Margaret E. "Fay Weldon." In *British Writers.* Supplement 4 in *Contemporary British Writers,* edited by George Stade and Carol Howard. New York: Scribner's, 1997. A very comprehensive study of Weldon's life and work. A lengthy but readable analysis is divided into sections on "Weldon's Feminism," "The Personal as Political," "Nature, Fate, and Magic," "Self and Solidarity," and "Fictions." Contains a biographical essay and a bibliography.

Weldon, Fay. "Towards a Humorous View of the Universe." In *Last Laughs: Perspectives on Women and Comedy,* edited by Regina Barreca. New York: Gordon and Breach, 1988. A short (three-page) article about humor as a protection against pain, with perceptive comments about class-related and gendered aspects of humor. Although Weldon herself does not draw the connections specifically, the reader can infer much from her comments about the role of humor in her own work.

Wilde, Alan. "'Bold, but Not Too Bold': Fay Weldon and the Limits of Poststructuralist Criticism." *Contemporary Literature* 29, no. 3 (1988): 403-419. The author focuses primarily not on Weldon's work but on literary theory, using *The Life and Loves of a She-Devil* as an arena to pit poststructuralism against New Criticism. The argument is at times obscure, but Wilde offers some useful comments regarding moderation versus extremism in this novel.

H. G. Wells

Born: Bromley, Kent, England; September 21, 1866
Died: London, England; August 13, 1946

Principal long fiction · *The Time Machine: An Invention,* 1895; *The Wonderful Visit,* 1895; *The Island of Dr. Moreau,* 1896; *The Wheels of Chance: A Holiday Adventure,* 1896; *The Invisible Man: A Grotesque Romance,* 1897; *The War of the Worlds,* 1898; *When the Sleeper Wakes: A Story of the Years to Come,* 1899; *Love and Mr. Lewisham,* 1900; *The First Men in the Moon,* 1901; *The Sea Lady,* 1902; *The Food of the Gods, and How It Came to Earth,* 1904; *Kipps: The Story of a Simple Soul,* 1905; *In the Days of the Comet,* 1906; *The War in the Air, and Particularly How Mr. Bert Smallways Fared While It Lasted,* 1908; *Tono-Bungay,* 1908; *Ann Veronica: A Modern Love Story,* 1909; *The History of Mr. Polly,* 1910; *The New Machiavelli,* 1910; *Marriage,* 1912; *The Passionate Friends,* 1913; *The Wife of Sir Isaac Harman,* 1914; *The World Set Free: A Story of Mankind,* 1914; *Bealby: A Holiday,* 1915; *The Research Magnificent,* 1915; *Mr. Britling Sees It Through,* 1916; *The Soul of a Bishop: A Novel—with Just a Little Love in It—About Conscience and Religion and the Real Troubles of Life,* 1917; *Joan and Peter: The Story of an Education,* 1918; *The Undying Fire: A Contemporary Novel,* 1919; *The Secret Places of the Heart,* 1922; *Men Like Gods,* 1923; *The Dream,* 1924; *Christina Alberta's Father,* 1925; *The World of William Clissold: A Novel at a New Age,* 1926 (3 volumes); *Meanwhile: The Picture of a Lady,* 1927; *Mr. Blettsworthy on Rampole Island,* 1928; *The King Who Was a King: The Book of a Film,* 1929; *The Autocracy of Mr. Parham: His Remarkable Adventure in This Changing World,* 1930; *The Buplington of Blup,* 1933; *The Shape of Things to Come: The Ultimate Resolution,* 1933; *The Croquet Player,* 1936; *Byrnhild,* 1937; *The Camford Visitation,* 1937; *Star Begotten: A Biological Fantasia,* 1937; *Apropos of Dolores,* 1938; *The Brothers,* 1938; *The Holy Terror,* 1939; *Babes in the Darkling Wood,* 1940; *All Aboard for Ararat,* 1940; *You Can't Be Too Careful: A Sample of Life, 1901-1951,* 1941.

Other literary forms · H. G. Wells's short stories appear in such collections as *The Stolen Bacillus and Other Incidents* (1895), *Tales of Space and Time* (1899), *The Country of the Blind and Other Stories* (1911), and *A Door in the Wall and Other Stories* (1911). *The Outline of History: Being a Plain History of Life and Mankind* (1920) and *Experiment in Autobiography: Discoveries and Conclusions of a Very Ordinary Brain Since 1866* (1934) extended his literary range. His sociological essays include *A Modern Utopia* (1905) and *Mind at the End of Its Tether* (1945).

Achievements · Wells is best known for his science-fiction novels, some having been adapted as popular films. A socialist and Fabian, he was a spokesman for women's rights and international peace movements, for which he wrote books of advocacy in essay and fictional form. He was also an effective novelist of social satire and comedy.

Biography · Herbert George Wells was born in 1866 at Bromley in Kent, England, to Joseph and Sarah Neal Wells. He attended a commercial academy from 1874 to 1880. Having run away from his apprenticeship in a drapery shop, he taught in a preparatory school. Then he attended the London Normal School of Science from

1884 to 1887, studying biology under T. H. Huxley. In 1891 he was married to Isabel Mary Wells, and he published "The Rediscovery of the Unique." *The Time Machine* brought him fame in 1895, the same year that he divorced Isabel to marry Amy Catherine Robbins.

In 1901, Wells's son George Philip was born; Frank Richard followed in 1903. In 1914, having visited Russia, Wells published a prophecy, *The War That Will End War*, that year his son Anthony West was born to Rebecca West. After visiting soldiers on the front lines of World War I, Wells supported a "League of Free Nations," and he entered the propaganda effort against Germany. In 1920 he made another trip to Russia, to

Library of Congress

meet Vladimir Ilich Lenin, and published *Russia in the Shadows.*

Wells was defeated as a Labour candidate for Parliament in 1922, and Amy Catherine died in 1927. He coauthored a book on biology before visiting Russia and the United States in 1934 to meet Joseph Stalin and President Franklin Delano Roosevelt. In 1935 he wrote film scenarios for *Things to Come* and *The Man Who Could Work Miracles.* In 1938 Orson Welles's radio broadcast of *The War of the Worlds* frightened people in the United States, paving the way for Wells's successful lecture tour there in 1940. Wells died in London on August 13, 1946.

Analysis · H. G. Wells's early scientific romances begin with *The Time Machine* (1895) and conclude with *The First Men in the Moon* (1901). His social satire and comic romance commence with *Kipps* (1905) and end with *The History of Mr. Polly* (1910). Didactic fiction dominated his last decades, from *Ann Veronica* (1909) to *You Can't Be Too Careful* (1941). Throughout is a struggle between science and socialism. Visions of doom alternate with calls for reform and renewal; individuals acquire knowledge of science but lose control of their destinies.

The Time Machine · Wells's early novels are journeys of ironic discovery. The enduring point of *The Time Machine* is in the Time-Traveller's frightening discovery in the year 802701. He encounters the Eloi, who have been terrorized by the Morlocks, molelike creatures who prey upon the flesh of the Upper-worlders. They are the fruits of an evolutionary process of separating capitalists from workers. Before he returns to his own time, the Time-Traveller accidentally moves even further into the future, to an Earth about to fall into a dying Sun.

The Island of Dr. Moreau · Edward Prendick, narrator of *The Island of Dr. Moreau*, is a castaway, grateful to reach Moreau's island—until he realizes its horrors. He thinks that Moreau is turning people into animals, but when he finds the Beast-people, he realizes his mistake. Moreau explains that pain is animality, and he excises pain to humanize animals, but they kill him as they revert to their animal natures. Prendick barely escapes becoming an animal before he returns to civilization, where he has anxiety attacks about people's animality.

Pessimism is never far from the surface of Wells's writing. Losing faith in reason, he turned to prophetic satire, as in *The Invisible Man*. In this story, Griffin, having failed to anticipate the awful effects of losing visibility, has lapsed in ethical responsibility because he had no training or economic opportunity to make better use of his knowledge. Lacking love, he lacks constructive purpose for his power. His invisibility represents knowledge itself, as either destructive or constructive. Knowledge and power combine without sympathy in *The War of the Worlds* to result in catastrophe. The narrator is a frightened man struggling to compete for survival of the fittest. He believes that the Martians are little more than brains, dispassionate reason threatening annihilation. All brain with no sympathy threatens civilization, but so does instinct with no brain. The Martians near success, when suddenly they die, ironically having succumbed to the tiniest life form, bacteria.

The First Men in the Moon · Wells reverses the cosmic journey in *The First Men in the Moon*, as Bedford accompanies eccentric scientist Cavor to mine the Moon, adding private enterprise to science. The heroes find an intoxicating mushroom, which prompts Bedford to speculate that his private motive for profit will produce public benefits—even for the Moon itself. This madly grandiose notion is subverted when Bedford and Cavor are captured by the antlike Selenites, who live under the surface of the Moon. When Bedford escapes alone to Earth, Cavor sends messages that he is to be executed to prevent Earth inhabitants from returning with their violent ways, to do to the Moon what Wells had envisioned in *The War of the Worlds*, where Earth was invaded by Martians.

The Food of the Gods, and How It Came to Earth · *The Food of the Gods, and How It Came to Earth* edges beyond science and humor into socialism and satire. Experiments with Boomfood on a chicken farm cause mass destruction through the creation of giant chickens, rats, and wasps; human babies become giants, and ordinary mortals grow terrified. Wells is on the giants' side, because they can make a new world by destroying the faults of the old. People accommodate to preserve old ways, but they shut their eyes to truth, eventually causing a crisis of choice between old and new. The story ends as the giants prepare for a war with the little people.

In the Days of the Comet · With *In the Days of the Comet* Wells presents a more optimistic view of changes that can be made in the world. Willie Leadford describes life before the great "change," when a comet turned Earth into paradise. The power of the novel, however, is in the rhythm of rage and hate that accelerates as Willie pursues the woman he loved, to kill her and her new lover. This momentum is accented by other accelerating events, including economic crisis and war with Germany. The comet changes all, including Willie and his beloved, Nettie, who offers to live with both lovers. In a new world, people learn to accept polygamy as natural and right.

Kipps · *Kipps: The Story of a Simple Soul* is a story like Charles Dickens's *Great Expectations* (1860-1861). The aunt and uncle who reared Kipps expected him to become a store clerk; Kipps has not been very skilled at anything he has undertaken, and he proves no better at handling an unexpected inheritance. Kipps has a dreary existence: He gains no real pleasure from life, not even from reading. Life in lower-middle-class commercial and shopkeeping society is without substance, imagination, or purpose. Kipps's first thought is to buy a banjo, though he cannot play it. Thinking more seriously of his prospects, he asks his art teacher to marry him, and she proceeds to teach him to speak and dress properly. Kipps tries and hopes, until he encounters an old love, Ann Pornick, working as a maid. He snubs her and in his guilt asks her forgiveness; she not only forgives him, but also marries him. Thus, Kipps has stumbled through mistake after mistake, from education to apprenticeship to courtship and marriage. Finally, when he loses most of his fortune, he and his wife resign themselves to a restricted life and open a bookshop.

Wells's satire is directed at Kipps for trying to be more than he can be, for misplacing values in a system of manners; indeed, Wells intensely scorns the social superficialities. The protagonist of *Tono-Bungay*, George Ponderevo, has much in common with Kipps, but George is less simple and more reflective. His early life is like Kipps's (and Wells's) in that he resists training for trade, shows a talent for science, marries above his class, divorces, and rediscovers a childhood romance, through scenes of satirical analysis of the social snobs, religious bigots, and capitalist cutthroats of England. More sympathetic is ambitious Uncle Teddy, who makes a fortune with Tono-Bungay, a bogus medicine, and launches a disastrous career in the "romance of modern commerce." George Ponderevo is more a master of his destiny than is Kipps. After the collapse of his uncle's financial empire, George turns to engineering as a means of commitment to scientific objectivity. He is beyond society and governments, as he is alone in the world of love.

Science triumphs over socialism and capitalism in *Tono-Bungay*, while individual vitality triumphs over all ideas in *The History of Mr. Polly*, another of Wells's best comic novels from his middle period. This story begins with a discontented middle-aged shopkeeper, Mr. Polly, contemplating his boredom, indigestion, and proud misuse of English. He decides to burn his shop and cut his throat. Having succeeded in his arson but having forgotten to cut his throat, he deserts his wife for happy obscurity as a fat woman's handyman, forgetting the life he detested. Although Mr. Polly is an absurd creature, surrounded by stupid, unambitious people, he is sympathetic because he rebels against that absurdity and stupidity. Wells rewards Mr. Polly well for his rebellion.

Ann Veronica · Wells also rewards the heroine of his infamous novel *Ann Veronica*, which takes up more fully themes of free love and women's rights. Ann Veronica Stanley rebels against her father's authority and flees to London, where she attends university lectures in biology. Having thrown herself into the cause of women's suffrage, she is arrested and imprisoned. Then she elopes with her biology instructor, a married man, to Switzerland. This unconventional woman, however, receives a very conventional reward: She marries her lover, has children, and becomes reconciled with her father.

Having put new ideas into old literary forms with *Ann Veronica*, Wells set the direction of his writing for the rest of his life. In his later novels, ideas, argument, debate, and intellectual analysis become prominent, often at the expense of literary form. Feminist causes give way to issues of world peace in books dealing with the world wars, the one that was and the one to come. *Mr. Britling Sees It Through* is one of the best, though it is a troubling confusion of political despair and comic resignation. Touches of good humor keep the book going with scenes of absurdity, as when

Mr. Britling tries to drive his car or Mr. Direck tries to understand British manners. This good humor erodes, however, under the pressure of the events of World War I. Mr. Britling's son is killed, his children's German tutor also is killed, and his private secretary is terribly wounded. The war nearly destroys Mr. Britling, but he sees it through, clinging to a religious hope of divine struggle through human suffering. He commits himself to the cause of world peace, but in the course of writing a letter to the German parents of his children's tutor, he gradually gives way to outrage against Germany and finally collapses in grief. The novel ends when Mr. Britling gets up from his writing to look out his window at the sunrise.

Such an ending hints of an uncertainty in Wells's own commitment to hope. His novels analyze the dead end of civilization and call for redirection through peaceful applications of scientific discoveries. Wells's bitterness at the barbarism of World War I emerges again in *Mr. Blettsworthy on Rampole Island*, whose hero, driven by an unhappy love affair and a failing business, travels to forget. This is one of Wells's most interesting later works, combining anthropology and psychology with experimentation in form. Mr. Blettsworthy's experience with cannibals on Rampole Island may be a fantasy of his madness or an insight into reality, but his experience on the battlefield of World War I is a plunge into an all-too-real madness. Blettsworthy's romantic life of optimism finally yields to a cynical discontent with reality. His perspective is not, however, Wells's final word, since Blettsworthy's business partner, Lyulph Graves, speaks at the end for a philosophy of "creative stoicism," like the attitude which is assumed by Mr. Britling and, perhaps, by Wells himself. Certainly there were differing points of view in Wells's imagination. These differences may express intellectual confusion, but they gave substance to his fiction and saved it from succumbing utterly to his tendency to preach.

The Autocracy of Mr. Parham · The opposition of Blettsworthy and Graves is repeated in the relationship of Mr. Parham with Sir Bussy Woodcock in *The Autocracy of Mr. Parham*, which envisions a time when humankind might destroy itself through another barbarous world war. Mr. Parham voices the Fascist call (by Benito Mussolini) to traditional discipline and order as a way to prevent self-destruction; Sir Bussy expresses suspicion of dictatorship, social discipline, and intellectual utopias. Wells employs an entertaining device for exposing the differences between his protagonists: He brings them into a fantasy of the future as the result of a séance.

Possessed by a Nietzschean force calling itself the "Master Spirit," Mr. Parham's ego is loosed upon the world as the British dictator Lord Paramount. He goes to war with the United States and Germany, aiming for Russia, but he cannot command the obedience of Sir Bussy, who refuses to use a powerful new gas to destroy the opposition. After the séance, Mr. Parham discovers that Sir Bussy has had a dream very much like his own fantasy. Wells's use of comic irony is very strong in the conclusion, as Mr. Parham is deflated by Sir Bussy's plans to preach peace through the very means by which Mr. Parham had hoped to reach the world himself: journalism. Mr. Parham is a smug intellectual who knows where the world ought to go, if it would only follow his instructions; Sir Bussy is a muddled businessman, limited by the contingencies of immediate events and satisfied with the disorganized vitality that distresses Mr. Parham. This difference between creative capitalism and intellectual autocracy is imaged as a difference in personalities caught in a play of life's ironies.

Wells's scientific romances display an optimistic hope for a future made better by scientific discoveries, countered by the pessimistic doubt that humankind could make the necessary choices for social and political progress. Wells shows sympathy and scorn for the stunted characters of his middle novels, for Kipps, George Ponderevo, and Mr. Polly; he exposes their inadequacies, largely as products of a narrow, stultifying environment, but he also rescues them in life-affirming conclusions. Finally, between the great wars, H. G. Wells, like his Mr. Britling, "saw it through," exercised the "creative stoicism" of Lyulph Graves, and occasionally managed to rise above his pamphleteering style to produce entertaining novels of lives muddled by uncertainty, conflict, and contradiction.

Richard D. McGhee

Other major works

SHORT FICTION: *The Stolen Bacillus and Other Incidents*, 1895; *The Plattner Story and Others*, 1897; *Thirty Strange Stories*, 1897; *Tales of Space and Time*, 1899; *The Vacant Country*, 1899; *Twelve Stories and a Dream*, 1903; *The Country of the Blind and Other Stories*, 1911; *A Door in the Wall and Other Stories*, 1911; *The Short Stories of H. G. Wells*, 1927; *The Favorite Short Stories of H. G. Wells*, 1937.

NONFICTION: *Text-Book of Biology*, 1893 (2 volumes); *Honours Physiography*, 1893 (with Sir Richard A. Gregory); *Certain Personal Matters*, 1897; *A Text-Book of Zoology*, 1898 (with A. M. Davis); *Anticipations of the Reaction of Mechanical and Scientific Progress upon Human Life and Thought*, 1902 (also known as *Anticipations*); *The Discovery of the Future*, 1902; *Mankind in the Making*, 1903; *A Modern Utopia*, 1905; *Socialism and the Family*, 1906; *The Future in America: A Search After Realities*, 1906; *This Misery of Boots*, 1907; *New Worlds for Old*, 1908; *First and Last Things: A Confession of Faith and Rule of Life*, 1908; *The Great State: Essays in Construction*, 1912 (also known as *Socialism and the Great State*); *The War That Will End War*, 1914; *An Englishman Looks at the World: Being a Series of Unrestrained Remarks upon Contemporary Matters*, 1914 (also known as *Social Forces in England and America*); *God, the Invisible King*, 1917; *The Outline of History: Being a Plain History of Life and Mankind*, 1920; *Russia in the Shadows*, 1920; *The Salvaging of Civilization*, 1921; *A Short History of the World*, 1922; *Socialism and the Scientific Motive*, 1923; *The Open Conspiracy: Blue Prints for a World Revolution*, 1928; *Imperialism and the Open Conspiracy*, 1929; *The Science of Life: A Summary of Contemporary Knowledge About Life and Its Possibilities*, 1929-1930 (with Julian S. Huxley and G. P. Wells); *The Way to World Peace*, 1930; *What Are We to Do with Our Lives?*, 1931 (revised edition of *The Open Conspiracy*); *The Work, Wealth, and Happiness of Mankind*, 1931 (2 volumes); *After Democracy: Addresses and Papers on the Present World Situation*, 1932; *Evolution, Fact and Theory*, 1932 (with Huxley and G. P. Wells); *Experiment in Autobiography: Discoveries and Conclusions of a Very Ordinary Brain Since 1866*, 1934 (2 volumes); *The New America: The New World*, 1935; *The Anatomy of Frustration: A Modern Synthesis*, 1936; *World Brain*, 1938; *The Fate of Homo Sapiens: An Unemotional Statement of the Things That Are Happening to Him Now and of the Immediate Possibilities Confronting Him*, 1939; *The New World Order: Whether It Is Obtainable, How It Can Be Attained, and What Sort of World a World at Peace Will Have to Be*, 1940; *The Common Sense of War and Peace: World Revolution or War Unending?*, 1940; *The Conquest of Time*, 1942; *Phoenix: A Summary of the Inescapable Conditions of World Reorganization*, 1942; *Science and the World Mind*, 1942; *Crux Ansata: An Indictment of the Roman Catholic Church*, 1943; *'42 to '44: A Contemporary Memoir upon Human Behaviour During the Crisis of the World Revolution*, 1944; *Mind at the End of Its Tether*, 1945.

CHILDREN'S LITERATURE: *The Adventures of Tommy*, 1929.

Bibliography

Bergonzi, Bernard. *The Early H. G. Wells: A Study of the Scientific Romances.* Manchester, England: University Press, 1961. Bergonzi examines Wells's *fin de siècle* milieu and analyzes the scientific romances to *The First Men in the Moon*; he concludes that the early writings deserve recognition. Includes a bibliography, an appendix providing texts of "A Tale of the Twentieth Century" and "The Chronic Argonauts," notes, and an index.

Costa, Richard Hauer. *H. G. Wells.* Rev. ed. Boston: Twayne, 1985. A sympathetic survey of Wells's career and influence, with an emphasis on the major novels in the context of literary traditions before and after Wells. A chronology, a review of contemporary trends in Wells criticism, notes, an annotated bibliography, and an index strengthen this helpful book.

Hammond, J. R. *An H. G. Wells Chronology.* New York: St. Martin's Press, 1999. A guide to Well's life and work. Includes bibliographical references and an index.

_____. *An H. G. Wells Companion.* New York: Barnes & Noble, 1979. Part 1 describes Wells's background and his literary reputation. Part 2 is an alphabetical listing and annotation of every title Wells published. Part 3 provides succinct discussions of his short stories; part 4 contains a brief discussion of book-length romances, and part 5 addresses individual novels. Part 6 is a key to characters and locations. There is also an appendix on film versions of Wells's fiction and a bibliography. An indispensable tool for the Wells scholar.

Haynes, Roslynn D. *H. G. Wells: Discoverer of the Future.* London: Macmillan, 1980. This is a thorough study of the influence of science on Wells's fiction and sociological tracts. It shows how science helped Wells to achieve an analytical perspective on the problems of his time, from art to philosophy. A bibliography and an index follow notes for the text.

Huntington, John, ed. *Critical Essays on H. G. Wells.* Boston: G. K. Hall, 1991. Essays on his major writings, including *Tono-Bungay* and *The History of Mr. Polly*, as well as discussions of his science fiction and his treatment of social change, utopia, and women. Includes an introduction but no bibliography.

Smith, David C. *H. G. Wells: Desperately Mortal: A Biography.* New Haven: Yale University Press, 1986. The most scholarly biography of Wells, covering, with authority, every aspect of his life and art. Includes very detailed notes and bibliography.

Paul West

Born: Eckington, England; February 23, 1930

Principal long fiction · *A Quality of Mercy*, 1961; *Tenement of Clay*, 1965; *Alley Jaggers*, 1966; *I'm Expecting to Live Quite Soon*, 1970; *Caliban's Filibuster*, 1971; *Bela Lugosi's White Christmas*, 1972; *Colonel Mint*, 1972; *Gala*, 1976; *The Very Rich Hours of Count von Stauffenberg*, 1980; *Rat Man of Paris*, 1986; *The Place in Flowers Where Pollen Rests*, 1988; *Lord Byron's Doctor*, 1989; *The Women of Whitechapel and Jack the Ripper*, 1991; *Love's Mansion*, 1992; *The Tent of Orange Mist*, 1995; *Sporting with Amaryllis*, 1996; *Terrestrials*, 1997; *Life with Swan*, 1999; *The Dry Danube: A Hitler Forgery*, 2000; *O.K.: The Corral, the Earps, and Doc Holliday*, 2000.

Other literary forms · Paul West is a remarkably prolific novelist whose literary interests also include poetry, criticism, and other nonfiction. In addition to his books of verse, *Poems* (1952), *The Spellbound Horses* (1960), and *The Snow Leopard* (1964), West has published memoirs: *I, Said the Sparrow* (1963) recounts his childhood in Derbyshire; *Words for a Deaf Daughter* (1969), one of West's most popular works, poignantly relates the experiences of his deaf daughter, Mandy; and *Out of My Depths: A Swimmer in the Universe* (1983) describes the author's determination to learn to swim at middle age. His short stories were collected in *The Universe and Other Fictions* in 1988. Besides his numerous essays and book reviews in dozens of periodicals, journals, and newspapers, West has published *The Growth of the Novel* (1959), *Byron and the Spoiler's Art* (1960), *The Modern Novel* (1963), *Robert Penn Warren* (1964), *The Wine of Absurdity: Essays in Literature and Consolation* (1966), and a series of books entitled *Sheer Fiction* (vol. 1, 1987; vol. 2, 1991; vol. 3, 1994). *A Stroke of Genius: Illness and Self-Discovery* was published in 1995, and *The Secret Lives of Words* was published in 2000.

Achievements · When West arrived on the literary scene as a novelist, he was regarded as an author who possessed a compelling voice but also as one who wrote grotesque and verbally complex fictions. The unevenness of critical reaction cannot overshadow, however, the regard with which serious readers have approached his work, and a list of his fellowships and awards clearly indicates a writer of significant stature: He is the recipient of a Guggenheim Fellowship (1962), a *Paris Review* Aga Kahn Prize for Fiction (1974), the National Endowment for the Humanities Summer Stipend for science studies (1975), the National Endowment for the Arts Fellowship in Creative Writing (1980), the Hazlett Memorial Award for Excellence in the Arts (1981), the American Academy and Institute of Arts and Letters Award in Literature (1985), and a National Endowment for the Arts Fellowship in Fiction (1985). In 1998 the French government decorated him Chevalier of the Order of Arts and Letters. Besides teaching at Pennsylvania State University from 1962 to 1995, West was a visiting professor and writer-in-residence at numerous American universities. As his fiction developed, West showed himself to be a highly imaginative, experimental, and linguistically sophisticated writer. Critics usually commend him for his original style and note the striking diversity of his oeuvre.

Biography · Paul Noden West was born in Eckington, Derbyshire, on February 23, 1930, one of two children, into a working-class family. After attending local elementary and grammar schools, West went to Birmingham University, then to Lincoln College, Oxford, and in 1952 to Columbia University on a fellowship. Although profoundly attracted to New York life, West was forced to return to England to fulfill his military service in the Royal Air Force and there began his writing career. Once he concluded his service, West taught English literature at the Memorial University of Newfoundland, wrote a volume of poems, and did considerable work for the Canadian Broadcasting Corporation. In 1962 he was awarded a Guggenheim Fellowship and returned to the United States, where he took up permanent residence. He was a member of the English and comparative literature faculties at Pennsylvania State University from 1962 to 1995, dividing his time each year between teaching and writing in New York. Upon his retirement, he devoted himself to writing and guest lectureships at Goucher College, University of Miami, Cornell University, and the United States Air Force Academy. He prefers the United States to England, and he has become an American citizen.

Analysis · Paul West has long insisted that what is most important to him as a writer is the free play of the imagination. What the imagination invents, he contends, becomes something independent and actual. West himself states the case most clearly when noting that "elasticity, diversity, openness, these are the things that matter to me most." Thus his fictions often revolve, both thematically and structurally, around the interplay between the individual and his or her imagination and an absurd, threatening universe. Often these fictions rely heavily upon dreams of one sort or another, with characters living in their dreams or living out their dreams or becoming confused about where dreams leave off and the world begins.

Consequently, West's fictions often abound with a sense of precariousness as characters who are constrained in one form or another struggle to free themselves and find their places in the world. Sanity frequently becomes the central issue in these lives, with protagonists taking on the forces of conventionality in their private wars with the drab and mundane. Typical West heroes are outsiders, often marginal or largely inconsequential figures, who will not or cannot conform to the forces about them and who, in striking out on their own, pay steep prices for their individuality.

A Quality of Mercy · *A Quality of Mercy*, West's first novel and a work which he largely disowns, deals with a collection of embittered and failed lives overseen by Camden Smeaton, the novel's central consciousness. The novel is otherwise unmemorable except insofar as it anticipates concerns West more successfully developed in later novels: alienation, immersion in dream and illusion, the idea of an irrational universe, and the use of stylistic fragmentation.

Tenement of Clay · On the other hand, *Tenement of Clay*, West's second novel, stands as a far more accomplished work, controlled, stylistically inventive, morally probing. Here West introduces the reader to the voices of two narrators, each of whom is compelling and unique. The work is divided into three chapters, the two shortest forming a frame offered by Pee Wee Lazarus, a dwarf wrestler whose direct idiom immediately assaults the reader and demands his attention. His desire is to "involve" the reader in his tale, a story that revolves around Papa Nick, narrator of the middle section, who along with Lazarus meets a taciturn giant he names Lacland. Lacland appears to have no home or clear destination, so Nick takes him back to his rooms, where Nick presides over a private flophouse for local bums. Kept in the darkened basement, Lacland soon develops, under Lazarus's perverse tutelage, a sexual appetite and his own abusive language. After a series of horrible misadventures, Lacland reverts to his despondency and silence and eventually becomes Nick's legal ward.

All these events, extreme and dramatic as they may appear, actually operate as a backdrop to Nick's personal turmoil. For years he has carried on a fitful relationship with Venetia, a former film actress, who exhorts him to abandon his altruism toward the derelicts and to run off with her to a life of leisure. When Nick physically collapses from the burden of Lacland and Lazarus's escapades, Venetia nurses him back to health, leaves him when he returns to his bums, and dies in a car crash in Florida.

The novel's soul comes in the form of Nick's constant ruminations, which offer a way of coping with and sometimes solving the dilemmas of his existence. Gradually the line between straight narration and Nick's hallucinations begins to dissolve; the two become one, and the reader learns something fundamental about this world: Dream and reality invade each other; there is no escaping one for the other.

The novel is furthermore important for the moral questions it raises. Perhaps the most telling of these involves one's responsibilities to other human beings; in particular terms, is Nick responsible for the lives he admits into his home? As Lacland and Lazarus demonstrate, Nick has assumed the role of a Dr. Frankenstein and created his own monsters, whom he has unwittingly unleashed upon the world. Is the answer to this dilemma incarceration? Lacland's temporary internment in the basement suggests that it is not.

For Nick, these are the questions that finally come with life itself, and his failure to arrive at any fixed solution suggests a form of authorial honesty about the complexity of modern existence. In this context, the epigraph from Samuel Beckett makes sense: "If there were only darkness, all would be clear. It is because there is not only darkness but also light that our situation becomes inexplicable."

The novel's title comes from a passage in John Dryden's *Absalom and Achitophel* (1681-1682), and certainly the images of tenements abound in the work: all the buildings in this metropolis Lazarus calls New Babylon, especially Nick's flophouse, the grave into which Venetia is lowered, and the human body itself, which contains and in many cases entraps the spirit. In their concerns with their corporeal selves, most of these characters miss the important questions Nick poses throughout. Life, then, amounts to inhabiting one vast tenement, and the point is never escape, but how one chooses to live that life.

Alley Jaggers · With his next novel, *Alley Jaggers*, West moved even further into depicting a consciousness at odds with the rest of the world. Alley is as compelling a narrator as Lazarus or Nick, and like them he speaks in a language that is distinct and unique, an idiom that oddly combines Irish brogue, Midlands accent, and personal argot.

Alley is a profoundly frustrated little man who realizes that his job and marriage are unfulfilling but who has no idea how to remedy his situation. He spends his most satisfying moments dreaming of horses and the elaborate names owners concoct for them and creating airplanes in his attic retreat. Alley wants desperately to make an impression of some kind, and one of his creations, an androgynous, semihuman form emitting a silent scream, both intrigues his fellow workers and stands as an effigy of his own condition.

Eventually his boredom and frustration explode into violence when he accidentally kills a young woman during an unsuccessful sexual tryst. In fear and confusion,
he wraps her body in plaster and makes a companion for his own statue. When the
police inevitably discover the body, Alley has finally and inadvertently stumbled into
prominence: In the police he finds his first willing audience in years.

West's purpose here is far more sophisticated than the old cliché of the criminal as
artist or as misunderstood noble creature. Instead, Alley represents the alienated
individual, the small person cut off from any meaningful existence who struggles in
hopeless confusion to make his life somehow mean something. Unfortunately, Alley
is locked in the prison of himself, both convict and jailer at once, and remains in
fundamental confusion about what to do. Nevertheless, his most vital moments are
spent in his imagination, which is infinitely more extravagant and vital than his
quotidian existence.

I'm Expecting to Live Quite Soon · The second novel in the Jaggers trilogy, *I'm
Expecting to Live Quite Soon*, represents an entirely different turn in West's career. Here
he not only shifts his attention from Alley to his much maligned wife, Dot, but also
creates a more controlled, straightforward type of narrative. The real daring in this
work comes in West's attempt to enter the consciousness of a woman, to take the same
world of the first novel and shift the perspective to see through the eyes of another
member of the family.

Where Alley was frustrated and irresponsible to anyone outside himself, Dot lives
a life of devotion and caring: attending to Alley's irascible mother, ministering to her
dying father in a nursing home, and visiting Alley in the mental hospital. Like Alley,
she needs a release from boredom and conventionality, which eventually she achieves
through immersion in her sensual self. The measure of her change can be seen in her
eventual decision to throw over her old life and run away to Birmingham with
Jimsmith Williams, a black bus-driver.

Bela Lugosi's White Christmas · *Bela Lugosi's White Christmas*, the final volume in the
trilogy, finds Alley (now referred to as AJ) in analysis with Dr. Withington (With) in
a state institution. Who is counseling whom becomes vague as With is drawn increasingly into AJ's fractured mind, and the two eventually reverse roles, thus effecting AJ's
temporary freedom and With's incarceration.

More than any of the previous novels, this one dramatically stakes its claim to
stylistic and linguistic experimentation. Attempting to enter AJ's mind as fully as
possible, West fashions one of his densest, most verbally complex fictions. While the
reader is often at a loss to understand the exact meaning of many passages, what one
does comprehend is AJ's indefatigable desire to experience as much as he can as
quickly as he can. The result is criminal melee with AJ commandeering a bulldozer
and digging up graves in search of his dead father, threatening customers in a bar,
sodomizing and murdering a cow, covering himself with the animal's blood and
sawdust, and starting a fire in a factory near his mother's home.

AJ's immersion in his own mind becomes so complete that, like a Beckett character, he reaches a state of almost total silence by the end of the novel. Once again, West
examines the line between madness and sanity, originality and convention, but like
all of his fictions, the work is no polemic; AJ is neither saint nor hopelessly depraved
misanthrope but a tortured human being who desperately wants "a bit of individuality." The work is also significant for the fact that West actually intrudes on the fiction

in spots, first in a long footnote in which he explains the eccentricities of his characters' names and ends by noting that "in this text, optical illusion is empirically sound," and later in another footnote announcing his own presence throughout the narrative. The point in both cases is to assert artifice as a fictional construct: Fictions are both stories about people and about fiction itself.

Caliban's Filibuster · West deals with some of these same concerns in *Caliban's Filibuster*, the novel that was published immediately before *Bela Lugosi's White Christmas*. This work represents West at his most experimentally extreme as he takes his deepest plunge into an individual's consciousness. Cal, the narrator, is yet another of West's profoundly frustrated protagonists, in this case a failed novelist-cum-screenwriter who chafes at bastardizing his talent for decidedly mercenary ends. As he travels over the Pacific Ocean with his companions Murray McAndrew, a ham actor, and Sammy Zeuss, a crass film producer and Cal's employer, voices representing various of Cal's divided selves carry on endless debates about his artistic aspirations. Thus the reader is not only taken fully into the character's mind but also given access to the dimensions of his troubled psyche.

To appease these voices and satisfy himself, Cal concocts three separate yet interdependent scenarios in which he and his companions play significant roles. In creating these tales, Cal attempts to convince himself of his abused talent and also to distance himself from his experience, like a viewer before a screen in a theater watching versions of his own life. Like Caliban, his Shakespearean namesake in *The Tempest* (1611), Cal seethes with revenge, cursing those who control him. On his behalf, however, readers must regard his filibuster as an attempt to retain his individuality, which he sees as being eroded by the sterile conventions of his profession.

One way to view the novel is as West's paean to language itself, for it abounds in extravagant verbal complexities: anagrams, puns, malapropisms, acronyms, rhymes, and alphabet games. Language operates not only as Cal's professional tool but also as his saving grace; it literally keeps him sane, affording him the diversity of experience that the world denies. Like so many of West's heroes, Cal feels himself trapped, contained by forces which inexorably press against and threaten to destroy him. Language becomes his one potent defense.

Colonel Mint · In *Colonel Mint*, West operated from a seemingly straightforward, but by no means uncomplicated, premise: An astronaut in space claims that he has seen an angel. Whether he has or not is beside the point; instead, the fact that he *thinks* he has and that others want to disabuse him of this belief becomes the subject of this alternately humorous and morally serious work. For his comment Mint is shunted off to the hinterlands of Washington State and is forced to undergo endless hours of interrogation. If he recants he can go free; otherwise, he must indefinitely remain a prisoner of the space program.

The more Mint refuses to cooperate, the more clever and depraved the methods used against him become. After threats, physical beatings, and sexual sadism fail to make Mint waver, his tormentor, General Lew R., begins–like Dr. With in *Bela Lugosi's White Christmas*–gradually to assume Mint's point of view. He wonders what it would be like to see an angel, what exactly an angel is, and finally he accepts, though he cannot empirically confirm, that Mint has seen an angel.

When the two men escape from the interrogation compound for the wilds of the surrounding woods, it appears they have defeated the forces of conformity and conventional thinking. As is the case in so many of West's fictions, however, those forces track the characters down and exact payment: Lew R. is shot and Mint is frozen. Thus, in this novel, to assert one's individuality becomes tantamount to political treason, and the response of the state is swift, final, and utterly unforgiving.

Stylistically the novel is far more straightforward than *Caliban's Filibuster*, but in at least one important respect it recalls a feature of *Bela Lugosi's White Christmas.* The tone of the novel, for all of its physical and psychological horror, is remarkably level, often nonchalant and conversational. Here the narrator, not necessarily the author, addresses the audience directly a number of times. For example, early in the work, when the reader begins to doubt the plausibility of Mint's abduction, the narrator anticipates one's objections by remarking, "You might ask, now, where is the humanity in all this; where sweet reason went. . . ." The effect here and later in the work, when the intrusions continue, is one of complicity; the audience cannot remain at the safe distance of voyeur but must participate, psychologically and emotionally, in the events that transpire. The forces of conformity involve everyone, and the audience becomes uncomfortably aware of this throughout the narrative.

Gala · In *Gala,* West extends the range of his experimentation but also returns to some familiar territory as he develops fictionally the situation described in *Words for a Deaf Daughter.* Here, novelist and amateur astronomer Wight Deulius and his deaf child Michaela construct a model of the Milky Way in their basement. The reader takes a stellar journey through the universe, moving increasingly toward what appear to be the limits of the imagination.

What is especially intriguing about this work is the form West's experimentation takes. Recalling the practice of earlier novels, but especially *Caliban's Filibuster*, West fashions a unique structure for the fiction. Where in the latter work he relies upon the International Date Line and the color spectrum (different sections of the novel are devoted primarily to different colors), in *Gala* elements of physics and the genetic code symbols offer the pattern for the story. West explains this practice when remarking, "I am a compulsive exotic and structural opportunist. I have no idea what structures I will choose next—although I do feel that they will probably be from nature rather than from society."

The Very Rich Hours of Count von Stauffenberg · In his ninth novel, *The Very Rich Hours of Count von Stauffenberg,* West once again shifted focus and style to re-create the details of one of Adolf Hitler's would-be assassins. The novel represents the best in historical fiction, a seemingly effortless blending of fact, elaboration, and pure fantasy, with the result that history becomes for the reader felt experience rather than a catalog of dry, distant details. As West points out in a preface, Stauffenberg is important not only for his public persona but also as someone whose military experience recapitulates, to greater or lesser degrees, that of West's father and all those who lived through World War II. Thus the reader comes to understand an important feature of this writer's fiction, which he expresses as follows: "Whatever I'm writing evinces the interplay between it and my life at the moment of writing, and the result is prose which, as well as being narrative and argumentative and somewhat pyrotechnical, is also symptomatic."

While the narrative, on the surface, seems markedly different from the novels which immediately precede it, one can also see characteristic West concerns emerging. For example, most of the novel places the audience squarely in Stauffenberg's mind as he copes with his war wounds, struggles to express the abiding love he feels for his wife and family, ponders the responsibilities that come with his social and military class, and rages increasingly at the psychopathic perversity of Hitler, the displaced paperhanger. West manages to avoid the obvious trap of the revisionist historian who might be tempted to make Stauffenberg into a martyr or saint. Instead, he emerges as a deeply committed, idealistic man but also one whose psyche is profoundly bruised and disturbed by the events of which he finds himself a part.

The structure of this novel is also just as experimental as that of earlier novels. West had been reading a number of medieval books of hours, lay breviaries that offer devotional prayers alongside richly illuminated paintings. Stauffenberg's rich hours are the last thirty-six of his life; the novel, however, does not stop with his execution. West imaginatively allows the count to speak to the audience from the grave, becoming, then, the most authoritative and omniscient of narrators describing those turbulent last months of the Third Reich.

Rat Man of Paris · *Rat Man of Paris*, his most popular novel, found West exploring yet again the effects of the Third Reich on the life of yet another alienated, marginal figure, in this case a boulevardier of modern Paris who spends his time accosting passersby with a rat he conceals in his overcoat. Étienne Poulsifer, the rat man, has survived the Nazi occupation and destruction of his childhood village, and he carries about with him the emotional and psychological baggage of his horrifying past, as well as the rats which serve as metaphor for that growing legacy.

When he learns of Klaus Barbie's extradition to France, Poulsifer confuses him with the Nazi commander responsible for his parents' death and goes on a personal campaign to become the conscience of an entire nation. Watching all this is Sharli Bandol, Rat Man's lover, who desperately tries to bring some order and love into the chaos of his condition. The birth of a son appears to temper Poulsifer's extremism, but to the end he retains his eccentricity and thus his individuality.

Like *The Very Rich Hours of Count von Stauffenberg*, *Rat Man of Paris* carefully examines the interplay between personal and public trauma, and as West puts it, "Everybody who's born gets the ontological shock, and some people get the historical shock as well, and he has both. Because he has the historical shock, he has the ontological shock even worse, and this has blighted his life." Thus the rat man stands as a contemporary Everyman, radically imperfect, overwhelmed by the world in which he finds himself, but tenaciously determined to make something of his existence.

Also like other of West's protagonists, Poulsifer demonstrates the vitality of the creative imagination. Were it not for his wild musings, the delight he takes in yoking utterly disparate things together in his mind, he would be consumed by history and dreary conventionality. In many ways he is the last free man, an essential primitive who refuses the definitions and restrictions of others for a life created on his own terms.

Terrestrials · West's seventeenth novel, *Terrestrials*, was actually a story over which he had labored for twenty years or more. It involves a pair of American pilots flying a secret reconnaissance jet over Africa. During one routine flight, they are forced to eject over the Danakili Desert. One of the men is put to work by members of a local tribe in the grueling duties of a salt-mining crew, while the other is stranded in his ejection capsule on the ledge of a nearby mountain. Miraculously they are both rescued, ferried off to Turkey, and "debriefed" by junior officers they despise who question their loyalty. They are then returned to the United States and are kept on a base for more questioning. Eventually they escape, open an air touring business, and evade an assassination attempt.

On the surface the plot may seem confusing and unspectacular; however, plotting is neither the novel's primary concern nor the source of its achievement. The novel is a bold attempt to evince some of what two minds undergo as a result of life-altering trauma. Each is oppressed with guilt, feeling that he has betrayed the other, and although the two are not actually friends, they are devoted to and dependent upon each other. They grow closer as a result of their shared experience. In many ways the novel can be seen as a paean to friendship and near-filial devotion, and it asserts the intimate interconnectedness of all life.

Life with Swan · Another intimate portrait can be found in *Life with Swan*, a *roman à clef* about West's early courtship and years with his spouse of more than twenty years, poet and naturalist Diane Ackerman (an anagram of her name—Ariada Mencken—is used for the female character's). Set in the 1970's, the novel follows a middle-aged professor as he falls in love with a younger woman, against the advice of many of his friends and colleagues. The two begin a life that saves him from his excesses. Their mutual fascination with astronomy develops into a full-blown passion and culminates with their being witnesses, at the behest of Raoul Bunsen (a character who is an echo of cosmologist Carl Sagan), to the launches of the Viking spacecraft to Mars and the Voyager to Jupiter. If *Terrestrials* is a paean to friendship, *Life with Swan* is a companion piece that examines and glorifies the saving grace of unselfish love. The prose is lush and extravagant, every page lovingly adorned with West's incomparable lyricism.

Throughout his career, West has drawn criticism for his own stylistic eccentricities and rich verbal texturings. The usual complaint holds that he is self-indulgent and willfully obscure. While indeed his fiction makes considerable demands of his audience, he is anything but deliberately perverse or obscure. In fact, West consistently attempts to reach and communicate with his audience, to involve them, in each of his rich fictional stories. His note at the beginning of *Tenement of Clay*, the interview appended to *Caliban's Filibuster*, the footnotes in *Bela Lugosi's White Christmas*, the moments of direct address in *Colonel Mint*, the announcement in the middle of *Gala* of the novel's particular structure, and the preface to *The Very Rich Hours of Count von Stauffenberg*—all demonstrate that West is fully aware of his audience and always desirous of its sympathetic participation in the fictional experience. West is committed to the proposition that writing matters and that good writing must present its own unique experience. As he says in his essay "In Defense of Purple Prose," "The ideal is to create a complex verbal world that has as much presence, as much apparent physical bulk, as the world around it. . . . This is an illusion, to be sure, but art *is* illusion, and what's needed is an art that temporarily blots out the real."

David W. Madden

Other major works
SHORT FICTION: *The Universe and Other Fictions*, 1988.
POETRY: *Poems*, 1952; *The Spellbound Horses*, 1960; *The Snow Leopard*, 1964.
NONFICTION: *The Growth of the Novel*, 1959; *Byron and the Spoiler's Art*, 1960, 2d ed. 1992; *I, Said the Sparrow*, 1963; *The Modern Novel*, 1963; *Robert Penn Warren*, 1964; *The*

Wine of Absurdity: Essays in Literature and Consolation, 1966; *Words for a Deaf Daughter,* 1969; *Out of My Depths: A Swimmer in the Universe,* 1983; *Sheer Fiction,* 1987; *Portable People,* 1990 (drawings by Joe Servello); *Sheer Fiction,* vol. 2, 1991; *Sheer Fiction,* vol. 3, 1994; *A Stroke of Genius: Illness and Self-Discovery,* 1995; *My Mother's Music,* 1995; *The Secret Lives of Words,* 2000.

EDITED TEXT: *Byron: Twentieth Century Views,* 1963.

Bibliography

Bryfonski, Dedria, and Laurie Lanza Harris, eds. *Contemporary Literary Criticism.* Vol. 14. Detroit: Gale Research, 1980. Contains extracts from reviews of West's works, including *Gala* and *Words for a Deaf Daughter,* from such sources as *The Washington Post, The New York Times Book Review,* and *The Nation.* Most of the reviews are favorable, addressing West's intelligent writing as both an advantage and a disadvantage. One reviewer praises *Words for a Deaf Daughter,* calling it a "sympathetic book for anyone who feels responsible for someone else." Another review describes *Gala* in terms of its "startling, dazzling meditations."

Lucas, John. "Paul West." In *Contemporary Novelists,* edited by James Vinson. London: St. James Press, 1976. Lucas discusses the Alley Jaggers sequence of novels, which "deservedly won his reputation as an original novelist," although he faults them for their lack of psychological study. Mentions West's highly acclaimed study of Lord Byron's poetry and *Bela Lugosi's White Christmas.* Lists West's works up to 1975 and includes a statement by West.

McGuire, Thomas G. "The Face(s) of War in Paul West's Fiction." *War, Literature, and the Arts: An International Journal of the Humanities* 10, no. 1 (Spring/Summer, 1998): 169-186. Traces the persistence of West's rumination on warfare and conflict. Three principal novels—*The Very Rich Hours of Count von Stauffenberg, The Place in Flowers Where Pollen Rests,* and *Rat Man of Paris*—form the basis of the argument. The journal also contains an interview with West and three of the author's short fictions.

Madden, David W. "Indoctrination to Pariahdom: Liminality in the Fiction of Paul West." *Critique* 40, no. 1 (Fall, 1998): 49-70. Examines five of West's novels to explain the confusions and violence found so frequently there. The essay argues that each novel presents characters suspended in a liminal state from which they have difficulties extracting themselves.

_____, ed. *The Review of Contemporary Fiction* 11, no. 1 (Spring, 1991). A special half-issue devoted to West. Contains thirteen essays, an interview, and a primary bibliography of West's work up to *The Women of Whitechapel,* examining his novels from a variety of perspectives. The collection also features three short fictions from West.

_____. *Understanding Paul West.* Columbia: University of South Carolina Press, 1993. A book-length study on West that provides an overview of his work through *The Women of Whitechapel.* Intended as an introductory study to West's life and fiction, it traces the development of the themes of identity, artistic creation, and imagination's freedom.

Pope, Dan. "A Different Kind of Post-Modernism." *The Gettysburg Review* 3, no. 4 (Autumn, 1990): 658-669. Looks at West's 1988 short-story collection, *The Universe and Other Fictions,* in the company of Rick DeMarinis's *The Coming Triumph of the Free World* and T. Coraghessan Boyle's *If the River Was Whiskey.* A fine sustained consideration of West's short fiction.

Saltzman, Arthur M. "Beholding Paul West and *The Women of Whitechapel.*" *Twentieth*

Century Literature: A Scholarly and Critical Journal 40, no. 2 (Summer, 1994): 256-271. Examines West's thirteenth novel in terms of the author's wit and inventive verbal energy and the uneasy balance between ontology and linguistic inventiveness.

West, Paul. "Paul West." In *Contemporary Authors: Autobiography Series,* edited by Mark Zadrozny. Vol. 7. Detroit: Gale Research, 1988. A beautifully written autobiography, filled with rich images and information about West's early life, his ideas about writing, and other writers who became his friends. Includes a bibliography of his works.

T. H. White

Born: Bombay, India; May 29, 1906
Died: Piraeus, Greece; January 17, 1964

Principal long fiction · *Dear Mr. Nixon*, 1931 (with R. McNair Scott); *First Lesson*, 1932 (as James Aston); *They Winter Abroad*, 1932 (as Aston); *Darkness at Pemberley*, 1932; *Farewell Victoria*, 1933; *Earth Stopped: Or, Mr. Marx's Sporting Tour*, 1934; *Gone to Ground*, 1935; *The Sword in the Stone*, 1938; *The Witch in the Wood*, 1939; *The Ill-Made Knight*, 1940; *Mistress Masham's Repose*, 1946; *The Elephant and the Kangaroo*, 1947; *The Master: An Adventure Story*, 1957; *The Candle in the Wind*, 1958; *The Once and Future King*, 1958 (tetralogy; includes *The Sword in the Stone*, *The Witch in the Wood*, *The Ill-Made Knight*, and *The Candle in the Wind*); *The Book of Merlyn: The Unpublished Conclusion to "The Once and Future King,"* 1977.

Other literary forms · T. H. White's first literary productions were two poetry collections. Several short stories enclosed within the satirical frame narrative of *Gone to Ground* were reprinted along with later items in the posthumously issued *The Maharajah and Other Stories* (1981). The majority of White's nonfiction books celebrate his strong interest in field sports; *The Goshawk* (1951), which describes his experiments in falconry, is the most notable. The title of *The Godstone and the Blackymor* (1959) refers to a legendary monument on the island of Inniskea. White also wrote two books on famous scandals, *The Age of Scandal: An Excursion Through a Minor Period* (1950) and *The Scandalmonger* (1952).

Achievements · White labored long and hard in relative obscurity before achieving literary success. His most successful work, *The Sword in the Stone*, was considered by many a children's book. White intended from the very beginning, however, that the story should be the introduction to a comprehensive modern rendering of the Arthurian legend, and the second and third volumes became increasingly adult in their concerns and much darker in their implications. The fourth part languished unpublished for nearly twenty years, but after it was finally revised to form the conclusion of *The Once and Future King* the collection was eventually recognized as a masterpiece of modern fantasy. Even that version lacked the original fifth part, however, which remained unpublished for another nineteen years—thirteen years after the author's death. Although the animated film of *The Sword in the Stone* (1963) and the film version of the *Once and Future King*-based stage musical *Camelot* (1967) have reached a far wider audience than the original novels, the Arthurian sequence can now be seen as a work comparable in ambition and quality to the similar endeavors of fantasy novelist J. R. R. Tolkien.

Biography · Terence Hanbury White was born in Bombay, the son of a district supervisor of police and the grandson of a judge. He spent his first five years on the Indian subcontinent before returning to England with his mother, Constance. His childhood was difficult because Constance—who eventually obtained a judicial separation from her husband but not the divorce that would have allowed her to marry her live-in lover—was mentally disturbed, and White was frightened of her. Removal to Cheltenham College in 1920 provided no relief; mistreatment from classmates maintained his misery, but he still won admission to Queen's College in Cambridge. He might have been happier there were it not for anxieties about his own condition, in which homosexual feelings and alcoholism were further confused by the total loss of his early religious faith and irrepressible sadomasochistic fantasies. As if this were not enough, he contracted tuberculosis while in his second year at Cambridge, and his teachers had to donate money to send him to Italy to convalesce; it was there that he wrote his first novel.

White returned from Italy in much better condition. His determination to stay fit and healthy cemented his interest in field sports, but his triumph over physical frailty was shadowed by an exaggerated awareness of his mortality, which added furious fuel to all his activities. After obtaining a first-class degree with distinction in 1929 he became a schoolmaster for a while—concluding with a four-year stint at one of England's best public schools, Stowe, in 1932-1936, before the autobiographical potboiler *England Have My Bones* (1936) sold well enough to win him a commission to deliver a book every year to his publisher, Collins. He rented a gamekeeper's cottage on the Stowe estate in order to pursue his new career.

Fearful of conscription into a war he desperately did not want to be involved in, White moved to Ireland (which remained neutral throughout World War II) in 1939, lodging in Doolistown in County Meath and at Sheskin Lodge in County Mayo. In these two locations, living as an exile, he wrote the fourth and fifth parts of the Arthurian series, but Collins ended the book-per-year arrangement after issuing *The Ill-Made Knight*; the subsequent hiatus in his career lasted until 1946. In that year he relocated to the Channel Islands, living briefly in Jersey before settling in Aldernay in 1947; he died in his cabin, apparently of heart failure, while on a Mediterranean cruise in 1964.

Analysis · White's first five novels, one of which was written in collaboration with R. McNair Scott and two of which were concealed under the pseudonym James Aston, were all naturalistic. The only one which is now remembered is his nostalgic panorama of the Victorian era, *Farewell Victoria*, which was also the only one not solidly rooted in his own experiences. The first he wrote, *They Winter Abroad*—the third published, under the Aston pseudonym—is of some interest for the insight it offers into his youthful state of mind.

Earth Stopped* and *Gone to Ground · *Earth Stopped* is a satiric comedy paying respectful homage to the works of English novelist Robert Smith Surtees, whose addiction to hunting, shooting, and fishing White shared. White's similarly addicted friend Siegfried Sassoon had introduced him to a reprint of Surtees' 1845 novel *Hillingdon Hall* in 1931. Sassoon's autobiographical novel *Memoirs of a Fox-Hunting Man* (1928) reflects sarcastically on the fact that he had been sent to a sanatorium to save him from a court-martial when he refused to return to the front after being wounded in action in 1917, and his influence on White's attitudes was profound. *Earth Stopped* introduces the inept revolutionary Mr. Marx into a Surtees-like party gathered for a weekend's sport at an English country house. The party remains blithely good humored until the final chapters, when a world war abruptly precipitated by the forces of communism and fascism breaks out, at which point "the universe split open like a pea-pod, informed by lightning but far transcending thunder."

The story continues in *Gone to Ground*, in which the survivors of the house party swap tall tales while they hide from the catastrophe, taking psychological refuge in fantasy while taking physical refuge underground. Although its prophetic pretensions were supposedly impersonal, this provided an ironic metaphorical account of the subsequent shape of White's life and career. The book ends with the conclusion of the final tale–reprinted in *The Maharajah and Other Stories* as "The Black Rabbit"–in which Keeper Pan, who was the inventor of panic as well as the god of nature, asserts his ultimate dominion over the objects of human sport.

The Once and Future King · Anticipation of a new world war, which many imaginative people expected to put an end to civilization, overwhelmed English fantastic fiction in the late 1930's. Other English writers were writing apocalyptic fantasies far more terrifying than *Earth Stopped*, but White decided to go in the opposite direction, becoming a connoisseur of playful escapism. The account of the boyhood and education of Arthur set out in *The Sword in the Stone* is as firmly rooted in personal experience as White's earliest novels are, but it is a calculated magical transformation of the oppressions that afflicted the author and his ultimate redemption from them.

The Sword in the Stone begins with an exotic schoolroom syllabus devised for the future Sir Kay by his governess, who cannot punish her noble student but can and does take out her frustrations on his whipping boy, "the Wart," who is not recognized as the future embodiment of England and the chivalric ideal until he acquires a far more inspiring tutor in Merlyn. The debt that White owed to his tutor at Cambridge and longtime correspondent L. J. Potts is acknowledged in the fact that Merlyn, whose prophetic gifts result from living his life in reverse, actually served as a Cambridge tutor in the twentieth century, which lay in his distant past.

The account of the childhood of Gareth and his brothers contained in *The Witch in the Wood* is far darker–in spite of comic relief provided by the alcoholic lapsed saint Toirdealbhach and King Pellinore's obsessive pursuit of the Questing Beast–because their lustful, neglectful, and unbalanced mother is a transfiguration of White's own. The characterization of Lancelot in *The Ill-Made Knight* probably owes something to Siegfried Sassoon as well as to White's perception of himself, and it is significant that the text explicitly compares the greatest of all the Arthurian knights to one of the great sportsmen of the late 1930's, the Australian cricketer Donald Bradman. Lancelot's obsessive anxiety that his forbidden love for Guenever will sap the strength that makes him England's champion and deny him the chance to find the Holy Grail is a transfiguration of White's anxieties about his homosexuality and terror of military service (both of which were implicated in his decision to live as a recluse as soon as it became economically viable).

Given the deep personal significance of the first three volumes, it is hardly surprising that the dourly harrowing *The Candle in the Wind*, which White wrote in the latter months of 1940, is saturated with his anxiety for the blitzkrieg-devastated England that he had left and the civilization that it represented. He wrote to Potts on December 6, 1940, that he had discovered that "the central theme of the *Morte d'Arthur* is to find an antidote to war." In the fifth volume, Arthur goes underground with his old tutor, and they analyze the dismal failure of the Grail quest and look for a new way forward. While they do so, in *The Book of Merlyn*, they are surrounded by the animals Arthur loved so much as a boy, and Keeper Pan is certainly present in spirit, if not in person. Two key sequences from *The Book of Merlyn* were transposed into the version of *The Sword in the Stone* contained in *The Once and Future King*, and other elements were grafted onto the new version of *The Candle in the Wind* to supply the sense of an ending, but these devices distorted the balance and meaning of the whole, which was not published in its intended form.

J. R. R. Tolkien set out to expand his children's fantasy *The Hobbit* (1937) into an epic at almost exactly the same time White began to elaborate *The Once and Future King*. Tolkien was a Catholic and an Old English scholar who carefully excluded everything that had arrived in Britain with the Norman conquest (1066) from the mythos of his fantastic secondary world, Middle Earth; however, it was precisely that imported tradition of chivalric romance that White chose for the heart of his own exercise. There is, therefore, a curious sense that the two resultant masterpieces of fantasy are as complementary and opposed as the universities of Oxford, which was Tolkien's home, and Cambridge, White's spiritual home, to which he remained anchored by his correspondence with L. J. Potts. One might also compare and contrast *The Once and Future King* with the fantasies of an older Cambridge man who was also troubled by inescapable sadomasochistic fantasies, John Cowper Powys, who eventually followed up the Grail epic *A Glastonbury Romance* (1932) with a more explicit transfiguration of Arthurian myth, *Porius* (1951), which was never issued in its entirety. Powys tackled the problem of designing a mythology for the much-conquered island of Britain by producing his own syncretism of Anglo-Saxon and Anglo-Norman elements with earlier Celtic and Greek myths.

All three of these writers were trying to construct or reconstruct a neomythological epic for an island that had somehow never contrived to produce a real one, which would also embody and allegorize the crisis at which the contemporary British nation had arrived in the pause between World War I and World War II. Of the three, White's is by far the most lighthearted but also—by virtue of its precipitous plunge into tragedy in *The Candle in the Wind*—the most emotional. It is perhaps ironic that Tolkien, who was not nearly as committed to the politics of escapism as White, should have become the parent of a whole genre of escapist fantasy, while White became best known as the inspirer of a Walt Disney film and a musical comedy. Thanks to the University of Texas edition of *The Book of Merlyn*, however, modern readers and critics have the opportunity to reconstruct White's masterpiece as he intended it to be read, and to judge its true worth as an epic for the isle of Britain.

Later novels · The three fantasies that White wrote after he recovered from the disappointment of Collins's initial refusal to publish *The Candle in the Wind* are best regarded as footnotes to the main sequence of his novels, displaying a gradual acceptance of the fact that he was seen as a children's writer. *The Elephant and the Kangaroo* is an allegorical comedy in which an English atheist in Ireland witnesses a visitation by the archangel Michael and sets out to build an ark in response to the threat of an impending second deluge. In *Mistress Masham's Repose*, a young girl discovers descendants of the Lilliputians of Jonathan Swift's *Gulliver's Travels* (1726) living on an island and sets out to defend them from commercial exploitation by Hollywood filmmakers. *The Master* is a science-fiction story for children, whose juvenile heroes thwart the eponymous island-based villain's plans for world domination.

Brian Stableford

Other major works

SHORT FICTION: *The Maharajah and Other Stories*, 1981.

POETRY: *Loved Helen and Other Poems*, 1929; *The Green Bay Tree: Or, The Wicked Man Touches Wood*, 1929.

NONFICTION: *England Have My Bones*, 1936 (autobiography); *The Age of Scandal: An Excursion Through a Minor Period*, 1950 (anecdotes); *The Goshawk*, 1951; *The Scandalmonger*, 1952 (anecdotes); *The Godstone and the Blackymor*, 1959 (autobiography); *America at Last*, 1965 (autobiography).

TRANSLATION: *The Book of Beasts*, 1954 (of medieval bestiary).

Bibliography

Brewer, Elisabeth. *T. H. White's "The Once and Future King."* Cambridge, England: D. S. Brewer, 1993. Examines White's work and other Arthurian romances, historical fiction, and fantastic fiction. Includes bibliography and an index.

Crane, John K. *T. H. White*. New York: Twayne, 1974. A competent overview of White's work. For the beginning student.

Irwin, Robert. "T. H. White." *The St. James Guide to Fantasy Writers*. Detroit: St. James Press, 1996. A good summary account of White's fantasies.

Kellman, Martin. *T. H. White and the Matter of Britain*. Lewiston, N.Y.: E. Mellen Press, 1988. The second volume of a series on the historical novel. Kellman studies the Arthurian legend in detail.

Manlove, C. N. *The Impulse of Fantasy Literature*. Kent, Ohio: Kent State University Press, 1983. The chapter on White carefully relates his work to the book's other subjects and the tradition of British fantasy.

Warner, Sylvia Townsend. *T. H. White: A Biography*. London: Cape/Chatto & Windus, 1967. A sensitive biography, whose central conclusions are summarized in Warner's introduction to *The Book of Merlyn*.

Oscar Wilde

Born: Dublin, Ireland; October 16, 1854
Died: Paris, France; November 30, 1900

Principal long fiction · *The Picture of Dorian Gray*, 1890 (serial), 1891 (expanded).

Other literary forms · Oscar Wilde wrote in a number of literary forms. His earliest works were poems published in various journals and collected in a volume entitled *Poems* in 1881. His later and longer poems, including *The Sphinx* (1894), were occasionally overwrought or contrived, but his final published poem, *The Ballad of Reading Gaol* (1898), is regarded by many as a masterpiece. Wilde wrote two collections of fairy tales, *The Happy Prince and Other Tales* (1888) and *A House of Pomegranates* (1891). He wrote several plays, most notably the comedies *Lady Windermere's Fan* (1892), *A Woman of No Importance* (1893), the successful farce *The Importance of Being Earnest* (1895), and the controversial and temporarily banned *Salomé* (1893). Finally, Wilde wrote a few short stories, including "The Canterville Ghost" (1887) and "Lord Arthur Savile's Crime" (1887).

Achievements · Oscar Wilde's works remain popular a century after his death. This is due in part to the enduring beauty of his poetry and his prose, as well as the timeless insight he offers about art and morality. Wilde's conclusions are presented with such easy elegance and wit that readers enjoy the seduction of the narrative. No doubt Wilde's provocative statements and iconoclastic poses, as well as the notoriety of his trial, helped to immortalize his life and thus to sustain interest in his writings for generations. Wilde received Trinity College's Berkeley Gold Medal for Greek in 1874, and he won the Newdigate Prize for Poetry in 1878.

Biography · Oscar Wilde was born to ambitious, successful Irish parents in Dublin in 1854. As a young man he attended Trinity College, and in 1874 (at age twenty) he entered Magdalen College, Oxford, on a scholarship. Wilde was drawn to art criticism and literature in his studies, and he was strongly influenced by several mentors, most notably writers John Ruskin and Walter Pater. At college Wilde discovered, developed, and began to refine his extraordinary gifts of creativity, analysis, and expression. These he pressed into the service of aestheticism, an iconoclastic artistic movement promoted by Pater, which advocated "the love of art for art's sake." Wilde would come to personify aestheticism, with all its intellectual refinement, provocative posing, and hedonistic excess.

Wilde married Constance Lloyd in 1884 and with her had two sons. Although throughout his short life Wilde evinced great love and devotion to his wife and sons, he grew increasingly involved in sexual liaisons with men. Most notably and tragically, Wilde became engrossed in an obsessive and rocky homosexual friendship with Lord Alfred Douglas, the son of the Marquis of Queensberry. Douglas helped to lead Wilde deeper into London's homosexual underworld. While Douglas at times seemed to genuinely love Wilde, he periodically became impatient, selfish, and abusive toward his older friend. Still, Wilde remained, with increasing recklessness, committed to Douglas.

Library of Congress

During the second half of the 1880's Wilde wrote poems, plays, and stories with increasing success. To a large extent, however, it was his provocative and radical remarks, made at public lectures and at the social functions he so frequently attended, that gained for him sustained public attention. Wilde was a gifted speaker with a keen sense of timing and an ability to lampoon societal standards with his humorous remarks.

The Victorian public's amusement with Wilde's contrarianism turned to contempt in 1895. In this year the Marquis of Queensberry, furious over the writer's continuing relationship with his son, accused Wilde of being a "sodomite." Wilde ill-advisedly sued for libel, maintaining that he was not, in fact, homosexual. The Marquis, to support his claim about Wilde's homosexuality, entered into court various letters and other pieces of evidence. When Queensberry's lawyer was about to produce as witnesses young male prostitutes who had had sexual relations with Wilde, Wilde's lawyer withdrew from the suit. Queensberry was acquitted by the jury. Almost immediately after the trial, Wilde was arrested for violation of England's sodomy laws. By now the public had all but deserted Wilde, and after his conviction even most of his friends disavowed him. Wilde spent two years in prison for his offenses.

Upon his release from prison in 1897 Wilde left England to live in exile, finally locating in Paris. He lived under the alias Sebastian Melmoth, attempting to expunge his notoriety as the humiliated Oscar Wilde. Yet his spirits and his health had been broken by his prison sentence, and Wilde died within three years, at age forty-six.

Analysis · Wilde began his literary efforts with poetry, which was a common approach in his day. He published *Ravenna* in 1878. He would write little poetry after the release of *Poems* in 1881. For the next several years he gave lectures in Europe and America, establishing his name on both sides of the Atlantic. He also assumed the editorship of a monthly magazine, *The Lady's World,* which was rechristened *The Woman's World.*

In the late 1880's Wilde wrote two collections of fairy tales, as well as a number of short stories, essays, and book reviews. He steadily gained attention as a writer, social critic, and, most of all, aesthete. Literary critics frequently were unenthusiastic, or even hostile, toward his works, finding them to be overly contrived or recklessly immoral. It is true that Wilde's writing can at times assume a baroque ornamentation and artificiality. There is no doubt that Wilde's characteristic indolence (which he exaggerated for show) constrained his ability to see his works through to the final stages of editing and polishing. It is true also that Wilde's writing frequently ridiculed social conventions, mores, and morals. Yet Wilde was indisputably an ingenious analyst of art and culture, possessing a mastery of prose and verse, and equipped with a keen sense of paradox.

The Picture of Dorian Gray · Oscar Wilde's only novel was published in its complete form in 1891. It is not a long book, and some of its features reflect the writer's haste or carelessness. However, the story is a fascinating and engaging one, at once depicting basic elements of human nature and conjuring fantastic, almost gothic images. Its plot is rather simple, but the ideas and issues that the narrative presents are complex and even profound. Perhaps for this reason the book has stood the test of time.

The story centers on three figures: an artist (Basil Hallward), his clever but impudent friend (Lord Henry Wotton), and a young, attractive, and impressionable man (Dorian Gray). Basil paints a full-length portrait of young Dorian and presents it to him as a gift. Lord Henry, who meets Dorian for the first time at Basil's studio, talks at length about the supreme value, but transience, of youth. Immediately drawn to Lord Henry's theories, Dorian observes the just-completed portrait of himself and remarks on "how sad it is" that he "shall grow old, and horrible, and dreadful. But this picture will remain always young. . . . If it were only the other way!" In the first section of the book, therefore, Wilde sets up a framework to examine some fundamental ideas about art and beauty: the transience of beauty, the inevitability of aging and death, the goal of the artist to "capture" beauty in art, and the corruptive influence of ideas, among others.

Wilde uses Lord Henry—whom Wilde later declared to be a depiction of how the public perceived Wilde—to provide the corruptive theories and ideas. Throughout the book Lord Henry utters clever aphorisms and paradoxes in Wilde's celebrated wordplay. Dorian is infatuated by Lord Henry and appears receptive to his theories and values. Readers soon see evidence of the corruptive influence of those theories and values in Dorian's behavior. Dorian becomes smitten by a young actress in a seedy theater. He returns with Basil and Lord Henry to watch her perform, but this time he is disappointed by her acting. After the performance the actress declares to Dorian that he has helped her see how false is her world of acting—the false world of the stage—and she declares her love for him. Dorian, however, spitefully dismisses her, claiming that she had thrown away her artistic genius and poetic intellect. Now, she "simply produce(s) no effect."

Upon returning home, Dorian observes a slight change in the portrait Basil had painted of him. Dorian notes a "touch of cruelty in the mouth." It becomes evident that the painting shows the outward signs of sin and of aging, while Dorian himself does not change appearance. Although first horrified by this, Dorian eventually learns to take advantage of the situation. The narrative traces an ever-worsening degradation of Dorian Gray's soul. He lives for sensations and self-gratification, without regard for the consequences of his actions upon others. He is seemingly unbound by any sense of morality—indeed, the very notion of violating moral strictures seems to be an attractive prospect for him. Near the climax of the story Dorian goes so far as to murder Basil.

The story thus raises provocative questions about morality and self-imposed restraint. If a person could be assured that any indulgences, including gluttony, sexual abandon, and avarice, would have no effect upon one's earthly body, would self-control survive? What opportunities and temptations are imposed upon one who possesses unusual and eternal beauty? What is the relationship between virtue and constraint? What are the consequences of unexposed moral degradation? Indeed, what are the causes of immorality?

The Picture of Dorian Gray aroused enormous indignation in Wilde's contemporaries, and it was treated especially harshly by most critics. There seemed to be a consensus that the book itself was immoral, that it could corrupt readers, and that it somehow promoted decadent behavior. Yet one can easily arrive at the opposite conclusion. The story clearly emphasizes the costs of self-indulgent, immoral behavior. It literally shows this in the changes that appear in the painting, which is understood to portray the condition of Dorian's soul. The story also makes a point of noting the harm done to others by Dorian's misbehavior: reputations ruined, hearts broken, suicides induced, murders committed. In no way does the book portray the corruption of Dorian Gray in a glamorous or seductive way. Instead, the effect is to repulse the reader.

The book might be somewhat corruptive in its suggestion that immorality may be less a choice than simply a product of circumstances. We have no reason to believe that Dorian Gray is intrinsically evil; rather, if the book's basic premise that one's soul is normally reflected in one's appearance, then the introduction of Dorian as possessing "youth's passionate purity" conveys the idea that he is especially innocent. Ironically, Wilde himself was accused of corrupting a young man (Lord Alfred

Douglas), and his writings (including *The Picture of Dorian Gray*) were held up as evidence of his dangerous ideas. That Wilde responded that he believed there was no such thing as an immoral book, only a badly written one, compounds the irony.

The fatalistic view of sin (which might be consistent with Wilde's religious upbringing, such as it was) is further evidenced when Dorian is unable to change his course toward the end of the book. He feels his past starting to catch up with him as people he has wronged, or their defenders, begin to identify him and his actions. Resolving to abandon his ways, Dorian decides to do a good deed; he cancels an arranged plan to go off with (and undoubtedly take advantage of) a young female acquaintance. Yet when he subsequently examines the portrait for evidence of his good deed, he detects only a smirk of hypocrisy.

In a conclusion laden with symbolism, Dorian considers his situation hopeless. He reflects that "there [is] a God who called upon men to tell their sins to earth as well as to heaven." Yet he cannot fathom how he could ever confess his sins, and he recognizes that even his attempt to do good sprung from a hypocritical desire to experience new sensations. In desperation, he decides to drive a knife into the loathsome painting, which reflects all his sins. The servants downstairs hear a scream, and when they enter the room they see the portrait, restored to its original beauty, hanging on the wall. Dorian Gray lies on the floor with a knife in his heart, looking just as the figure in the loathsome portrait had moments earlier.

The conclusion creates a striking and stark symmetry, although how it answers the questions raised earlier is unclear. Still, the ending is satisfying in that it allows reality to finally come out of hiding. The parallels to Wilde's life are exceptional. While Wilde noted that the character of the languid iconoclast Lord Henry reflected how people viewed Wilde, he also asserted that it was the artist, Basil, whom Wilde actually resembled, and that it was Dorian himself whom Wilde wanted to be.

Steve D. Boilard

Other major works

SHORT FICTION: "The Canterville Ghost," 1887; *The Happy Prince and Other Tales*, 1888; *The House of Pomegranates*, 1891; *Lord Arthur Savile's Crime and Other Stories*, 1891.

PLAYS: *Vera: Or, The Nihilists*, pb. 1880; *The Duchess of Padua*, pb. 1883; *Lady Windermere's Fan*, pr. 1892; *Salomé*, pb. 1893 (in French), pb. 1894 (in English); *A Woman of No Importance*, pr. 1893; *An Ideal Husband*, pr. 1895; *The Importance of Being Earnest: A Trivial Comedy for Serious People*, pr. 1895; *A Florentine Tragedy*, pr. 1906 (one act; completed by T. Sturge More); *La Sainte Courtisane*, pb. 1908.

POETRY: *Ravenna*, 1878; *Poems*, 1881; *Poems in Prose*, 1894; *The Sphinx*, 1894; *The Ballad of Reading Gaol*, 1898.

NONFICTION: *Intentions*, 1891; *De Profundis*, 1905; *Letters*, 1962 (Rupert Hart-Davies, editor).

MISCELLANEOUS: *Works*, 1908; *Complete Works of Oscar Wilde*, 1948 (Vyvyan Holland, editor); *Plays, Prose Writings, and Poems*, 1960.

Bibliography

Calloway, Stephen, and David Colvin. *Oscar Wilde: An Exquisite Life*. New York: Welcome Rain, 1997. A brief, heavily illustrated presentation of Wilde's life.

Ellmann, Richard. *Oscar Wilde*. New York: Alfred A. Knopf, 1988. A biography of Wilde, drawing much insight from Wilde's published works. The book is extensively documented and footnoted and makes use of many of Wilde's writings and recorded conversations. Includes bibliography and appendices.

Hardwick, Michael. *The Drake Guide to Oscar Wilde.* New York: Drake, 1973. A description, with excerpts, of a number of Wilde's writings. Also includes a brief biography and an alphabetical index of descriptions of the major characters in the stories and plays.

Harris, Frank. *Oscar Wilde.* New York: Carrol and Graf, 1997. A biography written by one of Wilde's dedicated friends. Although hardly an objective work, Harris's book, written in the first person, provides details and insights about Wilde's life that many books do not.

Hyde, H. Montgomery. *Oscar Wilde: A Biography.* New York: Farrar, Straus & Giroux, 1975. Detailed discussion of Wilde's life, with emphasis on his trials and his exile. Many passages in this book draw upon published essays, poems, letters, and even testimony at Wilde's trial. Includes bibliography.

A. N. Wilson

Born: Stone, England; October 27, 1950

Principal long fiction · *The Sweets of Pimlico*, 1977; *Unguarded Hours*, 1978; *Kindly Light*, 1979; *The Healing Art*, 1980; *Who Was Oswald Fish?*, 1981; *Wise Virgin*, 1982; *Scandal*, 1983; *Gentlemen in England*, 1985; *Love Unknown*, 1986; *Incline Our Hearts*, 1988; *A Bottle in the Smoke*, 1990; *Daughters of Albion*, 1991; *The Vicar of Sorrows*, 1993; *Hearing Voices*, 1995; *A Watch in the Night: Being the Conclusion of the Lampitt Chronicles*, 1996; *Dream Children*, 1998.

Other literary forms · Despite the regularity with which A. N. Wilson produces novels, he has never been limited to that form alone. He is one of the best-known journalists in Great Britain, having served as literary editor to *The Spectator*, the prestigious weekly journal of conservative social and political opinion, and as the literary editor of the *Evening Standard*. His own writing has not been confined to reviewing books, and he is often a commentator on social and political subjects. Wilson has a special interest in religion, and aside from his occasional essays on that subject, he published a study of the layman's dilemma in matters of Christian belief, *How Can We Know?* (1985), and historical biographies of Jesus and of the apostle Paul. He taught at the University of Oxford and wrote biographies of writers Sir Walter Scott, John Milton, Hilaire Belloc, Leo Tolstoy, and C. S. Lewis. He has also published volumes of essays and reviews, *Pen Friends from Porlock* (1988) and *Eminent Victorians* (1989), as well as children's books, mostly about cats, such as *Stray* (1987) and *The Tabitha Stories* (1997).

Achievements · *The Sweets of Pimlico* gained for Wilson the John Llewelyn Rhys Memorial Prize in 1978, and *The Healing Art* won three prizes, including the Somerset Maugham Award for 1980 and the Arts Council National Book Award for 1981. *Wise Virgin* brought him the W. H. Smith Annual Literary Award in 1983, and his study of Scott, *The Laird of Abbotsford: A View of Sir Walter Scott* (1980), won the Rhys prize for him once again. Another of his biographies, *Tolstoy* (1988), won the Whitbread Award in 1988.

There are several formidable writers in Wilson's generation, but it is possible to distinguish Wilson as one of the best of the satirists and, as such, one of the most perceptive commentators on Great Britain in the last quarter of the twentieth century. Given his talent, and his capacity to comment attractively (if sometimes improperly) on the excesses of his society, it is not surprising that he has become something of a public personality, the literary figure most often identified with the "Young Fogeys," that amorphous group of literary, social, and political figures who espouse the principles of landowning Toryism and look with nostalgia back to the old Empire and to the days when High Anglicanism was a spiritual power in the land. Part of their conservatism is sheer mischief-making, part of it a matter of temperament and class, but in Wilson's case, it is a love for the aesthetic detail of what he sees as a richer and more caring society (which does not stop him from making wicked fun of it).

Biography · Andrew Norman Wilson, born in Stone, Staffordshire, England, in 1950, was educated at Rugby, one of the great English public schools, and at New College, Oxford. He won the Chancellor's Essay Prize in 1971 and the Ellerton Theological Prize in 1975. He was a lecturer in English at New College and at St. Hugh's College, Oxford, from 1976 to 1981. He was then appointed literary editor of *The Spectator* for two years and later became the literary editor of the *Evening Standard.* In addition to his fiction, his nonfiction, and his children's books, he has published in *The Times Literary Supplement, New Statesman, Daily Mail, Observer,* and the *Sunday Telegraph.* In 1992, he narrated *Jesus Before Christ,* a presentation by Thames Television Production which presents a demythologized approach to Jesus' life. His declaration of loss of faith and departure from the Church of England in the early 1990's ran parallel with events in the lives of a number of major characters throughout the corpus of his fiction. His new understanding and interpretation of Jesus and Saint Paul are presented in his biographies, published in 1992 and in 1997 respectively, of those early Christian figures. During his second year of studies at Oxford, Wilson married Katherine Duncan-Jones, one of his tutors in English at Oxford's Somerville College and a specialist in Renaissance literature. Early in the marriage they became the parents of two daughters. After the marriage ended in divorce, he married Ruth Guilding, an art historian whom he met in 1989 when filming a television episode of *Eminent Victorians,* which he was narrating. Wilson was made a Fellow of the Royal Society of Literature in 1981 and is also a member of the American Academy of Arts and Letters.

Analysis · A. N. Wilson's novels are part of the tradition of sophisticated wittiness—sometimes comic, sometimes satiric—that explores the English caste system (with particular emphasis upon the middle and upper-middle classes), long a subject for English letters, particularly in the 1930's. The promise that World War II would not only stop international tyranny but also destroy the British social hierarchy did not, in fact, come true. Great Britain may have fallen on hard times economically, and may have become less important politically, but the class structure, though shaken, would prevail.

The Sweets of Pimlico · Evelyn Waugh was the foremost social satirist prior to the war and until his death in 1966, commenting on the dottier aspects of life among the well-born, the titled, the talented, and the downright vulgar climbers and thrusters, determined to ascend the greasy pole of social, political, and economic success. Wilson's first novel, *The Sweets of Pimlico,* might well have been written by a young Waugh. Thinly plotted, but written with astringent grace and wide-ranging peripheral insights into the fastidious improprieties of the privileged, it tells of the queer love life of Evelyn Tradescant (whose surname alone is appropriately bizarre, but whose credentials are established by the fact that her father is a retired diplomat, Sir Derek Tradescant, of some minor political reputation).

By chance, Evelyn tumbles (literally) into an association with a much older man, Theo Gormann—wealthy, pleased by the attentions of a young woman, and mysteriously ambiguous about his past, which seems to have involved close association with the Nazis before the war. While Theo urges his peculiar attentions on Evelyn, so does his closest friend, John "Pimlico" Price, and Evelyn learns that everybody seems to know one another in varyingly confusing ways. Her father and mother remember the Gormann of Fascist persuasion, and her brother, Jeremy, is also known to Theo through his connection with Pimlico, who proves to be an occasional male lover of

Jeremy, who in his last year at Oxford is doing little work but considerable loving, including a sudden excursion into incest with Evelyn. Wilson is teasingly and sometimes feelingly successful in exploring the sexual brink upon which Evelyn and Theo hover in their relationship and which convinces Theo to give part of his estate to Evelyn. Pimlico, the present heir, knows that someone is being considered as a joint recipient of the estate, but he never suspects Evelyn, and Theo dies before the will is changed. All is well, however, since Evelyn and Pimlico decide to marry. It is farce of high order in which coincidence, arbitrary behavior, and sophisticated silliness are mixed with moments of genuine tenderness (but not so tender as to overcome the sly mockery of money and influence in the smart set of south London).

Unguarded Hours and Kindly Light · In his next two novels, *Unguarded Hours* and *Kindly Light,* Wilson eschews the underplayed wit of *The Sweets of Pimlico* for comic excess, reminiscent of P. G. Wodehouse in its extravagant playfulness. These theological comedies are strongly cinematic in their incident and character and they display, if ridiculously, Wilson's strong interest in, and deep knowledge of, English Anglicanism and its constant flirtation with Roman Catholicism as well as his affectionate enthusiasm for the detail, the knickknackery of religious ceremony and trapping. The two novels ought to be read in the proper chronological order, since the hero escapes in a balloon at the end of *Unguarded Hours* and begins in the next one, having floated some distance away, once again trying to make his way into the clerical life.

The Healing Art · *The Healing Art,* one of Wilson's most admired works, reveals how wide his range can be, not only tonally but also thematically. The novel is a "black comedy" in the sense that acts which normally offend are portrayed in such a way that readers enjoy the improprieties without worrying about the moral consequences. Two women, one a university don, one a working-class housewife, meet while having surgery for breast cancer and comfort each other, despite the fact that they otherwise have nothing in common. Their doctor, overworked but peremptory, unfeeling, and vain, may have misread the women's X rays and deems one of them cured and the other in need of chemotherapy. The gifted, handsome, successful younger woman, informed of her possibly fatal condition, refuses treatment, energetically determined to live out her life quickly and to explore her personal relations with some fervor. In the process, she learns much about herself and her male friends and becomes involved in a love affair with the cast-off, occasional mistress of the man whom she presumed was, in fact, her lover (even if such love had not, to the moment, been consummated).

Wilson juxtaposes the range of experience open to a woman of the upper middle class, searching for some meaning for the last days of her life, surrounded by the many pleasures and alternatives of her world, to the life of a working-class woman, supposedly healthy, but obviously wasting away and ignored by family and by the medical profession as something of a nuisance. The cruelty of it all is subtly explored by Wilson, and the final ironies for both women are unnervingly sad and comic. Wilson proves with this novel that he is serious, and sensitive, particularly in dealing with the emotional lives of the two women.

Who Was Oswald Fish? · In *Who Was Oswald Fish?*, which might be called a contemporary black fairy tale, coincidence simply struts through the novel. The mysterious Oswald Fish, a turn-of-the-century architect and designer whose one church—a Gothic ruin in the working-class district of Birmingham—is to be the center of life and death for the parties drawn together to decide its fate, proves to be related to everyone who matters (and some who do not). In the retrieval of Fish's reputation from the neglect and indifference of twentieth century tastelessness and vulgarity, one suicide, one manslaughter, and two accidental deaths occur, the latter two in the rubble of his lovely old church. No one means any harm (although there are two children in this novel who could put the St. Trinian's gang to flight). Fanny Williams, former pop star and model and survivor of the English rock revolution of the early 1960's, is, in the late 1970's, famous again as the owner of a chain of trash-and-trend novelty shops dealing in Victorian nostalgia, and she is determined to protect the ruined church from demolition at the hands of soulless civic planners. Sexy, generous, and often charmingly silly, her life is an extravagant mess, a whirlpool of sensual, slapstick nonsense in which some survive and some, quite as arbitrarily, drown. Behind the farcical escapades lies Wilson's deep affection for the rich clutter of Victoriana juxtaposed to the new efficiency.

Wise Virgin · After the comic excesses of *Who Was Oswald Fish?*, Wilson pulled back into the narrower range of his early work in *Wise Virgin*. There has always been a sense that not only Waugh but also Iris Murdoch influenced him (*The Sweets of Pimlico* had been dedicated to her and to her husband, the literary critic John Bayley), particularly in the way in which she uses love as an unguided flying object, which can strike any character in the heart at any moment. Love tends to strike arbitrarily in Wilson's fiction, for he, like Murdoch enjoys tracing the madness of fools in love. Also reminiscent of Murdoch, Wilson works interesting technical detail into his novels, often of the religious world, but in *Who Was Oswald Fish?* his interest in Victorian architecture and objets d'art predominates and adds amusingly to the texture of the novel. In *Wise Virgin*, Wilson utilizes his own special knowledge as a literary scholar, since his protagonist, Giles Fox, is a medievalist, working on a definitive edition of an obscure text, *A Treatise of Heavenly Love*, on the relation of virginity and the holy life. Fox, irascible, snobbish, and sometimes vicious, has two virgins on his hands, his daughter, whom he has sought to educate without benefit of twentieth century influence, and his assistant, Miss Agar, who is determined to marry him.

Wilson has been accused of gratuitous cruelty in the way in which he allows his characters to comment upon the gracelessness of contemporary British society, and it is true that Fox is a master of the unfair comment and is insensitive to the possibility that some kinds of stupidities, particularly in the less privileged classes, are only innocent gaucheries. Certainly Fox is an unattractive protagonist, but he is also a man who has suffered much, having lost one wife in childbirth and another in a motor accident, and having himself gone blind in midcareer. He is something of a twentieth century Job (although more deserving of punishment), and the tone and plot of the novel suggest black comedy bordering on tragedy. On the lighter side, Wilson satirizes Fox's sister and brother-in-law, who, suffering from that peculiar kind of arrested development which strikes some people as cute, indulge interminably in the baby talk of the schoolboys whom the husband teaches in a public school, clearly based upon Wilson's own school, Rugby.

Gentlemen in England · *Gentlemen in England* takes place in the late Victorian period of which Wilson is so fond. With this work, Wilson has written a trick novel, partly in the tradition of Thomas Keneally and E. L. Doctorow, in which actual historical events and characters intrude on, and affect, the action. Wilson, however, refuses to use obvious historical allusions carefully chosen to satisfy the vanities of intelligent, well-informed readers. Much of the historical structure requires a deep knowledge of Victorian England. For example, although the novel definitely takes place in 1880, the exact date is never stated but must be gathered from certain facts mentioned by the characters. Allusions to George Eliot and Henry James might be easy to pick up, but those to public figures of the time, such as Charles Bradlaugh, E. B. Pusey, and Sir Charles Wentworth Dilke, require a formidable cultural memory.

The story centers on a father who has lost his Christian faith in the face of Darwinism; a son who is flirting with the late stages of the Oxford movement in religion, with the more theatrical experiments of High Anglicanism, and with the revival of the Roman Catholic Benedictine movement; and a daughter pursued by a disciple of Alma-Tadema, the popular painter of the time. Wilson recounts their family drama in a Victorian style, most reminiscent of the works of Anthony Trollope— slightly arch, witty, but restrainedly so, and inclined to overripe ironies. Like Victorian furniture and design, it is rich and heavy to the point of ponderousness.

Inside this lovingly detailed, historically accurate structure, Wilson plays out pure farce: A mother, still beautiful in early middle age, falls in love with a young painter, who falls in love with the daughter, who is half in love with her mother's old lover, who is half in love with both of them, and who is Wilson's way into the real world of London life. Called, with obvious intent, Chatterway, the former lover is intimately associated with the major figures of London life in that particularly lively year, 1880. *Gentlemen in England* is, in many ways, a work which illustrates Wilson's manipulative curiosity about the ways in which novels can be pushed and pulled about. Kingsley Amis has similar ideas, and his *Riverside Villas Murder* (1973) anticipated Wilson in its careful re-creation of a 1930's-style English murder mystery in which content, structure, and language were scrupulous imitations of the real thing.

This awareness of the novel as a form which could be used in many ways allows Wilson many humorous moments. In *Who Was Oswald Fish?*, he introduces, in a minor role, Jeremy Tradescant, who was the sexually confused brother of Evelyn, the heroine of *The Sweets of Pimlico*. He goes even further in making a comment on the fate of Evelyn's marriage to Pimlico Price, incomprehensible to all but those who have read the earlier novel. Wilson introduces into *Gentlemen in England* a genuinely thoughtful discussion of the problem of Christian faith, which is tonally at odds with the clutter of Victorian sexual high jinks. He has, in short, no sense of decorum, not because he does not know, but because he knows so well. Sometimes, as in *Scandal* and *Love Unknown*, he seems to have returned to social satire; the latter novel is puzzling until one recognizes that it is based upon the most pathetic kind of popular romance. Wilson is off again, manipulating the genre, enriching junk literature by imposing first-class literary technique on banality and turning it into something it hardly deserves.

The Lampitt Chronicles · In a vein similar to his other novels, Wilson's five novels that constitute the Lampitt Chronicles focus on a group of middle- and upper-class English whose lives become intertwined through a variety of typically Wilsonian "coincidences." With its ironic overview of twentieth century English society, this *roman-fleuve* quintet chronicles the life of the first-person narrator, Julian Ramsey, and the lives of several members of the upper-class Lampitt family.

The first two novels recount the early events in Julian's life. In *Incline Our Hearts*, a twelve-year-old orphaned Julian is living with his Uncle Roy, the vicar at Timplingham. Roy, obsessed with the Lampitt family, continuously recounts "Lampitt-lore" to Julian, who develops an interest in James Petworth ("Jimbo") Lampitt, a minor Edwardian writer whose death begins the novel. This hilarious commentary on English snobbery and English institutions follows Julian at school (the "English Gulag") and through his adolescence. *A Bottle in the Smoke*, a darker satire, records Julian's marriage to Anne, a Lampitt niece. Some of the exasperation, confusion, and emptiness over modern relationships between the sexes expressed in poet T. S. Eliot's *The Waste Land* (1922) is echoed here (and in the next three novels).

The satire continues in *Daughters of Albion*, as Julian becomes "Jason Grainger" on the nationally popular radio series *The Mulberrys*. Raphael Hunter (Jimbo's biographer, who outraged the family by presenting Jimbo as a homosexual) successfully sues a would-be Blakean poet, Albion Pugh, for accusing him of murdering Jimbo. Interspersed with his satire on the world of publishing, radio, and television, Wilson, through both the narrator and Pugh, presents ideas about myth, Christianity, Jesus, and Saint Paul, which later find their nonfiction counterparts in Wilson's religious biographies.

Hearing Voices is a mystery as well as a comedy of manners. Ramsey, asked to write an authorized biography of the Lampitts, goes to America to do research, and he marries for the second time (unsuccessfully). The murder of the American tycoon who had bought Jimbo's literary papers remains unsolved, as Wilson's emphasis continues to be on human interactions.

In *A Watch in the Night: Being the Conclusion of the Lampitt Chronicles*, Ramsey, in his late sixties and at peace with himself, addresses dramatist William Shakespeare—as Saint Augustine does God in his *Confessiones* (397-400; *Confessions*, 1620)—as he reflects on his life and its intersection with the lives of countless characters. This Proustian summary clarifies major and minor ambiguities in the earlier novels (and resolves the murders).

Although Wilson's satiric tone varies in his novels from caustic to gentle, his works are generally amusing, perceptive about the human condition, and memorable for their characters (despite their chaotic lives). His insight into English society and its institutions, past and present, reflects the deep confusions not only of contemporary England but also of twentieth century Western civilization. Whether he should be grouped primarily with Angus Wilson and Evelyn Waugh for serious farce, with Iris Murdoch and Joyce Cary for analytical comedy, or with Kingsley Amis for caustic irony, it is clear that Wilson is one of the twentieth century's major English authors.

Charles H. Pullen,
updated by Marsha Daigle-Williamson

Other major works

NONFICTION: *The Laird of Abbotsford: A View of Sir Walter Scott*, 1980; *The Life of John Milton*, 1983; *Hilaire Belloc*, 1984; *How Can We Know?*, 1985; *Pen Friends from Porlock*, 1988; *Tolstoy*, 1988; *Eminent Victorians*, 1989; *C. S. Lewis*, 1990; *Jesus*, 1992; *The Rise and Fall of the House of Windsor*, 1993; *Paul: The Mind of the Apostle*, 1997; *God's Funeral: The Decline of Faith in Western Civilization*, 1999.

CHILDREN'S LITERATURE: *Stray*, 1987; *The Tabitha Stories*, 1988; *Hazel the Guinea Pig*, 1989.

EDITED TEXTS: *The Faber Book of Church and Clergy*, 1992; *The Faber Book of London*, 1993.

Bibliography

CSL: The Bulletin of the New York C. S. Lewis Society 10, no. 8/9 (June/July, 1990): 1-16. Introduction is by Jerry L. Daniel, and articles are by John Fitzpatrick, George Sayer, and Eugene McGovern. The entire issue is devoted to reviews of Wilson's 1990 biography of C. S. Lewis, which are mostly unfavorable because of disagreement with his biographical approach and speculative interpretation.

Landrum, David W. "Is There Life After Jesus? Spiritual Perception in A. N. Wilson's *The Vicar of Sorrows.*" *Christianity and Literature* 44 (Spring/Summer, 1995): 359-368. A discussion of Wilson's first novel after he declared his unbelief in Christianity. Wilson deals much more seriously here with the problem of evil and other difficult religious questions than in his other fiction.

Weales, Gerald. "Jesus Who?" *The Gettysburg Review* 6, no. 4 (Autumn, 1993): 688-696. A comparison of Gore Vidal's treatment of Christ in his novel *Live from Golgotha* (1992) to Wilson's treatment of Christ in *Jesus*.

Weinberg, Jacob. "A. N. Wilson: Prolific to a Fault." *Newsweek* 112 (September 13, 1988): 75. A short but well-written essay, interspersed with comments by Wilson, on his novels and biographies. Also concerns Wilson as a "Young Fogey," a term used to describe young members of the Conservative party in England.

Wilson, A. N. "PW Interviews A. N. Wilson." Interview by Michele Field. *Publishers Weekly* 231 (May 15, 1987): 262-263. In the course of this interview, Wilson discusses his Anglo-Catholicism, the inevitable comparison of his works with those of Evelyn Waugh, the "cruel" nature of his novels, and his views on the writing of biography. Also contains much valuable biographical information.

Wolfe, Gregory. "Off Center, on Target." *Chronicles* 10, no. 10 (1986): 35-36. Wolfe's essay concerns Wilson's affinities with Evelyn Waugh, particularly in terms of their style and in their perspectives on Western Christianity. Sees Wilson as in the tradition of P. G. Wodehouse, who epitomized the light comic novel, but in Wilson's hands that novel becomes a vehicle for satire and social criticism.

Angus Wilson

Born: Bexhill, East Sussex, England; August 11, 1913
Died: Bury St. Edmunds, Suffolk, England; June 1, 1991

Principal long fiction · *Hemlock and After*, 1952; *Anglo-Saxon Attitudes*, 1956; *The Middle Age of Mrs. Eliot*, 1958; *The Old Men at the Zoo*, 1961; *Late Call*, 1964; *No Laughing Matter*, 1967; *As If by Magic*, 1973; *Setting the World on Fire*, 1980.

Other literary forms · Angus Wilson started his literary career in 1946, at the age of thirty-three, by writing short stories. The earliest stories were published in *Horizon*. *The Wrong Set and Other Stories* (1949), *Such Darling Dodos and Other Stories* (1950), and *A Bit off the Map and Other Stories* (1957) deal with the same problems and use the same imagery as his novels. Wilson also wrote drama, and in the 1970's, he became a leading reviewer of fiction. His literary journalism and criticism for *The Spectator, The Observer*, and *London Magazine* center mainly on the problem of the English novel. The range of writers he discussed in articles, introductions, or lectures is extremely wide and includes, among others, the Victorians, the Bloomsbury Group, Aldous Huxley, D. H. Lawrence, John Cowper Powys, Leo Tolstoy, Fyodor Dostoevski, Irving Shaw, Robert Penn Warren, and William Golding. He also published three full-length literary monographs: *Émile Zola: An Introductory Study of His Novels* (1952), *The World of Charles Dickens* (1970), and *The Strange Ride of Rudyard Kipling* (1977). Wilson's many lectures and articles display his concern with a wide range of problems relevant to the second half of the twentieth century. Most important for the study and understanding of his art is the volume *The Wild Garden: Or, Speaking of Writing* (1963), which contains lectures given in California in 1960. Some of his criticism was collected in *Diversity and Depth in Fiction: Selected Critical Writings of Angus Wilson* (1983). Travel pieces written over several decades are collected in *Reflections in a Writer's Eye* (1986).

Achievements · Most critics agree that by the 1980's, Wilson had secured a place among the most distinguished contemporary British novelists. He even became recognized outside the English-speaking world, particularly in France. In the 1960's and 1970's, the number of interviews with the artist increased, signifying his growing recognition among critics. Whether the critics use Stephen Spender's terminology of "modern" and "contemporary," or speak of experimental, psychological, aesthetic, or modern versus the traditional, sociological English novel, they all try to assess Wilson in relation to these categories. Some contend that Wilson's main concern rests with the sociological aspects of human life, but almost all critics concede that his interest goes beyond social issues. Without abandoning his commitment to depicting reality, Wilson was always committed to probing deeper into the dark depths of the human self. This concern with the inner self separates him sharply from the "angry" writers who also wrote in the 1950's: Kingsley Amis, John Wain, and Alan Sillitoe. Wilson, however, was dedicated to experimenting in both content and method. In his novels and critical writings, he emerged as a champion for a new type of novel, standing between the traditional and the experimental.

Biography · Angus Frank Johnstone Wilson was born in Bexhill, Sussex, on August 11, 1913, the sixth son of a middle-class family. His father was of Scottish extraction; his mother came from South Africa, and he spent some time there as a child. In constant financial troubles, his parents tried to maintain pretense and appearance, which left a deep impression on Wilson: At a very early age, he became aware of the chasm separating the real world and the world of fantasy into which many people escape to avoid the unpleasant facts of their lives. Frequently lonely (he was thirteen years younger than his next older brother), he realized that his clowning ability made him popular with the schoolchildren. He attended prep school in Seaford; from there he went to Westminster School and then to Merton College, Oxford. At the University of Oxford, his history training was on the Marxist line; that fact and his left-wing political activities in the 1930's account for his Labour sympathies.

In 1937, he started work at the British Museum, and, with an interruption during World War II, he stayed there until 1955. During the war, he was associated with an interservice organization attached to the Foreign Office, and for a while he lived in the country in a home with a Methodist widow and her daughter. During this time, he had a serious nervous breakdown; his psychotherapist suggested creative writing as therapy. In 1946, Wilson rejoined the staff at the British Museum and, at the same time, started writing seriously. His first published writing, the short story "Raspberry Jam" (1946), reflects his personal crisis and foreshadows the dark atmosphere of most of his work to come. The whole experience at the British Museum, situated in London's sophisticated Bloomsbury district, and especially his job as Deputy Superintendent at the Reading Room provided him with an understanding and knowledge of the cultural establishment and of the management of cultural institutions, which he used later in *The Old Men at the Zoo*. Also, observing scholars, book addicts, and eccentric visitors to the Reading Room gave him material for creating some of his fictional characters, such as Gerald Middleton in *Anglo-Saxon Attitudes.*

In 1952, he published his first novel, *Hemlock and After*, and a critical monograph, *Émile Zola*. He gave talks on the novel for the British Broadcasting Corporation that were later published in *The Listener*. In 1955, a contract with Secker and Warburg as well as his ongoing reviewing activity for *The Spectator* and *Encounter* made it possible for him to resign his post at the British Museum. He then retired to the Sussex countryside, thus reviving his childhood garden-dream. As a result of his freedom from job-related responsibilities, he published four novels in a rapid sequence: *Anglo-Saxon Attitudes, The Middle Age of Mrs. Eliot, The Old Men at the Zoo,* and *Late Call.* Furthermore, his participation in the cultural and literary life of England as a journalist, critic, and lecturer became more extensive. In 1963, he started his association with the University of East Anglia as a part-time lecturer, becoming professor in 1966. Also in 1966, he became Chairman of the Literary Panel of the Arts Council of Great Britain. In 1967, he lectured at Berkeley, California, as a Beckerman Professor, and in the same year *No Laughing Matter* appeared.

In 1968, he was made Commander of the British Empire and Honorary Fellow of Cowell College of the University of California at Santa Cruz. He honored the Dickens Centennial in 1970 with *The World of Charles Dickens*. Between 1971 and 1974, he served as Chairman of the National Book League while receiving two more distinctions in 1972, becoming a Companion of Literature and a Chevalier de l'Ordre des Arts et des Lettres, the latter a sign of his growing reputation in France. A sixth novel, *As If by Magic*, appeared in 1973; in it he made use of his teaching experience and involvement with young intellectuals. He continued to live in the country, his many activities including travel. His Asian journey resulted in his book *The Strange Ride of Rudyard Kipling.* He was John Hinkley Visiting Professor at The Johns Hopkins University in 1974, and, in 1977, Distinguished Visiting Professor at the University of Delaware; he also lectured at many other American universities. In 1980, he published another novel, *Setting the World on Fire.* His manuscripts, deposited at the Library of the University of Iowa, provide ample material for future researchers.

After suffering a stroke, Wilson died on June 1, 1991, in a nursing home in the southeast of England. He was seventy-seven years old.

Analysis · "Self-realization was to become the theme of all my novels," declared Angus Wilson in *The Wild Garden.* Self-realization does not take place in a vacuum; the process is closely linked with a person's efforts to face and to cope with the world. Wilson's childhood experience, among déclassé middle-class people living in a fantasy world, initiated the novelist's interest in the conflict between two worlds and in the possibility or impossibility of resolving the conflict. The rapidly changing scene in England as the Edwardian Age gave way to the postwar 1920's, with the cultural dominance of Bloomsbury, and then to the radical leftist 1930's, impressed on him the urgency of such a search. His encounter with Marxism at Oxford intensified Wilson's tendency to see the world as one of opposing forces. The dichotomy of town and country, of the classes, and of old and new forms the background of Wilson's fiction as the remnants of Edwardian England disappeared and the dissolution of the British Empire left the island nation searching for its place in the modern world.

In *The Wild Garden,* Wilson describes his creative-writing process in terms of a dialectic; he reveals that he "never felt called upon to declare allegiance to either fantasy or realism," but then he adds that "without their fusion I could not produce a novel." Wilson is desperately looking for syntheses to all kinds of conflicts and insists that self-realization is an absolute necessity to achieve them. His own breakdown as well as Sigmund Freud's impact on his generation pushed Wilson in the direction of psychoanalysis and the search for identity. In an age of tension, violence, and suffering, he insists on the necessity of self-realization in order to overcome despair.

Wilson's heroes all have crippled, wasted lives and broken families, and the novelist explores their "cherished evasions." Bernard Sand in *Hemlock and After* has to be shocked into self-knowledge by facing sadism in his own nature; Gerald Middleton, in *Anglo-Saxon Attitudes,* gets a new chance for a satisfactory, if not happy, life in old age when he is ready to resume responsibility as a scholar and to reveal a shameful hoax. Both these heroes are presented in their private and public lives because, in Wilson's view, both of these aspects of life are equally important to modern people. This view of human life in the dialectic of the private and the public is even more important for Meg Eliot, the heroine of *The Middle Age of Mrs. Eliot;* after many frustrations she emerges at the end of the novel as a career woman. Similarly, Sylvia Calvert in *Late Call* discovers a meaningful (retirement) life of her own, independent of her family.

Wilson was a very "British" writer with a subtle sense for the typical English understatement, while his Hegelian drive for reconciliation of conflicts agrees with the spirit of the traditional English compromise. He was constantly searching for ways to save the remnants of the liberal, humanistic values that have remained dear to him in a world that did not seem to have any use for them. His heroes and heroines, saved from final disintegration, are restored to some kind of meaningful life through self-knowledge and are brought closer to other people in defiance of loneliness and despair.

Hemlock and After · In his first novel, *Hemlock and After*, Wilson extends the exploration of the theme of self-knowledge to both the private and public life of his hero. The novel is about Bernard Sand's troubled conscience, a most private matter; but Bernard is an important public figure, described as "the country's own ambassador to the world outside," and a successful, self-confident novelist who organizes a subsidized writers' colony, Valden Hall, in order to support young talent. Overtly successful, his family life is in shambles. His wife, Ella, lives in "neurotic misery"; his son is a staunch conservative in strong disagreement with Bernard's liberal views; his unmarried daughter, a journalist, feels lonely and unhappy. As an indication of the overhanging disaster, Bernard's first novel is entitled *Nightmare's Image*.

In the title, "Hemlock" suggests poisonous wrong, evil, and even violence. Poisoning and violence occur in a "massacre of innocence," as related to Eric, Bernard's young homosexual partner, and to the little girl Elzie, whom the disreputable Mrs. Curry wants to make available to Hugh Rose. Wilson deliberately links the fate of the two young people by calling them both "rabbits." Rose and Mrs. Curry strike their deal at the "Lamb" Inn.

The word "After" in the title refers to the aftermath of knowledge: self-knowledge. A crucial scene occurs at the end of book 1 when a still complacent and self-confident Bernard watches the arrest of young homosexuals at Leicester Square and is shocked suddenly by the discovery that he experienced sadistic enjoyment in watching the terror in the eyes of those youths. This discovery has a devastating effect on Bernard's life and destroys not only him but also Valden Hall. The long-awaited opening of the young artists' colony becomes a total disaster, as its erupting violence grows into a symbol of the modern predicament. Wilson describes the scene as one of chaos, disorder, disappointment, strain, and hostility.

After this startling event, Bernard's life goes downhill very rapidly; self-knowledge paralyzes his will, and he is entirely unable to act. The discovery of sadistic tendencies makes him suspect of his own motives. He realizes with frightening clarity the abyss of the human soul and is driven to utter despair about the motivation behind any action. He has a horrifying vision of the subtle difference between intention and action, and as a consequence, Bernard loses his determination to deal with Mrs. Curry. At the same time, Ella almost miraculously recovers from her nervous breakdown and, after Bernard dies, acts on his behalf in arranging efficient management at Valden Hall and a prison sentence for Rose and Mrs. Curry. Rose commits suicide in prison, while Mrs. Curry earns an early release with her good behavior. It is briefly indicated that she might continue her former activity; thus the epilogue ends the novel on an ambiguous note of qualified optimism.

Anglo-Saxon Attitudes · The title *Anglo-Saxon Attitudes*, derived from Lewis Carroll's *Alice's Adventures in Wonderland* (1865), suggests a typically English atmosphere; it is Wilson's most Victorian novel, a broad social comedy. At the same time, it displays experimental technique in the use of the flashback, which provides all the background to Gerald Middleton's crisis in his private and public life. The hero, a sixty-year-old failure, is a historian. In the beginning of the novel, sitting by himself at a Christmas party given by his estranged wife, Inge, Gerald overhears broken sentences of conversation that remind him of the most significant episodes of his life. Wilson makes it very clear that self-knowledge is important for Gerald; it is both a psychological need to him and a matter of "intellectual honesty," a duty to the professional community of historians.

Gerald's crisis of conscience concerns a cruel hoax that occurred back in 1912 when he participated with a team in an excavation. Young Gilbert Stokeway, a disciple of T. H. Hulme and Wyndham Lewis and the son of the leader of the team, put a fake idol in the tomb under research at Melpham. His hoax was successful, and the fake came to be hailed as a pagan idol. At that time, Gerald was a Prufrock-like antihero: disabled physically by a sprained ankle, and disabled emotionally by his love for Gilbert's wife, Dollie. His affair with her played an important role in his silence about the fake idol. Gerald's feelings of guilt center on "the two forbidden subjects of his thoughts," his marriage and the hoax. His life, "rooted in evasion," appears to him empty, meaningless, and futile. His professional career fell victim to his decision not to reveal the hoax. Because of his affair with Dollie, he evaded dealing with Inge's inadequacies as a mother.

In fact, none of the minor characters has a happy, self-fulfilling life. While Gerald still believes in the liberal tradition, neither of his sons adheres to his beliefs. His elder son, Robert, a businessman, stands rather to the right and the younger son, John, is a radical, and they have violent clashes whenever they meet. Both sons are unhappy in their personal relationships as well. Robert is married to the conventional Marie-Hélène but loves the more modern Elvira Portway. John has a short-lived homosexual relationship with an unruly young Irishman, Larry, who is killed in a wild drive in which John loses a leg. Gerald's daughter, Kay, has a serious crisis in her marriage to the smart right-wing young sociologist, Donald. Wilson employs specific imagery to drive home to the reader the overwhelming atmosphere of frustration of all these people. Expressions such as "flat and dead" and "deadly heaviness" abound, referring to the behavior of people at parties when communication is impossible. Gerald's house is "noiseless as a tomb," and during the Christmas party at the home of the "Norse Goddess" Inge, all those present "shivered" in spite of the central heating.

Realizing the failure of his family, Gerald has to admit that he is to take the blame; when he selected Inge to be his wife, he decided for second-best. Yet, at the end, Gerald manages to pull himself out of his dead life. By revealing the hoax, he succeeds in restoring his professional status, and after a long silence, he becomes active again in research. The novel, however, like *Hemlock and After*, ends on a note of qualified optimism as Gerald remains estranged from his family. The picture of Gerald's life, combined with the divergent subplots, reveals a world in which relationships do not last, where options are limited.

The Middle Age of Mrs. Eliot ·Critics believe that they can recognize Wilson in most of his central characters; the novelist, however, admits the connection only in the case of Meg Eliot, the heroine of his third novel, *The Middle Age of Mrs. Eliot*. "Meg," he says, "is in large part modelled on myself," while David Parker's nursery recalled to Wilson childhood memories of a garden of a friendly family.

Meg Eliot, a well-to-do barrister's childless, worldly, spoiled wife, experiences sudden tragedy when her husband dies from a gunshot wound as he tries to protect a local minister. The novel depicts Meg's nervous breakdown and painful recovery: her journey to self-knowledge. She is first revealed to be holding desperately to her old friends; yet, their lives are no more secure than hers. Lady Pirie in her "decaying genteel jail" is preoccupied with her son only, bohemian Polly Robinson lives a kind of "animated death," and Jill Stokes is obsessed with the memory of her dead husband. These "lame ducks" cannot help Meg, nor can drugs. Meg's brother, David Parker, who runs the nursery with his homosexual partner, is sheltered in the pleasant quiet atmosphere, which suggests a return to lost innocence. Yet, Wilson is ambiguous about the validity of the garden image, since David's nursery is commercial, an irony in itself. Meg cannot share her brother's lifestyle, his abnegation of action and the human world. Wilson does not censure David for his contemplative lifestyle, but it is evident that he prefers Meg's choice "to be with people!"

Meg is determined to find meaning in life, in a life with people. She is strikingly reminiscent of George Eliot's heroines; similar to them, she used to live in self-delusion and is shocked into consciousness by the "remorse of not having made life count enough" for her husband. Moreover, again like the Victorian woman, she returns to a fuller life. Two factors are important in her recovery. First, she refuses any kind of opium, a George Eliot ideal; second, she is determined to build herself a meaningful, useful life. While she admits that she "used to be Maggie Tulliver," she also resembles Gwendolen Harleth from Eliot's *Daniel Deronda* (1876). She shares with her an unhappy childhood and the horrors of remorse, but she shares also in Gwendolen's way of redemption. Like the Victorian heroine, Meg too had to learn in a painful way that the outside world could intrude into her life at any time and destroy it if she is taken unaware. As she takes a paying secretarial job, Meg is full of confidence in her farewell letter to David: "At any rate in a few years at least, the modern world won't be able to take me by surprise so easily again."

The Old Men at the Zoo · From the omniscient narrator of his early works, Wilson shifts to a more modern device in *The Old Men at the Zoo* by creating a first-person narrator in Simon Carter. In the beginning of the novel, Simon is a gifted, dedicated yet disabled naturalist, very much like Gerald Middleton at the time of the excavation. He is prevented from continuing research in Africa because of amoebal dysentery. He joins the London Zoo as an administrator at a crucial time when the zoo itself becomes a battleground of conflicting ideas, reflecting a conflict of values in British politics. Wilson creates an armed conflict between England and Allied Europe, followed by a Fascist invasion of England when all standards of civilized behavior collapse and give way to brutality. When the war breaks out, the Fascists want to put on a spectacle with prisoners of war fighting the zoo animals. Simon is horrified, but as he later tries to drive the animals to safety, he finds himself killing his favorite badgers to feed a boy and his mother.

Almost an antihero, trying to avoid any kind of involvement with people, an administrator following orders, Simon emerges at the end of the novel ready to face the world, to be involved with people, even running for director. Because of his loyalty to the zoo under three different administrations, representing three different political ideologies, some are inclined to view him as a Vicar of Bray. In the twentieth century, however, many people had to face Simon's fundamental dilemma: whether to follow orders or to take up independent responsibility. Simon's American-born wife, Martha, disapproves of his behavior; she would like him to give up his job. Simon refuses, saying, "What do you think I am, a weathercock?" There is cruel irony in this remark; however, Wilson's irony is not pointed at Simon but rather at the general human predicament of a rapidly changing world in which choices are limited and people are continuously bombarded with dilemmas.

Simon's only independent action is his attempt to save the animals, which ends in disaster. In him, Wilson presents modern society struggling with despair in a desperate race to catch up with challenges. Simon's painful adjustment commands respect; he almost achieves heroic status when, after all the horrors and violence, he describes this modern world as "a demie-paradise." In this sense, *The Old Men at the Zoo* is Wilson's least pessimistic novel.

No Laughing Matter · *No Laughing Matter* is one of Wilson's most complex novels and requires close reading. The narrative is interwoven with dramas, enacted by the characters and reflecting various dramatic styles, including the absurd. Pastiches and parody of writers are important features of the novel, and literary references abound. John Galsworthy's 1922 *A Forsyte Saga*-like family chronicle of the Matthews family, the novel is also a historical document covering the twentieth century to 1967. The father, Billy Pop, a Micawber of the twentieth century, is a failure in his writing profession and ineffectual in his family life, letting his selfish wife dominate the children. All six of them have a crippled childhood and are deprived of privacy. By the end of the novel, they all achieve some kind of success in their professional lives; some even attain fame, such as Rupert, the actor, and Quentin, the political journalist, later a celebrated television commentator. Success does not make him lovable, and his cynicism, enjoyed by a million common viewers, questions the role of the media.

The final scene, in 1967, brings the whole clan together. While Margaret and her brother Marcus, a homosexual art dealer, are discussing and quarreling about Margaret's art, Hassan, who will inherit Marcus's cooperatively run scent factory, makes a final statement: the last words of the novel. He considers Marcus's ideas of a cooperative absurd. Hassan admires "ambition, high profit and determined management." His coldly calculating thoughts cast a dark shadow on the future; they underline once again Wilson's skepticism about the survival of liberal humanistic ideals in the modern world.

A strong moral sense links Wilson to George Eliot, and his sense of the caricature and the grotesque shows affinities with his favorite author, Charles Dickens. At the same time, his fiction is full of experiments into new literary methods. With almost each novel, Wilson made an important step forward in his search for new techniques. Tragedy and laughter coexist in his novels; there is tragedy in the private lives of the characters, but Wilson has a grotesque view of people's behavior, and his ability to create atmosphere through concentrating on speech habits promotes laughter.

In his commitment to duty, in his moral seriousness, Wilson is definitely akin to George Eliot, but he differs from the Victorian novelist in that he cannot believe in "meliorism." George Eliot firmly maintained that self-awareness would lead to self-improvement and in consequence, to the individual's improved performance in the human community. Wilson is much more skeptical. Like E. M. Forster, he, too, is painfully aware of the decline of liberal hopes. In *The Middle Age of Mrs. Eliot*, he came to the sad conclusion that "self-knowledge had no magic power to alter," and in his sixth novel, he killed magic with finality.

As If by Magic · In *As If by Magic*, magic, the ultimate evasion, is destroyed forever for the two central characters. Moreover, this time they are not middle-aged or elderly intellectuals paralyzed by frustration; they are young people. Wilson's teaching experience in Britain and America caused him to concentrate on the young, the future generation. Hamo Langmuir is a dedicated young scientist on a worldwide fact-finding tour to study the benevolent affects of his "magic" rice, destined to solve the problem of starvation in underdeveloped countries. His goddaughter, Alexandra Grant, in the company of her fellow hippies, is also on a world tour in search of an occult answer to all human problems. A bewildered Hamo must find out that his magic rice solution has introduced a farming method for which natives are not yet prepared and, consequently, it is causing more damage than good. Hamo falls victim to the anger of a crowd at a moment when he is ready to get involved in the human aspects of research. He, like Alexandra, who gets to Goa at the same time, had to learn through experience that the intrusion of Western ways into radically different cultures can cause disruption and many unnecessary tragedies. At the end of the novel, a sober Alexandra, cured of her hippie ways, resumes the responsibility of building a normal life for her son, a legacy of the hippie venture. A millionaire through an inheritance, she is ready to support and subsidize food research, but she knows by now that the possibilities are limited and that no easy answers are available; magic of any kind is only for the neurotics who are unable to face reality or for the power-hungry who use it to dominate others.

Setting the World on Fire · Wilson's concern with human nature and with what it means for the future of the world dominates *Setting the World on Fire*. This novel is a family chronicle like *No Laughing Matter* but more condensed, more limited in time (1948-1969) and in the number of characters. Indeed, the writer concentrates on two brothers, Piers and Tom, the last generation of an old aristocratic family. Literary references are replaced by other arts: theater, music, architecture, and painting. Piers hopes to dedicate his life to the theater, and as a promising student, he earns the admiration of family, friends, and teachers with his stage-managing and directing abilities. The final part of the novel is about the preparations for the first performance of a new play, with the younger brother Tom supporting Piers as best he can in the hectic work. Everything is set for success when, unexpectedly, Scotland Yard intervenes and orders the premises emptied because of a bomb threat. The author of the play, an old employee of the family, masterminded the plot, simultaneously aimed at the family and at the government.

Tom saves Piers's life by knocking him down, but he himself gets killed. On his way home from the hospital where Tom died, Piers is on the verge of a breakdown and about to give up hope as well as artistic ambitions, because what good are the wonders of art in "a chaotic universe"? He calms down, however, and decides to stage the play anyway; he must not "lose the power to ascend the towers of imagination," he says. The tragedy brought Piers to a fuller realization of his duty as an artist, which means doing the only thing left to him: to create in, and for, a world threatened by chaos, violence, and destruction.

Wilson, a mixture of a twentieth century Charles Dickens, George Eliot, and E. M. Forster, with an increasingly dark vision of the modern predicament, rededicated himself, the artist, to his moral obligation. He continued writing in a desperate attempt to impose some kind of order on chaos and, by making people aware, to try to save humankind from itself.

Anna B. Katona

Other major works

SHORT FICTION: *The Wrong Set and Other Stories,* 1949; *Such Darling Dodos and Other Stories,* 1950; *A Bit off the Map and Other Stories,* 1957; *Death Dance: Twenty-five Stories,* 1969.

PLAY: *The Mulberry Bush,* pr., pb. 1956.

NONFICTION: *Émile Zola: An Introductory Study of His Novels,* 1952; *For Whom the*

Cloche Tolls: A Scrapbook of the Twenties, 1953 (with Philippe Jullian); *The Wild Garden: Or, Speaking of Writing,* 1963; *Tempo: The Impact of Television on the Arts,* 1964; *The World of Charles Dickens,* 1970; *The Strange Ride of Rudyard Kipling,* 1977; *Diversity and Depth in Fiction: Selected Critical Writings of Angus Wilson,* 1983; *Reflections in a Writer's Eye,* 1986.

Bibliography

Conradi, Peter. *Angus Wilson.* Plymouth, England: Northcote House, 1997. A very fine introduction to Wilson's work, including a biographical outline, a section on his stories, chapters on his major novels, notes, and a very useful annotated bibliography.

Drabble, Margaret. *Angus Wilson: A Biography.* New York: St. Martin's Press, 1995. Written by a fine novelist and biographer, this book is a sympathetic, well-researched, and astute guide to Wilson's life and work. Includes notes and bibliography.

Faulkner, Peter. *Angus Wilson: Mimic and Moralist.* New York: Viking Press, 1980. Follows a chronological approach to Wilson's writings, including pertinent biographical background and evaluations of one or two main works each chapter in order to illustrate the evolution of Wilson's art. Also contains a bibliography of Wilson's major publications and selected secondary sources.

Gardner, Averil. *Angus Wilson.* Boston: Twayne, 1985. The first full-length study of Wilson published in the United States, representing a well-rounded introduction to Wilson's fiction. Includes a biographical sketch and analyses of Wilson's stories and novels through 1980. Contains a useful annotated bibliography of secondary sources.

Halio, Jay L. *Angus Wilson.* Edinburgh: Oliver & Boyd, 1964. The first full-length study of Wilson, this slender volume covers Wilson's writing through *The Wild Garden.* After a biographical sketch, Halio examines Wilson's fiction in chronological order. Concludes with a chapter on Wilson's literary criticism.

_____. ed. *Critical Essays on Angus Wilson.* Boston: G. K. Hall, 1985. Includes an overview of Wilson's writings, several reviews of his work, three interviews with the author, and fourteen essays that offer a diverse study of Wilson's individual works as well as his career as a whole. The selected bibliography draws readers' attention to further resources.

Stape, J. H., and Anne N. Thomas. *Angus Wilson: A Bibliography, 1947-1987.* London: Mansell, 1988. This thorough and indispensable resource includes a foreword by Wilson and a useful chronology of his life. Part 1 is a bibliography of works by Wilson, including books, articles, translations of his works, and interviews. Part 2 is a bibliography of works about Wilson.

P. G. Wodehouse

Born: Guildford, Surrey, England; October 15, 1881
Died: Southampton, Long Island, New York; February 14, 1975

Principal long fiction · *The Pothunters*, 1902; *A Prefect's Uncle*, 1903; *The Gold Bat*, 1904; *The Head of Kay's*, 1905; *Love Among the Chickens*, 1906; *Not George Washington*, 1907 (with Herbert Westbrook); *The White Feather*, 1907; *Mike: A Public School Story*, 1909 (also known as *Enter Psmith, Mike at Wrykyn*, and *Mike and Psmith*); *The Swoop: How Clarence Saved England*, 1909; *Psmith in the City: A Sequel to "Mike,"* 1910; *A Gentleman of Leisure*, 1910 (also known as *The Intrusion of Jimmy*); *The Prince and Betty*, 1912; *The Little Nugget*, 1913; *Something Fresh*, 1915 (also known as *Something New*); *Psmith Journalist*, 1915 (revision of *The Prince and Betty*); *Uneasy Money*, 1916; *Piccadilly Jim*, 1917; *Their Mutual Child*, 1919 (also known as *The Coming of Bill*); *A Damsel in Distress*, 1919; *The Little Warrior*, 1920 (also known as *Jill the Reckless*); *Indiscretions of Archie*, 1921; *The Girl on the Boat*, 1922 (also known as *Three Men and a Maid*); *The Adventures of Sally*, 1922 (also known as *Mostly Sally*); *The Inimitable Jeeves*, 1923 (also known as *Jeeves*); *Leave It to Psmith*, 1923; *Bill the Conqueror: His Invasion of England in the Springtime*, 1924; *Sam the Sudden*, 1925 (also known as *Sam in the Suburbs*); *The Small Bachelor*, 1927; *Money for Nothing*, 1928; *Summer Lightning*, 1929 (also known as *Fish Preferred and Fish Deferred*); *Very Good, Jeeves*, 1930; *Big Money*, 1931; *If I Were You*, 1931; *Doctor Sally*, 1932; *Hot Water*, 1932; *Heavy Weather*, 1933; *Thank You, Jeeves*, 1934; *Right Ho, Jeeves*, 1934 (also known as *Brinkley Manor: A Novel About Jeeves*); *Trouble Down at Tudsleigh*, 1935; *The Luck of the Bodkins*, 1935; *Laughing Gas*, 1936; *Summer Moonshine*, 1937; *The Code of the Woosters*, 1938; *Uncle Fred in the Springtime*, 1939; *Quick Service*, 1940; *Money in the Bank*, 1942; *Joy in the Morning*, 1946; *Full Moon*, 1947; *Spring Fever*, 1948; *Uncle Dynamite*, 1948; *The Mating Season*, 1949; *The Old Reliable*, 1951; *Barmy in Wonderland*, 1952 (pb. in U.S. as *Angel Cake*); *Pigs Have Wings*, 1952; *Ring for Jeeves*, 1953 (also known as *The Return of Jeeves*); *Jeeves and the Feudal Spirit*, 1954 (also known as *Bertie Wooster Sees It Through*); *French Leave*, 1956; *Something Fishy*, 1957 (also known as *The Butler Did It*); *Cocktail Time*, 1958; *Jeeves in the Offing*, 1960 (also known as *How Right You Are, Jeeves*); *Ice in the Bedroom*, 1961; *Service with a Smile*, 1961; *Stiff Upper Lip, Jeeves*, 1963; *Biffen's Millions*, 1964 (also known as *Frozen Assets*); *Galahad at Blandings*, 1965 (also known as *The Brinkmanship of Galahad Threepwood: A Blandings Castle Novel*); *Company for Henry*, 1967 (also known as *The Purloined Paperweight*); *Do Butlers Burgle Banks?* 1968; *A Pelican at Blandings*, 1969 (also known as *No Nudes Is Good Nudes*); *The Girl in Blue*, 1970; *Jeeves and the Tie That Binds*, 1971 (also known as *Much Obliged, Jeeves*); *Pearls, Girls and Monty Bodkin*, 1972 (also known as *The Plot That Thickened*); *Bachelors Anonymous*, 1973; *The Cat-Nappers: A Jeeves and Bertie Story*, 1974 (also known as *Aunts Aren't Gentlemen*); *Sunset at Blandings*, 1977.

Other literary forms · In addition to writing more than ninety novels, P. G. Wodehouse wrote hundreds of short stories, some eighteen plays (of which ten were published), the lyrics for thirty-three musicals, and a vast, uncollected body of essays, reviews, poems, and sketches. So much of Wodehouse's early work has been lost that it is impossible to measure his total literary output, and collections of his stories published under the title "Uncollected Wodehouse" are likely to appear with some frequency for the next twenty years. He also wrote two comic autobiographies, *Performing Flea: A Self-Portrait in Letters* (1953; revised as *Author! Author!*, 1962) and *America, I Like You* (1956; revised as *Over Seventy: An Autobiography with Digressions*, 1957).

Achievements · Wodehouse has always been regarded as a "popular" writer. The designation is just. "Every schoolboy," wrote Ogden Nash, "knows that no one can hold a candle to P. G. Wodehouse." His novels and short stories were among the best-selling works of their generation, but it should be remembered that Wodehouse's appeal transcended his popular audience. Many of the major writers of the twentieth century have professed a deep admiration for the art

Courtesy D.C. Public Library

of "Plum," as Wodehouse was known to his friends and family. T. S. Eliot, W. H. Auden, Bertrand Russell—all were fanatic enthusiasts of Wodehouse. Hilaire Belloc said that he was the greatest writer of the twentieth century, and Evelyn Waugh offered the following tribute to his genius: "Mr. Wodehouse's idyllic world can never stale. He will continue to release future generations from captivity that may be more irksome than our own." It is unfortunately true that critics and readers who expect high seriousness from their literary pleasures will never quite approve of one who makes a lighthearted mockery of most of England's and America's most sacred cows. F. R. Leavis, the celebrated English scholar, pointed to the awarding of an honorary doctorate to Wodehouse as proof of declining literary standards. Other critics have been even more emphatic in their deprecation of Wodehouse's lack of seriousness. For sheer enjoyment, however, or what Dr. Johnson called "innocent recreation," no one can touch P. G. Wodehouse.

Biography · Pelham Grenville Wodehouse was born in Guildford, Surrey, on October 15, 1881, the third of four sons born to Henry Ernest and Eleanor Deane Wodehouse. Wodehouse's father was a member of the English Civil Service and spent most of his working years in Hong Kong; indeed, it was a mere chance that Wodehouse was not born in Hong Kong. Whether it was miscalculation or the event was premature, his birth occurred during one of his mother's rare and rather brief visits to England.

Wodehouse was reared away from his parents; they were, he often remarked, like distant aunts and uncles rather than parents. Wodehouse entered Dulwich College at the age of twelve and remained there for the next six years. The school was not prominent in the sense that Harrow and Eton were prominent; it was simply a good middle-class school. The headmaster was the most impressive figure and may have served as the model for Wooster's nemesis, the Reverend Aubrey Upjohn; the headmaster was not impressed with his student. He once wrote to Wodehouse's parents: "He has the most distorted ideas about wit and humour. . . . One is obliged to like him in spite of his vagaries." The vagaries, apart from the student's drawing match figures in his classical texts, are unrecorded. In those final years at Dulwich, Wodehouse had found his vocation. He was appointed editor of the school paper and sold his first story to a boy's weekly, *The Public School Magazine.* The story won first prize for fiction in that year.

Following graduation in 1900, Wodehouse went to work for the London branch of the Hong Kong and Shanghai Bank. His work there was not a complete disaster for the banking industry, but very nearly so. Wodehouse was no good at checks and balances and served only as an unpleasant distraction for those who were. At night, he continued to write fiction and reviews or plays and was given a position on the *Globe* in 1902, the year the first of his many novels was published. *Punch* accepted an article from him the next year, and a second novel was also published in 1903. From that time, Wodehouse averaged more than a novel, several short stories, and either a play or musical a year. In 1914, Wodehouse married Ethel Rowley, a widow with one child. The marriage was a happy one, and the author frequently expressed his gratitude to his wife for the support she had given to his work. For the Wodehouse reader, however, the following year had a much greater significance: *Something New,* the first of the Blandings novels, was published. A few years later, *My Man Jeeves* (1919) appeared, the first of the Jeeves and Wooster saga.

Novels and stories appeared with an unfailing regularity, and in the next two decades, Wodehouse became an acknowledged master. In 1939, Oxford paid tribute to his greatness by conferring on him the honorary Doctorate of Letters (D.Litt.). The doctorate meant that Jeeves, Wooster, Emsworth, and the rest were accepted as part of the heritage of English literature. The London *Times* supported the Oxford gesture, noting that the praise given to Wodehouse the stylist was especially apt: "Style goes a long way in Oxford; indeed the purity of Mr. Wodehouse's style was singled out for particular praise in the Public Orator's happy Horatian summing up of Mr. Wode-house's qualities and achievements."

Wodehouse and his wife had lived in France throughout much of the 1930's, and though war with Germany was believed imminent, he returned to France after he received the doctorate at Oxford. In 1940, he was taken prisoner by the Germans. In various prison camps, he made a series of broadcasts over German radio which were interpreted as a form of collaboration with the enemy. Wodehouse was innocent of all the charges, but it was perhaps his innocence, the vital ingredient in most of his heroes, that almost undid him. The closest Wodehouse came to collaboration was his remark to the effect that he was not unhappy in prison, for he was able to continue his work. One scholar has called that broadcast "clearly indiscreet," but those who have read the Wodehouse letters know that he scarcely thought about anything else beside his work.

After his release, Wodehouse eventually returned to America, where he took permanent residence; he was naturalized in 1955. In 1973 he was knighted, and he died in 1975 at the age of ninety-three.

Analysis · Few of P. G. Wodehouse's novels are ever far from the school environment, for the plots of the later Jeeves and Blandings series of novels frequently derive from the desire of one schoolmate, usually Bertie Wooster, to help another. Yet the early school novels represent a distinct type within the body of Wodehouse's fiction.

The school novels · Perhaps, as one scholar has observed, these eight school novels are no more than "bibliographical curiosities," in that only the most ardent fan of Wodehouse would be led to read them after the later work had been written. Still, the works are different in tone and theme. The novels are set at Wrykyn College, which seems to closely resemble Dulwich, the author's alma mater. The emphasis is on sports, and this emphasis gives a serious tone to the work. Boys are measured largely by their athletic skills. One might suggest that the ever-present sports motif was a symbol of the particular virtues of youth: comradeship, loyalty, and perseverance. Enlarging upon these virtues, Wodehouse was following what was almost a cliché in the boy's fiction of the time. The cliché, however, was one particularly congenial to the author, who once noted that he would never be able to write his autobiography, for he had not had one of the essentials in the background of an autobiographer—"a hell of a time at his public school."

Wodehouse loved Dulwich College, and the eight school novels are a record of his affection. The schoolmasters are a decent group; the boys, with few exceptions, are generous and loyal; and the setting of the college is one of great beauty. The distinctive element in the novels is the happiness which pervades them, and the reader need only remember George Orwell's, Graham Greene's, and Evelyn Waugh's accounts of their own school days to notice the sharp difference between Wodehouse and many of his contemporaries. The only curiosity about the novels is not the absence of horror and malice, but that no one in the school novels seems to have learned anything at Wrykyn. It should also be remembered that many of Wodehouse's most celebrated idiots are graduates of Oxford and Cambridge.

Wodehouse once said of his work: "I believe there are two ways of writing novels. One is mine, making a sort of musical comedy without music and ignoring life altogether." The Blandings series of novels is perhaps the best example of the author's determined resistance to "real life." These twenty-odd novels are centered on the beautiful estate of Lord Emsworth, who serves as unwilling host to almost everyone who goes in and out of his ancestral home. Lord Emsworth is old and absentminded, and his affections are limited to his younger brother Galahad, his roses, and his pig, the Empress of Blandings. This pig, as Emsworth remarks several times in each of the novels, has won the silver prize for being the fattest in Shropshire County. Only Galahad can really appreciate the high distinction that has been conferred on the Empress, and one feels that even he is not very serious about the pig. Yet the Empress is very nearly the catalyst for all the actions that take place in the novels. She is stolen, which makes it imperative to effect a rescue; she is painted an outrageous color and introduced into strange bedrooms to make the recipients of such favors "more spiritual" in their outlook; and on one occasion, her portrait is done at the behest of Lord Emsworth.

The Blandings novels · This last episode in the life of the Empress occurs in one of the best of the Blandings novels and is a fair measure of the formula used by Wodehouse in the series. *Full Moon*, in which the portrait is commissioned, has all the characteristics of the Blandings novels. Emsworth has the insane idea that the pig's portrait should be done by an eminent painter, but they have all turned down his request. While this action is debated, Lady Constance, Emsworth's sister, has come to the castle with a young lady in tow. Her intent is to keep the young woman away from the man to whom she has become foolishly engaged, foolishly because the fellow does not have any money, which is the essential requisite for a good marriage in the mind of Lady Constance. Galahad arranges to have the young man invited to the castle on the pretext that he is Edwin Landseer, celebrated painter of animal pictures, including "Pig at Bey." Galahad's ruse works for a while, but the young man's painting is rejected by Emsworth, who complains that the painting makes the Empress look as if she had a hangover. The young man is ejected from Blandings but soon returns, wearing a beard resembling that of an Assyrian monarch. He makes a tragic mistake when he gives a love note to one of Emsworth's other sisters, thinking that she is a cook. He is again thrown out. By the novel's end, however, he has successfully won the hand of his beloved, and the sisters are all leaving the estate. Galahad has once more succeeded in spreading "sweetness and light" in all directions, except that of his usually irate sisters.

There are few variations in the Blandings series. At least one and sometimes as many as three courtships are repaired; the pig is safe from whatever threatens it; the sisters have been thwarted in usually about five ways by Galahad; and Lord Emsworth has the prospect of peace and quiet in front of him at the novel's end. Yet Emsworth, Galahad, the sisters, and a host of only slightly less important or interesting characters are among the most brilliant comic figures in the whole of English literature. In writing the Blandings novels, Wodehouse followed his own precept: "The absolute cast-iron rule, I'm sure, in writing a story is to introduce *all* your characters as early as possible—especially if they are going to play important parts later." Yet his other favorite maxim that a novel should contain no more than one "big" character—is seldom observed in the Blandings series. Each of the characters has his own element of fascination, and each is slightly crazy in one way or another. As absurd and funny as is Lord Emsworth's vanity about his pig, it is only a little more so than his sisters' vanity about their social position and wealth. If the formula for this series does not vary, neither does the uniform excellence of each novel in the series.

The Jeeves and Wooster novels · More than a dozen novels use Jeeves and Bertie Wooster as the main characters. These novels have commonly been regarded as Wodehouse's "crowning achievement," but the author once noted that the idea of the latent greatness of Jeeves came to him very slowly. In his first appearance in a short story, he barely says more than "Very good, Sir." Jeeves is the manservant to Bertie Wooster, who is preyed upon by aunts, friends, and women who wish to help him improve his mind as a prerequisite to marriage with him. Wooster has been dismissed as silly and very stupid. Compared to Jeeves, perhaps he is both, but he is also extremely generous with both his money and time, and it is his unfailing willingness to help others that invariably places him in the precarious situation that is the main plot. Wooster is an Oxford graduate, but detective novels are his most demanding reading. He never uses a word of more than two syllables without wondering whether he is using the word properly. Wooster is the "big" character in the Jeeves series, and such a character, according to Wodehouse, is worth "two of any other kind."

The marriage motif is very much a part of the Wooster and Jeeves saga, but frequently the central issue of this series is helping Bertie keep away from the wrong woman. It is not quite accurate to describe him as one of "nature's bachelors," for he has been engaged to nearly a score of females and is threatened with marriage in nearly every one of the novels in the series. Some of these women are insipid and poetic, others are coarse and athletic; the worst are intellectual women who want to improve his mind. He is assigned books to read that he finds boring and incomprehensible, told never to laugh aloud, and threatened, after marriage, with having his membership in the Drones Club revoked. Bertie is quite content with the state of his mind and soul. At the threat of marriage and all the other threats that the novels present, Jeeves comes to the rescue. In spite of Bertie's chronic need of Jeeves's aid, he is ostensibly the main character in the novels and one of Wodehouse's most brilliant creations. It is through the eyes of Bertie that the reader observes and passes judgment on what is taking place in the novel. Such a process was an enormous technical difficulty for his creator: Wooster must be stupid and generous in order for the plot to develop, but not so stupid that the reader casts him off.

The character of Jeeves, perfect as it is, is one of the most traditional aspects of Wodehouse's craft, for the wise servant of a stupid master is a hoary cliché. Jeeves has never been to Oxford, and he has no aristocratic blood flowing in his veins to spur him into action. His central motive for rescuing Bertie and the legions of others who come to him for counsel is a manifestation of what is called in this series of novels "the feudal spirit." Though not a university man, Jeeves knows French, Latin, and the whole of English literature. He quotes freely from the Shakespearean tragedies and even has at his disposal a host of obscure lines from obscure poets in Latin and English. He is not a gloomy person, but Benedictus de Spinoza is his favorite author. He is well acquainted with psychology, and his rescue of Bertie or others in trouble frequently derives from his knowledge of the "psychology" of the individuals in question. He is moved by the feudal spirit, but he is tipped in a handsome way by his employer for services rendered, and he accepts the just praises of all whom he serves.

The series is also distinguished by a host of lesser figures who threaten to jostle Bertie out of his role as the main character. Gussie Fink-Nottle is an old schoolmate of Bertie, and he is engaged to a particularly insipid woman, Madelaine Basset, a romantic intellectual. She has a poetic phrase for everything and drives Bertie and all who know her crazy merely by opening her mouth. Madelaine is one of Bertie's former girlfriends, and she imagines that Bertie is still in love with her. The hero's duty is to see that the pending nuptials between Gussie and Madelaine take place, but Gussie, who is even less intelligent than Bertie, keeps fouling things up. Bertie goes at once to his aid, but nothing works until Jeeves puts his brain to the trial.

Eulalie Soeurs · Jeeves never fails in his destined role as guardian angel to Wooster, but the plots frequently have an additional twist. Jeeves, though not omniscient as a character, has recourse to a body of information that none of the others shares. As a butler and member of a London club for butlers, he has access to a private collection of anecdotes supplied by other butlers about their masters. It is a point of honor for a manservant to supply all vital information about his employer—tastes, eccentricities, and even weaknesses—so that others will be well advised before taking employment with the same person. The collection has something about almost every rich male in England, and when affairs take on a desperate note, Jeeves is dispatched to London to find out something about the adversary that might serve as blackmail. Thus, one of the silliest of Wodehouse's creations, a proto-Fascist named Spode who is inclined to bully everyone and especially Wooster, is disarmed when it is discovered that he designs ladies' underwear. As Wooster is being threatened with decapitation by Spode, he mentions the name of Spode's company, *Eulalie Soeurs*, and the man is silent and servile, though it is only at the very end and with the bribe of a trip around the world that Jeeves tells Wooster the meaning of that magic phrase.

The Jeeves novels, then, have at least three plots running through them, and it is in his scrupulous concern for the development of the plot that the author exhibits one of his greatest talents. The key to Wodehouse's concerns for the logic and probability of his plots derives, perhaps, from his lifelong interest in detective novels; Wodehouse frequently avowed that they were his favorite kind of reading. The plots of the great Wodehouse comedies develop like that of a superb mystery: There is not an extraneous word or action in them.

The Psmith novels · For most Wodehouse readers, the Blandings and Jeeves series of novels represent the highest level of Wodehouse's art, but there are many other novels that do not fit into either category. In 1906, Wodehouse published *Love Among the Chickens*, which has in it the first of Wodehouse's several "nonheroes," Ukridge. Ukridge has almost no attractive qualities. He does not work; rather, he lives by his wits and is able to sponge off his friends and from many who scarcely know him. Another character who figures prominently in several novels is Psmith. The name is pronounced "Smith," and its owner freely admits that he added the *P* to distinguish himself from the vast number of Smiths. The name is one mark of the young man's condescending arrogance, but he is helpful toward all who seek his assistance. A Psmith novel usually ends with the marriage of a friend or simply a bit of adventure for the central figure. Psmith does not hold a regular job, and like many of the other young male protagonists in Wodehouse novels, he seems to be a textbook study in the antiwork ethic. The heroes in the Psmith series, like the central figure himself, are not ignorant or stupid men, but the novelist's emphasis is on their old school ties and on physical excellence. They are, as one critic noted, "strong, healthy animals." They are good at sports and they triumph over poets and other intellectual types. On occasion, they may drink heavily, but they make up for an infrequent binge by an excess of exercise.

Evelyn Waugh once suggested that the clue to Wodehouse's great success was the fact that he was unaware of the doctrine of original sin. In the Wodehouse novel, virtue is inevitably triumphant, and even vice is seldom punished with anything that might be called severity. In Wodehouse's catalog of bad sorts, one group alone stands out: intellectual snobs. In his frequent descriptions of such types, Wodehouse may have consciously been responding to the disdain with which intellectuals have usually treated his work; in turn, the author had almost no sympathy for the group that he often described as "eggheads." Whatever may have been his motivation, the athletes and the innocents invariably triumph over those who carry on about their own minds or some esoteric art form. It is therefore hard to agree with critics such as George Orwell who find elements of snobbery in the Wodehouse novels. It is true that the creator of Blandings Castle loved big houses and grand vistas, but the aristocrats are too obviously flawed in intellect or temper for any to assume Wodehouse was on their side. It may be, however, that Wodehouse was an inverse snob in his treatment of intellectuals, both male and female. None of them succeeds in his fiction.

There is nothing like a consensus over the source or qualities of Wodehouse's greatness as a writer. Scholars have traced Wooster and Jeeves back through English literature to authors such as Ben Jonson, but source studies do not account for Wodehouse's genius. He has been called the laureate of the Edwardian age, but there is little resemblance between the Edwardian world and that of P. G. Wodehouse. For most readers, the triumph of a Wodehouse novel is in its artistry of presentation. All the aspects of fiction–good story, effective characters, and dialogue which is often brilliant–are present. Wodehouse once summed up his career as well as anyone ever has: "When in due course Charon ferries me across the Styx and everyone is telling everyone else what a rotten writer I was, I hope at least one voice will be heard piping up: 'But he did take trouble.'" Wodehouse did indeed take trouble with his work, but given the rich abundance of that work and the incredible smoothness of each volume, the reader would never know.

John R. Griffin

Other major works

SHORT FICTION: *Tales of St. Austin's,* 1903; *The Man Upstairs, and Other Stories,* 1914; *The Man with Two Left Feet, and Other Stories,* 1917; *My Man Jeeves,* 1919; *The Clicking of Cuthbert,* 1922 (also known as *Golf Without Tears*); *Ukridge,* 1924 (also known as *He Rather Enjoyed It*); *Carry on, Jeeves!* 1925; *The Heart of a Goof,* 1926 (also known as *Divots*); *Meet Mr. Mulliner,* 1927; *Mr. Mulliner Speaking,* 1929; *Jeeves Omnibus,* 1931 (revised as *The World of Jeeves,* 1967); *Mulliner Nights,* 1933; *Blandings Castle and Elsewhere,* 1935 (also known as *Blandings Castle*); *Mulliner Omnibus,* 1935 (revised as *The World of Mr. Mulliner,* 1972); *Young Men in Spats,* 1936; *Lord Emsworth and Others,* 1937 (also known as *The Crime Wave at Blandings*); *Dudley Is Back to Normal,* 1940; *Eggs, Beans, and Crumpets,* 1940; *Nothing Serious,* 1950; *Selected Stories,* 1958; *A Few Quick Ones,* 1959; *Plum Pie,* 1966; *The Golf Omnibus: Thirty-one Golfing Short Stories,* 1973; *The World of Psmith,* 1974.

PLAYS: *A Gentleman of Leisure,* pr. 1911 (with John Stapleton); *Oh, Lady! Lady!,* pr. 1918; *The Play's the Thing,* pr. 1926 (adaptation of Ferenc Molnár); *Good Morning, Bill,* pr. 1927 (adaptation of László Fodor); *A Damsel in Distress,* pr. 1928 (with Ian Hay); *Baa, Baa, Black Sheep,* pr. 1929 (with Hay); *Candlelight,* pr. 1929 (adaptation of Siegfried Geyer); *Leave It to Psmith,* pr. 1930 (adaptation with Hay); *Anything Goes,* pr. 1934 (with Guy Bolton and others); *Carry On, Jeeves,* pb. 1956 (adaptation with Bolton).

NONFICTION: *William Tell Told Again,* 1904 (with additional fictional material); *Louder and Funnier,* 1932; *Bring on the Girls: The Improbable Story of Our Life in Musical Comedy, with Pictures to Prove It,* 1953 (with Guy Bolton); *Performing Flea: A Self-Portrait in Letters,* 1953 (revised as *Author! Author!* 1962; W. Townend, editor); *America, I Like You,* 1956 (revised as *Over Seventy: An Autobiography with Digressions,* 1957).

EDITED TEXTS: *A Century of Humour,* 1934; *The Best of Modern Humor,* 1952 (with Scott Meredith); *The Week-End Book of Humor,* 1952 (with Meredith); *A Carnival of Modern Humor,* 1967 (with Meredith).

Bibliography

Green, Benny. *P. G. Wodehouse: A Literary Biography.* New York: Rutledge Press, 1981. This very useful study, arranged chronologically, traces the connections between Wodehouse's personal experiences and his fictional creations. Illustrations, a chronology, notes, a bibliography, and an index are included.

Hall, Robert A., Jr. *The Comic Style of P. G. Wodehouse.* Hamden, Conn.: Archon Books, 1974. Provides a discussion of three types of Wodehouse's stories, including school tales and juvenilia, romances and farces, and the various sagas. The detailed analysis of Wodehouse's narrative techniques and linguistic characteristics is indispensable for anyone interested in understanding his style. Contains an index and a bibliography.

Phelps, Barry. *P. G. Wodehouse: Man and Myth.* London: Constable, 1992. Phelps has uncovered much new information in this sympathetic biography. He also provides an unusual number of useful appendices including a Wodehouse chronology, family tree, and bibliography.

Sproat, Iain. *Wodehouse at War.* New Haven, Conn.: Ticknor & Fields, 1981. This volume is necessary to those studying the sad war events that clouded Wodehouse's life and to those interested in exploring the individual psychology that produced such comic delight. Sproat, a politician as well as a fan, vindicates Wodehouse's innocence in the infamous Nazi broadcasts, which are reprinted here. Includes appendices of documents in the case.

Usborne, Richard. *After Hours with P. G. Wodehouse.* London: Hutchinson, 1991. A collection of entertaining pieces on Wodehouse's life and death written somewhat in the spirit of Wodehouse himself.

_____. *Wodehouse at Work to the End.* 1961. Rev. ed. London: Barrie & Jenkins, 1976. Includes individual chapters on Wodehouse's major series characters; very helpful appendices of lists of his books, plays, and films; and an index. For the diehard fan, each chapter is followed by a brief section called "Images," with humorous quotations from the works. The introduction refers to other secondary sources.

Voorhees, Richard J. *P. G. Wodehouse.* New York: Twayne, 1966. An excellent introductory volume on Wodehouse, with chapters on his life, his public school stories, his early novels, the development of his romantic and comic novels, a description of the Wodehouse world, and a discussion of the place of that world in British literature. A chronology, notes and references, and a bibliography of primary and secondary sources are provided.

Virginia Woolf

Born: London, England; January 25, 1882
Died: Rodmell, Sussex, England; March 28, 1941

Principal long fiction · *The Voyage Out,* 1915; *Night and Day,* 1919; *Jacob's Room,* 1922; *Mrs. Dalloway,* 1925; *To the Lighthouse,* 1927; *Orlando: A Biography,* 1928; *The Waves,* 1931; *Flush: A Biography,* 1933; *The Years,* 1937; *Between the Acts,* 1941.

Other literary forms · To say that Virginia Woolf lived to write is no exaggeration. Her output was both prodigious and varied; counting her posthumously published works, it fills more than forty volumes. Beyond her novels her fiction encompasses several short-story collections. As a writer of nonfiction, Woolf was similarly prolific, her book-length works including *Roger Fry: A Biography* (1940) and two influential feminist statements, *A Room of One's Own* (1929) and *Three Guineas* (1938). Throughout her life, Woolf also produced criticism and reviews; the best-known collections are *The Common Reader: First Series* (1925) and *The Common Reader: Second Series* (1932). In 1966 and 1967, the four volumes of *Collected Essays* were published. Additional books of essays, reviews, and sketches continue to appear, most notably the illuminating selection of autobiographical materials, *Moments of Being* (1976). Her letters–3,800 of them survive–are available in six volumes; when publication was completed, her diaries stood at five. Another collection, of Woolf's essays, also proved a massive, multivolume undertaking.

Achievements · From the appearance of her first novel in 1915, Virginia Woolf's work was received with respect—an important point, since she was extremely sensitive to criticism. Descendant of a distinguished literary family, member of the avant-garde Bloomsbury Group, herself an experienced critic and reviewer, she was taken seriously as an artist. Nevertheless, her early works were not financially successful; she was forty before she earned a living from her writing. From the start, the rather narrow territory of her novels precluded broad popularity, peopled as they were with sophisticated, sexually reserved, upper-middle-class characters, finely attuned to their sensibilities and relatively insulated from the demands of mundane existence. When in *Jacob's Room* she first abandoned the conventional novel to experiment with the interior monologues and lyrical poetic devices which characterize her mature method, she also began to develop a reputation as a "difficult" or "high-brow" writer, though undeniably an important one. Not until the brilliant fantasy *Orlando* was published did she enjoy a definite commercial success. Thereafter, she received both critical and popular acclaim; *The Years* was even a bona fide best-seller.

During the 1930's, Woolf became the subject of critical essays and two book-length studies; some of her works were translated into French. At the same time, however, her novels began to be judged as irrelevant to a world beset by growing economic and political chaos. At her death in 1941, she was widely regarded as a pioneer of modernism but also reviewed by many as the effete, melancholic "invalid priestess of Bloomsbury," a stereotype her friend and fellow novelist E. M. Forster dismissed at the time as wholly inaccurate; she was, he insisted, "tough, sensitive but tough."

Over the next twenty-five years, respectful attention to Woolf's work continued, but in the late 1960's, critical interest accelerated dramatically and has remained strong. Two reasons for this renewed notice seem particularly apparent. First, Woolf's feminist essays *A Room of One's Own* and *Three Guineas* became rallying documents in the growing women's movement; readers who might not otherwise have discovered her novels were drawn to them via her nonfiction and tended to read them primarily as validations of her feminist thinking. Second, with the appearance of her husband Leonard Woolf's five-volume autobiography from 1965-1969, her nephew Quentin Bell's definitive two-volume biography of her in 1972, and the full-scale editions of her own diaries and letters commencing in the mid-1970's, Woolf's life has become one of the most thoroughly documented of any modern author. Marked by intellectual and sexual unconventionality, madness, and suicide, it is for today's readers also one of the most fascinating; the steady demand for memoirs, reminiscences, and photograph collections relating to her has generated what is sometimes disparagingly labeled "the Virginia Woolf industry." At its worst, such insatiable curiosity is morbidly voyeuristic, distracting from and trivializing Woolf's achievement; on a more responsible level, it has led to serious, provocative reevaluations of the political and especially the feminist elements in her work, as well as to redefinitions of her role as an artist.

Biography · Daughter of the eminent editor and critic Sir Leslie Stephen and Julia Jackson Duckworth, both of whom had been previously widowed, Virginia Woolf was born in 1882 into a solidly late Victorian intellectual and social milieu. Her father's first wife had been William Makepeace Thackeray's daughter; James Russell Lowell was her godfather; visitors to the Stephens' London household included Henry James, George Meredith, and Thomas Hardy. From childhood on, she had access to her father's superb library, benefitting from his guidance and commentary on her rigorous, precocious reading. Nevertheless, unlike her brothers, she did not receive a formal university education, a lack she always regretted and that partly explains the anger in *Three Guineas*, where she proposes a "university of outsiders." (Throughout her life she declined all academic honors.)

In 1895, when Woolf was thirteen, her mother, just past fifty, suddenly died. Altruistic, self-sacrificing, totally devoted to her demanding husband and large family, the beautiful Julia Stephen fulfilled the Victorian ideal of womanhood and exhausted herself doing so; her daughter would movingly eulogize her as Mrs. Ramsay in *To the Lighthouse*. The loss devastated Woolf, who experienced at that time the first of four major mental breakdowns in her life, the last of which would end in death.

Leslie Stephen, twenty years his wife's senior and thus sanguinely expecting her to pilot him comfortably through old age, was devastated in another way. Retreating histrionically into self-pitying but deeply felt grief, like that of his fictional counterpart, Mr. Ramsay, he transferred his intense demands for sympathetic attention to a succession of what could only seem to him achingly inadequate substitutes for his dead wife: first, his stepdaughter Stella Duckworth, who herself died suddenly in 1897, then, Virginia's older sister Vanessa. The traditional feminine role would eventually have befallen Virginia had Leslie Stephen not died in 1904. Writing in her 1928 diary on what would have been her father's ninety-sixth birthday, Woolf reflects that, had he lived, "His life would have entirely ended mine. . . . No writing, no books;—inconceivable."

On her father's death, Woolf sustained her second incapacitating breakdown. Yet she also gained, as her diary suggests, something crucial: freedom, which took an immediate form. Virginia, Vanessa, and their brothers Thoby and Adrian abandoned the Stephen house in respectable Kensington to set up a home in the seedy bohemian district of London known as Bloomsbury. There, on Thursday evenings, a coterie of Thoby Stephen's Cambridge University friends regularly gathered to talk in an atmosphere of free thought, avant-garde art, and sexual tolerance, forming the nucleus of what came to be called the Bloomsbury Group. At various stages in its evolution over the next decade, the group included such luminaries as biographer Lytton Strachey, novelist E. M. Forster, art critic Roger Fry, and economist John Maynard Keynes. In 1911, they were joined by another of Thoby's Cambridge friends, a colonial official just returned from seven years in Ceylon, Leonard Woolf; Virginia Stephen married him the following year. Scarcely twelve months after the wedding, Virginia Woolf's third severe breakdown began, marked by a suicide attempt; her recovery took almost two years.

The causes of Woolf's madness have been much debated and the treatment she was prescribed—bed rest, milk, withdrawal of intellectual stimulation—much disputed, especially since she apparently never received psychoanalytic help, even though the Hogarth Press, founded by the Woolfs in 1917, was one of Sigmund Freud's earliest English publishers. A history of insanity ran in the Stephen family; if Virginia were afflicted with a hereditary nervous condition, it was thought, then, that must be accepted as unalterable. On the other hand, the timing of these three breakdowns prompts speculation about more subtle causes. About her parents' deaths she evidently felt strong guilt; of *To the Lighthouse*, the fictionalized account of her parents' relationship, she would later say, "I was obsessed by them both, unhealthily; and writing of them was a necessary act." Marriage was for her a deliberately sought yet disturbing commitment, representing a potential loss of autonomy and a retreat into what her would-be novelist Terence Hewet envisions in *The Voyage Out* as a walled-up, firelit room. She found her own marriage sexually disappointing, perhaps in part because she had been molested as both a child and a young woman by her two Duckworth stepbrothers.

In the late twentieth century, feminist scholars especially argued as a cause of Woolf's madness the burden of being a greatly talented woman in a world hostile to feminine achievement, a situation that Woolf strikingly depicts in *A Room of One's Own* as the plight of Wil-

Courtesy D.C. Public Library

liam Shakespeare's hypothetical sister. Indeed, the young Virginia Stephen might plunder her father's library all day, but by teatime she was expected to don the role of deferential Victorian female in a rigidly patriarchal household. Yet once she settled in Bloomsbury, she enjoyed unconventional independence and received much sympathetic encouragement of her gifts, most of all from her husband.

Leonard Woolf, himself a professional writer and literary editor, connected her madness directly with her genius, saying that she concentrated more intensely on her work than any writer he had ever known. Her books passed through long, difficult gestations; her sanity was always most vulnerable immediately after a novel was finished. Expanding on his belief that the imagination in his wife's books and the delusions of her breakdowns "all came from the same place in her mind," some critics go so far as to claim her madness as the very source of her art, permitting her to make mystical descents into inner space from which she returned with sharpened perception.

It is significant, certainly, that although Woolf's first publication, an unsigned article for *The Guardian*, appeared just two months after her 1904 move to Bloomsbury, her first novel, over which she labored for seven years, was only completed shortly after her marriage; her breakdown occurred three months after its acceptance for publication. Very early, therefore, Leonard Woolf learned to keep a daily record of his wife's health; throughout their life together, he would be alert for those signs of fatigue or erratic behavior that signaled approaching danger and the need for her customary rest cure. Rational, efficient, uncomplaining, Leonard Woolf has been condemned by some disaffected scholars as a pseudosaintly nurse who benignly badgered his patient into crippling dependency. The compelling argument against this extreme interpretation is Virginia Woolf's astonishing productivity after she recovered from her third illness. Although there were certainly periods of instability and near disaster, the following twenty-five years were immensely fruitful as she discarded traditional fiction to move toward realizing her unique vision, all the while functioning actively and diversely as a fine critic, too.

After Woolf's ninth novel, *The Years*, was finished in 1936, however, she came closer to mental collapse than she had been at any time since 1913. Meanwhile, a larger pattern of breakdown was developing in the world around her as World War II became inevitable. Working at her Sussex home on her last book, *Between the Acts*, she could hear the Battle of Britain being fought over her head; her London house was severely damaged in the Blitz. Yet strangely, that novel was her easiest to write; Leonard Woolf, ever watchful, was struck by her tranquility during this period. The gradual symptoms of warning were absent this time; when her depression began, he would recall, it struck her "like a sudden blow." She began to hear voices and knew what was coming. On February 26, 1941, she finished *Between the Acts*. Four weeks later, she went out for one of her usual walks across the Sussex downs, placed a heavy stone in her pocket, and stepped into the River Ouse. Within minutes Leonard Woolf arrived at its banks to find her walking stick and hat lying there. Her body was recovered three weeks later.

Analysis · In one of her most famous pronouncements on the nature of fiction—as a practicing critic, she had much to say on the subject—Virginia Woolf insists that "life is not a series of gig lamps symmetrically arranged; but a luminous halo, a semi-transparent envelope surrounding us from the beginning of consciousness to the end." In an ordinary day, she argues, "thousands of ideas" course through the human brain;

"thousands of emotions" meet, collide, and disappear "in astonishing disorder." Amid this hectic interior flux, the trivial and the vital, the past and the present, are constantly interacting; there is endless tension between the multitude of ideas and emotions rushing through one's consciousness and the numerous impressions scoring on it from the external world. Thus, even personal identity becomes evanescent, continually reordering itself as "the atoms of experience . . . fall upon the mind." It follows, then, that human beings must have great difficulty communicating with one another, for of this welter of perceptions that define individual personality, only a tiny fraction can ever be externalized in word or gesture. Yet, despite—in fact, because of—their frightening isolation as unknowable entities, people yearn to unite both with one another and with some larger pattern of order hidden behind the flux, to experience time standing still momentarily, to see matches struck that briefly illuminate the darkness.

Given the complex phenomenon of human subjectivity, Woolf asks, "Is it not the task of the novelist to convey this varying, this unknown and uncircumscribed spirit . . . with as little mixture of the alien and external as possible?" The conventional novel form is plainly inadequate for such a purpose, she maintains. Dealing sequentially with a logical set of completed past actions that occur in a coherent, densely detailed physical and social environment, presided over by an omniscient narrator interpreting the significance of it all, the traditional novel trims and shapes experience into a rational but falsified pattern. "Is life like this?" Woolf demands rhetorically. "Must novels be like this?"

In Woolf's first two books, nevertheless, she attempted to work within conventional modes, discovering empirically that they could not convey her vision. Although in recent years some critics have defended *The Voyage Out* and *Night and Day* as artistically satisfying in their own right, both novels have generally been considered interesting mainly for what they foreshadow of Woolf's later preoccupations and techniques.

The Voyage Out · *The Voyage Out* is the story of Rachel Vinrace, a naïve and talented twenty-four-year-old amateur pianist who sails from England to a small resort on the South American coast, where she vacations with relatives. There, she meets a fledgling novelist, Terence Hewet; on a pleasure expedition up a jungle river, they declare their love. Shortly thereafter, Rachel falls ill with a fever and dies. The novel's exotic locale, large cast of minor characters, elaborate scenes of social comedy, and excessive length are all atypical of Woolf's mature work. Already, however, many of her later concerns are largely emerging. The resonance of the title itself anticipates Woolf's poetic symbolism; the "voyage out" can be the literal trip across the Atlantic or up the South American river, but it also suggests the progression from innocence to experience, from life to death, which she later depicts using similar water imagery. Her concern with premature death and how survivors come to terms with it prefigures *Jacob's Room, Mrs. Dalloway, To the Lighthouse,* and *The Waves.* Most significant is her portrayal of a world in which characters are forever striving to overcome their isolation from one another. The ship on which Rachel "voyages out" is labeled by Woolf an "emblem of the loneliness of human life." Terence, Rachel's lover, might be describing his creator's own frustration when he says he is trying "to write a novel about Silence, the things people don't say. But the difficulty is immense."

Yet moments of unity amid seemingly unconquerable disorder do occur. On a communal level, one such transformation happens at a ball being held to celebrate the engagement of two English guests at the resort's small hotel. When the musicians go home, Rachel appropriates the piano and plays Mozart, hunting songs, and hymn tunes as the guests gradually resume dancing, each in a newly expressive, uninhibited way, eventually to join hands in a gigantic round dance. When the circle breaks and each member spins away to become individual once more, Rachel modulates to Bach; her weary yet exhilarated listeners sit quietly and allow themselves to be soothed by the serene complexity of the music. As dawn breaks outside and Rachel plays on, they envision "themselves and their lives, and the whole of human life advancing nobly under the direction of the music." They have transcended their single identities temporarily to gain a privileged glimpse of some larger pattern beyond themselves.

If Rachel through her art briefly transforms the lives of a small community, she herself privately discerns fleeting stability through her growing love for Terence. Yet even love is insufficient; although in the couple's newfound sense of union "divisions disappeared," Terence feels that Rachel seems able "to pass away to unknown places where she had no need of him." In the elegiac closing scenes of illness (which Woolf reworked many times and which are the most original as well as moving part of the novel), Rachel "descends into another world"; she is "curled up at the bottom of the sea." Terence, sitting by her bedside, senses that "they seemed to be thinking together; he seemed to be Rachel as well as himself." When she ceases breathing, he experiences "an immense feeling of peace," a "complete union" with her that shatters when he notices an ordinary table covered with crockery and realizes in horror that in this world he will never see Rachel again. For her, stability has been achieved; for him, the isolating flux has resumed.

Night and Day · Looking back on *The Voyage Out*, Woolf could see, she said, why readers found it "a more gallant and inspiring spectacle" than her next and least known book *Night and Day*. This second novel is usually regarded as her most traditional in form and subject—in its social satire, her obeisance to Jane Austen. Its dancelike plot, however, in which mismatched young couples eventually find their true loves, suggests the magical atmosphere of William Shakespeare's romantic comedies as well. References to Shakespeare abound in the book; for example, the delightfully eccentric Mrs. Hilbery characterizes herself as one of his wise fools, and when at the end she presides over the repatterning of the couples in London, she has just arrived from a pilgrimage to Stratford-upon-Avon. Coincidentally, *Night and Day* is the most conventionally dramatic of Woolf's novels, full of dialogue, exits and entrances; characters are constantly taking omnibuses and taxis across London from one contrived scene to the next.

Like *The Voyage Out*, *Night and Day* does point to Woolf's enduring preoccupations. It is, too, a novel depicting movement from innocence to maturity and escape from the conventional world through the liberating influence of love. Ralph Denham, a London solicitor from a large, vulgar, middle-class family living in suburban High-gate, would prefer to move to a Norfolk cottage and write. Katharine Hilbery measures out her days serving tea in her wealthy family's beautiful Chelsea home and helping her disorganized mother produce a biography of their forebear, a great nineteenth century poet. Her secret passions, however, are mathematics and astronomy. These seeming opposites, Ralph and Katharine, are alike in that both retreat at night to their rooms to pursue their private visions. The entire novel is concerned with such dualities—public selves and private selves, activity and contemplation, fact and imagination; but Woolf also depicts the unity that Ralph and Katharine can achieve, notwithstanding the social and intellectual barriers separating them. At the end, as the couple leaves Katharine's elegant but constraining home to walk in the open night air, "they lapsed gently into silence, travelling the dark paths side by side towards something discerned in the distance which gradually possessed them both."

The sustained passages of subtle interior analysis by which Woolf charts the couple's growing realization of their need for each other define her real area of fictional interest, but they are hemmed in by a tediously constrictive traditional structure. Except for her late novel, *The Years*, also comparatively orthodox in form, her first two books took the longest to finish and underwent the most extensive revisions, undoubtedly because she was writing against her grain. Nevertheless, they represented a necessary apprenticeship; as she would later remark of *Night and Day*, "You must put it all in before you can leave out."

Jacob's Room · Woolf dared to leave out a great deal in the short experimental novel she wrote next. Described in conventional terms, *Jacob's Room* is a *Bildungsroman* or "novel of formation" tracing its hero's development from childhood to maturity: Jacob Flanders is first portrayed as a small boy studying a tide pool on a Cornish beach; at twenty-six, he dies fighting in World War I. In structure, style, and tone, however, *Jacob's Room* defies such labeling. It does not move in steady chronological fashion but in irregular leaps. Of the fourteen chapters, two cover Jacob's childhood, two, his college years at Cambridge, the remainder, his life as a young adult working in London and traveling abroad. In length, and hence in the complexity with which various periods of Jacob's existence are treated, the chapters range from one to twenty-eight pages. They vary, that is, as the process of growth itself does.

Individual chapters are likewise discontinuous in structure, broken into irregular segments that convey multiple, often simultaneous perspectives. The ten-page chapter 8, for example, opens with Jacob slamming the door of his London room as he starts for work in the morning; he is then glimpsed at his office desk. Meanwhile, on a table back in his room lies his mother's unopened letter to him, placed there the previous night by his lover, Florinda; its contents and Mrs. Flanders herself are evoked. The narrator then discourses on the significance of letter-writing. Jacob is next seen leaving work for the day; in Greek Street, he spies Florinda on another man's arm. At eight o'clock, Rose Shaw, a guest at a party Jacob attended several nights earlier, walks through Holburn, meditating bitterly on the ironies of love and death. The narrator sketches London by lamplight. Then, Jacob is back in his room reading by the fire a newspaper account of the Prime Minister's speech on Home Rule; the night is very cold. The narrator abruptly shifts perspective from congested London to the open countryside, describing the snow that has been accumulating since mid-afternoon; an old shepherd crossing a field hears a distant clock strike. Back in London, Jacob also hears the hour chiming, rakes out his fire, and goes to bed. There is no story here in any conventional sense, no action being furthered; in the entire ten pages, only one sentence is direct dialogue. What Woolf delineates is the *texture* of an ordinary day in the life of Jacob and the world in which he exists. Clock time moves the chapter forward, while spatially the chapter radiates outward from the small area Jacob occupies. Simultaneously, in the brief reference to the Prime Minister, Woolf suggests the larger procession of modern history that will inexorably sweep Jacob to premature death.

Such indirection and understatement characterize the whole novel: "It is no use trying to sum people up," the narrator laments. "One must follow hints." Thus, Jacob is described mainly from the outside, defined through the impressions he makes on others, from a hotel chambermaid to a Cambridge don, and by his surroundings and possessions. Even his death is conveyed obliquely: Mrs. Flanders, half asleep in her Yorkshire house, hears "dull sounds"; it cannot be guns, she thinks, it must be the sea. On the next page, she stands in her dead son's London room, holding a pair of Jacob's old shoes and asking his friend pathetically, "What am I to do with these, Mr. Bonamy?" The novel ends.

To construct Jacob's ultimately unknowable biography out of such fragments, Woolf evolves not only a new structure but a new style. Long, fluid sentences contain precise physical details juxtaposed with metaphysical speculations on the evanescence of life and the impossibility of understanding another person. Lyrical descriptions of nature—waves, moths, falling snow, birds rising and settling—are interspersed to suggest life's beauty and fragility. Images and phrases recur as unifying motifs: Jacob is repeatedly associated with Greek literature and myth and spends his last fulfilling days visiting the Parthenon. Most important, Woolf begins to move freely in and out of her characters' minds to capture the flow of sense impressions mingling with memory, emotion, and random association, experimenting with that narrative method conveniently if imprecisely labeled "stream of consciousness."

Jacob's Room is not a mature work, especially with its intrusive narrator, who can be excessively chatty, archly pedantic, and sententious. Woolf protests the difficulties of her task ("In short, the observer is choked with observations") and cannot quite follow the logic of her new method; after an essay-like passage on the necessity of illusion, for example, she awkwardly concludes, "Jacob, no doubt, thought something in this fashion. . . ." Even the lovely passages of poetic description at times seem self-indulgent. The book definitely shows its seams. Woolf's rejection of traditional novel structure, however, and her efforts to eliminate "the alien and the external" make *Jacob's Room* a dazzling advance in her ability to embody her philosophic vision: "Life is but a procession of shadows, and God knows why it is that we embrace them so eagerly, and see them depart with such anguish, being shadows."

Mrs. Dalloway · Within three years, Woolf had resolved her technical problems superbly in *Mrs. Dalloway*. The intruding narrator vanishes; though the freedom with which point of view shifts among characters and settings clearly posits an omniscient intelligence, the narrator's observations are now subtly integrated with the thoughts of her characters, and the transitions between scenes flow organically. Woolf's subject is also better suited to her method: Whereas *Jacob's Room* is a story of youthful potential tragically cut off, *Mrs. Dalloway* is a novel of middle age, about what people have become as the result of choices made, opportunities seized or refused. Jacob Flanders had but a brief past; the characters in *Mrs. Dalloway* must come to terms with theirs, sifting and valuing the memories that course through their minds.

The book covers one June day in the life of Clarissa Dalloway, fifty-two years old, an accomplished London political hostess and wife of a Member of Parliament. A recent serious illness from which she is still recovering has made her freshly appreciate the wonder of life as she prepares for the party she will give that evening. Peter Walsh, once desperately in love with her, arrives from India, where he has had an undistinguished career; he calls on her and is invited to the party, at which another friend from the past, Sally Seton, formerly a romantic and now the conventional wife of a Manchester industrialist, will also unexpectedly appear. Running parallel with Clarissa's day is that of the mad Septimus Warren Smith, a surviving Jacob Flanders, shell-shocked in the war; his suicide in the late afternoon delays the arrival of another of Clarissa's guests, the eminent nerve specialist Sir William Bradshaw. Learning of this stranger's death, Clarissa must confront the inevitability of her own.

Mrs. Dalloway is also, then, a novel about time itself (its working title at one point was *The Hours*). Instead of using chapters or other formal sectioning, Woolf structures the book by counterpointing clock time, signaled by the obtrusive hourly tolling of Big Ben, against the subjective flow of time in her characters' minds as they recover the past and envision the future. Not only does she move backward and forward in time, however; she also creates an effect of simultaneity that is especially crucial in linking Septimus's story with Clarissa's. Thus, when Clarissa Dalloway, buying flowers that morning in a Bond Street shop, hears "a pistol shot" outside and emerges to see a large, official automobile that has backfired, Septimus is standing in the crowd blocked by the car and likewise reacting to this "violent explosion" ("The world has raised its whip; where will it descend?"). Later, when Septimus's frightened young Italian wife Rezia guides him to Regents Park to calm him before their appointment with Bradshaw, he has a terrifying hallucination of his dead friend Evans, killed just before the Armistice; Peter Walsh, passing their bench, wonders, "What awful fix had they got themselves in to look so desperate as that on a fine summer morning?" This atmosphere of intensely populated time and space, of many anonymous lives intersecting briefly, of the world resonating with unwritten novels, comic and tragic, accounts in part for the richly poignant texture of nearly all Woolf's mature work.

In her early thinking about *Mrs. Dalloway*, Virginia Woolf wanted to show a "world seen by the sane and the insane, side by side." Although the novel definitely focuses on Clarissa, Septimus functions as a kind of double, representing her own responses to life carried to an untenable extreme. Both find great terror in life and also great joy; both want to withdraw from life into blissful isolation, yet both want to reach out to merge with others. Clarissa's friends, and indeed she herself, sense a "coldness" about her, "an impenetrability"; both Peter and Sally believe she chose safety rather than adventure by marrying the unimaginative, responsible Richard Dalloway. The quiet attic room where she now convalesces is described as a tower into which she retreats nunlike to a virginal narrow bed. Yet Clarissa also loves "life; London; this moment of June"–and her parties. Though some critics condemn her partygiving as shallow, trivial, even corrupt (Peter Walsh could make her wince as a girl by predicting that she would become "the perfect hostess"), Clarissa considers her parties a form of creativity, "an offering," "her gift" of bringing people together. For Septimus, the war has destroyed his capacity to feel; in his aloneness and withdrawal, he finds "an isolation full of sublimity; a freedom which the attached can never know"–he can elude "human nature," "the repulsive brute, with the blood-red nostrils." Yet just watching leaves quivering is for him "an exquisite joy"; he feels them "connected by millions of fibres with his own body" and wants to reveal this unity to the world because "communication is health; communication is happiness."

Desperate because of his suicide threats, Septimus's wife takes him to see Sir William Bradshaw. At the center of the novel, in one of the most bitter scenes in all of Woolf's writing (certainly one with strong autobiographical overtones), is Septimus's confrontation with this "priest of science," this man of "lightning skill" and "almost infallible accuracy" who "never spoke of 'madness'; he called it not having a sense of proportion." Within three minutes, he has discreetly recorded his diagnosis on a pink card ("a case of complete breakdown . . . with every symptom in an advanced stage"); Septimus will be sent to a beautiful house in the country where he will be taught to rest, to regain proportion. Rezia, agonized, understands that she has been failed by this obtuse, complacently cruel man whom Woolf symbolically connects with a larger system that prospers on intolerance and sends its best young men to fight futile wars. Septimus's suicide at this point becomes inevitable.

The two stories fuse when Bradshaw appears at the party. Learning of the reason for his lateness, Clarissa, deeply shaken, withdraws to a small side room, not unlike her attic tower, where she accurately imagines Septimus's suicide: "He had thrown himself from a window. Up had flashed the ground; through him, blundering, bruising, went the rusty spikes. . . . So she saw it." She also intuits the immediate cause: Bradshaw is "capable of some indescribable outrage, forcing your soul, that was it"; seeing him, this young man must have said to himself, "they make life intolerable, men like that." Thus, she sees, "death was defiance," a means to preserve one's center from being violated, but "death was an attempt to communicate," and in death, Septimus's message that all life is connected is heard by one unlikely person, Clarissa Dalloway. Reviewing her own past as she has reconstructed it this day, and forced anew to acknowledge her own mortality, she realizes that "he had made her feel the beauty." Spiritually regenerated, she returns to her party "to kindle and illuminate" life.

To the Lighthouse · In her most moving, complexly affirmative novel, *To the Lighthouse*, Woolf portrays another woman whose creativity lies in uniting people, Mrs. Ramsay. For this luminous evocation of her own parents' marriage, Woolf drew on memories of her girlhood summers at St. Ives, Cornwall (here transposed to an island in the Hebrides), to focus on her perennial themes, the difficulties and joys of human communication, especially as frustrated by time and death.

The plot is absurdly simple: An expedition to a lighthouse is postponed, then completed a decade later. Woolf's mastery, however, of the interior monologue in this novel makes such a fragile plot line quite sufficient; the real "story" of *To the Lighthouse* is the reader's gradually increasing intimacy with its characters' richly depicted inner lives; the reader's understanding expands in concert with the characters' own growing insights.

Woolf again devises an experimental structure for her work, this time of three unequal parts. Approximately the first half of the novel, entitled "The Window," occurs during a single day at the seaside home occupied by an eminent philosopher, Mr. Ramsay, his wife, and a melange of children, guests, and servants, including Lily Briscoe, an amateur painter in her thirties, unmarried. Mrs. Ramsay's is the dominant consciousness in this section. A short, exquisitely beautiful center section, "Time Passes," pictures the house succumbing to time during the family's ten-year absence and then being rescued from decay by two old women for the Ramsays' repossession. Periodically interrupting this natural flow of time are terse, bracketed, clock-time announcements like news bulletins, telling of the deaths of Mrs. Ramsay, the eldest son Andrew (in World War I), and the eldest daughter Prue (of childbirth complications). The final third, "The Lighthouse," also covers one day; the diminished family and several former guests having returned, the lighthouse expedition can now be completed. This section is centered almost entirely in Lily Briscoe's consciousness.

Because Mr. and Mrs. Ramsay are both strong personalities, they are sometimes interpreted too simply. Particularly in some readings by feminist critics, Mr. Ramsay is seen as an insufferable patriarch, arrogantly rational in his work but almost infantile emotionally, while Mrs. Ramsay is a Victorian Earth Mother, not only submitting unquestioningly to her husband's and children's excessive demands but actively trying to impose on all the other female characters her unliberated way of life. Such readings are sound to some extent, but they undervalue the vivid way that Woolf captures in the couple's monologues the conflicting mixture of motives and needs that characterize human beings of either sex. For example, Mrs. Ramsay is infuriated that her husband blights their youngest son James's anticipation of the lighthouse visit by announcing that it will storm tomorrow, yet his unflinching pursuit of truth is also something she most admires in him. Mr. Ramsay finds his wife's irrational habit of exaggeration maddening, but as she sits alone in a reverie, he respects her integrity and will not interrupt, "though it hurt him that she should look so distant, and he could not reach her, he could do nothing to help her." Lily, a shrewd observer who simultaneously adores and resists Mrs. Ramsay, perceives that "it would be a mistake . . . to simplify their relationship."

Amid these typical contradictions and mundane demands, however, "little daily miracles" may be achieved. One of Woolf's finest scenes, Mrs. Ramsay's dinner, provides a paradigm (though a summary can scarcely convey the richness of these forty pages). As she mechanically seats her guests at the huge table, Mrs. Ramsay glimpses her husband at the other end, "all in a heap, frowning": "She could not understand how she had ever felt any emotion of affection for him." Gloomily, she perceives that not just the two of them but everyone is separate and out of sorts. For example, Charles Tansley, Mr. Ramsay's disciple, who feels the whole family despises him, fidgets angrily; Lily, annoyed that Tansley is always telling her "women can't paint," purposely tries to irritate him; William Bankes would rather be home dining alone and fears that Mrs. Ramsay will read his mind. They all sense that "something [is] lacking"–they are divided from one another, sunk in their "treacherous" thoughts. Mrs. Ramsay wearily recognizes that "the whole of the effort of merging and flowing and creating rested on her."

She instructs two of her children to light the candles and set them around a beautiful fruit centerpiece that her daughter Rose has arranged for the table. This is Mrs. Ramsay's first stroke of artistry; the candles and fruit compose the table and the faces around it into an island, a sheltering haven: "Here, inside the room, seemed to be order and dry land; there, outside, a reflection in which things wavered and vanished, waterily." All the guests feel this change and have a sudden sense of making "common cause against that fluidity out there." Then the maid brings in a great steaming dish of *boeuf en daube* that even the finicky widower Bankes considers "a triumph." As the guests relish the succulent food and their camaraderie grows, Mrs. Ramsay, serving the last helpings from the depths of the pot, experiences a moment of perfect insight: "There it was, all around them. It partook . . . of eternity." She affirms to herself that "there is a coherence in things, a stability; something, she meant, that is immune from change, and shines out . . . in the face of the flowing, the fleeting." As is true of so much of Woolf's sparse dialogue, the ordinary words Mrs. Ramsay then speaks aloud can be read both literally and symbolically: "Yes, there is plenty for everybody." As the dinner ends and she passes out of the room triumphantly–the inscrutable poet Augustus Carmichael, who usually resists her magic, actually bows in homage–she looks back on the scene and sees that "it had become, she knew . . . already the past."

The burden of the past and the coming to terms with it are the focus of part 3. Just as "a sort of disintegration" sets in as soon as Mrs. Ramsay sweeps out of the dining room, so her death has left a larger kind of wreckage. Without her unifying artistry, all is disorder, as it was at the beginning of the dinner. In a gesture of belated atonement for quarreling with his wife over the original lighthouse trip, the melo-dramatically despairing Mr. Ramsay insists on making the expedition now with his children James and Cam, although both hate his tyranny and neither wants to go. As they set out, Lily remains behind to paint. Surely mirroring the creative anxiety of Woolf herself, she feels "a painful but exciting ecstasy" before her blank canvas, knowing how ideas that seem simple become "in practice immediately complex." As she starts making rhythmic strokes across the canvas, she loses "consciousness of outer things" and begins to meditate on the past, from which she gradually retrieves a vision of Mrs. Ramsay that will permit her to reconstruct and complete the painting she left unfinished a decade ago, one in which Mrs. Ramsay would have been, and will become again, a triangular shadow on a step (symbolically echoing the invisible "wedge-shaped core of darkness" to which Mrs. Ramsay feels herself shrinking during her moments of reverie). Through the unexpectedly intense pain of recalling her, Lily also comprehends Mrs. Ramsay's significance, her ability "to make the moment something permanent," as art does, to strike "this eternal passing and flowing . . . into stability." Mrs. Ramsay is able to make "life stand still here."

Meanwhile, Mr. Ramsay and his children are also voyaging into the past; Cam, dreamily drifting her hand in the water, begins, as her mother did, to see her father as bravely pursuing truth like a tragic hero. James bitterly relives the childhood scene when his father thoughtlessly dashed his hopes for the lighthouse visit, but as they near the lighthouse in the present and Mr. Ramsay offers his son rare praise, James too is reconciled. When they land, Mr. Ramsay himself, standing in the bow "very straight and tall," springs "lightly like a young man . . . on to the rock," renewed. Simultaneously, though the boat has long since disappeared from her sight and even the lighthouse itself seems blurred, Lily intuits that they have reached their goal and she completes her painting. All of them have reclaimed Mrs. Ramsay from death, and she has unified them; memory can defeat time. "Yes," Lily thinks, "I have had my vision." Clearly, Woolf had achieved hers too and transmuted the materials of a painful past into this radiant novel.

Although Woolf denied intending any specific symbolism for the lighthouse, it resonates with almost infinite possibilities, both within the book and in a larger way as an emblem of her work. Like the candles at the dinner party, it can be a symbol of safety and stability amid darkness and watery flux, its beams those rhythmically occurring moments of illumination that sustain Mrs. Ramsay and by extension everyone. Perhaps, however, it can also serve as a metaphor for human beings themselves as Woolf portrays them. The lighthouse signifies what can be objectively perceived of an individual—in Mrs. Ramsay's words, "our apparitions, the things you know us by"; but it also signals invisible, possibly tragic depths, for, as Mrs. Ramsay knew, "beneath it is all dark, it is all spreading, it is unfathomably deep."

The Waves ·In *The Waves*, widely considered her masterpiece, Woolf most resolutely overcomes the limits of the traditional novel. Entirely unique in form, *The Waves* cannot perhaps be called a novel at all; Woolf herself first projected a work of "prose yet poetry; a novel and a play." The book is a series of grouped soliloquies in varying combinations spoken by six friends, three men and three women, at successive stages in their lives from childhood to late middle age. Each grouping is preceded by a brief, lyrical "interlude" (Woolf's own term), set off in italic type, that describes an empty house by the sea as the sun moves across the sky in a single day.

The texture of these soliloquies is extremely difficult to convey; the term "soliloquy," in fact, is merely a critical convenience. Although each is introduced in the same straightforward way ("Neville said," "Jinny said"), they obviously are unspoken, representing each character's private vision. Their style is also unvarying—solemn, formal, almost stilted, like that of choral figures. The author has deliberately translated into a rigorously neutral, dignified idiom the conscious and subconscious reality her characters perceive but cannot articulate on their own. This method represents Woolf's most ambitious attempt to capture the unfathomable depths of separate human personalities which defy communication in ordinary life, and in ordinary novels. The abstraction of the device, however, especially in combination with the flow of cosmic time in the interludes, shows that she is also concerned with depicting a universal pattern which transcends mere individuals. Thus, once more Woolf treats her theme of human beings' attempts to overcome their isolation and to become part of a larger stabilizing pattern; this time, however, the theme is embodied in the very form of her work.

It would be inaccurate, though, to say that the characters exist only as symbols. Each has definable qualities and unique imagery; Susan, as an example, farm-bred and almost belligerently maternal, speaks in elemental images of wood smoke, grassy paths, flowers thick with pollen. Further, the characters often evoke one another's imagery; the other figures, for example, even in maturity picture the fearful, solitary Rhoda as a child rocking white petals in a brown basin of water. They are linked by intricately woven threads of common experience, above all by their shared admiration for a shadowy seventh character, Percival. Their gathering with him at a farewell dinner before he embarks on a career in India is one of the few actual events recorded in the soliloquies and also becomes one of those miraculous moments of unity comparable to that achieved by Mrs. Ramsay for her dinner guests; as they rise to leave the restaurant, all the characters are thinking as Louis does: "We pray, holding in our hands this common feeling, 'Do not move, do not let the swing-door cut to pieces this thing that we have made, that globes itself here. . . .'" Such union, however, is cruelly impermanent; two pages later, a telegram announces Percival's death in a riding accident. Bernard, trying to make sense of this absurdity, echoes the imagery of encircling unity that characterized their thoughts at the dinner: "Ideas break a thousand times for once that they globe themselves entire."

It is Bernard—identified, significantly, throughout the book as a storyteller—who is given the long final section of *The Waves* in which "to sum up," becoming perhaps a surrogate for the author herself. (As a young man at school, worrying out "my novel," he discovers how "stories that follow people into their private rooms are difficult.") It is he who recognizes that "I am not one person; I am many people," part of his friends as they are part of him, all of them incomplete in themselves; he is "a man without a self." Yet it is also he who on the novel's final page, using the wave imagery of the universalizing interludes, passionately asserts his individuality: "Against you I will fling myself, unvanquished and unyielding, O Death!" Life, however obdurate and fragmented, must be affirmed.

The Waves is without doubt Woolf's most demanding and original novel, her most daring experiment in eliminating the alien and the external. When she vowed to cast out "all waste, deadness, and superfluity," however, she also ascetically renounced some of her greatest strengths as a novelist: her wit and humor, her delight in the daily beauty, variety, and muddle of material existence. This "abstract mystical eyeless book," as she at one point envisioned it, is a work to admire greatly, but not to love.

The six years following *The Waves* were a difficult period for Woolf both personally and artistically. Deeply depressed by the deaths of Lytton Strachey and Roger Fry, two of her oldest, most respected friends, she was at work on an "essay-novel," as she first conceived of it, which despite her initial enthusiasm became her most painfully frustrating effort—even though it proved, ironically, to be her greatest commercial success.

The Years · In *The Years*, Woolf returned to the conventional novel that she had rejected after *Night and Day*; she planned "to take in everything" and found herself "infinitely delighting in facts for a change." Whereas *The Waves* had represented the extreme of leaving out, *The Years* suggests the opposite one of almost indiscriminate putting in. Its very subject, a history of the Pargiter clan spanning fifty years and three generations, links it with the diffuse family sagas of John Galsworthy and Arnold Bennett, whose books Woolf was expressly deriding when she demanded, "Must novels be like this?"

Nevertheless, *The Years* is more original than it may appear; Woolf made fresh use of her experimental methods in her effort to reanimate traditional form. The novel contains eleven unequal segments, each standing for a year; the longest ones, the opening "1880" section and the closing "Present Day" (the 1930's), anchor the book; the nine intermediate sections cover the years between 1891 and 1918. Echoing *The Waves*, Woolf begins each chapter with a short panoramic passage describing both London and the countryside. Within the chapters, instead of continuous narrative, there are collections of vignettes, somewhat reminiscent of *Jacob's Room*, depicting various Pargiters going about their daily lives. Running parallel with the family's history are larger historical events, including Edward VII's death, the suffrage movement, the Irish troubles, and especially World War I. These events are usually treated indirectly, however; for example, the "1917" section takes place mainly in a cellar to which the characters have retreated, dinner plates in hand, during an air raid. It is here that Eleanor Pargiter asks, setting a theme that suffuses the rest of the novel, "When shall we live adventurously, wholly, not like cripples in a cave?"

The most pervasive effect of the war is felt in the lengthy "Present Day" segment, which culminates in a family reunion, where the youngest generation of Pargiters, Peggy and North, are lonely, cynical, and misanthropic, and their faltering elders are compromised by either complacency or failed hopes. Symbolically, Delia Pargiter gives the party in a rented office, not a home, underscoring the uprooting caused by the war. Yet the balancing "1880" section is almost equally dreary: The Pargiters' solid Victorian house shelters a chronically ailing mother whose children wish she would die, a father whose vulgar mistress greets him in hair curlers and frets over her dog's eczema, and a young daughter traumatized by an exhibitionist in the street outside. One oppressive way of life seems only to have been superseded by another, albeit a more universally menacing one.

The overall imagery of the novel is likewise unlovely: Children recall being scrubbed with slimy washcloths; a revolting dinner of underdone mutton served by Sara Pargiter includes a bowl of rotting, flyblown fruit, grotesquely parodying Mrs. Ramsay's *boeuf en daube* and Rose's centerpiece; London is populated with deformed violet-sellers and old men eating cold sausages on buses. Communication in such a world is even more difficult than in Woolf's earlier books; the dialogue throughout is full of incomplete sentences, and a central vignette in the "Present Day" section turns on one guest's abortive efforts to deliver a speech toasting the human race.

Despite these circumstances, the characters still grope toward some kind of transforming unity; Eleanor, the eldest surviving Pargiter and the most sympathetic character in the novel, comes closest to achieving such vision on the scale that Lily Briscoe and Clarissa Dalloway do. At the reunion, looking back over her life, she wonders if there is "a pattern; a theme recurring like music . . . momentarily perceptible?" Casting about her, trying to connect with her relatives and friends but dozing in the process, she suddenly wakes, proclaiming that "it's been a perpetual discovery, my life. A miracle." Answering by implication her question posed fifteen years earlier during the air raid, she perceives that "we're only just beginning . . . to understand, here and there." That prospect is enough, however; she wants "to enclose the present moment . . . to fill it fuller and fuller, with the past, the present and the future, until it shone, whole, bright, deep with understanding."

Even this glowing dream of eventual unity is muted, though, when one recalls how Eleanor's embittered niece Peggy half pities, half admires her as a person who "still believed with passion . . . in the things man had destroyed," and how her nephew North, a captain in the trenches of World War I, thinks, "We cannot help each other, we are all deformed." It is difficult not to read the final lines of this profoundly somber novel ironically: "The sun had risen, and the sky above the houses wore an air of extraordinary beauty, simplicity and peace."

Between the Acts · Woolf's final work, *Between the Acts*, also deals with individual lives unfolding against the screen of history, but her vision and the methods by which she conveys it are more inventive, complex, and successful than in *The Years*. Covering the space of a single day in June, 1939, as world war threatens on the Continent, *Between the Acts* depicts the events surrounding a village pageant about the history of England, performed on the grounds of Pointz Hall, a country house occupied by the unhappily married Giles and Isa Oliver. The Olivers' story frames the presentation of the pageant, scenes of which are directly reproduced in the novel and alternate with glimpses of the audience's lives during the intervals between the acts. The novel's title is hence richly metaphorical: The acts of the drama itself are bracketed by the scenes of real life, which in turn can be viewed as brief episodes in the long pageant of human history. Equally ambiguous, then, is the meaning of "parts," connoting clearly defined roles within a drama but also the fragmentation and incompleteness of the individuals who play them, that pervasive theme in Woolf's work.

In *The Years*, Woolf had focused on the personal histories of her characters; history in the larger sense made itself felt as it impinged on private lives. This emphasis is reversed in *Between the Acts*. Though the novel has interesting characters, Woolf provides scant information about their backgrounds, nor does she plumb individual memory in her usual manner. Instead, the characters possess a national, cultural, *communal* past—finally that of the whole human race from the Stone Age to the present. That Woolf intends her characters to be seen as part of this universal progression is clear from myriad references in the early pages to historical time. For example, from the air, the "scars" made by the Britons and the Romans can be seen around the village as can the Elizabethan manor house; graves in the churchyard attest that Mrs. Haines's family has lived in the area "for many centuries," whereas the Oliver family has inhabited Pointz Hall for "only something over a hundred and twenty years"; Lucy Swithin, Giles's endearing aunt, enjoys reading about history and imagining Piccadilly when it was a rhododendron forest populated by mastodons, "from whom, presumably, she thought . . . we descend."

The pageant itself, therefore, functions in the novel as more than simply a church fund-raising ritual, the product of well-meaning but hapless amateurs (though it exists amusingly on that level too). It is a heroic attempt by its author-director, the formidable Miss La Trobe, to make people see themselves playing parts in the continuum of British history. Thus, the audience has an integral role that blurs the lines "between the acts"; "Our part," says Giles's father, Bartholomew, "is to be the audience. And a very important part too." Their increasing interest in the pageant as they return from the successive intermissions signals their growing sense of a shared past and hence of an identity that both binds and transcends them as individuals.

The scenes of the pageant proceed from bathos to unnerving profundity. The first player, a small girl in pink, announces, "England am I," then promptly forgets her lines, while the wind blows away half the words of the singers behind her. Queen Elizabeth, splendidly decorated with six-penny brooches and a cape made of silvery scouring pads, turns out to be Mrs. Clark, the village tobacconist; the combined applause and laughter of delighted recognition muffle her opening speech. As the pageant progresses from a wicked though overlong parody of Restoration comedy to a satiric scene at a Victorian picnic, however, the audience becomes more reflective; the past is now close enough to be familiar, triggering their own memories and priming them for the last scene, Miss La Trobe's inspired experiment in expressionism, "The Present Time. Ourselves." The uncomprehending audience fidgets as the stage remains empty, refusing to understand that they are supposed to contemplate their own significance. "Reality too strong," Miss La Trobe mutters angrily from behind the bushes, "Curse 'em!" Then, "sudden and universal," a summer shower fortuitously begins. "Down it rained like all the people in the world weeping." Nature has provided the bridge of meaning Miss La Trobe required. As the rain ends, all the players from all the periods reappear, still in costume and declaiming fragments of their parts while flashing mirrors in the faces of the discomfited audience. An offstage voice asks how civilization is "to be built by orts, scraps and fragments like ourselves," then dies away.

The Reverend Streatfield, disconcerted like the rest of the audience, is assigned the embarrassing role of summing up the play's meaning. Tentatively, self-consciously, he ventures, "To me at least it was indicated that we are members of one another. . . . We act different parts; but are the same. . . . Surely, we should unite?" Then he abruptly shifts into a fund-raising appeal that is drowned out by a formation of war planes passing overhead. As the audience departs, a gramophone plays a valedictory: "Dispersed are we; we who have come together. But let us retain whatever made that harmony." The audience responds, thinking "There is joy, sweet joy, in company."

The qualified optimism of the pageant's close, however, is darkened by the bleak, perhaps apocalyptic postscript of the framing story. After the group disperses, the characters resume their usual roles. Lucy Swithin, identified earlier as a "unifier," experiences a typically Woolfian epiphany as she gazes on a fishpond, glimpsing the silver of the great carp below the surface and "seeing in that vision beauty, power and glory in ourselves." Her staunchly rational brother Bartholomew, a "separatist," goes into the house. Miss La Trobe, convinced that she has failed again, heads for the local pub to drink alone and plan her next play; it will be set at midnight with two figures half hidden by a rock as the curtain rises. "What would the first words be?"

It is the disaffected Giles and Isa, loving and hating each other, who begin the new play. In a remarkable ending, Woolf portrays the couple sitting silently in the dark before going to bed: "Before they slept, they must fight; after they had fought they would embrace." From that embrace, they may create another life, but "first they must fight, as the dog fox fights the vixen, in the heart of darkness, in the fields of night." The "great hooded chairs" in which they sit grow enormous, like Miss La Trobe's rock. The house fades, no longer sheltering them; they are like "dwellers in caves," watching "from some high place." The last lines of the novel are, "Then the curtain rose. They spoke."

This indeterminate conclusion implies that love and hate are elemental and reciprocal, and that such oppositions on a personal level are also the polarities that drive human history. Does Woolf read, then, in the gathering European storm, a cataclysm that will bring the pageant of history full circle, back to the primitive stage of prehistory? Or, like W. B. Yeats in "The Second Coming," does she envision a new cycle even more terrifying than the old? Or, as the faithful Lucy Swithin does, perhaps she hopes that "*all* is harmony could we hear it. And we shall."

Eight years earlier, Virginia Woolf wrote in her diary, "I think the effort to live in two spheres: the novel; and life; is a strain." Miss La Trobe, a crude alter ego for the author, is obsessed by failure but always driven to create anew because "a vision imparted was relief from agony . . . for one moment." In her brilliant experimental attempts to impart her own view of fragmented human beings achieving momentary harmony, discovering unity and stability behind the flux of daily life, Woolf repeatedly endured such anguish, but after *Between the Acts* was done, the strain of beginning again was too great. Perhaps the questions Virginia Woolf posed in this final haunting novel, published posthumously and unrevised, were answered for her in death.

Kristine Ottesen Garrigan

Other major works

SHORT FICTION: *Monday or Tuesday*, 1921; *A Haunted House and Other Short Stories*, 1943; *Mrs. Dalloway's Party*, 1973 (Stella McNichol, editor); *The Complete Shorter Fiction of Virginia Woolf*, 1985.

NONFICTION: *The Common Reader: First Series*, 1925; *A Room of One's Own*, 1929; *The Common Reader: Second Series*, 1932; *Three Guineas*, 1938; *Roger Fry: A Biography*, 1940; *The Death of the Moth and Other Essays*, 1942; *The Moment and Other Essays*, 1947; *The Captain's Death Bed and Other Essays*, 1950; *A Writer's Diary*, 1953; *Granite and Rainbow*, 1958; *Contemporary Writers*, 1965; *Collected Essays, Volumes 1-2*, 1966; *Collected Essays, Volumes 3-4*, 1967; *The London Scene: Five Essays*, 1975; *The Flight of the Mind: The Letters of Virginia Woolf, Vol. I, 1888-1912*, 1975 (pb. in U.S. as *The Letters of Virginia Woolf, Vol. I: 1888-1912*, 1975; Nigel Nicolson, editor); *The Question of Things Happening: The Letters of Virginia Woolf, Vol. II, 1912-1922*, 1976 (pb. in U.S. as *The Letters of Virginia Woolf, Vol. II: 1912-1922*, 1976; Nicolson, editor); *Moments of Being*, 1976 (Jeanne Schulkind, editor); *Books and Portraits*, 1977; *The Diary of Virginia Woolf*, 1977-1984 (5 volumes; Anne Olivier Bell, editor); *A Change of Perspective: The Letters of Virginia Woolf, Vol. III, 1923-1928*, 1977 (pb. in U.S. as *The Letters of Virginia Woolf, Vol. III: 1923-1928*, 1978; Nicolson, editor); *A Reflection of the Other Person: The Letters of Virginia Woolf, Vol. IV, 1929-1931*, 1978 (pb. in U.S. as *The Letters of Virginia Woolf, Vol. IV: 1929-1931*, 1979; Nicolson, editor); *The Sickle Side of the Moon: The Letters of Virginia Woolf, Vol. V, 1932-1935*, 1979 (pb. in U.S. as *The Letters of Virginia Woolf, Vol. V: 1932-1935*, 1979; Nicolson, editor); *Leave the Letters Til We're Dead: The Letters of Virginia Woolf, Vol. VI, 1936-1941*, 1980 (Nicolson, editor); *The Essays of Virginia Woolf*, 1987-1994 (4 volumes).

Bibliography

Abel, Elizabeth. *Virginia Woolf and the Fictions of Psychoanalysis.* Chicago: University of Chicago Press, 1989. With a focus upon symbolism and stylistic devices, this book comprehensively delineates the psychoanalytic connections between Woolf's fiction and Sigmund Freud's and Melanie Klein's theories. Sometimes difficult to follow, however, given Abel's reliance on excellent but extensive endnotes.

Baldwin, Dean R. *Virginia Woolf: A Study of the Short Fiction.* Boston: Twayne, 1989. Baldwin's lucid parallels between Woolf's life experiences and her innovative short-story techniques contribute significantly to an understanding of both the author and her creative process. The book also presents the opportunity for a comparative critical study by furnishing a collection of additional points of view in the final section. A chronology, a bibliography, and an index supplement the work.

Beja, Morris. *Critical Essays on Virginia Woolf.* Boston: G. K. Hall, 1985. In an excellent composite of literary analyses, Beja directs attention to both reviews and critical essays on Woolf's writings in order to demonstrate her universal and ageless appeal. Several critical disciplines are represented. Includes essay endnotes and an index.

Dowling, David. *Mrs. Dalloway: Mapping Streams of Consciousness.* Boston: Twayne, 1991. Divided into sections on literary and historical context and interpretations of the novel. Dowling explores the world of Bloomsbury, war, and modernism; the critical reception of the novel and how it was composed; Woolf's style, theory of fiction, handling of stream of consciousness, structure, characters, and themes. Includes a chronology and concordance to the novel.

Ginsberg, Elaine K., and L. M. Gottlieb, eds. *Virginia Woolf: Centennial Essays.* Troy, N.Y.: Whitston, 1983. Sixteen papers cover, among other topics, Woolf's style, gender consciousness, and feminist inclinations. Style, approach, and interpretation vary widely by presenter, and the text as a whole requires some familiarity with Woolf's writings. Notes on contributors, endnotes following each paper, and an index are provided.

Heilbrun, Carolyn G. *Women's Lives: The View from the Threshold.* Toronto: University of Toronto Press, 1999. This volume discusses George Eliot, Woolf, Willa Cather, and Harriet Beecher Stowe. Focuses on the female view and feminism in literature.

Lee, Hermione. *Virginia Woolf.* New York: Knopf, 1997. The most complete biography of Woolf so far, drawing on the latest scholarship and on primary sources. Includes family tree, notes, and bibliography.

Warner, Eric, ed. *Virginia Woolf: A Centenary Perspective.* New York: St. Martin's Press, 1984. With a nonpartisan approach, this text offers seven papers and two panel discussions from Fitzwilliam College's Virginia Woolf Centenary Conference in Cambridge, England. Notes at the end of each presentation, notes on the contributors, and an index are provided.

TERMS AND TECHNIQUES

Absurdism: A philosophical attitude pervading much of modern drama and fiction, which underlines the isolation and alienation that humans experience, having been thrown into what absurdists see as a godless universe devoid of religious, spiritual, or metaphysical meaning. Conspicuous in its lack of logic, consistency, coherence, intelligibility, and realism, the literature of the absurd depicts the anguish, forlornness, and despair inherent in the human condition. Counter to the rationalist assumptions of traditional humanism, absurdism denies the existence of universal truth or value.

Allegory: A literary mode in which a second level of meaning, wherein characters, events, and settings represent abstractions, is encoded within the surface narrative. The allegorical mode may dominate the entire work, in which case the encoded message is the work's primary excuse for being, or it may be an element in a work otherwise interesting and meaningful for its surface story alone. Elements of allegory may be found in Jonathan Swift's *Gulliver's Travels* (1726) and Thomas Mann's *The Magic Mountain* (1924).

Anatomy: Literally the term means the "cutting up" or "dissection" of a subject into its constituent parts for closer examination. Northrop Frye, in his *Anatomy of Criticism* (1957), uses the term to refer to a narrative that deals with mental attitudes rather than people. As opposed to the novel, the anatomy features stylized figures who are mouthpieces for the ideas they represent.

Antagonist: The character in fiction who stands as a rival or opponent to the *protagonist.*

Antihero: Defined by Seán O'Faoláin as a fictional figure who, deprived of social sanctions and definitions, is always trying to define himself and to establish his own codes. Ahab may be seen as the antihero of Herman Melville's *Moby Dick* (1851).

Archetype: The term "archetype" entered literary criticism from the psychology of Carl G. Jung, who defined archetypes as "primordial images" from the "collective unconscious" of humankind. Jung believed that works of art derived much of their power from the unconscious appeal of these images to ancestral memories. In his extremely influential *Anatomy of Criticism* (1957), Northrop Frye gave another sense of the term wide currency, defining the archetype as "a symbol, usually an image, which recurs often enough in literature to be recognizable as an element of one's literary experience as a whole."

Atmosphere: The general mood or tone of a work; it is often associated with setting but can also be established by action or dialogue. A classic example of atmosphere is the primitive, fatalistic tone created in the opening description of Egdon Heath in Thomas Hardy's *The Return of the Native* (1878).

Bildungsroman: Sometimes called the "novel of education," the *Bildungsroman* focuses on the growth of a young *protagonist* who is learning about the world and finding his or her place in life; typical examples are James Joyce's *A Portrait of the Artist as a Young Man* (1916) and Thomas Wolfe's *Look Homeward, Angel* (1929).

Biographical criticism: Criticism that attempts to determine how the events and experiences of an author's life influence his work.

Bourgeois novel: A novel in which the values, preoccupations, and accoutrements of middle-class or bourgeois life are given particular prominence. The heyday of the bourgeois novel was the nineteenth century, when novelists as varied as Jane Austen, Honoré de Balzac, and Anthony Trollope both criticized and unreflectingly transmitted the assumptions of the rising middle class.

Canon: An authorized or accepted list of books. In modern parlance, the literary canon comprehends the privileged texts, classics, or great books that are thought to belong permanently on university reading lists. Recent theory, especially feminist, Marxist, and poststructuralist, critically examines the process of canon formation and questions the hegemony of white male writers. Such theory sees canon formation as the ideological act of a dominant institution and seeks to undermine the notion of canonicity itself, thereby preventing the exclusion of works by women, minorities, and oppressed peoples.

Character: Characters in fiction can be presented as if they were real people or as stylized functions of the plot. Usually characters are a combination of both factors.

Classicism: A literary stance or value system consciously based on the example of classical Greek and Roman literature. While the term is applied to an enormous diversity of artists in many different periods and in many different national literatures, "classicism" generally denotes a cluster of values including formal discipline, restrained expression, reverence for tradition, and an objective rather than a subjective orientation. As a literary tendency, classicism is often opposed to *Romanticism,* although many writers combine classical and romantic elements.

Climax/Crisis: Whereas climax refers to the moment of the reader's highest emotional response, crisis refers to a structural element of plot. Crisis refers to a turning point in fiction, a point when a resolution must take place.

Complication: The point in a novel when the conflict is developed or when the already existing conflict is further intensified.

Conflict: The struggle that develops as a result of the opposition between the *protagonist* and another person, the natural world, society, or some force within the self.

Conventions: All those devices of stylization, compression, and selection that constitute the necessary differences between art and life. According to the Russian Formalists, these conventions constitute the "literariness" of literature and are the only proper concern of the literary critic.

Deconstruction: An extremely influential contemporary school of criticism based on the works of the French philosopher Jacques Derrida. Deconstruction treats literary works as unconscious reflections of the reigning myths of Western culture. The primary myth is that there is a meaningful world that language signifies or represents. The deconstructionist critic is most often concerned with showing how a literary text tacitly subverts the very assumptions or myths on which it ostensibly rests.

Detective story: The so-called classic detective story (or mystery) is a highly formalized and logically structured mode of fiction in which the focus is on a crime solved by a detective through interpretation of evidence and ratiocination; the most famous detective in this mode is Arthur Conan Doyle's Sherlock Holmes. Many modern practitioners of the genre, however, such as Dashiell Hammett, Raymond Chandler, and Ross Macdonald, have deemphasized the puzzlelike qualities of the detective story, stressing instead characterization, theme, and other elements of mainstream fiction.

Determinism: The belief that an individual's actions are essentially determined by biological and environmental factors, with free will playing a negligible role. (See *Naturalism.*)

Dialogue: The similitude of conversation in fiction, dialogue serves to characterize, to further the plot, to establish conflict, and to express thematic ideas.

Displacement: Popularized in criticism by Northrop Frye, the term refers to the author's attempt to make his or her story psychologically motivated and realistic, even as the latent structure of the mythical motivation moves relentlessly forward.

Dominant: A term coined by Roman Jakobson to refer to that which "rules, deter-mines, and transforms the remaining components in the work of a single artist, in a poetic canon, or in the work of an epoch." The shifting of the dominant in a *genre* accounts for the creation of new generic forms and new poetic epochs. For example, the rise of realism in the mid-nineteenth century indicates realistic conventions becoming dominant and romance or fantasy conventions becoming secondary.

Doppelgänger: A double or counterpart of a person, sometimes endowed with ghostly qualities. A fictional character's *Doppelgänger* often reflects a suppressed side of his or her personality. One of the classic examples of the *Doppelgänger* motif is found in Fyodor Dostoevski's novella *The Double* (1846); Isaac Bashevis Singer and Jorge Luis Borges, among others, offer striking modern treatments of the *Doppelgänger.*

Epic: Although this term usually refers to a long narrative poem that presents the exploits of a central figure of high position, the term is also used to designate a long novel that has the style or structure usually associated with an epic. In this sense, for example, Herman Melville's *Moby Dick* (1851) and James Joyce's *Ulysses* (1922) may be called epic.

Episodic narrative: A work that is held together primarily by a loose connection of self-sufficient episodes. *Picaresque novels* often have an episodic structure.

Epistolary novel: A novel made up of letters by one or more fictional characters. Samuel Richardson's *Pamela* (1740-1741) is a well-known eighteenth century example. In the nineteenth century, Bram Stoker's *Dracula* (1897) is largely epistolary. The technique allows for several different points of view to be presented.

Euphuism: A style of writing characterized by ornate language that is highly contrived, alliterative, and repetitious. Euphuism was developed by John Lyly in his *Euphues, an Anatomy of Wit* (1578) and was emulated frequently by writers of the Elizabethan Age.

Existentialism: A philosophical, religious, and literary term, emerging from World War II, for a group of attitudes surrounding the pivotal notion that existence precedes essence. According to Jean-Paul Sartre, "man is nothing else but what he makes himself." Forlornness arises from the death of God and the concomitant death of universal values, of any source of ultimate or a priori standards. Despair arises from the fact that an individual can reckon only with what depends on his or her will, and the sphere of that will is severely limited; the number of things on which he or she can have an impact is pathetically small. Existentialist literature is antideterministic in the extreme and rejects the idea that heredity and environment shape and determine human motivation and behavior.

Exposition: The part or parts of a fiction that provide necessary background informa-tion. Exposition not only provides the time and place of the action but also introduces readers to the fictive world of the story, acquainting them with the ground rules of the work.

Fantastic: In his study *The Fantastic* (1970), Tzvetan Todorov defines the fantastic as a *genre* that lies between the "uncanny" and the "marvelous." All three *genres* embody the familiar world but present an event that cannot be explained by the laws of the familiar world. Todorov says that the fantastic occupies a twilight zone between the uncanny, when the reader knows that the peculiar event is merely the result of an illusion, and the marvelous, when the reader understands that the event is supposed to take place in a realm controlled by laws unknown to humankind. Thus, the fantastic is essentially unsettling, provocative, even subversive.

Feminist criticism: A criticism advocating equal rights for women in a political, economic, social, psychological, personal, and aesthetic sense. On the thematic level, the feminist reader should identify with female characters and their concerns. The object is to provide a critique of phallocentric assumptions and an analysis of patriarchal ideologies inscribed in a literature that is male-centered and male-dominated. On the ideological level, feminist critics see gender, as well as the stereotypes that go along with it, as a cultural construct. They strive to define a particularly feminine content and to extend the *canon* so that it might include works by lesbians, feminists, and female writers in general.

Flashback: A scene in a fiction that depicts an earlier event; it can be presented as a reminiscence by a character in the story or it can simply be inserted into the narrative.

Foreshadowing: A device to create suspense or dramatic irony by indicating through suggestion what will take place in the future.

Genre: In its most general sense, the term "genre" refers to a group of literary works defined by a common form, style, or purpose. In practice, the term is used in a wide variety of overlapping and, to a degree, contradictory senses. Thus, tragedy and comedy are described as distinct genres; the novel (a form that includes both tragic and comic works) is a genre; and various subspecies of the novel, such as the *gothic* and the *picaresque*, are themselves frequently treated as distinct genres. Finally, the term *genre fiction* refers to forms of popular fiction in which the writer is bound by more or less rigid conventions. Indeed, all these diverse usages have in common an emphasis on the manner in which individual literary works are shaped by the expectations and conventions of a particular genre: this is the subject of genre criticism.

Genre fiction: Categories of popular fiction such as the mystery, the romance, and the Western. Although the term can be used in a neutral sense, "genre fiction" is often pejorative, used dismissively to refer to fiction in which the writer is bound by more or less rigid conventions.

Gothic novel: A form of fiction developed in the eighteenth century that focuses on horror and the supernatural. In his preface to *The Castle of Otranto* (1764), the first gothic novel in English, Horace Walpole claimed that he was trying to combine two kinds of fiction, with events and story typical of the medieval romance and character delineation typical of the realistic novel. Other examples of the form are Matthew Gregory Lewis's *The Monk* (1796) and Mary Wollstonecraft Shelley's *Frankenstein* (1818).

Grotesque: According to Wolfgang Kayser (*The Grotesque in Art and Literature*, 1963), the grotesque is an embodiment in literature of the estranged world. Characterized by a breakup of the everyday world by mysterious forces, the form differs from fantasy in that the reader is not sure whether to react with humor or with horror and in that the exaggeration manifested exists in the familiar world rather than in a purely imaginative world.

Hebraic/Homeric styles: Terms coined by Erich Auerbach in *Mimesis: The Representation of Reality in Western Literature* (1953) to designate two basic fictional styles: the Hebraic, which focuses only on the decisive points of narrative and leaves all else obscure, mysterious, and "fraught with background," and the Homeric, which places the narrative in a definite time and place and externalizes everything in a perpetual foreground.

Historical novel: A novel that depicts past historical events, usually public in nature, and features real as well as fictional people. Sir Walter Scott's Waverley novels established the basic type, but the relationship between fiction and history in the form varies greatly depending on the practitioner.

Implied author: According to Wayne Booth (*The Rhetoric of Fiction*, 1961), the novel often creates a kind of second self who tells the story, a self who is wiser, more sensitive, and more perceptive than any real person could be.

Interior monologue: Defined by Édouard Dujardin as the speech of a character designed to introduce the reader directly to the character's internal life, the form differs from other monologues in that it attempts to reproduce thought before any logical organization is imposed upon it. See, for example, Molly Bloom's long interior monologue at the conclusion of James Joyce's *Ulysses* (1922).

Irrealism: A term often used to refer to modern or postmodern fiction that is presented self-consciously as a fiction or a fabulation rather than a mimesis of external reality. The best-known practitioners of irrealism are John Barth, Robert Coover, and Donald Barthelme.

Marxist criticism: Based on the nineteenth century writings of Karl Marx and Friedrich Engels, Marxist criticism views literature as a product of ideological forces determined by the dominant class. However, many Marxists believe that literature operates according to its own autonomous standards of production and reception: It is both a product of ideology and able to determine ideology. As such, literature may overcome the dominant paradigms of its age and play a revolutionary role in society.

Metafiction: The term refers to fiction that manifests a reflexive tendency, such as Vladimir Nabokov's *Pale Fire* (1962) and John Fowles's *The French Lieutenant's Woman* (1969). The emphasis is on the loosening of the work's illusion of reality to expose the reality of its illusion. Such terms as *irrealism, postmodernist fiction,* "antifiction," and "surfiction" are also used to refer to this type of fiction.

Modernism: An international movement in the arts that began in the early years of the twentieth century. Although the term is used to describe artists of widely varying persuasions, modernism in general was characterized by its international idiom, by its interest in cultures distant in space or time, by its emphasis on formal experimentation, and by its sense of dislocation and radical change.

Motif: A conventional incident or situation in a fiction that may serve as the basis for the structure of the narrative itself. The Russian Formalist critic Boris Tomashevsky uses the term to refer to the smallest particle of thematic material in a work.

Motivation: Although this term is usually used in reference to the convention of justifying the action of a character from his or her psychological makeup, the Russian Formalists use the term to refer to the network of devices that justify the introduction of individual *motifs* or groups of *motifs* in a work. For example, compositional motivation refers to the principle that every single property in a work contributes to its overall effect; realistic motivation refers to the realistic devices used to make the work plausible and lifelike.

Multiculturalism: The tendency to recognize the perspectives of those traditionally excluded from the canon of Western art and literature. In order to promote multiculturalism, publishers and educators have revised textbooks and school curricula to incorporate material by and about women, minorities, non-Western cultures, and homosexuals.

Myth: Anonymous traditional stories dealing with basic human concepts and antinomies. Claude Lévi-Strauss says that myth is that part of language where the "formula *tradutore, tradittore* reaches its lowest truth value. . . . Its substance does not lie in its style, its original music, or its syntax, but in the story which it tells."

Myth criticism: Northrop Frye says that in myth, "we see the structural principles of literature isolated." Myth criticism is concerned with these basic principles of literature; it is not to be confused with mythological criticism, which is primarily concerned with finding mythological parallels in the surface action of the *narrative.*

Narrative: Robert Scholes and Robert Kellogg, in *The Nature of Narrative* (1966), say that by narrative they mean literary works that include both a story and a storyteller. Narrative usually implies a contrast to "enacted" fiction such as drama.

Narratology: The study of the form and functioning of narratives; it attempts to examine what all *narratives* have in common and what makes individual *narratives* different from one another.

Narrator: The character who recounts the *narrative,* or story. Wayne Booth describes various dramatized narrators in *The Rhetoric of Fiction* (1961): unacknowledged centers of consciousness, observers, narrator-agents, and self-conscious narrators. Booth suggests that the important elements to consider in narration are the relationships among the narrator, the author, the characters, and the reader.

Naturalism: As developed by Émile Zola in the late nineteenth century, naturalism is the application of the principles of scientific *determinism* to fiction. Although it usually refers more to the choice of subject matter than to technical conventions, those conventions associated with the movement center on the author's attempt to be precise and scientifically objective in description and detail, regardless of whether the events described are sordid or shocking.

Novel: Perhaps the most difficult of all fictional forms to define because of its multiplicity of modes. Edouard, in André Gide's *The Counterfeiters* (1926), says the novel is the freest and most lawless of all *genres*: he wonders if fear of that liberty is not the reason the novel has so timidly clung to reality. Most critics seem to agree that the novel's primary area of concern is the social world. Ian Watt (*The Rise of the Novel*, 1957) says that the novel can be distinguished from other fictional forms by the attention it pays to individual characterization and detailed presentation of the environment. Moreover, says Watt, the novel, more than any other fictional form, is interested in the "development of its characters in the course of time."

Novel of manners: The classic example of the form might be the novels of Jane Austen, wherein the customs and conventions of a social group of a particular time and place are realistically, and often satirically, portrayed.

Novella, novelle, nouvelle, novelette, novela: Although these terms often refer to the short European tale, especially the Renaissance form employed by Giovanni Boccaccio, the terms often refer to that form of fiction that is said to be longer than a short story and shorter than a novel. "Novelette" is the term usually preferred by the British, whereas "novella" is the term usually used to refer to American works in this *genre.* Henry James claimed that the main merit of the form was the "effort to do the complicated thing with a strong brevity and lucidity."

Phenomenological criticism: Although best known as a European school of criticism practiced by Georges Poulet and others, this so-called criticism of consciousness is also propounded in America by such critics as J. Hillis Miller. The focus is less on individual works and *genres* than it is on literature as an act; the work is not seen as an object, but rather as part of a strand of latent impulses in the work of a single author or an epoch.

Picaresque novel: A form of fiction that centers on a central rogue figure or picaro who usually tells his or her own story. The plot structure is normally *episodic*, and the episodes usually focus on how the picaro lives by his or her wits. Classic examples of the mode are Henry Fielding's *Tom Jones* (1749) and Mark Twain's *Adventures of Huckleberry Finn* (1884).

Plot/Story: Story is a term referring to the full narrative of character and action, whereas plot generally refers to action with little reference to character. A more precise and helpful distinction is made by the Russian Formalists, who suggest that plot refers to the events of a *narrative* as they have been artfully arranged in the literary work, subject to chronological displacement, ellipses, and other devices, while story refers to the sum of the same events arranged in simple, causal-chronological order. Thus, story is the raw material for plot. By comparing the two in a given work, the reader is encouraged to see the *narrative* as an artifact.

Point of view: The means by which the story is presented to the reader, or, as Percy Lubbock says in *The Craft of Fiction* (1921), "the relation in which the narrator stands to the story," a relation that Lubbock claims governs the craft of fiction. Some of the questions the critical reader should ask concerning point of view are Who talks to the reader? From what position does the narrator tell the story? At what distance does he or she place the reader from the story? What kind of person is he or she? How fully is he or she characterized? How reliable is he or she? For further discussion, see Wayne Booth, *The Rhetoric of Fiction* (1961).

Postcolonialism: Postcolonial literature emerged in the mid-twentieth century when colonies in Asia, Africa, and the Caribbean began gaining their independence from the European nations that had long controlled them. Postcolonial authors, such as Salman Rushdie and V. S. Naipaul, tend to focus on both the freedom and the conflict inherent in living in a postcolonial state.

Postmodernism: A ubiquitous but elusive term in contempory criticism, "postmodernism" is loosely applied to the various artistic movements that followed the era of so-called high modernism, represented by such giants as James Joyce and Pablo Picasso. In critical discussions of contemporary fiction, the term "postmodernism" is frequently applied to the works of writers such as Thomas Pynchon, John Barth, and Donald Barthelme, who exhibit a self- conscious awareness of their modernist predecessors as well as a reflexive treatment of fictional form.

Protagonist: The central character in a fiction, the character whose fortunes most concern the reader.

Psychological criticism: While much modern literary criticism reflects to some degree the impact of Sigmund Freud, Carl Jung, Jacques Lacan, and other psychological theorists, the term "psychological criticism" suggests a strong emphasis on a causal relation between the writer's psychological state, variously interpreted, and his or her works. A notable example of psychological criticism is Norman Fruman's *Coleridge, the Damaged Archangel* (1971).

Psychological novel: A form of fiction in which character, especially the inner life of characters, is the primary focus. The form has been of primary importance, at least since Henry James, and it characterizes much of the work of James Joyce, Virginia Woolf, and William Faulkner. For a detailed discussion, see *The Modern Psychological Novel* (1955) by Leon Edel.

Realism: A literary technique in which the primary convention is to render an illusion of fidelity to external reality. Realism is often identified as the primary method of the novel form: It focuses on surface details, maintains a fidelity to the everyday experiences of middle-class society, and strives for a one-to-one relationship between the fiction and the action imitated. The realist movement in the late nineteenth century coincides with the full development of the novel form.

Reception aesthetics: The best-known American practitioner of reception aesthetics is Stanley Fish. For the reception critic, meaning is an event or process; rather than being embedded in the work, it is created through particular acts of reading. The best-known European practitioner of this criticism, Wolfgang Iser, says indeterminacy is the basic characteristic of literary texts; the reader must "normalize" the text either by projecting his or her standards into it or by revising his or her standards to "fit" the text.

Rhetorical criticism: The rhetorical critic is concerned with the literary work as a means of communicating ideas and the means by which the work affects or controls the reader. Such criticism seems best suited to didactic works such as satire.

Roman à clef: A fiction wherein actual people, often celebrities of some sort, are thinly disguised.

Romance: The romance usually differs from the novel form in that the focus is on symbolic events and representational characters rather than on "as-if-real" characters and events. Richard Chase says that in the romance, character is depicted as highly stylized, a function of the plot rather than as someone complexly related to society. The romancer is more likely to be concerned with dreamworlds than with the familiar world, believing that reality cannot be grasped by the traditional novel.

Romanticism: A widespread cultural movement in the late eighteenth and early nineteenth centuries, the influence of which is still felt. As a general literary tendency, Romanticism is frequently contrasted with *classicism.* Although there were many varieties of Romanticism indigenous to various national literatures, the term generally suggests an assertion of the preeminence of the imagination. Other values associated with various schools of Romanticism include primitivism, an interest in folklore, a reverence for nature, and a fascination with the demoniac and the macabre.

Scene: The central element of narration; specific actions are narrated or depicted that make the reader feel he or she is participating directly in the action.

Science fiction: Fiction in which certain givens (physical laws, psychological principles, social conditions: any one or all of these) form the basis of an imaginative projection into the future or, less commonly, an extrapolation in the present or even into the past.

Semiotics: The science of signs and sign systems in communication. Roman Jakobson says that semiotics deals with the principles that underlie the structure of signs, their use in language of all kinds, and the specific nature of various sign systems.

Sentimental novel: A form of fiction popular in the eighteenth century in which emotionalism and optimism are the primary characteristics. The best-known examples are Samuel Richardson's *Pamela* (1740-1741) and Oliver Goldsmith's *The Vicar of Wakefield* (1766).

Setting: Setting refers to the circumstances and environment, both temporal and spatial, of a *narrative.*

Spatial form: An author's attempt to make the reader apprehend the work spatially in a moment of time rather than sequentially. To achieve this effect, the author breaks up the *narrative* into interspersed fragments. Beginning with James Joyce, Marcel Proust, and Djuna Barnes, the movement toward spatial form is concomitant with the modernist effort to supplant historical time in fiction with mythic time. For the seminal discussion of this technique, see Joseph Frank, *The Widening Gyre* (1963).

Stream of consciousness: The depiction of the thought processes of a character, insofar as this is possible, without any mediating structures. The metaphor of consciousness as a "stream" suggests a rush of thoughts and images governed by free association rather than by strictly rational development. The term "stream of consciousness" is often used loosely as a synonym for *interior monologue.* The most celebrated example of stream of consciousness in fiction is the monologue of Molly Bloom in James Joyce's *Ulysses* (1922); other notable practitioners of the stream-of-consciousness technique include Dorothy Richardson, Virginia Woolf, and William Faulkner.

Structuralism: As a movement of thought, structuralism is based on the idea of intrinsic, self-sufficient structures that do not require reference to external elements. A structure is a system of transformations that involves the interplay of laws inherent in the system itself. The study of language is the primary model for contemporary structuralism. The structuralist literary critic attempts to define structural principles that operate intertextually throughout the whole of literature as well as principles that operate in *genres* and in individual works. The most accessible survey of structuralism and literature is Jonathan Culler's *Structuralist Poetics* (1975).

Summary: Those parts of a fiction that do not need to be detailed. In *Tom Jones* (1749), Henry Fielding says "If whole years should pass without producing anything worthy of . . . notice . . . we shall hasten on to matters of consequence."

Thematics: Northrup Frye says that when a work of fiction is written or interpreted thematically, it becomes an illustrative fable. Murray Krieger defines thematics as "the study of the experiential tensions which, dramatically entangled in the literary work, become an existential reflection of that work's aesthetic complexity." See Krieger's *The Tragic Vision* (1960).

Tone: Tone usually refers to the dominant mood of the work. (See *Atmosphere.*)

Unreliable narrator: A narrator whose account of the events of the story cannot be trusted, obliging readers to reconstruct, if possible, the true state of affairs themselves. Once an innovative technique, the use of the unreliable narrator has become commonplace among contemporary writers who wish to suggest the impossibility of a truly "reliable" account of any event. Notable examples of the unreliable narrator can be found in Ford Madox Ford's *The Good Soldier* (1915) and Vladimir Nabokov's *Lolita* (1958).

Victorian novel: Although the Victorian period extended from 1837 to 1901, the term "Victorian novel" does not include the later decades of Queen Victoria's reign. The term loosely refers to the sprawling works of novelists such as Charles Dickens and William Makepeace Thackeray, works that frequently appeared first in serial form and are characterized by a broad social canvas.

Vraisemblance/Verisimilitude: Tzvetan Todorov defines vraisemblance as "the mask which conceals the text's own laws, but which we are supposed to take for a relation to reality." When one speaks of vraisemblance, one refers to the work's attempts to make the reader believe that it conforms to reality rather than to its own laws.

Charles E. May

Time Line

Date and place of birth	Name
Early 15th cent.: Warwickshire (?), England	Sir Thomas Malory
Nov. 1628: Elstow, England	John Bunyan
July (?), 1640: England	Aphra Behn
1660: London, England	Daniel Defoe
Nov. 30, 1667: Dublin, Ireland	Jonathan Swift
July 31 (?), 1689: Derbyshire, England	Samuel Richardson
Apr. 22, 1707: Sharpham Park, Somersetshire, England	Henry Fielding
Sept. 18, 1709: Lichfield, Staffordshire, England	Samuel Johnson
Nov. 24, 1713: Clonmel, Ireland	Laurence Sterne
Mar. 19, 1721 (baptized): Dalquhurn, Scotland	Tobias Smollett
Nov. 10, 1728 or 1730: Pallas, County Longford(?), Ireland	Oliver Goldsmith
June 13, 1752: King's Lynn, England	Fanny Burney
1762: Portsmouth, England	Susanna Rowson
July 9, 1764: London, England	Ann Radcliffe
Jan. 1, 1767: Black Bourton, England	Maria Edgeworth
Aug. 15, 1771: Edinburgh, Scotland	Sir Walter Scott
July 9, 1775: London, England	Matthew Gregory Lewis
Dec. 16, 1775: Steventon, England	Jane Austen
Sept. 25, 1780: Dublin, Ireland	Charles Robert Maturin
Oct. 18, 1785: Weymouth, England	Thomas Love Peacock
Aug. 30, 1797: London, England	Mary Wollstonecraft Shelley
Sept. 29, 1810: Chelsea, London, England	Elizabeth Gaskell
July 18, 1811: Calcutta, India	William Makepeace Thackeray
Feb. 7, 1812: Portsmouth, England	Charles Dickens
Aug. 28, 1814: Dublin, Ireland	Joseph Sheridan Le Fanu
Apr. 24, 1815: London, England	Anthony Trollope
Apr. 21, 1816: Thornton, Yorkshire, England	Charlotte Brontë
July 30, 1818: Thornton, Yorkshire, England	Emily Brontë
Nov. 22, 1819: Chilvers Coton, England	George Eliot
Jan. 8, 1824: London, England	Wilkie Collins
Feb. 12, 1828: Portsmouth, England	George Meredith
Jan. 27, 1832: Daresbury, Cheshire, England	Lewis Carroll

Date and place of birth	Name
Dec. 4, 1835: Langar Rectory, England	Samuel Butler
Aug. 4, 1839: London, England	Walter Pater
June 2, 1840: Higher Bockhampton, England	Thomas Hardy
Nov. 13, 1850: Edinburgh, Scotland	Robert Louis Stevenson
Oct. 16, 1854: Dublin, Ireland	Oscar Wilde
Nov. 22, 1857: Wakefield, England	George Gissing
Dec. 3, 1857: Near Berdyczów, Poland	Joseph Conrad
May 22, 1859: Edinburgh, Scotland	Arthur Conan Doyle
Dec. 30, 1865: Bombay, India	Rudyard Kipling
Sept. 21, 1866: Bromley, Kent, England	H. G. Wells
May 27, 1867: Shelton, near Hanley, England	Arnold Bennett
Aug. 14, 1867: Kingston Hill, England	John Galsworthy
Apr. 25, 1873: Charlton, Kent, England	Walter de la Mare
May 17, 1873: Berkshire, England	Dorothy Richardson
Dec. 17, 1873: Merton, England	Ford Madox Ford
Jan. 25, 1874: Paris, France	W. Somerset Maugham
May 29, 1874: London, England	G. K. Chesterton
Jan. 1, 1879: London, England	E. M. Forster
Aug. 1, 1881: Rugby, England	Rose Macaulay
Oct. 15, 1881: Guildford, Surrey, England	P. G. Wodehouse
Jan. 25, 1882: London, England	Virginia Woolf
June 5, 1884: Pinner, England	Ivy Compton-Burnett
Sept. 11, 1885: Eastwood, Nottinghamshire, England	D. H. Lawrence
Dec. 7, 1888: Londonderry, Ireland	Joyce Cary
Sept. 15, 1890: Torquay, England	Agatha Christie
Jan. 3, 1892: Bloemfontein, South Africa	J. R. R. Tolkien
June 13, 1893: Oxford, England	Dorothy L. Sayers
July 26, 1894: Laleham, near Godalming, Surrey, England	Aldous Huxley
Aug. 24, 1894: Roseau, Dominica Island, West Indies	Jean Rhys
Sept. 13, 1894: Bradford, England	J. B. Priestley
July 24, 1895: Wimbledon, England	Robert Graves
Dec. 30, 1895: Whittlesea, England	L. P. Hartley
July 19, 1896: Cardross, Scotland	A. J. Cronin
Nov. 29, 1898: Belfast, Northern Ireland	C. S. Lewis
June 7, 1899: Dublin, Ireland	Elizabeth Bowen
June 25, 1903: Motihari, India	George Orwell

Date and place of birth	Name
Oct. 28, 1903: London, England	Evelyn Waugh
Oct. 2, 1904: Berkhamsted, England	Graham Greene
Sept. 4, 1905: London, England	Mary Renault
Sept. 5, 1905: Budapest, Hungary	Arthur Koestler
Oct. 15, 1905: Leicester, England	C. P. Snow
Dec. 21, 1905: London, England	Anthony Powell
May 29, 1906: Bombay, India	T. H. White
May 13, 1907: London, England	Daphne Du Maurier
July 28, 1909: Liscard, England	Malcolm Lowry
Sept. 19, 1911: St. Columb Minor, Cornwall, England	William Golding
Feb. 27, 1912: Julundur, India	Lawrence Durrell
June 2, 1913: Oswestry, England	Barbara Pym
Aug. 11, 1913: Bexhill, East Sussex, England	Angus Wilson
Feb. 25, 1917: Manchester, England	Anthony Burgess
Dec. 16, 1917: Minehead, Somerset, England	Arthur C. Clarke
Feb. 1, 1918: Edinburgh, Scotland	Muriel Spark
July 15, 1919: Dublin, Ireland	Iris Murdoch
Oct. 22, 1919: Kermanshah, Persia	Doris Lessing
May 9, 1920: Newbury, England	Richard Adams
Aug. 3, 1920: Oxford, England	P. D. James
Apr. 16, 1922: London, England	Kingsley Amis
June 4, 1923: Birmingham, England	Elizabeth Jolley
Mar. 14, 1925: Stoke-on-Trent, Staffordshire, England	John Wain
Mar. 31, 1926: Leigh-on-Sea, England	John Fowles
May 7, 1927: Cologne, Germany	Ruth Prawer Jhabvala
July 16, 1928: London, England	Anita Brookner
Feb. 23, 1930: Eckington, England	Paul West
Nov. 15, 1930: Shanghai, China	J. G. Ballard
Sept. 22, 1931: Alvechurch, England	Fay Weldon
Oct. 19, 1931: Poole, England	John le Carré
Mar. 17, 1933: Cairo, Egypt	Penelope Lively
June 5, 1939: Sheffield, England	Margaret Drabble
May 7, 1940: Eastbourne, Sussex, England	Angela Carter
Jan. 19, 1946: Leicester, England	Julian Barnes
Aug. 25, 1949: Oxford, England	Martin Amis
Oct. 27, 1950: Stone, England	A. N. Wilson

Index